...AND YOUR POINT?

sixth edition

Reading
Thinking
Composing

laura d. knight
w. james franklin

Cover Design by Lawrence Petraccaro
Page Design and Layout by Lynn Holl

Cover art adapted from *Feast in the House of Levi* (1573) by Il Veronese–Paolo Caliari–(1528-1588), Galleria della Academia, Venice.

Printed in the United States of America

10 9 8 7 6

Windsor Press and Publishing L.L.C.
PO Box 248
Adelphia, NJ 07710
http://windsorpress.net/
732-577-6327
windsorpp@att.net

...AND YOUR POINT?

ACKNOWLEDGEMENTS

When we starting writing this book many years ago as a reaction against the traditional composition textbooks of the time, we had no idea that we would be sending the sixth edition to print. This book has grown, evolved and benefited from the thoughtful suggestions of many instructors and students. Your comments and advice have been invaluable.

As in past editions, we remain grateful to many people who helped make the book not just possible, but better. Special thanks go to Larry Petraccaro for his inspired cover designs; Lynn Holl her fine work (and infinite patience) designing the inside pages; the MCCC librarians, especially Martin Crabtree, for being able to find anything we ask; and our colleagues at Mercer County Community College, especially Robin Schore, for your continued support.

TABLE OF CONTENTS

PART TWO
READINGS

PART THREE
GRAMMAR AND MECHANICS

PART FOUR
IMPROVING SENTENCES

PART FIVE
PUNCTUATION

PART SIX
USAGE

WRITING: PROCESS AND PRODUCT

WHY WE WRITE

Humans are the only creatures on earth who write. We write to describe, to tell stories, to define, to explain, to persuade, to teach, to learn.... We write because we are human. "Talking" with one another—either orally or in writing—is the basis for all human communication.

On a practical note, we write for other reasons. We write to communicate with an audience, one that we don't have to be in front of. For example, the authors of your college textbooks communicate with thousands of people whom they will never meet. In business, executives write memos, letters, and reports. In police work, officers write reports. (A former student who is now a police officer says that writing his reports is the most important part of his job.) Artists write proposals. Nurses write reports. Some of you take courses via the internet and write your responses on your course web page. And so the list goes on. In our society, people in every profession need to write for one reason or another. This is the age of written communication.

In most academic institutions, the curriculum is broken down into three areas: the natural sciences (the world of nature that humans do not control); the social sciences (how groups of people interact); and the humanities (areas that deal with works created by humans—such as art, music, dance and literature). You'll be reading and writing in all these areas throughout your college career. The readings and writing assignments in this textbook address these areas.

This text emphasizes the three critically important elements of communication: writing, reading and speaking. Because writing doesn't have the face-to-face contact, it is a more formalized way of expressing yourself, employing certain conventions that informed readers expect you to follow, such as capital letters to start sentences. Writings can reach millions of people over a span of ages (think of the Bible and Shakespeare). Good writing is effective when it makes a point, follows standard conventions and uses clear language. These are your goals and this text will help you achieve them.

THE ESSAY

Most of the writing you will do in college is in the form of an essay. Essays have certain characteristics: they are fairly brief, they are non-fiction, they make a point, and they are interesting to read.

- **They are fairly brief.** Essays generally run from two pages to around twenty-five pages—long enough to develop the point adequately, yet short enough to read in one sitting.

- **They are non-fiction.** Essayists aim to tell the truth. Stories, facts, and statistics are not made up for embellishment, nor are they created for effect. Personal opinions are kept to a minimum and they are backed by facts.

- **They are interesting to read.** Maybe you've always thought or perhaps you've been told that academic writing has to be long-winded, boring, and stuffy. This is not the case. In fact, it's just the opposite: if your writing is interesting, people will *want* to read it and your ideas will be heard. Keep in mind, however, that interesting writing does not mean sloppy writing.

- **They make a point.** Essayists explain, persuade, or support or refute a point that is directly, not incidentally, about the topic.

Your goal is to choose your words, points, style and tone to achieve the maximum effect on the reader. When you write your essays, you should focus on being engaging, honest, and convincing.

Essays are created through a writing process of creation and revision (re-seeing) that allows you to approach the essay in parts, working on each until you achieve your purpose.

Short essays typically follow this structure:

ESSAY OUTLINE
INTRODUCTION
    Introduce the general topic
    Introduce the specific topic
    Title (if essay is based on a specific text)
    Author (if essay is based on a specific text)
    Thesis Statement (Argument)

FIRST BODY PARAGRAPH (1st supporting reason)
    Topic Sentence
    Expand and give specific details
    Evidence → Quote from text or example
    Analysis (analyze/connect evidence to supporting reason
    and argument)

SECOND BODY PARAGRAPH (2nd supporting reason)
    Topic Sentence
    Expand and give specific details
    Evidence → Quote from text or example
    Analysis (analyze/connect evidence to supporting reason
    and argument)

THIRD BODY PARAGRAPH (3rd supporting reason)
    Topic Sentence
    Expand and give specific details
    Evidence → Quote from text or example
    Analysis (analyze/connect evidence to supporting reason
    and argument)
Continue for as many supporting reasons as necessary

CONCLUSION
    Restate thesis
    Summarize supporting reasons
    Concluding thoughts

PURPOSE, AUDIENCE, TONE & LEVEL OF LANGUAGE

PURPOSE

Baseball Hall of Fame catcher Yogi Berra said, "You've got to be very careful if you don't know where you're going because you might not get there." Knowing "where you are going"—your purpose for writing—is essential. If you don't know your purpose, you'll wander around and around hoping to find your destination. You probably won't succeed. For an essay, you'll write and write, but you'll never make a point. Whenever you write, you have a purpose. Are you trying to describe someone or something, tell a story, show the differences or similarities between two things, or persuade your readers to see your point of view? Before you begin writing, ask yourself—"Why am I writing this?" "What am I trying to accomplish?" "What point am I trying to make?" When you determine this, write it at the top of your paper. It will always be there for you to see and to keep you on the right track.

AUDIENCE

The audience is the people for whom you are writing—the people who will read your essay. You need to know who they are so you can direct your writing to them—your audience.

Suppose for a moment that you were explaining an assignment to a kindergarten class. Think of the words and sentences that you would use: simple and appropriate for five-year olds. Now think of explaining the assignment to your college composition class. Would you use the same words and sentence structure? Obviously not. What if you were writing a letter to your friend at another college about an unfair traffic law? What if you wrote a letter to your senator about the same law? Since your audience is different, your writing would be different. Even though you're writing about the same subject, your word choices, sentence structure and tone would need to be appropriate for the audience.

Another point to consider is how much your audience already knows about the subject. If you were writing an essay about cars for other car enthusiasts, you wouldn't have to explain the terms. For example, does your audience know what a catalytic converter does? You would have to explain if your audience was unfamiliar with the mechanics of a car. Generally in academic writing, your audience is your instructor and your classmates, unless you are told otherwise, so direct your writing to them.

TONE

Tone is the author's attitude toward the subject matter and the audience.

It is the way your essay "sounds" to a reader. Often tone is described by the use of adjectives: *humorous, serious, nasty, businesslike, friendly* or *obsequious*. The tone reflects your essay's mood or attitude as revealed by its language. Is your subject matter serious or humorous, scary or light? Is the writing formal or informal?

Look at these two passages written by the same author—Mark Twain. Which piece denotes a seriousness of purpose and which is intended to make us laugh?

1. "'At the great baseball match on Tuesday, while I was engaged in hurrahing, a small boy walked off with an English-made brown silk umbrella belonging to me, and forgot to bring it back. I will pay $5 for the return of that umbrella in good condition to my house on Farmington Avenue. I do not want the boy (in an active state) but will pay two hundred dollars for his corpse.' *Samuel L. Clemens*." (published in the *Hartford Courant*, 1875)

2. "That is the basest of all instincts, passions, vices—the most hateful. That one thing puts [man] below the rats, the grubs, the trichinae. He is the only creature that inflicts pain for sport, knowing it to *be* pain. But if the cat knows she is inflicting pain when she plays with the frightened mouse, then we must make an exception here; we must grant that in one detail man is the moral peer of the cat. *All* creatures kill—there seems to be no exception; but of the whole list, man is the only one that kills for fun; he is the only one that kills in malice, the only one that kills for revenge." (From *Mark Twain's Autobiography*, "The Nature of Man.")

If you read carefully, you heard the humor in the first example and the seriousness in the second example.

LEVEL OF LANGUAGE

If you have ever sent an email or text message, or posted to a discussion board, or blogged or twittered, you are familiar with the shortcuts and informality of the writing. For example, "LOL" and "R" and "U" and "K" are all common abbreviations when using these formats. Slang is common as is relaxed sentence structure. However, no matter how familiar you are with these shortcuts or how much fun they are to write, they are never acceptable in the papers you write in your college courses. It would be like wearing jeans to a job interview or a bikini to a wedding reception—inappropriate. So save these abbreviations and other lack of conventions for your Facebook or blog or email, and remember to chose the appropriate level of language for the occasion.

Your tone determines your level of language. This, in turn, helps you to determine your word choice, sentence and essay structure, and level of documentation, among other areas. Although there are many levels of language, the three basic levels are informal, middle, and formal. By analyzing your subject matter and your audience, you will be able to choose which level of language to use.

- **Formal** prose follows all the rules of usage; does not use contractions, slang, or first or second person; and is properly documented. In a formal essay the writer is a silent presence behind the words.
- **Middle-level** prose also follows the rules of usage, does not use slang or first or second person and uses informal documentation, but contractions are generally accepted. The writer is also silent presence behind the words but to a lesser degree in the middle-level essay.
- **Informal** writing has a relaxed style and follows a less rigid structure. It tends to be more personal than the formal or middle, expressing subjective opinions. In an informal essay the writer speaks directly to the reader in a conversational style.

PRACTICE 1 LEVEL OF LANGUAGE: Suppose you get a ticket for speeding, but you think it is unfair because the speed limit is not posted from where you exited the highway onto the road. You decide to write to your friend at another college about it, use it as a subject for a class essay, and write to your state's Secretary of Transportation complaining about the lack of a posted speed sign. Here's how portions of the letters might be written. For the following three passages determine which is informal, middle, and formal:

Essay 2—English Comp. 1
On my way home after dropping a friend off at her house, I saw red lights flashing in my rear view mirror. I pulled over to see what the police officer wanted. I was stopped by for speeding—going 45 m.p.h. in a 35 m.p.h. zone. Although I explained to the officer that the speed limit wasn't posted since I entered the road five miles before, he gave me a ticket anyway. This is an example of local towns setting up speed traps to gain money. It's wrong and speed traps ought to be illegal.

1. _____

Mario,
You're not going to believe what happened last Friday after I dropped Joanie off at her place. Remember I met her last week at the club? Well, a cop pulled me over for speeding (I was only going 45 after getting off the highway). I got busted with a $60 ticket. It wasn't even posted and I had traveled on that road for about 5 miles already. How was I to know it was a 35 m.p.h. speed zone? Now I'm going to have to go to court to fight this. What a speed trap! What a night!

2. _____

To the Honorable Chairman Edgardo Rivera:
This letter is to inform you of a "speed trap" located on Route 565 in Elktown. Last Friday evening, April 15, I received a speeding ticket for traveling at 45 m.p.h. in a 35 m.p.h. zone; however, from where I exited the Turnpike to where I was stopped, a distance of five miles, no speed limit sign was posted.

3. _____

Choosing the right level of language for your audience is important. If you had used the formal tone to write to your friend, he or she might have thought you had been abducted by aliens and replaced with an English teacher. And if you had used the informal tone for your composition essay or letter to the Secretary of Transportation, you would have scored one strike against your case with the inappropriate level of language and tone.

READING

In this textbook, you will read works from different parts of the world conveying ideas from many different time periods and cutures. You may be familiar with some of the authors or topics, or they may all be new to you. In either case, view the readings in this text as a way to see and understand parts of the world without traveling around the world or back in time.

Before you settle into your favorite chair, you need to learn how to read. Of course you know how to decipher the sounds on the page into words and also to read for pleasure. That's not what we mean by reading on a college level. In the academic world the reading you do for your classes requires you to not only read the words, but also to comprehend their meaning by using critical thinking. You read to *understand* the material—the author's point.

ANNOTATING THE TEXT

Always grab a pen or pencil before you start to read. You should write right in the book—usually in the margins of the piece you are reading. Although this may go against everything you've been taught about books, marking the text while you read is not only all right, but it is one of the most important steps in your understanding of the material. Marking the text will focus you on the reading and your thought processes. You will be engaging with the author's words, thoughts, and ideas. There is a connection between you and the text.

Here is a chart of markings you may want to use in this and your other textbooks:

Mark	Meaning
?	I don't understand this; ask the professor
!	What?! This material is surprising.
*	Note this; this is important.

You may also want to underline passages or words or use a highlighter. However, you should use care with underlining and highlighting so that only the important ideas—not most of the text—is accented. By marking the text every time you read an assignment, the important passages will stand out and you will be more easily able to contribute to and understand the discussion of the piece. You have engaged the text in a meaningful manner.

READING CRITICALLY

In the academic world, the reading you do for your classes requires you to not only read the words but also to analyze and interpret their meaning by reading critically. When you are looking only for facts, you read non-critically. The nursing student might read a book to learn anatomy of the human body, the engineering student might read a book to learn mathematical formulas for bridge construction, and the geography student might read a book to learn the longitude and latitude of countries. When reading non-critically, you may also be looking for an accepted interpretation of an event, for example in history. In these cases, you find the facts and can restate them. Reading critically, however, goes beyond this.

The critical reader, having understood what a writing states, looks at what a text does (the structure) and what the text means (interpretation). You, the critical reader, analyze the structure: Is it showing causes? Is it making an argument? Does it use pathos? Is it finding a connection by comparing, or is it contrasting to make a point? Then you analyze and interpret the writer's thoughts and information from the text to determine what it means and evaluate it on its own merits without interjecting your opinions or prior knowledge.

Critical reading and critical thinking work in concert. Critical thinking depends on critical reading because only when you have understood the text can you think about it critically. When you examine a text critically, you examine the logical inferences and think about the validity of what you have read. Your decision about the text is based on your evaluation of the evidence supplied. Here's an example: "Teen arrestees often test positive for recent drug use. The National Institute of Justices Arrestee and Drug Monitoring System (ADAM) drug testing program found that 66 percent of underage male arrestees tested positive for marijuana." Did you ask yourself what "often" means or how many teens were in the sample of the 66 percent or what geographic area it covered? You may or may not find that the information is valid; however, if you are not reading critically, you are not analyzing nor evaluating the information, and you will not know if it accurately represents the information.

Here's another example. Let's say that a friend of yours says to you in a casual conversation, "You know, the AIDS epidemic was started by the U.S. government. The virus was developed in a government lab at a military base and then spread around in inner-city neighborhoods to cut the population of young minority men." Depending on your background, experiences and cultural influences, your response might be, "That's stupid. The United States government would never do something like that!" Or you might say, "Makes sense to me. I'm not surprised the government did that considering all the other stuff they've done to people over the years."

One of the goals of your college professors is to encourage you to question and not to accept at face value statements like the AIDS example above and to examine with a critical eye ideas that might appear to be valid but after critically thinking about them may not be.

In the example above, let's assume you're the one who immediately said, "That's stupid. The United States government would never do anything like that," and now you're told about the experiments carried out by the U.S. Public Health Service (PHS) on 399 poor, black sharecroppers in Tuskegee, Alabama from 1932 until 1972. The men, most of whom were illiterate, were all in the late stages of syphilis. They were told they were being treated for "bad blood," but they were not being treated at all. Rather, the PHS was waiting for them to die so that autopsies could be performed to determine if syphilis affected blacks differently from whites. Respected news anchor Harry Reasoner of *Sixty Minutes* said the experiment "used human beings as laboratory animals in a long and inefficient study of how long it takes syphilis to kill someone." Can you still be so certain that "the United States government would never do something like that"?

Conversely, if you're the one who fully believes the allegation that the U.S. government committed this heinous act, shouldn't you be asking yourself why the government would unleash a deadly virus that it had no hope of controlling once it was "out of the bottle," much like the first time the Germans used poison gas in World War One and the wind shifted, blowing the gas back and killing their own soldiers. Wouldn't the government be aware of that kind of potential backlash? Also, if the intent was to cut the population of young minority men, why did the virus, when it was first identified in 1981, hit white middle-class homosexual males with such devastating effect?

Today, with the research tools that we have at our disposal, especially the internet, we are in a position as never before in history to be able to critically examine the claims and counter-claims of all those who have a certain agenda they want us to buy into. In the 2000 presidential primaries, when some supporters of one of John McCain's opponents said that McCain had fathered a mixed-race baby out of wedlock, how much time did it take for people to discover that the "mixed-race baby" was actually a Bangladeshi child that McCain and his wife Cindi had adopted? In the presidential race of 2008, how difficult was it to determine that Barrack Obama is a Baptist and not a Muslim?

If you know where and how to look and research, you have a power that no demagogue or slick salesman can take away from you. But first you have to train your critical reading and critical thinking skills to meet the challenge. This critical scholarship is well described by Sir Francis Bacon, an English statesman, philosopher and author: "For myself, I found that I was fitted for nothing so well as for the study of Truth; as having a mind nimble and versatile enough to catch the resemblances of things ... and at the same time steady enough to fix and distinguish their subtler differences; as being gifted by nature with desire to seek, patience to doubt, fondness to meditate, slowness to assert, readiness to consider, carefulness to dispose and set in order; and as being a man that neither affects what is new nor admires what is old, and that hates every kind of imposture."

THE WRITING PROCESS

WRITING—the very word may scare you or make you uncomfortable. Perhaps the only writing you've ever done has been in the form of a school assignment or something for your boss. Many people share your discomfort because they think they need to write perfectly the first time they address a subject. Few successful writers have ever achieved this. Writers think about their subject, prewrite in some form, outline, draft, edit, draft, revise, and draft and edit again until the words say what the writers mean. And then they have to proofread. This is called the **WRITING CYCLE** or the **WRITING PROCESS**.

THE WRITING CYCLE

The writing cycle consists of prewriting, organizing, drafting, revising, editing and proofreading. The process is not linear, but rather cyclic in that you might go back two steps before going forward one. For example, after revising you may realize you need to explain more in paragraph three, so you go back to your prewriting strategies to get more ideas. You would then draft them, and again edit. This cycle continues until you are pleased with what you've written (or as a friend who rewrites constantly says, you run out of time).

PREWRITING

Several ways to get your ideas flowing and down on paper include freewriting, brainstorming, the six questions, and mapping.

FREEWRITING (also known as nonstop writing or speedwriting) is an effective cure for writer's block. It consists of writing on a subject **without stopping** for ten minutes. Either at a computer or with a piece of paper, you sit quietly for a minute thinking about your topic; then after setting your timer for ten minutes you begin to write. There is one main rule: DON'T STOP. If you make a mistake, don't go back to correct it. <u>Spelling, grammar, punctuation, neatness do not count</u>. If you run out of ideas, repeat the last thing you wrote, you wrote, you wrote, until the next idea pops into your head, and it will. Ideas *will* come to you from deep down inside. At the end of ten minutes, stop writing.

Here's an example on the topic "Conspicuous Consumption in the US":

So I have to write this I don't know what to write lots of things come to mind cars furs mcmansions. We have a lot of money here but this stuff is part of our society it is who we are. eEveryone has cell phones and mpc players and dvds and big cars. We think these things are necessary ubt we also use them to show how successful we are. Guys show they make money to get girls and women do it show they are successful and kids want to fit in. The poor kid swho doesn't have the latest things get teased. Even if a guy is a gcreep we admire him if he shows off his stuff in what he has bought and then its okay. I ageee that we don't show off our good qualities as much as we sow off what we've acquired.

This freewrite has the beginning ideas for the writer's topic. She's established that she agrees there is conspicuous consumption in the United States and has written some reasons why.

You can also freewrite if you need to think of a topic for an essay assignment. You do it the same way, except that you have no definite topic on which you are concentrating. If you can't stop thinking about what happened at work last night, you need to clear your mind before beginning to write; otherwise, you won't be able to concentrate on your essay assignment. Freewriting will get it off your mind so you'll be free to concentrate on your schoolwork.

BRAINSTORMING is thinking about your topic and then writing down every word or phrase that comes to mind in the form of a list. Don't stop until you have about 15 words or phrases on your list. Don't worry if the words aren't related, and don't try to write sentences.

Here's a brainstorm on "The Effects of Civil War":
1. generals make decisions
2. civilians have to leave their houses
3. the sniper killed his brother
4. the town got bombed
5. civilians are accidentally bombed
6. the city has machine guns
7. the women have no where to go
8. they lose all their possessions
9. civilians die
10. the soldiers are young men
11. the old woman informer dies
12. the woman is shrieking in anguish
13. the painting shows chaos
14. the sniper feels remorse
15. baby dead
16. family against family

This list becomes the starting point for the ideas you'll write about in your essay. You can also brainstorm when you need to think of a topic, instead of being assigned one. The same principles apply—open your mind and start listing all the things that come to you.

THE SIX QUESTIONS are based on the questions journalists ask to gather the facts for a story: Who? What? Where? Why? When? and How? By answering these questions, you'll generate ideas.

<u>Who:</u>   the women in stories
<u>What:</u>   repressed
<u>Where:</u> in their homes, specifically
<u>Why:</u>   the husbands think they are "helping" their wives
<u>When:</u> Victorian era, 19th century
<u>How:</u>   by not letting them think for themselves or do what they want

MAPPING is a visual depiction of your ideas and their relationship. In the center of the map is your topic or main idea. The circles coming off this topic are the main ideas, and the next level of circles contains the details of the main ideas.

ORGANIZING

Once you are satisfied with your prewriting efforts and you have a sufficient number of ideas about your topic, you should organize your material in the most effective way possible.

A rough outline does not have the same structure of a formal outline, but it is similar in that it gives you a form to follow. Outlines are easier to change than drafts and once they are finished, you don't have to think about what comes next because it's right there in the outline.

INFORMAL OUTLINING

Here's a sample rough outline for the topic "Jonathan Swift's Use of Irony in 'A Modest Proposal.'" The writer has chosen to argue that Swift's use of irony was an effective tool to make people aware of the problems confronting the Irish in the 1700's.

1. Intro—Use statistics of Ireland during 1700's. Add transition. Thesis: Swift's use of irony is an effective tool to highlight the plight of the Irish in the 1700's.
2. English absentee landlords/gentlemen
   - Hunting youths instead of deer
   - Live in England to avoid paying tithes to the church
   - Will encourage to purchase Irish goods
3. Shopkeepers
   - Will charge fair prices
   - Profit from new dish
   - Will increase business/profit
4. Husband
   - Inducement to marriage
   - Treat pregnant wives as well as their farm animals
   - Will stay around and care for their children
5. Conclusion—tie into thesis, give concluding thoughts

You can see at a glance what the basic ideas for the essay are going to be.

FORMAL OUTLINING

Many writers find a formal outline useful for keeping their writing on track. A formal outline establishes degrees of importance: it subordinates certain ideas to others by indenting them and using a different set of number or letters to rank them.

Suppose, for instance, you are writing an essay on UFO sightings and you have many points you want to bring up. A formal outline would help you to sort out all the factors.

I.   Introduction: use quotations, transition, thesis statement
II. Belief in UFOs remain popular
   A. Over a fifty-year period, thousands of sightings have been reported
   B. Much of the public and astronomers take UFOs seriously
   C. Television shows and movies about UFOs are top-rated
   D. Some government officials believe UFOs are real
III. No reliable reasons for believing in UFOs have been presented
   A. Reports of UFOs do not address other explanations
      1. Swamp gas
      2. Tricks of light
      3. Airplane lights
      4. Weather balloons
   B. Reports don't provide independent chains of evidence
   C. Believers rely on faulty logic—"government conspiracy" theory
IV. Conclusion: Belief in UFOs relies on faith rather than scientific explanation.

DRAFTING

Now that you've thought about your topic, done some prewriting, and written your rough outline and perhaps formal outline, it's time to write your rough draft. Using your prewriting (freewrite, map, outline) as your guide, write a draft of the essay. You are taking the information from your prewriting, phrasing it in complete sentences, and filling in the gaps with transitions and your own understanding of the subject.

SOME TIPS ABOUT DRAFTING:

• **Drafts are for the writer**: Your brain is processing the information and making connections as you write down your ideas. You may also find yourself discovering new ideas as you are writing your first drafts. Because of this, you may need to change your thesis or supporting information. Remember, you are really drafting for yourself—to understand your ideas and put them into words. You might be unhappy with your early results. Don't agonize over every word and sentence. Just get your ideas down on paper even if they sound silly or awkward. You can always go back and fix them later – that's what revision is for.

• **Drafting takes time:** The more complicated your writing task is, the more time you should allow yourself for drafting. As you discover new ideas and connections, you need the time to incorporate them into your plan. Don't procrastinate; rather work consistently on your essay.

• **Save your drafts:** Writing early drafts on the computer makes revising and editing much easier. Whether you are word-processing or handwriting, save all of your drafts because you might come back to ideas that you previously discarded.

REVISING

If drafting is for the writer, revision is for the reader. During revision you consider your writing from your audience's point of view. In fact, to revise means literally to "re-see" or "re-look" at your writing. When you revise, you are looking at the parts of your essay and making sure that each part works together to make a coherent whole. You may need to change the order of your information, expand on certain sections, or cut irrelevant information in others. Often, you will need to go back to the drafting stage and re-work parts of your paper.

Most writers find it helpful to have someone else read their writing at this stage. A reader who is unfamiliar with your essay can help you identify which parts are working and which parts are still unclear. Also, revision works best when you have some time to let your writing sit. You will be better able to look at your writing with a reader's eye if you can put it aside for a while before working on it again.

NOTE: Prewriting, drafting and revising are not independent steps but rather stages within a cyclical process. Good writers move back and forth between planning, drafting, and revising many times during the course of creating a single document.

EDITING/PROOFREADING

Producing a clean, error-free final draft isn't easy. Even the most carefully edited professional publications occasionally contain errors. Most readers understand this and aren't bothered by such infrequent problems. However, repeated or numerous errors undermine your authority and disrupt your communication with the reader. To edit well, it helps to know the basics of grammar and mechanics, but equally important are good editing practices, which require patience and attention to detail.

1. **Know your common errors**. What types of errors do you tend to make most often? Do you have problems with subject-verb agreement or with run-ons? Look for patterns in your errors and focus on eliminating the more serious and higher frequency errors first. Then check for less obvious ones.

2. **Edit your "hard" copy**. If you're writing at the computer, check your work quickly on the screen and run a spell-check. Then print out a copy to go over meticulously, looking for anything you may have missed, keeping in mind that the spell-check will not catch all errors and sometimes may replace the correct

word with the wrong word. Don't rely on the grammar checker. It is unreliable for many errors.

3. **Edit actively**. Go through your draft carefully, pen in hand. Actually touch each word with your pen. Look especially at word endings. Have you dropped any *s* or *ed* endings? Does each pronoun have a clear antecedent?

4. **Edit with a partner**. Read your draft slowly aloud while your partner, pen in hand, reads another copy of the draft. Have your partner stop you whenever there might be a difference from what you read to what is on your paper. Discuss each questionable difference, such as punctuation mark or word choice.

All this may seem tedious at first, but it is worth the effort. A well-edited final draft makes a good impression; it shows you care about your writing. When readers sense you care, they'll care, also.

Use this checklist to evaluate your essay before submitting it to your professor:

Can you point to a **thesis statement** in the essay? Is it clearly stated? If not, does the **body** of the paper need revising, or does the thesis statement need to be polished to reflect your ideas?
Are the ideas in the essay clearly **organized**? If the reader had to, could he or she write an **outline** from your essay?
Are there any serious fallacies in the **logic** of your argument? Does each point flow logically to the next? Have you used clear **transitions** to go from one idea to the next?
Are **paragraphs adequately developed?** Does each sentence **support** the point of that paragraph? Do the body paragraphs fulfill the **purpose** of the thesis statement?
Is your **word choice** specific? Does each word mean what you think it means? Have you considered the **connotation** of each word?
Is the **introduction** clear and developed? Have you drawn in your reader? Does the **conclusion** do what you want it to? Does the conclusion reflect the thesis statement (but not too simplistically)?
Is the **tone** consistent and appropriate for your audience and the subject? Have you avoided slang and informality? At the other extreme, have you avoided sounding pretentious?
Personal Grammatical Issues: Have you paid special attention to your areas of writing weakness and checked these areas for their correctness?

When you've finished with the checklist, go through the essay again on the computer screen and hard copy—just in case you changed something and created a new error where one did not exist before. A word of caution: don't be one of those students who show up late for class empty-handed, tearfully explaining that the printer in the library broke down or your printer at home jammed five minutes before class. Leave time for such emergencies. They don't happen often, but when they do, they always happen at the worst possible time.

AN OVERVIEW OF THE WRITING PROCESS

1. After you've read the assignment, grab a blank sheet or two of paper, and use one of the prewriting strategies to collect your thoughts about the assignment. Do this for ten to fifteen minutes. Some students prefer to type and turn off the monitors on their computers to type their ideas without the distraction of a grammar or spelling checker. Either way, don't worry about what you write— just let yourself go. Remember not to stop writing the entire time; don't cross out words as you go; don't police yourself in anyway. Most of all, don't be afraid of what you're writing; no one else will ever see it. After 10 or 15 minutes, stop. Read what you've written.

2. What you're looking at are raw materials for building your essay. Underline, circle or put checks in the margins next to those ideas you think you should keep and see if you can piece together a scratch outline. If you find you don't have enough ideas to support your thesis, you'll need to use a prewriting strategy again. If so, repeat step one until you have enough information.

3. Once your prewriting is complete, begin to assemble your outline. This will be the blueprint for your essay. If you get stuck filling in some of the blanks (more support for paragraph 2? a better point for paragraph 3?), go back to step one and try one of the other prewriting activities. Make sure the outline is "solid" and that you can write your essay based upon it. Ask yourself: Is my thesis strong? How are my topic sentences? Does each support the thesis? Do I have enough support in each of my paragraphs? Are my ideas presented in a logical order? If you can answer "yes" to these questions, you are ready for step four.

4. Once your planning is complete, you start writing. Following your outline, write your first draft. If you follow through on this, you will feel superb—a sense of accomplishment. Feel free to share your draft with your classmates or a trusted friend. Maybe you're unsure of a line you've written or perhaps you think a paragraph is under-developed. Ask your classmates or friends for their opinion.

5. Now comes revision. Print your draft and look it over critically. This means **honestly** evaluating its strengths and weakness. Look at your word choice, sentence structure, organization, and coherence. Ask yourself if you would want to read this essay.

6. Next you need to edit/proofread your essay for the details (did you accidentally write the same same word twice? Or did you transpose lettres?). Go over it several times (hopefully you've left enough time to take a break in between readings), looking just for those little errors. Be sure you are reading the paper copy, and not the computer screen. If you are pleased with what you've written, you are ready to hand it in knowing that you've given it your best effort.

THE PARAGRAPH

Learning to write clear, well-developed paragraphs is important step because paragraphs are the basic building blocks of essays. In the same way that a combination of letters can create a word and words come together to create a sentence, paragraphs are put together to form an essay. In academic writing, a paragraph is a group of sentences that discuss the same topic. ALL of the sentences are relevant to the topic of the paragraph. In other words, no sentence is about anything else.

Just the way essays are held together by thesis statements, paragraphs are governed by topic sentences. Think of topic sentences as "mini thesis statements." Accordingly, they must follow the same criteria established for thesis statements: no announcements, not too broad, not too narrow. Topic sentences usually are not in the form of a question.

You arrive at a topic sentence the same way you arrive at a thesis statement, by having a point to make. Your topic sentences emerge from your prewriting in the form of ideas you've come up with to support your thesis.

Each paragraph should have enough supporting sentences and details to substantiate the topic sentence. Let's look at this paragraph's development:

For the unfortunate M. Lantin of "The False Gems," emotional distress stems from the betrayal by his first wife and the reflection it casts against his own desire. He begins the story finding joy with a woman he falsely believes to be virtuous (260-261). After her death, he discovers she was not who he thought she was (263). He then falls victim to the shallow trappings of the rich by buying things and going places he never did with his first wife (264). The tale ends with him being made miserable by second wife (265). Lantin began this story happy with a lie and ultimately resigned himself to a depressing truth.

It has a topic sentence (the first sentence) and it appears to have adequate support. However, if you look carefully at the supporting sentences, you will see that no specific information is given; it is all vague allusions and generalizations. With specific quotes and points from the reading added, the writer's support is stronger and more convincing.

Here is the same paragraph with the addition of more effective supporting detail:

For the unfortunate M. Lantin of "The False Gems," emotional distress stems from the betrayal by his first wife and the reflection it casts against his own desire. He begins the story finding joy with a woman he falsely believes to be virtuous. We learn that "[t]he young girl was a perfect type of the virtuous woman whom every sensible young man dreams of one day winning for life" and that she has "the charm of angelic modesty" (260). After her death, he discovers she was not who he thought she was. While trying to pawn her "paste" jewels, he discovers that they were real and expensive presents from an admirer, and he wonders "a present from whom? For what?" (263). After getting the money for the gems, he then falls victim to the shallow trappings of the rich by buying things and going places he never did with his first wife. He "lunched at Voisin's and drank wine worth twenty francs a bottle," and he "was not bored at the theater" (264). The tale ends with him being made miserable by second wife, "a very virtuous woman, with a violent temper" (265). Lantin began this story happy with a lie and ultimately resigned himself to a depressing truth.

Here is another example of a well-supported body paragraph:

Another application in literature of Charles Darwin's theory of "Natural Selection, or Survival of the Fittest," in which a species' evolution requires that the strong survive and the weak perish, occurs in Jack London's short story, "To Build a Fire." The primary reason for his "law," as Darwin calls it, is to ensure that future generations of the species in question will possess only the favorable traits of their ancestors and will thus survive and flourish, and the weak or inferior specimens will fall by the wayside. We see this natural filtration process at work early in the story as London tells us that "the man" (he is never named — simply an anonymous representative of the species *Homo sapiens*), a newcomer to the Yukon territory, is in trouble because he doesn't understand his surroundings. London says " . . . the absence of sun from the sky, the tremendous cold, and the strangeness and weirdness of it all made no impression on the man. The trouble with him was that he was without imagination"(518-519). Here the author is setting the stage for the man's destruction because the man lacks the necessary Darwinian skills to survive—while the dog, the "lower" species, a "dumb animal," knows instinctually how to cope with the harsh environment: "The animal was depressed by the tremendous cold. It knew that it was no time for traveling. Its instinct told it a truer tale than was told to the man by the man's judgment (519)." As the story plays out to its conclusion, the man's misunderstanding of the environment causes him to make mistake after deadly mistake while the dog watches—and waits. Ultimately, as the last little flame flickers out, dooming the man, the dog's Darwinian instinct for survival engages. Leaving the frozen body of the man in the snow, " . . . [the dog] turned and trotted up the trail in the direction of the camp where, it knew, were the other food-providers and fire-providers (530)."

All topic sentences (as well as thesis statements) have two things in common: they have a SUBJECT and a JUDGMENT about that subject. In this example, the subject of the thesis statement in the introductory paragraph (the last sentence) is Darwinian survival of the fittest, and the judgment is an assertion that Jack London's short story demonstrates how it works. The subject of the topic sentence is the man and the judgment is that he is in trouble because of his lack of understanding of his environment. The supporting sentences use quotes from the story to provide specific evidence in support of the topic sentence.

As for length, paragraphs should be as long as they need to be to fully cover the topic presented. This means there is no set length for a paragraph; you should have a sense of when more needs to be said or when you've said enough. Having said that, however, a general guideline for a body paragraph is six to ten sentences.

PRACTICE 2 DEVELOPING PARAGRAPHS: Indicate by placing the appropriate letter in the blank whether each of the following paragraphs has an adequate topic sentence (T) or whether the topic sentence is missing (M).

_____1. American children watch an average of three to fours hours of television daily (Hirschberg 455). They watch thousands of commercials each year, many of which are for alcohol, junk food and toys. According to the American Academy of Child and Adolescent Psychiatry, children who watch a lot of television, defined as more than two hours a day, are more likely to suffer adverse effects than those who watch fewer than two hours of television. They have lower grades in school, read fewer books, exercise less, and are more likely to be overweight (456). Violence, sexuality, race and gender stereotypes, drug and alcohol abuse are common themes of television programs. Young children are impressionable and may assume that what they see on television is "typical, safe, and acceptable" (458). They often cannot tell the difference between the fantasies presented on television and the realities of everyday life.

_____2. According to Des Kennedy in "Rats–Who's Racing Whom?" one pair of rats is capable of producing 359 million offspring in one year if all survive. Yet, it is not in the interests of the rat colony to produce so many, and rats have evolved with the advantage of birth control; females are capable of spontaneous abortion as well as the ability to physiologically "terminate already fertilized embryos and absorb them back into the body" (469). Females will also kill members of the litter if there is overcrowding in the colony, and weak young may not be fed or be forced out of the litter. Further, rats will not hesitate to fight to the death and cannibalism is common, which leads to "an average rat life expectancy of three months, with less than 10 percent of rats surviving more than a year" (469). And yet rats continue to keep pace with the human population.

_____3. Although many studies have shown that watching television can be detrimental to a child's development, other studies have indicated that watching certain types of television programs can actually be beneficial to the children who watch them. Shows such as *Sesame Street* and *Barney* help teach young children how to spell and master arithmetical concepts. Bernard McAfee's study, for example, showed that many pre-school children were fascinated by "The Count" on *Sesame Street*, leading to an understanding of the role of numbers (147). Other educational shows such as *Bob the Builder* and *Thomas the Tank Engine* combine interesting stories with lessons about how to socialize and face problems in life. Children are just learning how to interact with others, and these shows give them guidelines on how to do this successfully.

_____4. In Liam O'Flaherty's short story "The Sniper," the experiences of the central character highlight O'Flaherty's theme of the particular inhumanity of a civil war. In the opening of the story, we learn that "heavy guns roared" and "machine-guns and rifles broke the silence of the night" (506). The main character, the Republican sniper, is described as having "the eyes of a man who is used to looking at death" (506). As the plot evolves, the sniper does not flinch when he shoots the opposing group's soldier whose head was now "hanging lifelessly over the turret" or even an old woman, an informer, who falls "with a shriek to the ground" (507). The sniper "smiled" when taking the shot that would kill the opposing side's sniper. Only when he sees his enemy's body falling did he feel "the lust of battle [die] in him" and he was "bitten by remorse...cursing the war, cursing himself, cursing everybody" (508). But this is short-lived and the "cloud of fear scattered from his mind and he laughed" (508). O'Flaherty depicts this character as a young man whose human emotions, including his relationships with his fellow countrymen, have been totally deadened by this war.

_____5. The 2006 United Nations report on World Population estimates the earth's human population will be 9.2 billion in 2050 (600). The world population trend is spiraling downward, yet 97 percent of growth will take place in less developed regions, "with the African population increase estimated at 17 million per year, giving it the highest growth rate of 2.36 percent" (603). Africa's share in population growth will be 55 percent in 2045-2050, and its "total share of world population is projected at 19.8 percent in 2050" (603). Ten countries will account for "[s]ixty percent of the world population increase (605). India will grow by 21 percent, and China will grow by 15 percent (605). On the other hand, Europe's and Northern America's "share of the world total decreased to 17.5 in 1998"; the report predicts this decrease will continue "to 11.5 in 2050" (605). In addition, in these regions, "the number of older persons exceeded that of children for the first time" (601).

_____ 6. In "The Story of an Hour," Louise Mallard, a woman living in the 1890's—a period when women were still seen as no more than extensions of their husbands—looks forward to the freedom she will now have as an individual. After hearing of her husband's untimely death, she, at first, retreats to her bedroom sobbing. But in the quiet of her room, she "abandons" herself to the thought that she is now "free, free, free!"; she relishes the thought that "she would live for herself" (517). She looks forward to the "long procession of years to come that would belong to her absolutely" and she "opened and spread her arms out to them in welcome" (517). She had wished that life would be short, but now she "breathed a quick prayer that life might be long" (518). Although she loved her husband "sometimes," she reasons "[w]hat could love ...count for in the face of this possession of self-assertion" and she "recognized [it] as the strongest impulse of her being" (517). She descends the stairs with "triumph in her eyes...like a goddess of Victory" (518).

ORGANIZATION

All well-written essays have some type of organization—a logical plan with a coherent flow of ideas.

THE INTRODUCTION

Introductions typically have two parts: the "grabber" opener and the thesis statement.

THE "GRABBER" OPENER

An interesting introduction is one that "grabs" the reader's attention. You should make a point to write an engaging introduction, one that makes the reader want to continue reading. There are several ways to spice up your intro-duction: personal narrative, quotation, current event, related fact or statistic, or question.

PERSONAL NARRATIVE relates a strong or dramatic or surprising story about the topic. The story should be no more than a paragraph long and come from an event that you have personally lived through, or you know someone who has and you are relating his or her story. A good strong narrative captures the reader's attention. However, don't make one up; readers can usually sense that you aren't being sincere, and the bond of trust necessary for writers to com-municate to their readers will be broken. If the reader can't believe you about this, why should he or she believe you about the rest of your essay? Here's an example:

> My mother enrolled me in dancing school when I was thirteen years old, and I distinctly remember my first class. I walked into a room filled with fifteen other girls, all stragers to me. I felt scared and alone and butterflies entered in my stomach as I sat with the other girls who would soon become my closest friends. My dance instructor, Ms. Joyce, told us she was a very strong and independent woman, and she hoped that we would also come feel the same way about ourselves. Back then this made no sense at all to me. But as I grew older, I began to realize just how much those words would play an important role in my life. Although my inspiration came from dancing class, all young women need some strong role model who will guide them to achieve the goals they set for themselves. (This was the introduction to an essay about how roles models are important to develop-ing young women's self-esteem.)

A QUOTATION, from a famous or not-so-famous person, your grandmother, for example, is a skillful way to grab your reader's attention as long as it relates to your thesis. Quotations can be humorous or serious, poetry or prose, modern or ancient. There are many good books of quotations published, for example, *Bartlett's Familiar Quotations*; having one in your personal library is a good idea. Here are some examples:

> My grandmother had numerous sayings all meant to keep her family safe: "Throw salt over your shoulder to keep away the 'evil eye.'" "Don't walk under ladders. You'll get bad luck." "Have some chicken soup. It will make your cold go away." She might not be right about the first two, but science has now proven that many homeopathic remedies, including chicken soup for a cold, do work. (This was the introduction for an essay about homeo-pathic cures.)

A CURRENT EVENT is a recent, important event reported in the news, and because of this it would be familiar to your readers. You can use more than one event if they are about the same issue. After relating the incident or incidents, you tie it (or them) into your thesis.

> Last week an Oregon jury ordered the tobacco giant Phillip Morris to pay $81 million to the family of a smoker who died of lung cancer. Two months ago a San Francisco jury awarded $50 million to a former smoker with inoperable lung cancer. Last year, the tobacco industry and 40 states reached a $206 billion settlement to end lawsuits. These large verdicts are putting an end to the era of the "glamorous" and "harmless" cigarette and forcing tobacco manufacturers to admit their history of lying to the public about the dangers of cigarette smoking. (This was the introduction for an essay about the history of cigarette manufacturers glamorizing smoking while they knew the dangers.)

A FACT OR STATISTIC from a reliable source, a newspaper or journal for example, can catch your reader's attention if it is unusual or startling.

> Although earning on average $17,000 less than their white counterparts, black graduates of Ivy League colleges earn twice as much as black graduates and over $20,000 more than white graduates from non-Ivy League colleges. Removing Affirmative Action would raise white enrollment by only one percent according to the former presidents of Princeton and Harvard Universities. Also, more so than their white peers, black graduates of Ivy League colleges are likely to become active in their community as civic leaders (*Newsweek* 49). These statistics strongly argue for maintaining our present system of leveling the playing field for minorities through Affirmative Action. (This was the introduction for an essay about why Affirmative Action should be retained.)

AN INTERESTING QUESTION can be asked and then later answered in your essay's body or conclusion. When a rhetorical question is asked for effect, no answer is actually expected. This type of question is meant to get your reader thinking about an idea that you'll present in your thesis statement.

> Can you imagine a place where you can catch and cook a trout without moving a step or taking the fish off the line? Would you like to see a place where tens of thousand of gallons of hot water roar 150 feet high, and the cold water hurtles down 308 feet at a speed of about 60,000 gallons per second? If these are still not interesting you, how about the excitement of observing grizzly bears walking right outside your car or even your tent? This place is Yellowstone, the first national park in the world. Yellowstone

is so famous in the world that recent immigrants know of Yellowstone even before they know the English language. Yellowstone National Park embodies all one needs for a relaxing or exciting vacation. (This was the introduction for an essay about why Yellowstone is the ideal vacation spot.)

THE THESIS STATEMENT

The thesis statement is the sentence that explains what your essay will be about. Like the topic sentence in a paragraph, it always has two features: a *subject* and a *judgment* about that subject. It serves as the structure or blueprint for the essay, and tells the reader what point you are going to make. Sometimes, it also shows how you are going to support that point or some elements within that point. Usually, but not always, it is placed at the end of the introductory paragraph.

Sometimes students run into trouble with their thesis statement because they don't have a firm idea of what their paper is about. So they write a vague thesis statement and, of course, the rest of the paper rambles about, hoping to make a point. Before you can formulate a thesis, you must know about your intended subject. This is where prewriting activities come into play. If you are unsure of the purpose or point of your essay, then return to prewriting until you are have a firm subject and something to say about it.

Let's say you have used prewriting strategies, and you know what you want to write about and which points you will use to support your thesis. Before you commit your ideas to paper, ask yourself some questions:

1. Is this point worth my reader's time?
2. Is it too vague or narrow?
3. Is the point too obvious?
4. Can this point be effectively supported?
5. Does it announce the subject rather than making a statement about it? (It shouldn't. Don't write "I am going to write about how Polonius's advice to Hamlet is still applicable today." Just write it.)

Announcing your subject is comfortable for many students; however, it is a weak way to start your essay and you should avoid using it. When you announce your subject you place yourself in the subject position. In the example in #5 above, the subject of the essay isn't "I"; it is Polonius. The best way to eliminate announcements is to cross out all the words before the actual subject, in this case "I am going to write about." Now your thesis reads, "Polonius's advice to Hamlet is still applicable today." This is stronger, tighter, more interesting writing.

Once you've determined you have a strong point that can be covered in the number of pages assigned with sufficient evidence that does not belittle your reader's intelligence, you have the "green light" to write the thesis.

WEAK: *The Producers*, a popular 1968 movie, was made into a Broadway play. (Has a subject—*"The Producers"* but doesn't have a judgment.)

BETTER: *The Producers*, a popular 1968 movie, was successfully transformed into a Broadway play. (Has both a subject, *"The Producers,"* and judgment "successfully transformed into a Broadway play" but is still too vague.)

BEST: *The Producers*, a popular 1968 movie, was successfully transformed into a Broadway play because of the set design, screenplay, and acting. (Has both a subject, *"The Producers,"* and a judgment "successfully transformed into a Broadway play"). The author tells us that she will write about set design, screenplay, and acting —*in that order*.

PRACTICE 3 EVALUATING THESIS STATEMENTS: Write **A** in the blank in front of sentences that are announcements rather than thesis statements and **T** in front of sentences that establish and advance a point that could be developed into a coherent essay.

_____ 1. Physician-assisted suicide should be banned on the basis of moral, religious and medical considerations.

_____ 2. In this essay, I will tell you about the businesses that encourage high standards of corporate behavior and why this is important for Americans.

_____ 3. Richmond Redmond was an anomaly: a gentleman, a scholar— and a drunk living in a refrigerator carton on New York City's Bowery.

_____ 4. This report will explain the causes and effects of thermal pollution in the waters adjacent to nuclear power generating plants.

_____ 5. Mary Cassatt's painting style and subject matter changed greatly because of her association with the Impressionists.

_____ 6. The main point I want to get across in this essay is that the problem of poverty in America affects people in all racial and ethnic groups from both urban and rural areas, the native-born

more than the immigrant
SOME MYTHS ABOUT THESIS STATEMENTS

- *A thesis statement must come at the end of the first paragraph.* This is a natural position for a statement of focus, but it's not the only one. Some theses can be stated in the opening sentences of an essay; others need a paragraph or two of introduction; others can't be fully formulated until the end of the essay.

- *A thesis statement must be one sentence in length, no matter how many clauses it contains.* Clear writing is more important than rules like these. Use two or three sentences if you need them. A complex argument may require a whole tightly knit paragraph to make its initial statement of position.

- *You can't start writing an essay until you have a perfect thesis statement.* It may be advisable to draft a hypothesis or tentative thesis statement near the start of a big project, but changing and refining a thesis is acommon occurence as you of think your way through your idea.

- *A thesis statement must have three points of support.* The thesis statement should indicate that the essay will explain and give evidence for its assertion, but points don't need to come in any specific number.

PRACTICE 4 EVALUATING THESIS STATEMENTS: Write an **X** in the blank in front of the thesis statements that are too broad or too narrow to be developed into a college-level essay, and a √ in front of those that can be developed effectively. Remember to check for a subject and a judgment about the subject.

_____1. John T. Scopes, a high school biology teacher in the small, rural town of Dayton, Tennessee, was found guilty on July 21, 1925 of teaching evolution in the classroom and fined $100.00.

_____2. Herman Melville's *Moby Dick* is a great novel with many interesting characters and a lot of exciting events.

_____3. Approximately 10,000 books are published each month in the United States, and many of them are sold on the internet.

_____4. Inner city schools that lack up-to-date computer labs fail to prepare their students for college, the workplace, and a society that is dependent upon computer literacy.

_____5. Because herbal teas containing senna, aloe, buckthorn, and other plant-derived laxatives promote rapid weight loss that results in the loss of muscle and lean body mass, they pose a potential danger to those who drink them.

_____6. Physics is the study of the science of matter and energy and of the interactions between the two that affect everything in the universe, including the Milky Way, which is Earth's galaxy.

_____7. An Italian sonnet is a fourteen-line poem in iambic pentameter with a carefully patterned rhyme scheme that usually follows an a-b-b-a, a-b-b-a pattern in the first eight lines.

_____8. College students who major in psychology and then graduate with a Bachelor of Science degree or a Bachelor of Arts degree from an accredited college or university can, after further graduate study, possibly pursue a career as a clinical psychologist.

_____9. If film and the internet are the communications tools of the 21st century, then together these two media create a powerful means for making connections among diverse people and cultures of the world.

_____10. The fall of the Roman Empire had many causes, including the growth of a powerful military caste, reliance on foreign mercenaries in the Roman Legions, and the decay of political morality; the major reason for the fall of Rome, however, was bad economic policy.

SOME DOs and DON'Ts FOR INTRODUCTIONS

DO

- use an interesting opener
- have a transition to your point (thesis)
- write an identifiable thesis statement
- follow the order of organization you list, if you give one

DON'T

- announce your topic ("I am going to write about . . ." "This paper is about . . .")
- rely on your title to be the subject of the first sentence of the introduction. (Title: Recycling   Opening Paragraph: "It is very important for the environment." "It, as the first word of the essay, doesn't have a noun to refer to—the title doesn't count.)

BODY

The body contains paragraphs with the ideas that support your thesis statement. These also have an organization: spatial—left to right, top to bottom; chronological—time order; or order of importance—usually going from the least important to the most.

Each body paragraph is held together by its topic sentence, the statement that explains the paragraph. Like the thesis statement, the topic sentence contains a subject and an opinion. All of the following sentences that follow in that paragraph explain the point made in the topic sentence.

The body may also contain transitional paragraphs. These are one- or two-sentence paragraphs that act as a bridge between the ideas in the main paragraphs. Sometimes the transitions are in the last sentence of the paragraph or within the next paragraph's topic sentence.

In the following a student essay on the similarities between humans and rats, the writer introduces the subject in the thesis and then supports it with specific examples summarized in the topic sentences. Notice the transitional phrases that lead the reader from topic to topic, as a bridge does from landmass to landmass.

The "Rat Race" of Human Existence: More than Just a Cliché
JUSTIN AQUAVIVA

The image of the common rat, Chinese zodiac notwithstanding, conjures up a terrible image in the imaginations of most humans. They are pests. They are parasites. They are vermin. What's worse, their mere presence seems to exact a grave toll on the human population. The rat is the poster child for the disease, filth and despair—this is the opinion prominent not only in the undeveloped nations of the earth, but the arena of squalid urban decay as well. Des Kennedy in his essay "Rats: Who's Racing Whom" writes, "There's no question that rats spread disease. Food contaminated with their droppings can cause salmonella or food poisoning as well as leptospiral jaundice" (182).

Charles Darwin introduced his theory of evolution in 1859 amid a hail of scandal and controversy. Darwin thought that humanity as we now know it grew out of—or to be more specific, evolved from—lesser, more primitive species. He purported that all animal life on earth came into being in this fashion, citing such unusual adaptations as the tortoise and finch species of the Galapagos Island as examples. In his writings, he put forth the intertwined notions of "Natural Selection" and "Survival of the Fittest." Darwin's notion maintains that those individuals of a species who exhibit the qualities that best enable them to survive in their environment will survive to sire the next generation. Those who lack these traits will perish. Therefore, desirable traits for the survival of an organism will be passed on to the later generations, thus strengthening the species as a whole.

To the untrained, the human being and the common rat are certain to appear most dissimilar. One is the pre-eminent species on earth, erecting vast cities and other great technological marvels as an enduring monument to his own sense of importance. The other is one of the "lower" beasts, living out its existence in the cracks and crevices of human society, feeding off its waste and ever-expanding in its shadow. In reality, the human and the rat share a strange and perhaps disturbing parallel; the two are remarkably similar, always competing and oddly complementary.

Man has long held himself as the "dominant" species—the pinnacle of evolution, so far removed from the lower creatures. Yet in reality, humanity and the common rat stand in direct opposition, exploding in our populations and directly competing for many of the same resources necessary to sustain life. Both human and rat cover the globe, spread by both colonization and transplantation. Wherever we have journeyed, the rat has come with us—welcome or not. Kennedy explains that rats have "become communal species, living in or near our buildings and feeding off our food, following us wherever we've settled" (181). We both adapt to our terrain, climate and circumstances with remarkable ease. From a Darwinian standpoint, we are both the pinnacle of our order.

Des Kennedy in his essay addresses the traits that have allowed society's most notorious vermin to not only survive but thrive. Calling the creatures "the most successful biological opponents of humans on earth," (181), Kennedy states that the rat population of the planet totals approximately 4 billion— roughly one for every human alive (at the time of his writing). Following the population of both the common Black Rat and the Norway Rat, the author exposes a system that not only follows the basic tenets of Darwin's theory, but also parallels the expansion of the human race. Kennedy states that rats are omnivorous, easily adaptable to almost any climate or ecosystem and readily transplantable to almost any areas where humans unwittingly bring them. Wherever humankind has traveled, it seems, we bring with us the rat. As human culture has expanded throughout Europe, Asia and the Americas, the rats have followed—and prospered in our wake (181).

Rat society offers an amazing series of parallels to our own. Rats live in a rigid, "organized social hierarchy" (182) and in "'their behavior towards members of their own community... rats are 'the model of social virtue,'" writes Konrad Lorenz in *On Aggression* (183). This society is as quick and effective in the management of its own population growth as it is brutal and ruthless in its willingness to dispose of any external threat. If a stray rat wanders into the burrow, an alarm is spread throughout the rat colony of the unfamiliar rat is brutally attacked. Like humans, rats practice the "traditional passing-on of acquired experience" (184); for example, if a rat finds some food with which the pack is unfamiliar, it will communicate to the other rats by screaming or soiling that it to show that it should not be eaten. "Their capacity for survival is the stuff of legend," notes Kennedy (184), and citing Lornez he states, "The difficulty of successfully combating, the brown rat, ...lies chiefly in the fact that the rat operates basically with the same methods as those of man, by traditional transmission of experience and its dissemination within the close community (185)." Like humans, they are prolific, cunning and difficult to defeat; rat society serves as an ideal example of the Darwinian Theory.

The fertile, prolific nature of the human species also comes under scrutiny in a report published by the United Nations Department of Economic and Social Affairs. In their report, "World Population Nearing 6 Billion," researchers examine the numerical explosion of the human race and the impact this nearly unchecked growth is sure to have on the planet as an ecosystem. At the time of the report (1998), UN researchers placed the human population at approximately 5.9 Billion. They theorized that if current trends continue, the human race would number 6 billion by 1999 and as many as 9 billion by 2050. Experts cite that the current rate of expansion exceeds the death rate. In addition, population growth also more than exceeds the 2.1 births per child-bearing woman that is required to replace lost members of the previous generation. In an expected parallel, the growth of the human population closely mirrors that of the rat species in one very important area: the largest percentage of both human and rat population growth occurs in the less-developed areas of the globe. Human and rat numbers swell the greatest in Asia, India and rural Africa. In both cases, such growth stems directly from the high fertility of both populations, the availability of resources and the relatively low effects of those factors that can significantly escalate mortality (World Population 226).

The correlations, then, are easy to recognize: The rat population closely mirrors human society, following human expansion wherever it may lead. The rats thrive on our waste and compete directly with humanity for both space and resource. Humans, in turn, transplant the rat species into whatever areas we see fit to colonize or populate. We spread out into the uncharted areas of the world, unwittingly bringing our closest, most dire competition in tow. So human and rat continue to struggle for dominance on earth. Both survive. Both adapt. Both would surely make Darwin proud.

PRACTICE 5 THESIS STATEMENT AND TOPIC SENTENCE:
Underline the thesis statement and topic sentences in the above essay.

CONCLUSION
The concluding paragraph reiterates the main ideas of the essay and gives the essay its sense of closure. Every essay needs some type of closure. Usually the conclusion echoes the idea in the thesis, but in different words. It may take an idea from the introduction and come back to it, this time with the reader having the additional knowledge supplied in the body paragraphs. Here is an example of a conclusion echoing the introduction:

Introduction:

When one thinks of rats, a slew of miserable and disgusting images come to mind. Rats infest the dark places of the Earth, lurking in the shadows and scavenging what others discard. They bring to mind images of disease, pestilence, and revulsion. Rats have an all-powerful will to survive, a complex and rigid social model, and an unrivaled ferocity and adaptability that make them the perfect evolutionary species. Their habits and behavior, like humans, parallel those theories offered by Charles Darwin regarding the Earth's system of nature and the origin of all species.

Conclusion:

As disturbing as it may be, one can easily draw many parallels between the behavior of rats and of humans. In fact, these parallels could extend—some quite accurately—to many of the other numerous species that inhabit the Earth. However, one would be hard pressed to find a species that so succinctly and perfectly demonstrates the behaviors and instincts inherent to Darwin's theories. As repulsive as they may be, rats are the perfect evolutionary species.

SOME DO's AND DON'Ts FOR CONCLUSIONS

DO

- write your conclusion knowing your reader is now familiar with your points.
- try to tie in an aspect of your introduction into the conclusion.
- feel free to make recommendations or a "call for action" based upon the points made in the body of your essay.

DON'T

- write "In conclusion …" Since it's the last paragraph, the reader already knows that it's the end.
- add new information. If you've discovered a wonderful point, add it to the body of the essay.
- repeat your introduction point for point. That's just plain boring.

LANGUAGE

BEING SPECIFIC

We have certain expectations in our use of language. When someone routinely uses in speech expressions such as "She don't care" or "He ain't here" or "I seen Amy today," educated Americans will mark that person as under- or uneducated. When the speaker's or writer's use of language doesn't meet the expectations of "correct" English that educated Americans use in their daily conversation and writing, a negative impression of the speaker or writer may be formed.

As a college student, you should be concerned about your use of the English language, partly because a well-educated person should write well and sound good, but also because good writers and careful speakers go further in their careers. Most jobs do require both good writing and speaking skills. When you misuse words, you confuse your readers. You appear as if you don't know the meaning of the words you use. The media don't help; many people who work in mass media, for example, don't know that the word *media* is plural. Here are some faulty expressions recently read in newspapers or magazines or heard on the radio or television:

- **It's *déjà vu* all over again**—All over again? Not if you know what *déjà vu* means.
- **The accident victim was successfully rescued from the fire.** If the victim was rescued, then the attempt was successful. How can someone be *unsuccessfully* rescued?
- **Dr. Smith, who is the past and former president of the American Psychological Association . . .** This is redundant. *Past* and *former* mean the same thing, so the radio announcer who spoke this certainly sounded like a fool.
- **The grand jury indicted he and his partner.** The grand jury indicted *he*?
- **She was flustrated . . .** *Flustered* or *frustrated*? Make a decision.

Sometimes the way words are put together causes the reader to pause because the words seem to have two meanings, as do these headlines from various American newspapers:

- **Kids Make Nutritious Snacks**—Yikes! The town is promoting cannibalism?
- **Chef Throws His Heart into Helping Feed Needy**—He'll only do that once!
- **Arson Suspect Held in Massachusetts Fire**—Gee, what will they do to him if he's found guilty?
- **New Vaccine May Contain Rabies**—So does the writer mean contain as in *holds* or contain as in *to harness*?

And sometimes words are used to confuse their meaning. When we accept these terms, we allow the language to be manipulated for questionable purposes.

- **Friendly fire**—This actually means accidentally killing your own men and women. The fire isn't *friendly* to those who die.
- **Extermination of the Jews**—We usually use the word exterminate to describe killing bugs and vermin. This term was used by Nazis to make their murders seem less horrible, as if they weren't killing humans.
- **He was "erased"**—This is a term used by mobsters to describe the murder of someone. Notice how *erase* seems so non-violent and cleansing.
- **Ethnic Cleansing**—This term has been used in the Balkans to describe the attempted genocide of an ethnic group. Cleansing sounds beneficial, but murdering an entire people never is.

How you treat the language will determine your success in communicating. All of what you've learned so far about **how** to express yourself effectively goes back to the words you choose. Carefully choosing your words makes your points clear, eliminates confusion, and shows that you control the language.

PRACTICE 6 USING SPECIFIC LANGUAGE: The more specific the words you choose (keeping in mind their connotation as well as their denotation), the clearer your writing will be. Each of the sentences below is vague. Underline the subject and the verb in each sentence and substitute a more specific term. If possible, add a descriptive word or phrase.

1. The car hit an object. _____

2. The animal ate its food. _____

3. The store sells stuff. _____

4. A man went into a building. _____

5. The parent held the child. _____

CONNOTATION AND DENOTATION

From Latin *de* meaning apart and *notatio/notationis* meaning marking, denotation is the literal meaning of a word; think of it as the "dictionary meaning." From the Latin *con* meaning together, connotation is the attitude we associate with a word, the emotion. For example, the word "mother" literally means a woman who has borne a child. This is its denotation. For most people, the connotation of the word mother brings to mind the feelings of loving, kindness and helpfulness.

Another way to get a feel for the connotations of words and improve your word choice is by practicing shifting your viewpoint so that you can describe the same object both favorably and unfavorably. You can do this by first using words with a positive connotation and then switching to words with a negative connotation.

PRACTICE 7 CONNOTATION: For the descriptions below, write a sentence that has a favorable connotation and then a sentence that has an unfavorable connotation. For example, you might describe a ripe banana as sweet or you might describe it as mushy, depending on the desired connotation.

1. A wet street after a rainstorm _____

_____

_____

_____

_____

_____

2. A difficult college course _____

_____

_____

_____

_____

_____

3. The location of the parking lots _____

_____

_____

_____

_____

_____

RHETORICAL MODES

Rhetorical modes, also known as modes of discourse, are methods of developing and ordering your ideas. Although some essays make use of one rhetorical mode for an entire essay, most essays use of combination of these modes.

DESCRIPTION

One way to communicate well is to use descriptive, vivid language. When you think of descriptive language, you should think of the five senses: seeing, touching, tasting, smelling, and hearing. Through these senses you process the world and explain your world to others. As writers, we each have a responsibility to "transport" our readers into our world—the scene, the place, event, even emotion that we are describing. This is done through **VIVID** language.

The key to writing good description is word choice. Vague words leave vague impressions. So to write, "The dog came toward us" leaves the reader with a picture of a dog but little else. The noun "dog" and verb "came" tell us unclearly who the subject is or how he acted. We want to know: What type of dog? Size? Coloring? Compare these two sentences: "The Saint Bernard bounded toward us." "The terrier crept toward us." These are two different images that elicit contrary feelings, both of which could have come from the original sentence.

Are you using boring verbs (*sat, ran* and *looked* instead of **slouched, bolted** and **glared**)? So instead of writing, "She WALKED into the garden" you might write, "She TIPTOED into the garden" (if, indeed, she did). Look at your nouns and how they are modified: "A lone middle-aged woman with fire-engine-red hair picked over the tee shirts in the bargain bin."

As you read the essays and short stories by the authors in this text, identify and think about the various types of imagery they use.

READING A DESCRIPTION ESSAY

Let's look at the student essay "Accident in the Barn"; the assignment was to write a short in-class essay describing a specific event.

ACCIDENT IN THE BARN
LAURIE ELDER

The clouds cover the moon; darkness surrounds the barn. Cicada bugs screech with increasing speed: my body tenses. The ground is a thick mud-hay mixture, giving my footsteps a slimy sucking sound. As I walk towards the barn, I hear the sirens wailing in the distance becoming closer.

As I open the door, a foul smell is released, making me nauseous. The intense odor of dirty chickens, animal feces, and blood fills the old barn. I pass the horse stalls, proceeding with caution. Suddenly, I can see, illuminated by the blue and red ambulance lights, a tall, bony mid-sixties man sitting upright. He is held in this position by a pitchfork, which had pierced through his worn overalls and frail back, exiting his worn-in pale blue and white flannel shirt near his nipples. Each prong is covered slightly with brownish blood, thick from the heat. His suspenders are blood-soaked around each prong, and blood has dripped down his legs to a pool that soaks the underneath of his overalls. Flies, nesting in the fresh corpse, cluster in his wounds and blood pool.

My stomach turns so I take my eyes off the torso. I look at the sweat-covered face with its blank expression—the thin, chapped lips slightly parted revealing blood-stained teeth—and notice his small, pale blue eyes staring at me. Quickly I look away, only to be face to face with a huge man. I gasp—the paramedic. Passing me, he rushes to the corpse. Many other uniformed men and women hustle into the barn. After touching his fingers to the old man's neck, the paramedic shakes his head. Backing away from the commotion, I take one last look at the body. My eyes are drawn to his head, slumped on his left shoulder; I notice his thinning silver hair. The crown is sweat-soaked. My eyes glance down his left arm to a wrinkled, yet hard-working hand, limp in the same dark pool of blood.

Turning to leave the barn, I hear the crackling of breaking bones as they separate the frail dead body from the blood-covered pitchfork. I bolt out through the large barn doors to escape the sound and breathe in the dead still, but fresh, midnight air.

PRACTICE 8   ANALYZING THE ESSAY: Answer the following questions about the essay you just read.

1.   In this story, the writer sets the scene in the first paragraph. What are some the vivid sights and sounds?

_____

_____

_____

2.   In the beginning of the second paragraph, we read about smell. What is the olfactory image that she uses?

_____

_____

3.   All these descriptions not only set the scene, but also establish the tone.

What is the tone?

_____

_____

4. Next we see the old man. Notice the detail with which he is described. The nouns and verbs and adjectives are specific, leaving us with a clear picture of this macabre scene. Find at least five descriptive details that describe the dead man.

A. _____

B. _____

C. _____

D. _____

E. _____

5. How does the conclusion wrap up the essay? Is there a tie-in to the introduction? If so, what is it?

_____

_____

_____

NARRATION

We mentioned earlier that a short narration can be used as a lead-in to the thesis statement. Sometimes, however, the entire essay is a narration. Events that are told in stories don't have to be monumental—earthquakes or murder. Often the best stories are ones that have the most meaning to the teller. To write a successful narration, you must begin by selecting a topic from the many hundreds, probably thousands, in your memory. When deciding on the order in which you will write your narration, remember that the most natural order is chronological, telling a story from the first incident to the last.

READING A NARRATION ESSAY

Let's look at the essay "Melanie and Scratchy" to determine what makes it a successful narrative.

MELANIE AND SCRATCHY
SIR SIDNEY WEINSTEIN

Since I was a pupil there more than sixty years ago, the images of most of my friends from Charles Sumner Junior High School have long since been merely deposited in my memory; my friends have all either moved away or physically ceased to exist. Every experience in a child's life, even when it appears commonplace, reflects a microcosm; each teaches us something— sometimes enduring, and sometimes only ephemeral. Unknowingly, Scratchy Itzkowitz and Melanie Wilson deposited a strong memory in the storage banks of my cortex, and it obviously remains because it contains something of emotional significance to me.

When Scratchy called me recently, I was shocked; it had been forty years since we had spoken. We chatted for a few minutes, and I asked whether he recalled an incident concerning our algebra teacher, Miss Melanie Wilson, which specifically involved him. When he said that he didn't, I related the one that was very unusual. I was surprised that his memory of it was hazy; mine surely was not. Bizarre as this incident was, it differed little, except for its extreme nature, from other grotesque occurrences that we encountered daily at Charles Sumner Junior High School.

The teachers (and several students) could be considered a collection of bizarre personalities often found in textbooks of abnormal behavior, and Charles Dickens would have relished the inventory for his novels. Mrs. Connelly was a fastidious, pedantic disciplinarian who wore *pinz nez* glasses; Miss Ferrante, the opposite of Mrs. Connelly, was weak and ineffectual, always being harried by the pupils; and Mr. Beckhardt, a small, wizened French teacher, saved one-inch sized pencils, "bad-boy pencils," for those who had forgotten to bring their own. My memories of them, and many others, remain strong.

Although it would be difficult to rank them in order of their peculiarities, among the most bizarre was Miss Melanie Wilson, a prim, white-haired lady, a misplaced belle from the Old South, who was inordinately proud of her name and Southern heritage. Melanie, she informed us, was a true Southern belle's name, and she carefully instructed us on its pronunciation: the stress was on the first syllable. But along with her outward show of gentility, Mrs. Wilson was most intolerant of sounds of any sort unrelated to the lesson of the day, and she harbored an unexpected leaning toward violence. While we were occupied by her algebra tests, she would patrol the aisles, cupping her hand behind her ear to amplify the sound as she passed each pupil.

"I'll get the hummer; I'll get the tapper," she would drone on slowly in her southern drawl, "and when I do [drawn out in almost two syllables 'd-yew'] . . . ."

But she left her threat unfinished; she never actually clarified just what she would "d-yew," leaving the hummer and tapper's fate to our fertile imaginations. Woe unto the student so immersed in thought that he unthinkingly tapped his pencil while seeking the answer to an equation. A sharp rap on the nape of his neck with a ruler would bring him back to the reality of that class: silence was more important than problem solving.

But one day we understood the magnitude of her threat of what she would "d-yew." Sam Heimbender was a smaller-than-usual boy in the seventh grade, but he made up for his diminutive stature with brazen behavior, usually exemplified by the most blatant, resounding, and prolonged nature of his belch. This achievement that could make the walls reverberate was a skillful performance always available on request. We all would have liked to emulate his proficiency, but we knew we didn't have the slightest possibility of success. He was widely known for this talent, and those who knew him would request a performance frequently; we would even encourage him to display his prowess for the few who were not aware of his proficiency.

One afternoon while we sat attentively in Miss. Wilson's algebra class, as she was writing some equations on the blackboard, Sam Heimbender, for reasons still a mystery to me, delivered the granddaddy of all eructations: an abrupt rendering that nowadays might be termed "the mother of all belches." It resounded like a peal from Mt. Olympus, proclaiming the end of the world and reverberating for what seemed an eternity. It must have started somewhere deep in his feet, gathering speed and resonance as it cannonballed along, rising within his organs until, Vesuvius-like, it erupted violently, almost shattering the walls. There was no doubt of its premeditation and deliberate attempt to provoke Mrs. Wilson, who remained facing the blackboard with her back to us for several seconds, paralyzed by the enormity of the audacity.

We were, naturally, shocked by the brazenness of this diminutive boy, especially in the classroom of a woman who had threatened that even a hum or a pencil tap would bring forth uncertain, but undoubtedly grisly, repercussions. Slowly, she turned to face us and, with an expression that left no doubt of her rage, snarled, "Hands behind your backs!" a command given that demanded the abject surrender of slaves to their mistress.

We obeyed immediately, placing our hands behind our backs and sitting silently erect, while she stalked the aisles like a tigress, seeking a clue to the transgressor.

We all knew the perpetrator—he was too famous to be anonymous—it had to be Sam Heimbender, master eructologist! But we wondered just what Mrs. Wilson would or could do. Surely Sam would never voluntarily confess, and it was getting close to three o'clock when school ended. We assumed she would stalk about with threatening expressions, perhaps berating the unknown belch-master as a degenerate debauchee and, when the bell rang, we would leave as her anger dissipated.

Shocked as we were by the enormity of Sam's act, we were also highly amused. How could he have the gall to exhibit his prowess in front of (or actually behind) the martinet of the seventh grade? But we continued to suppress any overt signs of our delectation, except for one uncontrolled reaction by one hapless boy, Scratchy, a cheerful soul much delighted by such impromptu diversions. As Mrs. Wilson continued to prowl in search of the miscreant, we all remained silent (perhaps allowing ourselves a tiny smile when she was facing away). Scratchy, however, could not restrain his exhilaration for Sam's *piece de resistance*. He could not contain a small chortle that proved to be his undoing. Without a second's delay, our tigress pounced.

I can't determine whether the outrage expressed by Mrs. Wilson was greater after Sam's grandiose performance or Scratchy's post-exhibition expression of appreciation, but she instantly ran toward Scratchy and dragged him by the hair to the front of the room. There, he remained, an evil eleven-year-old, caught in the unforgivable act of showing admiration for an unforgivable abomination, a burp. He stood frozen in terror.

As he stood there immobile, Mrs. Wilson lurched to the blackboard, snatched a rubber-tipped wooden pointer used to indicate geographical sites on maps, and proceeded literally to flog him with it. The lashes were brutal and numerous, landing on his shoulders, back, and arms, and Scratchy, protecting his head with his arms, was predictably soon sobbing in pain and humiliation. Blood began seeping through the back of his shirt, and, probably more from her own exhaustion than pity, she finally stopped thrashing him.

We were now, of course, no longer amused. Sam's original performance was over and although we now had the subsequent vicious punishment of an innocent student to contemplate, we were too frightened to do or say anything. So, when the bell rang ending the "algebra lesson," Mrs. Wilson released us from the class and we scurried away lest she find another student inadvertently showing appreciation for the humiliation she had experienced.

Since it was our last class most of us ran home, probably speedier than usual. I walked along with Scratchy because we were friends and lived across the street from one another. Although Mrs. Wilson's brutality was both inappropriate and surely illegal, these were the days when one did not complain of the misdeeds of teachers, no matter how inappropriate, for fear of the reactions of parents who automatically assumed their children to be culpable, and, therefore, deserving perhaps of another beating.

Scratchy sneaked past his mother, who was at her usual place at the sink or stove, quickly removed his bloody shirt and washed it in the bathroom sink before his parents could see it. He quickly donned another, allowing the bloody one to dry in his room.

The next day at school, the incident was hardly mentioned, and school returned to the "normal," schizophrenic, hurly burly with which we were accustomed. Although Scratchy's memory may have been hazy, my memory of this incident, however, remains intact to this day.

PRACTICE 9 ANALYZING THE ESSAY: Answer the following questions about the essay you just read.

1. The introduction gives the reader some background information. Why we are hearing this story? What else does the author accomplish in the introduction? In which paragraph does the story actually start?

_____

_____

_____

_____

2. The author changes tone in the essay. What are the tones he uses? What, if anything, is the benefit of changing the tone?

_____

_____

_____

_____

3. The author uses many descriptive details to bring the reader into the story and allow the reader to "be in the classroom." List three descriptive details that you think are effective.

A. _____

B. _____

C. _____

4. The conclusion wraps up an essay—gives it its sense of closure. What does the author write to let you know that the story is over? Is it effective? Why or why not?

_____

_____

_____

EXAMPLES/ILLUSTRATION

Examples (also known as illustration) help a writer put general or abstract thoughts into specifics. We all respond to concrete instances or illustrations when we are trying to understand a point. You probably already know the importance of giving examples as a way of explaining or presenting information. Every time you explain why you believe something to be true and you give more than one case to back up your reasoning, you are using examples. The example/illustration essay is the most straightforward essay form you will encounter. It is also the one you will always continue to use in writing your essays because all essays, whether argumentative or informational, need the support that good illustrations provide. When you present examples to support your thesis or topic sentence, you need several reasons that lead you to that conclusion. A single isolated example would not convince anyone easily.

READING AN EXAMPLE ESSAY

Let's look at the student essay "Visits at Trenton State Prison"; the assignment was to write a short essay describing a specific place.

VISITS AT TRENTON STATE PRISON
DAVID WILLETTS

One of the major complaints of both visitors and inmates about Trenton State Prison is that its visiting facilities and regulations are archaic and inhumane. The old and inadequate visiting booths, the short and inequitable amounts of time allowed, and the lack of human contact with the reactions it brings makes the visiting situation at the prison almost intolerable. Dostoevsky once wrote that "the degree of civilization in a society can be judged by entering its prisons." If this be the case, Trenton State Prison certainly speaks poorly of New Jersey.

One first notices the deplorable physical conditions of the visiting booths. Visits at the prison are held in small booths, with the inmate on one side and the visitor on the other. The main elements of each booth are a stool to sit on, a telephone through which the conversation is held, and an eighteen by twenty-four-inch plate of glass through which the prisoner and visitor view each other. In many cases the glass is cracked, and in almost all cases filthy. There are sixteen such booths in the visiting room, although usually only thirteen or fourteen are functioning. There are 1,360 inmates at Trenton, and the ratio of operable booths to prisoners is approximately one booth per one hundred men.

In his attempt to secure a booth in the crowded visiting room, the visitor realizes a further injustice: inequitable and short visiting periods. He is permitted to talk to the inmate for a period of thirty minutes to two hours, depending upon which officers are on duty and the prisoner's popularity with them and the prison administration. Prison regulations allow a visitor to come once a week on a weekday and visit for a period of one hour. Visitors who come on weekends are allowed one half hour once a month. Unfortunately, the majority of men in Trenton Prison come from low-income groups whose family or friends are in the working class. In many cases their visitors are forced to come on weekends since they cannot afford the financial loss which would result from taking a weekday off to visit an inmate. Thus, the affluent may enjoy more and longer visits than the less affluent.

There is still a greater injustice concerning the visits at Trenton, and that is the total lack of contact between the inmates and their visitors. Of all of New Jersey's state penal institutions, the prison at Trenton is the only one that does not have contact visits. This means that a man who is unfortunate enough to be in Trenton rather than any other reformatory or prison in the state is subjected to an additional cruel punishment. He is completely separated from physical contact with his family, friends, and outside life. In too many cases this has a drastic effect on the prisoner and his thinking. Some feel themselves inadequate while others turn to homosexuality to fulfill their need for physical affection. Almost all harbor some bitterness. The lack of contact deprives the inmate of one of the most basic human needs, the need to give and receive human physical affection. A scene constantly repeated is that of a husband and wife looking lovingly into each other's eyes and unconsciously reaching out to touch hands, and then their hands are halted by an inch of glass. The look of love quickly transforms into an expression of agony and frustration. This situation increases family break-ups and is probably the most inhumane aspect of visits at the prison.

All of the problems with the visiting situation at the prison could be ended without great effort, and surely should be. As visits are conducted now, they are inequitable and inhumane and serve not to help an inmate toward readjustment and rehabilitation, but rather to make him embittered and hostile. The visiting regulations at Trenton State Prison do not advance the progressive and civilized image New Jersey projects and desires.

PRACTICE 10   ANALYZING THE ESSAY: Answer the following questions about the essay you just read.

1.   Which sentence is the thesis statement?

_____

_____

2. What method of "grabber" introduction does the author use?

    _____

    _____

3. Who is Dostoevsky? Why do you think the author used a quote by him?

    _____

    _____

4. In the second paragraph (the first body paragraph) what specific information does the author give to support his point?

    _____

    _____

5. In the third paragraph, which is the topic sentence? What specific information does the author give to support his point?

    _____

    _____

6. In the fourth paragraph, which is the topic sentence? What specific information does the author give to support his point?

    _____

    _____

7. Notice the transitions. *"One first notices…"* is the first one. What are the other ones?

    _____

    _____

8. The conclusion refers to the introduction. What does the author write that brings the reader back to the conclusion? Write the sentence here.

    _____

    _____

If you read the essay carefully, you saw the numerous, specific examples that the author gives to support his thesis. You, too, must give specific examples if you want to convince your readers of the validity of your point.

COMPARE AND CONTRAST

Comparison and contrast is a way of analyzing similarities and differences between two or more subjects. Comparison looks at how things, people, or ideas are the same; contrast looks at their differences. In writing, comparing and contrasting is often the best way to explain something. An object, person or idea is often better understood when its features stand next to those of another object, person or idea. For example, if you were looking at the way a student dresses, let's say a hippie, and you stood her next to someone in business attire, the contrast would be more obvious than if she stood alone.

When planning your essay, ask yourself some questions: How are they alike? How are they different? Write two lists, one for similarities and one for differences. After you create the lists, look for items in the same category: that is, you need to compare the same things (character to character or setting to setting, for example).

POINT-BY POINT METHOD OF ORGANIZATION

I.   Introduction
II. Love (point 1)
     A. "The Story of an Hour"
        1. Mr. Mallard
        2. Mrs. Mallard
     B. "The Yellow Wallpaper"
        1. John
        2. The narrator

III. Illness and death (point 2)
     A. "The Story of an Hour"
        1. Mr. Mallard
        2. Mrs. Mallard
     B. "The Yellow Wallpaper"
        1. John
        2. The narrator
IV. Control of destiny (point 3)
     A. "The Story of an Hour"
        1. Mr. Mallard
        2. Mrs. Mallard
     B. "The Yellow Wallpaper"
        1. John
        2. The narrator
V.   Conclusion

BLOCK ORGANIZATION

I.   Introduction
II. "The Story of an Hour"
     A. Love (point 1)
        1. Mr. Mallard
        2. Mrs. Mallard
     B. Illness and death (point 2)
        1. Mr. Mallard
        2. Mrs. Mallard
     C. Control of destiny (point 3)
        1. Mr. Mallard
        2. Mrs. Mallard
III. "The Yellow Wallpaper"
     A. Love (point 1)
        1. John
        2. The narrator
     B. Characters (point 2)
        1. John
        2. The narrator
     C. Control of destiny (point 3)
        1. John
        2. The narrator
IV. Conclusion

The two ways to organize your essay are point-by-point or block. In point-by-point, the organization is determined by the similarities/difference. In the block method, each item being compared/contrasted sets the organization.

Use specific examples to support your points. If you use the exact language from a story, you must put it in quotation marks.

READING A COMPARISON AND CONTRAST ESSAY

Let's look at the student essay "Love versus Domination in 'The Story of an Hour,' 'The Yellow Wallpaper' and 'The False Gems.'"

LOVE VS DOMINATION IN "THE STORY OF AN HOUR," "THE YELLOW WALLPAPER" AND "THE FALSE GEMS"
JODY BRITT

"We often speak of love when we really should be speaking of the drive to dominate or to master, so as to confirm ourselves as active agents, in control of our own destinies and worthy of respect from others," wrote Thomas Szasz in *Love, The Second Sin* (1973). The sentiments in this quote apply to the female characters of three stories "The Yellow Wallpaper" by Charlotte Perkins Gilman, "The False Gems" by Guy deMaupassant, and "The Story of an Hour" by Kate Chopin. Each female character is seeking to assert herself either within or despite a loving relationship. However, the manner, as well as the circumstances, in which each character attempts her assertion is quite different.

Love, its power or irrelevance to affect self-realization, is a factor in all three stories. It is undeniable that the husbands in all three stories truly love their wives, and it is acknowledged in the stories. In "The Yellow Wallpaper," the narrator explains how the couple are extending themselves financially to rent the house because John, her husband, is so concerned about her health. She states, "Dear John! He loves me dearly and hates to have me sick" (614). Yet, despite his intentions, the smothering over-protective effect of her husband's love prevents the narrator of "The Yellow Wallpaper" from regaining her health and control of her life. The narrator in "The False Gems" states " ... six years after their marriage M. Lantin discovered that he loved his wife even more than the first days of his honeymoon" (262). The power of M. Lantin's love for his "virtuous wife" blinds him to the circumstances of his finances and her source of income, but this also allows Mme. Lantin the freedom to control her life. She goes off to the theater without her husband and fulfills her "desire to adorn her person" (263) despite her husband's entreaties to the opposite. In "The Story of an Hour," Mrs. Mallard reflects on her husband's "face that never looked save with love upon her." Mrs. Mallard knows that "she would weep again when she saw the kind, tender hands folded in death" (517). However, she sees his love and her own for him as irrelevant, as she asserts, "What could love, the unsolved mystery, count for in the face of this possession of self-assertion..." (517).

Death and illness represent the ultimate loss of control. Illnesses and/or death and their imagery add dramatic impact to the points that the storytellers want to make, and all three stories use this literary device. The narrator of the "Yellow Wallpaper" descends into madness, powerless to take of control of her life. By the end of the story she sees a woman in the wallpaper of her room trying to escape: "And she is all the time trying to climb through. But nobody could climb through that pattern—it strangles so" (618). The reader realizes that "she" is all the trapped women and "that pattern" is the society of men that keep her trapped, just as in her situation. Her only way of coping is to lose her mind in symbolic freeing herself by pulling down "that pattern" of the wallpaper. In "The False Gems," we learn that Mme. Lantin "attended the opera, and on her return was chilled through and through. The next morning she coughed, and eight days later she died" (263). Mme. Lantin dies young and unexpectedly, losing control of her carefully amassed fortune. And having one of the main characters die in the middle of the story certainly adds dramatic impact: we wonder where the story now will lead us. We discover that M. Lantin apparently loses his mind and finances at the end; he quits his job, thinks he's rich and tells everyone he has different amounts of net worth. He then marries a woman after knowing her for only six months because he thinks since she is virtuous (unlike his first wife). He has compromised love for the control he thinks he will have over his life. He is wrong. The last line of the story tells us, "She made his life miserable" (267). Mrs. Mallard in "The Story of an Hour" dies from a heart attack when confronted with the fact that her husband is not dead and her dreams to control her destiny are shattered. She can no longer return to her former way of life after her new-found realizations. The irony is that "[w]hen the doctors came they said she had died of heart disease—of joy that kills" (518). We know better. She dies because she cannot return to her former life.

The freedom to shape and control one's destiny is a basic human desire. In the three stories, each female character is in a different position of ability to assert herself. In the "The Yellow Wallpaper," the narrator is ill and is manipulated and controlled by her overbearing but well-meaning husband. She agrees to take the nursery as her bedroom rather than the beautiful downstairs bedroom; she has to sneak her writing as "he hates to have me write a word" (610) and she is denied the company of her friends even though she finds it "so discouraging not to have any advice and companionship" (611). She writes, "Personally, I believe that congenial work, with excitement and change, would do me good. But what is one to do?" (608). She sublimates her will and power to his, even though she knows what he is doing on her behalf is not working. She is not in control. Unlike the other women, in "The False Gems," Mme. Lantin is in control. She has the freedom to live her own life on her terms. She establishes her own financial independence and runs the household, deciding for herself what she will do with her time. But because of the social restraints of the time, she has to take this control in an illicit way. M. Lantin realizes this when he goes to sell her "paste" jewelry and finds out that they are, in fact, real and presents from men: "A horrible doubt entered his mind—she? Then all the other gems must have been presents too!" (265). In "The Story of an Hour," Mrs. Mallard is at a crossroads in her life, a transitional stage of control. She is about to take control of her future and assert her freedom. She thinks, "There would be no powerful will bending hers in that blind persistence with which men and women believe they have a right to impose a private will upon a fellow creature" (517). She dreams of "a long procession of years to come that would belong to her absolutely" (517). But she is denied that possibility by the return of her husband.

The three stories show that loving relationships can inhibit freedom. Each female character in these stories is loved, yet it isn't enough. Love can be a destructive force if people are not allowed to be active agents in control of their destiny. As Szasz tells us, we need to be "active agents, in control of our own destinies and worthy of respect from others."

PRACTICE 11 ANALYZING THE ESSAY: Answer the following questions about the essay you just read.

1. Introductions should be engaging—that is, they should draw in the reader. Which method of introduction does the author use to draw in his readers? Do you find it effective?

_____

_____

2. List the three similarities the author uses to make his case. What is the one contrast?

_____

_____

3. What purpose do the quotes in the story serve? Are they effective? Why or why not?

_____

_____

4. Which method of organization does the author use?

_____

_____

CAUSE AND EFFECT

Cause and effect essays try to explain why events occur or what the results (or expected results) of a chain of happenings might be. Cause-and-effect looks for connections between things and the reasons behind them. It identifies conditions (the causes) and determines results or consequences (the effects). Your writing will be strengthened by your ability to point out why something is so. The causes are the reasons and the effects are the the consequences or results.

READING A CAUSE-AND-EFFECT ESSAY

Let's look at the student essay "Confessions of a Teen-Aged Alcoholic."

CONFESSIONS OF A TEEN-AGED ALCOHOLIC
JOHN M.

My name is John, and I'm a nineteen-year-old alcoholic. When I was fourteen years old, I discovered the magic of alcohol while my parents were out at a party, and I sampled some of the contents of their liquor cabinet. By the time I was eighteen, I was a full-blown alcoholic, drinking every day and getting totally wiped out every weekend. Finally, my life had become such a mess that I gave in to my parents and spent 28 days in a rehab in Pennsylvania. What I found out there about alcohol and alcoholism helped me turn my life around.

I can still remember the first high that I got when I was fourteen. I loved the feeling that alcohol gave me. I was kind of a loner at school with only a few close friends, and I realize now that alcohol helped mask my feelings of isolation. The more I drank, the better I felt. It wasn't long before I became addicted to the idea that alcohol was my best friend. I became a daily drinker, usually starting before I left the house for school with a quick nip on the vodka bottle in my parents' liquor cabinet. I soon found the other kids at school who liked to get high, and I was always able to get all the booze I needed in one way or another. I had a part-time job in a gas station where the boss was a heavy hitter, so he never noticed—or cared—that I always came to work with a buzz.

Between the money from my job and my allowance, I always had enough money to buy liquor. The group of kids at school that I eventually hooked up with had a lot of contacts to get drugs (mainly marijuana) and alcohol for us. I sometimes smoked grass with my friends, but I always preferred the effects of alcohol.

The first signal that I might be having a problem with booze came when my girlfriend, Annie, confronted me about my drinking. She told me that she was tired of going to parties with me and watching me act like a jerk when I had too many. Several times she told me I had come onto other girls at parties while she was watching me. I didn't believe her. I had no recollection of any of the things Annie said I had supposedly done. I thought she was making up these stories just to get me to slow down on my drinking. I later found out in rehab that I was in alcoholic blackouts when I did those things my girlfriend was talking about. She wasn't making them up. I just couldn't remember what had happened after I got to a certain (unpredictable) point in my drinking.

Then I noticed that my grades in school had started to slip. Before I started drinking, I wasn't the smartest or hardest-working student, but I usually maintained about a B average with a moderate amount of effort. By my junior year, my grade point average had slipped to between a C and a D, and I had failed math twice. My parents saw what was happening and talked to me about it, but I lied to them and said that I was trying my best but the work was just too hard for me. They knew I was lying, but I think they were afraid to hear the truth. They continued to enable me to drink by not taking a stand and confronting me.

I also gave up sports so that I could drink. When I was younger, I had loved soccer and baseball, and I was good in both. In junior high school I had been one of the best players on a travel team in our local soccer league. My coaches said that if I continued to develop, I could probably eventually get a scholarship to an NCAA Division I college. In baseball, I won MVP awards in both Little League and Babe Ruth. I had natural talent, and I loved the thrill of competition. After a few years of drinking, I realized that I couldn't keep getting drunk and still play sports, so I had to make a choice. I chose liquor.

By my senior year of high school I had lost almost everything that had once been important to me. Annie had ditched me in our junior year. I was so out of shape from drinking that competitive sports were out of the question— plus I had no interest in them anyway. My parents thought I was a lazy bum who would rather hang out with my "worthless friends" than try to get good grades and go on to college. I would rather drink than eat, so my weight had dropped to 130 pounds, and I looked like death warmed over. All of that was bad enough, but the worst effect of the alcohol was on my mental state. I was constantly depressed and suicidal. I felt as though I had fallen into a deep pit with slippery, muddy sides and no matter how hard I tried, I couldn't get out. I felt doomed. I frequently considered killing myself, but my brain was so muddled with booze that I couldn't figure out how to do it so that it would look like an accident and it would be a clean kill, not leaving me a vegetable in a hospital bed, living off a respirator.

Finally, my parents, a couple of my teachers and some of my real friends got together and did an intervention. They confronted me in the living room of my house and for two brutal hours they laid out the gory details of what my life had become during the past four years—years that I had essentially lost because I had been in an alcoholic fog.. When they were finished, I was too. I cried and told them that I was ready to do whatever it took to get my life back.

My dad had already checked out the details with his medical insurance carrier where he worked, and within a few hours of the intervention, I was in an alcohol and drug rehabilitation center in rural Pennsylvania. When I arrived at the rehab, I didn't know what to expect; I just knew that I needed to be there and felt as though a heavy burden had been lifted off my back. Every day was filled with therapy sessions with fellow alcoholics and drug abusers in the morning followed in the afternoon by classes on the physical, psychological and social effects of drug and alcohol abuse. In the evening we attended Alcoholics Anonymous or Narcotics Anonymous meetings.

In the afternoon sessions we listened to lectures by doctors, psychologists and social workers, and we were given a lot of material to read. I learned that alcoholism is a chronic disease with no known cure, much like diabetes (Jellinek 3). While normal drinkers have a "thermostat" that tells them when they've had enough alcohol before they get to the stage of acting drunk and stupid, the alcoholic doesn't seem to know when to stop. Scientists aren't sure why some drinkers become alcoholics and others don't, just as we don't know why some smokers get lung cancer and others don't. There are three basic theories of the causes of alcoholism: 1) a personality disorder usually marked by a low tolerance for frustration, a strong sense of rebellion, a tendency to act impulsively and a feeling of isolation; 2) a chemical imbalance that "short circuits" the cut-off mechanism in the alcoholic's brain as soon as alcohol enters his or her system; or 3) a genetic predisposition to alcoholism inherited from alcoholic family members (Diethelm 17).

Many non-alcoholics view the alcoholic as "weak-willed" or someone who drinks to have fun and raise hell. In fact, once a drinker has crossed what Alcoholics Anonymous calls the "invisible line" into alcoholism, he or she usually becomes incapable of stopping drinking without some kind of help (AA: *Young People*). And, since alcohol is not a stimulant (as most people mistakenly believe) but a depressant, inside, alcoholics are not the cheerful, happy drunks like Norm in *Cheers*; instead, they are often depressed and suicidal. The longer a person drinks, the more the cells of the body depend on the alcohol until a point is reached where removing the alcohol can have serious effects, such as hallucinations (the "DTs") or seizures (AAAS 3).

While I was in rehab, I learned that alcoholic drinking has both physical and mental effects. When alcohol is absorbed from the digestive tract into the bloodstream, it is quickly distributed throughout the body and affects nearly all of the cells, especially those of the brain. Different levels of concentrations of alcohol affect different parts of the brain. In an average-sized male, drinking two or three ounces of whiskey will result in a blood-alcohol level of 0.05 percent, which affects the highest brain centers, those concerned with judgment and inhibition (AAAS 4). This is the point at which the non-alcoholic's "thermostat" will click off, and he or she will usually not want to have any more to drink. The alcoholic (like me), however, is just getting started.

At 0.1 percent blood-alcohol level (four to six one-ounce shots of whiskey), the motor-control areas of the brain, especially those concerned with speech, balance and manual dexterity are affected. This is why most states use the 0.1-level as the legal definition of driving while under the influence of alcohol (DWI). When the alcohol level in the bloodstream reaches 0.45 percent—the equivalent for an average-sized male of drinking a little under a quart of whiskey in about an hour—the entire area of the brain controlling perception is affected, and the drinker falls into a coma. At a level of 0.7, about a quart and a half in a short period of time, the centers of the brain controlling heartbeat and breathing are depressed to the point of stopping altogether and the drinker dies (as happened to a fraternity pledge recently at MIT).

If a person drinks long and hard enough, say, a quart of whiskey a day for 15 or 20 years, he or she will usually develop a red, puffy face with prominent dark red and purple veins in the cheeks, and a swollen, enlarged nose ("whiskey nose"). Other problems will develop, including gastritis (a chronic irritation of the lining of the stomach) accompanied by nausea and vomiting; pancreatitis; liver disease (cirrhosis); and, finally, esophageal varices, a bursting of the blood vessels in the throat that will cause a person to drown in his own blood within minutes (AAAS 5).

If a person continues to drink long enough, he or she will also develop various mental disorders. At the very least, the active alcoholic is usually mentally "fogged up," selfish and obnoxious to other people. A constant intake of alcohol kills off millions of brain cells until eventually the alcoholic becomes a drooling, incontinent "wet brain" confined to a mental hospital. One of the psychologists told us of visiting a chronic alcoholic ward in a Veterans Administration hospital in New Jersey. The psychologist said that the "wet brains" were kept naked (so they could be hosed off when they defecated and urinated on themselves), strapped to wheelchairs until they died of liver failure or other illnesses caused by their drinking.

When I left rehabilitation, I no longer had any doubts about what I needed to do. The first night I was home, I went to a local AA meeting and stuck out my hand to everyone I met. "Hi," I said. "I'm John, and I'm a grateful recovering alcoholic."

Works Cited

American Association for the Advancement of Science (AAAS), Publication No. 47: *Alcoholism, Basic Aspects and Treatment*. Washington, D.C., 1997.

Alcoholics Anonymous World Services, Inc. *Three Talks to Medical Societies by Bill W.* New York, 1990.

Alcoholics Anonymous World Services, Inc. *This is A.A.* New York, 1991.

Alcoholics Anonymous World Services, Inc. *Young People and A.A.* New York, 2002.

Alcoholics Anonymous World Services, Inc. *The A.A. Member and Drug Abuse*. New York, 2001.

Diethelm, Oskar, *Etiology of Chronic Alcoholism: Investigations into Its Causes*. Springfield, Illinois, 1995.

Jellinek, Elvin M., *The Disease Concept of Alcoholism*. Yale University Press. New Haven, Connecticut, 1999.

PRACTICE 12 ANALYZING THE ESSAY: Answer the following questions about the essay you just read.

1. Which technique does the writer use for his introduction?
   __ Personal Narrative   __ Fact or Statistic   __ Current Event
   __ Quotation   __ Question   __ Thesis Statement

2. In the first several paragraphs the writer's diction establishes an informal tone. From the first three body paragraphs, list six colloquial words or expressions the writer uses to maintain this informal tone.

   _____ _____ _____

   _____ _____ _____

3. Write the first sentence of the paragraph in which the writer makes a transition from personal narrative to text supported by the use of outside sources.

   _____

   _____

4. The writer cites three possible causes for alcoholism. What are they?

   A. _____

   B. _____

   C. _____

5. The writer cites several effects of alcoholism. List three.

   A. _____

   B. _____

   C. _____

6. At what point does the writer return to a personal narrative? Why?

   _____

   _____

ARGUMENTATION

Argumentation is showing others the soundness of your viewpoint on a topic of controversy. An **argument** is not the same thing as a quarrel. The goal of an argument is not to attack your opponent. The goal of an argument is to offer good **reasons** in support of your **conclusion**, reasons that all parties to your dispute can accept. It is an art. An important first step is recognizing your "opponent" as a worthy adversary; if you don't there is no point in discussing or arguing a point. Also, realize that most issues are not black or white, but a shade of gray. You are trying to advance a position (your point) so that readers can clearly understand it and perhaps be swayed to change, not condemn those who disagree with you.

When you want to convince your readers of a point, you can't expect your readers to believe you on faith or because you say so. You have to appeal to their logic and common sense, showing that your thesis is based on sound reasoning and established facts. You'll have to examine the sub-issues of the topic, compare and contrast the merits of the two opposing positions, look at any cause-and-effect relationships, and explain your reasoning.

PREMISES AND CONCLUSIONS

Logic is the way we make judgments from statements we are willing to accept as facts. These judgments or conclusions are based on premises, stated and assumed. Some common premise flags are the words **because, since, given that** and **for**. These words usually come right before a premise. Here are two examples:

- **Because** euthanasia is murder, it is always morally wrong.
- **Given that** euthanasia is a common medical practice, the state legislatures ought to legalize it and set up regulations to prevent abuse.

Some common conclusion flags are the words **thus, therefore, hence, it follows that, so** and **consequently**. These words usually come right before a conclusion. Here are two examples that follow the premises above:

- Euthanasia involves choosing to die rather than to struggle on to see what life may bring. **Thus**, euthanasia is giving up on life, and it is **therefore** cowardly and despicable.
- Euthanasia is a personal choice between the patient and his or her physician; **consequently**, the state should not pass laws preventing this medical practice.

Premises and conclusions follow a classical chain of reasoning: a logical conclusion is reached by finding the connection that exists between the two premises. The questions of importance here is—"Is the conclusion true?" Yes, if it was validly drawn from true premises. No, if the second premise excludes other possibilities or if the stated or assumed premise is faulty. Look at this chain of reasoning:

- *Premise stated:*
  The decay of American culture is growing every year.
- *Premise assumed:*
  Judeo-Christian morals and values guide America.
- *Conclusion:*
  Judeo-Christian morals and values are responsible for the decay of American culture.

This is not a logical chain of reasoning because some would question if Americans adhere to Judeo-Christian morals and values as much as they did in the past and if other reasons might be responsible for the decay of American culture (if in fact it *is* decaying at all!).

Your argument must pass some tests if it is to be convincing. The first of these tests apply to any sort of essay you write: is your essay direct and well organized? If not, you have erected a barrier that may prevent your readers from sympathizing with your position. Next, is your argument well supported with detail in the form of evidence? This can be statistical, from personal experience, or from well-respected sources. If not, your argument will be difficult to believe—people want to be shown how something is true or logical, not simply told that it *is*.

LOGICAL FALLACIES

Also, you need to examine your ideas for "logical fallacies"—errors in logic or thinking. Here are some examples:

- ***Argumentum ad antiquitatem* (the argument to antiquity or tradition).** This is the familiar argument that some policy, behavior, or practice is right or acceptable because "it's always been done that way." This is an extremely popular fallacy in debate rounds; for example, "Every great civilization in history has provided state subsidies for art and culture." But that fact does not justify continuing the policy.
- **"*Ad hominem*"** means in Latin "to the man [or woman]" which means attacking the person rather than his/her argument. You can find some great examples of this sort of logical fallacy if you examine the quotes in newspapers from the opposing candidates in any political campaign. Here's an example: "My opponent, Mr. Cenekofsky, will certainly not make a good mayor. In the past the man has spoken out against an ordinance about minority women; therefore, he is sexist and racist." This statement is clearly meant as a smear against Mr. Cenekofsky without considering whether the ordinance is practical or cost-effective. *Argumentum ad*

hominem also occurs when someone's arguments are discounted merely because they stand to benefit from the policy they advocate—such as Bill Gates arguing against antitrust, rich people arguing for lower taxes, white people arguing against affirmative action, minorities arguing for affirmative action, etc. In all of these cases, the relevant question is not who makes the argument, but whether the argument is valid.

- **"Begging the question"** assumes that readers share basic assumptions and beliefs with the writer when in fact they don't necessarily. When you read—"Everyone knows," "We all agree," "It's obvious that"—you've encountered a question-begging argument. The writer is trying to pass off as a fact a statement that is nothing more than an opinion. Here's an example: An art student arguing for an exemption from a science requirement might claim that artists don't need a science requirement since they'll never use it. "Everyone knows that art students are not interested in the sciences." The problem with this argument is that not all art majors are uninterested in the sciences and that majoring in the humanities doesn't exclude one's relationship to the natural sciences; the assertion is inaccurate. This argument "begs the question" of the importance of requiring science for college graduation.

- **"Hasty generalizations"** draw conclusions from too little evidence. For example: "It's not safe to travel in the United States because of the terrorist attacks on the World Trade Center and the Pentagon." Although certainly these attacks have had a immense impact on our society, these incidents do not give enough evidence to make a general statement about travel safety in the United States. Be careful of absolute terms—*always*, *never*, *everyone*, *no one*, *all*, and *none*. These are rarely accurate.

- A *"Non Sequitur"* (Latin for "it does not follow") proposes a cause-and-effect link between two events or conditions that aren't necessarily connected. Here are two examples: "Rasheed's parents are well-to-do since he goes away for the entire summer and winter break every year." This statements **MAY** be true, but neither draws any direct connection between claims. It reflects clichéd or simplistic thinking rather than reasoning. Rasheed may be staying with friends or relatives or each of his parents may have worked two jobs.

Make sure your arguments follow logic. Think your argument through and ask: "On what are my claims based?"

ORGANIZATION

When you write an argumentation paper, you must address the opposing arguments or the paper will seem to evade key points. Keep in mind that counter arguments can make the structure of the paper more complex. You can either incorporate the counter arguments in the first body paragraph or into each paragraph where they are appropriate. For example:

I.   Introduction: Thesis
II. Counter arguments 1, 2, and 3
III. Your argument 1
    A.   Examples
    B.   Illustrations
IV. Your argument 2
    A.   Examples
    B.   Illustrations
V.   Your argument 3
    A.   Examples
    B.   Illustrations
VI. Conclusion

OR

I.   Introduction: Thesis
II. Your Argument 1
    A.   Counter Argument (if one for this point)
    B.   Your Examples
    C.   Your Illustrations
III. Your Argument 2
    A.   Counter Argument (if one for this point)
    B.   Your Examples
    C.   Your Illustrations
IV. Your Argument 3
    A.   Your Counter Argument (if one for this point)
    B.   Your Examples
    C.   Your Illustrations
V.   Your Argument 4 (this is optional)
    A.   Counter Argument (if one for this point)
    B.   Your Examples
    C.   Your Illustrations
VI. Conclusion

This is an essay for which you must plan carefully before you write. List all the points on your side; then list all the opposing views. Pick out the most convincing of each and discuss them in reverse order of importance—least to most important.

THE THESIS

An area to concentrate on is your thesis. Your thesis should state your position clearly. For example: "Although television certainly has its mind-numbing or violent shows, by parents carefully selecting television programs, television can educate and entertain responsibly." Don't announce your subject with "I'm going to write about television and how it harms children's values." Don't use "I" or "you."

Be sure your thesis doesn't contain broad generalizations: *any, all, none, always, never, only, no one,* and *everyone.* These "all-inclusive" words are a sign of faulty generalization where the writer assumes because something happens some of the time, it happens all the time. For example, if you write: "There is no reason to withhold a national health insurance program." The reader will immediately wonder, as should you, "Are there *no* reasons to withhold a national health insurance policy?" If your reader can think of at least one reason, and he or she surely will, then your credibility is compromised.

Another area to watch is writing a thesis that reflects your personal experience only. If your thesis mirrors only your experience, then you are relying on guesswork and an obviously inadequate sample of one case. For example, if you write, "College professors are not sympathetic to their students' complicated lives," what you really mean is "I had an ugly experience in Introduction to Biology when my professor wouldn't let me make up a test." Personal experience can be helpful to illustrate an argumentative essay, but you shouldn't allow it to be the only element of your thesis.

CONCLUSION

In your conclusion, you can make a suggestion. Here's an example from an essay on television watching: "So Americans should feel free to enjoy their television programs." Or you can write a "call for action": "So Americans should shut off the television and take a walk with their children." Of course, this is just one sentence of the three or four that make-up your conclusion, and conclusions for argumentation persuasion follow the other rules for conclusion writing.

READING AN ARGUMENT ESSAY

Let's look at the student essay "Television: Junk Food, Not Brain Food."

TELEVISION: JUNK FOOD, NOT BRAIN FOOD
MAUREEN WELLS

"Kevin, dinner's ready." No response. "Kevin, come and get it." Still no response. "Kevin, do you hear me?" Silence. "Kevin, it's getting cold!" Once more, no reply. What has happened to Kevin? Has he been abducted? Of course not, I can see him in the living room. Is he asleep? No, his eyes are wide open. Has he gone deaf? Maybe. What is wrong? Kevin has, in a sense, been abducted—taken against his parents' will to another place, another dimension—the unreal fantasy world of television. Physically present but mentally, intellectually, and even socially, Kevin is somewhere else, and these chilling effects of watching television—mental, intellectual and social—are frightening and statistically staggering.

Far from being "participatory," as technology guru Marshall McLuhan affirms in an interview with talk show host Tom Snyder, television viewing creates a passive mental attitude where the only real participation is to keep one's eyes open. Brain waves of viewers around the globe are being altered each day in the corporate action of television viewing. The body is relaxed in front of a continuously blinking screen; a hypnotic effect begins as alpha brain waves increase. A series of non-stop images made up of thousands upon thousands of dots flash before staring eyes. The viewer is mentally carried to a scene, along with millions or even billions of other viewers where they witness a predetermined scenario with a predetermined outcome. At regular intervals, eyes and minds are treated to an onslaught of high-tech advertising images and mantras or slogans (McLuhan). This is one global village meeting we can do without. The individual mind is at risk. Even McLuhan, one of television's greatest proponents, confirms this in the same interview where he states, "But one of the effects of television is to remove people's private identity. They become corporate peer group people just by watching. They lose interest in being individual, private individuals. And this is one of the hidden and perhaps insidious effects of television" (McLuhan).

This collective consciousness concept is alarming when we consider just who chooses what that collective consciousness will be focused on, whose values are advocated and whose ideals will be upheld. We are slowly becoming a one-world mind, learning what is and is not politically or otherwise correct from television. From the content of the evening news to issues broached on sit-coms, our thought processes are directed subtly, and sometimes not so subtly. Jerry Mander, a successful advertising executive who left his vocation after working with and researching the actual technology of television, wrote *Four Arguments for the Elimination of Television*, an expose of the pitfalls of television watching. He states, "Television images are not sought, they just arrive in a direct channel, all on their own, from cathode to brain . . . . We may have entered an era when information is fed directly into the mass subconscious."

Mander continues, "Television viewing may then qualify as a stranger's dream, from a faraway place, though it plays against the screen of your mind" (Mander 156).

A common justification for the merits of television is that it is intellectually stimulating. W. Cordellan in *Television and Children: Towards the Millennium* states that "aspects of the 'structure' of screen messages: their pace, absence of silence, visual tricks such as fades, dissolves, and time devices such as flashbacks might produce positive results on skills of visual inference and interpretation of spatial relations between objects." The same study continues on to say that "viewing is an active experience for children, and one from which they can, and often do, derive benefit." However, Fred Emery at the Center for Continuing Education, Australian National University at Canberra, said after his study on the neurophysiology of television viewing that "the technology of television and the inherent nature of the viewing experience actually inhibit learning as we usually think of it. Very little cognitive, recallable, analyzable, thought-based learning takes pace while watching TV" (253). Furthermore, the report says, "The evidence is that television not only destroys the capacity of the viewer to attend, it also, by taking over a complex of direct and indirect neural pathways, decreases vigilance—the general state of arousal which prepares the organism for action should its attention be drawn to specific stimulus" (254). The report says that since the viewer is physically removed from the action, "he must inhibit the neural pathways between visual data and the autonomic nervous system, which stimulates movement and mental attention. The viewer is left in a passive but also frustrated state" (254). According to the report *Strong Families, Strong Schools*, from the U.S. Dept. of Education, December 1994, "Academic achievement drops sharply for children who watch more than 10 hours a week of TV, or an average of two hours a day" (7). In light of this evidence, it is clear that television viewing not only decreases the potential for any real long-term learning but decreases mental awareness.

TV watching has had profound effects on society from national elections to the core family unit. *The Television Project* by Mediascape asserts that 98% of American homes have television and that 78% of Americans believe TV violence causes real life mayhem. They continue with "America, the nation with the highest homicide rate in the developed world, has seen violence soar to epidemic levels over the past several decades. The average child sees 8,000 murders on TV by the time he finishes elementary school." These statistics are impressive and disconcerting.

Are we Americans rushing home to meet with *Oprah* and *Rosie*—or our families? Are we spending "quality time" with our children by watching TV with them? Is *watching* a baseball game with Dad an adequate replacement for *playing* baseball with Dad? Television images are someone else's representation of reality. This cost to society is inestimable in terms of family life and relationships. A report, *Volume IV of Television and Social Behavior,* prepared by the National Institute of Mental Health of the Dept. of Health, Education and Welfare, reports that a majority of adults, nearly as high as the percentage as children, use television to learn how to handle specific life problems: family routines, relationships with fellow workers (260). Is television our family's source of wisdom?

Society also suffers because our political and news processes are corrupted through the manipulation of news. Elections are fought and won via television "sound bytes." The "talking heads" of so-called news shows are, in reality, mouthpieces of special interest groups reciting carefully worded morsels that the public is expected to, and often does, swallow. Style and persona have replaced content. The person with the most "charisma" wins, with character and content taking second place. The news we see on TV is chosen for us, edited for us, disseminated and explained to us. Mander, writing of television news coverage during the Vietnam War in 1964, gives an extreme example of news filtering. He says, "The Gulf of Tonkin incident never happened, but it was carried as legitimate news by every news outlet. That convinced both Congress and the public and gave Johnson the approval he needed to escalate the Vietnam War" (261).

So, if you don't mind becoming hypnotized on a regular basis and becoming part of a directed global consciousness with your awareness so dulled that learning is limited and your social/family life impaired while you are mentally assaulted and manipulated by producers, writers, government officials and advertising moguls, then – just stayed tuned.

Works Cited

Cordellan, W. *Television and Children: Towards the Millennium.* Communication 2 Research Trends, Vol. 10, 1990, No. 3 <www.cyfc.umn.edu> March 12, 2005.

Emery, Fred. Volume IV of Television and Social Behavior. National Institute of Mental Health. Dept. of Health and Human Services.

Mander, Jerry. *Four Arguments for the Elimination of Television.* New York: Morrow, 1978.

Quill, 1996. McLuhan Video, Inc. <www.videomcluhan.com/harcourt> March 14, 2005.

Strong Families, Strong Schools. U.S. Dept. of Education, December 1994,

The Television Project by Mediascape <www.mediascape.com> March 18, 2005.

PRACTICE 13   ANALYZING THE ESSAY: Answer the following questions about the essay you just read.

1. The author catches our attention in the opening sentences. What method of introduction does she use? Does she use more than one method?

_____

_____

_____

2. After the method to catch our attention, the author writes a transition, one that takes us from the opener to the thesis. What is the transition sentence(s)?

_____

_____

3. What is the thesis statement? What are the points she will discuss?

_____

_____

_____

4. To support her point of view, the writer cites several authorities. List three of them and their credentials.

_____

_____

_____

5. The authorities that the writer cites support her argument against television watching. What are three specific arguments she gives against television watching?

_____

_____

_____

6. Most good arguments give the other side's points and either acknowledge them as valid or refute them. Give at least one example where the author gives the other side's point. Then state whether she refutes the argument or acknowledges it as valid.

_____

_____

_____

7. In the conclusion, the author sums up her essay. What does she use to reinforce her thesis and show closure?

_____

_____

_____

SUMMARY WRITING

One of the most valuable ways to respond to a writer's story or article is through your own writing. Your purpose in writing a summary is twofold: to respond to the story or article by showing your understanding of what you have read and to do this in approximately 1/10th of the words of the original. In a summary you demonstrate that you can identify and **describe the main ideas** or thesis or controlling ideas and the major details **without adding any opinions of your own**.

Sometimes summary writing can be difficult because one requirement is that you cannot copy the exact words from the piece you are summarizing. You must come up with your own words to express the full message of the reading. Remember, a summary should be short, including only the main and important points. For example, a summary of a 1,000-word article would be about 100-150 words. A shorter reading would have a shorter summary while the summary of a longer reading would be longer.

Here are the steps to follow for good summary writing:

1. After reading the story or article, ask yourself who or what this is about. Once you have discovered that, write it down.
2. Next, ask yourself what major problem or idea is being discussed and write it down. At this point you have identified the main idea or thesis of the story or article.
3. This next step is crucial because it is here that you must decide what important details the writer discusses that support his/her article or story. Read each paragraph as a unit of thought and underline the main idea for each paragraph. As you reread or review the article or short story, look for these underlines in the text and add them to your notes.
4. Once you have identified these major points, write them in your own words. Do not "cheat" at this point and "borrow" the author's words. This is plagiarism. Also, do not make judgments or conclusions about the work. Your opinions about the topic are not relevant here.
5. You are almost finished with the summary, but you still have two more important steps. Read all your notes and underlines, and stop to think. (It isn't the product but the process. If you spend 5-10 minutes, maybe more, thinking about what you have read and looking at your writing from summary steps 1-3, you will be ready to write your summary.)
6. Based on your notes, write the first draft of your summary. Begin with the title and author of the original.
7. Revise your summary, exclude non-essential detail, and use your own words without adding your opinion, checking to see that you have included all the main points.

WRITING AN ESSAY EXAMINATION

You may often be asked in college to take essay exams. In certain ways, the same principles for writing good out-of-class essays apply to writing good in-class essays as well. For example, both kinds of essays are more successful when you take into consideration your purpose, audience and information; when you develop a thesis with support; when you prove your assertions with evidence; when you guide your readers with transitions, and so forth.

However, there are some differences to keep in mind as you prepare to write. The most important one is the purpose for writing. You write essay exams to demonstrate your knowledge. You are not only conveying information, but also proving to your audience — the examiner — that you have mastered reading and writing critically. In other words, your purpose is both informative and persuasive. Keeping this purpose in mind will help you both prepare for and write the essay.

PREPARING FOR THE EXAM

When you are reading the essays for the exam, pay attention to the connections between ideas. The evaluators are not looking for a collection of unrelated pieces of information. Rather, they want to see that you can write about the whole picture — how your thesis creates the framework for the specific facts, and how the examples or details fill in the gaps. If your instructor has given you the question in advance, practice answering that question. Outline your essay and then actually write it out, timing yourself. Remember that it's not simply what you say or the amount you write, but HOW you say it that's important. You want to show the evaluators that you have mastered the material of writing effectively.

Read the question thoroughly. Read the question carefully to determine exactly what you are being asked to do. Most essay exam questions, or "prompts," are carefully worded and contain specific instructions about WHAT you are to write about as well as HOW you should organize your answer. The prompt may use one or more of the following terms. If you see one of these terms, try to organize your essay to respond to the question or questions indicated.

compare:	What are the similarities among these ideas?
contrast:	What are the differences between these ideas?
critique:	What are the strengths and weaknesses of this idea?
describe:	What are the important characteristics or features of this idea?
evaluate:	What are the arguments for and against this idea? Which arguments are stronger?
explain:	Why is this the case?
interpret:	What does this idea mean? Why is it important?
justify:	Why is this correct? Why is this true?

Plan your answer. Jot down the main points you intend to make as you think through your answer. Then, use your list to help you stick to the topic and plan your outline. In an exam situation, it's easy to forget points if you don't write them down.

TAKING THE EXAM

Write out your essay, using good writing techniques. As was said earlier, in-class essay exams are like other essays, so use the same good writing strategies you use for other kinds of writing. Create a thesis for your essay that you can defend. Often, you can turn the prompt into an answer and use it as your thesis. Then, explain, develop, and support your thesis, drawing upon materials from readings. Be sure to support any and all generalizations with concrete evidence, relevant facts, and specific details that will convince your reader that your thesis is valid. Make your main points stand out by writing distinct paragraphs, and indicate the relationship between them with transitions. Finally, sum up your essay with a brief conclusion that lends your essay a clear sense of closure.

Proofread your answer. Reserve a few minutes after completing your essay to proofread it carefully. First, make sure you stick to the question. Always answer exactly the question asked without digressing. If you find you have digressed, neatly cross out the words or paragraphs. It's better to cross out a paragraph that is irrelevant (and to replace it with a relevant one if you have time) than to allow it to stand. In this context at least, quality is always preferable to quantity. Also check sentence structure, spelling and punctuation.

OVERVIEW

1. Read the question carefully.
2. Plan out your answer, including an outline and practice essay.
3. Support what you say with specific examples from the readings. For instance, if you say that the writer uses many metaphors, give some examples of these.
4. Do not pad your answer, but answer all parts of the question.
5. Use all the time provided.
6. Proofread your answer.

One final piece of advice is to **plan, plan, plan** and budget your time wisely. Show the evaluators your best work.

PART 2

READINGS

ACCEPTANCE SPEECH, NOVEMBER 4, 2008
BARACK OBAMA

Barack Hussein Obama, Jr. (1961-) is the 44th president of the United States, and the first African-American to hold the office. After graduating from Harvard Law School, he moved to Chicago to work as a civil rights attorney and teach constitutional law at the University of Chicago. He was elected to three terms in the Illinois Senate (1997-2004) and then served as the junior United States Senator from Illinois from 2005-2008 until his election as president November 4, 2008. He was inaugurated January 20, 2009. The following is his acceptance speech after his victory over Senator John McCain.

[1]Hello, Chicago. If there is anyone out there who still doubts that America is a place where all things are possible, who still wonders if the dream of our founders is alive in our time, who still questions the power of our democracy, tonight is your answer.

[2]It's the answer told by lines that stretched around schools and churches in numbers this nation has never seen, by people who waited three hours and four hours, many for the first time in their lives, because they believed that this time must be different, that their voices could be that difference. It's the answer spoken by young and old, rich and poor, Democrat and Republican, black, white, Hispanic, Asian, Native American, gay, straight, disabled and not disabled and Americans who sent a message to the world that we have never been just a collection of individuals or a collection of red states and blue states. We are, and always will be, the United States of America. It's the answer that led those who've been told for so long by so many to be cynical and fearful and doubtful about what we can achieve to put their hands on the arc of history and bend it once more toward the hope of a better day. It's been a long time coming, but tonight, because of what we did on this date in this election at this defining moment change has come to America.

[3]A little bit earlier this evening, I received an extraordinarily gracious call from Senator McCain. Senator McCain fought long and hard in this campaign. And he's fought even longer and harder for the country that he loves. He has endured sacrifices for America that most of us cannot begin to imagine. We are better off for the service rendered by this brave and selfless leader. I congratulate him; I congratulate Governor Palin for all that they've achieved. And I look forward to working with them to renew this nation's promise in the months ahead.

[4]I want to thank my partner in this journey, a man who campaigned from

his heart, and spoke for the men and women he grew up with on the streets of Scranton and rode with on the train home to Delaware, the vice president-elect of the United States, Joe Biden. And I would not be standing here tonight without the unyielding support of my best friend for the last 16 years, the rock of our family, the love of my life, the nation's next first lady, Michelle Obama. Sasha and Malia, I love you both more than you can imagine. And you have earned the new puppy that's coming with us to the new White House. And while she's no longer with us, I know my grandmother's watching, along with the family that made me who I am. I miss them tonight. I know that my debt to them is beyond measure. To my sister Maya, my sister Alma, all my other brothers and sisters, thank you so much for all the support that you've given me. I am grateful to them. And to my campaign manager, David Plouffe, the unsung hero of this campaign, who built the best — the best political campaign, I think, in the history of the United States of America; to my chief strategist David Axelrod who's been a partner with me every step of the way; to the best campaign team ever assembled in the history of politics—you made this happen, and I am forever grateful for what you've sacrificed to get it done.

[5]But above all, I will never forget who this victory truly belongs to. It belongs to you. It belongs to you. I was never the likeliest candidate for this office. We didn't start with much money or many endorsements. Our campaign was not hatched in the halls of Washington. It began in the backyards of Des Moines and the living rooms of Concord and the front porches of Charleston. It was built by working men and women who dug into what little savings they had to give $5 and $10 and $20 to the cause. It grew strength from the young people who rejected the myth of their generation's apathy, who left their homes and their families for jobs that offered little pay and less sleep. It drew strength from the not-so-young people who braved the bitter cold and scorching heat to knock on doors of perfect strangers, and from the millions of Americans who volunteered and organized and proved that more than two centuries later a government of the people, by the people, and for the people has not perished from the Earth. This is your victory. And I know you didn't do this just to win an election. And I know you didn't do it for me. You did it because you understand the enormity of the task that lies ahead. For even as we celebrate tonight, we know the challenges that tomorrow will bring are the greatest of our lifetime — two wars, a planet in peril, the worst financial crisis in a century. Even as we stand here tonight, we know there are brave Americans waking up in the deserts of Iraq and the mountains of Afghanistan to risk their lives for us. There are mothers and fathers who will lie awake after the children fall asleep and wonder how they'll make the mortgage or pay their doctors' bills or save enough for their child's college education.

[6]There's new energy to harness, new jobs to be created, new schools to build, and threats to meet, alliances to repair. The road ahead will be long. Our

climb will be steep. We may not get there in one year or even in one term. But, America, I have never been more hopeful than I am tonight that we will get there. I promise you, we as a people will get there.

[7]There will be setbacks and false starts. There are many who won't agree with every decision or policy I make as president. And we know the government can't solve every problem. But I will always be honest with you about the challenges we face. I will listen to you, especially when we disagree. And, above all, I will ask you to join in the work of remaking this nation, the only way it's been done in America for 221 years — block by block, brick by brick, calloused hand by calloused hand.

[8]What began 21 months ago in the depths of winter cannot end on this autumn night. This victory alone is not the change we seek. It is only the chance for us to make that change. And that cannot happen if we go back to the way things were. It can't happen without you, without a new spirit of service, a new spirit of sacrifice. So let us summon a new spirit of patriotism, of responsibility, where each of us resolves to pitch in and work harder and look after not only ourselves but each other. Let us remember that, if this financial crisis taught us anything, it's that we cannot have a thriving Wall Street while Main Street suffers.

[9]In this country, we rise or fall as one nation, as one people. Let's resist the temptation to fall back on the same partisanship and pettiness and immaturity that has poisoned our politics for so long. Let's remember that it was a man from this state who first carried the banner of the Republican Party to the White House, a party founded on the values of self-reliance and individual liberty and national unity. Those are values that we all share. And while the Democratic Party has won a great victory tonight, we do so with a measure of humility and determination to heal the divides that have held back our progress. As Lincoln said to a nation far more divided than ours, we are not enemies but friends. Though passion may have strained, it must not break our bonds of affection.

[10]And to those Americans whose support I have yet to earn, I may not have won your vote tonight, but I hear your voices. I need your help. And I will be your president, too. And to all those watching tonight from beyond our shores, from parliaments and palaces, to those who are huddled around radios in the forgotten corners of the world, our stories are singular, but our destiny is shared, and a new dawn of American leadership is at hand. To those — to those who would tear the world down: We will defeat you. To those who seek peace and security: We support you. And to all those who have wondered if America's beacon still burns as bright: Tonight we proved once more that the true strength of our nation comes not from the might of our arms or the scale of our wealth, but from the enduring power of our ideals: democracy, liberty, opportunity and unyielding hope. That's the true genius of America: that America can change. Our union can be perfected. What we've already achieved gives

us hope for what we can and must achieve tomorrow.

[11]This election had many firsts and many stories that will be told for generations. But one that's on my mind tonight's about a woman who cast her ballot in Atlanta. She's a lot like the millions of others who stood in line to make their voice heard in this election except for one thing: Ann Nixon Cooper is 106 years old. She was born just a generation past slavery; a time when there were no cars on the road or planes in the sky; when someone like her couldn't vote for two reasons — because she was a woman and because of the color of her skin.

[12]And tonight, I think about all that she's seen throughout her century in America — the heartache and the hope; the struggle and the progress; the times we were told that we can't, and the people who pressed on with that American creed. At a time when women's voices were silenced and their hopes dismissed, she lived to see them stand up and speak out and reach for the ballot. When there was despair in the Dust Bowl and depression across the land, she saw a nation conquer fear itself with a New Deal, new jobs, a new sense of common purpose. When the bombs fell on our harbor and tyranny threatened the world, she was there to witness a generation rise to greatness and a democracy was saved. She was there for the buses in Montgomery, the hoses in Birmingham, a bridge in Selma, and a preacher from Atlanta who told a people that We Shall Overcome. A man touched down on the moon, a wall came down in Berlin, a world was connected by our own science and imagination. And this year, in this election, she touched her finger to a screen, and cast her vote, because after 106 years in America, through the best of times and the darkest of hours, she knows how America can change. Yes we can.

[13]America, we have come so far. We have seen so much. But there is so much more to do. So tonight, let us ask ourselves — if our children should live to see the next century; if my daughters should be so lucky to live as long as Ann Nixon Cooper, what change will they see? What progress will we have made?

[14]This is our chance to answer that call. This is our moment. This is our time, to put our people back to work and open doors of opportunity for our kids; to restore prosperity and promote the cause of peace; to reclaim the American dream and reaffirm that fundamental truth, that, out of many, we are one; that while we breathe, we hope. And where we are met with cynicism and doubts and those who tell us that we can't, we will respond with that timeless creed that sums up the spirit of a people: Yes, we can.

[15]Thank you. God bless you. And may God bless the United States of America.

Vocabulary

[2] cynical   [5] apathy   [10] parliament   [12] tyranny

[4] unsung hero   [9] partisanship   [12] Dust Bowl   [14] creed

[4] strategist   [9] values

Discussion Questions

1. To what is Obama referring in paragraph 1? Extend your answer beyond the obvious.

2. Obama addresses many people and groups in his speech. List them. Why would he address these particular people/groups in his speech?

3. What is Obama referring to when he says that John McCain "endured sacrifices that most of us cannot begin to imagine"?

4. What is the significance of Obama's reference in paragraph 6 to "alliances to repair"?

5. What is he saying to the individual groups in paragraphs 9 and 10?

6. Why does Obama discuss Ann Nixon Cooper? Do you think this is an effective device? Explain.

7. Obama uses several metaphors in this speech (for example, "the rock of our family") to make his points. Pick three and discuss what they mean.

THE ACHIEVEMENT OF DESIRE
FROM *HUNGER OF MEMORY*

RICHARD RODRIQUEZ

Richard Rodriquez (1944-   ), a prominent Mexican-American writer, is an associate editor with Pacific News Service in San Francisco, a contributing editor of Harper's *and the* Los Angeles Times, *and a regular essayist on the* Jim Lehrer News Hour. *He is the author of* Brown: The Last Discovery of America *(2003);* Days of Obligation: An Argument with My Mexican Father *(1992); and* Hunger of Memory: The Education of Richard Rodriquez *(1983), from which this excerpt is taken.*

¹I stand in the ghetto classroom—"the guest speaker"—attempting to lecture on the mystery of the sounds of our words to rows of diffident students. "Don't you hear it? Listen! The music of our words. *'Sumer is i-cumen in . . . .'* And songs on the car radio. We need Aretha Franklin's voice to fill plain words with music—her life." In the face of their empty stares, I try to create an enthusiasm. But the girls in the back row turn to watch some boy passing outside. There are flutters of smiles, waves. And someone's mouth elongates heavy, silent words through the barrier of glass: Silent words—the lips straining to shape each voiceless syllable: *"Meet meee later errr."* By the door, the instructor smiles at me, apparently hoping that I will be able to spark some enthusiasm in the class. But only one student seems to be listening. A girl, maybe fourteen. In this gray room her eyes shine with ambition. She keeps nodding and nodding at all that I say; she even takes notes. And each time I ask a question, she jerks up and down in her desk like a marionette, while her hand waves over the bowed heads of her classmates. It is myself (as a boy) I see as she faces me now (a man in my thirties).

²The boy who first entered a classroom barely able to speak English, twenty years later concluded his studies in the stately quiet of the reading room in the British Museum. Thus with one sentence I can summarize my academic career. It will be harder to summarize what sort of life connects the boy to the man.

³With every award, each graduation from one level of education to the next, people I'd meet would congratulate me. Their refrain was always the same: "Your parents must be very proud." Sometimes then they'd ask me how I managed it—my "success." (How?) After a while, I had several quick answers to give in reply. I'd admit, for one thing, that I went to an excellent grammar

school. (My earliest teachers, the nuns, made my success their ambition.) And my brother and both my sisters were very good students. (They often brought home the shiny school trophies I came to want.) And my mother and father always encouraged me. (At every graduation they were behind the stunning flash of the camera when I turned to look at the crowd.)

⁴As important as these factors were, however, they account inadequately for my academic advance. Nor do they suggest what an odd success I managed. For although I was a very good student, I was also a very bad student. I was a "scholarship boy," a certain kind of scholarship boy. Always successful, I was always unconfident. Exhilarated by my progress. Sad. I became the prized student—anxious and eager to learn. Too eager, too anxious—an imitative and unoriginal pupil. My brother and two sisters enjoyed the advantages I did, and they grew to be as successful as I, but none of them ever seemed so anxious about their schooling. A second-grade student, I was the one who came home and corrected the "simple" grammatical mistakes of our parents. ("Two negatives make a positive.") Proudly I announced—to my family's startled silence—that a teacher had said I was losing all trace of a Spanish accent. I was oddly annoyed when I was unable to get parental help with a homework assignment. The night my father tried to help me with an arithmetic exercise, he kept reading the instructions, each time more deliberately, until I pried the textbook out of his hands, saying, "I'll try to figure it out some more by myself."

⁵When I reached the third grade, I outgrew such behavior. I became more tactful, careful to keep separate the two very different worlds of my day. But then, with ever-increasing intensity, I devoted myself to my studies. I became bookish, puzzling to all my family. Ambition set me apart. When my brother saw me struggling home with stacks of library books, he would laugh, shouting: "Hey, Four Eyes!" My father opened a closet one day and was startled to find me inside, reading a novel. My mother would find me reading when I was supposed to be asleep or helping around the house or playing outside. In a voice angry or worried or just curious, she'd ask: "What do you see in your books?" It became the family's joke. When I was called and wouldn't reply, someone would say I must be hiding under my bed with a book.

⁶(How did I manage my success?)

⁷What I am about to say to you has taken me more than twenty years to admit: *A primary reason for my success in the classroom was that I couldn't forget that schooling was changing me and separating me from the life I enjoyed before becoming a student.* That simple realization! For years I never spoke to anyone about it. Never mentioned a thing to my family or my teachers or classmates. From a very early age, I understood enough, just enough about my classroom experiences to keep what I knew repressed, hidden beneath layers of embarrassment. Not until my last months as a graduate student, nearly thirty years old, was it possible for me to think much about the reasons for my aca-

demic success. Only then. At the end of my schooling, I needed to determine how far I had moved from my past. The adult finally confronted, and now must publicly say, what the child shuddered from knowing and could never admit to himself or to those many faces that smiled at his every success. ("Your parents must be very proud....")

[8]At the end, in the British Museum (too distracted to finish my dissertation) for weeks I read, speed-read, books by modern educations theorists, only to find infrequent and slight mention of students like me . . . . Then one day, leafing through Richard Hoggart's *The Uses of Literacy,*[a] I found, in his description of the scholarship boy, myself. For the first time I realized that there were other students like me, and so I was able to frame the meaning of my academic success, its consequent price—the loss.

[9]Hoggart's description is distinguished, at least initially, by deep understanding. What he grasps very well is that the scholarship boy must move between environments, his home and the classroom, which are at cultural extremes, opposed. With his family, the boy has the intense pleasure of intimacy, the family's consolation in feeling public alienation. Lavish emotions texture home life. *Then*, at school, the instruction bids him to trust lonely reason primarily. Immediate needs set the pace of his parents' lives. From his mother and father the boy learns to trust spontaneity and non-rational ways of knowing. *Then*, at school, there is mental calm. Teachers emphasize the value of a reflectiveness that opens a space between thinking and immediate action:

[10]Years of schooling must pass before the boy will be able to sketch the cultural differences in his day as abstractly as this. But he senses those differences early. Perhaps as early as the night he brings home an assignment from school and finds the house too noisy for study.

[11]"He has to be more and more alone, if he is going to 'get on.' He will have, probably unconsciously, to oppose the ethos of the hearth, the intense gregariousness of the working-class family group. Since everything centres upon the living-room, there is unlikely to be a room of his own; the bedrooms are cold and inhospitable, and to warm them or the front room, if there is one, would not only be expensive, but would require an imaginative leap—out of the tradition—which most families are not capable of making. There is a corner of the living-room table. On the other side Mother is ironing, the wireless is on, someone is singing a snatch of song or Father says intermittently whatever comes to his head. The boy has to cut himself off mentally, so as to do his homework, as well as he can" (Hoggart).

[12]The next day, the lesson is as apparent at school. There are even rows of desks. Discussion is ordered. The boy must rehearse his thoughts and raise

---

[a] Richard Hoggart, *The Uses of Literacy* (London: Chatto and Windus, 1957), chapter 10.

his hand before speaking out in a loud voice to an audience of classmates. And there is time enough, and silence, to think about ideas (big ideas) never considered at home by his parents.

[13]Not for the working-class child alone is adjustment to the classroom difficult. Good schooling requires that any student alter early childhood habits. But the working-class child is usually least prepared for the change. And, unlike many middle-class children, he goes home and sees in his parents a way of life not only different but starkly opposed to that of the classroom. (He enters the house and hears his parents talking in ways his teachers discourage.)

[14]Without extraordinary determination and the great assistance of others—at home and at school—there is little chance for success. Typically most working-class children are barely changed by the classroom. The exception succeeds. The relative few become scholarship students. Of these, Richard Hoggart estimates, most manage a fairly graceful transition. Somehow they learn to live in the two very different worlds of their day. There are others, however, those Hoggart pejoratively terms "scholarship boys," for whom success comes with special anxiety. Scholarship boy: good student, troubled son. The child is "moderately endowed," intellectually mediocre, Hogart supposed—though it may be more pertinent to note the special qualities of temperament in the child. High strung child. Brooding. Sensitive. Haunted by the knowledge that one *chooses* to become a student. (Education is not an inevitable or natural step in growing up.) Here is a child who cannot forget that his academic success distances him from a life he loved, even from his own memory of himself.

[15]Initially, he wavers, balances allegiance. (Hoggart says, "The boy is himself [until he reaches, say, the upper forms] very much of *both* the worlds of home and school. He is enormously obedient to the dictates of the world of school, but emotionally still strongly wants to continue as part of the family circle.") Gradually, necessarily, the balance is lost. The boy needs to spend more and more time studying, each night enclosing himself in the silence permitted and required by intense concentration. He takes his first step toward academic success, away from his family.

[16]He cannot afford to admire his parents. (How could he and still pursue such a contrary life?) He permits himself embarrassment at their lack of education. And to evade nostalgia for the life he has lost, he concentrates on the benefits education will bestow upon him. He becomes especially ambitious. Without the support of old certainties and consolations, almost mechanically, he assumes the procedures and doctrines of the classroom. The kind of allegiance the young student might have given his mother and father only days earlier, he transfers to the teacher, the new figure of authority.

Vocabulary

[1]diffident	[8]dissertation	[11]ethos	[14]pejoratively
[1]marionette	[9]lavish	[11]gregariousness	[15]dictates
[4]exhilarated	[9]spontaneity	[11]inhospitable	[16]nostalgia
[5]tactful	[10]abstractly	[11]intermittently	

Discussion Questions

1. What does Rodriquez mean when he talks about using language differently in public and private life?

2. In what ways does Rodriquez's experience with education create a "gulf" between himself and his family?

3. Describe the "scholarship boy."

4. What does Rodriquez say he gains and loses by pursuing education?

5. Explain the title of Rodriquez's book, *Hunger of Memory: The Education of Richard Rodriquez*, from which this excerpt is taken.

6. Some people think that as immigrant populations assimilate to American culture they will lose touch with their roots and their "voices." Do you agree? Explain.

7. Compare Rodriquez's essay with Mark Twain's essay "Two Views of the Mississippi" on page 553 of this text. What similarities do you find?

8. Look at Judith Ortiz Cofer's essay "The Myth of the Latin Woman" on page 423 of this text. In what ways are the experiences of the two writers similar? Which areas of their experiences with American culture does each of the two writers emphasize?

ADDRESS TO THE NATION 9/11/01
GEORGE W. BUSH

*At 8:46 a.m. on Tuesday September 11, 2001 the first of two commercial airliners hijacked by fundamentalist Islamic terrorists crashed into one of the two towers of the World Trade Center in New York City. Approximately 20 minutes later a second hijacked aircraft, piloted by Al-Qaeda-linked terrorists, crashed into the other WTC tower. During the next few hours, the two towers collapsed, another hijacked plane was flown into the Pentagon and a fourth crashed in a field in Pennsylvania as passengers attempted to overpower the hijackers Excluding the 19 hijackers, 2,974 people, mostly civilians, died in the attacks. At 8:30 that evening President **George W. Bush** went on nationwide television to speak to Americans about the events of the day.*

[1]Good evening. Today, our fellow citizens, our way of life, our very freedom came under attack in a series of deliberate and deadly terrorist acts. The victims were in airplanes or in their offices: secretaries; businessmen and women; military and federal workers; moms and dads; friends and neighbors. Thousands of lives were suddenly ended by evil, despicable acts of terror.

[2]The pictures of airplanes flying into buildings, fires burning, huge structures collapsing have filled us with disbelief, terrible sadness, and a quiet, unyielding anger. These acts of mass murder were intended to frighten our nation into chaos and retreat. But they have failed; our country is strong.

[3]A great people has been moved to defend a great nation. Terrorist attacks can shake the foundations of our biggest buildings, but they cannot touch the foundation of America. These acts shattered steel, but they cannot dent the steel of American resolve.

[4]America was targeted for attack because we're the brightest beacon for freedom and opportunity in the world. And no one will keep that light from shining.

[5]Today, our nation saw evil, the very worst of human nature. And we responded with the best of America—with the daring of our rescue workers, with the caring for strangers and neighbors who came to give blood and help in any way they could.

[6]Immediately following the first attack, I implemented our government's emergency response plans. Our military is powerful, and it's prepared. Our emergency teams are working in New York City and Washington, D.C. to help with local rescue efforts.

[7]Our first priority is to get help to those who have been injured, and to take every precaution to protect our citizens at home and around the world from further attacks.

[8]The functions of our government continue without interruption. Federal agencies in Washington which had to be evacuated today are reopening for essential personnel tonight, and will be open for business tomorrow. Our financial institutions remain strong, and the American economy will be open for business, as well.

[9]The search is underway for those who are behind these evil acts. I've directed the full resources of our intelligence and law enforcement communities to find those responsible and to bring them to justice. We will make no distinction between the terrorists who committed these acts and those who harbor them.

[10]I appreciate so very much the members of Congress who have joined me in strongly condemning these attacks. And on behalf of the American people, I thank the many world leaders who have called to offer their condolences and assistance.

[11]America and our friends and allies join with all those who want peace and security in the world, and we stand together to win the war against terrorism. Tonight, I ask for your prayers for all those who grieve, for the children whose worlds have been shattered, for all whose sense of safety and security has been threatened. And I pray they will be comforted by a power greater than any of us, spoken through the ages in Psalm 23: "Even though I walk through the valley of the shadow of death, I fear no evil, for You are with me."

[12]This is a day when all Americans from every walk of life unite in our resolve for justice and peace. America has stood down enemies before, and we will do so this time. None of us will ever forget this day. Yet, we go forward to defend freedom and all that is good and just in our world.

[13]Thank you. Good night, and God bless America.

Discussion Questions

1. President Bush addresses several different groups of people in this speech. Identify by paragraph number the various groups being addressed.

2. What is Bush's purpose in addressing the different groups?

3. Which specific parts of government does Bush bring into his remarks? Why do you think he did this?

4. Bush repeats the words "steel" and "foundation" in paragraph 3. Why do you think he does this?

5. Describe the tone of President Bush's remarks here. Compare Bush's tone to that of President Franklin Roosevelt in his speech to Congress following the attack on Pearl Harbor on page 223 of this text.

6. Compare this speech to President Roosevelt's speech. In what ways are they similar? How are they different?

ADVICE TO LAERTES
FROM *HAMLET*

WILLIAM SHAKESPEARE

*Although **William Shakespeare** (c. 1564-1616) is considered by many to be the greatest English-speaking playwright, we know very little about him We do know that
he married Anne Hathaway in 1582 and fathered three
children. He wrote or collaborated on 38 plays, although
scholars debate the exact number. In 1611, he retired from
writing and returned to his home in Stratford, England.
The first folio of his work was published in 1623.*

Polonius. Yet here, Laertes? Aboard, aboard, for shame!   1
    The wind sits in the shoulder of your sail,
    And you are stayed for. There—my blessing with thee,
    And these few precepts in thy memory
    Look thou character. Give thy thoughts no tongue,   5
    Nor any unproportioned thought his act.
    Be thou familiar, but by no means vulgar.
    Those friends thou hast, and their adoption tried,
    Grapple them unto thy soul with hoops of steel,
    But do not dull thy palm with entertainment   10
    Of each new-hatched, unfledged comrade. Beware
    Of entrance to a quarrel; but being in,
    Bear't that th' opposed may beware of thee.
    Give every man thine ear, but few thy voice;
    Take each man's censure, but reserve thy judgment.   15
    Costly thy habit as thy purse can buy,
    But not expressed in fancy; rich, not gaudy,
    For the apparel oft proclaims the man,
    And they in France of the best rank and station
    Are of a most select and generous chief in that.   20
    Neither a borrower nor a lender be,
    For loan oft loses both itself and friend,
    And borrowing dulleth the edge of husbandry.
    This above all, to thine own self be true,
    And it must follow, as the night the day,   25
    Thou canst not then be false to any man.
    Farewell. My blessing season this in thee!

Vocabulary

[4]precepts   [11]unfledged   [16]habit   [23]husbandry

[9]grapple   [15]censure   [17]gaudy

Discussion Questions

1. Polonious is Laertes's father. In this speech from *Hamlet,* he is giving Laertes advice before Laertes leaves for France. Transcribe this advice into modern English.

2. Shakespeare uses figurative language throughout this speech. Find three examples of figurative language, write what they mean, and then discuss the effectiveness of their use.

3. Choose one piece of advice that Polonius gives Laertes that you think is applicable to a young person going away from home today. Explain why you chose this piece of advice.

4. Compare this advice to Franklin's "Advice to a Young Man" on the next page or Jamaica Kincaid's "Girl" on page 274.

ADVICE TO A YOUNG MAN

BENJAMIN FRANKLIN

Benjamin Franklin *(1706-1790), among other accomplishments, wrote* Poor Richard's Almanack, *performed electrical studies, was designated the first postmaster general of the United States and helped draft the Declaration of Independence. He organized Philadelphia's Union Fire Company, the first in the city, and invented the heat-efficient Franklin stove (still in use today), refusing to obtain a patent for it because it benefitted society. He also invented swim fins and bifocals.*

PHILADELPHIA, *25 June, 1745.*

¹To My DEAR FRIEND: I know of no Medicine fit to diminish the violent natural Inclinations you mention; and if I did, I think I should not communicate it to you. Marriage is the proper remedy. It is the most natural state of Man, and therefore the State in which you are most likely to find solid Happiness. Your reasons against entering into it at present appear to me to be not well founded. The Circumstantial Advantages you have in View by postponing it, are not only uncertain, but they are small in comparison with that of the Thing itself, the being married and settled. It is the Man and Woman united that makes the complete human Being. Separate, she wants his force of Body and Strength of Reason, he her Softness, Sensibility and acute Discernment. Together they are more likely to succeed in the World. A single Man has not nearly the Value he would have in the State of Union. He is an incomplete Animal. He resembles the odd Half of a pair of Scissors.

²If you get a prudent, healthy Wife, your Industry in your Profession, with her good economy, will be a Fortune sufficient.

³But if you Will not take this Counsel, and persist in thinking a Commerce with the Sex inevitable, then I repeat my former Advice that in all your Amours you should prefer old Women to young ones. You call this a Paradox, and demand my reasons. They are these:

⁴1. Because they have more Knowledge of the World, and their minds are better stored with Observations, their Conversation is more improving and more lastingly agreeable.

⁵2. Because when Women cease to be handsome, they study to be good. To maintain their Influence over Men, they supply the Diminution of Beauty by an Augmentation of Utility. They learn to do a thousand Services, small and great; and are the most tender and useful of all Friends when you are sick. Thus they continue amiable. And hence there is hardly such a thing to be found as an old Woman who is not a good Woman.

⁶3. Because there is no Hazard of Children, which irregularly produced may be attended with much Inconvenience.

[7]4. Because through more Experience they are more prudent and discreet in conducting an Intrigue to prevent Suspicion. The Commerce with them is therefore safer with regard to your reputation. And with regard to theirs, if the Affair should happen to be known, considerate People might be rather inclined to excuse an old Woman, who would kindly take care of a young Man, form his manners by her good Counsels, and prevent his ruining his Health and Fortune among mercenary Prostitutes.

[8]5. Because in every Animal that walks upright, the Deficiency of the Fluids that fill the Muscles appears first in the highest Part. The Face first grows lank and wrinkled, then the neck, then the Breast and Arms, the lower Parts continuing to the last as plump as ever; so that covering all above with a Basket, and regarding only what is below the Girdle, it is impossible of two Women to know an old one from a young one. And as in the Dark all Cats are grey, the Pleasure of Corporal Enjoyment with an old Woman is at least equal and frequently superior; every Knack being by Practice capable of Improvement.

[9]6. Because the sin is less. The Debauching a Virgin may be her Ruin, and make her for Life unhappy.

[10]7. Because the Compunction is less. The having made a young girl miserable may give you frequent bitter Reflections; none of which can attend making an old Woman happy.

[11]8th, and lastly. They are so grateful!

[12]Thus much for my Paradox. But still I advise you to marry immediately; being sincerely,

Your affectionate Friend,
BENJAMIN FRANKLIN

Vocabulary

[3]amours	[5]augmentation	[7]intrigue	[9]debauching
[3]paradox	[5]utility	[7]mercenary	[10]compunction
[5]diminution	[5]amiable		

Discussion Questions

1. This is a fictional letter written to a fictional young man. What is the main point in this letter?

2. Discuss the framework that Franklin uses to lead into his main point.

3. Franklin uses irony to make his point. Define irony and give an example from the reading.

4. Which of the six reasons that Franklin cites are applicable to today's young man.

5. Did you find this letter sexist? Explain.

6. Compare this advice to Polonius's "Advice to Laertes" on page 83 or to Jamaica Kincaid's "Girl" on page 274 of this text.

ALLEGORY OF THE CAVE

PLATO

Plato (428 BC-347 BC), who studied under Socrates, is one of the most important Greek philosophers. He founded the Academy in Athens, considered the first university. Devoted to research and instruction in philosophy, mathematics and the sciences, it produced numerous scientific and mathematical innovations. Plato was a prolific writer. "The Allegory of the Cave" is from Book VII of his Republic *and is an extended metaphor for the state of human existence. Here Socrates is talking to a young follower of his named Glaucon.*

¹And now, I said, let me show in a figure how far our nature is enlightened or unenlightened:—Behold! human beings living in an underground den, which has a mouth open towards the light and reaching all along the den; here they have been from their childhood, and have their legs and necks chained so that they cannot move, and can only see before them, being prevented by the chains from turning round their heads. Above and behind them a fire is blazing at a distance, and between the fire and the prisoners there is a raised way; and you will see, if you look, a low wall built along the way, like the screen which marionette players have in front of them, over which they show the puppets.

²I see.

³And do you see, I said, men passing along the wall carrying all sorts of vessels, and statues and figures of animals made of wood and stone and various materials, which appear over the wall? Some of them are talking, others silent.

⁴You have shown me a strange image, and they are strange prisoners.

⁵Like ourselves, I replied; and they see only their own shadows, or the shadows of one another, which the fire throws on the opposite wall of the cave?

⁶True, he said; how could they see anything but the shadows if they were never allowed to move their heads?

⁷And of the objects which are being carried in like manner they would only see the shadows?

⁸Yes, he said.

⁹And if they were able to converse with one another, would they not suppose that they were naming what was actually before them?

¹⁰Very true.

¹¹And suppose further that the prison had an echo which came from the other side, would they not be sure to fancy when one of the passers-by spoke

that the voice which they heard came from the passing shadow?

[12]No question, he replied.

[13]To them, I said, the truth would be literally nothing but the shadows of the images.

[14]That is certain.

[15]And now look again, and see what will naturally follow if the prisoners are released and disabused of their error. At first, when any of them is liberated and compelled suddenly to stand up and turn his neck round and walk and look towards the light, he will suffer sharp pains; the glare will distress him, and he will be unable to see the realities of which in his former state he had seen the shadows; and then conceive some one saying to him, that what he saw before was an illusion, but that now, when he is approaching nearer to being and his eye is turned towards more real existence, he has a clearer vision,—what will be his reply? And you may further imagine that his instructor is pointing to the objects as they pass and requiring him to name them,—will he not be perplexed? Will he not fancy that the shadows which he formerly saw are truer than the objects which are now shown to him?

[16]Far truer.

[17]And if he is compelled to look straight at the light, will he not have a pain in his eyes which will make him turn away to take refuge in the objects of vision which he can see, and which he will conceive to be in reality clearer than the things which are now being shown to him?

[18]True, he said.

[19]And suppose once more, that he is reluctantly dragged up a steep and rugged ascent, and held fast until he is forced into the presence of the sun himself, is he not likely to be pained and irritated? When he approaches the light his eyes will be dazzled, and he will not be able to see anything at all of what are now called realities.

[20]Not all in a moment, he said.

[21]He will require to grow accustomed to the sight of the upper world. And first he will see the shadows best, next the reflections of men and other objects in the water, and then the objects themselves; then he will gaze upon the light of the moon and the stars and the spangled heaven; and he will see the sky and the stars by night better than the sun or the light of the sun by day?

[22]Certainly.

[23]Last of all he will be able to see the sun, and not mere reflections of him in the water, but he will see him in his own proper place, and not in another; and he will contemplate him as he is.

[24]Certainly.

[25]He will then proceed to argue that this is he who gives the season and the years, and is the guardian of all that is in the visible world, and in a certain way the cause of all things which he and his fellows have been accustomed to behold?

[26]Clearly, he said, he would first see the sun and then reason about him.

[27]And when he remembered his old habitation, and the wisdom of the den and his fellow-prisoners, do you not suppose that he would felicitate himself on the change, and pity them?

[28]Certainly, he would.

[29]And if they were in the habit of conferring honors among themselves on those who were quickest to observe the passing shadows and to remark which of them went before, and which followed after, and which were together; and who were therefore best able to draw conclusions as to the future, do you think that he would care for such honors and glories, or envy the possessors of them? Would he not say with Homer,

[30]Better to be the poor servant of a poor master, [a]

and to endure anything, rather than think as they do and live after their manner?

[31]Yes, he said, I think that he would rather suffer anything than entertain these false notions and live in this miserable manner.

[32]Imagine once more, I said, such a one coming suddenly out of the sun to be replaced in his old situation; would he not be certain to have his eyes full of darkness?

[33]To be sure, he said.

[34]And if there were a contest, and he had to compete in measuring the shadows with the prisoners who had never moved out of the den, while his sight was still weak, and before his eyes had become steady (and the time which would be needed to acquire this new habit of sight might be very considerable), would he not be ridiculous? Men would say of him that up he went and down he came without his eyes;[b] and that it was better not even to think of ascending; and if any one tried to loose another and lead him up to the light, let them only catch the offender, and they would put him to death.[c]

[35]No question, he said.

[36]This entire allegory, I said, you may now append, dear Glaucon, to the previous argument; the prison-house is the world of sight, the light of the fire is the sun, and you will not misapprehend me if you interpret the journey upwards

---

[a]This refers to a passage in Homer's *Odyssey* in which the ghost of the great hero Achilles, when asked if he is not proud of the fame his deeds have spread throughout the world, answers that he would rather be a slave on a worn-out farm than king over all of the famous dead.

[b]The comic playwright Aristophanes had mocked Plato's teacher, Socrates, as a foolish intellectual with his head in the clouds.

[c]Plato is alluding to the Athenians, who had condemned Socrates to death. Plato considered Socrates to be supremely enlightened.

to be the ascent of the soul into the intellectual world according to my poor belief, which, at your desire, I have expressed whether rightly or wrongly God knows. But, whether true or false, my opinion is that in the world of knowledge the idea of good appears last of all, and is seen only with an effort; and, when seen, is also inferred to be the universal author of all things beautiful and right, parent of light and of the lord of light in this visible world, and the immediate source of reason and truth in the intellectual; and that this is the power upon which he who would act rationally, either in public or private life must have his eye fixed.

[37] I agree, he said, as far as I am able to understand you.

[38] Moreover, I said, you must not wonder that those who attain to this beatific vision are unwilling to descend to human affairs; for their souls are ever hastening into the upper world where they desire to dwell; which desire of theirs is very natural, if our allegory may be trusted.

[39] Yes, very natural.

[40] And is there anything surprising in one who passes from divine contemplations to the evil state of man, misbehaving himself in a ridiculous manner; if, while his eyes are blinking and before he has become accustomed to the surrounding darkness, he is compelled to fight in courts of law, or in other places, about the images or the shadows of images of justice, and is endeavoring to meet the conception of those who have never yet seen absolute justice?

[41] Anything but surprising, he replied.

[42] Any one who has common sense will remember that the bewilderments of the eyes are of two kinds, and arise from two causes, either from coming out of the light or from going into the light, which is true of the mind's eye; and he who remembers this when he sees any one whose vision is perplexed and weak, will not be too ready to laugh; he will first ask whether that soul of man has come out of the brighter life, and is unable to see because unaccustomed to the dark, or having turned from darkness to the day is dazzled by excess of light. And he will count the one happy in his condition and state of being, and he will pity the other; or, if he have a mind to laugh at the soul which comes from below into the light, there will be more reason in this than in the laugh which greets him who returns from above out of the light into the den.

[43] That, he said, is a very just distinction.

[44] But then, if I am right, certain professors of education must be wrong when they say that they can put a knowledge into the soul which was not there before, like sight into blind eyes.

[45] They undoubtedly say this, he replied.

[46] Whereas our argument shows that the power and capacity of learning exists in the soul already; and that just as the eye was unable to turn from darkness to light without the whole body, so too the instrument of knowledge can only by the movement of the whole soul be turned from the world of becoming

into that of being, and learn by degrees to endure the sight of being and of the brightest and best of being, or in other words, of the good.

Vocabulary

[3]vessel   [15]perplexed   [36]append   [36]inferred

[15]disabused   [27]felicitate   [36]misapprehend   [38]beatific

[15]compelled   [28]confer

Discussion Questions

1. What does the sun symbolize in the allegory?

2. The cave is an allegory for everyday reality. Who are the prisoners and what kinds of activities do they engage in?

3. Describe other "caves" in modern life in which people might be "imprisoned" or feel "imprisoned."

4. Is a resident of the cave likely to want to make the ascent to the outer world? Why or why not?

5. If a prisoner is released from the cave and compelled to look toward the light, what will he experience? Why?

6. What are the stages of the liberated prisoner's experience outside the cave?

7. If the liberated prisoner goes back to the cave and tries to explain to his former fellow prisoners, what kind of reaction will he get? Why?

8. What is truth according to Plato in this allegory?

9. To what extent do you find Plato's point about human tendency to confuse "shadows" with "reality" relevant today?

10. What could be the elements that prevent people from seeing the truth, or regarding "shadow" as the "truth"?

11. We have two very different models of education: blank slate information delivery (i.e., the prisoners in the cave who learn the names of the shadows through repetition) and the discovery process in which the prisoner is forced to experience and explore realities outside of his comfort zone. Which model did your school system use? Was it effective? Why or why not?

AMERICA:
THE MULTINATIONAL SOCIETY

ISHMAEL REED

Ishmael Scott Reed (1938-   ) is a poet, essayist, and novelist whose work is often critical of American political culture. Reed graduated from the University of Buffalo and taught for 35 years at the University of California, Berkeley. Among his nine novels, four collections of poetry, six plays,and four collections of essays, he is probably best known for two of his satirical novels, Yellow Back Broke-Down *(1969) and* Mumbo-Jumbo *(1972), which literary critic Harold Bloom characterized as one of the 500 most important works in Western literature.*

"At the annual Lower East Side Jewish Festival yesterday, a Chinese woman ate a pizza slice in front of Ty Thuan Duc's Vietnamese grocery store. Beside her a Spanish-speaking family patronized a cart with two signs: "Italian Ices" and "Kosher by Rabbi Alper." And after the pastrami ran out, everybody ate knishes."—New York *Times* 23 June 1983

[1]On the day before Memorial Day, 1983, a poet called me to describe a city he had just visited. He said that one section included mosques, built by the Islamic people who dwelled there. Attending his reading, he said, were large numbers of Hispanic people, forty thousand of whom lived in the same city. He was not talking about a fabled city located in some mysterious region of the world. The city he'd visited was Detroit.

[2]A few months before, as I was leaving Houston, Texas, I heard it announced on the radio that Texas's largest minority was Mexican-American, and though a foundation recently issued a report critical of bilingual education, the taped voice used to guide the passengers on the air trams connecting terminals in Dallas Airport is in both Spanish and English. If the trend continues, a day will come when it will be difficult to travel through some sections of the country without hearing commands in both English and Spanish; after all, for some western states, Spanish was the first written language and the Spanish style lives on in the western way of life.

[3]Shortly after my Texas trip, I sat in an auditorium located on the campus of the University of Wisconsin at Milwaukee as a Yale professor—whose original work on the influence of African cultures upon those of the Americas has led to his ostracism from some monocultural intellectual circles—walked up and down the aisle, like an old-time southern evangelist, dancing and drum-

ming the top of the lectern, illustrating his points before some serious Afro-American intellectuals and artists who cheered and applauded his performance and his mastery of information. The professor was "white." After his lecture, he joined a group of Milwaukeeans in a conversation. All of the participants spoke Yoruban,[a] though only the professor had ever traveled to Africa.

[4]One of the artists told me that his paintings, which included African and Afro-American mythological symbols and imagery, were hanging in the local McDonald's restaurant. The next day I went to McDonald's and snapped pictures of smiling youngsters eating hamburgers below paintings that could grace the walls of any of the country's leading museums. The manager of the local McDonald's said, "I don't know what you boys are doing, but I like it," as he commissioned the local painters to exhibit in his restaurant.

[5]Such blurring of cultural styles occurs in everyday life in the United States to a greater extent than anyone can imagine and is probably more prevalent than the sensational conflict between people of different backgrounds that is played up and often encouraged by the media. The result is what the Yale professor, Robert Thompson, referred to as a cultural bouillabaisse, yet members of the nation's present educational and cultural Elect[b] still cling to the notion that the United States belongs to some vaguely defined entity they refer to as "Western civilization," by which they mean, presumably, a civilization created by the people of Europe, as if Europe can be viewed in monolithic terms. Is Beethoven's *Ninth Symphony*, which includes Turkish marches, a part of Western civilization, or the late nineteenth- and twentieth-century French paintings, whose creators were influenced by Japanese art? And what of the cubists, through whom the influence of African art changed modern painting, or the surrealists, who were so impressed with the art of the Pacific Northwest Indians that, in their map of North America, Alaska dwarfs the lower forty-eight in size?

[6]Are the Russians, who are often criticized for their adoption of "Western" ways by Tsarist dissidents in exile,[c] members of Western civilization? And what of the millions of Europeans who have black African and Asian ancestry,

---

[a]Yoruban (or Yoruba) is the third most spoken African language and is associated with populations in the Nigeria-Togo-Benin region of West Africa. Traces of the language are also found in Brazil and Cuba.

[b]The "Elect" here refers to a "cultural elite," that is, those who are seen as setting the standards for literature, art, music, language and so on in American culture. Reed repeats the term in a different context in paragraph 11 where it refers to the belief in some Protestant sects, based upon biblical interpretation, that a chosen few believers, the "called, justified, adopted, sanctified, and saved," have been chosen (elected) by God to go to heaven while everyone else will suffer eternal damnation.

[c]"Tsarist dissidents" is a reference to followers in exile of the Tsar (or Czar) of Russia who was deposed and killed by the Bolsheviks in the Russian Revolution of 1917.

black Africans having occupied several countries for hundreds of years? Are these "Europeans" members of Western civilization, or the Hungarians, who originated across the Urals in a place called Greater Hungary, or the Irish, who came from the Iberian Peninsula?[d]

[7]Even the notion that North America is part of Western civilization because our "system of government" is derived from Europe is being challenged by native American historians who say that the founding fathers, Benjamin Franklin especially, were actually influenced by the system of government that had been adopted by the Iroquois hundreds of years prior to the arrival of large numbers of Europeans.

[8]Western civilization, then, becomes another confusing category like Third World, or Judeo-Christian culture, as man attempts to impose his small-screen view of political and cultural reality upon a complex world. Our most publicized novelist recently said that Western civilization was the greatest achievement of mankind, an attitude that flourishes on the street level as scribbles in public restrooms: "White Power," "Niggers and Spics Suck," or "Hitler was a prophet," the later being the most telling, for wasn't Adolph Hitler the archetypal monoculturalist who, in his pigheaded arrogance, believed that one way and one blood was so pure that it had to be protected from alien strains at all costs? Where did such an attitude, which has caused so much misery and depression in our national life, which has tainted even our noblest achievements, begin? An attitude that caused the incarceration of Japanese-American citizens during World War II, the persecution of Chicanos and Chinese-Americans, the near-extermination of the Indians, and the murder and lynchings of thousands of Afro-Americans.

[9]Virtuous, hardworking, pious, even though they occasionally would wander off after some fancy clothes, or rendezvous in the woods with the town prostitute, the Puritans are idealized in our schoolbooks as "a hardy band" of no-nonsense patriarchs whose discipline razed the forest and brought order to the New World (a term that annoys Native American historians). Industrious, responsible, it was their "Yankee ingenuity" and practicality that created the work ethic. They were simple folk who produced a number of good poets, and they set the tone for the American writing style, of lean and spare lines, long before Hemingway. They worshipped in churches whose colors blended in with the New England snow, churches with simple structures and ornate lecterns.

[10]The Puritans were a daring lot, but they had a mean streak. They hated the theater and banned Christmas. They punished people in a cruel and inhuman manner. They killed children who disobeyed their parents. When they came in contact with those whom they considered heathens or aliens, they be-

---

[d]The Iberian Peninsula is the southwestern tip of Europe containing Spain, Portugal and a small piece of Southern France.

haved in such a bizarre and irrational manner that this chapter in the American history comes down to us as a late-movie horror film. They exterminated the Indians, who taught them how to survive in a world unknown to them, and their encounter with the calypso culture of Barbados[e] resulted in what the tourist guide in Salem's Witches' house refers to as the Witch-craft Hysteria.[f] The Puritan legacy of hard work and meticulous accounting led to the establishment of a great industrial society; it is no wonder that the American industrial revolution began in Lowell, Massachusetts, but there was the other side, the strange and paranoid attitudes toward those different from the Elect.

[11]The cultural attitudes of that early Elect continue to be voiced in everyday life in the United States: the president of a distinguished university, writing a letter to the *Times,* belittling the study of African civilizations; the television network that promoted its show on the Vatican art with the boast that this art represents "the finest achievements of the human spirit." A modern up-tempo state of complex rhythms that depends upon contacts with an international community can no longer behave as if it dwelled in a "Zion Wilderness"[g] surrounded by beasts and pagans.

[12]When I heard a schoolteacher warn the other night about the invasion of the American educational system by foreign curriculums, I wanted to yell at the television set, "Lady, they're already here." It has already begun because the world is here. The world has been arriving at these shores for at least ten thousand years from Europe, Africa, and Asia. In the late nineteenth and early twentieth centuries, large numbers of Europeans arrived, adding their cultures to those of the European, African, and Asian settlers who were already here, and recently millions have been entering the country from South America and the Caribbean, making Yale Professor Bob Thompson's bouillabaisse richer and thicker.

[13]One of our most visionary politicians said that he envisioned a time

---

[e]Calypso music of the Caribbean, including Barbados and especially Trinidad, was introduced into the United States in the 1930's, but the culture that Reed refers to traces its roots back to rhythms and traditions brought to America by African slaves beginning in the 17th century.

[f]Reed's connecting of "Calypso culture" to the Salem Witch Trials probably refers to the role of Tituba in that event. The origins of Tituba, who was one of the first three people accused of witchcraft, are obscure, but it is generally believed that she migrated to Massachusetts from Barbados. Some religious traditions with origins in Africa that were practiced in the Caribbean, as well as those of the Native Americans, were viewed by some Puritans (notably Cotton Mather) as witchcraft.

[g]"Zion Wilderness," a reference to the language of the Book of Isaiah of the Hebrew Bible (the Christian Old Testament), is used here in the sense of America acting as if it were the ancient land of Israel (sometimes referred to as the Land of Zion), isolating and protecting itself from other lands that harbor "beasts and pagans."

when the United States could become the brain of the world, by which he meant the repository of all of the latest advanced information systems. I thought of that remark when an enterprising poet friend of mine called to say that he had just sold a poem to a computer magazine and that the editors were delighted to get it because they didn't carry fiction or poetry. Is that the kind of world we desire? A humdrum homogeneous world of all brains and no heart, no fiction, no poetry; a world of robots with human attendants bereft of imagination, of culture? Or does North America deserve a more exciting destiny? To become a place where the cultures of the world crisscross. This is possible because the United States is unique in the world: The world is here.

Vocabulary

[3]ostracism	[6]dissidents	[9]razed	[11]pagans
[3]lectern	[8]archetypal	[9]Yankee	[13]repository
[5]prevalent	[8]monoculturalist	[9]ingenuity	[13]humdrum
[5]bouillabaisse	[8]Chicanos	[9]ornate	[13]homogeneous
[5]monolithic	[9]pious	[10]heathens	[13]bereft
[5]cubism	[9]rendezvous	[10]meticulous	
[5]surrealism	[9]patriarchs		

Discussion Questions

1. What is Reed's purpose in putting the quote from the New York *Times* at the beginning of his essay?

2. Summarize Reed's thesis in one or two sentences.

3. Reed says in paragraph 5 that " . . . conflict between people of different backgrounds . . . is played up and often encouraged by the media." Do you agree with Reed's assessment of American media's handling of conflicts between people of "different backgrounds"? Support your answer and give an example.

4. Cite an example from your own experience of Robert Thompson's "cultural bouillabaisse."

5. What does Reed mean by "small-screen view" in paragraph 8.

6. Reed ends paragraph 8 with a list. What, specifically, is he referring to in each of the items on the list?

7. What is the tone of the topic sentence of paragraph 9—positive or negative? Explain your answer.

8. Reed uses the term "the Elect" several times in this essay. To whom is he referring and do you think he approves or disapproves of them?

9. Why, according to Reed, is the United States "unique in the world" and does he see this as a positive or a negative?

10. Compare this essay written in 1988 to the one written in 1894 by Theodore Roosevelt ("True Americanism") located on page 537 in this text. In what ways are the two writers' messages the same or different?

THE ANT AND THE GRASSHOPPER
W. SOMERSET MAUGHAM

W. Somerset Maugham (1874-1965) was supposed to become a lawyer; instead he became a playwright, novelist, travel writer, essayist, and short story writer. He published over fifty books in his lifetime. Many of his works, including Of Human Bondage *(1915) and* The Razor's Edge *(1944), were made into movies. His experiences as a spy for the British during World War I are reflected in his novel* Amenden: Or the British Agent *(1928), a work that strongly influenced such later writers as Graham Greene, Ian Fleming and John le Carre.*

¹When I was a very small boy I was made to learn by heart certain of the fables of La Fontaine, and the moral of each was carefully explained to me. Among those learned was *The Ant and the Grasshopper,* which is devised to bring home to the young the useful lesson that in an imperfect world industry is rewarded and giddiness punished. In this admirable fable (I apologise for telling something which everyone one is politely, but inexactly, supposed to know) the ant spends a laborious summer gathering its winter store, while the grasshopper sits on a blade of grass singing to the sun. Winter comes and the ant is comfortably provided for, but the grasshopper has an empty larder: he goes to the ant and begs for a little food. Then the ant gives him her classic answer:

²"What were you doing in the summer time?"

³"Saving your presence, I sang. I sang all day, all night."

⁴"You sang. Why, then go, and dance."

⁵I do not ascribe it to perversity on my part, but rather to the inconsequence of childhood, which is deficient in moral sense, that I could never quite reconcile myself to the lesson. My sympathies were with the grasshopper and for some time I never saw an ant without putting my foot on it. In this summary (and as I have discovered since, entirely human) fashion I sought to express my disapproval of prudence and common-sense.

⁶I could not help thinking of this fable when the other day I saw George Ramsay lunching by himself in a restaurant. I never saw anyone wear an expression of such deep gloom. He was staring into space. He looked as though the burden of the whole world sat upon his shoulders. I was sorry for him: I suspected at once that his unfortunate brother had been causing trouble again. I went up to him and held out my hand.

⁷"How are you?" I asked.

[8]"I'm not in hilarious spirits," he answered.

[9]"Is it Tom again?"

[10]He sighed.

[11]"Yes, it's Tom again."

[12]"Why don't you chuck him? You've done everything in the world for him. You must know by now that he's quite hopeless."

[13]I suppose every family has a black sheep. Tom had been a sore trial to his for twenty years. He had begun life decently enough: he went into business, married and had two children. The Ramsays were perfectly respectable people and there was every reason to suppose that Tom Ramsay would have a useful and honourable career.

[14]But one day, without warning, he announced that he didn't like work and that he wasn't suited for marriage. He wanted to enjoy himself. He would listen to no expostulations. He left his wife and his office. He had a little money and he spent two happy years in various capitals of Europe. Rumours of his doings reached his relations from time to time and they were profoundly shocked. He certainly had a very good time. They shook their heads and asked what would happen when his money was spent. They soon found out: he borrowed. He was charming and unscrupulous. I have never met anyone to whom it was more difficult to refuse a loan. He made a steady income from his friends and he made friends easily. But he always said that the money you spent on necessities was boring; the money that was amusing to spend was the money you spent on luxuries. For this he depended on his brother George. He did not waste his charm on him.

[15]George was respectable. Once or twice he fell to Tom's promises of amendment and gave him considerable sums in order that he might make a fresh start. On these Tom bought a motorcar and some very nice jewelry. But when circumstances forced George to realise that his brother would never settle down and he washed his hands of him, Tom, without a qualm, began to blackmail him. It was not very nice for a respectable lawyer to find his brother shaking cocktails behind the bar of his favourite restaurant or to see him waiting on the box-seat of a taxi outside his club. Tom said that to serve in a bar or to drive a taxi was a perfectly decent occupation, but if George could oblige him with a couple of hundred pounds he wouldn't mind for the honour of the family giving it up. George paid.

[16]Once Tom nearly went to prison. George was terribly upset. He went into the whole discreditable affair. Really Tom had gone too far. He had been wild, thoughtless and selfish, but he had never before done anything dishonest, by which George meant illegal; and if he were prosecuted he would assuredly be convicted. But you cannot allow your only brother to go to gaol. The man Tom had cheated, a man called Cronshaw, was vindictive. He was determined to take the matter into court; he said Tom was a scoundrel and should be pun-

ished. It cost George an infinite deal of trouble and five hundred pounds to settle the affair. I have never seen him in such a rage as when he heard that Tom and Cronshaw had gone off together to Monte Carlo the moment they cashed the cheque. They spent a happy month there.

[17]For twenty years Tom raced and gambled, philandered with the prettiest girls, danced, ate in the most expensive restaurants, and dressed beautifully. He always looked as if he had just stepped out of a bandbox. Though he was forty-six you would never have taken him for more than thirty-five. He was a most amusing companion and though you knew he was perfectly worthless you could not but enjoy his society. He had high spirits, an unfailing gaiety and incredible charm. I never grudged the contributions he regularly levied on me for the necessities of his existence. I never lent him fifty pounds without feeling that I was in his debt. Tom Ramsay knew everyone and everyone knew Tom Ramsay. You could not approve of him, but you could not help liking him.

[18]Poor George, only a year older than his scapegrace brother, looked sixty. He had never taken more than a fortnight's holiday in the year for a quarter of a century. He was in his office every morning at nine-thirty and never left it till six. He was honest, industrious and worthy. He had a good wife, to whom he had never been unfaithful even in thought, and four daughters to whom he was the best of fathers. He made a point of saving a third of his income and his plan was to retire at fifty-five to a little house in the country where he proposed to cultivate his garden and play golf. His life was blameless. He was glad that he was growing old because Tom was growing old too. He rubbed his hands and said:

[19]"It was all very well when Tom was young and good looking, but he's only a year younger than I am. In four years he'll be fifty. He won't find life too easy then. I shall have fifty thousand pounds by the time I'm fifty. For twenty-five years I've said that Tom would end in the gutter. And we shall see how he likes that. We shall see if it really pays best to work or be idle."

[20]Poor George! I sympathised with him. I wondered now as I sat down beside him what infamous thing Tom had done. George was evidently very much upset.

[21]"Do you know what's happened now?" he asked me.

[22]I was prepared for the worst. I wondered if Tom had got into the hands of the police at last. George could hardly bring himself to speak.

[23]"You're not going to deny that all my life I've been hard working, decent, respectable and straightforward. After a life of industry and thrift I can look forward to retiring on a small income in gilt-edged securities. I've always done my duty in that state of life in which it has pleased Providence to place me."

[24]"True."

[25]"And you can't deny that Tom has been an idle, worthless, dissolute

and dishonourable rogue. If there were any justice he'd be in the workhouse."

[26]"True."

[27]George grew red in the face.

[28] "A few weeks ago he became engaged to a woman old enough to be his mother. And now she's died and left him everything she had. Half a million pounds, a yacht, a house in London and a house in the country."

[29] George Ramsay beat his clenched fist on the table.

[30] "It's not fair, I tell you, it's not fair. Damn it, it's not fair."

[31] I could not help it. I burst into a shout of laughter as I looked at George's wrathful face. I rolled in my chair; I very nearly fell on the floor. George never forgave me. But Tom often asks me to excellent dinners in his charming house in Mayfair, and if he occasionally borrows a trifle from me, that is merely from force of habit. It is never more than a sovereign.

Vocabulary

[1]LaFontaine	[14]expostulations	[17]philandered	[25]dissolute
[1]giddiness	[14]unscrupulous	[17]bandbox	[25]rogue
[1]larder	[15]qualm	[18]scapegrace	[31]wrathful
[5]perversity	[16]discreditable	[18]fortnight	[31]trifle
[5]inconsequence	[16]gaol	[23]gilt-edged	[31]sovereign
[5]reconcile	[16]vindictive		

Discussion Questions

1. How does the narrator introduce the story he is going to tell?

2. During the telling of the story, the narrator shifts time frames. Identify the two shifts and explain their importance to the story.

3. What is the setting–place and time–of this story? What clues contained in the text led you to this conclusion?

4. Discuss Tom's character. Be specific in your assessment of him.

5. What is the "blackmail" described in paragraph 15? Do you think this would work in America today? Explain the reasons for your answer.

6. Discuss George's character. What in his sense of self convinces him to keep helping Tom?

7. Discuss the narrator's feelings toward the fable he tells at the beginning of the story in connection to the story's conclusion.

8. George or Tom?—With whom would you rather be friends? Explain.

9. Look at the original fable in poetic form on the next page. What do you see in this version that adds to Maugham's prose summary of the fable?

THE GRASSHOPPER AND THE ANT

[1]The Grasshopper having sung
All the summer long,
Found herself lacking food
When the North Wind began its song.
Not a single little piece
Of fly or grub did she have to eat.

[2]She went complaining of hunger
To the Ant's home, her neighbour,
Begging there for a loan
Of some grain to keep herself alive
Til the next season should arrive.
"I shall pay you," she said,
"Before next August, on my word as an animal.
I'll pay both interest and principal."

[3]The Ant was not so inclined:
this not being one of her faults.
"What did you do all summer?"
Said she to the grasshopper.

[4]"Night and day I sang,
I hope that does not displease you."

[5]"You sang? I will not look askance.
But now my neighbour it's time to dance."

FROM **THE ANTICHRIST**

FRIEDRICH NIETZSCHE

Friedrich Nietzsche (1844-1900) was born in Röcken, Germany. Both of his grandfathers and his father were Lutheran ministers. A brilliant student, Nietzsche studied at the University of Bonn where he began to turn against the religious teachings of his father and grandfathers. Nietzsche was appointed professor of classical philology at the University of Basel, Switzerland at the age of 24—before he had finished his doctoral studies. At the age of 46 he suffered a nervous breakdown from which he never fully recovered; he died in Weimar, Germany. His notable works include Thus Spake Zarathustra *(1883-85);* Beyond Good and Evil *(1886); and* The Antichrist *(1888).*

PREFACE

[1]This book belongs to the rarest of men. Perhaps not one of them is yet alive. It is possible that they may be among those who understand my *Zarathustra*:[a] how *could* I confound myself with those who are now sprouting ears? First, the day after tomorrow must come for me. Some men are born posthumously.

[2]The conditions under which anyone understands me, and *fully* understands me—I know them only too well. Even to endure my seriousness, my passion, he must carry intellectual integrity to the verge of hardness. He must be accustomed to living on mountain tops—and to looking upon the wretched gabble of politics and nationalism as *beneath* him. He must have become indifferent; he must never ask of the truth whether it brings profit to him or a fatality to him. He must have an inclination, born of strength, for questions that no one has the courage for; the courage for the *forbidden;* predestination for the labyrinth. The experience of seven solitudes. New ears for new music. New eyes for what is most distant. A new conscience for truths that have hitherto remained unheard. *And* the will to economize in the grand manner—to hold together his strength, his enthusiasm. Reverence for self; love of self; absolute freedom of self. Very well, then! of that sort only are my readers, my true readers, my readers foreordained: of what account are the *rest?*—The rest are merely humanity.—One must make one's self superior to humanity, in power, in *loftiness* of soul,—in contempt.

FRIEDRICH W. NIETZSCHE

---

[a] *Zarathustra* is a reference to one of Nietzsche's primary works, *Thus Spake Zarathustra,* in which the philosopher develops the ideas of "eternal recurrence," (all events that have happened will happen again, infinitely) and the role of the *ubermensch* (translated as "overman" or " superman"). Man is viewed as merely a bridge between animals and the overman.

2.

[3]What is good?—Whatever augments the feeling of power, the will to power, power itself, in man.

[4]What is evil?—Whatever springs from weakness.

[5]What is happiness?—The feeling that power *increases*—that resistance is overcome.

[6]Not contentment, but more power; not peace at any price, but war; *not* virtue, but efficiency (virtue in the Renaissance sense, *virtu,* virtue free of moral acid).

[7]The weak and the botched shall perish: first principle of *our* charity. And one should help them to it.

[8]What is more harmful than any vice?—Practical sympathy for the botched and the weak—Christianity.

3.

[9]The problem that I set here is not what shall replace mankind in the order of living creatures (man is an end) but what type of man must be *bred,* must be *willed,* as being the most valuable, the most worthy of life, the most secure guarantee of the future.

[10]This more valuable type has appeared often enough in the past: but always as a happy accident, as an exception, never as deliberately *willed.* Very often this higher type has been precisely the most feared; hitherto it has been almost *the* terror of terrors—and out of that terror the contrary type has been willed, cultivated and *attained:* the domestic animal, the herd animal, the sick brute-man—the Christian.

4.

[11]Mankind surely does *not* represent an evolution toward a better or stronger or higher level, as progress is now understood. This "progress" is merely a modern idea, which is to say, a false idea. The European of today, in his essential worth, falls far below the European of the Renaissance; the process of evolution does *not* necessarily mean elevation, enhancement, strengthening.

[12]True enough, it succeeds in isolated and individual cases in various parts of the earth and under the most widely different cultures, and in these cases a *higher* type certainly manifests itself; something which, compared to mankind in the mass, appears as a sort of superman.[b] Such happy strokes of

---

[b] "Superman" is Nietzsche's concept of the superior being, the person who is above conventional morality. In popular culture, when the comic book hero Superman was first created by Jerry Siegal and Joe Shuster in 1932, he was originally a villain modeled on Nietzsche's concept. As the comic book series progressed, Superman became a hero and Lex Luthor took on the characteristics of the ultimate villain who is above all constraints of societal values.

high success have always been possible, and will remain possible, perhaps, for all time to come. Even whole races, tribes and nations may occasionally represent such lucky accidents.

5.

[13]We should not deck out and embellish Christianity: it has waged a war to the death against this *higher* type of man, it has put all the deepest instincts of this type under its ban, it has developed its concept of evil, of the Evil One himself, out of these instincts—the strong man as the typical reprobate, the "outcast among men." Christianity has taken the part of all the weak, the low, the botched; it has made an ideal out of *antagonism* to all the self-preservative instincts of sound life; it has corrupted even the faculties of those natures that are intellectually most vigorous, by representing the highest intellectual values as sinful, as misleading, as full of temptation. The most lamentable example: the corruption of Pascal,[c] who believed that his intellect had been destroyed by original sin, whereas it was actually destroyed by Christianity!

6.

[14]It is a painful and tragic spectacle that rises before me: I have drawn back the curtain from the *rottenness* of man. . . . As you probably surmise, I understand rottenness in the sense of *decadence:* my argument is that all the values on which mankind now fixes its highest aspirations are *decadence*-values.

[15]I call an animal, a species, an individual corrupt, when it loses its instincts, when it chooses, when it *prefers,* what is injurious to it. A history of the "higher feelings," the "ideals of humanity"—and it is possible that I'll have to write it—would almost explain why man is so degenerate. Life itself appears to me as an instinct for growth, for survival, for the accumulation of forces, for *power:* whenever the will to power fails there is disaster. My contention is that all the highest values of humanity have been emptied of this will—that the values of *decadence,* of *nihilism,* now prevail under the holiest names.

---

[c] Blaise Pascal was a 17th century French philosopher, scientist and mathematician who experienced two great religious conversions later in his life. Here, Nietzsche is being critical of Pascal, the rational scientist and mathemetician, for "betraying" rationality and embracing Christianity. Pascal is known for formulating "Pascal's Wager," which says a) It is possible that the Christian God exists and it is possible that the Christian God does not exist; b) If one believes in the Christian God and He exists, then one receives an infinitely great reward and if He does not exist, then one loses little or nothing; 3) If one does not believe in the Christian God and He exists, then one receives an infinitely great punishment, but if He does not exist, then one gains little or nothing.; 4) It is better to receive an infinitely great reward or lose little or nothing than it is to receive an infinitely great punishment or gain little or nothing; 5) Therefore, it is better (more rational) to believe in the Christian God than it is not to believe in the Christian God.

7.

[16]Christianity is called the religion of *pity.*—Pity stands in opposition to all the tonic passions that augment the energy of the feeling of aliveness; it is a depressant. Anyone who pities loses power. Suffering is made contagious by pity; under certain circumstances it may lead to a total sacrifice of life and living energy—a loss out of all proportion to the magnitude of the cause (the case of the death of the Nazarene). . . . Pity thwarts the whole law of evolution, which is the law of natural selection. It preserves whatever is ripe for destruction; it fights on the side of those disinherited and condemned by life; by maintaining life in so many of the botched of all kinds, it gives life itself a gloomy and dubious aspect. Mankind has ventured to call pity a virtue (in every *superior* moral system it appears as a weakness); going still further, it has been called *the* virtue, the source and foundation of all other virtues—but let us always bear in mind that this was from the standpoint of a philosophy that was nihilistic, and upon whose shield *the denial of life* was inscribed.

[17]Schopenhauer[d] was right in this: that by means of pity life is denied. . . . Let me repeat: this depressing and contagious instinct stands against all those instincts which work for the preservation and enhancement of life: in the role of *protector* of the miserable, it is a prime agent in the promotion of *decadence—pity* persuades to extinction. Of course, one doesn't say "extinction": one says "the other world," or "God," or "the *true* life," or Nirvana, salvation, blessedness. This innocent rhetoric, from the realm of religious-ethical balderdash, appears a *good deal less innocent* when one reflects upon the tendency that it conceals beneath sublime words: the tendency to *destroy life.* Nothing is more unhealthy, amid all our unhealthy modernism, than Christian pity. To be the doctors *here,* to be unmerciful *here,* to wield the knife *here*—all this is *our* business, all this is *our* sort of humanity.

****

9.

[18]Upon this theological instinct I make war: I find the tracks of it everywhere. Whoever has theological blood in his veins is shifty and dishonorable in all things. The pathetic thing that grows out of this condition is called *faith:* in other words, closing one's eyes upon one's self once and for all, to avoid suffering the sight of incurable falsehood. People erect a concept of morality, of vir-

---

[d] Arthur Schopenhauer (1788 – 1860) was a German philosopher who influenced Nietzsche. Schopenhauer favored a lifestyle of closely controlling human desires, similar to the priciples of living found in Buddhism.

tue, of holiness upon this false view of all things; they ground good conscience upon faulty vision; they argue that no other sort of vision has value any more, once they have made theirs sacrosanct with the names of "God," "salvation" and "eternity."

[19]I unearth this theological instinct in all directions: it is the most widespread and the most *subterranean* form of falsehood to be found on earth. Whatever a theologian regards as true *must* be false: there you have almost a criterion of truth. His profound instinct of self-preservation stands against truth ever coming into honor in any way, or even getting stated. Wherever the influence of theologians is felt there is a transvaluation of values, and the concepts "true" and "false" are forced to change places: whatever is most damaging to life is there called "true," and whatever exalts it, intensifies it, approves it, justifies it and makes it triumphant is there called "false." When theologians, working through the "consciences" of princes (or of peoples), stretch out their hands for power, there is never any doubt as to the fundamental issue: the will to make an end, the *nihilistic* will exerts that power.

****

14.

[20]We have unlearned something. We have become more modest in every way. We no longer derive man from the "spirit," from the "god-head"; we have dropped him back among the beasts. We regard him as the strongest of the beasts because he is the craftiest; one of the results thereof is his intellectuality. On the other hand, we guard ourselves against a conceit which would assert itself even here: that man is the great second thought in the process of organic evolution. He is, in truth, anything but the crown of creation: beside him stand many other animals, all at similar stages of development. And even when we say that, we say a bit too much, for man, relatively speaking, is the most botched of all the animals and the sickliest, and he has wandered the most dangerously from his instincts—though for all that, to be sure, he remains the most *interesting!* . . .

15.

[21]Under Christianity, neither morality nor religion has any point of contact with actuality. It offers purely imaginary *causes* ("God" "soul," "ego," "spirit," "free will" . . .), and purely imaginary *effects* ("sin" "salvation" "grace," "punishment," "forgiveness of sins"). Intercourse between imaginary *beings* ("God," "spirits," "souls"); an imaginary *natural history* (anthropocentric; a total denial of the concept of natural causes); an imaginary *psychology* (misunderstandings of self, misinterpretations of agreeable or disagreeable general

feelings—for example, of the states of the *nervus sympathicus*[e] with the help of the sign-language of religio-ethical balderdash—"repentance," "pangs of conscience," "temptation by the devil," "the presence of God"); an imaginary *teleology* (the "kingdom of God," "the last judgment," "eternal life").

[22]This purely *fictitious world,* greatly to its disadvantage, is to be differentiated from the world of dreams; the later at least reflects reality, whereas the former falsifies it, cheapens it and denies it. Once the concept of "nature" had been opposed to the concept of "God," the word "natural" necessarily took on the meaning of "abominable"—the whole of that fictitious world has its sources in hatred of the natural (—the real!—), and is no more than evidence of a profound uneasiness in the presence of reality. *This explains everything.* Who alone has any reason for living his way out of reality? The one who suffers under it. But to suffer from reality one must be a *botched* reality. The preponderance of pains over pleasures is the cause of this fictitious morality and religion: but such a preponderance also supplies the formula for *decadence.*

****

17.

[23]Wherever the will to power begins to decline, in whatever form, there is always an accompanying decline physiologically, a *decadence.* The divinity of this *decadence,* shorn of its masculine virtues and passions, is converted perforce into a god of the physiologically degraded, of the weak. Of course, they do not *call* themselves the weak; they call themselves "the good." . . . .

18.

[24]The Christian concept of a god—the god as the patron of the sick, the god as a spinner of cobwebs, the god as a spirit—is one of the most corrupt concepts that has ever been set up in the world: it probably touches low-water mark in the ebbing evolution of the god-type. God degenerated into the *contradiction of life.* Instead of being its transfiguration and eternal Yea!, in him war is declared on life, on nature, on the will to live! God becomes the formula for every slander upon the "here and now," and for every lie about the "beyond"! In him nothingness is deified, and the will to nothingness is made holy!

19.

[25]The fact that the strong races of northern Europe did not repudiate this

---

[e] *nervus sympathicus* is a part of the autonomous nervous system that makes organs function without the voluntary input of the organism as, for example, the digestive system. Here, Nietzsche is saying that religion encourages us to attribute natural physiological feelings (e.g., a stomach ache) to a supernatural cause.

Christian god does little credit to their gift for religion—and not much more to their taste. They ought to have been able to make an end of such a moribund and worn-out product of the *decadence*. A curse lies upon them because they were not equal to it; they made illness, decrepitude and contradiction a part of their instincts—and since then they have not managed to *create* any more gods. Two thousand years have come and gone—and not a single new god! Instead, there still exists, and as if by some intrinsic right—as if he were the *ultimatum* and *maximum* of the power to create gods, of the *creator spiritus* in mankind— this pitiful god of Christian monotono-theism! This hybrid image of decay, conjured up out of emptiness, contradiction and vain imagining, in which all the instincts of *decadence,* all the cowardices and wearinesses of the soul find their sanction!

20.

[26]In my condemnation of Christianity I surely hope I do no injustice to a related religion with an even larger number of believers: I allude to *Buddhism.* Both are to be reckoned among the nihilistic religions—they are both *decadence* religions—but they are separated from each other in a very remarkable way. For the fact that he is able to *compare* them at all the critic of Christianity is indebted to the scholars of India. Buddhism is a hundred times as realistic as Christianity. It is part of its living heritage that it is able to face problems objectively and coolly; it is the product of long centuries of philosophical speculation. The concept, "god," was already disposed of before it appeared. Buddhism is the only genuinely *positive* religion to be encountered in history . . . . It does not speak of a "struggle with sin," but, yielding to reality, of the "struggle with suffering." Sharply differentiating itself from Christianity, it puts the self-deception that lies in moral concepts behind it; it is, in my phrase, *beyond* good and evil.

[27]The two physiological facts upon which Buddhism grounds itself and upon which it bestows its chief attention are, *first,* an excessive sensitiveness to sensation, which manifests itself as a refined susceptibility to pain; and *second,* an extraordinary spirituality, a too- protracted concern with concepts and logical procedures, under the influence of which the instinct of personality has yielded to a notion of the "impersonal. . . . " These physiological states produced a *depression,* and Buddha tried to combat it by hygienic measures. Against it he prescribed a life in the open, a life of travel; moderation in eating and a careful selection of foods; caution in the use of intoxicants; the same caution in arousing any of the passions that foster a bilious habit and heat the blood; finally, no *worry,* either on one's own account or on account of others.

[28]He encourages ideas that make for either quiet contentment or good cheer—he finds means to combat ideas of other sorts. He understands good, the state of goodness, as something which promotes health. *Prayer* is not included,

and neither is *asceticism*. There is no categorical imperative[f] nor are there any disciplines, even within the walls of a monastery (it is always possible to leave). . . . For the same reason he does not advocate any conflict with unbelievers; his teaching is antagonistic to nothing so much as to revenge, aversion, resentment ("enmity never brings an end to enmity": the moving refrain of all Buddhism). And in all this he was right, for it is precisely these passions which, in view of the main purpose of his regimen, are *unhealthful*. The mental fatigue that he observes, already plainly displayed in too much "objectivity" (that is, in the individual's loss of interest in himself, in loss of balance and of "egoism"), he combats by strong efforts to lead even the spiritual interests back to the *ego*. In Buddha's teaching, egoism is a duty. The "one thing needful," the question "how can you be delivered from suffering," regulates and determines the whole spiritual diet. (Perhaps one will here recall that Athenian who also declared war upon pure "scientificality," to wit, Socrates, who also elevated egoism to the estate of a morality).

21.

[29]The things necessary to Buddhism are a very mild climate, customs of great gentleness and liberality, and *no* militarism; moreover, it must get its start among the higher and better educated classes. Cheerfulness, quiet and the absence of desire are the chief attributes, and they are *attained*. Buddhism is not a religion in which perfection is merely an object of aspiration: perfection is actually normal.

[30]Under Christianity the instincts of the subjugated and the oppressed come to the fore: it is only those who are at the bottom who seek their salvation in it. Here the prevailing pastime, the favorite remedy for boredom is the discussion of sin, self-criticism, the inquisition of conscience; here the emotion produced by *power* (called "God") is pumped up (by prayer); here the highest good is regarded as unattainable, as a gift, as "grace." Here, too, open dealing is lacking; concealment and the darkened room are Christian. Here body is despised and hygiene is denounced as sensual; the church even ranges itself against cleanliness (the first Christian order after the banishment of the Moors closed the public baths, of which there were 270 in Cordova alone).[g]

---

[f] "Categorical imperative" is a term coined by German philosopher Immanuel Kant. It is the core concept of his moral philosophy, or ethics, and may be stated as "Act only according to that maxim whereby you can at the same time will that it should become a universal law." In other words, for any decision you make as to whether an act is right or wrong, ask yourself what would happen if everyone in the world committed the act.

[g] "Banishment of the Moors" refers to the North African Muslims driven out of Spain in the 15th century by Christians after nearly eight centuries of occupation.

[31]Christian, too; is a certain cruelty toward one's self and toward others; hatred of unbelievers; the will to persecute. . . . And Christian is all hatred of the intellect, of pride, of courage of freedom, of intellectual liberty; Christian is all hatred of the senses, of joy in the senses, of joy in general . . .

****

24.

[32]Here I barely touch upon the problem of the *origin* of Christianity. The first thing necessary to its solution is this: that Christianity is to be understood only by examining the soil from which it sprang—it is not a reaction against Jewish instincts; it is their inevitable product; it is simply one more step in the awe-inspiring logic of the Jews. In the words of the Saviour, "salvation is of the Jews." The second thing to remember is this: that the psychological type of the Galilean is still to be recognized, but it was only in its most degenerate form . . . that it could serve in the manner in which it has been used: as a type of the *Saviour* of mankind.

[33]The Jews are the most remarkable people in the history of the world, for when they were confronted with the question, "to be or not to be," they chose, with perfectly unearthly deliberation, to be *at any price;* this price in-volved a radical *falsification* of all nature, of all naturalness, of all reality, of the whole inner world, as well as of the outer. They put themselves against all those conditions under which, hitherto, a people had been able to live, or had even been *permitted* to live; out of themselves they evolved an idea which stood in direct opposition to *natural* conditions—one by one they distorted religion, civilization, morality, history and psychology until each became a contradiction of its *natural significance.*

[34]We meet with the same phenomenon later on, in an incalculably exag-gerated form, but only as a copy: the Christian church, put beside the "people of God," shows a complete lack of any claim to originality. Precisely for this reason the Jews are the most *fateful* people in the history of the world: their influence has so falsified the reasoning of mankind in this matter that today the Christian can cherish anti-Semitism without realizing that it is no more than the *final consequence of Judaism. . . .*

[35]To the sort of men who reach out for power under Judaism and Chris-tianity, that is to say, to the *priestly* class, *decadence* is no more than a means to an end. Men of this sort have a vital interest in making mankind sick, and in confusing the values of "good" and "bad," "true" and "false" in a manner that is not only dangerous to life, but also slanders it.

****

26.

[36]The concept of god falsified; the concept of morality falsified; but even

here Jewish priestcraft did not stop. The whole history of Israel ceased to be of any value: out with it!–These priests accomplished that miracle of falsification of which a great part of the Bible is the documentary evidence; with a degree of contempt unparalleled, and in the face of all tradition and all historical reality, they translated the past of their people into religious terms, which is to say, they converted it into an idiotic mechanism of salvation, whereby all offenses against Jahveh[h] were punished and all devotion to him was rewarded.

[37]We would regard this act of historical falsification as something far more shameful if familiarity with the ecclesiastical interpretation of history for thousands of years had not blunted our inclinations for uprightness in the historical record. And the philosophers support the church: the lie about a "moral order of the world" runs through the whole of philosophy, even the newest. What is the meaning of a "moral order of the world"? That there is a thing called the will of God which, once and for all time, determines what man ought to do and what he ought not to do; that the worth of a people, or of an individual thereof, is to he measured by the extent to which they or he obey this will of God; that the destinies of a people or of an individual are controlled by this will of God, which rewards or punishes according to the degree of obedience manifested.

[38]In place of all that pitiable lie, reality has this to say: the priest, a parasitical variety of man who can exist only at the cost of every sound view of life, takes the name of God in vain: he calls that state of human society in which he himself determines the value of all things, "the kingdom of God"; he calls the means whereby that state of affairs is attained "the will of God"; with cold-blooded cynicism he estimates all peoples, all ages and all individuals by the extent of their subservience or opposition to the power of the priestly order.

[39]One observes him at work: under the hand of the Jewish priesthood the great age of Israel became an age of decline; the Exile, with its long series of misfortunes, was transformed into a punishment for that great age, during which priests had not yet come into existence. Out of the powerful and wholly free heroes of Israel's history they fashioned, according to their changing needs, either wretched bigots and hypocrites or men entirely "godless." They reduced every great event to the idiotic formula: "obedient or disobedient to God."

[40]They went a step further: the "will of God" (in other words some means necessary for preserving the power of the priests) had to be determined—and to this end they had to have a "revelation." In plain English, a gigantic literary fraud had to be perpetrated, and "holy scriptures" had to be concocted—and so, with the utmost hierarchical pomp, and days of penance and much lamentation over the long days of "sin" now ended, they were duly published.

[41]The "will of God," it appears, had long stood like a rock; the trouble was that mankind had neglected the "holy scriptures." But the "will of God"

---

[h]Jahveh (pronounced Ya-vay) is a Judeo-Christian reference to God (also Jehovah).

had already been revealed to Moses. What happened? Simply this: the priest had formulated, once and for all time and with the strictest meticulousness, what tithes were to be paid to him, from the largest to the smallest (not forgetting the most appetizing cuts of meat, for the priest is a great consumer of beefsteaks); in brief, he let it be known just what he wanted, what "the will of God" was. From this time forward, things were so arranged that the priest became indispensable everywhere; at all the great natural events of life, at birth, at marriage, in sickness, at death, not to say at the "sacrifice" (that is, at meal-times), the holy parasite put in his appearance, and proceeded to denaturize it—in his own phrase, to "sanctify" it. . . .

[42]Disobedience to God, which actually means to the priest, to "the law," now gets the name of "sin"; the means prescribed for "reconciliation with God" are, of course, precisely the means which bring one most effectively under the thumb of the priest; he alone can "save." Psychologically considered, "sins" are indispensable to every society organized on an ecclesiastical basis; they are the only reliable weapons of power; the priest lives upon sins; it is necessary to him that there be "sinning." Prime axiom: "God forgiveth him that repenteth"–in plain language, him that submitteth to the priest.

****

62.

[43]With this I come to a conclusion and pronounce my judgment. I condemn Christianity; I bring against the Christian church the most terrible of all the accusations that an accuser has ever had in his mouth. It is, to me, the greatest of all imaginable corruptions; it seeks to work the ultimate corruption, the worst possible corruption. The Christian church has left nothing untouched by its depravity; it has turned every value into worthlessness, and every truth into a lie, and every integrity into baseness of soul. Let anyone dare to speak to me of its "humanitarian" blessings! Its deepest necessities range it against any effort to abolish distress; it lives by distress; it creates distress to make itself immortal.

[44]For example, the worm of sin: it was the church that first enriched mankind with this misery!–The "equality of souls before God"–this fraud, this pretext for the rancunes[i] of all the base-minded–this explosive concept, ending in revolution, the modern idea, and the notion of overthrowing the whole social order—this is Christian dynamite.

[45]The "humanitarian" blessings of Christianity forsooth![j] To breed out of

---

[i]*rancune* is a French word for "bitterness," "rancor" or "grudge."

[j]forsooth! indeed!

humanitas a self-contradiction, an art of self-pollution, a will to lie at any price, an aversion and contempt for all good and honest instincts! All this, to me, is the "humanitarianism" of Christianity!

[46]Parasitism as the only practice of the church; with its anemic and "holy" ideals, sucking all the blood, all the love, all the hope out of life; the beyond as the will to deny all reality; the cross as the distinguishing mark of the most subterranean conspiracy ever heard of,—against

health, beauty, well-being, intellect, kindness of soul–against life itself.

[47]This eternal accusation against Christianity I shall write upon all walls, wherever walls are to be found—I have letters that even the blind will be able to see. I call Christianity the one great curse, the one great intrinsic depravity, the one great instinct of revenge, for which no means are venomous enough, or secret, subterranean and small enough—I call it the one immortal blemish upon the human race.

Vocabulary

[1]confound	[16]augment	[24]deified	[30]subjugated
[1]posthumously	[16]the Nazarene	[25]repudiate	[30]inquisition
[2]wretched	[18]sacrosanct	[25]moribund	[32]the Galilean
[2]gabble	[19]theologian	[25]decrepitude	[34]incalculably
[2]predestination	[20]conceit	[25]intrinsic	[37]ecclesiastical
[2]labyrinth	[21]intercourse	[25]conjured	[38]parasitical
[3]augment	[21]anthropocentric	[26]allude	[38]cynicism
[10]hitherto	[21]religio-ethical	[27]protracted	[38]subservience
[13]embellish	[21]balderdash	[27]bilious	[40]hierarchical
[13]reprobate	[21]teleology	[28]asceticism	[40]pomp
[13]lamentable	[22]preponderance	[28]aversion	[40]penance
[14]decadence	[23]physiologically	[28]enmity	[41]meticulousness
[15]contention	[23]perforce	[28]regimen	[41]tithes
[15]nihilism	[24]transfiguration	[29]aspiration	[43]depravity
[16]tonic			

Discussion Questions

1. "Some men are born posthumously" (paragraph 1) is a rather remarkable statement. What do you think Nietzsche means by it?

2. In the second paragraph of the preface, how does Nietzsche characterize those who read his work? And those who don't?

3. What is Nietzsche's definition of "good" in Section 2? Evil? Do you agree or disagree with his opinion?

4. In Section 2 Nietzsche establishes his attitude toward Christianity and society's less-fortunate members. Summarize his position.

5. In Section 3 Nietzsche says that "man is an end." Would Darwin agree?

6. What are the implications in Section 3 of "[this] type of man must be *bred*, must be *willed*"? Who are some possible historical examples of this "higher type of man"?

7. In the selection from *Origin of Species* on page 434 of this text, Charles Darwin says, ". . . as natural selection works solely by and for the good of each being, all corporal and mental endowments will tend to progress toward perfection." What does Nietzsche say about this in Sections 3 and 4?

8. In Section 4, Nietzsche says, "Even whole races, tribes and nations may occasionally represent such lucky accidents." The Nazis adapted many of Nietzcshe's ideas to their political philosophy. How does this quote support Nazi ideology?

9. What is Nietzsche saying about the traditions of Christian theology in the first sentence of Section 5?

10. What is Nietzsche saying about Christianity and Darwinism in Sections 6 and 7?

11. What does Nietzsche say about the place of humans in the animal kingdom in Section 14?

12. What does Nietzsche say about the Christian concept of heaven in Section 18?

13. Nietzsche makes up the word "monotono-theism" in Section 19. What does he mean by it?

14. What does Nietzsche mean when he says that in Buddhism, "The concept, 'god,' was already disposed of before it appeared." What is Nietzsche's opinion of Buddhism?

15. Compare what Nietzsche says about Buddhism in Section 20 with the introductory material on Buddhism beginning on page 171 of this text. Are Nietzsche's observations correct? Explain.

16. What is Nietzsche's view of "sin" and "salvation" as expressed in Section 26?

17. In Section 24 Nietzsche discusses the origins of Christianity. Where does he say it came from?

18. Read "The Sermon on the Mount" on page 489 of this text. Based upon what he has written here, how would Nietzsche view the sentiments expressed in the sermon?

19. What do you think Nazi party members thought of the ideas Nietzsche expressed in Sections 24 and 26?

Grafitto in New York City Subway

God is dead!
                Nietzsche

Nietzsche is dead.
                God

APACHE CREATION STORY
TRANSLATED BY EDWARD S. CURTIS

Edward Sheriff Curtis (1868-1952) was a noted photographer and ethnographer of the Native American tribes of the western United States. He was the official photographer on the Harriman Expedition to Alaska in 1899 and photographer for President Theodore Roosevelt and family. Funded by the business tycoon J. P. Morgan, Curtis wrote 20 volumes of ethnographic text illustrated with photoengravings, The North American Indian, *which documented all of the tribes west of the Mississippi that to a certain degree still maintained their native life-ways and customs*
 The **Apache Native Americans** *are a part of the North American Indian tribes of the Southwest. The Apache as known in historic times were dependent upon hunting game and gathering roots. They were especially known for their fierce fighting ability, which allowed them to resist the advancement of Spanish colonization and American advancement to the west until the early twentieth century. Famous Apache leaders include Cochise, Geronimo, Mangas Coloradas and Victorio. The Apache now live primarily on reservations in Arizona.*

[1]There was a time when nothing existed to form the universe—no earth, no sky, and no sun or moon to break the monotony of the illimitable darkness. But as time rolled on, a spot, a thin circular disc no larger than the hand, yellow on one side and white on the other, appeared in midair. Inside the disc sat a bearded man but little larger than a frog, upon whom was to fall the task of creating all things. Kútĕrastan, The One Who Lives Above, is the name by which he is now known, though some call him Yŭádĭstan, Sky Man.

[2]Kútĕrastan, as if waking from a long sleep, sat up and rubbed his face and eyes with both hands. Then bending forward, he looked up into the endless darkness, and lo! light appeared everywhere above him. He then looked down, and all below became a sea of light. A glance to the east created yellow streaks of dawn, another to the west the saffron tints of the dying day, both soon becoming obscured by numerous clouds of many hues, formed by his looking around and about in all directions.

[3]Again with both hands Kútĕrastan wiped his eyes and sweating face and, rubbing his hands together as if he were rolling a small pebble between the palms, suddenly parted them with a quick downward fling, and there before him on a shining, vaporless, mirage-like cloud sat a little girl no larger than a doll. Kútĕrastan directed her to stand up, asking where she intended to go, but she replied not. He cleared his vision once more with his hands, then proffered his right hand to the girl, Stĕnátlĭhăⁿ, Woman Without Parents, who grasped it,

with the greeting "Whence came you?"

⁴For reply Kúterastan merely repeated her question, adding, "Look to the east, it is light! There will be light in the south, in the west, and in the north." And as she looked she saw light. He then came out upon the cloud.

⁵"Where is the earth?" asked Stěnátlῑhă, to which Kúterastan replied by asking:

⁶"Where is the sky?" Then requesting that he be not disturbed, he began to sing: "I am thinking, thinking, thinking, thinking what shall I do next." Four times he thus sang, at the end of the fourth time brushing his face with his hands, which he rubbed briskly together and parted quickly; and there before him stood Chuganaái, the Sun. Raising his left hand to his brow, from the sweat thereon, which he rolled in his hands as before, Kúterastan let drop from his right palm a small boy, Hádῑntῑn Skhῑn.

⁷The four sat upon that still cloud for a time as if in reverie, the first to break the silence being he who commenced the creation: "What shall we do next? I do not like this cloud to live upon, but we are to rule and must stay together. How dreary it is here! I wish we had some place to go." And then he set to work again, creating Nacholécho, the Tarantula, who was later to help in completing the earth, and Nôkusé, the Big Dipper, whose duty it would be to befriend and to guide. The creation of Nῑlchídῑlhkῑzn, the Wind, Ndídῑlhkῑzn, the Lightning Maker, and the clouds in the west to house Ndísâgocha, Lightning Rumbler, whom he placed in them at the same time, next occupied his attention. Then turning to Stěnátlῑhă, Kúterastan said, "Truly this is not a fit place in which to live; let us make the earth." And so saying he at once began to sing, "I am thinking of the earth, the earth, the earth; I am thinking of the earth," which he repeated four times. As he ceased, Stěnátlῑhă, Chuganaái, and Hádῑntῑn Skhῑn each shook hands with him. Sweat from their hands adhered to his. He at once began rubbing his palms, when suddenly there slipped from between them a small brown body, no larger than a bean. Kúterastan kicked it and it expanded; Stěnátlῑhă then kicked it and its size further increased; Chuganaái next gave it a severe blow with his foot and it became larger still; a kick from Hádῑntῑn Skhῑn made it greater yet. Nῑlchídῑlhkῑzn, the Wind, was told to go inside and blow outward in all directions. This he did, greatly expanding the dimensions of that body, now so wide that they could hardly see its edge. The Lightning was next directed to exert his strength, so with a terrific flash and roar he penetrated the body to its centre, spreading it still wider. Then Tarantula was called on to assist, and accordingly he started off to the east, spinning a strong black cord, on which he pulled with all his might; another cord of blue was spun out to the south, a third of yellow to the west, and a fourth of glistening white to the north. A mighty pull on each of these stretched the surface of that dark brown body to almost immeasurable size. Finally Kúterastan directed all to cover their eyes with their hands, and when they opened them a moment later

they beheld Nigostú☐n, the Earth, complete in extent. No hills or mountains were there in sight, nothing but a smooth, treeless, reddish-brown plain.

[8]Nĭlchídĭlhkĭzn, the Wind, scratched his chest and rubbed his fingers together, when out from between them flew Dátĭlyĕ, the Humming-bird. Dátĭlyĕ was told to make a circuit of the earth and report what he saw. He started off toward the east, circled south, west, north, and back from the east. All was well; the earth was most beautiful, very smooth, and covered with water on the western side.

[9]But the Earth was not still; it kept shifting and rolling and dancing up and down, so Kútĕrastan made four great posts—colored black, blue, yellow, and white—to support it. Then he directed Stĕnátlĭhă to sing a song. She sang, "The world is made and will soon sit still." These two then stood and faced Chuganaái and Hádĭntĭn Skhĭn, when into their midst came Nĭlchídĭlhkĭzn, who dashed away to the cardinal points with the four posts, which he placed under the sides of the earth; and upon them it sat and was still. This pleased Kútĕrastan, so he sang a song, repeating, "The world is now made and sits still."

[10]Then Kútĕrastan began another song, referring to the sky. None existed as yet, and he felt there ought to be one. Four times he chanted the song, at the end of the fourth time spreading his hands wide before him, when lo! there stood twenty-eight men and women ready to help make a sky to cover the earth. He next chanted a song for the purpose of making chiefs for the sky and the earth, and at its close sent Ndídĭlhkĭzn, the Lightning Maker, to encircle the world. Ndídĭlhkĭzn departed at once, but returned in a short time with three very uncouth persons, two girls and a boy, whom he had found in the sky in a large turquoise bowl. Not one of them had eyes, ears, hair, mouth, nose, or teeth, and though they had arms and legs, they had neither fingers nor toes.

[11]Chuganaái at once sent for Doh, the Fly, to come and erect a *kaché☐*, or sweat-house. It took but a short time to put up the framework, which Stĕnátlĭhă covered closely with four heavy clouds: a black cloud on the east, a blue one on the south, a yellow one on the west, and a white one on the north. Out in front of the doorway, at the east, she spread a soft red cloud for a foot-blanket after the sweat. Twelve stones were heated in a fire, and four of them placed in the *kaché☐*. Kútĕrastan, Stĕnátlĭhă, Chuganaái, and Hádĭntĭn Skhĭn each inspected the sweat-house and pronounced it well made. The three newcomers were bidden to enter and were followed by Chuganaái, Nĭlchídĭlhkĭzn, Ndídĭlhkĭzn, Nôkusé, and Doh. The eight sang songs as their sweat began. Chuganaái led, singing four songs, and each of the others followed in turn with the same number. They had had a good sweat by the time the songs were finished, so Stĕnátlĭhă removed the black cloud and all came out. She then placed the three strangers on the red-cloud blanket, and under the direction of Kútĕrastan made for them fingers, toes, mouth, eyes, ears, hair, and nose. Then Kútĕrastan bade them welcome, making the boy, whom he called Yádĭlhkĭh Skhĭn, Sky Boy, chief of the sky and its people. The second he named Nigostú☐n Nalí☐n, Earth

Daughter, and placed her in charge of the earth and its crops; while to the third, Hádĭnĭn Nalí☐n, Pollen Girl, was assigned the care of the health of the earth's people. This duty also devolved upon Hádĭntĭn Skhĭn, but each looks more to the welfare of his own sex than to that of the other.

[12]The earth was smooth, flat, and barren, so Kútĕrastan made a few animals, birds, trees, and a hill. Then he sent Ágocho, the Pigeon, to see how the world looked. Four days later Ágocho returned and said all was beautiful, but that in four days more the water on the opposite side would rise and flood the land. Kútĕrastan at once created a piñon tree. This Stĕnátlĭhă̆ skillfully tended until it grew to be of gigantic size at the end of four days. Then with four great limbs as a framework she made a very large water bottle, *tus*, covering it with gum from the piñon. When the water appeared as predicted, Kútĕrastan went up on a cloud, taking his twenty-eight helpers with him, while Stĕnátlĭhă̆ summoned all the others and put them into the *tus*, into which she climbed last, closing the mouth at the top.

[13]The flood completely submerged the earth for twelve days. Then the waters subsided, leaving the *tus* on the summit of the hill Kútĕrastan had made. The rush of the waters had changed the once smooth, level plain into series of mountains, hills, rivers, and valleys, so that Stĕnátlĭhă̆ hardly knew where they were when she opened the *tus* and came out. Tázhĭ, the Turkey, and Gắgĕ, the Crow, were the first to make a tour of the land. At the base of the hill they descended into a small muddy alkaline creek, in which the Turkey got the tips of his tail-feathers whitened, and they have been white ever since. On return they reported that all looked beautiful as far as they had travelled. Stĕnátlĭhă̆ then sent Ágocho to make a complete circuit and let her know how things appeared on all sides. He came back much elated, for he had seen trees, grass, mountains, and beautiful lakes and rivers in every direction.

[14]Directing the others to remain where she left them, Stĕnátlĭhă̆ summoned Hádĭntĭn Skhĭn, Hádĭntĭn Naln, Ndídĭlhkĭzn, and Ágocho, and took them up in a cloud, in which they drifted until they met Kútĕrastan and his band of workers, who had completed the sky during the time of the flood. The two clouds floated to the top of the hill on which stood the *tus*. All descended to the valley below, where Stĕnátlĭhă̆ marshalled them into line, that Kútĕrastan might talk to them. He briefly told them that he was going to leave them and wished each one to do his part toward making the world perfect and happy. "You, Ndísâgocha, shall have charge of the clouds and the water. You, Yádĭlhkĭh Skhĭn, I leave in charge of the sky. Nigostú☐n Nalí☐n, you are to look after the crops of our people; and you, Hádĭntĭn Skhĭn, must care for their health and guide them." He then called Stĕnátlĭhă̆[n] to him and placed her in charge of all.

[15]The people stood in line facing their god, with hands extended as if in supplication. Kútĕrastan and Stĕnátlĭhă̆[n] stood facing each other. Each rubbed their thighs with their hands, then cast their hands downward, and there arose between them a great pile of wood. Stĕnátlĭhă̆ knelt and slipped a hand under

it, and as she did so Kútĕrastan passed his hand over the top. Great white bil-lowy clouds of smoke at once issued forth, rising straight skyward. Into these Kútĕrastan disappeared. All the other gods and goddesses soon followed, leav-ing the twenty-eight whom Kútĕrastan had made to build the sky to remain upon the earth and people it. Chuganaái went east to travel with the sun; Stĕnátlĭhă departed westward to make her home in clouds on the horizon, while Hádĭntĭn Skhĭn and Hádĭntí□n Nalín sought homes among the clouds in the south, and Nôkusé may still be seen in the northern sky at night.

Vocabulary

¹illimitable	²hues	⁷adhered	¹²piñon
²saffron	³proffered	⁹cardinal	¹³alkaline
²obscure	⁷reverie	¹⁰uncouth	¹⁴marshalled

Discussion Questions

1. Describe the progression of the Creator's handiwork.

2. There are several instances of cause and effect in the creations. Pick one and discuss the cause and effect relationship.

3. Read the excerpt from the Judeo/Christian story of Genesis on page 271 of this text. Discuss the similarities between Genesis and Apache Creation Story. Do the same for the Hindu Aitareya Upanishad on pages 148-152 and the Qur'an, Suras 7 and 11 on pages 451 and 455 of this text.

4. How is the account of the creation of humans here similar to or different from the Judeo-Christian story of Adam and Eve in Genesis on page 271 of this text?

5. Read what Richard Dawkins says in paragraph 20 on page 316. How does what he says relate to this reading and the others mentioned in question 3, above?

FROM **ARGUMENT FOR THE EXISTENCE OF GOD**

ST. THOMAS AQUINAS

St. Thomas Aquinas (1225-1274) was an Italian Roman Catholic priest of the Dominican Order. Nearly eight centuries after his birth, Aquinas is still thought by many Catholics to be the Church's greatest scholar and theologian; he is considered to be the model teacher for those studying for the priesthood. Aquinas's works had a significant influence on Western thought, with much of modern philosophical thought either a reaction against or an agreement with his ideas, particularly in regard to ethics, natural law and theology. The excerpt below is from his Summa Theologica, *which he worked on from 1265 until his death in 1274. Aquinas was canonized a saint in 1323.*

NOTE: The argument that Aquinas proposes here is an early form of the "intelligent design" argument for the existence of God and the origins of the universe that are frequently cited today in objections to Darwinism. In their respective scriptures, Islam, Judaism, Hinduism and Christianity all make references to a creative force as a "first mover" or a "grand designer." Thomas's Fifth Way (paragraph 18 below) is often referred to as a basis for an argument supporting intelligent design.

PREFACE

[1]Because the chief aim of sacred doctrine is to teach the knowledge of *God*, not only as He is in Himself, but also as He is the beginning of things and their last end, and especially of rational creatures, therefore, in our endeavor to expound this science, we shall discuss 1) *Whether it can be demonstrated that God exists; and* 2) *Whether God exists.*

WHETHER IT CAN BE DEMONSTRATED THAT *GOD* EXISTS

[2]*Objection* 1: It seems that the existence of *God* cannot be demonstrated, for it is an article of faith that *God exists.* But what is of faith cannot be demonstrated because a demonstration produces scientific knowledge; whereas faith is of the unseen. Therefore it cannot be demonstrated that *God exists.*

[3]*Objection* 2: We cannot know in what *God's* essence consists, but solely in what it does not consist; therefore, we cannot demonstrate that *God exists.*

[4]*Objection* 3: Further, if the existence of *God* were demonstrated, this could only be from His effects. But His effects are not proportionate to Him, since He is infinite and His effects are finite; and between the finite and infinite there is no

proportion. Therefore, since a cause cannot be demonstrated by an effect not proportionate to it, it seems that the existence of *God* cannot be demonstrated.

[5]*On the contrary,* The Apostle says: "The invisible things of Him are clearly seen, being understood by the things that are made." But this would not be unless the existence of *God* could be demonstrated through the things that are made; for the first thing we must know of anything is, *whether it exists.*

[6]*I answer that,* Demonstration can be made thus: When an effect is better known to us than its cause, from the effect we proceed to the knowledge of the cause. And from every effect the existence of its proper cause can be demonstrated, so long as its effects are better known to us; because since every effect depends upon its cause, if the effect *exists,* the cause must pre-exist. Hence the existence of *God*, in so far as it is not self-evident to us, can be demonstrated from those of His effects which are known to us.

[7]*Reply to Objection* 1: The existence of *God* and other like truths about *God*, which can be known by natural reason, are not articles of faith, but are preambles to the articles; for faith presupposes natural knowledge, even as grace presupposes nature, and perfection supposes something that can be perfected. Nevertheless, there is nothing to prevent someone who cannot grasp a proof, accepting, as a matter of faith, something which in itself is capable of being scientifically known and demonstrated.

[8]*Reply to Objection* 2: When the existence of a cause is demonstrated from an effect, this effect takes the place of the definition of the cause in proof of the cause's existence. This is especially the case in regard to *God*, because, in order to prove the existence of anything, it is necessary to accept as a middle term the meaning of the word, and not its essence, for the question of its essence follows on the question of its existence. Now the names given to *God* are derived from His effects; consequently, in demonstrating the existence of *God* from His effects, we may take for the middle term the meaning of the word "God."

[9]*Reply to Objection* 3: From effects not proportionate to the cause no perfect knowledge of that cause can be obtained. Yet from every effect the existence of the cause can be clearly demonstrated, and so we can demonstrate the existence of *God* from His effects; though from them we cannot perfectly know *God* as He is in His essence.

WHETHER GOD EXISTS

[10]*Objection* 1: It seems that *God* does not exist because if one of two contraries be infinite, the other would be altogether destroyed. But the word "*God*" means that He is infinite goodness. If, therefore, *God* existed, there would be no evil discoverable; but there is evil in the world. Therefore *God* does not exist.

[11]*Objection* 2: Further, it is superfluous to suppose that what can be accounted for by a few principles has been produced by many. But it seems that

everything we see in the world can be accounted for by other principles, supposing *God* did not exist. For all natural things can be reduced to one principle, which is nature; and all voluntary things can be reduced to one principle, which is human reason, or will. Therefore there is no need to suppose *God*'s existence.

[12]*On the contrary,* It is said in the person of *God*: *I am Who am.* (Exodus iii. 14).

[13]*I answer that,* The existence of *God* can be proved in five ways:

1) [14]The first and more manifest way is the argument from motion. It is certain, and evident to our senses, that in the world some things are in motion. Now whatever is in motion is put in motion by another, for nothing can be in motion except it is in potentiality to that towards which it is in motion; whereas a thing moves inasmuch as it is in act. For motion is nothing else than the reduction of something from potentiality to actuality. But nothing can be reduced from potentiality to actuality, except by something in a state of actuality. Thus that which is actually hot, as fire, makes wood, which is potentially hot, to be actually hot, and thereby moves and changes it. Now it is not possible that the same thing should be at once in actuality and potentiality in the same respect, but only in different respects. For what is actually hot cannot simultaneously be potentially hot; but it is simultaneously potentially cold. It is therefore impossible that in the same respect and in the same way a thing should be both mover and moved, *i.e.,* that it should move itself. Therefore, whatever is in motion must be put in motion by another. If that by which it is put in motion be itself put in motion, then this also must needs be put in motion by another, and that by another again. But this cannot go on to infinity because then there would be no first mover, and, consequently, no other mover; seeing that subsequent movers move only inasmuch as they are put in motion by the first mover; as the staff moves only because it is put in motion by the hand. Therefore it is necessary to arrive at a first mover, put in motion by no other; and this everyone understands to be *God.*

2) [15]The second way is from the nature of the efficient cause. In the world of sense we find there is an order of efficient causes. There is no case known (neither is it, indeed, possible) in which a thing is found to be the efficient cause of itself; for so it would be prior to itself, which is impossible. Now in efficient causes it is not possible to go on to infinity because in all efficient causes following in order, the first is the cause of the intermediate cause, and the intermediate is the cause of the ultimate cause, *whether* the intermediate cause be several or one only. Now to take away the cause is to take away the effect. Therefore, if there be no first cause among efficient causes, there will be no ultimate, nor any intermediate cause. But if in efficient causes it is possible to go on to infinity, there will be no first efficient cause; neither will there be an ultimate effect, nor any intermediate efficient causes, all of which is plainly false. Therefore it is necessary to admit a first efficient cause, to which everyone gives the name of *God*.

3) [16]The third way is taken from possibility and necessity and runs thus: we find in nature things that are possible to be and not to be, since they are found to be generated, and to corrupt, and consequently they are possible to be and not to be. But it is impossible for these always to exist, for that which is possible not to be at some time is not. Therefore, if everything is possible not to be, then at one time there could have been nothing in existence. Now if this were true, even now there would be nothing in existence because that which does not exist only begins to exist by something already existing. Therefore, if at one time nothing was in existence, it would have been impossible for anything to have begun to exist; and thus even now nothing would be in existence—which is absurd. Therefore, not all beings are merely possible, but there must exist something the existence of which is necessary. But every necessary thing either has its necessity caused by another, or not. Now it is impossible to go on to infinity in necessary things which have their necessity caused by another, as has been already proved in regard to efficient causes. Therefore we cannot but postulate the existence of some being having of itself its own necessity and not receiving it from another, but rather causing in others their necessity. This everyone speaks of as *God*.

4) [17]The fourth way is taken from the gradation to be found in things. Among beings there are some more and some less good, true, noble, and the like. But "more" and "less" are predicated of different things, according as they resemble in their different ways something which is the maximum, as a thing is said to be hotter according as it more nearly resembles that which is hottest; so that there is something which is truest, something best, something noblest, and, consequently, something which is uttermost being; for those things that are greatest in truth are greatest in being, as it is written in *Metaphysics*. ii[a]. Now the maximum in any genus is the cause of all in that genus; as fire, which is the maximum of heat, is the cause of all hot things. Therefore there must also be something which is to all beings the cause of their being, goodness, and every other perfection; and this we call *God*.

5) [18]The fifth way is taken from the governance of the world. We see that things which lack intelligence, such as natural bodies, act for an end, and this is evident from their acting always, or nearly always, in the same way, so as to

---

[a]*Metaphysics ii* is a reference to *Metaphysics, "Book II"* written by Aristotle in 350 BC in which the Greek philosopher says, ". . . evidently there is a first principle, and the causes of things are neither an infinite series nor infinitely various in kind. . . ." and "By 'as the man comes from the boy' we mean 'as that which has come to be from that which is coming to be' . . . ."

obtain the best result. Hence it is plain that not fortuitously, but designedly, do they achieve their end. Now whatever lacks intelligence cannot move towards an end, unless it be directed by some being endowed with knowledge and intelligence, just as the arrow is shot to its mark by the archer. Therefore some intelligent being *exists* by whom all natural things are directed to their end; and this being we call *God*.

Vocabulary

[1]expound   [14]manifest   [17]predicated
[11]superfluous   [17]gradation   [18]fortuitous

Discussion Questions

1. What was Aquinas's purpose in writing this piece?

2. Summarize Objection 1 (paragraph 2) in "Whether It Can Be Demonstrated That *God* Exists."

3. What are the two opposing forces in Objection 1? Are these two forces still in opposition nearly eight centuries after this was written, or have they come to an agreement?

4. In essence, what is Aquinas attempting to do in this section ("Whether It Can Be Demonstrated That *God* Exists")?

5. What examples do you think Aquinas would give of the "effects" in paragraph 6 that would prove the cause must be God?

6. Summarize the "first mover" argument (paragraph 14) in your own words.

7. Summarize the "first cause" argument (paragraph 15) in your own words.

8. What is the difference between first mover and first cause?

9. In paragraph 16, the third argument, Aquinas says that everything that exists has not always existed, that everything had to come from nothingness to a state of existence. How does he then conclude this argument? Cite an example to support his argument.

10. In the fifth argument, Aquinas uses "the arrow shot to its mark by the archer" as a supporting example. Research William Paley's 1802 "watch on a beach" example and explain how this fits with Thomas's fifth argument.

11. In his recent book, *The Evolution of God*, Robert Wright compares God to an electron, saying scientists know the electron is there because scientific experiments show its effects, but the scientists don't know what an electron looks like or what its properties are. How does Wright's analogy relate to Aquinas's argument?

THE BEDCHAMBER MYSTERY

C.S. FORESTER

*C S Forester, pen name of British author **Cecil Smith** (1899-1966), is best known for his Horatio Hornblower series. He also wrote thirty-five novels, two plays, five biographies and three children's books as well as histories and other works. During the opening years of World War II, before the bombing of Pearl Harbor, he went to Hollywood to write and produce films intended to convince U.S. filmgoers to support the British and their allies in the war in Europe.*

[1]Now that a hundred years have passed, one of the scandals in my family can be told. It is very doubtful if in 1843 Miss Forester (she was Eulalie, but being the eldest daughter unmarried, she, of course, was Miss Forester) and Miss Emily Forester and Miss Eunice Forester ever foresaw the world of 1943 to which their story would be told; in fact it is inconceivable that they could have believed that there ever would be a world in which their story could be told blatantly in public print. At that time it was the sort of thing that could only be hinted at in whispers during confidential moments in feminine drawing rooms; but it was whispered about enough to reach, in the end, the ears of my grandfather, who was their nephew, and my grandfather told it to me.

[2]In 1843 Miss Forester and Miss Emily and Miss Eunice Forester were already maiden ladies of a certain age. The old-fashioned Georgian house in which they lived kept itself modestly retired, just like its inhabitants, from what there was of bustle and excitement in the High Street of the market town. The ladies indeed led a retired life; they went to church a little, they visited those of the sick whom it was decent and proper for maiden ladies to visit, they read the more colorless of the novels in the circulating library, and sometimes they entertained other ladies at tea.

[3]And once a week they entertained a man. It might almost be said that they went from week to week looking forward to those evenings. Dr. Acheson was (not one of the old ladies would have been heartless enough to say "fortunately," but each of them felt it) a widower, and several years older even than my great-great-aunt Eulalie. Moreover, he was a keen whist player and a brilliant one, but in no way keener or more brilliant than were Eulalie, Emily, and Eunice. For years now the three nice old ladies had looked forward to their weekly evening of whist—all the ritual of setting out the green table, the two hours of silent cut-and-thrust play, and the final twenty minutes of conversation with Dr. Acheson as he drank a glass of old Madeira before bidding them good night.

[4]The late Mrs. Acheson had passed to her Maker somewhere about 1830, so that it was for thirteen years they had played their weekly game of whist before the terrible thing happened. To this day we do not know whether it happened to Eulalie or Emily or Eunice, but it happened to one of them. The three of them had retired for the night, each to her separate room, and had progressed far toward the final stage of getting into bed. They were not dried-up old spinsters; on the contrary they were women of weight and substance, with the buxom contours even married women might have been proud of. It was her weight which was the undoing of one of them, Eulalie, Emily, or Eunice.

[5]Through the quiet house that bedtime there sounded the crash of china and a cry of pain, and two of the sisters—which two we do not know—hurried in their dressing gowns to the bedroom of the third—her identity is uncertain—to find her bleeding profusely from severe cuts in the lower part of the back. The jagged china fragments had inflicted severe wounds, and, most unfortunately, just in those parts where the injured sister could not attend to them herself. Under the urgings of the other two she fought down her modesty sufficiently to let them attempt to deal with them, but the bleeding was profuse, and the blood of the Foresters streamed from the prone figure face downward on the bed in terrifying quantity.

[6]"We shall have to send for the doctor," said one of the ministering sisters; it was a shocking thing to contemplate.

[7]"Oh, but we cannot!" said the other ministering sister.

[8]"We must," said the first.

[9]"How terrible!" said the second.

[10]And with that the injured sister twisted her neck and joined in the conversation. "I will not have the doctor," she said. "I would die of shame."

[11]"Think of the disgrace of it!" said the second sister. "We might even have to explain to him how it happened!"

[12]"But she's bleeding to death," protested the first sister.

[13]"I'd rather die!" said the injured one, and then, as a fresh appalling thought struck her, she twisted her neck even further. "I could never face him again. And what would happen to our whist?"

[14]That was an aspect of the case which until then had occurred to neither of the other sisters, and it was enough to make them blench. But they were of stern stuff. Just as we do not know which was the injured one, we do not know which one thought of a way out of the difficulty, and we shall never know. We know that it was Miss Eulalie, as befitted her rank as eldest sister, who called to Deborah the maid to go and fetch Dr. Acheson at once, but that does not mean to say that it was not Miss Eulalie who was the injured sister—injured or not, Miss Eulalie was quite capable of calling to Deborah and telling her what to do.

[15]As she was bid, Deborah went and fetched Dr. Acheson and conducted him to Miss Eunice's bedroom, but, of course, the fact that it was Miss Eunice's

bedroom is really no indication that it was Miss Eunice who was in there. Dr. Acheson had no means of knowing; all he saw was a recumbent form covered by a sheet. In the center of the sheet a round hole a foot in diameter had been cut, and through the hole the seat of the injury was visible.

[16]Dr. Acheson needed no explanations. He took his needles and his thread from his little black bag and he set to work and sewed up the worst of the cuts and attended to the minor ones. Finally he straightened up and eased his aching back..

[17]"I shall have to take those stitches out," he explained to the still and silent figure which had borne the stitching stoically without a murmur. "I shall come next Wednesday and do that."

[18]Until the next Wednesday the three Misses Forester kept to their rooms. Not one of them was seen in the streets of the market town, and when on Wednesday Dr. Acheson knocked at the door, Deborah conducted him once more to Miss Eunice's bedroom. There was the recumbent form, and there was the sheet with the hole in it. Dr. Acheson took out the stitches.

[19]"It has healed very nicely," said Dr. Acheson. "I don't think any further attention from me will be necessary."

[20]The figure under the sheet said nothing, nor did Dr. Acheson expect it. He gave some concluding advice and went his way. He was glad later to receive a note penned in Miss Forester's Italian hand:

> Dear Dr. Acheson,
> We will all be delighted if you will come to whist this week as usual.

[21]When Dr. Acheson arrived he found that the "as usual" applied only to his coming, for there was a slight but subtle change in the furnishings of the drawing room. The stiff, high-backed chairs on which the three Misses Forester sat bore, each of them, a thick and comfortable cushion upon the seat. There was no knowing which of the sisters needed it.

Vocabulary

[1]inconceivable	[3]whist	[6]prone	[13]appalling
[2]blatantly	[3]Madeira	[6]ministering	[14]blench
[2]Georgian	[4]buxom	[6]contemplate	[15]recumbent
[3]keen	[5]profusely		

Discussion Questions

1. From what you have read, determine the time period and the country in which the story takes place. Why is knowing the time and place important to understanding the story?

2. In the first sentence, the narrator describes what happened as a "scandal." Why do you think he considers it as such? Why did the sisters consider it a scandal? How does knowing the time period and country influence your answer?

3. Can you surmise how the sister was injured?

4. Why does the narrator use the term "seat of the injury" in paragraph 15?

5. Which sister do you think was injured? What information from the story led you to this conclusion?

6. Do you think women today would react with this sense of mystery and coyness for a similar injury?

BELIEVING IN FAIRIES
THE REV. DR. MYKEL JOHNSON

The Reverend Dr. Mykel Johnson received her B.A. in Religious Studies and Psychology from Aquinas College in Grand Rapids, Michigan and her Master of Divinity degree from Chicago Theological Seminary. She earned a Doctor of Ministry degree in Feminist Liberation Theology and Ministry at Episcopal Divinity School, Cambridge, MA, in 1991. She is active in many causes, including equality for same-sex relationships and the co-existence of religion and evolution. She has been the pastor of Allen Avenue Unitarian Universalist Church in Portland, ME since August, 2005. This selection was originally delivered as a sermon by Dr. Johnson to her congregation and has since been reprinted in a number of publications.

[1]A friend of mine heard a story while she was visiting Ireland. A short time before, an airport had been planning to build a new runway. On the proposed site of this runway there was an old oak tree. It was gnarled and majestic, and the people in that area understood it to be an ancient fairy tree. Unfortunately, the airport managers didn't care about this: they made plans for it to be removed. However, when they tried to hire someone to do the job, none of the local workers was willing to cut it down.

[2]Still thinking like a corporation, the airport managers decided to bring in outside workers. The workers arrived, and one man gathered some of their equipment and started out toward the tree. When he got close to it, he tripped and fell. The other workers found him gripping his right arm in pain. It was broken. His buddies brought him into the local hospital for treatment, and then went back to their own town. The airport managers decided to change the plans and move the runway. The fairy tree was not cut down.

[3]Believing in fairies. . . Could it be that the tree actually was a fairy tree? Did the beliefs of the people make it so? I remember watching the movie *Peter Pan* as a child. There comes a moment when a tiny fairy, Tinker Bell, begins to fade and she appeals to all of us in the audience, "Clap if you believe in fairies." "Clap if you believe in fairies." Perhaps, like Tinker Bell, fairies cannot exist in our reality unless we believe in them.

[4]This year will be the twenty-third anniversary of my coming out as a lesbian. I never cease to be amazed by that transformation. When lesbian women came into my life, my whole reality changed. It was like enough people clapping and Tinker Bell springing into view. Someone was celebrating lesbian existence and I, too, began to be able to exist as a lesbian. To claim the word *lesbian* for myself was to leap over a vast chasm, or to cut through a thick bar-

rier. To claim the word *lesbian* was to cross a raging river into an entirely new creation.

⁵I came out at the late age of 31, after a five-year process of struggle and transformation. In the reality I knew in my younger days, gay people, like fairies, did not exist. In fact, when I was growing up, during the 1950s and 60s, I never even heard the word, *lesbian*, and *gay* only meant happy. I never saw us on TV, read about us in a book or newspaper, or learned about us in school. As a girl in a Catholic family there were two possibilities for my life path: I could become a wife and mother, or I could become a nun. I never even imagined the possibility of lesbian.

⁶The Jewish feminist poet Adrienne Rich has written,

> "the whole chorus throbbing at our ears
> like midges, told us nothing, nothing
> of origins, nothing we needed
> to know, nothing that could re-member us.
> Only: that it is unnatural
> the homesickness for a woman, for ourselves..."[a]

⁷Only: that it is unnatural. . . When I went to college, one of my best friends slowly revealed to those close to him that he was homosexual. This was a great torment for him and for all of us who loved him, because according to Catholic teaching, homosexuality was against the laws of nature. Gay people were never meant to exist. And if we did exist, we were identified as unnatural, a disorder, a mistake, a problem.

⁸So much has changed in the years since I was a teenager and young adult. Now it is hard to imagine that I didn't know about the existence of lesbians or gay men. Now we are easily found in books and newspapers, and prime time television. There are supportive high school groups for Gay, Lesbian, Bisexual, Transgender, Questioning, and Straight youth. In 2004, Massachusetts became the first state in the U.S. to allow same-sex couples to be legally married. Several other states have granted civil unions to same-sex couples, and here in Maine we can be recognized as domestic partners.

⁹So much has changed. For me, it seems like a miracle—in fact, a triple miracle. One, I can still be amazed that I exist as a lesbian at all. Two, it is amazing that we who are queer can celebrate being queer. And three, it is amazing that there are communities in which people of every sexual orientation celebrate together. When I came to the Allen Avenue Unitarian Universalist Church two and a half years ago to be your minister, you welcomed me and my

---

[a] Adrienne Rich, "Transcendental Etude," in *The Dream of a Common Language: Poems 1974-1977*, (New York: Norton, 1978), pp. 75-76.

partner Margy with open arms. There are still very many people who condemn us as unnatural. But in all our various identities, as gay men, lesbians, bisexuals, as transgender or transsexual, or as straight allies, we are creating realities where we believe in each other and ourselves, and that is changing everything.

[10]How did we go from being outcasts to celebrating and believing in ourselves? How did we go from being outcasts, to demanding that reality make a place for us? To celebrate ourselves as queer we often have had to risk every other valuable thing in our lives. We've risked family, jobs, friends, safety. Yet this thing which was considered a problem became the pearl of great price. And this was amazing to see!

[11]We couldn't have done it without the foundations laid before us. I am thinking about all the great liberation struggles of this last century. I am reminded of that powerful moment in the sixties when the rallying cry for African Americans became "Black is beautiful!" They claimed the power to name what was valuable. They claimed the power to believe in themselves. They went from being the supporting players in someone else's drama to being the stars of their own. And it was like wildfire sparks lighting up so many more transformations among the ragged communities of outcast people.

[12]This past summer, Margy and I met David Bermudez Velasco, who was part of the Stonewall Rebellion in 1969. The police had raided the gay bar, the Stonewall Inn, many, many times before. But in the early morning hours of June 28th, the drag queens started fighting back, and others joined them. The crowd started chanting, "Gay Power, Gay Power." The rebellion continued for five days, and was completely ignored by the media, but it was the spark that energized the modern GLBT movement.[b] We claimed the power to name what is valuable. We claimed the power to believe in ourselves. The location of ultimate value had shifted. Liberation theology expresses it this way: The divine itself is revealed in the struggle of oppressed people for liberation.

[13]That is what happened for me, too. I found the divine in the midst of the women celebrating lesbian existence. Some of us called her goddess. Some of us had no name to describe it. But we experienced a sacred and holy power when we seized the courage to kiss the body of another woman. Something shifted. It no longer mattered whether we were welcome at the table of the society that excluded us. We were in a new reality and could no longer be denied.

[14]Adrienne Rich celebrated that moment when lesbian women call each other into existence. She wrote:

> "This is what she was to me, and this
> is how I can love myself--
> as only a woman can love me.
> ...two women, eye to eye

---

[b]GLBT is shorthand for Gay, Lesbian, Bisexual and Transgender.

> measuring each other's spirit, each other's
> limitless desire,
> a whole new poetry beginning here."[c]

[15]Even language became transformed. Words like *lesbian*, or *queer*—once painful putdowns—were reclaimed as words of honor. I hold vivid images in my mind of young activists marching and shouting: "We're here, we're queer, get used to it." And then in 2002, there was the great Simpson's episode on Fox TV, when Lisa Simpson is watching the Springfield Gay Pride Parade and listening to that very chant. She says to the marchers, "You do this every year. We are used to it." Maybe it is we older queer folk who still are not quite used to it.

[16]Was the tree in Ireland actually a fairy tree? Or did the beliefs of the people make it so? Those of us who believe in queer people are in a battle over reality. There is something going on here which is more than a simple tolerance for diversity. Those of us who believe in queer people are like sailors in a mutiny—and the ship over which we struggle is reality itself.

[17]Queer people have more in common with fairies than just the name gay men are sometimes called. Those of us who exist at the edges of reality have learned that reality is not an immutable and solid thing. Reality is capable of being turned inside out, toppled and tossed upside down. There are more realities than we know, not only what we can already see. But reality is definitely linked to what we believe in.

[18]African-American lesbian poet Audre Lorde wrote, "We were never meant to survive."[d] Years ago, I received a letter from one of my younger sisters. Her words were words that too many of us have heard from the people closest to us, from the institutions of our society. She wrote: "I pray for you night after night . . . I do not believe people are born gay or homosexual. It is a lie from the devil . . . . Homosexuality is wrong! And as your sister I don't want to lose you to the devil." Another sister refused to let me to stay in her home because she didn't want her children to know about gay people.

[19]Those of us who believe in gay people are in a battle over reality. We are often under assault even from those who are closest to us. How much guilt, despair, and shame have gay people carried in our guts because of their definition of reality? How many gay people have killed themselves in the pain of that reality? How many gay people have been killed, through the violence and hate of a society that has refused to include us in their definition of reality?

---

[c] Adrienne Rich, pp. 75-76.

[d] Audre Lorde, "A Litany for Survival," in *The Black Unicorn: Poems,* (New York: Norton, 1978), p. 31.

[20]The stronger we grow, the more we also face a backlash. When Maine legislators passed a civil rights bill that included sexual orientation and gender expression, the right wing waged a referendum campaign to repeal the law. It took twenty years to finally succeed. When Massachusetts legalized same-sex marriage, many other states changed their constitutions to prohibit it. There is something about being queer that threatens everything my sister, and others like her, believe in.

[21]Why is it so frightening? Sometimes it seems so silly to me. When I look at my life and love, and that of my other lesbian, gay, bisexual and transgender friends, we seem so ordinary and gentle. Nothing to be scared about. Much of the gay rights movement has been trying to convince people that we are just like everyone else.

[22]On the other hand, I don't want to so easily sacrifice the power and mystery of our difference. As much as we claim our connections, what we really have to fight for is the necessity of our difference. We are not the same as everyone else. We never will be. Most of us, like the name of a Boston band, are "adult children of heterosexuals." We will always be a minority, coming into our families like changelings, because we do not quite resemble our parents. By its very nature, queerness will always be linked to the mystery of difference. And that can be a frightening thing for all of us.

[23]Paula Gunn Allen, a lesbian of Laguna Pueblo and Sioux heritage, speaks of the "life-long liminality" that is part of being queer. The word "liminal" describes those things which are at the threshold, the place where we cross over into another place. She says this "is what constitutes the sacred moment, the process of changing from one condition to another."[e] Queer people are sacred inasmuch as we are involved in the shifting of reality.

[24]There is power and mystery in our difference. Think about the diversity of life on earth. All of life, every species of plant and animal, from virus and bacteria to the largest whales in the sea, are formed from the same inner codes of DNA, like a four-letter alphabet. But that DNA spells out billions of different words. According to evolutionary theories, the diversity of life grew from small mutations in the code, maybe happening just one in a million times. One science documentary described them as small spelling errors. That caught my attention. All of the diversity of creation sprang from small spelling mistakes.

[25]It reminded me of the rugs made by the Navajo, or Dine, people. It is traditional for the Dine weavers to purposefully leave a small flaw in each rug. The Dine understand this as a way of expressing respect, that only the Creator can make perfect things. But the meaning I was wondering about was different. If the great diversity of creation is born of the small flaws, then perhaps it is the Creator who causes so-called "mistakes" to come into being. The mistakes are

---

[e] Jane Caputi, "Interview with Paula Gunn Allen," in *Trivia*, Vol. 16/17, p. 56.

the seeds of the next new thing. The mistakes themselves are sacred and holy.

[26]There is a parable here for the deviance of queer existence. Rather than trying to get everyone to see how ordinary we are, rather than trying to make sure we fit in, what might happen if we believed in the power of our difference? I don't mean that we shouldn't have all the rights and freedoms of straight people. But what might change if we stopped seeing the so-called mistakes as problems? What might change if we were open to the sacredness of aberration? What might happen if we truly believed in ourselves and in each other?

[27]And this is a question not just for gay, lesbian, bisexual, or transgender people. This is a question for anyone who doesn't quite match the norm. Anyone with disabilities. Anyone who isn't white. Anyone who is deaf or hard of hearing. Anyone who is "too fat" or "too thin." Anyone who is on the edges, out of a job, homeless. Anyone who is not exactly perfect. Anyone who feels caught between realities, who doesn't really fit the way we are supposed to.

[28]According to Chicana lesbian writer Gloria Anzaldua, primal cultures saw "a magic aspect in abnormality and so-called deformity. Maimed, mad, and sexually different people were believed to possess supernatural powers."[f] In the Jewish and Christian Scriptures, we read, "The stone which the builders rejected has become the keystone."[g]

[29]When we believe in each other, all of reality begins to shift. When we believe in each other, in all of the mystery of our differences, we align ourselves with the ancient evolutionary power of creation. The power that brings forth new forms out from the material of the old. The power that experiments, mutates, transforms. When we believe in each other, we reveal a vision of the divine as an ever changing, ever creating force. When we believe in each other, we are like a spelling mistake on the way to creating a new reality. When we believe in each other, anything can happen.

[30]*Closing Words*

When you are wounded and bruised by the battles in your reality,
When your light is in danger of going out,
May you always find someone to believe in you.

By believing in each other,
May we know the presence of the divine
within our midst.
Blessed be.

---

[f]Gloria Anzaldua, *Borderland/La Frontera: The New Mestiza*, (San Francisco: Spinsters/Aunt Lute, 1987), p. 19.

[g]Psalm 118:22 is the original, and it is often quoted in other locations as well, eg. Luke 20:17.

Vocabulary

[1]gnarled	[17]immutable	[26]parable	[28]Chicana
[4]chasm	[22]changelings	[26]deviance	[28]primal
[8]transgender	[23]liminality	[26]aberration	

Discussion Questions

1. What point is Johnson making in connecting clapping for Tinker Bell and her understanding of being a lesbian?

2. Johnson cites several examples of homosexuals being invisible when she was younger. What are these? Why does she bring these up?

3. In paragraph 12 Johnson defines "liberation theology." Research this term and explain why some critics call it "Marxist." How does liberation theology relate to Johnson's discussion of homosexuality?

4. What does Johnson mean when she writes in paragraph 17 , "But reality is definitely linked to what we believe in"?

5. What are Johnson's sisters' "reality"?

6. What is Johnson's view of being different?

7. To support her points, Johnson incorporates the words and traditions of people of various religions and cultures. Why do you think she cites them? What do they add to her point?

8. What is Johnson's main argument in this sermon? (Hint: it is not about being lesbian.)

FROM THE BHAGAVAD GITA AND THE UPANISHADS

Hinduism, with its vast gallery of gods and goddesses, is one of the oldest religions in the world, tracing its origins back approximately 5,000 years. As the dominant religion of India, Hinduism is practiced in one form or another by approximately 80 percent of the Indian population.

The Bhagavad Gita (commonly referred to simply as the Gita) is a Sanskrit text taken from the Mahābhārata epic, one of the longest epic poems in the world. The Mahābhārata, consisting of 74,000 verses, long prose passages and about 1.8 million words, is one of the two major Sanskrit epics of ancient India, the other being the Rāmāyaṇa.

The Mahābhārata is of immense importance to the culture of India and is a major text of Hinduism. The Bhagavad Gita, consisting of 18 chapters, opens with blind King Dhritarashtra asking his secretary, Sanjaya, to describe to him the battle between Dhritarashtra's sons, the Kauravas, and their cousins, the Pandavas. Lord Krishna, (the Supreme Personality of Godhead and one of the ten incarnations of Vishnu), out of affection for his devotee, the Pandava prince Arjuna, has agreed to drive his chariot onto the battlefield. As Arjuna takes up his bow and prepares to fight, he sees the sons of Dhritarashtra drawn up and ready to go into battle. Arjuna asks the infallible Krishna to draw his chariot between the two fighting forces. There in the midst of both armies, Arjuna expresses his fears and doubts about the coming battle and carries on a dialogue with Krishna. Foreseeing the imminent deaths of his relatives and friends, Arjuna throws down his bow and arrows and decides not to fight.

In the excerpts from the later chapters presented here, Lord Sri Krishna is seen as a great personality with human characteristics, but at the same time we recognize that He is the Supreme Lord with control over the universal affairs of material nature. When we see wonderful things happening in the cosmos, we should know that behind this cosmic manifestation is a supreme controller.

The Upanishads, a part of the Vedas, are an essential element of the Hindu scriptures, focusing primarily on the nature of God, philosophy and meditation.

BHAGAVAD GITA

FROM Chapter 11: Of the Manifesting of the One and Manifold

[1]*Arjuna[a] said:* This, for my soul's peace, have I heard from Thee,

---

[a]Arjuna, whose name means "bright," "shining" is a great warrior and archer. He is a heroic figure in the *Mahabharata*, from which the Bhagavad Gita is taken.

The unfolding of the Mystery Supreme,
Comprehending which
My darkness is dispelled; for now I know—O Lotus-eyed!—whence is the birth of men,
And whence their death, and the majesties
Of Thine immortal rule.

[2]Thus would I see,
As thou Thyself declare it, Sovereign Lord!
The likeness of that glory of Thy Form
 Wholly revealed. O Thou Divinest One!
Make Thyself visible, Lord of all prayers!
Show me Thy very self, the Eternal God!

[3]*Krishna said:* Gaze, then, thou Son of Pritha![b] I manifest for thee
Those hundred thousand thousand shapes that clothe my Mystery;
I show thee all my forms, infinite, rich, divine.
See! in this face of mine,
Adityas, Vasus, Rudras, Aswins, Maruts and the other demigods;[c] see
Wonders unnumbered, Indian Prince! revealed to none save thee.

[4]Thou canst not see!—not with human eyes, Arjuna!
Therefore I give thee sense divine. Have other eyes, new light!
And, look! This is My glory, unveiled to mortal sight!

[5]*Sanjaya*[d] *said:* Then, the King— O God!—so saying,
Stood, to Arjuna, displaying
All the splendor, wonder, dread
Of His vast Almighty head.
Out of countless eyes beholding,

---

[b]Pritha is Arjuna's mother; she is also known as Kunti. As a child she was given a *mantra* (here meaning a wish or prediction) giving her the power to summon any god and have a child by him. To test the mantra, she summoned Surya, the sun god, and had a child by him. She later abandoned the child in a basket in a river.

[c]Hinduism embraces many gods in addition to the supreme ruler, Vishnu (Krishna is one of the ten avatars of Vishnu). The Aswins, for example, are the twin sons of the sun god Surya; the Vasus are eight lesser gods who attend Vishnu and represent elements of the natural world, such as the wind, sky and moon.

[d] Sanjaya (also known as Sanjay) is the narrator in the epic *Mahabharata* who describes the action of the great battle to the blind king Dhritarashtra and relates the conversation between Krishna and Arjuna. Many passages in the epic begin with the Sanskrit "*Sanjay uvaacha,*" "Sanjay said . . . ."

Out of countless mouths commanding,
Countless mystic forms enfolding
In one Form: supremely standing
Countless radiant glories wearing,
Countless heavenly weapons bearing,
Boundless, beautiful—all spaces
With His all-regarding faces;
So He showed! If there should rise
Suddenly within the skies
Sunburst of a thousand suns
Flooding earth with beams undeemed-of,
Then might be that Holy One's
Majesty and radiance dreamed of!

⁶So did Arjuna behold
God of Gods, the Never-Ending
Deity!

⁷Then, thrilled, amazed,
Overfilled, dazzled, and dazed,
Arjuna knelt; and bowed his head,
And clasped his palms; and cried, and said: 'Yea! I have seen! I see!
Lord! all is wrapped in Thee!
The gods are in Thy glorious frame! the creatures
Of earth, and heaven, and hell
In Thy Divine form dwell.

⁸Infinite King! I see
The diadem on Thee,
The Fount whence Life's stream draws
All waters of all rivers of all being:
The One Unborn, Unending:
Unchanging and Unblending!
With might and majesty, past thought, past seeing!

⁹O Mystic, All-Powerful One!
At sight of Thee, made known,
The Three Worlds quake; the lower gods draw nigh Thee;
They fold their palms, and bow
Body, and breast, and brow,
And, whispering worship, laud and magnify Thee!

[10]Rishis and Siddhas[e] cry
"Hail! Highest Majesty!
From sage and singer breaks the hymn of glory
In sweet harmony,
Sounding the praise of Thee;
While the demigods take up the story,

[11]The Rudras, who ride the storms,
The Adityas' shining forms,
Vasus and Sadhyas, Viswas, Ushmapas;
Maruts, and those great Twins
The heavenly, fair, Aswins,
Gandharvas, Rakshasas, Siddhas, and Asuras,—

[12]These see Thee, and revere
In sudden-stricken fear;
The Three wide Worlds before Thee
Adore, as I adore Thee,
Quake, as I quake, to witness so much splendor!

[13]I see Thee strike the skies
With power, in wondrous wise;
O Eyes of God! O Head!
My strength of soul is fled,
Gone is heart's force, rebuked is mind's desire!
When I behold Thee so,
With awful brows a-glow,
With burning glance, and lips lighted by fire

[14]Fierce as those flames which shall
Consume, at close of all,
Earth, Heaven! Ah me! I see no Earth and Heaven!
Thee, Lord of Lords! I see,
Thee only—only Thee!
Now let Thy mercy unto me be given,

[15]Thou Refuge of the World!
Lo! to the cavern hurled
Of Thy wide-opened throat, and white lips on-rushed,

---

[e]Rishis are poets. Siddhas are "perfected masters" who, through persistent meditation, have
   achieved mastery of mind over body and perfection of spirit.

I see our noblest ones,
Great Dhritarashtra's sons,
Bhishma, Drona, and Karna,[f] caught and crushed!

[16]The Kings and Chiefs drawn in,
That gaping gorge within;
The best of both these armies torn and riven!
Between Thy jaws they lie
Mangled full bloodily,
Ground into dust and death! Like streams

[17]Like moths which in the night
Flutter towards a light,
Drawn to their fiery doom, flying and dying,
So to their death still throng,
Blind, dazzled, borne along
Ceaselessly, all those multitudes, wild flying!

[18]Thou, that hast fashioned men,
Devourest them again,
One with another, great and small, alike!
The creatures whom Thou makest,
With flaming jaws Thou takest,
Lapping them up! Lord God! Thy terrors strike

[19]From end to end of earth,
Filling life full, from birth
To death, with deadly, burning, lurid dread!
Ah, Vishnu![g] make me know
Why is Thy visage so?
Who art Thou, feasting thus upon Thy dead?

[20]*Krishna said:* Thou seest Me as Time who kills,
Time who brings all to doom,
The Slayer Time, Ancient of Days, come hither to consume;
Excepting thee, of all these hosts of hostile chiefs arrayed,
There stands not one shall leave alive the battlefield! Dismayed

---

[f]Bhishma, Drona, and Karna are three of the 100 sons of King Dhritarashtra, all of whom are
   killed in the battle being described to the king by Sanjaya.

[g]In this context, Vishnu may be seen as another name for Krishna.

Sanjaya said: Hearing mighty Keshav's[h] word,
Trembling that helmeted Lord[i]
Clasped his lifted palms, and—praying
Grace of Krishna—stood there, saying,
With bowed brow and accents broken,
These words, timorously spoken:

[21]*Arjuna:* Worthily, Lord of Might!
The whole world hath delight
In Thy surpassing power, obeying Thee;
The Rakshasas,[j] in dread
At sight of Thee, are sped
To all four quarters; and the company

[22]Of Siddhas sound Thy name.
How should they not proclaim
Thy Majesties, Divinest, Mightiest?
Thou Brahm, than Brahma[k] greater!
Thou Infinite Creator!
Thou God of gods, Life's Dwelling-place and
Rest. Who knoweth all, and art
Wisdom Thyself! O Part
In all, and All; for all from Thee have risen
Numberless now I see
The aspects are of Thee!
He who keeps the prison

---

[h]Keshav is another name for Krishna.

[i]The "helmeted lord" is Arjuna.

[j]Rakshashas are demons, said by some to be particularly wicked humans in their previous incarnations. They are notorious for desecrating graves, harassing priests and possessing humans. They have venom in their fingernails and feed on human flesh and rotten food.

[k]In Hindu cosmology, Brahma, the "Great Creator," is one of the "Hindu triad" (also known as the "Great Trinity") along with Vishnu, the maintainer or preserver, and Shiva, the destroyer or transformer. Here, Arjuna seems to be saying that Krishna is greater than even the "Great Creator."

[23]Of Narak, Yama[l] dark;
And Agni's shining spark;
Varuna's waves are Thy waves. Moon and starlight
Are Thine! Prajapati[m]
Art Thou, and 'tis to Thee
They knelt in worshipping the old world's far light,
The first of mortal men.

[24]For Thou art All! Yea, Thou!
Guru of Gurus; more
To reverence and adoration
Than all which is adorable and high!
How, in the wide worlds there
Should any equal be?
Should any other share Thy Majesty?

[25]Therefore, with body bent
And reverent intent,
I praise, and serve, and seek Thee, asking grace.
As father to a son,
As friend to friend, as one
Who loveth to his lover, turn Thy face

[26]In gentleness on me!
Good is it I did see
This unknown marvel of Thy Form! But fear
Mingles with joy! Retake,
Dear Lord! for pity's sake
Thine earthly shape, which earthly eyes may bear!

[27]Be merciful, and show
The visage that I know;

---

[l]Narak is a rough equivalent of the hell found in Christian and Islamic religious tradition, a place
in the afterlife of punishment and suffering. Yama, the Lord of Justice, determines appropriate punshments, if warranted, for human beings after death, such as being boiled in oil. *Yama
Loka*, the dwelling place of Yama, is viewed as more like the purgatory of Roman Catholicism
rather than a place of eternal punishment. Yama's divine assistant, Lord Chitragupta, keeps
records of the deeds and misdeeds of every person in the world, and based on these records,
sends the soul of the deceased either to Svarga (heaven) or to the various levels of Narak according to the nature and seriousness of their sins.

[m]Agni is the god of fire; Varuna is the god of sky, rain and ocean; Prajapati is the god of procreation and the protector of life.

Let me regard Thee, as of yore, arrayed
With disc and forehead-gem,
With mace and diadem,
Thou who sustainest all things!

[28]Undismayed
Let me once more behold
The form I loved of old,
Thou of the thousand arms and countless eyes!
This frightened heart is fain
To see restored again
My Charioteer, in Krishna's kind disguise.

[29]*Krishna said*: Yea! thou hast seen, Arjuna! because I loved thee well,
The secret countenance of Me, revealed by mystic spell,
Shining, and wonderful, and majestic, manifold,
Which none save thou in all the years had favor to behold;
For not by Vedas[n] cometh this, nor sacrifice, nor alms,
Nor works well-done, nor penance long, nor prayers, nor chanted psalms,
That mortal eyes should bear to view the Immortal Soul unclad,
Prince of the Kurus![o] This was kept for thee alone! Be glad!
Let no more trouble shake thy heart, because thine eyes have seen
My terror with My glory. As I before have been
So will I be again for thee; with lightened heart behold!
Once more I am thy Krishna, the form thou knew'st of old!

[30]*Sanjaya said*: These words to Arjuna spake
Krishna, and straight did take
Back again the semblance dear
Of the well-loved charioteer;
Peace and joy it did restore
When the Prince beheld once more
Mighty BRAHMA'S form and face
Clothed in Krishna's gentle grace.

[31]*Arjuna said*: Now that I see come back, Janardana![p]

---

[n]Vedas are the oldest form of Sanskrit literature and the oldest sacred texts of Hinduism.

[o]The Kurus were an Indo-Aryan tribe dating back to approximately the tenth century BC and were located in the modern state of Harayana in northern India near the Punjab region.

[p]Janardana, another name for Krishna, has been translated as "He who punishes evil people."

This friendly human frame, my mind can think
Calm thoughts once more; my heart beats still again!

[32]*Krishna said*: Yea! it was wonderful and terrible
To view me as thou didst, dear Prince! The gods
Dread and desire continually to view!
Yet not by Vedas, nor from sacrifice,
Nor penance, nor gift-giving, nor with prayer
Shall any so behold, as thou hast seen!
Only by fullest service, perfect faith,
And uttermost surrender am I known
And seen, and entered into, Indian Prince!
Who doeth all for Me; who findeth Me
In all; adoreth always; loveth all
Which I have made, and Me, for Love's sole end,
That man, Arjuna! unto Me doth come.

Chapter 12: Of the Religion of Faith

[1]*Arjuna said*: Lord! of the men who serve Thee true in heart
As God revealed;
Which take the better way of faith and life?

[2]*Krishna said*: Whoever serve Me as I show Myself, and who are constantly
true, in full devotion fixed,
Those I hold very holy. But those who
Worship Me—The One, The Invisible,
The Unrevealed, Unnamed, Unthinkable,
The Unchangeable, Fixed and Immovable,
Beyond the perception of the senses,
Who thus adore Me, mastering their own senses,
Of one set mind and doing good for all,
These blessed souls come unto Me.

[3]Yet, hard the task is
For such as bend their minds to reach
The Unmanifest—the Unworldly. That viewless path
Shall scarce be trod by man bearing the flesh!

[4]But whereso any doeth all his deeds

Renouncing self for Me, full of Me, fixed
To serve only the Highest, night and day
Musing on Me—those will I swiftly lift
Forth from life's ocean of distress and death,
Whose soul clings fast to Me. Cling thou to Me!

⁵Clasp Me with heart and mind! so shalt thou dwell
Surely with Me on high. But if thy thought
Droops from such height; if thou be weak to set
Body and soul upon Me constantly,
Despair not! Give Me lower service! Seek
To reach Me, worshipping with steadfast will;

⁶And, if thou canst not meditate upon Me steadfastly,
Work for Me, toil in works pleasing to Me!
For he that labor right for love of Me
Shall finally attain! But, if in this
Thy faint heart fails, bring Me thy failure! Find refuge in Me! let fruits of
labor go,
Renouncing hope for Me, with lowliest heart,
So shalt thou come; for, though to know is more
Than diligence, yet worship better is
Than knowing, and renouncing better still.
Near to renunciation—very near—
Dwelleth Eternal Peace!
⁷Who hateth nothing,
Of all which lives, living himself benign,
Compassionate, from arrogance exempt,
Exempt from love of self, unchangeable
By good or ill; patient, contented, firm
In faith, mastering himself, true to his word,
Seeking Me, heart and soul; vowed unto Me,—
That one I love! Who troubleth not his kind,
And is not troubled by them; clear of wrath,
Living too high for gladness, grief, or fear,
That one I love! Who, dwelling quiet-eyed,
Stainless, serene, well-balanced, unperplexed,
Working with Me, yet from all works detached,
That one I love! Who, fixed in faith on Me,
Dotes upon none, scorns none; rejoices not,
And grieves not, letting good or evil
Land where it will, and when it will depart,

That one I love! Who, unto friend and foe
Keeping an equal heart, with equal mind
Bears shame and glory; with an equal peace
Takes heat and cold, pleasure and pain; abides
Quit of desires, hears praise or blame
In passionless restraint, unmoved by each;
Linked by no ties to earth, steadfast in Me,
That one I love!
[8]But most of all I love
Those happy ones to whom 'tis life to live
In single fervid faith and love unseeing,
Drinking the blessed Amrit[a] of my Being!

---

[a]Amrit is a holy nectar, that is, a sweet fruit drink, the life-giving drink of the gods.

AITAREYA UPANISHAD

[1]Om![a] May my speech be in accord with the mind;
May my mind be in accord with my speech.
O Self-effulgent[b] One, reveal Thyself to me.
May both speech and mind be the carriers of the Veda[c] to me.
May not all that I have heard depart from me.
I shall join together day
And night through this study.
I shall utter what is verbally true;
I shall utter what is mentally true.
May Brahman[d] protect me;
May that protect the speaker, may that protect me;
Om! Peace! Peace! Peace!

---

[a]Om (also aum) is a sacred syllable in Hindu, Jain and Buddhist religions that is placed at the beginning of most Hindu texts as a sacred exclamation to be uttered at the beginning and end of a reading. The symbol is written on the tongues of children in honey when they are born.

[b]Self-effulgent One is one who is full of radiant splendor, here apparently addressed to the chief deity.

[c]Vedas are the oldest form of Sanskrit literature and the oldest sacred texts of Hinduism.

[d]Brahman is the unchanging, infinite and transcendent reality, which is the divine basis for all matter, energy time, space and being. It is associated with the creator god Brahma.

[2]In the beginning this was but the absolute Self alone. There was nothing else whatsoever that winked. He thought, "Let Me create the worlds."

[3]He created these worlds: ambhas, marici, mara, apah. That which is beyond heaven is ambhas. Heaven is its support. The sky is marici. The earth is mara. The worlds that are below are the apah.

[4]He thought, "These then are the worlds. Let Me create the protectors of the worlds." Having gathered up a lump of the human form from the water itself, He gave shape to it.

[5]He deliberated with regard to him (Virat) of the human form. As Virat was being deliberated on, his mouth parted, just as an egg does. From the mouth emerged speech; from speech came Fire. The nostrils parted; from the nostrils came out the sense of smell; from the sense of smell came Air (Vayu). The two eyes parted; from the eyes emerged the sense of sight; from the sense of sight came the Sun. The two ears parted; from the ears came the sense of hearing; from the sense of hearing came the Directions. The skin emerged; from the skin came out hair (the sense of touch); from the sense of touch came the Herbs and Trees. The heart took shape; from the heart issued the internal organ (mind); from the internal organ came the Moon. The navel parted; from the navel came out the organ of ejection; from the organ of ejection issued Death. The seat of the procreative organ parted; from that came the procreative organ; from the procreative organ came out Water.

****

[6]These deities that had been created fell into this vast ocean. He subjected Virat to hunger and thirst. They said to the Creator, "Provide an abode for us where we can eat food."

[7]For them the Creator brought a cow. They said, "This one is certainly not adequate for us." For them He brought a horse. They said, "This one is certainly not adequate for us."

[8]For them He brought a man. They said "This one is well formed; man indeed is a creation of God Himself." To them He said, "Enter into your respective abodes."

[9]Fire entered into the mouth, taking the form of the organ of speech; Air entered into the nostrils, assuming the form of the sense of smell; the Sun entered into the eyes as the sense of sight; the Directions entered into the ears by becoming the sense of hearing; the Herbs and Trees entered into the skin in the form of hair, the sense of touch; the Moon entered into the heart in the shape of the mind; Death entered into the navel in the form of Apana (the vital energy that presses down); Water entered into the limb of generation in the form of semen (the organ of procreation).

[10]To Him Hunger and Thirst said, "Provide for us an abode." To them He said, "I provide your livelihood among these very gods; I make you share in their portions." Therefore when oblation is taken up for any deity whichsoever, Hunger and Thirst become verily sharers with that deity.

****

[11]He thought, "These, then, are the senses and the deities of the senses. Let Me create food for them.

[12]He deliberated with regard to the water. From the water, thus brooded over, evolved a form. The form that emerged was verily food.

[13]This food, that was created, turned back and attempted to run away. He tried to take it up with speech. He did not succeed in taking it up through speech. If He had succeeded in taking it up with the speech, then one would have become contented merely by talking of food.

[14]He tried to grasp that food with the sense of smell. He did not succeed in grasping it by smelling. If He had succeeded in grasping it by smelling, then everyone should have become contented merely by smelling food.

[15]He wanted to take up the food with the eye. He did not succeed in taking it up with the eye. If He had taken it up with the eye, then one would have become satisfied by merely seeing food.

[16]He wanted to take up the food with the ear. He did not succeed in taking it up with the ear. If He had taken it up with the ear, then one would have become satisfied by merely by hearing of food.

[17]He wanted to take it up with the sense of touch. He did not succeed in taking it up with the sense of touch. If He had taken it up with touch, then one would have become been satisfied merely by touching food.

[18]He wanted to take it up with the mind. He did not succeed in taking it up with the mind. If He had taken it up with the mind, then one would have become satisfied by merely thinking of food.

[19]He wanted to take it up with the procreative organ. He did not succeed in taking it up with the procreative organ. If He had taken it up with the procreative organ, then one would have become satisfied by merely ejecting food.

[20]He wanted to take it up with Apana. He caught it. This is the devourer of food. That vital energy which is well known as dependent of food for its subsistence is this vital energy called *Apana*.

[21]He thought, "How indeed can it be there without Me?" He thought, "Through which of the two ways should I enter?" He thought, "If utterance is done by the organ of speech, smelling by the sense of smell, seeing by the eye, hearing by the ear, feeling by the sense of touch, thinking by the mind, the act of drawing in (or pressing down) by Apana, ejecting by the procreative organ, then who or what am I ?"

²²Having split up this very end, He entered through this door. This entrance is known as *vidriti*, the chief entrance. Hence it is delightful. Of Him there are three abodes – three states of dream. This one is an abode, this one is an abode. This one is an abode.

²³Being born, He manifested all the beings; for did He speak of or know anything else? He realized this very Purusha[e] as Brahman, the most pervasive, thus: "I have realized this."

²⁴Therefore His name is Idandra.[f] He is verily known as Idandra. Although He is Idandra, they call Him indirectly Indra; for the gods are verily fond of indirect names.

---

[e]Purusha is the "self" that pervades the universe. In one school of Hindu philosophy, Purusha is our true identity, pure consciousness, as opposed to the material.

[f]In early Hinduism, Indra is mentioned as the chief deity, the king of the gods. His role has diminished in modern Hinduism.

****

²⁵In man indeed is the soul first conceived. That which is the semen is extracted from all the limbs as their vigor. He holds that self of his in his own self. When he sheds it into his wife, then he pocreates it. That is its first birth.

²⁶That becomes non-different from the wife, just as much as her own limb is. Therefore the fetus does not hurt her. She nourishes this self of his that has entered her in her womb.

²⁷She, the nourisher, becomes fit to be nourished. The wife bears that embryo before the birth. He, the father, protects the son at the very start, soon after his birth. That he protects the son at the very beginning, just after birth, thereby he protects his own self for the sake of the continuance of these worlds. For thus is the continuance of these worlds ensured. That is his second birth.

²⁸This self of his, the son, is substituted by the father for the performance of virtuous deeds. Then this other self of his (that is, the father of the son), having got his duties ended and having advanced in age, departs. As soon as he departs, he takes birth again. That is his son's third birth.

²⁹This fact was stated by the seer: "Even while lying in the womb, I came to know of the birth of all the gods. A hundred iron citadels held me down. Then, like a hawk, I forced my way through by dint of knowledge of the Self." Vamadeva[g] said this while still lying in the mother's womb.

---

[g]Vamadeva is the name of the "preserver" aspect of the god Shiva.

[30]He who had known thus had become identified with the Supreme, and attained all desirable things, even here; and having then ascended higher up after the destruction of the body, he became immortal, in the world of the Self. He became immortal.

****

[31]What is It that we worship as this Self? Which of the two is the Self? Is It that by which one sees, or that by which one hears, or that by which one smells odor, or that by which one utters speech, or that by which one tastes the sweet or the sour ?

[32]It is this heart (intellect) and this mind that were stated earlier. It is sentience, rulership, secular knowledge, presence of mind, retentiveness, sense-perception, fortitude, thinking, genius, mental suffering, memory, ascertainment resolution, life-activities, desiring, passion and such others. All these verily are the names of Consciousness.

[33]This One is the inferior Brahman; this is Indra, this is Prajapati;[h] this is all these gods; and this is these five elements, viz. earth, air, space, water, fire; and this is all these big creatures, together with the small ones, that are the procreators of others and referable in pairs—to wit, those that are born of eggs, of wombs, of moisture of the earth, viz. horses, cattle, men, elephants, and all the creatures that there are which move or fly and those which do not move. All these have Consciousness as the giver of their reality; all these are impelled by Consciousness; the universe has Consciousness as its eye and Consciousness is its end. Consciousness is Brahman.

[34]Through this Self that is Consciousness, he ascended higher up from this world, and getting all desires fulfilled in that heavenly world, he became immortal.

Here ends the Aitareyopanishad, as contained in the Rig-Veda.

---

[h]Prajapati is the god who presides over procreation and protects life.

Vocabulary

Chapter 11

[1]dispelled	[12]revere	[20]hosts	[28]fain
[1]whence	[13]rebuked	[20]arrayed	[29]manifold
[6]deity	[16]gorge	[20]timorously	[29]alms
[8]diadem	[16]riven	[24]guru	[29]penance
[8]fount	[19]lurid	[27]yore	[29]psalms
[9]laud	[19]visage	[27]mace	

Chapter 12

[3]trod	[6]renunciation	[7]wrath	[7]abides
[4]musing	[7]benign	[7]perplexed	[7]quit (of desires)
[5]steadfast	[7]exempt	[7]dotes	[8]fervid
[6]diligence			

Aitareya Upanishad

[5]procreative	[12]brooded	[30]dint	[33]fortitude
[6]abode	[34]impelled	[33]sentience	[33]ascertainment
[10]oblation	[21]subsistence	[33]secular	[34]viz
[10]verily	[30]seer	[33]retentiveness	[34]impelled

Discussion Questions
Chapter 11

1. In Verse 1 Arjuna tells Krishna that from their dialogue in earlier chapters he, Arjuna, now knows about the birth and death of men and of Krishna's "immortal rule." In verse 3, what essentially is Krishna telling Arjuna of His, Krishna's, "manifest form"?

2. How does Sanjaya describe Krishna in Verse 5? From your knowledge of or research into the traditions of Islam, Judaism, Christianity, how does this description of Krishna compare to descriptions of "God" in these other major religious traditions?

3. Again, looking at the other major religions for comparison, what do you think is meant by the "three worlds" in Verse 9?

4. Keeping in mind the introductory notes that say the *Gita* is an epic poem about a battle between Arjuna and his relatives, what appears to be happening in Verses 16-19?

5. In Verse 20, Krishna describes himself as "Time who kills." Explain this concept.

6.   Research the meaning of "Guru" and explain the reference in Verse 24.

7.   What is Arjuna asking Krishna to do in Verses 26-28?

8.   In what way does Verse 32 serve as a transition into the content of Chapter 12?

Chapter 12

1. What is the essential theme of Chapter 12?

2. What are the similarities and differences between Chapter 12 here and The Sermon on the Mount found on page 489 of this text?

3. Which of the two works, Chapter 12 or Sermon on the Mount, seems to give more specific suggestions on attaining salvation? Explain.

4. Look at The Eightfold Path beginning on page 178 of this text, Leviticus beginning on page 377, Sura 2 of the Holy Qur'an beginning on page 451, and the Sermon on the Mount on page 489. Compare these works to this chapter of the Gita and explain what they all have in common.

Aitareya Upanishad

1. This text contains other versions of stories similar to this one. Pick one of the other ones and point out the similarities and differences between the other story and this one.

BHAGAVAD GITA
IN COMIC BOOK FORMAT

India has a rich tradition in book publishing, and, as in the United States, comic books are an important segment of the publishing industry with many of the popular titles having a religious content. On the following pages, this excerpt from "The Gita" in comic book format presents several key elements of Hinduism in a simplified format designed to appeal to children.

The Avatar, for example, an essential concept in Hinduism, is illustrated in the last panel of this excerpt when Arjuna asks Krishna to manifest himself in worldly form. The comic book illustrator blends "the whole of [human] creation" in with some of the avatars of the ten incarnations of Vishnu within the image of Krishna.

Vishnu, a mighty male god who plays several roles for his followers, is one of a "trinity" of Hindu gods (with Brahma and Shiva) who is the creator of the cosmos, its sustainer, and, ultimately, its destroyer. On earth he has appeared in ten different avatars, that is, forms or manifestations, which are sometimes compared to the stages of development of Homo sapiens in Charles Darwin's theory of evolution. The avatar concept, the cornerstone of Hindu theology, has the Supreme Power manifesting itself in animal or human form on earth with the divine misssion of cleansing the world of periodically increasing evil.

The ten incarnations of Vishnu are 1) Matsya, the Fish 2) Kurma, the Tortoise 3) Varaha, the Boar 4) Narasimha, Half Man, Half Lion 5) Vamanna, the Dwarf 6) Parashurama 7) Rama 8) Krishna, the Original Godhead 9) Buddha 10) Kalki. The final incarnation of Vishnu, Kalki, is the only one that has not yet occurred and may be seen to be similar to the coming of a messiah in Judaic-Christian theosophy. Kalki's arrival will signal the end of the Kali period, a period of great hardship and destruction. At the conclusion of the Kali Age, the minds of the people will become as pure as flawless crystal, and they will be awakened as if at the conclusion of night.

In the other panels, the concepts of Dharma (duty) and Karma (retribution and rebirth) are illustrated as in the first panel Krishna argues with Arjuna, explaining that it is his duty (Dharma) to go to war with his cousins. The second and third panels illustrate the concept of Samsara, the cycle of life, which is in turn related to Karma. Karma means "deed" or "act," but in broader terms is the universal principle of cause and effect—what the individual does in this life will affect the soul's journey and ultimate destiny. See pages 176-177 of this text for a further explanation of Samsara and Karma.

THE GITA

ARJUNA, YOU CANNOT KILL BHEESHMA OR DRONA. NOR CAN YOU KILL DURYODHANA OR YOUR OTHER COUSINS.

WHAT DO YOU MEAN? WON'T MY ARROWS KILL THEM?

"IT IS ONLY THE BODY OF MAN THAT IS SUBJECT TO CHANGES LIKE...

BIRTH...

...CHILDHOOD...

...YOUTH...

...OLD AGE...

...AND DEATH.

THE SOUL IN MAN IS NEITHER BORN NOR DOES IT DIE. WEAPONS CANNOT CUT IT. FIRE CANNOT BURN IT. WATER CANNOT WET IT; WIND CANNOT DRY IT. WHAT MAKES YOU THINK YOU CAN KILL THE SOUL?

"JUST AS A MAN DISCARDS OLD CLOTHES AND WEARS NEW ONES...

...THE ETERNAL SOUL SHEDS A DEAD BODY...

...AND ENTERS ANOTHER.

BECAUSE YOU THINK THE SOUL OF MAN AND HIS BODY ARE ONE, YOU BELIEVE YOU CAN KILL OR BE KILLED. TRULY I TELL YOU, THE SOUL IS NOT SUBJECT TO ANY CHANGE.

WHAT YOU SAY MAY BE TRUE, KRISHNA. BUT I FAIL TO PERCEIVE THE TRUTH IN YOUR STATEMENT.

16

158

AS ARJUNA LOOKED UP, THE LIGHT DAZZLED HIM. HE SAW IN IT ALL BEINGS. IT SEEMED TO HIM AS IF HE WERE LOOKING AT CREATION; THE WHOLE OF CREATION; EVERYTHING IN CREATION; LOOKING AT THE WHOLE OF THE PAST; THE WHOLE OF THE PRESENT AND THE WHOLE OF THE FUTURE — ALL AT ONCE. IT WAS A SIGHT NO MAN HAD SEEN BEFORE. IT STAGGERED AND STUPEFIED HIM. HE WAS AS IF THE OBSERVER OF THE WHOLE DRAMA OF LIFE.

BODY RITUAL AMONG THE NACIREMA
HORACE MINER

Horace Miner (1912-1993) is the author of numerous books and articles on sociology and anthropology. He received his Ph.D. from the University of Chicago (1939) and did his post-graduate work at Columbia University (1941-42). He taught at the University of Detroit, University of Michigan and the University of Chicago, where he also was the Senior Scientific Researcher from 1980-1993.

[1]Ed. Note: Most cultures exhibit a particular configuration or style. A single value or pattern of perceiving the world often leaves its stamp on several institutions in the society. Examples are "machismo" in Spanish-influenced cultures, "face" in Japanese culture, and "pollution by females" in some highland New Guinea cultures. Here Horace Miner demonstrates that "attitudes about the body" have a pervasive influence on many institutions in Nacirema society. [1]

[2]The anthropologist has become so familiar with the diversity of ways in which different people behave in similar situations that he is not apt to be surprised by even the most exotic customs. In fact, if all of the logically possible combinations of behavior have not been found somewhere in the world, he is apt to suspect that they must be present in some yet undescribed tribe. The point has, in fact, been expressed with respect to clan organization by Murdock. [2] In this light, the magical beliefs and practices of the Nacirema present such unusual aspects that it seems desirable to describe them as an example of the extremes to which human behavior can go.

[3]Professor Linton [3] first brought the ritual of the Nacirema to the attention of anthropologists twenty years ago, but the culture of this people is still very poorly understood. They are a North American group living in the territory between the Canadian Cree, the Yaqui and Tarahumare of Mexico, and the Carib and Arawak of the Antilles. Little is known of their origin, although tradition states that they came from the east.

[4]Nacirema culture is characterized by a highly developed market economy which has evolved in a rich natural habitat.

[5]While much of the people's time is devoted to economic pursuits, a large part of the fruits of these labors and a considerable portion of the day are spent in ritual activity. The focus of this activity is the human body, the appearance and health of which loom as a dominant concern in the ethos of the

people. While such a concern is certainly not unusual, its ceremonial aspects and associated philosophy are unique. The fundamental belief underlying the whole system appears to be that the human body is ugly and that its natural tendency is to debility and disease. Incarcerated in such a body, man's only hope is to avert these characteristics through the use of ritual and ceremony. Every household has one or more shrines devoted to this purpose. The more powerful individuals in the society have several shrines in their houses and, in fact, the opulence of a house is often referred to in terms of the number of such ritual centers it possesses. Most houses are of wattle and daub construction, but the shrine rooms of the more wealthy are walled with stone. Poorer families imitate the rich by applying pottery plaques to their shrine walls.

[6]While each family has at least one such shrine, the rituals associated with it are not family ceremonies but are private and secret. The rites are normally only discussed with children, and then only during the period when they are being initiated into these mysteries. I was able, however, to establish sufficient rapport with the natives to examine these shrines and to have the rituals described to me.

[7]The focal point of the shrine is a box or chest which is built into the wall. In this chest are kept the many charms and magical potions without which no native believes he could live. These preparations are secured from a variety of specialized practitioners. The most powerful of these are the medicine men, whose assistance must be rewarded with substantial gifts. However, the medicine men do not provide the curative potions for their clients, but decide what the ingredients should be and then write them down in an ancient and secret language. This writing is understood only by the medicine men and by the herbalists who, for another gift, provide the required charm. The charm is not disposed of after it has served its purpose, but is placed in the charmbox of the household shrine. As these magical materials are specific for certain ills, and the real or imagined maladies of the people are many, the charm-box is usually full to overflowing. The magical packets are so numerous that people forget what their purposes were and fear to use them again. While the natives are very vague on this point, we can only assume that the idea in retaining all the old magical materials is that their presence in the charmbox, before which the body rituals are conducted, will in some way protect the worshipper.

[8]Beneath the charm-box is a small font. Each day every member of the family, in succession, enters the shrine room, bows his head before the charm-box, mingles different sorts of holy water in the font, and proceeds with a brief rite of ablution. [4] The holy waters are secured from the Water Temple of the community, where the priests conduct elaborate ceremonies to make the liquid ritually pure.

[9]In the hierarchy of magical practitioners, and below the medicine men in prestige, are specialists whose designation is best translated as "holy-mouth-

men." The Nacirema have an almost pathological horror of and fascination with the mouth, the condition of which is believed to have a supernatural influence on all social relationships. Were it not for the rituals of the mouth, they believe that their teeth would fall out, their gums bleed, their jaws shrink, their friends desert them, and their lovers reject them. They also believe that a strong relationship exists between oral and moral characteristics. For example, there is a ritual ablution of the mouth for children which is supposed to improve their moral fiber.

[10]The daily body ritual performed by everyone includes a mouth-rite. Despite the fact that these people are so punctilious [5] about care of the mouth, this rite involves a practice which strikes the uninitiated stranger as revolting. It was reported to me that the ritual consists of inserting a small bundle of hog hairs into the mouth, along with certain magical powders, and then moving the bundle in a highly formalized series of gestures. [6]

[11]In addition to the private mouth-rite, the people seek out a holy-mouth-man once or twice a year. These practitioners have an impressive set of paraphernalia, consisting of a variety of augers, awls, probes, and prods. The use of these items in the exorcism of the evils of the mouth involves almost unbelievable ritual torture of the client.

[12]The holy-mouth-man opens the client's mouth and, using the above-mentioned tools, enlarges any holes which decay may have created in the teeth. Magical materials are put into these holes. If there are no naturally occurring holes in the teeth, large sections of one or more teeth are gouged out so that the supernatural substance can be applied.

[13]In the client's view, the purpose of these ministrations [7] is to arrest decay and to draw friends. The extremely sacred and traditional character of the rite is evident in the fact that the natives return to the holy-mouth-men year after year, despite the fact that their teeth continue to decay.

[14]It is to be hoped that, when a thorough study of the Nacirema is made, there will be careful inquiry into the personality structure of these people. One has but to watch the gleam in the eye of a holy-mouth-man, as he jabs an awl into an exposed nerve, to suspect that a certain amount of sadism is involved. If this can be established, a very interesting pattern emerges, for most of the population shows definite masochistic tendencies. It was to these that Professor Linton referred in discussing a distinctive part of the daily body ritual which is performed only by men. This part of the rite includes scraping and lacerating the surface of the face with a sharp instrument.

[15]Special women's rites are performed only four times during each lunar month, but what they lack in frequency is made up in barbarity. As part of this ceremony, women bake their heads in small ovens for about an hour. The theoretically interesting point is that what seems to be a preponderantly masochistic people have developed sadistic specialists.

[16]The medicine men have an imposing temple, or latipso, in every community of any size. The more elaborate ceremonies required to treat very sick patients can only be performed at this temple. These ceremonies involve not only the thaumaturge [8] but a permanent group of vestal maidens who move sedately about the temple chambers in distinctive costume and headdress.

[17]The latipso ceremonies are so harsh that it is phenomenal that a fair proportion of the really sick natives who enter the temple ever recover. Small children whose indoctrination is still incomplete have been known to resist attempts to take them to the temple because "that is where you go to die." Despite this fact, sick adults are not only willing but eager to undergo the protracted ritual purification, if they can afford to do so.

[18]No matter how ill the supplicant or how grave the emergency, the guardians of many temples will not admit a client if he cannot give a rich gift to the custodian. Even after one has gained and survived the ceremonies, the guardians will not permit the neophyte to leave until he makes still another gift.

[19]The supplicant entering the temple is first stripped of all his or her clothes. In everyday life the Nacirema avoids exposure of his body and its natural functions. Bathing and excretory acts are performed only in the secrecy of the household shrine, where they are ritualized as part of the body-rites. Psychological shock results from the fact that body secrecy is suddenly lost upon entry into the latipso. A man, whose own wife has never seen him in an excretory act, suddenly finds himself naked and assisted by a vestal maiden while he performs his natural functions into a sacred vessel. This sort of ceremonial treatment is necessitated by the fact that the excreta are used by a diviner to ascertain the course and nature of the client's sickness. Female clients, on the other hand, find their naked bodies are subjected to the scrutiny, manipulation and prodding of the medicine men.

[20]Few supplicants in the temple are well enough to do anything but lie on their hard beds. The daily ceremonies, like the rites of the holy-mouth-men, involve discomfort and torture. With ritual precision, the vestals awaken their miserable charges each dawn and roll them about on their beds of pain while performing ablutions, in the formal movements of which the maidens are highly trained. At other times they insert magic wands in the supplicant's mouth or force him to eat substances which are supposed to be healing. From time to time the medicine men come to their clients and jab magically treated needles into their flesh. The fact that these temple ceremonies may not cure, and may even kill the neophyte, in no way decreases the people's faith in the medicine men.

[21]There remains one other kind of practitioner, known as a "listener." This witchdoctor has the power to exorcise the devils that lodge in the heads of people who have been bewitched. The Nacirema believe that parents bewitch

their own children. Mothers are particularly suspected of putting a curse on children while teaching them the secret body rituals. The counter-magic of the witchdoctor is unusual in its lack of ritual. The patient simply tells the "listener" all his troubles and fears, beginning with the earliest difficulties he can remember. The memory displayed by the Nacirema in these exorcism sessions is truly remarkable. It is not uncommon for the patient to bemoan the rejection he felt upon being weaned as a babe, and a few individuals even see their troubles going back to the traumatic effects of their own birth.

[22]As a last observation, mention must be made of certain practices which have their base in native esthetics but which depend upon the pervasive aversion to the natural body and its functions. There are ritual fasts to make fat people thin and ceremonial feasts to make thin people fat. Still other rites are used to make women's breasts larger if they are small, and smaller if they are large. General dissatisfaction with breast shape is symbolized in the fact that the ideal form is virtually outside the range of human variation. A few women afflicted with almost inhuman hyper-mammary development are so idolized that they make a handsome living by simply going from village to village and permitting the natives to stare at them for a fee.

[23]Reference has already been made to the fact that excretory functions are ritualized, routinized, and relegated to secrecy. Natural reproductive functions are similarly distorted. Intercourse is taboo as a topic and scheduled as an act. Efforts are made to avoid pregnancy by the use of magical materials or by limiting intercourse to certain phases of the moon. Conception is actually very infrequent. When pregnant, women dress so as to hide their condition. Parturition takes place in secret, without friends or relatives to assist, and the majority of women do not nurse their infants.

[24]Our review of the ritual life of the Nacirema has certainly shown them to be a magic-ridden people. It is hard to understand how they have managed to exist so long under the burdens which they have imposed upon themselves. But even such exotic customs as these take on real meaning when they are viewed with the insight provided by Malinowski [9] when he wrote:

[25]Looking from far and above, from our high places of safety in the developed civilization, it is easy to see all the crudity and irrelevance of magic. But without its power and guidance early man could not have mastered his practical difficulties as he has done, nor could man have advanced to the higher stages of civilization.

---

1 All footnotes were added by Prof. John A. Dowell, University of Minnesota.

2 George Peter Murdock (1897-1985), famous ethnographer.

3 Ralph Linton (1893-1953), best known for studies of enculturation (maintaining that all culture is learned rather than inherited; the process by which a society's culture is transmitted from one generation to the next), claiming culture is humanity's "social heredity."

4 A washing or cleansing of the body or a part of the body. From the Latin *abluere*, to wash away.

5 Marked by precise observance of the finer points of etiquette and formal conduct.

6 It is worthy of note that since Prof. Miner's original research was conducted, the Nacirema have almost universally abandoned the natural bristles of their private mouth-rite in favor of oil-based polymerized synthetics. Additionally, the powders associated with this ritual have generally been semi-liquefied. Other updates to the Nacirema culture shall be eschewed in this document for the sake of parsimony.

7 Tending to religious or other important functions.

8 A miracle-worker.

9 Bronislaw Malinowski (1884-1942), famous cultural anthropologist best known for his argument that people everywhere share common biological and psychological needs and that the function of all cultural institutions is to fulfill such needs.

Vocabulary

[1]machismo [9]pathological [16]thaumaturge [21]weaned
[1]pervasive [10]punctilious [16]sedately [22]esthetics
[4]habitat [11]exorcism [18]neophyte [22]aversion
[5]debility [13]ministrations [19]supplicant [22]hyper-mammary
[5]wattle [14]sadism [19]excretory [23]relegated
[5]daub [14]masochistic [19]excreta [23]taboo
[6]rapport [15]barbarity [19]diviner [23]parturition
[8]ablution [15]preponderantly [19]ascertain

Discussion Questions

1. From the description in the article, determine where the Nacirema live.

2. Discuss the tone Miner uses in this article. How does it add or detract from the credibility of the article?

3. Pick three body rituals from the article. Are there any rituals that you find similar to your customs? Explain.

4. Explain the quote from Malinowski at the end of the article.

5. When did you "get it"? Explain. How does knowing this information change the meaning of the article for you?

6. What do you think Miner is trying to tell us, i.e., what was his purpose in writing this article?

BORN OF MAN AND WOMAN

RICHARD MATHESON

Richard Matheson (1926-) had his first story, "Born of Man and Woman," published in The Magazine of Fantasy and Science Fiction *in 1950. His works include* I Am Legend *(1954),*The Shrinking Man *(1956),* The Last Man on Earth *(1964 screenplay),* What Dreams May Come *(1978), and episodes of* Twilight Zone, Night Gallery *and* Star Trek. *He is the recipient of many awards for his writing, including the Bram Stoker Award and the Edgar Allan Poe Award.*

[1]X—This day when it had light mother called me a retch. You retch she said. I saw in her eyes the anger. I wonder what it is a retch.

[2]This day it had waterfalling from upstairs. It fell all around. I saw that. The ground of the back I watched from the little window. The ground it sucked up the water like thirsty lips. It drank too much and it got sick and runny brown. I didn't like it.

[3]Mother is a pretty thing I know. In my bed place with cold walls around I have a paper things that was behind the furnace. It says on it SCREEN-STARS. I see in the pictures faces like of mother and father. Father says they are pretty. Once he said it.

[4]And also mother he said. Mother so pretty and me decent enough. Look at you he said and didn't have the nice face. I touched his arm and said it is alright father. He shook and pulled away where I couldn't reach.

[5]Today mother let me off the chain a little so I could look out the little window. That's how I saw the water falling from upstairs.

[6]XX—This day it had goldness in the upstairs. As I know when I looked at it my eyes hurt. After I looked at it the cellar is red.

[7]I think this was church. They leave the upstairs. The big machine swallows them and rolls out past and is gone. In the back part is the little mother. She is much small than me. I am big. It is a secret but I have pulled the chain out of the wall. I can see out the little window all I like.

[8]In this day when it got dark I had eat my food and some bugs. I hear laughs upstairs. I like to know why there are laughs for. I took the chain from the wall and wrapped it around me. I walked squish to the stairs. They creak when I walk on them. My legs slip on them because I don't want on stairs. My feet stick to the wood.

[9]I went up and opened the door. It was a white place. White as white jewels that come from upstairs sometime. I went in and stood quiet. I hear the

laughing some more. I walk to the sound and look through to the people. More people than I thought was. I thought I should laugh with them.

[10]Mother came out and pushed the door in. It hit me and hurt. I fell back on the smooth floor and the chain made noise. I cried. She made a hissing noise into her and put her hand on her mouth. Her eyes got big.

[11]She looked at me. I heard father call. What fell he called. She said a iron board. Come help pick it up she said. He came and said now is *that* so heavy you need me. He saw me and grew big. The anger came in his eyes. He hit me. I spilled some of the drip on the floor from one arm. It was not nice. It made ugly green on the floor.

[12]Father told me to go to the cellar. I had to go. The light it hurt now in my eyes. It is not like that in the cellar.

[13]Father tied my legs and arms up. He put me on my bed. Upstairs I heard laughing while I was quiet there looking on a black spider that was swinging down to me. I thought what father said. Ohgod he said. And only eight.

[14]XXX—This day father hit in the chain again before it had light. I have to try to pull it out again. He said I was bad to come upstairs. He said never do that again or he would beat me hard. That hurts.

[15]I hurt. I slept the day and rested my head against the cold wall. I thought of the white place upstairs.

[16]XXXX—I got the chain from the wall out. Mother was upstairs. I heard little laughs very high. I looked out the window. I saw all little people like the little mother and little fathers too. They are pretty.

[17]They were making nice noise and jumping around the ground. Their legs was moving hard. They are like mother and father. Mother says all right people look like they do.

[18]One of the little fathers saw me. He pointed at the window. I let go and slid down the wall in the dark. I curled up as they would not see. I heard their talks by the window and foots running. Upstairs there was a door hitting. I heard the little mother call upstairs. I heard heavy steps and I rushed to my bed place. I hit the chain in the wall and lay down on my front.

[19]I heard mother come down. Have you been at the window she said. I heard the anger. *Stay* away from the window. You have pulled the chain out again.

[20]She took the stick and hit me with it. I didn't cry. I can't do that. But the drip ran all over the bed. She saw it and twisted away and made a noise. Oh mygod mygod she said why have you *done* this to me? I heard the stick go bounce on the stone floor. She ran upstairs. I slept the day.

[21]XXXXX—This day it had water again. When mother was upstairs I heard the little one come slow down the steps. I hidded myself in the coal bin for mother would have anger if the little mother saw me.

[22]She had a little live thing with her. It walked on the arms and had pointy ears. She said things to it.

[23]It was all right except the live thing smelled me. It ran up the coal and looked down at me. The hairs stood up. In the throat it made an angry noise. I hissed but it jumped on me.

[24]I didn't want to hurt. I got fear because it bit me harder than the rat does. I hurt and the little mother screamed. I grabbed the live thing tight. It made sounds I never heard. I pushed it all together. It was lumpy and red on the black coal.

[25]I hid there when mother called. I was afraid of the stick. She left. I crept over the coal with the thing. I hid it under my pillow and rested on it. I put the chain in the wall again.

[26]X—This is another times. Father chained me tight. I hurt because he beat me. This time I hit the stick out of his hands and made noise. He went away and his face was white. He ran out of my bed place and locked the door.

[27]I am not so glad. All day it is cold in here. The chain comes slow out of the wall. And I have a bad anger with mother and father. I will show them. I will do what I did that once.

[28]I will screech and laugh loud. I will run on the walls. Last I will hang head down by all my legs and laugh and drip green all over until they are sorry they didn't be nice to me. If they try to beat me again I'll hurt them. I will.

Discussion Questions

1. What point of view does Matheson use in this story? Do you find it to be effective? Why or why not?

2. How old is the narrator? How do you know?

3. What is the significance of the X's?

4. If we assume the narrator has been confined to the cellar all these years, how has he/she/it been able to develop a command of language to be able to communicate thoughts so that we understand them?

5. What is meant by "the little mother"? Why would the narrator use that term?

6. How do you explain "my feet stick on the wood" of the stairs and "I will run on the walls"?

7. What is the "drip green" reference?" Does the narrator know colors?

8. What do you think the "live thing" is in paragraph 23?

9. Would you classify this story as natural or supernatural? Why?

THE BOY WHO DREW CATS
FROM A Japanese folktale retold by

LAFCADIO HEARN

Lafcadio Hearn (1850–1904) was educated in Ireland, England, and France before emigrating to the United States in 1869. Hearn is admired for his sensitive use of language in writing about the macabre. In 1890 he went to Japan to write a series of articles for an American publisher. He spent the rest of his life in Japan writing his best work. In 1895 he became a Japanese citizen, taking the name Yakumo Koizumi. Of the twelve books he wrote during this period, Glimpses of Unfamiliar Japan *(1894),* Kokoro *(1896),* Japanese Fairy Tales *(1902), and* Japan: An Attempt at Interpretation *(1904) are most memorable.*

[1] A long, long time ago, in a small country village in Japan, there lived a poor farmer and his wife, who were very good people. They had a number of children and they found it hard to feed them all. The elder son was strong enough when only fourteen years old to help his father; and the little girls learned to help their mother almost as soon as they could walk.

[2] But the youngest child, a little boy, did not seem to be fit for hard work. He was very clever—cleverer than all his brothers and sisters, but he was quite weak and small, and people said he could never grow very big. So his parents thought it would be better for him to become a priest than to become a farmer. They took him to the village temple one day, and asked the good old priest who lived there if he would have their little boy as their pupil, and teach him all that a priest ought to know.

[3] The priest spoke kindly to the boy and asked him several hard questions. The priest was astonished at the boy's keen understanding and the imaginative answers which he gave. Then the old priest agreed to take the boy as an acolyte, with the understanding that the boy would obey him in everything.

[4] The boy learned very quickly what the old priest taught him, and the boy tried very hard to obey, but he had one failing. When he should have been studying his lessons on his own, the boy drew cats instead. He could not help himself, for he was an artist at heart. He drew big cats and small cats, fat cats and thin cats, tall cats and short cats, sweet cats and ferocious cats. He drew cats on his lessons, he drew cats on the floor, he drew cats on the walls and, worst of all, he drew cats on the big, white, rice paper screens in the temple itself.

[5] The old priest was angry at first, and told the boy that drawing cats when he should be studying was wrong. But then the priest became sadder and sadder

because the boy continued to draw cats when he should have been working on his lessons. The old priest said to him, "My boy, you must go away from this temple at once. You will never make a good priest, but maybe you will become a great artist. Now let me give you a last piece of advice, and be sure you never forget it. *Avoid large places at night; keep to small!*"

⁶The boy did not know what the priest meant by saying, *"Avoid large places at night, keep to small."* Then the priest went into his room and closed the door. The boy did not understand what the priest meant, but he was afraid to knock on the door to ask for an explanation. He packed his few belongings into a bundle.

⁷He left the temple very sorrowfully and began to wonder what he should do. He thought, "If I go home, my parents will be angry and will punish me for being disobedient to the priest." All at once he remembered that in the city, twelve miles away, there was a very big temple. He had heard that there were several priests at that temple; he made up his mind to go to them and ask them to take him as their acolyte.

⁸No one had told the boy that the grand temple in the city had been closed. The boy took his time and enjoyed the walk to the city, looking at the fields and birds and butterflies. It was dark when the boy arrived at the city gates, and everyone was in bed asleep. There was no one to tell him that an evil goblin had taken over the temple and chased all the priests and acolytes away. There was no one to tell him that many soldiers had tried to rid the temple of the goblin rat, but had failed.

⁹Boldly, he walked up to the temple door and knocked on it. Because there was no answer, he knocked several more times. When there still was no answer, he turned the handle and pushed on the door. It swung wide open, and the boy walked in calling, "Is anyone here?" No one answered him, but he thought that a priest would come by eventually. The boy saw that there was a little room near the door, so he went in and sat down to wait.

¹⁰Now the goblin always left a light burning in the temple in order to lure strangers in at night. But the little boy had never heard this, so he just waited and inspected the room he was in. It was very dusty and dirty, and he thought that the priests really needed an acolyte to keep it neat and clean. While he was looking around, he opened the drawer in a table and found some rice paper, pens and ink. Soon he was filling the paper with drawings of cats. When he ran out of paper, he drew cats on the floor. And then he just couldn't help himself. He had to draw cats on the white, paper screens in the temple. He drew and drew until they were covered with cats.

¹¹When he had filled the screens with pictures of every kind of cat he could imagine, the little boy was very tired. He started to lie down next to one of the screens. But just then the words of the old priest ran through his mind. "Avoid large places, keep to small." The temple was enormous, so the boy

looked around for a small place. He found a tiny cupboard in the little room near the door and climbed into it with his parcel of clothes. He shut the cabinet door and was soon fast asleep on a shelf, with his bundle for a pillow. In the middle of the night, the boy heard a loud sound of fighting. It sounded like yowling and running and thumping and bumping and growling. He peeked out of his cubbyhole, but it was too dark. He couldn't see anything and he was so frightened that he just closed the cabinet door and stayed inside.

[12]In the morning the boy opened the cupboard and crawled out. He tiptoed out of the little room and peeked into the temple. What a surprise! The immense, evil goblin was dead, lying on the temple floor. Who could have killed him? Then the little boy looked at the temple screens. Each cat that he had drawn had a little circle of red around its mouth. Then the boy knew that his cats had attacked and killed the goblin. And he now understood what the priest meant when he said, "Avoid large places, keep to small."

[13]When the people of the city discovered that the goblin had been defeated, they proclaimed the boy a hero. The soldiers went into the temple to drag the dead goblin away.

[14]The priests of that temple would have been happy to take him as an acolyte, but the little boy had changed his mind. He did not become an acolyte or a priest. He became an artist instead, and his paintings of cats were famous in all of Japan. Perhaps the next time you go there, you will see one of his beautiful cats.

Vocabulary
[3]acolyte

Discussion Questions

1. How is the boy in the story different from those around him?

2. Why do you think the boy in the story isn't named? Is this important? Why or why not?

3. How does the priest treat the boy? Use examples from the story to support your answer.

4. How does the boy defeat the goblin?

5. What does the story imply about people who are different?

6. What qualities make the boy a hero?

7. In what ways does the story support the importance of being true to oneself?

FROM **BUDDHA: THE WORD**
A TRANSLATION OF THE
TEACHINGS OF THE BUDDHA
TRANSLATION BY PAUL CARUS (1852-1919)

*Though some people question whether Buddhism may properly be called a religion since it is not based upon a belief in and worship of a creator/ supreme being, it is generally listed as the fourth largest religion in the world with approximately 365 million followers—six percent of the world's population. Buddhism is exceeded in the number of followers only by Christianity, Islam and Hinduism. Buddhism was founded in Northern India in the sixth century BC by **Siddhartha Gautama**, who professed to have achieved enlightenment and assumed the title of Lord Buddha (the Awakened One). Buddhism subsequently all but died out in India but over many centuries spread throughout other areas of Asia including Sri Lanka, Tibet, and large portions of China and Japan.*

The excerpt from the Buddha's teachings presented here is from a translation by Paul Carus of works by disciples of the Buddha written down at various times during the two centuries following Gautama's death. Carus was the founder of Open Court Press, a publishing company that specialized in works of eastern philosophy and theology.

Since Buddhists strive to overcome a cycle of rebirths and to achieve nirvana, a state of perfect enlightenment, they follow a set of firm guiding principles as the path to spiritual perfection. Buddhists believe their present existence was shaped by—and their future existence will be shaped by—the karma ("action" or "making") they create based upon how closely they adhere to the principles set forth in "The Four Noble Truths," "The Eightfold Path" and "The Middle Way" as outlined below.

THE FOUR NOBLE TRUTHS

[1]THUS has it been said by the Buddha, the Enlightened One: It is through not understanding, not realizing four things, that I, Disciples, as well as you, had to wander so long through this round of rebirths. And what are these four things? They are the Noble Truth of Suffering, the Noble Truth of the Origin of Suffering, the Noble Truth of the Extinction of Suffering, the Noble Truth of the Path that Leads to the Extinction of Suffering.

[2]As long as the absolutely true knowledge and insight as regards these

Four Noble Truths was not quite clear in me, so long was I not sure whether I had won that supreme Enlightenment which is unsurpassed in all the world with its heavenly beings, evil spirits and gods, amongst all the hosts of ascetics and priests, heavenly beings and men. But as soon as the absolutely true knowledge and insight as regards these Four Noble Truths had become perfectly clear in me, there arose in me the assurance that I had won that supreme Enlightenment unsurpassed.

³And I discovered that profound truth, so difficult to perceive, difficult to understand, tranquilizing and sublime, which is not to be gained by mere reasoning, and is visible only to the wise. The world, however, is given to pleasure, delighted with pleasure, enchanted with pleasure. Verily, such beings will hardly understand the law of conditionality, the Dependent Origination of every thing; incomprehensible to them will also be the end of all formations, the forsaking of every substratum of rebirth, the fading away of craving; detachment, extinction, Nirvana.

⁴Yet there are beings whose eyes are only a little covered with dust: they will understand the truth.

FIRST TRUTH: THE NOBLE TRUTH OF SUFFERING

⁵WHAT, now, is the Noble Truth of Suffering?

⁶Birth is suffering; Decay is suffering; Death is suffering; Sorrow, Lamentation, Pain, Grief, and Despair are suffering; not to get what one desires is suffering; in short: the Five Groups of Existence are suffering.

⁷What, now, is Birth? The birth of beings belonging to this or that order of beings, their being born, their conception and springing into existence, the manifestation of the groups of existence, the arising of sense activity—this is called Birth.

⁸And what is Decay? The decay of beings belonging to this or that order of beings; their getting aged, frail, grey, and wrinkled; the failing of their vital force, the wearing out of the senses—-this is called Decay.

⁹And what is Death? The parting and vanishing of beings out of this or that order of beings, their destruction, disappearance, the completion of their life-period, dissolution of the groups of existence, the discarding of the body—this is called Death.

¹⁰And what is Sorrow? The sadness arising through this or that loss or misfortune which one encounters, the worrying of oneself, the state of being alarmed, inward sadness, inward woe—this is called Sorrow.

¹¹And what is Lamentation? Whatsoever, through this or that loss or misfortune which befalls one, is wail and sorrow, mourning and crying, grieving and weeping and the state of woe—this is called Lamentation.

[12]And what is Pain? The bodily discomfort and unpleasantness, the sore, aching and unpleasant feeling produced by bodily contact—this is called Pain.

[13]And what is Grief? The mental discomfort and unpleasantness, the painful and disagreeable feeling produced by mental contact—this is called Grief.

[14]And what is Despair? Suffering and hopelessness arising through this or that loss or misfortune which one encounters, distress and desperation—this is called Despair.

[15]And what is the "suffering of not getting what one desires?" To beings subject to birth there comes the desire: "O that we were not subject to birth! O that no new birth was before us!"

[16]Subject to decay, disease, death, sorrow, lamentation, pain, grief, and despair, the desire comes to them: "O that we were not subject to these things! O that these things were not before us!" But this cannot be got by mere desiring; and not to get what one desires, is suffering.

THE THREE CHARACTERISTICS OF EXISTENCE

[17]All formations are "transient"; all formations are "subject to suffering"; all things are "without a Self-entity (Ego)." Corporeality is transient, feeling is transient, perception is transient, mental formations are transient, consciousness is transient.

[18]And that which is transient is subject to suffering; and of that which is transient, and subject to suffering and change, one cannot rightly say: "This belongs to me; this am I; this is my Ego."

[19]Therefore, whatever there be of corporeality, of feeling, perception, mental formations, or consciousness, whether one's own or external, whether gross or subtle, lofty or low, far or near, one should understand, according to reality and true wisdom: "This does not belong to me; this am I not; this is not my Ego."

[20]Suppose someone who is not blind were to behold the many bubbles on the Ganges as they are driving along; and should watch them and carefully examine them. After he carefully examines them, they will appear to him empty, unreal, and unsubstantial. In exactly the same way does the monk behold all the corporeal phenomena, feelings, perceptions, mental formations, and states of consciousness—whether they be of the past, the present or the future, far, or near.

[21]And he watches them and examines them carefully; and, after carefully examining them, they appear to him empty, void, and without an Ego. Whoso delights in corporeality, or feeling, or perception, or mental formations, or consciousness, he delights in suffering; and whoso delights in suffering will not be freed from suffering. Thus I say

[22]How can you find delight and mirth,
Where there is burning without end?
In deepest darkness you are wrapped!
Why do you not seek for the light?

[23]Look at this puppet here, well rigged,
A heap of many sores, piled up,
Diseased, and full of greediness,
Unstable, and impermanent!

[24]Devoured by old age is this frame,
A prey of sickness, weak and frail;
To pieces breaks this putrid body,
All life must truly end in death.

THE THREE WARNINGS

[25]Did you never see in the world a man, or a woman, eighty, ninety, or a hundred years old, frail, crooked as a gable roof, bent down, resting on crutches, with tottering steps, infirm, youth long since fled, with broken teeth, grey and scanty hair, or bald-headed, wrinkled, with blotched limbs? And did the thought never come to you that also you are subject to decay, that also you cannot escape it?

[26]Did you never see in the world a man, or a woman, who being sick, afflicted, and grievously ill, and wallowing in his own filth, was lifted up by some people and put to bed by others? And did the thought never come to you that also you are subject to disease, that also you cannot escape it?

[27]Did you never see in the world the corpse of a man, or a woman, one, or two, or three days after death, swollen up, blue-black in color, and full of corruption? And did the thought never come to you that also you are subject to death, that also you cannot escape it?

SECOND TRUTH:
THE NOBLE TRUTH OF THE ORIGIN OF SUFFERING

[28]WHAT, now, is the Noble Truth of the Origin of Suffering? It is that craving which gives rise to fresh rebirth, and, bound up with pleasure and lust, now here, now there, finds ever fresh delight.

HEAPING UP OF PRESENT SUFFERING

[29]Verily, due to sensuous craving, conditioned through, impelled by, entirely moved by sensuous craving, kings fight with kings, princes with princes, priests with priests, citizens with citizens; the mother quarrels with the son, the son with the mother, the father with the son, the son with the father; brother quarrels with brother, brother with sister, sister with brother, friend with friend. Thus, given to dissension, quarreling and fighting, they fall upon one another with fists, sticks, or weapons.

[30]And thereby they suffer deadly pain or death.

[31]And further, due to sensuous craving, conditioned through, impelled by, entirely moved by sensuous craving, people break into houses, rob, plunder, pillage whole houses, commit highway robbery, seduce the wives of others. Then, the rulers have such people caught and inflict on them various forms of punishment. And thereby they incur deadly pain or death. Now, this is the misery of sensuous craving, the heaping up of suffering in this present life, due to sensuous craving, conditioned through, caused by, entirely dependent on sensuous craving.

HEAPING UP OF FUTURE SUFFERING

[32]And further, people take the evil way in deeds, words and thoughts; and by taking the evil way in deeds, words, and thoughts, at the dissolution of the body after death, they fall into a downward state of existence, a state of suffering, into perdition, and the abyss of hell. But, this is the misery of sensuous craving, the heaping up of suffering in the future life, due to sensuous craving, conditioned through, caused by and entirely dependent on sensuous craving.

[33]Not in the air, nor ocean-midst,
Nor hidden in the mountain clefts,
Nowhere is found a place on earth,
Where man is freed from evil deeds.

THIRD TRUTH:
THE NOBLE TRUTH OF THE EXTINCTION OF SUFFERING

[34]WHAT, now, is the Noble Truth of the Extinction of Suffering? It is the complete fading away and extinction of this craving, its forsaking and giving up, the liberation and detachment from it.

[35]But where may this craving vanish, where may it be extinguished? Wherever in the world there are delightful and pleasurable things, there this craving may vanish, there it may be extinguished.

[36]Be it in the past, present, or future, whosoever of the monks or priests regards the delightful and pleasurable things in the world as "impermanent," "miserable," and "without Ego," as a disease and cancer; it is he who overcomes the craving.

[37]And released from Sensual Craving, released from the Craving for Existence, he does not return, does not enter again into existence.

FOURTH TRUTH: THE NOBLE TRUTH OF THE PATH THAT LEADS TO THE EXTINCTION OF SUFFERING

THE TWO EXTREMES AND THE MIDDLE PATH

[38]To give oneself up to indulgence in sensual pleasure, the base, common, vulgar, unholy, unprofitable; and also to give oneself up to self-mortification, the painful, unholy, unprofitable: both these two extremes the Perfect One has avoided, and found out the Middle Path, which makes one both to see and to know, which leads to peace, to discernment, to enlightenment, to Nirvana.

SAMSARA (THE WHEEL OF EXISTENCE)

[39]Inconceivable is the beginning of this Samsara;[1] not to be discovered is any first beginning of beings, who, obstructed by ignorance, and ensnared by craving, are hurrying and hastening through this round of rebirths.

[40]Which do you think is the more: the flood of tears, which, weeping and wailing, you have shed upon this long way—hurrying and hastening through this round of rebirths, united with the undesired, separated from the desired this, or the waters of the four oceans?

[41]Long have you suffered the death of father and mother, of sons, daughters, brothers, and sisters. And whilst you were thus suffering, you have, verily, shed more tears upon this long way than there is water in the four oceans.

[42]And thus have you long time undergone suffering, torment, and misfortune, and filled the graveyards full; verily, long enough to be dissatisfied with all the forms of existence, long enough to turn away, and free yourselves from them all.

---

[1]Samsara—the Wheel of Existence; literally, the "Perpetual Wandering"—is the name designating the sea of life ever restlessly heaving up and down, the symbol of this continuous process of ever again and again being born, growing old, suffering, and dying. More precisely put: Samsara is the unbroken chain of the fivefold Khandha—combinations, which, constantly changing from moment to moment, follow continuously one upon the other through inconceivable periods of time. Of this Samsara, a single lifetime constitutes only a vanishingly tiny fraction; hence, to be able to comprehend the First Noble Truth, one must let one's gaze rest upon the Samsara, upon this frightful chain of rebirths, and not merely upon one single lifetime, which, of course, may be sometimes not very painful. [Note by Carus]

KARMA (THE INHERITANCE OF DEEDS)

[43]For, owners of their deeds are the beings, heirs of their deeds; their deeds are the womb from which they sprang; with their deeds they are bound up; their deeds are their refuge.

[44]Whatever deeds they do—good or evil—of such they will be the heirs.

[45]Verily, because beings, obstructed by delusion and ensnared by craving, now here, now there, seek ever-fresh delight, therefore such action comes to ever-fresh rebirth. However, through the fading away of delusion, through the arising of wisdom, through the extinction of craving, no future rebirth takes place again.

[46]And the action that is done out of greed, anger and delusion, the action that springs from them, has its source and origin there; this action ripens wherever one is reborn; and wherever this action ripens, there one experiences the fruits of this action, be it in this life, or the next life, or in some future life.

[47]For the actions which are not done out of greed, anger and delusion, which have not sprung from them, which have not their source and origin there—such actions are rooted out, like a palm-tree torn out of the soil, destroyed, and not liable to spring up again.

[48]In this respect one may rightly say of me that I teach annihilation, that I propound my doctrine for the purpose of annihilation, and that I herein train my disciples; for, certainly, I do teach annihilation—the annihilation, namely, of greed, anger and delusion, as well as of the manifold evil and unwholesome things.

[49]There will come a time when the mighty ocean will dry up, vanish, and be no more. There will come a time when the mighty earth will be devoured by fire, perish, and be no more. Yet, there will be no end to the suffering of beings, who, obstructed by ignorance and ensnared by craving, are hurrying and hastening through this round of rebirths.

NIRVANA (PERFECT ENLIGHTENMENT)

[50]This, truly, is the Peace, this is the Highest, namely the end of all formations, the forsaking of every substratum of rebirth, the fading away of craving: detachment, extinction—Nirvana.

[51]Enraptured with lust, enraged with anger, blinded by delusion, overwhelmed, with mind ensnared, man aims at his own ruin, at others' ruin, at the ruin of both parties, and he experiences mental pain and grief. But, if lust, anger, and delusion are given up, man aims neither at his own ruin, nor at others' ruin, nor at the ruin of both parties, and he experiences no mental pain and grief. Thus is Nirvana immediate, visible in this life, inviting, attractive, and comprehensible to the wise.

[52]The extinction of greed, the extinction of anger, the extinction of delusion: this, indeed, is called Nirvana.

THE EIGHTFOLD PATH

[53]It is the Noble Eightfold Path, the way that leads to the extinction of suffering, namely:
1. Right Understanding,
2. Right Mindedness, which together are Wisdom.
3. Right Speech,
4. Right Action,
5. Right Living, which together are Morality.
6. Right Effort,
7. Right Attentiveness,
8. Right Concentration, which together are Concentration.

[54]This is the Middle Path which the Perfect One has found out, which makes one both to see and to know, which leads to peace, to discernment, to enlightenment, to Nirvana.

[55]Free from pain and torture, free from groaning and suffering is this path; it is the perfect path.

[56]Truly, like this path there is no other path to the purity of insight. If you follow this path, you will put an end to suffering.

[57]But each one has to struggle for himself; the Perfect Ones have only pointed out the way.

[58]Give ear, then, for the Immortal is found. I reveal, I set forth the Truth. As I reveal it to you, so act! And that supreme goal of the holy life, for the sake of which sons of good families rightly go forth from home to the homeless state: this you will, in no long time, in this very life, make known to yourself, realize, and make your own.

FIRST STEP: RIGHT UNDERSTANDING

[59]WHAT, now, is Right Understanding? It is understanding the Four Noble Truths. To understand suffering; to understand the origin of suffering; to understand the extinction of suffering; to understand the path that leads to the extinction of suffering: This is called Right Understanding

[60]Or, when the loyal disciple understands what is the root of unwholesome karma, then he has Right Understanding.

[61]What, now, is unwholesome karma?

[62]Unwholesome karma is every volitional act of body, speech, or mind rooted in greed, hatred, or delusion, and produces evil and painful results in this or any future form of existence.

[63]In Bodily Action it is destruction of living beings; stealing; and unlawful sexual intercourse. In Verbal Action it is lying; tale-bearing; harsh language; and frivolous talk. In Mental Action it is covetousness; ill-will; and wrong views.

[64]And what is the root of unwholesome karma? Greed is a root of unwholesome karma; Anger is a root of unwholesome karma; Delusion is a root of unwholesome karma.

[65]The state of greed, as well as that of anger, is always accompanied by delusion; and delusion, ignorance, is the primary root of all evil.

[66]Therefore, I say, these demeritorious actions are of three kinds: either due to greed, or due to anger, or due to delusion.

[67]What, now, is wholesome karma?

[68]In Bodily Action it is to abstain from killing; to abstain from stealing; and to abstain from unlawful sexual intercourse.

[69]In Verbal Action it is to abstain from lying; to abstain from tale-bearing; to abstain from harsh language; and to abstain from frivolous talk.

[70]In Mental Action it is absence of covetousness; absence of ill-will; and right understanding.

[71]And what is the root of wholesome karma? Absence of greed (unselfishness) is a root of wholesome karma; absence of anger (benevolence) is a root of wholesome karma; absence of delusion (wisdom) is a root of wholesome karma.

[72]Or, when one understands that corporeality, feeling, perception, mental formation, and consciousness, are transient (subject to suffering and without an Ego), also in that case one possesses Right Understanding.

SECOND STEP: RIGHT MINDEDNESS

[73]WHAT, now, is Right Mindedness? It is thoughts free from lust; thoughts free from ill-will; thoughts free from cruelty. This is called right mindedness.

[74]Now, Right Mindedness, let me tell you, is of two kinds: 1) Thoughts free from lust, from ill-will, and from cruelty—this is called "Worldly Right Mindedness," which yields worldly fruits and brings good results; 2) But, whatsoever there is of thinking, considering, reasoning, thought, ratiocination, application—the mind being holy, being turned away from the world, and conjoined with the path, the holy path being pursued—these "Verbal Operations" of the mind are called "Unworldly Right Mindedness," which is not of the world, but is above and apart from the worldly and conjoined with the paths.

[75]Now, in understanding wrong-mindedness as wrong, and right-mindedness as right, one practices Right Understanding (1st step); and in making efforts to overcome evil-mindedness, and to arouse right-mindedness, one practices Right Effort (6th step); and in overcoming evil-mindedness with attentive mind, and dwelling with attentive mind in possession of right-mindedness, one practices Right Attentiveness (7th step).

THIRD STEP: RIGHT SPEECH

[76]WHAT, now, is Right Speech? It is abstaining from lying; abstaining from tale-bearing; abstaining from harsh language; abstaining from vain talk.

[77]There, someone avoids lying and abstains from it. He speaks the truth, is devoted to the truth, reliable, worthy of confidence, is not a deceiver of people. Being at a meeting, or amongst people, or in the midst of his relatives, or in a society, or in the royal court, and called upon and asked as witness to tell what he knows, he answers, if he knows nothing: "I know nothing"; and if he knows, he answers: "I know"; if he has seen nothing, he answers: "I have seen nothing,"
and if he has seen, he answers: "I have seen." Thus, he never knowingly speaks a lie, neither for the sake of his own advantage, nor for the sake of another person's advantage, nor for the sake of any advantage whatsoever.

[78]He avoids tale-bearing and abstains from it. What he has heard here, he does not repeat there, so as to cause dissension there; and what he heard there, he does not repeat here, so as to cause dissension here. Thus he unites those that are divided; and those that are united, he encourages. Concord gladdens him; he delights and rejoices in concord, and it is concord that he spreads by his words.

[79]He avoids harsh language and abstains from it. He speaks such words as are gentle, soothing to the ear, loving, going to the heart, courteous and dear, and agreeable to most.

[80]I said to the monks: "Even should robbers and murderers saw through your limbs and joints, whoso gave way to anger thereat, would not be following my advice. For thus ought
you to train yourselves: Undisturbed shall our mind remain, no evil words shall escape our lips; friendly and full of sympathy shall we remain, with heart full of love, and free from any hidden malice; and that person shall we penetrate with loving thoughts, wide, deep, boundless, freed from anger and hatred."

[81]He avoids vain talk, and abstains from it. He speaks at the right time, in accordance with facts, speaks what is useful, speaks about the law and the discipline; his speech is like a treasure, at the right moment accompanied by arguments, moderate and full of sense.

[82]This is called right speech.

FOURTH STEP: RIGHT ACTION

[83]WHAT, now, is Right Action? It is abstaining from killing; abstaining from stealing; abstaining from unlawful sexual intercourse.

[84]There, someone avoids the killing of living beings and abstains from it. Without stick or sword, conscientious, full of sympathy, he is anxious for the welfare of all living beings.

[85]He avoids stealing and abstains from it; what another person possesses

of goods and chattels in the village or in the wood, that he does not take away with thievish intent.

⁸⁶He avoids unlawful sexual intercourse and abstains from it. He has no intercourse with such persons as are still under the protection of father, mother, brother, sister or relatives, nor with married women, nor female convicts, nor, lastly, with betrothed girls.

⁸⁷This is called Right Action.

FIFTH STEP: RIGHT LIVING

⁸⁸WHAT, now, is Right Living? When the noble disciple, avoiding a wrong way of living, gets his livelihood by a right way of living, this is called Right Living.

⁸⁹Now, right living, let me tell you, is of two kinds: 1) When the loyal disciple, avoiding wrong living, gets his livelihood by a right way of living—this is called the "Worldly Right Living," which yields worldly fruits and brings good results; 2) but the abhorrence of wrong living, the abstaining, withholding, refraining therefrom—the mind being holy, being turned away from the world, and conjoined with the path, the holy path being pursued—this is called "Unworldly Right Living," which is not of the world and is conjoined with the paths.

SIXTH STEP: RIGHT EFFORT

⁹⁰WHAT, now, is Right Effort? There are Four Great Efforts: the effort to avoid, the effort to overcome, the effort to develop, and the effort to maintain.

⁹¹What, now, is the effort to avoid? There, the disciple incites his mind to avoid the arising of evil, demeritorious things that have not yet arisen; and he strives, puts forth his energy, strains his mind and struggles.

⁹²Thus, when he perceives a form with the eye, a sound with the ear, an odor with the nose, a taste with the tongue, a contact with the body, or an object with the mind, he adheres neither to the whole, nor to its parts. And he strives to ward off that through which evil and demeritorious things, greed and sorrow, would arise if he remained with unguarded senses; and he watches over his senses, restrains his senses.

⁹³Possessed of this noble "Control over the Senses," he experiences inwardly a feeling of joy, into which no evil thing can enter. This is called the effort to avoid.

⁹⁴What, now, is the effort to overcome? There, the disciple incites his mind to overcome the evil, demeritorious things that have already arisen; and he strives, puts forth his energy, strains his mind and struggles.

⁹⁵He does not retain any thought of sensual lust, ill-will, or grief, or any other evil and demeritorious states that may have arisen; he abandons them, dispels them, destroys them, causes them to disappear. If, whilst regarding a cer-

tain object, there arise in the disciple, on account of it, evil and demeritorious thoughts connected with greed, anger and delusion, then the disciple should, by means of this object, gain another and wholesome object. Or, he should reflect on the misery of these thoughts: "Unwholesome, truly, are these thoughts! Blameable are these thoughts! Of painful result are these thoughts!" Or, he should pay no attention to these thoughts. Or, he should consider the compound nature of these thoughts. Or, with teeth clenched and tongue pressed against the gums, he should, with his mind, restrain, suppress and root out these thoughts; and in doing so, these evil and demeritorious thoughts of greed, anger and delusion will dissolve and disappear; and the mind will inwardly become settled and calm, composed and concentrated. This is called the effort to overcome.

[96]What, now, is the effort to develop? There the disciple incites his will to arouse meritorious conditions that have not yet arisen; and he strives, puts forth his energy, strains his mind and struggles. Thus he develops the "Elements of Enlightenment," bent on solitude, on detachment, on extinction, and ending in deliverance, namely: Attentiveness, Investigation of the Law, Energy, Rapture, Tranquility, Concentration, and Equanimity. This is called the effort to develop.

[97]What, now, is the effort to maintain? There, the disciple incites his will to maintain the meritorious conditions that have already arisen, and not to let them disappear, but to bring them to growth, to maturity and to the full perfection of development; and he strives, puts forth his energy, strains his mind and struggles

SEVENTH STEP: RIGHT ATTENTIVENESS

[98]WHAT, now, is Right Attentiveness? The only way that leads to the attainment of purity, to the overcoming of sorrow and lamentation, to the end of pain and grief, to the entering upon the right path and the realization of Nirvana, is the "Four Fundamentals of Attentiveness."

[99]And which are these four? In them, the disciple dwells in contemplation of the body, in contemplation of feeling, in contemplation of the mind, in contemplation of the mind-objects, ardent, clearly conscious and attentive, after putting away worldly greed and grief.

[100]But, how does the disciple dwell in contemplation of the body? There, the disciple retires to the forest, to the foot of a tree, or to a solitary place, sits himself down, with legs crossed, body erect, and with attentiveness fixed before him.

[101]With attentive mind he breathes in, with attentive mind he breathes out. When making a long inhalation, he knows: "I make a long inhalation" and when making a short inhalation, he knows: "I make a short inhalation." Thus he trains himself, clearly perceiving the entire breath-body, calming this bodily

function. He dwells in contemplation of the body, either with regard to his own person or to other persons or to both. He beholds how the body arises and how it passes away. Thus does the disciple dwell in contemplation of the body.

[102]But how does the disciple dwell in contemplation of the feelings? In experiencing feelings, the disciple knows: "I have an indifferent agreeable feeling," or "I have a disagreeable feeling," or "I have an indifferent feeling." Thus he dwells in contemplation of the feelings, either with regard to his own person or to other persons or to both. He beholds the arising and passing away of the feelings. This clear consciousness is present in him, because of his knowledge and mindfulness; and he lives independent, unattached to anything in the world. Thus does the disciple dwell in contemplation of the feelings.

[103]But how does the disciple dwell in contemplation of the mind? The disciple knows the greedy mind as greedy, and the not-greedy mind as not greedy; knows the angry mind as angry, and the not-angry mind as not angry; knows the deluded mind as deluded, and the undeluded mind as undeluded. He knows the cramped mind as cramped, and the scattered mind as scattered; knows the developed mind as developed, and the undeveloped mind as undeveloped; knows the surpassable mind as surpassable, and the unsurpassable mind as unsurpassable; knows the concentrated mind as concentrated, and the unconcentrated mind as unconcentrated; knows the freed mind as freed, and the unfreed mind as unfreed.

[104]But how does the disciple dwell in contemplation of the mind-objects? First, the disciple dwells in contemplation of the phenomenon of the "Five Hindrances." He knows when there is lust, anger, torpor and drowsiness, restlessness and mental worry, and when there are doubts in him. He knows how they come to arise and knows how, once arisen, they are overcome; he also knows how, once overcome, to prevent their rise again in the future.

EIGHTH STEP: RIGHT CONCENTRATION

[105]WHAT, now, is Right Concentration? Fixing the mind to a single object ("Singleness of mind"): this is concentration.

[106]The four Fundamentals of Attentiveness (seventh step): these are the objects of concentration.

[107]The four Great Efforts (sixth step): these are the requisites for concentration.

[108]The practicing, developing and cultivating of these things: this is the "Development" of concentration.

Vocabulary

[2]ascetics
[3]sublime
[3]incomprehensible
[3]substratum
[6]lamentation
[7]manifestation
[9]dissolution
[17]transient
[17]corporeality

[20]Ganges
[20]phenomena
[22]mirth
[24]putrid
[26]afflicted
[26]wallowing
[27]corruption
[29]impelled
[31]incur

[32]dissolution
[32]perdition
[32]abyss
[33]clefts
[38]indulgence
[38]base
[38]mortification
[38]discernment
[48]annihilation

[48]propound
[51]enraptured
[62]volitional
[63]frivilous
[66]demeritorious
[74]ratiocination
[96]equanimity
[99]ardent

Discussion Questions

1. At what point in paragraph 1 does Buddha begin speaking to his disciples? What is the first word of his instructions to his followers?

2. What does Buddha mean by "round of rebirths" in paragraph 1?

3. Look at the introductory material at the top of the first page of this selection. When Buddha mentions "heavenly beings, evil spirits and gods," in paragraph 2, what religion is he probably referring to?

4. How would you characterize Buddha's view of his own place in the world based upon what he says in paragraphs 2 and 3?

5. Who do you suppose are the "beings whose eyes are only a little covered with dust" mentioned in paragraph 4?

6. How does Buddha define suffering in paragraph 16?

7. Explain the purpose of the "bubbles on the Ganges" analogy used in paragraph 20.

8. What does Buddha say is responsible for the origin of suffering in paragraphs 28 and 29?

9. How, then does one bring about the extinction of suffering?

10. What is the Middle Path and where does it lead? What does one find upon arriving at this destination?

11. Explain each of the following in your own words: 1) Samsara; 2) Karma; 3) Nirvana. How does each fit into the overall philosophy of Buddhism?

12. What is "unwholesome karma," and where does it come from? (See paragraphs 61-66.)

13. How do you think step seven is accomplished by Buddha's followers? Does this have any place in our modern world?

14. Look at Chapter 12 of the Bhagavad Gita beginning on page 144 of this text, Leviticus beginning on page 377, Sura 2 of the Holy Qur'an beginning on page 451, and the Sermon on the Mount on page 489. Compare these works to the Eightfold Path and explain what they all have in common.

THE BUTTERFLY

JAMES HANLEY

*The author of over 50 books, **James Hanley** (1901-1985) was born in Ireland and brought up in Liverpool but considered himself Welsh, having lived in North Wales for years. He was a boy seaman and fought in World War 1, experiences that he used in his short stories and novels. Among his works are* Drift *(1930),* Boy *(1931),* The Secret Journey *(1936),* Sailor's Song *(1943),* Levine *(1956),* Say Nothing *(1962), and* A Kingdom *(1978).*

[1]Brother Timothy's cassock made a peculiar swishing noise as he strode up and down the passage. His face was red, his mouth twitched, whilst his fingers pulled nervously at the buttons upon the cassock. There was something wild, even a little aimless, about this pacing up and down, a kind of clue as to the chaos of his thoughts. One could see at a glance that he was angry. From time to time he muttered to himself, and when he did this he always cast a quick and furtive glance at a stout wooden door that opened onto the middle of the dark and musty corridor. His thoughts had neither shape nor order. He was a bewildered man. He simply could not understand the boy. Every time the name Cassidy came into his mind the blood mounted to his forehead. It was the boy's silence that was the enraging thing, his infernal silence; and what was even worse was the something serene that this silence betokened. Curse him for his silence, his serenity, and his content. The boy must have no conscience at all.

[2]Suddenly he stopped and stared at the stout door. He knew it would be getting dark in there. He listened. Not a sound. Perhaps the fellow had fallen asleep, but perhaps he had not. He might indeed be standing behind it now, listening, yes, even thinking that he would be let out. Ambitious and fancy thought indeed. Brother Timothy laughed then. What a hope. That boy would stay there until he explained himself. It wasn't the flouting of authority, though that itself manifested a danger looming black upon the horizon of all order and obedience. No; it was this silence, this calm indifference. It wasn't innocence; no, not that. Such a thing was already confounded by his action. Silence was like ignorance, a stout wall, but this boy Cassidy, his was a steel wall, impenetrable.

[3]How to break it down then? Yes, one must try to think.

[4]He continued his wild pacing up and down the passage for about five minutes; then he stopped again at the door. He knocked loudly upon it and called out, "Cassidy! You there, Cassidy?" There was no answer. A muttered

exclamation came from Brother Timothy. Confound it! He really believed the boy was asleep. What right had he to be asleep? He drew a key from his pocket, opened the door and went inside. The door shut silently behind him. The boy was sitting on the bed. He looked up at the Brother, but something in the other's glance made him hurriedly drop his eyes again.

⁵"Well, Cassidy," said Brother Timothy, "have you come to your senses yet?" The veins in his neck stood out. The silence galled him. "Answer me, I tell you," he shouted. "Answer me, you insolent, you villainous, you..." But words failed him. He stood looking down at the culprit. After a while he drew a chair and sat down opposite the boy.

⁶"I repeat," he began, "I repeat that you have not yet offered any explanation of your outrageous conduct. Listen to me. Look at me, you young.... Yesterday you missed the mass, you and this other wretch Byrne; you went off together, but where? And why did you do it? Did I say you could go? Answer me, will you? Did you ask permission, even supposing that I should ever think of granting your request? Why did you play truant? Why were you so unlike the others, you and this other wretch? I repeat that you will be kept here until you offer an explanation. And now, listen further: This silence, d'you hear me, this silence I will not stand. You've the devil in you; it's he who has trapped your tongue. But I'll break you. Do you hear me? I ask you for the last time, why did you miss the mass?"

⁷Cassidy, a boy of fifteen, looked up at the Brother. His lips moved, but he made no sound. When the Brother struck him across the face he said slowly, "Brother Timothy, I told you yesterday."

⁸"You are determined then. Very well. You will remain here, you will have your meals sent up, but out of this room you won't go until you open that mouth of yours." Suddenly he gripped the boy by the shoulders and shook him. "You have no right to do it. You have no right. And when you have explained to me you will go to confession, and you will there make an act of contrition. Do you understand me? You have no right to be silent." Then he got up and strode out of the room.

⁹Cassidy smiled. The door banged, the key turned. He undressed and got into bed. In the morning when he woke the sun was streaming through the window. It filled him with an intense longing for the open air, to be free of this room, free of the sound of those well-known footsteps, from the sight of that face, which mirrored rage and defeat. He reflected that he meant no harm. He had simply gone into the lanes with Byrne, they had become absorbed in the strange life that abounded in the hedges and ditches, they had not heard the bell. And here he was stuck in this musty room for two days because he would not explain. "But I have explained," he kept saying to himself. "I have explained."

¹⁰From his pocket he took a cardboard box pinned with airholes. He re-

moved the lid. Slowly a green caterpillar crept out and along his finger. Cassidy watched its slow graceful movements down his hand. He lowered his head and stared hard at it. What a lovely green it was. And one day it would turn into a beautiful butterfly. How marvelous. He stroked it gently with his finger. The sun came out, it poured through the window, filled the room, the long green caterpillar was bathed in the light.

[11]"I think I'll call you Xavier," he said to the insect, and smiled. For two whole days he had had it in the cardboard box. It made him happy knowing it was there, in the room with him. It made him forget Brother Timothy, forget many things. He knew he would be happy whilst he had the green caterpillar. If it could speak he would explain to it why he was kept in the stuffy room by Brother Timothy. Perhaps this long smooth green thing did know, perhaps it looked at him.

[12]"Oh!" he exclaimed, and the box dropped to the floor. He had heard footsteps in the corridor. A moment later the door was opened and Brother Timothy stepped into the room.

[13]"Well, Cassidy," he said. "Have you come to your senses?" But the boy appeared not to hear him. He was standing with his back to the brother, the sunlight on his face, and he was gently laying the caterpillar on a bit of moss in the cardboard box. He gave the green insect a final stroke and put the lid on.

[14]"Cassidy!" roared the man behind him, and the boy turned round. "What have you there?"

[15]"Nothing—I mean—Brother Timothy, it's a—"

[16]"What! And this is how you spend your time. Aren't you sorry for your sin?"

[17]"Sin? Brother Timothy, I—I mean he's only a little caterpillar."

[18]If silence had been poisonous, this was worse. He pulled the boy's ear.

[19]"Is this how you think upon your conscience? Is this how you think out your explanation? Outrageous, boy! Give me that at once."

[20]"But it's only a caterpillar, Brother Timothy, a little green one. Soon it'll be a butterfly. It's so green and soft, and it crawls up my finger as though it knew me. Please, Brother—while I was sitting here all by myself it made me happy, I liked having it, I—"

[21]"How dare you!" Brother Timothy grabbed the box and turned out the caterpillar. It fell to the floor and slowly began to crawl.

[22]"You have no right to miss the mass and you have no right to be happy or anything else. D'you hear me?" and with a quick movement of his broad foot he trod on the insect and crushed out its life. Cassidy looked up at the Brother. Then he burst into tears.

Vocabulary

[1]cassock	[2]flouting	[2]confounded	[6]wretch
[1]furtive	[2]manifested	[5]galled	[8]contrition
[1]infernal	[2]indifference	[5]culprit	[11]Xavier
[1]betokened			

Discussion Questions

1. Describe Brother Timothy in your own words. Be sure to look at Brother Timothy throughout the entire story before responding.

2. Describe Cassidy's temperament.

3. What is the significance of Cassidy's naming the caterpillar Xavier? (Hint: Research saints of the Roman Catholic Church.)

4. Xavier is Cassidy's pet caterpillar, but it is also a symbol. Look up the meaning of symbolism and then discuss what Xavier symbolizes.

5. "The Butterfly" does not have any butterflies in it. Explain the title of the story.

6. The final paragraph in the story suggests a change in Cassidy. Explain what you think this change will be.

THE CAPTURE OF ATLANTA
FROM *THE MEMOIRS OF GENERAL WILLIAM T. SHERMAN*

GENERAL WILLIAM T. SHERMAN

William Tecumseh Sherman (1820-1891) is considered the first modern general for his philosophy that "War is cruelty and you cannot refine it." During the Civil War Sherman and his 62,000 men made their famous march to the sea from Atlanta through Georgia and then the Carolinas, forcing the surrender of the last major Confederate forces. When asked to run for president in 1884, he answered with "I will not accept if nominated and will not serve if elected," an oft-quoted refusal since then.

[1]The success at Atlanta made the election of Mr. Lincoln certain. Among the many letters of congratulation received, those of Mr. Lincoln and General Grant seem most important:

Executive Mansion
Washington, D. C., September 3, 1864

[2]The national thanks are rendered by the President to Major General W.T. Sherman and the gallant officers and soldiers of his command before Atlanta for the distinguished ability and perseverance displayed in the campaign in Georgia, which under Divine favor, has resulted in the capture of Atlanta. The marches, battles, sieges, and other military operations that have signaled the campaign, must render it famous in the annals of war, and have entitled those who have participated therein to the applause and thanks of the nation.

ABRAHAM LINCOLN,
President of the United States

Major-General SHERMAN:
[3]I have just received your dispatch announcing the capture of Atlanta. In honor of your great victory, I have ordered a salute to be fired with *shotted* guns from every battery bearing upon the enemy. The salute will be fired within an hour amid great rejoicing.

U.S. GRANT, *Lieutenant General.*

[4]I resolved not to attempt at that time a further pursuit of Hood's army, but slowly and deliberately to move back, occupy Atlanta, enjoy a short period of rest, and to think well over the next step required in the progress of events. I rode back to Jonesboro on the 6th, and there inspected the rebel hospital, full of wounded officers and men left by Hardee in his retreat.

[5]In Atlanta, I took up my headquarters at the house of Judge Lyons, which stood opposite one corner of the courthouse square, and at once set about a measure already ordered, of which I had thought much and long, that is, to remove the entire civil population of Atlanta, and to deny to all civilians from the rear the expected profits of civil trade.

[6]Hundreds of merchants and traders were waiting at Nashville and Chattanooga, greedy to reach Atlanta with their wares and goods, with which to drive a profitable trade with the inhabitants. I gave positive orders that none of these traders, except three (one for each separate army), should be permitted to come nearer than Chattanooga; and, moreover, I peremptorily required that all the citizens and families resident in Atlanta should go away, giving to each the option to go south or north, as their interests or feelings dictated.

[7]I was resolved to make Atlanta a pure military garrison or depot, with no civil population to influence military measures. I had seen Memphis, Vicksburg, Natchez and New Orleans, all captured from the enemy, and each one was garrisoned by a full division of troops, if not more, so that success was actually crippling our armies in the field by detachments to guard and protect the interests of a hostile population.

[8]I gave notice of this purpose, as early as the 4th September to General Halleck in a letter concluding with these words:

[9]If the people raise a howl against my barbarity and cruelty, I will answer that war is war, and not popularity-seeking. If they want peace, they and their relatives must stop the war.

[10]I knew, of course, that such a measure would be strongly criticized, but made up my mind to do it with the absolute certainty of its justness, and that time would sanction its wisdom. I knew that the people of the South would read in this measure two important conclusions: one, that we were in earnest; and the other, if they were sincere in their common and popular clamor "to die in the last ditch," that the opportunity would soon come.

[11]Soon after our reaching Atlanta, General Hood had sent in by a flag of truce a proposition, offering a general exchange of prisoners. I would not exchange for his prisoners because I knew that ours would have to be sent to their own regiments, away from my army, whereas all we would give him could at once be put to duty in his immediate army.

[12]Quite an angry correspondence grew up between us, which was published at the time in the newspapers, but it is not to be found in any book of which I have present knowledge and is therefore given here.

Headquarters of the Army
Washington, September 16, 1864

General W. T. Sherman, *Atlanta, Georgia.*

MY DEAR GENERAL:

[13]Your very interesting letter of the 4th is just received. Its perusal has given me the greatest pleasure. I have not written before to congratulate you on the capture of Atlanta, the objective point of your brilliant campaign, for the reason that I have been suffering from my annual attack of hay-fever. It affects my eyes so much that I can scarcely see to write.

[14]As you suppose, I have watched your movements most attentively and critically, and I do not hesitate to say that your campaign has been the most brilliant of the war.

[15]You must have been very considerably annoyed by the State Negro recruiting agents. Your letter was a capital one, and did much good. The law was a ridiculous one; it was opposed by the War Department, but passed through the influence of Eastern manufacturers who hoped to escape the draft in that way. They were making immense fortunes out of the war and could well afford to purchase Negro recruits, and thus save their employees at home.

[16]Hooker certainly made a mistake in leaving before the capture of Atlanta. I understand that, when here, he said that you would fail; your army was discouraged and dissatisfied. He is most unmeasured in his abuse of me. The funny part of the business is that I had nothing whatever to do with his being relieved on either occasion.

[17]His animosity arises from another source. He is aware that I know some things about his character and conduct in California, and, fearing that I may use that information against him, he seeks to ward off its effect by making it appear that I am his personal enemy and jealous of him, etc. I know of no other reason for his hostility to me.

[18]He is welcome to abuse me as much as he pleases; I don't think it will do him much good or me much harm.

[19]With many thanks for your kind letter and wishes for your future, yours truly,

H.W. Halleck

Headquarters Military Division of the Mississippi
Atlanta Georgia, September 20, 1864.

Major-General Halleck, *Chief of Staff, Washington, D. C.*

GENERAL:

[20]I have the honor herewith to submit copies of a correspondence between General Hood, of the Confederate Army, the Mayor of Atlanta, and myself, touching the removal of the inhabitants of Atlanta.

[21]In explanation of the tone which marks some of these letters, I will only call your attention to the fact that, after I had announced my determination, General Hood took upon himself to question my motives.

[22]It is sufficient for my Government to know that the removal of the inhabitants has been made with liberality and fairness, that it has been attended with no force, and that no women or children have suffered, unless for want of provisions by their natural protectors and friends.

[23]My real reasons for this step were:

[24]We want all the houses of Atlanta for military storage and occupation.

[25]We want to contract the lines of defense, so as to diminish the garrison to the limit necessary to defend its narrow and vital parts, instead of embracing, as the lines do now, the vast suburbs. This contraction of the lines, with the necessary citadels and redoubts, will make it necessary to destroy the very houses used by families as residences.

[26]Atlanta is a fortified town, was stubbornly defended, and fairly captured. As captors, we have a right to it.

[27]The residence here of a poor population would compel us, sooner or later, to feed them or to see them starve under our eyes.

[28]The residence here of the families of our enemies would be a temptation and a means to keep up a correspondence dangerous and hurtful to our cause; a civil population calls for provost-guards, and absorbs the attention of officers in listening to everlasting complaints and special grievances that are not military.

[29]These are my reasons; and, if satisfactory to the Government of the United States, it makes no difference whether it pleases General Hood and his people or not. I am, with respect, your obedient servant,

W.T. Sherman,
Major-General commanding.

Headquarters Military
Division of the Mississippi
In the Field, Atlanta, Georgia,
September 7, 1864

General Hood, *commanding, Confederate Army*

GENERAL:

[30]I have deemed it to the interest of the United States that the citizens now residing in Atlanta should remove, those who prefer it to go south, and the rest north. That their removal may be made with as little discomfort as possible, it will be necessary for you to help transport the families.

[31]If you consent, I will undertake to remove all the families in Atlanta who prefer to go south with all their movable effects, including clothing, trunks, reasonable furniture, bedding, etc., with their servants, white and black, with the proviso that no force shall be used toward the blacks, one way or the other. If they want to go with their masters or mistresses, they may do so; otherwise, they will be sent away, unless they be men, when they may be employed by our quartermaster.

[32]Atlanta is no place for families or non-combatants, and I have no desire to send them north if you will assist in conveying them south.

[33]If this proposition meets your views, I will consent to a truce. Each of us might send a guard of, say, one hundred men to maintain order, and limit the truce to, say, two days after a certain time appointed.

[34]I have authorized the mayor to choose two citizens to convey to you this letter, with such documents as the mayor may forward in explanation, and shall await your reply. I have the honor to be your obedient servant,

W.T. Sherman, *Major-General commanding.*

Headquarters, Army of Tennessee
Office of Chief of Staff
September 9, 1864

Major-General W. T. Sherman, *commanding United States Forces in Georgia.*

GENERAL:
[35]Your letter of yesterday's date, borne by James M. Ball and James R. Crew, citizens of Atlanta, is received. You say therein, "I deem it to be to the interest of the United States that the citizens now residing in Atlanta should remove," etc. I do not consider that I have any alternative in this matter. I therefore accept your proposition to declare a truce of two days, or such time as may be necessary to accomplish the purpose mentioned, and shall render all assistance in my power to expedite the transportation of citizens in this direction.

[36]And now, sir, permit me to say that the unprecedented measure you propose transcends, in studied and ingenious cruelty, all acts ever before brought to my attention in the dark history of war.

[37]In the name of God and humanity, I protest, believing that you will find that you are expelling from their homes and firesides the wives and children of a brave people. I am, general, very respectfully, your obedient servant,

J.B. Hood, *General.*

*****

Headquarters, Military Division of the Mississippi
In the Field, Atlanta, Georgia
September 10, 1864

General J. B. Hood, *commanding Army of Tennessee, Confederate Army.*

GENERAL:
[38]I have the honor to acknowledge the receipt of your letter of this date, consenting to the arrangements I had proposed to facilitate the removal of the people of Atlanta. I enclose a copy of my orders, which will, I am satisfied, accomplish my purpose perfectly.

[39]You style the measures proposed "unprecedented," and appeal to the dark history of war for a parallel, as an act of "studied

and ingenious cruelty." It is not unprecedented, for General Johnston himself, however wisely and properly, removed the families all the way from Dalton down, and I see no reason why Atlanta should be excepted. Nor is it necessary to appeal to the dark history of war, when recent and modern examples are so handy.

[40]You yourself burned dwelling-houses along your parapet, and I have seen today fifty houses that you rendered uninhabitable because they stood in the way of your forts and men. You defended Atlanta on a line so close to town that every cannon-shot and many musket-shots from our line of investment, that overshot their mark, went into the habitations of women and children.

[41]General Hardee did the same at Jonesboro, and General Johnston did the same last summer at Jackson, Mississippi. I have not accused you of heartless cruelty, but merely instance these cases of very recent occurrence, and could go on and on and enumerate hundreds of others, and challenge any fair man to judge which of us has the heart of pity for the families of a "brave people."

[42]I say that it is kindness to these families of Atlanta to remove them now, at once, from scenes that women and children should not be exposed to, and the "brave people" should scorn to commit their wives and children to the rude barbarians who thus, as you say, violate the laws of war, as illustrated in the pages of its dark history.

[43]If we must be enemies, let us be men, and fight it out as we propose to do, and not deal in such hypocritical appeals to God and humanity. God will judge us in due time, and he will pronounce whether it be more humane to fight with a town full of women and the families of a brave people at our back, or to remove them in time to places of safety around their own friends and people.

[44]I am, very respectfully, your obedient servant,

W.T. Sherman, *Major-General commanding.*

Headquarters Army of Tennessee
September 12,1864.

Major-General W. T. Sherman, *commanding Military Division of the Mississippi.*

GENERAL:

[45]I have the honor to acknowledge the receipt of your letter of the 9th inst., with its enclosure in reference to the women, children, and others, whom you have thought proper to expel from their homes in the city of Atlanta.

[46]I feel no other emotion than pain in reading that portion of your letter which attempts to justify your shelling Atlanta without notice under pretense that I defended Atlanta upon a line so close to town that every cannon-shot and many musket-balls from your line of investment, that overshot their mark, went into habitations of women and children. I made no complaint of your firing into Atlanta in any way you thought proper.

[47]I make none now, but there are a hundred thousand witnesses that you fired into the habitations of women and children for weeks, firing far above and miles beyond my line of defense. I have too good an opinion, founded both upon observation and experience, of the skill of your artillerists, to credit the insinuation that they for several weeks unintentionally fired too high for my modest field-works, and slaughtered women and children by accident and want of skill.

[48]You order into exile the whole population of a city; drive men, women and children from their homes at the point of the bayonet, under the plea that it is to the interest of your government, and on the claim that it is an act of "kindness to these families of Atlanta." Butler only banished from New Orleans the registered enemies of his government, and he acknowledged that he did it as a punishment. You issue a sweeping edict, covering all the inhabitants of a city, and add insult to the injury heaped upon the defenseless by assuming that you have done them a kindness.

[49]You say, "Let us fight it out like men." To this my reply is—for myself, and I believe for all the true men, ay, and women and children, in my country—we will fight you to the death! I better die a thousand deaths than submit to live under you or your Government and your Negro allies!

[50]Respectfully, your obedient servant,

J. B. Hood, *General.*

Atlanta, Georgia
September 11, 1864.

Major-General W. T. Sherman.

Sir:

[51]We the undersigned, Mayor and two of the Council for the city of Atlanta, for the time being the only legal organ of the people of the said city, to express their wants and wishes, ask leave most earnestly but respectfully to petition you to reconsider the order requiring them to leave Atlanta.

[52]At first view, it struck us that the measure would involve extraordinary hardship and loss, but since we have seen the practical execution of it so far as it has progressed, and the individual condition of the people, and heard their statements as to the inconveniences, loss, and suffering attending it, we are satisfied that the amount of it will involve in the aggregate consequences appalling and heart-rending.

[53]Many poor women are in advanced state of pregnancy, others now having young children, all whose husbands for the greater part are either in the army, prisoners, or dead. Some say, "I have such a one sick at my house; who will wait on them when I am gone?" Others say: "What are we to do? We have no house to go to, and no means to buy, build, or rent any; no parents, relatives, or friends to go to."

[54]Another says: "I will try and take this or that article of property, but such and such things I must leave behind, though I need them much." We reply to them: "General Sherman will carry your property to the south and General Hood will take it thence on." And they will reply to that: "But I want to leave the railroad at such a place, and cannot get conveyance from there on."

[55]We only refer to a few facts, to try to illustrate in part how this measure will operate in practice. As you advanced, the people north of this city fell back; and before your arrival here, a large portion of the people had retired south, so that the country south of here is already crowded, and without houses enough to accommodate the people, and we are informed that many are now straying in churches and other out-buildings.

[56]This being so, how is it possible for the people still here (mostly women and children) to find any shelter? And how can they live through the winter in the woods—no shelter or subsistence, in the midst of strangers who know them not, and without the power to assist them much, if they were willing to do so?

[57]This is but a feeble picture of the consequences of this measure. You know the woe, the horrors, and the suffering cannot be described by words; imagination can only conceive of it, and we ask you to take these things into consideration.

[58]We most earnestly and solemnly petition you to reconsider this order, or modify it, and let this unfortunate people remain at home and enjoy what little means they have.

Respectfully submitted:
James M. Calhoun, *Mayor*
E.E. Rawson, *Councilman*
S.C. Wells, *Councilman*

*****

Headquarters Military Division of the Mississippi
In the Field, Atlanta, Georgia
September 12, 1864

James M. Calhoun, *Mayor*,
E.E. Rawson, S.C. Wells, *Representing City Council of Atlanta*

Gentlemen:
[59]I have your letter of the 11th, in the nature of a petition to revoke my orders removing all the inhabitants from Atlanta. I have read it carefully and give full credit to your statement of the distress that will be occasioned and yet shall not revoke my orders because they were not designed to meet the humanities of the case, but to prepare for the future struggles in which millions of good people outside of Atlanta have a deep interest.

[60]We must have peace, not only at Atlanta, but in all America. To secure this, we must stop the war that now desolates our once happy and favored country. To stop war, we must defeat the rebel armies which are arrayed against the laws and constitution that all must respect and obey. To defeat those armies, we must prepare the way to reach them in their recesses, provided with the arms and instruments which enable us to accomplish our purpose.

[61]You might as well appeal against the thunderstorm as against these terrible hardships of war. They are inevitable, and the only way the people of Atlanta can hope once more to live in peace and quiet at home is to stop the war, which can only be done by admitting that it began in error and is perpetuated in pride.

[62]We don't want your Negroes, your horses, your houses, or your lands, or anything you have, but we do want and will have a just obedience to the laws of the United States. That we will have, and, if it involves the destruction of your property, we cannot help it.

[63]I want peace and believe it can only be reached through union and war,
and I will ever conduct war with a view to perfect and early success.

[64]But, my dear sirs, when peace does come, you may call on me for anything. Then will I share with you the last cracker and watch with you to shield your homes and families against danger from every quarter.

[65]Now you must go, and take with you the old and feeble, feed and nurse them, and build for them, in more quiet places, proper habitations to shield them against the weather until the mad passions of men cool down and allow the Union and peace once more to settle over your old homes at Atlanta.

Yours in haste,
W.T. Sherman., *Major-General commanding*.

*****

Headquarters, Military Division of the Mississippi
In the Field
Atlanta, Georgia
September 14, 1864

General J. B. Hood, *commanding Army of the Tennessee, Confederate Army.*

GENERAL:

[66]Yours of September 12th is received and has been carefully perused. I agree with you that this discussion by two soldiers is out of place and profitless; but you must admit that you began the controversy by characterizing an official act of mine in unfair and improper terms.

[67]I reiterate my former answer, and to the only new matter contained in your rejoinder add: We have no "Negro allies" in this army; not a single Negro soldier left Chattanooga with this army, or is with it now. There are a few guarding Chattanooga, which General Steedman sent at one time to drive Wheeler out of Dalton.

[68]I was not bound by the laws of war to give notice of the shell-

ing of Atlanta, a "fortified town, with magazines, arsenals, foundries, and public stores"; you were bound to take notice. See the books.

[69]This is the conclusion of our correspondence, which I did not begin, and terminate with satisfaction. I am, with respect, your obedient servant,

W.T. Sherman, *Major-General commanding.*

*****

Headquarters of the Army
Washington
September 28, 1864

Major-General Sherman, *Atlanta, Georgia*
GENERAL:
[70]Your communications of the 20th in regard to the removal of families from Atlanta, and the exchange of prisoners, and also the official report of your campaign, are just received. I have not had time as yet to examine your report. The course which you have pursued in removing rebel families from Atlanta, and in the exchange of prisoners, is fully approved by the War Department.

[71]Not only are you justified by the laws and usages of war in removing those people, but I think it was your duty to your own army to do so. Moreover, I am fully of the opinion that the nature of your position, the character of the war, the conduct of the enemy (and especially of non-combatants and women of the territory which we have heretofore conquered and occupied), will justify you in gathering up all the forage and provisions which your army may require, both for a siege of Atlanta and for your supply in your march farther into the enemy's country.

[72]Let the disloyal families of the country, thus stripped, go to their husbands, fathers and natural protectors, in the rebel ranks; we have tried three years of conciliation and kindness without any reciprocation; on the contrary, those thus treated have acted as spies and guerrillas in our rear and within our lines. The safety of our armies, and a proper regard for the lives of our soldiers require that we apply to our inexorable foes the severe rules of war.

Very respectfully, your obedient servant,

H. W. Halleck, *Major-General, Chief of Staff.*

[73]In order to effect the exchange of prisoners, to facilitate the exodus of the people of Atlanta and to keep open communication with the South, we established a neutral camp at and about the railroad station next south of Atlanta, known as "Rough and Ready," to which point I dispatched Lieutenant Colonel Willard Warner of my staff with a guard of one hundred men, and General Hood sent Colonel Clare of his staff with a similar guard; these officers and men harmonized perfectly, and parted good friends when the work was done.

[74]By the middle of September all these matters were in progress, the reports of the past campaign were written up and dispatched to Washington, and our thoughts began to turn toward the future.

Vocabulary

[2]perseverance	[27]compel	[36]transcends	[52]aggregate
[2]annals	[31]proviso	[36]ingenious	[52]heart-rending
[6]peremptorily	[32]non-combatants	[40]parapet	[66]perused
[10]clamor	[35]borne	[40]investment	[72]inexorable
[25]redoubts	[35]expedite	[47]insinuation	

Discussion Questions

1. What "real" reasons does General Sherman give for the removal of the inhabitants from Atlanta? Paraphrase the reasons. Do you think these reasons are sufficient for evacuating the city? Explain.

2. What reasons does General Hood give for opposing Sherman's removal of the inhabitants? Do you think his reasons are strong? Explain why or why not.

3. What are Calhoun, Rawson and Wells's point of view on Sherman's order?

4. Sherman makes several statements about the nature of war. Choose one that you think best describes your understanding of war and explain why you agree with that viewpoint.

5. Discuss the style and tone of the letters between the two sides. Why do you think they were written in that manner?

CAT IN THE RAIN

ERNEST HEMINGWAY

Ernest Hemingway (1899-1961) is one of the most impor-tant American writers of the twentieth century. During the 1920s, Hemingway became a member of the group of expa-triate Americans in Paris dubbed "The Lost Generation," which he described in his first important work, The Sun Also Rises *(1926). His other novels include* A Farewell to Arms *(1929),* For Whom the Bell Tolls *(1940) and* The Old Man and the Sea *(1952).*

[1]There were only two Americans stopping at the hotel. They did not know any of the people they passed on the stairs on their way to and from their room. Their room was on the second floor facing the sea. It also faced the pub-lic garden and war monument. There were big palms and green benches in the public garden. In the good weather there was always an artist with his easel.

[2]Artists liked the way the palms grew and the bright colors of the hotels facing the sea. Italians came from a long way off to look up at the war monu-ment. It was made of bronze and glistened in the rain. It was raining. The rain dripped from the palm trees. Water stood in pools on the gravel paths. The sea broke in a long line in the rain. The motor cars were gone from the square by the war monument. Across the square in the doorway of the cafe a waiter stood looking out at the empty square.

[3]The American wife stood at the window looking out. Outside right un-der their window a cat was crouched under one of the dripping green tables. The cat was trying to make herself so compact that she would not be dripped on.

[4]"I'm going down and get that kitty," the American wife said.

[5]"I'll do it," her husband offered from the bed.

[6]"No, I'll get it. The poor kitty is out trying to keep dry under the table."

[7]The husband went on reading, lying propped up with the two pillows at the foot of the bed.

[8]"Don't get wet," he said.

[9]The wife went downstairs and the hotel owner stood up and bowed to her as she passed the office. His desk was at the far end of the office. He was an old man and very tall.

[10]"*Il piove*," the wife said. She liked the hotelkeeper.

[11]"*Si, si, Signora, brutto tempo*. It is very bad weather."

[12]He stood behind his desk in the far end of the dim room. The wife liked him. She liked the way he wanted to serve her. She liked the way he felt about being a hotel-keeper. She liked his old, heavy face and big hands.

[13]Liking him, she opened the door and looked out. It was raining harder. A man in a rubber cape was crossing the empty square to the cafe. The cat would be around to the right. Perhaps she could go along to the eaves. As she stood in the doorway an umbrella opened behind her. It was the maid who looked after their room.

[14]"You must not get wet," she smiled, speaking Italian. Of course, the hotel-keeper had sent her.

[15]With the maid holding the umbrella over her, she walked along the gravel path until she was under their window. The table was there, washed bright green in the rain, but the cat was gone. She was suddenly disappointed. The maid looked up at her.

[16]"*Ha perduto qualque cosa*, Signora?"

[17]"There was a cat," said the American girl.

[18]"A cat?"

[19]"*Si, il gatto.*"

[20]"A cat?" the maid laughed. "A cat in the rain?"

[21]"Yes," she said, "under the table." Then, "Oh, I wanted it so much. I wanted a kitty."

[22]When she talked English the maid's face tightened.

[23]"Come, *Signora*," she said. "We must get back inside. You will be wet."

[24]"I suppose so," said the American girl.

[25]They went back along the gravel path and passed in the door. The maid stayed outside to close the umbrella. As the American girl passed the office, the *padrone* bowed from his desk. Something felt very small and tight inside the girl. The *padrone* made her feel very small and at the same time really important. She had a momentary feeling of being of supreme importance. She went on up the stairs. She opened the door of the room. George was on the bed, reading.

[26]"Did you get the cat?" he asked, putting the book down.

[27]"It was gone."

[28]"Wonder where it went to," he said, resting his eyes from reading.

[29]She sat down on the bed.

[30]"I wanted it so much," she said. "I don't know why I wanted it so much. I wanted that poor kitty. It isn't any fun to be a poor kitty out in the rain."

[31]George was reading again.

[32]She went over and sat in front of the mirror of the dressing table looking at herself with the hand glass. She studied her profile, first one side and then the other. Then she studied the back of her head and her neck.

[33]"Don't you think it would be a good idea if I let my hair grow out?" she asked, looking at her profile again.

[34]George looked up and saw the back of her neck, clipped close like a boy's.

[35]"I like it the way it is."

[36]"I get so tired of it," she said. "I get so tired of looking like a boy."

[37]George shifted his position in the bed. He hadn't looked away from her since she started to speak.

[38]"You look pretty darn nice," he said.

[39]She laid the mirror down on the dresser and went over to the window and looked out. It was getting dark.

[40]"I want to pull my hair back tight and smooth and make a big knot at the back that I can feel," she said. "I want to have a kitty to sit on my lap and purr when I stroke her."

[41]"Yeah?" George said from the bed.

[42]"And I want to eat at a table with my own silver and I want candles. And I want it to be spring and I want to brush my hair out in front of a mirror and I want a kitty and I want some new clothes."

[43]"Oh, shut up and get something to read," George said. He was reading again.

[44]His wife was looking out of the window. It was quite dark now and still raining in the palm trees.

[45]"Anyway, I want a cat," she said, "I want a cat. I want a cat now. If I can't have long hair or any fun, I can have a cat."

[46]George was not listening. He was reading his book. His wife looked out of the window where the light had come on in the square.

[47]Someone knocked at the door.

[48]"*Avanti*," George said. He looked up from his book. In the doorway stood the maid. She held a big tortoise-shell cat pressed tight against her and swung down against her body.

[49]"Excuse me," she said, "the *padrone* asked me to bring this for the *Signora*."

Discussion Questions

1. In 30 words or fewer, summarize what this story is about.

2. Where does the story take place? Is this important to understanding the story?

3. How is the wife portrayed? The husband?

4. What is the relationship between George and his wife? What does it say about Hemingway's view of men and women?

5. Why do you think only the husband is given a name — George — but not the wife? Look at paragraphs 26 and 27 of "Kew Gardens" beginning on page 349 of this text. How does that relate to what is happening in this story?

6. In what way does this story address the nature of human longing?

7. What do you think the cat symbolizes? The rain?

8. Do you think the cat brought to the wife at the end of the story is the same one that she sees earlier? Explain your answer.

CONCESSION SPEECH, NOVEMBER 4, 2008
JOHN MCCAIN

John Sidney McCain III (1936-) is the senior sena-tor from Arizona. A graduate of the United States Naval Academy and flight school, he volunteered for service in Vietnam as a pilot. McCain's plane was shot down in 1967 and he spent five and one-half years as a prisoner of war. He served in the U.S. House of Representatives from 1982-1986 and the U.S. Senate from 1986 to the present. Mc-Cain lost the 2000 Republican Party presidential primary nomination to George W. Bush. He won the nomination in 2008 but lost in the general election to the Democratic Party nominee, Senator Barack Obama. The following is his 2008 concession speech.

[1]Thank you. Thank you, my friends. Thank you for coming here on this beautiful Arizona evening. My friends, we have come to the end of a long journey. The American people have spoken, and they have spoken clearly. A little while ago, I had the honor of calling Senator Barack Obama to congratulate him on being elected the next president of the country that we both love.

[2]In a contest as long and difficult as this campaign has been, his success alone commands my respect for his ability and perseverance. But that he managed to do so by inspiring the hopes of so many millions of Americans who had once wrongly believed that they had little at stake or little influence in the election of an American president is something I deeply admire and commend him for achieving. This is a historic election, and I recognize the special significance it has for African-Americans and for the special pride that must be theirs tonight. I've always believed that America offers opportunities to all who have the industry and will to seize it. Senator Obama believes that, too.

[3]But we both recognize that, though we have come a long way from the old injustices that once stained our nation's reputation and denied some Americans the full blessings of American citizenship, the memory of them still has the power to wound. A century ago, President Theodore Roosevelt's invitation of Booker T. Washington to dine at the White House was taken as an outrage in many quarters. America today is a world away from the cruel and frightful bigotry of that time. There is no better evidence of this than the election of an African-American to the presidency of the United States.

[4]Let there be no reason now for any Americans to fail to cherish their citizenship in this, the greatest nation on earth. Senator Obama has achieved a great thing for himself and for his country. I applaud him for it, and offer him my sincere sympathy that his beloved grandmother did not live to see this day though our faith assures us she is at rest in the presence of her creator and so very proud of the good man she helped raise.

[5]Senator Obama and I have had and argued our differences, and he has prevailed. No doubt many of those differences remain. These are difficult times for our country. And I pledge to him tonight to do all in my power to help him lead us through the many challenges we face. I urge all Americans who supported me to join me in not just congratulating him, but offering our next president our good will and earnest effort to find ways to come together to find the necessary compromises to bridge our differences and help restore our prosperity, defend our security in a dangerous world, and leave our children and grandchildren a stronger, better country than we inherited. Whatever our differences, we are fellow Americans. And please believe me when I say no association has ever meant more to me than that.

[6]It's natural tonight to feel some disappointment. But tomorrow, we must move beyond it and work together to get our country moving again. We fought—we fought as hard as we could. And though we fell short, the failure is mine, not yours. I am so deeply grateful to all of you for the great honor of your support and for all you have done for me. I wish the outcome had been different, my friends. The road was a difficult one from the outset, but your support and friendship never wavered. I cannot adequately express how deeply indebted I am to you.

[7]I'm especially grateful to my wife, Cindy, my children, my dear mother and all my family, and to the many old and dear friends who have stood by my side through the many ups and downs of this long campaign. I have always been a fortunate man and never more so for the love and encouragement you have given me. You know, campaigns are often harder on a candidate's family than on the candidate, and that's been true in this campaign. All I can offer in compensation is my love and gratitude and the promise of more peaceful years ahead.

[8]I am also—I am also, of course, very thankful to Governor Sarah Palin, one of the best campaigners I've ever seen, and an impressive new voice in our party for reform and the principles that have always been our greatest strength [and] her husband Todd and their five beautiful children for their tireless dedication to our cause, and the courage and grace they showed in the rough and tumble of a presidential campaign. We can all look forward with great interest to her future service to Alaska, the Republican Party and our country.

[9]To all my campaign comrades, from Rick Davis and Steve Schmidt and Mark Salter, to every last volunteer who fought so hard and valiantly, month after month, in what at times seemed to be the most challenged campaign in modern times, thank you so much. A lost election will never mean more to me than the privilege of your faith and friendship. I don't know—I don't know what more we could have done to try to win this election. I'll leave that to others to determine. Every candidate makes mistakes, and I'm sure I made my share of them. But I won't spend a moment of the future regretting what might have

been. This campaign was and will remain the great honor of my life, and my heart is filled with nothing but gratitude for the experience and to the American people for giving me a fair hearing before deciding that Senator Obama and my old friend Senator Joe Biden should have the honor of leading us for the next four years.

[10]I would not—I would not be an American worthy of the name should I regret a fate that has allowed me the extraordinary privilege of serving this country for a half a century. Today, I was a candidate for the highest office in the country I love so much. And tonight, I remain her servant. That is blessing enough for anyone, and I thank the people of Arizona for it. Tonight, more than any night, I hold in my heart nothing but love for this country and for all its citizens, whether they supported me or Senator Obama.

[11]I wish Godspeed to the man who was my former opponent and will be my president. And I call on all Americans, as I have often in this campaign, to not despair of our present difficulties, but to believe, always, in the promise and greatness of America, because nothing is inevitable here. Americans never quit. We never surrender. We never hide from history. We make history.

[12]Thank you, and God bless you, and God bless America. Thank you all very much.

Vocabulary

[4]cherish

[5]prevailed

[6]wavered

[9]valiantly

[11]Godspeed

[11]inevitable

Discussion Questions

1. Who are John McCain's primary audiences for this speech? What is his purpose in addressing these particular groups?

2. Why does McCain call this "a historic election"?

3. What do you think McCain's purpose is in bringing up President Theodore Roosevelt's invitation to Booker T. Washington to dine at the White House?

4. How do Senator McCain's remarks here compare to or contrast with Theodore Roosevelt's observations regarding "True Americanism" located on page 537 in this text?

5. Political analysts have said that this speech "sets the tone for reconciliation." What evidence from the speech supports this? Do you agree with this analysis? Why or why not?

CONSPICUOUS CONSUMPTION
FROM *THE THEORY OF THE LEISURE CLASS*

THORSTEIN VEBLEN

Thorstein B. Veblen (1837-1929) was an economist and sociologist who criticized American society from an evolutionary and urbane point of view. He taught at the University of Chicago, Stanford University, the University of Missouri, and New School of Social Research. Among his many works are The Theory of the Leisure Class *(1899),* The Higher Learning in America *(1918), and* Essays in Our Changing Order *(1934). He is credited for adding the term "conspicuous consumption" to our language.*

[1]In what has been said of the evolution of the leisure class and its differentiation from the general body of the working classes, reference has been made to a further division of labour—that between different gradations *within* the working class.

[2]One portion of the working class, chiefly those persons whose occupation allows them to accumulate wealth and rise within the class, come to undertake a new, subsidiary range of duties—the consumption of goods. The most obvious form in which this consumption occurs is seen in the wearing of fine clothing and the occupation of spacious quarters. Another form of consumption, and a much more widely prevalent one, is the consumption of food, clothing, dwelling, and furniture.

[3]But already at a point in economic evolution far antedating the emergence of this grade of the working class, specialized consumption of goods as an evidence of pecuniary strength had begun to work out in a more or less elaborate system. The beginning of a differentiation in consumption even antedates the appearance of anything that can fairly be called pecuniary strength. It is traceable back to the initial phase of predatory culture, and there is even a suggestion that an incipient differentiation in this respect lies back of the beginnings of the predatory life.

[4]This most primitive differentiation in the consumption of goods is like the later differentiation with which we are all so intimately familiar, in that it is largely of a ceremonial character, but unlike the latter it does not rest on a difference in accumulated wealth. The utility of consumption as an evidence of wealth is to be classed as a derivative growth. It is an adaptation to a new end, by a selective process, of a distinction previously existing and well established in people's habits of thought.

[5]In the earlier phases of the predatory culture the only economic differentiation is a broad distinction between an honorable superior class made up of the able-bodied men on the one side, and a base inferior class of laboring women on the other. According to the ideal scheme of life in force at that time it is the office of the men to consume what the women produce. Such consumption as falls to the women is merely incidental to their work; it is a means to their continued labor and not a consumption directed to their own comfort and fullness of life.

[6]Unproductive consumption of goods is honorable, primarily as a mark of prowess and a perquisite of human dignity; secondarily it becomes substantially honorable in itself, especially the consumption of the more desirable things. The consumption of choice articles of food, and frequently also of rare articles of adornment, becomes taboo to the women and children; and if there is a base (servile) class of men, the taboo holds also for them.

[7]When the quasi-peaceable stage of industry is reached, with its fundamental institution of chattel slavery, the general principle, more or less rigorously applied, is that the base, industrious class should consume only what may be necessary to their subsistence. In the nature of things, luxuries and the comforts of life belong to the leisure class. Under the taboo, certain victuals, and more particularly certain beverages, are strictly reserved for the use of the superior class.

[8]The ceremonial differentiation of the dietary is best seen in the use of intoxicating beverages and narcotics. If these articles of consumption are costly, they are felt to be noble and honorific. Therefore the base classes, primarily the women, practice an enforced continence with respect to these stimulants, except in countries where they are obtainable at a very low cost. From archaic times down through all the length of the patriarchal regime, it has been the office of the women to prepare and administer these luxuries, and it has been the perquisite of the men of gentle birth and breeding to consume them.

[9]Drunkenness and the other pathological consequences of the free use of stimulants therefore tend in their turn to become honorific, as being a mark of the superior status of those who are able to afford the indulgence. Infirmities induced by overindulgence are among some peoples freely recognized as manly attributes.

[10]Where the example set by the leisure class retains its imperative force in the regulation of the conventionalities, it is observable that the women still in great measure practice the same traditional continence with regard to stimulants.

[11]The greater abstinence of women is in some part due to an imperative conventionality; and this conventionality is, in a general way, strongest where the patriarchal tradition—the tradition that the woman is a chattel—has retained its hold in greatest vigor. In a sense which has been greatly qualified in scope

and the process of gradual amelioration which takes place in the articles of his consumption, the motive principle and the proximate aim of innovation is no doubt the higher efficiency of the improved and more elaborate products for personal comfort and well-being. But that does not remain the sole purpose of their consumption. The canon of reputability is at hand and seizes upon such innovations as are, according to its standard, fit to survive. Since the consumption of these more excellent goods is an evidence of wealth, it becomes honorific; and conversely, the failure to consume in due quantity and quality becomes a mark of inferiority and demerit.

[12]This growth of punctilious discrimination as to qualitative excellence in eating, drinking, etc., presently affects not only the manner of life, but also the training and intellectual activity of the gentleman of leisure. He is no longer simply the successful, aggressive male, the man of strength, resource, and intrepidity. In order to avoid stultification he must also cultivate his tastes, for it now becomes incumbent on him to discriminate with some nicety between the noble and the ignoble in consumable goods. He becomes a connoisseur in creditable viands of various degrees of merit, in manly beverages and trinkets, in seemly apparel and architecture, in weapons, games, dances, and narcotics.

[13]Conspicuous consumption of valuable goods is a means of reputability to the gentleman of leisure. As wealth accumulates on his hands, his own unaided effort will not avail to sufficiently put his opulence in evidence by this method. The aid of friends and competitors (vicarious consumers) is therefore brought in by resorting to the giving of valuable presents and expensive feasts and entertainments.

[14]With the disappearance of servitude, the number of vicarious consumers attached to any one gentleman tends, on the whole, to decrease. The like is true in the number of dependents who perform vicarious leisure for him. In a general way, though not wholly nor consistently, these two groups coincide. The dependent who was first delegated for these duties is the wife, or the chief wife; and, as would be expected, in the later development of the institution when the number of persons by whom these duties are customarily performed gradually narrows, the wife remains the last.

[15]In the higher grades of society, a large volume of both of these kinds of service is required; and here the wife is still assisted in the work by a more or less numerous corps of menials. But as we descend the social scale, the point is presently reached where the duties of vicarious leisure and consumption devolve upon the wife alone. In the communities of the Western culture, this point is at present found among the lower middle class.

[16]Conspicuous consumption claims a relatively larger portion of the income of the urban than of the rural population, and the claim is also more imperative. The result is that, in order to keep up a decent appearance, the former habitually live hand-to-mouth to a greater extent than the latter. So it comes, for

instance, that the American farmer and his wife and daughters are notoriously less modish in their dress, as well as less urbane in their manners, than the city worker's family with an equal income.

[17]It is not that the city population is by nature much more eager for the peculiar complacency that comes of a conspicuous consumption, nor has the rural population less regard for pecuniary decency. But the provocation to this line of evidence, as well as its transient effectiveness, is more decided in the city. This method is therefore more readily resorted to, and in the struggle to outdo one another the city population push their normal standard of conspicuous consumption to a higher point, with the result that a relatively greater expenditure in this direction is required to indicate a given degree of pecuniary decency in the city. The requirement of conformity to this higher conventional standard becomes mandatory. The standard of decency is higher, class for class, and this requirement of decent appearance must be lived up to on pain of losing caste.

[18]Throughout the entire evolution of conspicuous expenditure, whether of goods or of services or human lives, runs the obvious implication that in order to effectually mend the consumer's good fame it must be an expenditure of superfluities. In order to be reputable it must be wasteful. No merit would accrue from the consumption of the bare necessities of life, except by comparison with the abjectly poor who fall short even of the subsistence minimum; and no standard of expenditure could result from such a comparison except the most prosaic and unattractive level of decency.

Vocabulary

[1]gradations	[7]subsistence	[11]amelioration	[13]opulence
[2]subsidiary	[7]victuals	[11]proximate	[14]vicarious
[2]prevalent	[8]honorific	[11]innovation	[15]menials
[3]antedating	[8]continence	[11]canon	[15]devolve
[3]pecuniary	[8]archaic	[11]reputability	[15]modish
[3]predatory	[8]patriarchal	[12]punctilious	[15]urbane
[3]incipient	[8]regime	[12]qualitative	[17]transient
[3]differentiation	[9]pathological	[12]intrepidity	[17]caste
[4]derivative	[9]honorific	[12]stultification	[18]superfluities
[6]prowess	[9]infirmities	[12]incumbent	[18]accrue
[6]perquisite	[10]imperative	[12]nicety	[18]abjectly
[6]servile	[10]conventionalities	[12]ignoble	
[7]chattel	[11]abstinence	[12]viands	

Discussion Questions

1. Thorstein Veblen says that he is discussing a portion of the working class "whose occupation allows them to accumulate wealth and rise within the class." Can you give some specific examples of people in the American "working class" who have accumulated such wealth?

2. Veblen says that showing off one's possessions is not a new phenomenon; in fact, it "even antedates the appearance of anything that can fairly be called pecuniary strength." What does he mean by this?

3. Veblen further states that a display of "wealth" goes back to early predatory cultures and may even be behind "the beginnings of the predatory life." What does this mean? How does this manifest itself in modern American culture?

4. When Veblen speaks of "base classes" of people, to whom is he referring? What is their function in society as he describes it?

5. What point does Veblen make about "Drunkenness and the other pathological consequences of the free use of stimulants"? Is this still true today? If so, give a specific example from your own knowledge and experience.

6. Veblen talks about the "greater abstinence of women" in regard to the use of intoxicating beverages and stimulants. Why was this true in his day? Is it still true in the United States today? Discuss with your classmates.

7. Do you think city dwellers show off their wealth and possessions more than people in rural areas? Why or why not?

8. Do you agree with Veblen's assessment of the role of conspicuous consumption in American society? If you do, cite some examples. If you don't, explain why not.

THE CRUCIFIXION AND RESURRECTION OF JESUS OF NAZARETH

THE APOSTLE LUKE

The physical resurrection of Jesus Christ after he had been condemned by the Hebrew high priests and put to death on the cross by the Romans is a core event in Christian theology and is the basis for the celebration of Easter. The story of the events leading up to the crucifixion is also known as "The Passion of Christ" and is the basis for "passion plays" conducted in cutures around the world. Christians believe that Jesus died to atone for the sins of all mankind and that his rising from the dead gives them the promise of their own physical resurrection at the time of the Last Judgment.

Most Christians accept as historical fact the accounts of the resurrection as reported by the Apostles Matthew, Mark, Luke and John since these gospel narratives were written so soon after the event, from approximately thirty-five to sixty years after the crucifixion.

CHAPTER 22

¹Now the Feast of Unleavened Bread, called the Passover, was approaching, ²and the chief priests and the teachers of the law were looking for some way to get rid of Jesus, for they were afraid of the people. ³Then Satan entered Judas, called Iscariot, one of the Twelve. ⁴And Judas went to the chief priests and the officers of the temple guard and discussed with them how he might betray Jesus. ⁵They were delighted and agreed to give him money.ᵃ ⁶He consented, and watched for an opportunity to hand Jesus over to them when no crowd was present.

The Last Supper

⁷Then came the day of Unleavened Bread on which the Passover lamb had to be sacrificed. ⁸Jesus sent Peter and John, saying, "Go and make preparations for us to eat the Passover."

⁹"Where do you want us to prepare for it?" they asked.

¹⁰He replied, "As you enter the city, a man carrying a jar of water will meet you. Follow him to the house that he enters, ¹¹and say to the owner of the house, 'The Teacher asks: Where is the guest room, where I may eat the Passover with my disciples?' ¹²He will show you a large upper room, all furnished. Make preparations there."

ᵃThe Gospel of Matthew Chapter 26, Verse 15 says the chief priests paid Judas "thirty silver coins."

¹³They left and found things just as Jesus had told them. So they prepared the Passover.

¹⁴When the hour came, Jesus and his apostles reclined at the table. ¹⁵And he said to them, "I have eagerly desired to eat this Passover with you before I suffer. ¹⁶For I tell you, I will not eat it again until it finds fulfillment in the kingdom of God."

¹⁷After taking the cup, he gave thanks and said, "Take this and divide it among you. ¹⁸For I tell you I will not drink again of the fruit of the vine until the kingdom of God comes."

¹⁹And he took bread, gave thanks and broke it, and gave it to them, saying, "This is my body given for you; do this in remembrance of me."

²⁰In the same way, after the supper he took the cup, saying, "This cup is the new covenant in my blood, which is poured out for you.ᵇ ²¹But the hand of him who is going to betray me is with mine on the table. ²²The Son of Man will go as it has been decreed,ᶜ but woe to that man who betrays him."

²³They began to question among themselves which of them it might be who would do this.

²⁴Also a dispute arose among them as to which of them was considered to be greatest. ²⁵Jesus said to them, "The kings of the Gentiles lord it over them; and those who exercise authority over them call themselves Benefactors. ²⁶But you are not to be like that. Instead, the greatest among you should be like the youngest, and the one who rules like the one who serves. ²⁷For who is greater, the one who is at the table or the one who serves? Is it not the one who is at the table? But I am among you as one who serves. ²⁸You are those who have stood by me in my trials. ²⁹And I confer on you a kingdom, just as my Father conferred one on me, ³⁰so that you may eat and drink at my table in my kingdom and sit on thrones, judging the twelve tribes of Israel.

³¹"Simon, Simon, Satan has asked to sift you as wheat. ³²But I have prayed for you, Simon, that your faith may not fail. And when you have turned back, strengthen your brothers."

³³But he replied, "Lord, I am ready to go with you to prison and to death."

³⁴Jesus answered, "I tell you, Peter,ᵈ before the rooster crows today, you will deny three times that you know me."

³⁵Then Jesus asked them, "When I sent you without purse, bag or sandals, did you lack anything?" "Nothing," they answered.

ᵇ"The body and blood of Christ" in this passage is the basis for the rite of Holy Communion in Christian tradition.

ᶜ". . . as it has been decreed," is a reference to a number of places in the Protestant Old Testament (Hebrew Tanakh) that Christians believe foretold the details of the death of Jesus, including his betrayal by Judas Iscariot.

ᵈPeter is the same person as Simon whom Jesus addresses in verses 31 and 32 above; his full name is Simon Peter and Jesus uses both names alternately.

[36]He said to them, "But now if you have a purse, take it, and also a bag; and if you don't have a sword, sell your cloak and buy one. [37]It is written: 'And he was numbered with the transgressors'; and I tell you that this must be fulfilled in me. Yes, what is written about me is reaching its fulfillment."

[38]The disciples said, "See, Lord, here are two swords." "That is enough," he replied.

Jesus Prays on the Mount of Olives

[39]Jesus went out as usual to the Mount of Olives, and his disciples followed him. [40]On reaching the place, he said to them, "Pray that you will not fall into temptation." [41]He withdrew about a stone's throw beyond them, knelt down and prayed, [42]"Father, if you are willing, take this cup from me; yet not my will, but yours be done." [43]An angel from heaven appeared to him and strengthened him. [44]And being in anguish, he prayed more earnestly, and his sweat was like drops of blood falling to the ground.

[45]When he rose from prayer and went back to the disciples, he found them asleep, exhausted from sorrow. [46]"Why are you sleeping?" he asked them. "Get up and pray so that you will not fall into temptation."

Jesus Arrested

[47]While he was still speaking a crowd came up, and the man who was called Judas, one of the Twelve, was leading them. He approached Jesus to kiss him,[e] [48]but Jesus asked him, "Judas, are you betraying the Son of Man[f] with a kiss?"

[9]When Jesus' followers saw what was going to happen, they said, "Lord, should we strike with our swords?" [50]And one of them struck the servant of the high priest, cutting off his right ear.

[51]But Jesus answered, "No more of this!" And he touched the man's ear and healed him.

[52]Then Jesus said to the chief priests, the officers of the temple guard, and the elders, who had come for him, "Am I leading a rebellion, that you have come with swords and clubs? [53]Every day I was with you in the temple courts, and you did not lay a hand on me. But this is your hour—when darkness reigns."

---

[e]The gospels of Matthew, Mark and John point out that Judas had earlier arranged with the chief priests to identify Jesus by walking up to him and kissing him. This is the origin of the expression, "The kiss of death."

[f]The expression "Son of Man" is used extensively in the New Testament to refer to Jesus and is the subject of varied interpretations by biblical scholars. Some view it as Jesus using it to express his humility; others regard its use to connect Jesus with mankind and humanity in general.

Peter Disowns Jesus

[54]Then seizing him, they led him away and took him into the house of the high priest. Peter followed at a distance. [55]But when they had kindled a fire in the middle of the courtyard and had sat down together, Peter sat down with them. [56]A servant girl saw him seated there in the firelight. She looked closely at him and said, "This man was with him."

[57]But he denied it. "Woman, I don't know him," he said.

[58]A little later someone else saw him and said, "You also are one of them." "Man, I am not!" Peter replied.

[59]About an hour later another asserted, "Certainly this fellow was with him, for he is a Galilean."[g]

[60]Peter replied, "Man, I don't know what you're talking about!" Just as he was speaking, the rooster crowed. [61]The Lord turned and looked straight at Peter. Then Peter remembered the word the Lord had spoken to him: "Before the rooster crows today, you will disown me three times." [62]And he went outside and wept bitterly.

The Guards Mock Jesus

[63]The men who were guarding Jesus began mocking and beating him. [64]They blindfolded him and demanded, "Prophesy! Who hit you?" [65]And they said many other insulting things to him.

Jesus Before Pilate and Herod

[66]At daybreak the council of the elders of the people, both the chief priests and teachers of the law, met together, and Jesus was led before them.

[67]"If you are the Christ,"[h] they said, "tell us."

Jesus answered, "If I tell you, you will not believe me, [68]and if I asked you, you would not answer. [69]But from now on, the Son of Man will be seated at the right hand of the mighty God."

[70]They all asked, "Are you then the Son of God?" He replied, "You are right in saying I am."

[71]Then they said, "Why do we need any more testimony? We have heard it from his own lips."

---

[g]"Galilean" refers to the area around the Sea of Galilee where Jesus was living and preaching.

[h]"Christ" is the English word for the Greek "Khristos," meaning "the annointed one."

CHAPTER 23

[1]Then the whole assembly rose and led him off to Pilate.[i] [2]And they began to accuse him, saying, "We have found this man subverting our nation. He opposes payment of taxes to Caesar[j] and claims to be Christ, a king."

[3]So Pilate asked Jesus, "Are you the king of the Jews?" "Yes, it is as you say," Jesus replied.

[4]Then Pilate announced to the chief priests and the crowd, "I find no basis for a charge against this man."

[5]But they insisted, "He stirs up the people all over Judea by his teaching. He started in Galilee and has come all the way here."

[6]On hearing this, Pilate asked if the man was a Galilean. [7]When he learned that Jesus was under Herod's[k] jurisdiction, he sent him to Herod, who was also in Jerusalem at that time.

[8]When Herod saw Jesus, he was greatly pleased because for a long time he had been wanting to see him. From what he had heard about him, he hoped to see him perform some miracle. [9]He plied him with many questions, but Jesus gave him no answer. [10]The chief priests and the teachers of the law were standing there, vehemently accusing him. [11]Then Herod and his soldiers ridiculed and mocked him. Dressing him in an elegant robe, they sent him back to Pilate. [12]That day Herod and Pilate became friends—before this they had been enemies.

[13]Pilate called together the chief priests, the rulers and the people, [14]and said to them, "You brought me this man as one who was inciting the people to rebellion. I have examined him in your presence and have found no basis for your charges against him. [15]Neither has Herod, for he sent him back to us; as you can see, he has done nothing to deserve death. [16]Therefore, I will punish him and then release him."

[18]With one voice they cried out, "Away with this man! Release Barabbas to us!"[l] [19](Barabbas had been thrown into prison for an insurrection in the city, and for murder.)

---

[i]Pontious Pilate was the Roman Prefect of Judea (Israel) and acted as judge, hearing the charges against Jesus.

[j]Tiberius Julius Caesar Augustus (42 BC-37 AD), second Roman emperor. Judea/Israel was conquered by the Romans in 63 BC and remained under Roman domination for approximately 500 years.

[k]Herod Antipas (20 BC-c. AD 40), tetrarch of Galilee and Peraea. A tetrarch was a king or prince in a province conquered by Rome who was allowed to remain as ruler of his people, under Roman supervision.

[l]The Apostle Matthew's Gospel says, ". . . it was the governor's custom at the Feast to release a prisoner chosen by the crowd."

[20]Wanting to release Jesus, Pilate appealed to them again. [21]But they kept shouting, "Crucify him! Crucify him!"

[22]For the third time he spoke to them: "Why? What crime has this man committed? I have found in him no grounds for the death penalty. Therefore I will have him punished and then release him."

[23]But with loud shouts they insistently demanded that he be crucified, and their shouts prevailed. [24]So Pilate decided to grant their demand. [25]He released the man who had been thrown into prison for insurrection and murder, the one they asked for, and surrendered Jesus to their will.

The Crucifixion

[26]As they led him away, they seized Simon from Cyrene, who was on his way in from the country, and put the cross on him and made him carry it behind Jesus. [27]A large number of people followed him, including women who mourned and wailed for him. [28]Jesus turned and said to them, "Daughters of Jerusalem, do not weep for me; weep for yourselves and for your children. [29]For the time will come when you will say, 'Blessed are the barren women, the wombs that never bore and the breasts that never nursed!' [30]Then they will say to the mountains, 'Fall on us!' and to the hills, 'Cover us!' [31]For if men do these things when the tree is green, what will happen when it is dry?"

[32]Two other men, both criminals, were also led out with him to be executed. [33]When they came to the place called the Skull,[m] there they crucified him, along with the criminals—one on his right, the other on his left. [34]Jesus said, "Father, forgive them, for they do not know what they are doing." And they divided up his clothes by casting lots.

[35]The people stood watching, and the rulers even sneered at him. They said, "He saved others; let him save himself if he is the Christ of God, the Chosen One."

[36]The soldiers also came up and mocked him. They offered him wine vinegar [37]and said, "If you are the king of the Jews, save yourself."

[38]There was a written notice above him, which read: THIS IS THE KING OF THE JEWS.[n]

[39]One of the criminals who hung there hurled insults at him: "Aren't you the Christ? Save yourself and us!"

[40]But the other criminal rebuked him. "Don't you fear God," he said,

---

[m]The Gospels of Matthew, Mark and John use the name "Golgotha," Aramaic for "Place of the Skull."

[n]This is the source of the inscription INRI seen in many artworks depicting the crucifixion. INRI is an acronym for the Latin IESVS·NAZARENVS·REX·IVDÆORVM, "Jesus of Nazareth, King of the Jews."

"since you are under the same sentence? [41]We are punished justly, for we are getting what our deeds deserve. But this man has done nothing wrong."

[42]Then he said, "Jesus, remember me when you come into your kingdom."

[43]Jesus answered him, "I tell you the truth, today you will be with me in paradise."

Jesus' Death

[44]It was now about the sixth hour, and darkness came over the whole land until the ninth hour, [45]for the sun stopped shining. And the curtain of the temple was torn in two.[o] [46]Jesus called out with a loud voice, "Father, into your hands I commit my spirit." When he had said this, he breathed his last.

[47]The centurion, seeing what had happened, praised God and said, "Surely this was a righteous man." [48]When all the people who had gathered to witness this sight saw what took place, they beat their breasts and went away. [49]But all those who knew him, including the women who had followed him from Galilee, stood at a distance, watching these things.

Jesus' Burial

[50]Now there was a man named Joseph, a member of the Council, a good and upright man, [51]who had not consented to their decision and action. He came from the Judean town of Arimathea and he was waiting for the kingdom of God. [52]Going to Pilate, he asked for Jesus' body. [53]Then he took it down, wrapped it in linen cloth and placed it in a tomb cut in the rock, one in which no one had yet been laid. [54]It was Preparation Day, and the Sabbath[p] was about to begin.

CHAPTER 24
The Resurrection

[1]On the first day of the week, very early in the morning, the women took the spices they had prepared and went to the tomb. [2]They found the stone rolled away from the tomb, [3]but when they entered, they did not find the body of the Lord Jesus. [4]While they were wondering about this, suddenly two men

---

[o]The Gospels of Matthew and Mark report that at this point Jesus called out, "Eloi, Eloi, lama sabachthani?"— "My God, my God, why have you forsaken me?"

[p]The Sabbath is a weekly day of rest and/or time of worship in Judaism and Christianity based upon the story of the creation in the Hebrew Bible's Book of Genesis. It derives from the Hebrew *shabbat* and refers to the seventh day of the Creation when God rested.

in clothes that gleamed like lightning stood beside them. [5]In their fright the women bowed down with their faces to the ground, but the men said to them, "Why do you look for the living among the dead? [6]He is not here; he has risen! Remember how he told you, while he was still with you in Galilee: [7]'The Son of Man must be delivered into the hands of sinful men, be crucified and on the third day be raised again.'" [8]Then they remembered his words.

[9]When they came back from the tomb, they told all these things to the Eleven[q] and to all the others. [10]It was Mary Magdalene, Joanna, Mary the mother of James, and the others with them who told this to the apostles. [11]But they did not believe the women, because their words seemed to them like nonsense. [12]Peter, however, got up and ran to the tomb. Bending over, he saw the strips of linen lying by themselves, and he went away, wondering to himself what had happened.

On the Road to Emmaus

[13]Now that same day two of them were going to a village called Emmaus, about seven miles from Jerusalem. [14]They were talking with each other about everything that had happened. [15]As they talked and discussed these things with each other, Jesus himself came up and walked along with them; [16]but they were kept from recognizing him.

[17]He asked them, "What are you discussing together as you walk along?"

They stood still, their faces downcast. [18]One of them, named Cleopas, asked him, "Are you only a visitor to Jerusalem and do not know the things that have happened there in these days?"

[19]"What things?" he asked. "About Jesus of Nazareth," they replied. "He was a prophet, powerful in word and deed before God and all the people. [20]The chief priests and our rulers handed him over to be sentenced to death, and they crucified him; [21]but we had hoped that he was the one who was going to redeem Israel. And what is more, it is the third day since all this took place. [22]In addition, some of our women amazed us. They went to the tomb early this morning [23]but didn't find his body. They came and told us that they had seen a vision of angels, who said he was alive. [24]Then some of our companions went to the tomb and found it just as the women had said, but him they did not see."

[25]He said to them, "How foolish you are, and how slow of heart to believe all that the prophets have spoken! [26]Did not the Christ have to suffer these things and then enter his glory?" [27]And beginning with Moses and all the Prophets, he explained to them what was said in all the Scriptures concerning himself.

[28]As they approached the village to which they were going, Jesus acted

---

[q]The Eleven are the twelve apostles minus Judas Iscariot.

as if he were going farther. [29]But they urged him strongly, "Stay with us, for it is nearly evening; the day is almost over." So he went in to stay with them.

[30]When he was at the table with them, he took bread, gave thanks, broke it and began to give it to them. [31]Then their eyes were opened and they recognized him, and he disappeared from their sight. [32]They asked each other, "Were not our hearts burning within us while he talked with us on the road and opened the Scriptures to us?"

[33]They got up and returned at once to Jerusalem. There they found the Eleven and those with them, assembled together [34]and saying, "It is true! The Lord has risen and has appeared to Simon." [35]Then the two told what had happened on the way, and how Jesus was recognized by them when he broke the bread.

Jesus Appears to the Disciples

[36]While they were still talking about this, Jesus himself stood among them and said to them, "Peace be with you."

[37]They were startled and frightened, thinking they saw a ghost. [38]He said to them, "Why are you troubled, and why do doubts rise in your minds? [39]Look at my hands and my feet. It is I myself! Touch me and see; a ghost does not have flesh and bones, as you see I have."

[40]When he had said this, he showed them his hands and feet. [41]And while they still did not believe it because of joy and amazement, he asked them, "Do you have anything here to eat?" [42]They gave him a piece of broiled fish, [43]and he took it and ate it in their presence.

[44]He said to them, "This is what I told you while I was still with you: Everything must be fulfilled that is written about me in the Law of Moses, the Prophets and the Psalms."

[45]Then he opened their minds so they could understand the Scriptures. [46]He told them, "This is what is written: The Christ will suffer and rise from the dead on the third day, [47]and repentance and forgiveness of sins will be preached in his name to all nations, beginning at Jerusalem. [48]You are witnesses of these things. [49]I am going to send you what my Father has promised; but stay in the city until you have been clothed with power from on high."

The Ascension

[50]When he had led them out to the vicinity of Bethany, he lifted up his hands and blessed them. [51]While he was blessing them, he left them and was taken up into heaven. [52]Then they worshiped him and returned to Jerusalem with great joy. [53]And they stayed continually at the temple, praising God.

Vocabulary

CHAPTER 22		CHAPTER 23	CHAPTER 24
[1]unleavened	[25]Gentiles	[10]vehemently	[19]prophet
[1]Passover	[29]confer	[29]barren	[32]scriptures
[14]apostles	[37]transgressor	[29]womb	[47]repentance
[20]covenant	[39]disciple	[40]rebuke	
[22]decreed	[53]reigns	[47]centurion	

Discussion Questions

CHAPTER 22

1. This section of the Christian Bible focuses on the concept of resurrection. How do the excerpts in this text from the other major world religions, Judaism, Islam, Buddhism, Hinduism, address this concept, if at all?

2. Verse 1 says the chief priests and teachers of the law were "afraid of the people." Based upon the events of the story, what do you think the priests and teachers feared from the people?

3. Verse 3 says "Satan entered Judas." Who is Satan? Do you think this is to be taken literally? Explain.

4. In verse 37 Jesus says the prophesies said, "And he was numbered with the transgressors." What does this mean?

5. In verse 42 Jesus asks God, if it is possible, to take the cup from him. What is Jesus really asking here?

6. What do you verses 54-61 tell us about Peter?

7. In verse 71 the priests and teachers seem to conclude that Jesus is guilty of something. What is it?

CHAPTER 23

8. Why would Jesus' answer to Pilate's question in verse 3 be more upsetting to the priests and teachers than to Pilate?

9. Why didn't Jesus speak to Herod and respond to the charges against him?

10. Why do you think Pilate was reluctant to condemn Jesus?

CHAPTER 24

11. Much of religion depends upon a willingness to believe in the supernatural—to accept certain things on faith alone. What are some examples of the supernatural found in this chapter?

"DAY OF INFAMY" SPEECH

FRANKLIN DELANO ROOSEVELT

*This speech was delivered to the United States Congress by **President Franklin Delano Roosevelt** (1880-1945) on Monday, December 8, 1941, the day after an attack by naval and air forces of the Empire of Japan against U.S. military installations at Pearl Harbor, Hawaii. Approximately 2,400 Americans were killed and 1,300 wounded in the attack. President Roosevelt is asking the Congress, as required by the United States Constitution, for a declaration of war against Japan. Within an hour, the Congress, with one dissenting vote, had given the president the authority to go to war.*

Mr. Vice President, Mr. Speaker, members of the Senate and the House of Representatives:

[1]Yesterday, December 7, 1941—a date which will live in infamy—the United States of America was suddenly and deliberately attacked by naval and air forces of the Empire of Japan.

[2]The United States was at peace with that Nation and, at the solicitation of Japan, was still in conversation with its Government and its Emperor looking toward the maintenance of peace in the Pacific. Indeed, one hour after Japanese air squadrons had commenced bombing in Oahu, the Japanese Ambassador to the United States and his colleague delivered to the Secretary of State a formal reply to a recent American message. While this reply stated that it seemed useless to continue the existing diplomatic negotiations, it contained no threat or hint of war or armed attack.

[3]It will be recorded that the distance of Hawaii from Japan makes it obvious that the attack was deliberately planned many days or even weeks ago. During the intervening time the Japanese Government had deliberately sought to deceive the United States by false statements and expressions of hope for continued peace.

[4]The attack yesterday on the Hawaiian Islands has caused severe damage to American naval and military forces. Very many American lives have been lost. In addition American ships have been reported torpedoed on the high seas between San Francisco and Honolulu.

[5]Yesterday the Japanese Government also launched an attack against Malaya.

[6]Last night Japanese forces attacked Hong Kong.

[7]Last night Japanese forces attacked Guam.

[8]Last night Japanese forces attacked the Philippine Islands.

[9]Last night the Japanese attacked Midway Island.

[10]Japan has, therefore, undertaken a surprise offensive extending throughout the Pacific area. The facts of yesterday speak for themselves. The people of the United States have already formed their opinions and well understand the implications to the very life and safety of our Nation.

[11]As Commander-in-Chief of the Army and Navy I have directed that all measures be taken for our defense.

[12]Always will we remember the character of the onslaught against us.

[13]No matter how long it may take us to overcome this premeditated invasion, the American people in their righteous might will win through to absolute victory.

[14]I believe I interpret the will of the Congress and of the people when I assert that we will not only defend ourselves to the uttermost but will make very certain that this form of treachery shall never endanger us again.

[15]Hostilities exist. There is no blinking at the fact that our people, our territory, and our interests are in grave danger.

[16]With confidence in our armed forces—with the unbounded determination of our people—we will gain the inevitable triumph—so help us God.

[17]I ask that the Congress declare that since the unprovoked and dastardly attack by Japan on Sunday, December seventh, a state of war has existed between the United States and the Japanese Empire.

Franklin D. Roosevelt
The White House, December 8, 1941

Vocabulary

[1]infamy   [2]solicitation   [13]premeditated   [17]dastardly

Discussion Questions

1. Compare Roosevelt's sentence structure in paragraph 1 to paragraphs 5, 6, 7, 8 and 9. Why in paragraph 1 did he say, "The United States was attacked . . ." while in the other paragraphs he says, "Japanese forces attacked Hong Kong, etc."?

2. What is Roosevelt's purpose in including the details he presents in paragraphs 2 and 3?

3. In paragraphs 5 through 9 why do you think Roosevelt kept repeating "Japanese Forces attacked . . ." instead of simply saying, "Last night Japanese forces attacked Hong Kong, Guam, the Philippine Islands and Midway Island"?

4. What is the tone of this speech? What does the tone convey?

5. Look carefully at Roosevelt's diction—his choice of words. Which words strike you as being aggresively forceful?

6. Compare this speech to the one made by President George W. Bush after the 9/11/01 attacks included on page 81 of this text. How are they similar? How are they different?

THE DECLARATION OF INDEPENDENCE
THOMAS JEFFERSON AND OTHERS

*Helped by John Adams and Benjamin Franklin, **Thomas Jefferson** (1743-1826) was the primary author of the Declaration of Independence, whose ideas, in turn, he borrowed from Thomas Paine. He is considered the most conspicuous champion of political and religious freedom in American history. Among other accomplishments, he was the third president of the Untied States.*

[1]When in the Course of human events, it becomes necessary for one people to dissolve the political bands which have connected them with another, and to assume among equal station to which the Laws of Nature and of Nature's God entitle them, a decent respect to the opinions of mankind requires that they should declare the causes which impel them to the separation.

[2]We hold these truths to be self-evident, that all men are created equal, that they are endowed by their Creator with certain un-alienable Rights, that among these are Life, Liberty and the pursuit of Happiness. That to secure these rights, Governments are instituted among Men, deriving their just powers from the consent of the governed. That whenever any Form of Government becomes destructive of these ends, it is the Right of the People to alter or to abolish it, and to institute new Government, laying its foundation on such principles and organizing its powers in such form, as to them shall seem most likely to effect their Safety and Happiness. Prudence, indeed, will dictate that Governments long established should not be changed for light and transient causes; and accordingly all experience hath shewn, that mankind are more disposed to suffer, while evils are sufferable, than to right themselves by abolishing the forms to which they are accustomed. But when a long train of abuses and usurpations, pursuing invariably the same Object evinces a design to reduce them under absolute Despotism, it is their right, it is their duty, to throw off such Government, and to provide new Guards for their future security. Such has been the patient sufferance of these Colonies; and such is now the necessity which constrains them to alter their former Systems of Government. The history of the present King of Great Britain is a history of repeated injuries and usurpations, all having in direct object the establishment of an absolute Tyranny over these States. To prove this, let Facts be submitted to a candid world.

[3]He has refused his Assent to Laws, the most wholesome and necessary for the public good.

[4]He has forbidden his Government to pass Laws of immediate and press-

ing importance, unless suspended in their operation till his Assent should be obtained; and when so suspended, he has utterly neglected to attend to them.

[5]He has refused to pass other Laws for the accommodation of large districts of people, unless those people would relinquish the right of Representation in the Legislature, a right inestimable to them and formidable to tyrants only.

[6]He has called together legislative bodies at places unusual, uncomfortable, and distant from the depository of their Public Records, for the sole purpose of fatiguing them into compliance with his measures.

[7]He has dissolved Representative Houses repeatedly, for opposing with manly firmness his invasions on the rights of the people.

[8]He has refused for a long time, after such dissolutions, to cause others to be elected; whereby the Legislative Powers, incapable of Annihilation, have returned to the People at large for their exercise; the State remaining in the mean time exposed to all the dangers of invasion from without, and convulsions within.

[9]He has endeavoured to prevent the population of these States; for that purpose obstructing the Laws for Naturalization of Foreigners; refusing to pass others to encourage their migration hither, and raising the conditions of new Appropriations of Lands.

[10]He has obstructed the Administration of Justice, by refusing his Assent to Laws for establishing Judiciary Powers.

[11]He has made Judges dependent on his Will alone, for the tenure of their offices, and the amount and payment of their salaries.

[12]He has erected a multitude of New Offices, and sent hither swarms of Officers to harass our People, and eat out their substance.

[13]He has kept among us, in times of peace, Standing Armies without the Consent of our legislature.

[14]He has affected to render the Military independent of and superior to the Civil Power.

[15]He has combined with others to subject us to a Jurisdiction foreign to our constitution, and unacknowledged by our laws; giving his Assent to their acts of pretended legislation:

[16]For quartering large bodies of armed troops among us:

[17]For protecting them, by a mock Trial, from Punishment for any Murders which they should commit on the Inhabitants of these States:

[18]For cutting off our Trade with all parts of the world:

[19]For imposing taxes on us without our Consent:

[20]For depriving us in many cases, of the benefits of Trial by Jury;

[21]For transporting us beyond Seas to be tried for pretended offences:

[22]For abolishing the free System of English Laws in a neighbouring Province, establishing therein an Arbitrary government, and enlarging its Boundar-

ies so as to render it at once an example and fit instrument for introducing the same absolute rule into these Colonies:

[23]For taking away our Charters, abolishing our most valuable Laws, and altering fundamentally the Forms of our Governments:

[24]For suspending our own Legislature, and declaring themselves invested with Power to legislate for us in all cases whatsoever.

[25]He has abdicated Government here, by declaring us out of his Protection and waging War against us.

[26]He has plundered our seas, ravaged our Coasts, burnt our towns, and destroyed the lives of our people.

[27]He is at this time transporting large armies of foreign mercenaries to compleat the works of death, desolation and tyranny, already begun with circumstances of Cruelty & perfidy scarcely paralleled in the most barbarous ages, and totally unworthy the Head of a civilized nation.

[28]He has constrained our fellow Citizens taken Captive on the high Seas to bear Arms against their Country, to become the executioners of their friends and Brethren, or to fall themselves by their Hands.

[29]He has excited domestic insurrections amongst us, and has endeavoured to bring on the inhabitants of our frontiers, the merciless Indian Savages, whose known rule of warfare, is an undistinguished destruction of all ages, sexes and conditions.

[30]In every stage of these Oppressions We have Petitioned for Redress in the most humble terms: Our repeated Petitions have been answered only by repeated injury. A Prince, whose character is thus marked by every act which may define a Tyrant, is unfit to be the ruler of a free People.

[31]Nor have We been wanting in attention to our British brethren. We have warned them from time to time of attempts by their legislature to extend an unwarrantable jurisdiction over us. We have reminded them of the circumstances of our emigration and settlement here. We have appealed to their native justice and magnanimity, and we have conjured them by the ties of our common kindred to disavow these usurpations, which would inevitably interrupt our connections and correspondence. They too have been deaf to the voice of justice and of consanguinity. We must, therefore, acquiesce in the necessity, which denounces our Separation, and hold them, as we hold the rest of mankind, Enemies in War, in Peace Friends.

[32]We, THEREFORE, the Representatives of the UNITED STATES OF AMERICA, in General Congress, Assembled, appealing to the Supreme judge of the world for the rectitude of our intentions, do, in the Name, and by Authority of the good People of these Colonies, solemnly publish and declare, That these United Colonies are, and of Right ought to be FREE AND INDEPENDENT STATES; that they are Absolved from all Allegiance to the British Crown and that all political connection between them and the State of Great Britain, is and ought to be totally

dissolved; and that as Free and Independent States, they have full Power to levy War, conclude Peace, contract Alliances, establish Commerce, and to do all other Acts and Things which Independent States may of right do. And for the support of this Declaration, with a firm reliance on the Protection of Divine Providence, we mutually pledge to each other our Lives, our Fortunes, and our sacred Honor.

Vocabulary

[1]impel
[2]candid
[10]judiciary
[30]magnanimity

[2]unalienable
[3]assent
[11]tenure
[30]conjured

[2]deriving
[5]inestimable
[23]invested
[30]kindred

[2]transient
[5]formidable
[24]abdicated
[30]disavow

[2]usurpations
[6]depository
[26]perfidy
[30]consanguinity

[2]evinces
[8]dissolutions
[27]brethren
[30]acquiesce

[2]despotism
[8]annihilation
[29]redress
[31]rectitude

[2]constrains
[9]hither
[30]emigration
[31]absolved

[2]tyranny

Discussion Questions

1. In the first paragraph of this document, what reason does Jefferson give for the publication of this declaration?

2. For what specific audiences are Jefferson and the other authors publishing this document?

3. List ten of the specific grievances against the King of Great Britain that Jefferson and the others cite as part of their reason for declaring their independence.

4. Is the Declaration of Independence a radical document? Explain.

5. What issues of equality did the Declaration of Independence fail to resolve?

6. In modern political terms, would Jefferson be considered a liberal or a conservative? Explain.

7. What overall impact has the Declaration of Independence had on our country? On the nations of the world?

DECLARATION OF SENTIMENTS
Adopted by the Seneca Falls Convention, 1848

ELIZABETH CADY STANTON AND OTHERS

Elizabeth Cady Stanton (1815-1902) was the driving force behind the 1848 Women's Suffragette Convention, and for the next fifty years played a leading role in the women's rights movement. Stanton co-authored with Matilda Joslyn Gage and Susan B. Anthony the first three volumes of A History of Woman Suffrage. She married reformer Henry Stanton in 1840, insisting that the word "obey" be omitted from their wedding vows; they had seven children.

[1]When, in the course of human events, it becomes necessary for one portion of the family of man to assume among the people of the earth a position different from that which they have hitherto occupied, but one to which the laws of nature and of nature's God entitle them, a decent respect to the opinions of mankind requires that they should declare the causes that impel them to such a course.

[2]We hold these truths to be self-evident: that all men and women are created equal; that they are endowed by their Creator with certain inalienable rights; that among these are life, liberty, and the pursuit of happiness; that to secure these rights governments are instituted, deriving their just powers from the consent of the governed. Whenever any form of government becomes destructive of these ends, it is the right of those who suffer from it to refuse allegiance to it, and to insist upon the institution of a new government, laying its foundation on such principles, and organizing its powers in such form, as to them shall seem most likely to effect their safety and happiness.

[3]Prudence, indeed, will dictate that governments long established should not be changed for light and transient causes and accordingly all experience hath shown that mankind are more disposed to suffer, while evils are sufferable, than to right themselves by abolishing the forms to which they were accustomed. But when a long train of abuses and usurpations, pursuing invariably the same object, evinces a design to reduce them under absolute despotism, it is their duty to throw off such government, and to provide new guards for their future security. Such has been the patient sufferance of the women under this government, and such is now the necessity which constrains them to demand the equal station to which they are entitled.

[4]The history of mankind is a history of repeated injuries and usurpations on the part of man toward woman, having in direct object the establishment of

an absolute tyranny over her. To prove this, let facts be submitted to a candid world.

[5]He has never permitted her to exercise her inalienable right to the elective franchise.

[6]He has compelled her to submit to laws, in the formation of which she had no voice.

[7]He has withheld from her rights which are given to the most ignorant and degraded men—both natives and foreigners.

[8]Having deprived her of this first right of a citizen, the elective franchise, thereby leaving her without representation in the halls of legislation, he has oppressed her on all sides.

[9]He has made her, if married, in the eye of the law, civilly dead.

[10]He has taken from her all right in property, even to the wages she earns.

[11]He has made her, morally, an irresponsible being, as she can commit many crimes with impunity, provided they be done in the presence of her husband. In the covenant of marriage, she is compelled to promise obedience to her husband, he becoming, to all intents and purposes, her master—the law giving him power to deprive her of her liberty, and to administer chastisement.

[12]He has so framed the laws of divorce, as to what shall be the proper causes, and in case of separation, to whom the guardianship of the children shall be given, as to be wholly regardless of the happiness of women—the law, in all cases, going upon a false supposition of the supremacy of man, and giving all power into his hands.

[13]After depriving her of all rights as a married woman, if single, and the owner of property, he has taxed her to support a government which recognizes her only when her property can be profitable to it.

[14]He has monopolized nearly all the profitable employments, and from those she is permitted to follow, she receives but a scanty remuneration. He closes against her all the avenues to wealth and distinction which he considers most honorable to himself. As a teacher of theology, medicine, or law, she is not known.

[15]He has denied her the facilities for obtaining a thorough education, all colleges being closed against her.

[16]He allows her in Church, as well as State, but a subordinate position, claiming Apostolic authority for her exclusion from the ministry, and, with some exceptions, from any public participation in the affairs of the Church.

[17]He has created a false public sentiment by giving to the world a different code of morals for men and women, by which moral delinquencies which exclude women from society, are not only tolerated, but deemed of little account in man.

[18]He has usurped the prerogative of Jehovah himself, claiming it as his right to assign for a sphere of action, when that belongs to conscience and to her God.

[19]He has endeavored, in every way that he could, to destroy her confidence in her own powers, to lessen her self-respect, and to make willing to lead a dependent and abject life. Now, in view of this entire disfranchisement one-half the people of this country, their social and religious degradation—in view of the unjust laws above mentioned, and because women do feel themselves aggrieved, oppressed, and fraudulently deprived of their most sacred rights, we insist that they have immediate admission to all the rights and privileges which belong to them as citizens of the United States.

[20]In entering upon the great work before us, we anticipate no small amount of misconception, misrepresentation, and ridicule; but we shall use every instrumentality within our power to effect our object. We shall employ agents, circulate tracts, petition the State and National legislatures, and endeavor to enlist the pulpit and the press in our behalf. We hope this Convention will be followed by a series of Conventions embracing every part of the country.

Signed: Lucretia Mott, Harriet Cady Eaton, Margaret Pryor, Elizabeth Cady Stanton, Eunice Newton Foote, Mary Ann McClintock, Margaret Schooley, Martha C. Wright, Jane C. Hunt, Amy Post, Catharine F. Stebbins, Mary Ann Frink, Lydia Mount, Delia Mathews, Catharine C. Paine, Elizabeth W. McClintock, Malvina Seymour, Phoebe Mosher, Catharine Shaw, Deborah Scott, Sarah Hallowell, Mary McClintock, Mary Gilbert, Sophrone Taylor, Cynthia Davis, Hannah Plant, Lucy Jones, Sarah Whitney, Mary H. Hallowell, Elizabeth Conklin, Sally Pitcher, Mary Conklin, Susan Quinn, Mary S. Mirror, Phebe King, Julia Ann Drake, Charlotte Woodward, Martha Underhill, Dorothy Mathews, Eunice Barker, Sarah R. Woods, Lydia Gild, Sarah Hoffman, Elizabeth Leslie, Martha Ridley, Rachel D. Bonnel, Betsey Tewksbury, Rhoda Palmer, Margaret Jenkins, Cynthia Fuller, Mary Martin, P. A. Culvert , Susan R. Doty, Rebecca Race, Sarah A. Mosher, Mary E. Vail, Lucy Spalding, Lavinia Latham, Sarah Smith, Eliza Martin, Maria E. Wilbur, Elizabeth D. Smith, Caroline Barker, Ann Porter, Experience Gibbs, Antoinette E. Segur, Hannah J. Latham, Sarah Sisson.

The following are the names of the gentlemen present in favor of the movement: Richard P. Hunt, Samuel D. Tillman, Justin Williams, Elisha Foote, Frederick Douglass, Henry Seymour, Henry W. Seymour, David Spalding, William G. Barker, Elias J. Doty, John Jones, William S. Dell, James Mott, William Burroughs, Robert Smallbridge, Jacob Mathews, Charles L. Hoskins, Thomas McClintock, Saron Phillips, Jacob P. Chamberlain, Jonathan Metcalf, Nathan J. Milliken, S.E. Woodworth, Edward F. Underhill, George W. Pryor, Joel D. Bunker, Isaac Van Tassel, Thomas Dell, E. W. Capron, Stephen Shear, Henry Hatley, Azaliah Schooley.

Vocabulary

[1]hitherto   [3]evinces   [11]compel   [16]Apostolic

[1]impel   [3]despotism   [11]covenant   [19]abject

[2]inalienable   [3]constrain   [11]chastisement   [19]aggrieved

[2]deriving   [3]station   [12]supposition   [20]instrumentality

[3]transient   [5]elective franchise   [14]remuneration   [20]tract

[3]usurpations   [11]impunity

Discussion Questions

1. The Declaration of Sentiments contains a list of 12 "repeated injuries and usurpations on the part of man toward woman." Choose three of these and explain what the grievances mean. What are your own thoughts about them?

2. Two of the women who wrote the declaration were Lucretia Mott and Elizabeth Cady Stanton. What were their backgrounds? What future contributions did they make to the suffrage movement?

3. Compare the first four paragraphs of the "Declaration of Sentiments" to the first two paragraphs of the Declaration of Independence. Why do you think the women wrote their document in such a similar fashion? Which words are the same and which are different? Discuss.

4. Using sources other than your textbook, explain the effect that this work had on American society. Did it achieve what the writers and signers intended it to accomplish?

DEVOLUTION

H. ALLEN ORR

*Noted evolutionary geneticist **H. Allen Orr** is University Professor and Shirley Cox Kearns Professor of Biology at the University of Rochester in upstate New York. Professor Orr is widely published in leading scientific journals, including* Nature *and* Science, *and is the coauthor of* Speciation, *a work that discusses the genetics of adaptation and the role of natural and sexual selection in the development of species. Dr. Orr is a prominent figure in discussions about the relationship between science, religion and philosophy and has been a leading figure among scientists opposed to the "Intelligent Design" movement. This article originally appeared in the* New Yorker *magazine, May 30, 2005.*

[1]If you are in ninth grade and live in Dover, Pennsylvania, you are learning things in your biology class that differ considerably from what your peers just a few miles away are learning. In particular, you are learning that Darwin's theory of evolution provides just one possible explanation of life, and that another is provided by something called intelligent design. You are being taught this not because of a recent breakthrough in some scientist's laboratory but because the Dover Area School District's board mandates it. In October, 2004, the board decreed that "students will be made aware of gaps/problems in Darwin's theory and of other theories of evolution including, but not limited to, intelligent design."[a]

[2]While the events in Dover have received a good deal of attention as a sign of the political times, there has been surprisingly little discussion of the science that's said to underlie the theory of intelligent design, often called I.D.

---

[a]Professor Orr refers to a resolution passed 6-3 by the Dover, PA Board of Education requiring a statement to be read in ninth grade science classes at Dover High School that said in part,

Because Darwin's Theory is a theory, it is still being tested as new evidence is discovered. The Theory is not a fact. Gaps in the Theory exist for which there is no evidence. A theory is defined as a well-tested explanation that unifies a broad range of observations.
Intelligent design is an explanation of the origin of life that differs from Darwin's view. The reference book, *Of Pandas and People* is available for students to see if they would like to explore this view in an effort to gain an understanding of what intelligent design actually involves.
As is true with any theory, students are encouraged to keep an open mind. The school leaves the discussion of the origins of life to individual students and their families.

The three Board members who voted against the resolution resigned in protest when it passed, and

Many scientists avoid discussing I.D. for strategic reasons. If a scientific claim can be loosely defined as one that scientists take seriously enough to debate, then engaging the intelligent-design movement on scientific grounds, they worry, cedes what it most desires: recognition that its claims are legitimate scientific ones.

[3]Meanwhile, proposals hostile to evolution are being considered in more than twenty states; earlier this month, a bill was introduced into the New York State Assembly calling for instruction in intelligent design for all public-school students. The Kansas State Board of Education is weighing new standards, drafted by supporters of intelligent design, that would encourage schoolteachers to challenge Darwinism. Senator Rick Santorum, a Pennsylvania Republican, has argued that "intelligent design is a legitimate scientific theory that should be taught in science classes." An I.D.-friendly amendment that he sponsored to the No Child Left Behind Act—requiring public schools to help students understand why evolution "generates so much continuing controversy"—was overwhelmingly approved in the Senate. (The amendment was not included in the version of the bill that was signed into law, but similar language did appear in a conference report that accompanied it.) In the past few years, college students across the country have formed Intelligent Design and Evolution Awareness chapters. Clearly, a policy of limited scientific engagement has failed. So just what is this movement?

[4]First of all, intelligent design is not what people often assume it is. For one thing, I.D. is not Biblical literalism. Unlike earlier generations of creationists—the so-called Young Earthers and scientific creationists—proponents of intelligent design do not believe that the universe was created in six days, that Earth is ten thousand years old, or that the fossil record was deposited during Noah's flood. (Indeed, they shun the label "creationism" altogether.) Nor does I.D. flatly reject evolution: adherents freely admit that some evolutionary change occurred during the history of life on Earth. Although the movement

district science teachers refused to read the statement to their classes, believing it to be "false information." A school administrator read it to the classes. Subsequently eleven parents of Dover students, supported by attorneys from the American Civil Liberties Union (ACLU), sued the Board in an effort to overturn the requirement on the basis of inappropriately bringing religion into the classroom. Initially, the Discovery Institute had been advising the Board, but when the case went to trial, they curtailed their support, essentially because some members of the Board had made statements confirming their religious motivation in passing the resolution. After a six-week trial in federal district court, Judge John E. Jones ruled against the Board and the requirement to read the statement was overturned in December 2005. The six Board members who voted for the requirement were all voted off the Board in the 2005 school election, and the new Board indicated it would not pursue an appeal since it disagreed with the policy. The new Board was required to pay just over $1,000,000 in settlement costs and plaintiff legal fees.

is loosely allied with, and heavily funded by, various conservative Christian groups—and although I.D. plainly maintains that life was created—it is generally silent about the identity of the creator.

[5]The movement's main positive claim is that there are things in the world, most notably life, that cannot be accounted for by known natural causes and show features that, in any other context, we would attribute to intelligence. Living organisms are too complex to be explained by any natural—or, more precisely, by any mindless—process. Instead, the design inherent in organisms can be accounted for only by invoking a designer, and one who is very, very smart.

[6]All of which puts I.D. squarely at odds with Darwin. Darwin's theory of evolution was meant to show how the fantastically complex features of organisms—eyes, beaks, brains—could arise without the intervention of a designing mind. According to Darwinism, evolution largely reflects the combined action of random mutation and natural selection. A random mutation in an organism, like a random change in any finely tuned machine, is almost always bad. That's why you don't, screwdriver in hand, make arbitrary changes to the insides of your television. But, once in a great while, a random mutation in the DNA that makes up an organism's genes slightly improves the function of some organ and thus the survival of the organism. In a species whose eye amounts to nothing more than a primitive patch of light-sensitive cells, a mutation that causes this patch to fold into a cup shape might have a survival advantage. While the old type of organism can tell only if the lights are on, the new type can detect the *direction* of any source of light or shadow. Since shadows sometimes mean predators, that can be valuable information. The new, improved type of organism will, therefore, be more common in the next generation. That's natural selection. Repeated over billions of years, this process of incremental improvement should allow for the gradual emergence of organisms that are exquisitely adapted to their environments and that look for all the world as though they were designed. By 1870, about a decade after "The Origin of Species" was published, nearly all biologists agreed that life had evolved, and by 1940 or so most agreed that natural selection was a key force driving this evolution.

[7]Advocates of intelligent design point to two developments that in their view undermine Darwinism. The first is the molecular revolution in biology. Beginning in the nineteen-fifties, molecular biologists revealed a staggering and unsuspected degree of complexity within the cells that make up all life. This complexity, I.D.'s defenders argue, lies beyond the abilities of Darwinism to explain. Second, they claim that new mathematical findings cast doubt on the power of natural selection. Selection may play a role in evolution, but it cannot accomplish what biologists suppose it can.

[8]These claims have been championed by a tireless group of writers, most of them associated with the Center for Science and Culture at the Dis-

covery Institute, a Seattle-based think tank that sponsors projects in science, religion, and national defense, among other areas. The center's fellows and advisers—including the emeritus law professor Phillip E. Johnson, the philosopher Stephen C. Meyer, and the biologist Jonathan Wells—have published an astonishing number of articles and books that decry the ostensibly sad state of Darwinism and extol the virtues of the design alternative. But Johnson, Meyer, and Wells, while highly visible, are mainly strategists and popularizers. The scientific leaders of the design movement are two scholars, one a biochemist and the other a mathematician. To assess intelligent design is to assess their arguments.

[9]Michael J. Behe, a professor of biological sciences at Lehigh University (and a senior fellow at the Discovery Institute), is a biochemist who writes technical papers on the structure of DNA. He is the most prominent of the small circle of scientists working on intelligent design, and his arguments are by far the best known. His book *Darwin's Black Box* (1996) was a surprise best-seller and was named by *National Review* as one of the hundred best nonfiction books of the twentieth century. (A little calibration may be useful here; "The Starr Report" also made the list.)[b]

[10]Not surprisingly, Behe's doubts about Darwinism begin with biochemistry. Fifty years ago, he says, any biologist could tell stories like the one about the eye's evolution. But such stories, Behe notes, invariably began with cells, whose own evolutionary origins were essentially left unexplained. This was harmless enough as long as cells weren't qualitatively more complex than the larger, more visible aspects of the eye. Yet when biochemists began to dissect the inner workings of the cell, what they found floored them. A cell is packed full of exceedingly complex structures—hundreds of microscopic machines, each performing a specific job. The "Give me a cell and I'll give you an eye" story told by Darwinists, he says, began to seem suspect: starting with a cell was starting ninety per cent of the way to the finish line.

[11]Behe's main claim is that cells are complex not just in degree but in kind. Cells contain structures that are "irreducibly complex." This means that if you remove any single part from such a structure, the structure no longer functions. Behe offers a simple, nonbiological example of an irreducibly complex object: the mousetrap. A mousetrap has several parts—platform, spring, catch, hammer, and hold-down bar—and all of them have to be in place for the trap to work. If you remove the spring from a mousetrap, it isn't slightly worse at killing mice; it doesn't kill them at all. So, too, with the bacterial

---

[b] "The Starr Report" was a 445-page document delivered to the U.S. Congress Sept. 11, 1998 by Independent Counsel Kenneth Starr. The report contained details of Democratic President Bill Clinton's sexual relationship with 22-year-old White House intern Monica Lewinsky. The *National Review* is a politically conservative publication.

flagellum, Behe argues. This flagellum is a tiny propeller attached to the back of some bacteria. Spinning at more than twenty thousand r.p.m.s, it motors the bacterium through its aquatic world. The flagellum comprises roughly thirty different proteins, all precisely arranged, and if any one of them is removed the flagellum stops spinning.

[12]In *Darwin's Black Box*, Behe maintained that irreducible complexity presents Darwinism with "unbridgeable chasms." How, after all, could a gradual process of incremental improvement build something like a flagellum, which needs *all* its parts in order to work? Scientists, he argued, must face up to the fact that "many biochemical systems cannot be built by natural selection working on mutations." In the end, Behe concluded that irreducibly complex cells arise the same way as irreducibly complex mousetraps—someone designs them. As he put it in a recent *Times* Op-Ed piece: "If it looks, walks, and quacks like a duck, then, absent compelling evidence to the contrary, we have warrant to conclude it's a duck. Design should not be overlooked simply because it's so obvious." In *Darwin's Black Box*, Behe speculated that the designer might have assembled the first cell, essentially solving the problem of irreducible complexity, after which evolution might well have proceeded by more or less conventional means. Under Behe's brand of creationism, you might still be an ape that evolved on the African savanna; it's just that your cells harbor micro-machines engineered by an unnamed intelligence some four billion years ago.

[13]But Behe's principal argument soon ran into trouble. As biologists pointed out, there are several different ways that Darwinian evolution can build irreducibly complex systems. In one, elaborate structures may evolve for one reason and then get co-opted for some entirely different, irreducibly complex function. Who says those thirty flagellar proteins weren't present in bacteria long before bacteria sported flagella? They may have been performing other jobs in the cell and only later got drafted into flagellum-building. Indeed, there's now strong evidence that several flagellar proteins once played roles in a type of molecular pump found in the membranes of bacterial cells.

[14]Behe doesn't consider this sort of "indirect" path to irreducible complexity—in which parts perform one function and then switch to another—terribly plausible. And he essentially rules out the alternative possibility of a direct Darwinian path: a path, that is, in which Darwinism builds an irreducibly complex structure while selecting all along for the same biological function. But biologists have shown that direct paths to irreducible complexity are possible, too. Suppose a part gets added to a system merely because the part improves the system's performance; the part is not, at this stage, essential for function. But, because subsequent evolution builds on this addition, a part that was at first just advantageous might *become* essential. As this process is repeated through evolutionary time, more and more parts that were once merely beneficial become necessary. This idea was first set forth by H. J. Muller, the Nobel Prize-

winning geneticist, in 1939, but it's a familiar process in the development of human technologies. We add new parts like global-positioning systems to cars not because they're necessary but because they're nice. But no one would be surprised if, in fifty years, computers that rely on G.P.S. actually drove our cars. At that point, G.P.S. would no longer be an attractive option; it would be an essential piece of automotive technology. It's important to see that this process is thoroughly Darwinian: each change might well be small and each represents an improvement.

[15]Design theorists have made some concessions to these criticisms. Behe has confessed to "sloppy prose" and said he hadn't meant to imply that irreducibly complex systems "by definition" cannot evolve gradually. "I quite agree that my argument against Darwinism does not add up to a logical proof," he says—though he continues to believe that Darwinian paths to irreducible complexity are exceedingly unlikely. Behe and his followers now emphasize that, while irreducibly complex systems can in principle evolve, biologists can't reconstruct in convincing detail just how any such system did evolve.

[16]What counts as a sufficiently detailed historical narrative, though, is altogether subjective. Biologists actually know a great deal about the evolution of biochemical systems, irreducibly complex or not. It's significant, for instance, that the proteins that typically make up the parts of these systems are often similar to one another. (Blood clotting—another of Behe's examples of irreducible complexity—involves at least twenty proteins, several of which are similar, and all of which are needed to make clots, to localize or remove clots, or to prevent the runaway clotting of all blood.) And biologists understand why these proteins are so similar. Each gene in an organism's genome encodes a particular protein. Occasionally, the stretch of DNA that makes up a particular gene will get accidentally copied, yielding a genome that includes two versions of the gene. Over many generations, one version of the gene will often keep its original function while the other one slowly changes by mutation and natural selection, picking up a new, though usually related, function. This process of "gene duplication" has given rise to entire families of proteins that have similar functions; they often act in the same biochemical pathway or sit in the same cellular structure. There's no doubt that gene duplication plays an extremely important role in the evolution of biological complexity.

[17]It's true that when you confront biologists with a particular complex structure like the flagellum, they sometimes have a hard time saying which part appeared before which other parts. But then it can be hard, with any complex historical process, to reconstruct the exact order in which events occurred, especially when, as in evolution, the addition of new parts encourages the modification of old ones. When you're looking at a bustling urban street, for example, you probably can't tell which shop went into business first. This is partly be-

cause many businesses now depend on each other and partly because new shops trigger changes in old ones (the new sushi place draws twenty-somethings who demand wireless Internet at the café next door). But it would be a little rash to conclude that all the shops must have begun business on the same day or that some Unseen Urban Planner had carefully determined just which business went where.

[18]The other leading theorist of the new creationism, William A. Dembski, holds a Ph.D. in mathematics, another in philosophy, and a master of divinity in theology. He has been a research professor in the conceptual foundations of science at Baylor University and was recently appointed to the new Center for Science and Theology at Southern Baptist Theological Seminary. (He is a longtime senior fellow at the Discovery Institute as well.) Dembski publishes at a staggering pace. His books—including *The Design Inference*; *Intelligent Design*; *No Free Lunch;* and *The Design Revolution*—are generally well written and packed with provocative ideas.

[19]According to Dembski, a complex object must be the result of intelligence if it was the product neither of chance nor of necessity. The novel "Moby Dick," for example, didn't arise by chance (Melville didn't scribble random letters), and it wasn't the necessary consequence of a physical law (unlike, say, the fall of an apple). It was, instead, the result of Melville's intelligence. Dembski argues that there is a reliable way to recognize such products of intelligence in the natural world. We can conclude that an object was intelligently designed, he says, if it shows "specified complexity"—complexity that matches an "independently given pattern." The sequence of letters "jkxvcjudoplvm" is certainly complex: if you randomly type thirteen letters, you are very unlikely to arrive at this particular sequence. But it isn't *specified:* it doesn't match any independently given sequence of letters. If, on the other hand, I ask you for the first sentence of "Moby Dick" and you type the letters "callmeishmael," you have produced something that is both complex and specified. The sequence you typed is unlikely to arise by chance alone, and it matches an independent target sequence (the one written by Melville). Dembski argues that specified complexity, when expressed mathematically, provides an unmistakable signature of intelligence. Things like "callmeishmael," he points out, just don't arise in the real world without acts of intelligence. If organisms show specified complexity, therefore, we can conclude that they are the handiwork of an intelligent agent.

[20]For Dembski, it's telling that the sophisticated machines we find in organisms match up in astonishingly precise ways with recognizable human technologies. The eye, for example, has a familiar, cameralike design, with recognizable parts—a pinhole opening for light, a lens, and a surface on which to project an image—all arranged just as a human engineer would arrange them. And the flagellum has a motor design, one that features recognizable O-rings, a

rotor, and a drive shaft. Specified complexity, he says, is there for all to see.

[21]Dembski's second major claim is that certain mathematical results cast doubt on Darwinism at the most basic conceptual level. In 2002, he focused on so-called No Free Lunch, or N.F.L., theorems, which were derived in the late nineties by the physicists David H. Wolpert and William G. Macready. These theorems relate to the efficiency of different "search algorithms." Consider a search for high ground on some unfamiliar, hilly terrain. You're on foot and it's a moonless night; you've got two hours to reach the highest place you can. How to proceed? One sensible search algorithm might say, "Walk uphill in the steepest possible direction; if no direction uphill is available, take a couple of steps to the left and try again." This algorithm insures that you're generally moving upward. Another search algorithm—a so-called blind search algorithm—might say, "Walk in a random direction." This would sometimes take you uphill but sometimes down. Roughly, the N.F.L. theorems prove the surprising fact that, averaged over all possible terrains, no search algorithm is better than any other. In some landscapes, moving uphill gets you to higher ground in the allotted time, while in other landscapes moving randomly does, but on average neither outperforms the other.

[22]Now, Darwinism can be thought of as a search algorithm. Given a problem—adapting to a new disease, for instance—a population uses the Darwinian algorithm of random mutation plus natural selection to search for a solution (in this case, disease resistance). But, according to Dembski, the N.F.L. theorems prove that this Darwinian algorithm is no better than any other when confronting all possible problems. It follows that, over all, Darwinism is no better than blind search, a process of utterly random change unaided by any guiding force like natural selection. Since we don't expect blind change to build elaborate machines showing an exquisite coordination of parts, we have no right to expect Darwinism to do so, either. Attempts to sidestep this problem by, say, carefully constraining the class of challenges faced by organisms inevitably involve sneaking in the very kind of order that we're trying to explain— something Dembski calls the displacement problem. In the end, he argues, the N.F.L. theorems and the displacement problem mean that there's only one plausible source for the design we find in organisms: intelligence. Although Dembski is somewhat noncommittal, he seems to favor a design theory in which an intelligent agent programmed design into early life, or even into the early universe. This design then unfolded through the long course of evolutionary time, as microbes slowly morphed into man.

[23]Dembski's arguments have been met with tremendous enthusiasm in the I.D. movement. In part, that's because an innumerate public is easily impressed by a bit of mathematics. Also, when Dembski is wielding his equations, he gets to play the part of the hard scientist busily correcting the errors of those soft-headed biologists. (Evolutionary biology actually features an

extraordinarily sophisticated body of mathematical theory, a fact not widely known because neither of evolution's great popularizers—Richard Dawkins and the late Stephen Jay Gould—did much math.) Despite all the attention, Dembski's mathematical claims about design and Darwin are almost entirely beside the point.

[24]The most serious problem in Dembski's account involves specified complexity. Organisms aren't trying to match any "independently given pattern": evolution has no goal, and the history of life isn't trying to get anywhere. If building a sophisticated structure like an eye increases the number of children produced, evolution may well build an eye. But if destroying a sophisticated structure like the eye increases the number of children produced, evolution will just as happily destroy the eye. Species of fish and crustaceans that have moved into the total darkness of caves, where eyes are both unnecessary and costly, often have degenerate eyes, or eyes that begin to form only to be covered by skin—crazy contraptions that no intelligent agent would design. Despite all the loose talk about design and machines, organisms aren't striving to realize some engineer's blueprint; they're striving (if they can be said to strive at all) only to have more offspring than the next fellow.

[25]Another problem with Dembski's arguments concerns the N.F.L. theorems. Recent work shows that these theorems don't hold in the case of co-evolution, when two or more species evolve in response to one another. And most evolution is surely co-evolution. Organisms do not spend most of their time adapting to rocks; they are perpetually challenged by, and adapting to, a rapidly changing suite of viruses, parasites, predators, and prey. A theorem that doesn't apply to these situations is a theorem whose relevance to biology is unclear. As it happens, David Wolpert, one of the authors of the N.F.L. theorems, recently denounced Dembski's use of those theorems as "fatally informal and imprecise." Dembski's apparent response has been a tactical retreat. In 2002, Dembski triumphantly proclaimed, "The No Free Lunch theorems dash any hope of generating specified complexity via evolutionary algorithms." Now he says, "I certainly never argued that the N.F.L. theorems provide a direct refutation of Darwinism."

[26]Those of us who have argued with I.D. in the past are used to such shifts of emphasis. But it's striking that Dembski's views on the history of life contradict Behe's. Dembski believes that Darwinism is incapable of building anything interesting; Behe seems to believe that, given a cell, Darwinism might well have built you and me. Although proponents of I.D. routinely inflate the significance of minor squabbles among evolutionary biologists (did the peppered moth evolve dark color as a defense against birds or for other reasons?), they seldom acknowledge their own, often major differences of opinion. In the end, it's hard to view intelligent design as a coherent movement in any but a political sense.

[27]It's also hard to view it as a real research program. Though people often picture science as a collection of clever theories, scientists are generally staunch pragmatists: to scientists, a good theory is one that inspires new experiments and provides unexpected insights into familiar phenomena. By this standard, Darwinism is one of the best theories in the history of science: it has produced countless important experiments (let's re-create a natural species in the lab—yes, that's been done) and sudden insight into once puzzling patterns (*that's* why there are no native land mammals on oceanic islands). In the nearly ten years since the publication of Behe's book, by contrast, I.D. has inspired no nontrivial experiments and has provided no surprising insights into biology. As the years pass, intelligent design looks less and less like the science it claimed to be and more and more like an extended exercise in polemics.

[28]In 1999, a document from the Discovery Institute was posted, anonymously, on the Internet. This "Wedge Document," as it came to be called, described not only the institute's long-term goals but its strategies for accomplishing them. The document begins by labeling the idea that human beings are created in the image of God "one of the bedrock principles on which Western civilization was built." It goes on to decry the catastrophic legacy of Darwin, Marx, and Freud—the alleged fathers of a "materialistic conception of reality" that eventually "infected virtually every area of our culture." The mission of the Discovery Institute's scientific wing is then spelled out: "nothing less than the overthrow of materialism and its cultural legacies." It seems fair to conclude that the Discovery Institute has set its sights a bit higher than, say, reconstructing the origins of the bacterial flagellum.

[29]The intelligent-design community is usually far more circumspect in its pronouncements. This is not to say that it eschews discussion of religion; indeed, the intelligent-design literature regularly insists that Darwinism represents a thinly veiled attempt to foist a secular religion—godless materialism—on Western culture. As it happens, the idea that Darwinism is yoked to atheism, though popular, is also wrong. Of the five founding fathers of twentieth-century evolutionary biology—Ronald Fisher, Sewall Wright, J. B. S. Haldane, Ernst Mayr, and Theodosius Dobzhansky—one was a devout Anglican who preached sermons and published articles in church magazines, one a practicing Unitarian, one a dabbler in Eastern mysticism, one an apparent atheist, and one a member of the Russian Orthodox Church and the author of a book on religion and science. Pope John Paul II himself acknowledged in a 1996 address to the Pontifical Academy of Sciences that new research "leads to the recognition of the theory of evolution as more than a hypothesis." Whatever larger conclusions one thinks *should* follow from Darwinism, the historical fact is that evolution and religion have often coexisted. As the philosopher Michael Ruse observes, "It is simply not the case that people take up evolution in the morning, and become atheists as an encore in the afternoon."

[30]Biologists aren't alarmed by intelligent design's arrival in Dover and elsewhere because they have all sworn allegiance to atheistic materialism; they're alarmed because intelligent design is junk science. Meanwhile, more than eighty per cent of Americans say that God either created human beings in their present form or guided their development. As a succession of intelligent-design proponents appeared before the Kansas State Board of Education earlier this month, it was possible to wonder whether the movement's scientific coherence was beside the point. Intelligent design has come this far by faith.

Vocabulary

[2]cede	[9]calibration	[16]genome	[28]catastrophic
[5]inherent	[10]invariably	[18]divinity	[29]circumspect
[6]mutation	[11]qualitative	[21]algorithm	[29]eschews
[6]arbitrary	[11]comprises	[22]constrain	[29]foist
[6]incremental	[12]chasm	[22]noncommital	[29]secular
[6]exquisite	[13]co-opt	[24]crustaceans	[29]Pontifical
[8]emeritus	[14]plausible	[27]pragmatist	[29]hypothesis
[8]decry	[14]advantageous	[27]phenomena	[30]coherence
[8]ostensibly	[14]geneticist	[27]polemics	
[8]extol	[15]concession		

Discussion Questions

1. According to Professor Orr why have most scientists avoided entering into debates about Intelligent Design?

2. On page 446 in this text is a reproduction of the front page of a newspaper carrying a story about the "Scopes Monkey Trial." Research some details of that trial and explain any connections you see between that trial and the Dover Board of Education trial explained in footnote [a] above.

3. What do you think Orr's motivation was for writing this article and submitting it to the *New Yorker* magazine for publication?

4. What is the underlying point (or connotation) of the statement "[evolution] generates so much continuing controversy" in paragraph 3?

5. Explain "Intelligent Design" as you understand it.

6. Explain the differences between biblical literalism and Intelligent Design (paragraph 4).

7. Also in paragraph 4, what does Orr say is the stance of Intelligent Design proponents regarding the appearance of life on earth?

8. Summarize Darwin's explanation of the development of life on earth (see pages 439-440).

9. What is "irreducible complexity"? What analogy does Professor Behe use to clarify this term?

10. Orr says in paragraph 22 that while Professor Dembski "is somewhat noncommittal, he seems to favor" which design theory?

11. Compare Behe's and Dembski's views on the origin and development of human life.

12. What does Orr mean when he says that scientists are "generally staunch pragmatists" in paragraph 27?

13. What point does Orr make in paragraph 29?

14. Explain the significance of the Discovery Institute's "Wedge Document" to the points Professor Orr makes in this article about the motivation of those who advocate Intelligent Design as a legitimate scientific theory.

15. How does Professor Orr conclude his essay? Is it effective? Explain.

THE DISCOVERY OF THE BRAIN AREA
THAT CONTROLS INTELLIGENCE
SIR SIDNEY WEINSTEIN

Sir Sidney Weinstein (1921-   ) earned his Ph.D. from New York University. He is the author of over 100 scholarly articles and books, and inventor of the Weinstein-Semmes Athesiometer, a device that tests for peripheral nervous system damage associated with diagnosing diabetes, leprosy and amyotropic lateral sclerosis (Lou Gehrig's disease) among other disorders. In 1994 he was knighted by the Knights of Malta for his "contributions to humanity," and currently serves as the editor-in-chief of the International Journal of Neuroscience.

[1]For me research is the job that is the most fun and yields the most rewards. It deals with discovery of unknown and often quite unexpected facts. I must confess what exhilarated me most one day was the discovery of the part of the brain that was most concerned with intelligence. Most people think the entire brain is sort of one large bowl of porridge, with trillions of cells that all interconnect and act in unison, but that is just not true. There are very specific areas that are concerned with movement, others with smell, and still others with hearing or vision. But are there areas that are used to help us think? Is there a specific area dedicated to intelligence"?

[2]This problem continued to intrigue me and one day I was fortunate to acquire the material to solve that problem. Two basic sets of data became available to me: the surgeons' drawings of the brain areas of combat veterans that had been injured during the war in a group of men I was studying. These were usually rapid drawings and notes of gunshot wounds that the surgeons had cleaned and bandaged after the injuries. The other critical data were the AGCT scores that the men had completed before they went into battle and the AGCT scores they achieved after they were wounded. The AGCT stands for Army General Classification Test, and is basically considered an intelligence test because it correlates very highly with the best known and most frequently used test of intelligence, The Wechsler Bellevue Test.

[3]I contacted the Army and requested the AGCT scores of all the men I was studying. Unfortunately, of the hundreds of medical records of men who had brain wounds, most had been thrown away by an eager major who wanted the space for other materials he considered more valuable. But I was lucky that 63 AGCT scores were still available. I was able to subtract the post-gunshot-

injury score for each man from the normal one they achieved when they first entered the Army, and using a statistical technique, selected those records of those who had sustained a severe loss of intelligence.

[4]Now I had two separate lists: a list of the men whose intelligence had been impaired and a list of men who had also been wounded in their brain but whose intelligence, nevertheless, remained intact. The next thing to do was separate them into two separate groups: those who had lost a significant degree of intelligence, and those whose intelligence remained intact despite their brain wounds. I then drew a diagram of the wound of each man on a separate transparent plastic sheet which showed the basic outline of the brain and the major outlines of the four major lobes: frontal, parietal, temporal and occipital. Naturally, there were separate left and right hemisphere diagrams to show where the lesions were.

[5]I sat in silence at my desk; there was a radio playing soft classical music, and the hour was getting late. My wife was already sound asleep in the bedroom, and I was not only alone but also with a sense of impending expectancy. Would anything appear of all the work I had done, or was this just another day of seeking impossible relationships?

[6]I placed the pile of transparent brain injury drawings of all the men whose IQ had been impaired in one pile and the drawings of those whose IQs remained normal in separate piles. A feeling of heightened expectancy came over me. What would I find—something of scientific interest or just another hodge-podge of meaningless nonsense?

[7]I carefully positioned all the brain injury transparencies of the IQ-impaired men one over the other, and discovered that every one of the injuries was on the left side of the brain. As I looked closer, I could see, despite the fair degree of overlap of the diagrams, that all of them showed an injury in one very specific area: the juncture of the tempero-parietal region—an area that included a bit of both the temporal and parietal lobes, and all on the left side of the brain. Now came the critical test: where would the brain lesions be of those whose IQ was not impaired? My palms sweated as I picked up one transparency after the other and placed them on blank right and left charts of the brain. I felt a quickening sense of excitement as I noted that so far most of the normal charts were on the right side of the brain – so far so good – none of the impaired ones were on the right, but what about the few that were on the left side? Indeed, there were some, but they all seemed to be on the periphery, outside the temporoparietal area. But, would the remaining 20 or so non-impaired also stay out of that critical area? I could hardly wait as I carefully placed one after the other over the standard charts.

[8]Eureka! As I finished placing the last non-impaired chart, down, I could barely restrain my excitement – none of the lesions of the non-IQ-impaired men infringed on the left tempero-parietal area where all the impaired

men were, yet every one of the impaired ones hit that area. I had found a double dissociation: all the impaired ones were in one very specific area, yet none of the unimpaired ones were in that area. I had discovered for the first time, an area that seemed critical to maintaining intelligence. I must confess at that moment I felt like Henry Hudson peering down on the river that would one day bear his name. I had made a discovery that no one had ever been privy to.

[9]I had truly discovered a cause-and-effect phenomenon: a lesion to the left tempero-parietal area of the brain causes loss of intelligence; whereas no brain lesion outside this area does. And I had been fortunate to be the first to make that scientific discovery, and lucky that the prestigious scientific journal, *Science*, decided to publish it.

Vocabulary

[1]exhilarated	[4]lobe	[4]occipital	[7]periphery
[1]unison	[4]parietal	[4]lesions	[8]dissociation
[2]intrigue	[4]temporal	[5]impending	[9]privy

Discussion Questions

1. Discuss Weinstein's tone and writing style. Be specific. Do you find it effective? Why or why not?

2. Does the writing style fit your expectation of a paper about science? Explain.

3. Describe the setting. How does knowing this information add to the narrative?

4. In paragraph 2 Weinstein mentions "the war." To what war do you think he is referring?

5. Discuss the cause and effect relationship Weinstein discovers.

6. Weinstein tells how he made a scientific discovery. Did this fit your idea of how scientific discoveries are made? Discuss your image of how scientific discoveries happen.

THE DISSOLUTION
OF THE OEDIPUS COMPLEX

SIGMUND FREUD

*Sigmund Freud (1856-1939) was the Austrian origina-
tor of psychoanalysis for the treatment of psychological
and emotional disorders. This marked the beginning of a
modern understanding of unconscious mental processes,
neurosis, the sexual life of infants, and the interpretation of
dreams. Psychoanalysis became the dominant modern theory of human psychology, as well as an important method
of psychiatric treatment. Through his theories of the unconscious in the framework of dream analysis, Freud introduced the concept of the id, the ego and the superego.*

AUTHOR'S NOTE: This paper, written in the early months of 1924, was in its
essence an elaboration of a passage in "The Ego and the Id." It further claims our
special interest as laying emphasis for the first time on the different course taken by
the development of sexuality in boys and in girls.

¹To an ever-increasing extent the Oedipus[a] complex[b] reveals its importance as the central phenomenon of the sexual period of early childhood. After
that, its dissolution takes place; it succumbs to repression, as we say, and is
followed by the latency period. It has not yet become clear, however, what it is
that brings about its destruction. Analyses seem to show that it is the experience
of painful disappointments. The little girl likes to regard herself as what her
father loves above all else; but the time comes when she has to endure a harsh
punishment from him and she is cast out of her fool's paradise.

²The boy regards his mother as his own property; but he finds one day
that she has transferred her love and solicitude to a new arrival. Reflection must
deepen our sense of the importance of those influences, for it will emphasize
the fact that distressing experiences of this sort, which act in opposition to the
content of the complex, are inevitable. Even when no special events occur, like
those we have mentioned as examples, the absence of the satisfaction hoped for
must in the end lead the small lover to turn away from his hopeless longing. In

---

[a]Oedipus (pronounced Ed' uh pess)—the main character in the Greek tragedy *Oedipus the King*
by Sophocles (496-406 B.C.). Through a series of complex plot twists, Oedipus fulfills a
prophecy by unknowingly killing his father and marrying his mother.

[b]Oedipus complex—Freud's theory that young boys go through a stage of wanting to marry and
have sex with their mothers.

this way the Oedipus complex would go to its destruction from its lack of success, from the effects of its internal impossibility.

[3]Another view is that the Oedipus complex must collapse because the time has come for its disintegration, just as the milk-teeth fall out when the permanent ones begin to grow.

[4]Although the majority of human beings go through the Oedipus complex as an individual experience, it is a phenomenon determined and laid down by heredity and is bound to pass away when the next pre-ordained phase of development sets in.

[5]We have lately been made clearly aware that a child's sexual development advances to a certain phase at which the genital organ has already taken over the leading role. But this genital is the male one only, the penis; the female genital remains undiscovered. This phallic phase, which is contemporaneous with the Oedipus complex, is then submerged and is succeeded by the latency period. The termination of the phallic phase takes place in a typical manner and in conjunction with events that are of regular recurrence.

[6]When the (male) child's interest turns to his genitals, he betrays the fact by manipulating them frequently; he then finds that the adults do not approve of this behavior. More or less plainly, more or less brutally, a threat is pronounced that this part of him which he values so highly will be taken away from him. Usually the threat emanates from women; very often they seek to strengthen their authority by a reference to the father or the doctor, who, so they say, will carry out the punishment.

[7]In a number of cases the women will themselves mitigate the threat in a symbolic manner by telling the child that what is to be removed is not his genital, which actually plays a passive part, but his hand, which is the active culprit. It happens particularly often that the little boy is threatened with castration, not because he plays with his penis with his hand, but because he wets his bed every night and cannot be gotten clean. Those in charge of him behave as if this nocturnal incontinence was the result and the proof of his being unduly concerned with his penis, and they are probably right. In any case, long-continued bed-wetting is to be equated with the emissions of adults. It is an expression of the same excitation of the genitals which has impelled the child to masturbate at this period.

[8]Now it is my view that what brings about the destruction of the child's phallic-genital organization is this threat of castration. Not immediately, it is true, and not without other influences being brought to bear as well. For to begin with the boy does not believe in the threat or obey it in the least. Psychoanalysis has recently attached importance to two experiences which all children go through and which, it is suggested, prepare them for the loss of highly valued parts of the body. These experiences are the withdrawal of the mother's breast, at first intermittently and later for good, and the daily demand on them to give

up the contents of the bowel. But there is no evidence to show that, when the threat of castration takes place, those experiences have any effect. It is not until a fresh experience comes his way that the child begins to reckon with the possibility of being castrated, and then only hesitatingly and unwillingly, and not without making efforts to depreciate the significance of something he has himself observed.

⁹The observation which finally breaks down his unbelief is the sight of the female genitals. Sooner or later, the child, who is so proud of his possession of a penis, has a view of the genital region of a little girl and cannot help noting the absence of a penis in a creature who is so like himself. With this, the loss of his own penis becomes imaginable, and the threat of castration takes its deferred effect.

¹⁰We should not be as short-sighted as the person in charge of the child who threatens him with castration, and we must not overlook the fact that at this time masturbation by no means represents the whole of his sexual life. As can be clearly shown, he stands in the Oedipus attitude to his parents; his masturbation is only a genital discharge of the sexual excitation belonging to the complex, and throughout his later years will owe its importance to that relationship. The Oedipus complex offered the child two possibilities of satisfaction, an active and a passive one. He could put himself in his father's place in a masculine fashion and have intercourse with his mother as his father did, in which case he would soon have felt the latter as a hindrance; or he might want to take the place of his mother and be loved by his father, in which case his mother would become superfluous.

¹¹The child may have only very vague notions as to what constitutes a satisfying erotic intercourse; but certainly the penis must play a part in it, for the sensations in his own organ is evidence of that. So far he had had no occasion to doubt that women possessed a penis. But now his acceptance of the possibility of castration, his recognition that women were castrated, made an end of both possible ways of obtaining satisfaction from the Oedipus complex. For both of them entailed the loss of his penis—the masculine one as a resulting punishment and the feminine one as a precondition

¹²If the satisfaction of love in the field of the Oedipus complex is to cost the child his penis, a conflict is bound to arise between his narcissistic interest in that part of his body and the sexual desire exhibited toward his parental objects. In this conflict the first of these forces normally triumphs: the child's ego turns away from the Oedipus complex. The authority of the father or the parents is impressed upon the child's ego, and there it forms the nucleus of the super-ego, which takes over the severity of the father and perpetuates his prohibition against incest, and so prevents the ego from returning to the contemplation of sexual activity with the parent. The libidinal trends belonging to the Oedipus complex are desexualized and sublimated and changed into impulses of affection.

[13]The whole process has, on the one hand, preserved the genital organ—has averted the danger of its loss—and, on the other, has paralyzed it—has removed its function. This process ushers in the latency period, which now interrupts the child's sexual development. I see no reason for denying the name of a "repression" to the ego's turning away from the Oedipus complex, although later repressions come about for the most part with the participation of the super-ego, which in this case is only just being formed. But the process we have described is more than a repression. It is equivalent, if it is ideally carried out, to a destruction and an abolition of the complex.

[14]Analytic observation enables us to recognize the connections between the phallic organization, the Oedipus complex, the threat of castration, the formation of the super-ego and the latency period. These connections justify the statement that the destruction of the Oedipus complex is brought about by the threat of castration.

[15]The process which has been described refers, as has been expressly said, to male children only. How does the corresponding development take place in little girls? At this point our material—for some incomprehensible reason—becomes far more obscure and full of gaps. The female sex, too, develops an Oedipus complex, a super-ego and a latency period. May we also attribute a phallic organization and a castration complex to it? The answer is in the affirmative; but these things cannot be the same as they are in boys. Here the feminist demand for equal rights for the sexes does not take us far, for the morphological distinction is bound to find expression in differences of psychical development.

[16]"Anatomy is Destiny," to vary a saying of Napoleon's. The little girl's clitoris behaves just like a penis to begin with; but, when she makes a comparison with a playfellow of the other sex, she perceives that she has "come off badly," and she feels this as a wrong done to her and is a ground for inferiority. For a while still she consoles herself with the expectation that later on, when she grows older, she will acquire just as big an appendage as the boy's. Here the masculinity complex of women branches off.

[17]A female child, however, does not understand her lack of a penis as being a sex character; she explains it by assuming that at some earlier date she had possessed an equally large organ and had then lost it by castration. She seems not to extend this inference from herself to other, adult females, but, entirely on the lines of the phallic phase, to assume that they possess large and complete—that is to say, male-genitals. The essential difference thus comes about that the girl accepts castration as an accomplished fact, whereas the boy fears the possibility of its occurrence.

[18]The fear of castration being thus excluded in the little girl, a powerful motive also drops out for the setting-up of a superego and for the breaking-off of the infantile genital organization. In her, far more than in the boy, these

changes seem to be the result of upbringing and of intimidation from outside which threatens her with a loss of love. The girl's Oedipus complex is much simpler than that of the small bearer of the penis; in my experience, it seldom goes beyond the taking of her mother's place and the adopting of a feminine attitude towards her father.

[19]Renunciation of the penis is not tolerated by the girl without some attempt at compensation. She slips—along the line of a symbolic equation, one might say—from the penis to a baby. Her Oedipus complex culminates in a desire, which is long retained, to receive a baby from her father as a gift—to bear him a child. One has an impression that the Oedipus complex is then gradually given up because this wish is never fulfilled. The two wishes—to possess a penis and a child—remain strongly embedded in her unconscious and help to prepare the female for her later sexual role.

[20]I have no doubt that the chronological and causal relations described here between the Oedipus complex, sexual intimidation (the threat of castration), the formation of the super-ego and the beginning of the latency period are of a typical kind; but I do not wish to assert that this type is the only possible one. Variations in the chronological order and in the linking-up of these events are bound to have a very important bearing on the development of the individual.

Vocabulary

[1]phenomenon	[5]conjunction	[9]deferred	[12]sublimated [1]dis-
solution	[5]recurrence	[10]hindrance	[13]averted
[1]repression	[7]castration	[10]superfluous	[13]abolition
[1]latency	[7]nocturnal	[11]erotic	[15]incomprehensible
[2]solicitude	[7]incontinence	[12]narcissistic	[15]affirmative
[2]reflection	[7]unduly	[12]ego	[15]morphological
[2]inevitable	[7]equated	[12]nucleus	[15]psychical
[4]pre-ordained	[7]emissions	[12]super-ego	[16]clitoris
[5]genital	[7]impelled	[12]perpetuates	[16]appendage
[5]phallic	[8]intermittently	[12]contemplation	[17]inference
[5]contemporaneous	[8]depreciate	[12]libidinal (libido)	[19]renunciation

Discussion Questions

1. How does Freud describe the Oedipus Complex? What are its characteristics?

2. Freud indicates that researchers are unclear as to why the Oedipus complex dissipates. What are two possible reasons that he cites?

3. Do girls go through an Oedipus complex? If so, what is it? If not, why not?

4. What, according to Freud, brings about "the destruction of the child's phallic-genital organization"? (Paragraph 8)

5. What then reinforces the boy's idea that castration may actually be carried out?

6. What "forms the nucleus of the super-ego"? (Paragraph 12)

7. According to Freud how are bedwetting and masturbating connected?

8. What does Freud mean when he states, "Anatomy is Destiny"? (Paragraph 16)

9. According to Freud, how does a girl compensate for not having a penis?

10. Why does Freud believe that understanding these events that occur in childhood is important?

11. Compare this essay to Edward O. Wilson's "Sex" beginning on page 493 of this text. What connections do you find?

GUERNICA
PABLO PICASSO

Pablo Picasso (1881-1973) is considered to be the most influential artist of the 20th century. He started painting at age 10 and continued for the next 82 years, producing over 20,000 works in his lifetime. He is known for his Blue Period, Rose Period, Cubism, and, later in his life, his use of all manner of media to produce art. He is the only artist to have had his work in the Louvre while alive.

DOCTRINE AND MAGIC:
PICASSO'S *GUERNICA*
FROM *MODERN FRENCH PAINTING*

SAM HUNTER

Emeritus professor of art history at Princeton University,
Sam Hunter *is a noted critic and historian of modern
art. He has written numerous books, including* Modern
Art: Painting, Sculpture, Architecture *(2000);* Robert
Rauschenberg *(1999);* Michael Delacroix: Eternal Paris
(1998); Figure and Form: Present, Past, and Personal
(1998); The Museum of Modern Art, New York: The
History and the Collection *(1997);* Marino Marini *(1993);*
Larry Rivers *(1990); and* American Art of the 20th Cen-
tury *(1972).*

[1]One of Picasso's greatest creations, *Guernica* is a painting inspired by the fascist bombing of a Basque town during the Spanish civil war.

[2]Picasso was a Loyalist partisan in the civil war and accepted from the Republican government an appointment as director of the Prado, although he was never able to go to Spain to assume any official duties. He fought his personal war against fascism, however, in pictures that were the most eloquent indictments of organized brutality in modern times. In 1937 he did a series of etchings, *The Dream and Lie of Franco*, and wrote a violent Surrealist poem to accompany the sequence of plates. Franco is described as "an evil-omened polyp . . . his mouth full of the cinch-bug jelly of his words," and he emerges in the drawings as a hairy, three-pronged turnip with carious teeth and a pa-per-hat crown. The rape of Spain is shown in an episodic sequence of scenes and images: a dead horse, human cadavers, women fleeing with dead children. Franco the "polyp" turns into a horse in one episode and is disemboweled by an avenging bull. In another the majestic head of a bull confronts Franco's animal-vegetable incarnation and seems to dazzle and shrivel it by its presence.

[3]In the same year, Picasso painted his tragic mural, *Guernica*, a huge canvas (11 feet by nearly 26 feet). The wartime agony of death and sense-less destruction is emphasized by the stark black, white, and gray composition; there is no color. A broken, mangled form of a warrior at the base of the com-position with his features askew; a woman with a dead child; a disemboweled horse at the center with a spear-point tongue; another woman whose breast nipples have become bolts and who is crazed and cross-eyed with pain and grief—all these images and the expressive distortions suggest cruel affliction.

Two forms dominate the composition: the fierce bull and the dying horse. From the right, out of a window, flows the fearful face of a woman and a long arm like a hallucination. She holds a candle over the scene, and it seems to be a symbol of the conscience of a horrified humanity.

[4]Picasso explained the symbolism of the work simply, declaring that the bull "is brutality and darkness ... the horse represents the people." The painting has the impact of a nightmare, the melodrama and simplicity of presentation of the comic strip, and extreme psychological subtlety. By his strict decorative form and strong figurative conventions, Picasso has managed to intensify the emotions he wished to convey. *Guernica* has been criticized on the ground that its conventions are too private to excite general public emotion. If that is true, it is not so much Picasso's fault as our own and is a measure of the depletion of our artistic frame of reference.

[5]Picasso, in fact, has both deliberately simplified familiar classical figurative conventions and tried to fuse them with the convention of the comic strip to increase their clarity and legibility. The broken warrior at the bottom of the panel is a combination of a Greek hero derived from a classical bust and Kilroy or L'il Abner. Picasso multiplies terror by achieving it within decorum; his formalization gives horror the stark lineaments of classical tragedy. We may better appreciate the power and purity of Picasso's drama if we compare it to the hysteria and sentimentalism of German Expressionists who have treated similar themes.

[6]Much of *Guernica's* force derives from the significant and cruel distortions of the predatory bull, the stricken horse, and the scarecrow human figures. In these forms Picasso found a subjective equivalent for public chaos and aggression. By disorganizing and dissociating the anatomies of his protagonists he expressed some of our deepest fears and terrors. Many writers have pointed out the resemblance of drawings and paintings of the insane to some of Picasso's inventions: the disorganized anatomy, the double-profile, the aggressive, compulsive repetition of ornamental pattern. One of the profoundly tragic meanings of *Guernica* is the projection, by controlled symbolism, of a kind of mass insanity and in the language almost of psychotic drawing. Goya, in his *Caprices*, had written as a note to one of his etchings that "the dream of reason produces monsters." Picasso added an up-to-date, clinical postscript to Goya's vision of man's inhumanity to man.

[7]Few in the modern generation rose to the heights of expression and feeling attained by Picasso in the *Guernica* period. To achieve these heights Picasso gambled recklessly with the esthetic harmony and hedonistic intent of oil painting. For the sake of expression and as a criticism of the life of his time, he pushed art to an extreme point of human disenchantment, to a point almost of no return. It has been a measure of his greatness that he could sustain such an extreme point of view with no loss of either coherence or quality.

Vocabulary

[1]fascist	[2]cinch-bug	[4]depletion	[6]dissociating
[2]partisan	[2]carious	[5]Kilroy	[6]protagonist
[2]indictment	[2]disemboweled	[5]L'il Abner	[7]esthetic
[2]Surrealist	[2]incarnation	[5]decorum	[7]hedonistic
[2]polyp	[3]askew	[5]lineaments	[7]disenchantment
[2]cadaver	[4]melodrama	[6]predatory	

Discussion Questions

1. About what conflict did Picasso paint *Guernica*? Where did you find this information?

2. Professor Hunter analyzes Picasso's painting *Guernica*. What important points does Hunter make about *Guernica*? List them.

3. In paragraph 5 Hunter mentions Kilroy and L'il Abner. Who are they and why does Hunter allude to them?

4. What does Hunter mean when he says in paragraph 5 that Picasso has "simplified familiar classical figurative conventions" and fused "them with the convention of the comic strip"?

5. At the end of paragraph 5 Hunter mentions German Expressionism. Research this term and explain why Hunter refers to it.

6. In paragraph 7 Hunter says, ". . . as a criticism of the life of his time [Picasso] pushed art to an extreme point of human disenchantment." Cite specific features of the painting that support that statement.

7. What did you find particularly helpful in the essay to better understand the painting *Guernica*? In what ways was it helpful?

8. Look up the meaning of "symbolism." What symbols does Hunter discuss? Explain the symbolism of the bull and the horse.

THE EXACT SCIENCE OF MATRIMONY

O. HENRY

O. Henry (1862-1910), the pen name of William Sydney Porter, is one of America's most popular short story writers, best known for his ironic twists and surprise endings. O. Henry began writing seriously in a Texas federal prison while serving a sentence for embezzlement, though critics believe he was innocent of the crime. O. Henry's most famous stories are "The Gift of the Magi," "The Furnished Room," and "The Ransom of Red Chief." He published ten collections of stories during a period that spanned barely ten years.

[1]"As I have told you before," said Jeff Peters, "I never had much confidence in the perfidiousness of women. As partners or coeducators in the most innocent line of graft they are not trustworthy."

[2]"They deserve the compliment," said I. "I think they are entitled to be called the honest sex."

[3]"Why shouldn't they be?" said Jeff. "They've got the other sex either grafting or working overtime for 'em. They're all right in business until they get their emotions or their hair touched up too much. Then you want to have a flat-footed, heavy-breathing man with sandy whiskers, five kids and a building and loan mortgage ready as an understudy to take her desk. Now there was that widow lady that me and Andy Tucker engaged to help us in that little matrimonial agency scheme we floated out in Cairo.

[4]"When you've got enough advertising capital—say a roll as big as the little end of a wagon tongue—there's money in matrimonial agencies. We had about $2,000 and we expected to double it in two months, which is about as long as a scheme like ours can be carried on without taking out a New Jersey charter.

[5]"We fixed up an advertisement that read about like this:

[6]'Charming widow, beautiful, home loving, 32 years, possessing $2,000 cash and owning valuable country property, would remarry. Would prefer a poor man with affectionate disposition to one with means, as she realizes that the solid virtues are oftenest to be found in the humble walks of life. No objection to elderly man or one of homely appearance if faithful and true and competent to manage property and invest money with judgment. Address, with particulars,

Lonely,
Care of Peters & Tucker, agents,
Cairo, Ill.'

[7]"'So far, so pernicious,' says I, when we had finished the literary concoction. 'And now,' says I, 'where is the lady?'

[8]"Andy gives me one of his looks of calm irritation.

[9]"'Jeff,' says he, 'I thought you had lost them ideas of realism in your art. Why should there be a lady? When they sell a lot of watered stock on Wall Street would you expect to find a mermaid in it? What has a matrimonial ad got to do with a lady?'

[10]"'Now listen,' says I. 'You know my rule, Andy, that in all my illegitimate inroads against the legal letter of the law the article sold must be existent, visible, producible. In that way and by a careful study of city ordinances and train schedules I have kept out of all trouble with the police that a five-dollar bill and a cigar could not square. Now, to work this scheme we've got to be able to produce bodily a charming widow or its equivalent with or without the beauty, hereditaments and appurtenances set forth in the catalogue and writ of errors, or hereafter be held by a justice of the peace.'

[11]"'Well,' says Andy, reconstructing his mind, 'maybe it would be safer in case the post office or the Peace Commission should try to investigate our agency. But where,' he says, 'could you hope to find a widow who would waste time on a matrimonial scheme that had no matrimony in it?'

[12]"I told Andy that I thought I knew of the exact party. An old friend of mine, Zeke Trotter, who used to draw soda water and teeth in a tent show, had made his wife a widow a year before by drinking some dyspepsia cure of the old doctor's instead of the liniment that he always got boozed up on. I used to stop at their house often, and I thought we could get her to work with us.

[13]"Twas only sixty miles to the little town where she lived, so I jumps out on the I.C. and finds her in the same cottage with the same sunflowers and roosters standing on the washtubs. Mrs. Trotter fitted our ad first rate except, maybe, for beauty and age and property valuation. But she looked feasible and praiseworthy to the eye, and it was a kindness to Zeke's memory to give her the job.

[14]"'Is this an honest deal you are putting on, Mr. Peters?' she asks me when I tell her what we want.

[15]"'Mrs. Trotter,' says I, 'Andy Tucker and me have computed the calculation that 3,000 men in this broad and fair country will endeavor to secure your fair hand and ostensible money and property through our advertisement. Out of that number something like thirty hundred will expect to give you in exchange, if they should win you, the carcass of a lazy and mercenary loafer, a failure in life, a swindler and contemptible fortune seeker.

[16]"'Me and Andy,' says I, 'propose to teach these preyers upon society a lesson. It was with difficulty,' says I, 'that me and Andy could refrain from forming a corporation under the title of the Great Moral and Millenial Malevolent Matrimonial Agency. Does that satisfy you?'

[17]"'It does, Mr. Peters,' says she. 'I might have known you wouldn't have gone into anything that wasn't opprobrious. But what will my duties be? Do I have to reject personally these 3,000 rapscallions you speak of, or can I throw them out in bunches?'

[18]"'Your job, Mrs. Trotter,' says I, 'will be practically a cynosure. You will live at a quiet hotel and will have no work to do. Andy and I will attend to all the correspondence and business end of it.

[19]"'Of course,' says I, 'some of the more ardent and impetuous suitors who can raise the railroad fare may come to Cairo to personally press their suit or whatever fraction of a suit they might be wearing. In that case you will be probably put to the inconvenience of kicking them out face to face. We will pay you $25 per week and hotel expenses.'

[20]"'Give me five minutes,' says Mrs. Trotter, 'to get my powder rag and leave the front door key with a neighbor and you can let my salary begin.'

[21]"So I conveys Mrs. Trotter to Cairo and establishes her in a family hotel far enough away from mine and Andy's quarters to be unsuspicious and available, and I tell Andy.

[22]"'Great,' says Andy. 'And now that your conscience is appeased as to the tangibility and proximity of the bait, and leaving mutton aside, suppose we revenoo a noo fish.'

[23]"So, we began to insert our advertisement in newspapers covering the country far and wide. One ad was all we used. We couldn't have used more without hiring so many clerks and marcelled paraphernalia that the sound of the gum chewing would have disturbed the Postmaster-General.

[24]"We placed $2,000 in a bank to Mrs. Trotter's credit and gave her the book to show in case anybody might question the honesty and good faith of the agency. I knew Mrs. Trotter was square and reliable and it was safe to leave it in her name.

[25]"With that one ad Andy and me put in twelve hours a day answering letters.

[26]"About one hundred a day was what came in. I never knew there was so many large hearted but indigent men in the country who were willing to acquire a charming widow and assume the burden of investing her money.

[27]"Most of them admitted that they ran principally to whiskey and lost jobs and were misunderstood by the world, but all of 'em were sure that they were chock full of affection and manly qualities that the widow would be making the bargain of her life to get 'em.

[28]"Every applicant got a reply from Peters & Tucker informing him that the widow had been deeply impressed by his straightforward and interesting letter and requesting them to write again stating more particulars; and enclosing photograph if convenient. Peters & Tucker also informed the applicant that their fee for handing over the second letter to their fair client would be $2, enclosed therewith.

[29]"There you see the simple beauty of the scheme. About 90 percent of them domestic foreign noblemen raised the price somehow and sent it in. That was all there was to it. Except that me and Andy complained an amount about being put to the trouble of slicing open them envelopes, and taking the money out.

[30]"Some few clients called in person. We sent 'em to Mrs. Trotter and she did the rest; except for three or four who came back to strike us for carfare. After the letters began to get in from the r.f.d. districts Andy and me were taking in about $200 a day.

[31]"One afternoon when we were busiest and I was stuffing the twos and ones into cigar boxes and Andy was whistling 'No Wedding Bells for Her' a small, slick man drops in and runs his eye over the walls like he was on the trail of a lost Gainesborough painting or two. As soon as I saw him I felt a glow of pride, because we were running our business on the level.

[32]"'I see you have quite a large mail today,' says the man.

[33]"I reached and got my hat.

[34]"'Come on,' says I. 'We've been expecting you. I'll show you the goods. How was Teddy when you left Washington?'

[35]"I took him down to the Riverview Hotel and had him shake hands with Mrs. Trotter. Then I showed him her bank book with the $2,000 to her credit.

[36]"'It seems to be all right,' says the Secret Service.

[37]"'It is,' says I. 'And if you're not a married man I'll leave you to talk a while with the lady. We won't mention the two dollars.'

[38]"'Thanks,' says he. 'If I wasn't, I might. Good day, Mr. Peters.'

[39]"Toward the end of three months we had taken in something over $5,000, and we saw it was time to quit. We had a good many complaints made to us; and Mrs. Trotter seemed to be tired of the job. A good many suitors had been calling to see her, and she didn't seem to like that.

[40]"So we decides to pull out, and I goes down to Mrs. Trotter's hotel to pay her last week's salary and say farewell and get her check for $2,000.

[41]"When I get there I hear crying like a kid that doesn't want to go to school.

[42]"'Now, now,' says I, 'what's it all about? Somebody sassed you or you getting home-sick?'

[43]"'No, Mr. Peters,' says she. 'I'll tell you. You was always a friend of Zeke's, and I don't mind. Mr. Peters, I'm in love. I just love a man so hard I can't bear not to get him. He's just the ideal I've always had in mind.'

[44]"'Then take him,' says I. 'That is, if it's a mutual case. Does he return the sentiment according to the specifications and painfulness you have described?'

[45]"'He does,' says she. 'But he's one of the gentlemen that's been coming to see me about the advertisement and he won't marry me unless I give him

the $2,000. His name is William Wilkinson.' And then she goes off again in the agitations and hysterics of romance.

⁴⁶"'Mrs. Trotter,' says I, 'there's no man more sympathizing with a woman's affections than I am. Besides, you was once a life partner of one of my best friends. If it was left to me I'd say take this $2,000 and the man of your choice and be happy.

⁴⁷"'We could afford to do that, because we have cleaned up over $5,000 from these suckers that wanted to marry you. But,' says I, 'Andy Tucker is to be consulted.'

⁴⁸"I goes back to our hotel and lays the case before Andy.

⁴⁹"'I was expecting something like this all the time,' says Andy. 'You can't trust a woman to stick by you in any scheme that involves her emotions and preferences.'

⁵⁰"'It's a sad thing, Andy,' says I, 'to think that we've been the cause of the breaking of a woman's heart.'

⁵¹"'It is,' says Andy, 'and I tell you what I'm willing to do, Jeff. You've always been a man of a soft and generous disposition. Perhaps I've been too hard and worldly and suspicious. For once I'll meet you half way. Go to Mrs. Trotter and tell her to draw the $2,000 from the bank and give it to this man she's infatuated with and be happy.'

⁵²"I jumps and shakes Andy's hand for five minutes, and then I goes back to Mrs. Trotter and tells her, and she cries as hard for joy as she did for sorrow.

⁵³"Two days afterward me and Andy packed to go.

⁵⁴"'Wouldn't you like to go down and meet Mrs. Trotter once before we leave?' I asks him. 'She'd like mightily to know you and express her encomiums and gratitude.'

⁵⁵"'Why, I guess not,' says Andy. 'I guess we'd better hurry and catch that train.'

⁵⁶"I was strapping our capital around me in a memory belt like we always carried it, when Andy pulls a roll of large bills out of his pocket and asks me to put 'em with the rest.

⁵⁷"'What's this?' says I.

⁵⁸"'It's Mrs. Trotter's $2,000,' says Andy.

⁵⁹"'How do you come to have it?' I asks.

⁶⁰"'She gave it to me,' says Andy. 'I've been calling on her three evenings a week for more than a month.'

⁶¹"'Then you are William Wilkinson?' says I.

⁶²"'I was,' says Andy."

Vocabulary

[1]perfidiousness	[12]dyspepsia	[17]opprobrious	[23]paraphernalia
[1]graft	[13]feasible	[17]rapscallions	[26]indigent
[7]pernicious	[15]ostensible	[18]cynosure	[31]Gainesborough
[7]concoction	[15]mercenary	[19]ardent	[51]infatuated
[10]inroads	[15]prey	[19]impetuous	[54]encomiums
[10]appurtenances	[15]carcass	[22]tangibility	
[10]writ	[16]malevolent	[22]proximity	

Discussion Questions

1. When Jeff Peters says, "I never had much confidence in the perfidiousness of women" what exactly is he saying about women? Remember the context in which he says this. For example, how do Jeff and Andy make their living?

2. Explain "They've got the other sex either grafting or working overtime for 'em." What does this tell us about Jeff's attitude toward women?

3. At the beginning of the story, Jeff says "They're all right in business until they get their emotions or their hair touched up too much." Who are "they"? What is Jeff saying about "them"? In what way does the end of the story confirm this statement that Jeff makes at the beginning?

4. What is the tone of this story? Is it intended to be serious or comic? Support your view with specific passages from the text.

5. Can you surmise what is meant by "taking out a New Jersey charter"? Hint: It has to do with becoming incorporated as a company.

6. What is the implication of ". . . I have kept out of all trouble with the police that a five-dollar-bill and a cigar could not square"?

7. In what way do you think that Porter's time in prison influenced his writing style? Support your answer with specific references to the text.

8. Jeff describes Andy and himself as "coeducators" in a "line of graft." In what way can Andy and Jeff be seen as being "educators"?

9. Do you feel any sympathy for the men who are bilked by this scheme? Why or why not? How about Mrs. Trotter? Do you feel sorry for her? Why, why not?

THE FALSE GEMS

GUY DE MAUPASSANT

*Trained by novelist Gustave Flaubert, French writer **Guy de Maupassant** (1850-1893) was a master of the short story. Some of his important stories include "Ball of Fat" (1880), "Mademoiselle Fifi" (1882) and "The Necklace" (1884). During the 1880's de Maupassant wrote approximately 300 short stories, six novels, three travel books and one volume of poetry. His stories often use the theme of the cruelty of human beings to one another.*

¹M. Lantin had met the young woman at a *soiree*, at the home of the assistant chief of his bureau at the Ministry of the Interior, and at first sight had fallen madly in love with her.

²She was the daughter of a country physician who had died some months previously. She had come to live in Paris, with her mother, who visited much among her acquaintances, in the hope of making a favorable marriage for her daughter. They were poor and honest, quiet, and unaffected.

³The young girl was a perfect type of the virtuous woman whom every sensible young man dreams of one day winning for life. Her simple beauty had the charm of angelic modesty, and the imperceptible smile which constantly hovered about her lips seemed to be the reflection of a pure and lovely soul. Her praises resounded on every side. People were never tired of saying: "Happy the man who wins her love! He could not find a better wife."

⁴Now M. Lantin enjoyed a snug little income of three thousand francs and, thinking he could safely assume the responsibility of matrimony, proposed to this model young girl and was accepted.

⁵He was unspeakably happy with her; she governed his household so cleverly and economically that they seemed to live in luxury. She lavished the most delicate attentions on her husband, coaxed and fondled him, and the charm of her presence was so great that six years after their marriage M. Lantin discovered that he loved his wife even more than the first days of his honeymoon.

⁶He only felt inclined to blame her for two things: her love of the theater, and a taste for false jewelry. Her friends (she was acquainted with some officers' wives) frequently procured for her a box at the theater, often for the first representations of the new plays; and her husband was obliged to accompany her, whether he willed or not, to these amusements, though they bored him excessively, after a day's labor at the office.

⁷After a time, M. Lantin begged his wife to get some lady of her acquain-

tance to accompany her. She was at first opposed to such an arrangement; but after much persuasion on his part, she finally consented—to the infinite delight of her husband.

[8]Now, with her love for the theater came also the desire to adorn her person. True, her costumes remained as before simple, and in the most correct taste; but she soon began to ornament her ears with huge rhinestones, which glittered and sparkled like real diamonds. Around her neck she wore strings of false pearls, and on her arms bracelets of imitation gold.

[9]Her husband frequently remonstrated with her, saying, "My dear, as you cannot afford to buy real diamonds, you ought to appear adorned with your beauty and modesty alone, which are the rarest ornaments of your sex."

[10]But she would smile sweetly, and say: "What can I do? I am so fond of jewelry. It is my only weakness. We cannot change our natures."

[11]Then she would roll the pearl necklaces around her fingers, and hold up the bright gems for her husband's admiration, gently coaxing him:

[12]"Look! Are they not lovely? One would swear they were real."

[13]M. Lantin would then answer, smilingly:

[14]"You have Bohemian tastes, my dear."

[15]Often of an evening, when they were enjoying a *tête-à-tête* by the fireside, she would place on the tea table the leather box containing the "trash," as M. Lantin called it She would examine the false gems with a passionate attention, as though they were in some way connected with a deep and secret joy; and she often insisted on passing a necklace around her husband's neck, and laughing heartily would exclaim: "How droll you look!" Then she would throw herself into his arms and kiss him affectionately.

[16]One evening in winter, she attended the opera, and on her return was chilled through and through. The next morning she coughed, and eight days later she died.

[17]M. Lantin's despair was so great that his hair became white in one month. He wept unceasingly; his heart was torn with grief, and his mind was haunted by the remembrance, the smile, the voice—by every charm of his beautiful, dead wife.

[18]Time, the healer, did not assuage his grief. Often during office hours, while his colleagues were discussing the topics of the day, his eyes would suddenly fill with tears, and he would give vent to his grief in heartrending sobs. Everything in his wife's room remained as before her decease; and here he was wont to seclude himself daily and think of her who had been his treasure—the joy of his existence.

[19]But life soon became a struggle. His income, which in the hands of his wife had covered all household expenses, was now no longer sufficient for his own immediate wants; and he wondered how she could have managed to purchase such excellent wines and such rare delicacies, things which he could

no longer procure with his modest resources.

²⁰He incurred some debts and was soon reduced to absolute poverty. One morning, finding himself without a cent in his pocket, he resolved to sell something, and immediately the thought occurred to him of disposing of his wife's paste jewels. He cherished in his heart a sort of rancor against the false gems. They had always irritated him in the past, and the very sight of them spoiled somewhat the memory of his lost darling.

²¹To the last days of her life, she had continued to make purchases, bringing home new gems almost every evening. He decided the heavy necklace which she seemed to prefer, and which, he thought, ought to be worth six or seven francs; for although paste it was, nevertheless, of very fine workmanship.

²²He put it in his pocket and started out in search of a jeweler's shop. He entered the first one he saw, feeling a little ashamed to expose his misery and also to offer such a worthless article for sale.

²³He approached the merchant. "Sir," he said, "I would like to know what this is worth."

²⁴The man took the necklace, examined it, turned it over, called his clerk and made some remarks in low tones; then he placed the ornament back on the counter, and looked at it carefully from a distance to judge of the effect.

²⁵M. Lantin was annoyed by all this detail, and was on the point of saying: "Oh! I know well enough it isn't worth anything," when the jeweler said: "Sir, that necklace is worth between twelve and fifteen thousand francs; but I could not buy it unless you tell me now whence it comes."

²⁶The widower opened his eyes wide and remained gaping, not comprehending the merchant's meaning. Finally he stammered, "You say—are you sure?" The other replied dryly: "You can search elsewhere and see if anyone will offer you more. I consider it worth fifteen thousand at the most. Come back here if you cannot do better."

²⁷M. Lantin, beside himself with astonishment, took up the necklace and left the store. He wished time for reflection.

²⁸Once outside, he felt inclined to laugh, and he said to himself: "The fool! Had I only taken him at his word! That jeweler cannot distinguish real diamonds from paste."

²⁹A few minutes after, he entered another jewelry store on the Rue de la Paix. As soon as the proprietor glanced at the necklace, he cried out:

³⁰"Of course! I know it well; it was bought here!"

³¹M. Lantin was disturbed and asked, "How much is it worth?"

³²"Well, I sold it for twenty thousand francs. I am willing to take it back for eighteen thousand when you inform me, according to our legal formality, how it comes to be in your possession."

³³This time M. Lantin was dumbfounded.

[34]He replied: "But—but—examine it well. Until this moment, I was under the impression that it was paste."

[35]The jeweler said: "What is your name, sir?"

[36]"Lantin—I am in the employ of the Ministry of the Interior. I live at 16 Rue des Martyrs."

[37]The merchant looked through his books, found the entry, and said, "That necklace was sent to Mme. Lantin's address, 16 Rue des Martyrs, on July 20, 1876."

[38]The two men looked into each other's eyes—the widower speechless; the jeweler scenting a thief. The latter broke the silence by saying:

[39]"Would you leave this necklace here for twenty-four hours? I'll give you a receipt."

[40]"Certainly," answered M. Lantin, hastily. Then putting the ticket into his pocket, he left the store.

[41]He wandered aimlessly through the streets, his mind in a state of dreadful confusion. He tried to reason, to understand. He could not afford to purchase such a costly ornament. Certainly not! But, then, it must have been a present!—a present!—a present from whom? For what?

[42]He stopped and remained standing in the middle of the street. A horrible doubt entered his mind—she? Then all the other gems must have been presents too! The earth seemed to tremble beneath him,—the tree before him was falling—throwing up his arms, he fell to the ground, unconscious. He recovered his senses in a pharmacy into which passers-by had carried him, and was then taken to his home. When he arrived, he shut himself up in his room and wept until nightfall. Finally overcome with fatigue, he threw himself on the bed, where he passed an uneasy, restless night.

[43]The following morning he arose and prepared to go to his office. It was hard to work after such a shock. He sent a letter to his employer requesting to be excused. Then he remembered that he had to return to the jeweler's. He did not like the idea; but he could not possibly leave the necklace with that man. So he dressed and went out.

[44]It was a lovely day; a clear blue sky smiled on the busy city below, and men of leisure were strolling about with their hands in their pockets.

[45]Observing them, M. Lantin said to himself: "The rich indeed are happy. With money it is possible to forget even the deepest sorrow. One can go where one pleases, and in travel find that distraction which is the surest cure for grief. Oh! if only I were really rich!"

[46]He began to feel hungry, but his pockets were empty. He again remembered the necklace. Eighteen thousand francs! Eighteen thousand francs! What a fortune!

[47]He soon arrived in the Rue de la Paix, opposite the jeweler's. Eighteen thousand francs! Twenty times he resolved to go in, but shame kept him back.

He was still hungry, however—very hungry, and he had not a cent in his pocket. He decided quickly, raced across the street so as not to give himself time to think, and entered the store.

⁴⁸The proprietor immediately came forward, and politely offered him a chair; the clerks glanced at him knowingly.

⁴⁹"I have made inquiries, M. Lantin," said the jeweler, "and if you are still resolved to dispose of the gems, I am ready to pay you the price I offered."

⁵⁰"Certainly, sir," stammered M. Lantin.

⁵¹Whereupon the proprietor took from a drawer eighteen large notes, counted them, gave them to M. Lantin, who signed a receipt and with trembling hand put the money into his pocket.

⁵²As he was about to leave the store, he turned toward the merchant, who still wore the same knowing smile, and lowering his eyes, said:

⁵³"I have—I have some other gems—which I have received from the same source. Would you buy them also?"

⁵⁴The merchant bowed: "Certainly, sir."

⁵⁵One of the partners barely stifled a laugh, while the other was forced to leave the room to hide his mirth.

⁵⁶Lantin said gravely: "I will bring them to you." An hour later he returned with the gems.

⁵⁷The large diamond earrings were worth twenty thousand francs; the bracelets, thirty-five thousand; the rings, sixteen thousand; a set of emeralds and sapphires, fourteen thousand; a gold chain with solitaire pendant, forty thousand—making the sum of one hundred forty-three thousand francs.

⁵⁸The jeweler remarked jokingly: "There was a person who invested all her earnings in precious stones."

⁵⁹M. Lantin replied seriously: "It is only another way of investing one's money!"

⁶⁰That day he lunched at Voisin's and drank wine worth twenty francs a bottle. Then he hired a carriage and made a tour of the Bois de Boulogne, and as he scanned the various gleaming carriages with a contemptuous air he could hardly refrain from crying out to the occupants:

⁶¹"I, too, am rich!—I am worth two hundred thousand francs!"

⁶²Suddenly, he thought of this employer. He drove up to the office, and entered gaily, saying:

⁶³"Sir, I have to resign my position. I have just inherited three hundred thousand francs."

⁶⁴He shook hands with his former colleagues, and confided to them of his projects for the future. Then he went off to dine at the Cafe Anglais.

⁶⁵He seated himself alongside a gentleman of aristocratic bearing, and during the meal informed the latter confidentially that he had just inherited four hundred thousand francs.

[66]For the first time in his life he was not bored at the theater, and he spent the night carousing.

[67]Six months afterward he married again. His second wife was a very virtuous woman, with a violent temper. She made his life miserable.

Vocabulary

[1]*soiree*	[9]remonstrated	[18]wont	[27]reflection
[2]unaffected	[14]Bohemian	[20]incurred	[33]dumbfounded
[3]imperceptible	[15]droll	[20]rancor	[55]stifled
[6]procured	[18]assuage	[26]gaping	[55]mirth
			[57]pendant

Discussion Questions

1. When and where does this story take place? How do you know?

2. Describe Mme. Lantin's character. How is she presented at the beginning of the story? How do you view her at the end of the story?

3. Discuss M. Lantin's character. Does his character change through the course of the story or remain consistent throughout?

4. Look up the meaning of "irony." Discuss the irony presented in the story.

5. What does M. Lantin do for a living? If he were working in the United States, in what city would he probably be working? How much would his annual salary probably be? Can you calculate the worth of the gems in today's dollars based upon this information?

6. Does knowing the real worth of the gems change the meaning of the story for you? If so, how?

7. Mme. Lantin dies toward the beginning of the story in one abrupt sentence. Discuss why, as the writer of this short story, de Maupassant might have done this.

8. Contrast M. Lantin's first and second wives. With whom do you think he would rather spend the rest of his life? Why? Which of the two women appeals more to you? Why?

9. Based upon the five-word sentence with which de Maupassant ends the story, what might the author be saying about the nature of relationships?

10. English poet Thomas Gray wrote, "Where ignorance is bliss,/ 'Tis folly to be wise." How might this famous quote apply to this story?

GENESIS
FROM THE TORAH

The Torah consists of the five books of Moses, a central text of the Jewish religion and a significant part of the Christian Old Testament. Genesis is the first book. These opening sections tell how the world was created.

1 In the beginning God created the heaven and the earth. [2]Now the earth was unformed and void, and darkness was on the face of the deep; and the spirit of God hovered over the face of the waters. [3]And God said, "Let there be light." And there was light. [4]God saw the light, that it was good; and God divided the light from the darkness. [5]And God called the light Day, and the darkness He called Night. And there was evening and there was morning, a first day!

[6]And God said, "Let there be a firmament in the midst of the waters, and let it divide the waters from the waters." [7]God made the firmament, and divided the waters which were under the firmament from the waters which were above the firmament; and it was so. [8]God called the firmament Heaven. And there was evening and there was morning, a second day.

[9]And God said, "Let the waters under the heaven be gathered together unto one place, and let the dry land appear." And it was so. [10]God called the dry land Earth, and the gathering together of the waters He called Seas; and God saw that it was good. [11]And God said, "Let the earth put forth vegetation: seed-bearing plants, fruit trees after their kind wherein is the seed thereof upon the earth." And it was so. [12]The earth brought forth vegetation: seed-bearing plants of every kind, and trees of every kind bearing fruit with the seed in it; and God saw that it was good. [13]And there was evening and there was morning, a third day.

[14]And God said, "Let there be lights in the firmament of the heaven to divide the day from the night; and they shall serve as signs for the set times—the days, the seasons and the years; [15]and let them be for lights in the firmament of the heaven to give light upon the earth." And it was so. [16]God made the two great lights, the greater light to rule the day and the lesser light to rule the night, and the stars. [17]And God set them in the firmament of the heaven to shine upon the earth, [18]to rule over the day and over the night, and the stars, and to divide the

light from darkness. And God saw that it was good. [19]And there was evening and there was morning, a fourth day.

[20]And God said, "Let the waters bring forth swarms of living creatures, and let birds fly above the earth in the open firmament of the heaven." [21]God created the great sea monsters, and every living creature that creeps, which the waters brought forth in swarms; and all the winged birds of every kind. And God saw that it was good. [22]God blessed them, saying, "Be fruitful and multiply, and fill the waters in the seas, and let the birds multiply on the earth." [23]And there was evening and there was morning, a fifth day.

[24]And God said, "Let the earth bring forth the living creature after its kind: cattle, and creeping things, and wild beasts of every kind." And it was so. [25]God made wild beasts of every kind and cattle of every kind, and all kinds of creeping things of the earth. And God saw that it was good. [26]And God said, "Let us make man in our image, after our likeness; and let them have dominion over the fish of the sea, the birds of the sky, the cattle, and over all the earth, and all the creeping things that creep on earth." [27]And God created man in His own image, in the image of God He created him; male and female He created them. [28]And God blessed them and God said unto them, "Be fruitful and multiply, and replenish the earth, and subdue it; and rule the fish of the sea, the birds of the sky, and all the living things that creep on earth."

[29]And God said, "Behold, I have given you every seed-bearing plant that is upon all the earth, and every tree that has seed-bearing fruit; they shall be yours for food. [30]And to every beast on the earth, to all the birds of the sky, and to everything that creeps on earth, wherein there is a living soul, I have given all the green plants for food." And it was so. [31]And God saw that every thing that He had made, and behold, it was very good. And there was evening and there was morning, the sixth day.

2 The heaven and the earth were finished, and all the host of them. [2]On the seventh day God finished His work which He had made, and He rested on the seventh day from all His work which He had made. [3]And God blessed the seventh day and declared it holy, because on it God rested from all the work of creation which He had done. [4]Such is the story of heaven and earth when they were created.

Vocabulary

[2]hovered   [6]firmament   [24]dominion

Discussion Questions

1. In Genesis, the creation of heaven and earth follows a pattern. List the order in which the world is created.

2. Discuss why you think the creator chose this order. Would another order have worked as well? Discuss why or why not.

3. Look up the word "cadence." Discuss the cadence you find in this piece.

4. Read the Apache Creation Story on page 117 of this text, Aitareya Upanishad on page 148 and Suras 7, 5 and 11 from the Qur'an beginning on page 451. Discuss the similarities and differences you find. Share these with your classmates.

GIRL
FROM *AT THE BOTTOM OF THE RIVER*

JAMAICA KINCAID

*Born Elaine Potter Richardson, **Jamaica Kincaid** (1949-) is a Caribbean-American whose work focuses on mother/ daughter relationships as well as immigration and the experience of colonization. Her works have appeared in* the New Yorker, Harpers, The Paris Review *and* Rolling Stone. *She has published a collection of short stories,* At The Bottom of the River *(1983); two novels,* Annie John *(1985) and* The Autobiography of My Mother *(1996); one book of essays about Antigua,* A Small Place *(1988); and one fictionalized memoir,* My Brother *(1997).*

Wash the white clothes on Monday and put them on the stone heap; wash the color clothes on Tuesday and put them on the clothesline to dry; don't walk bareheaded in the hot sun; cook pumpkin fritters in very hot sweet oil; soak your little clothes right after you take them off; when buying cotton to make yourself a nice blouse, be sure that it doesn't have gum on it, because that way it won't hold up well after a wash; soak salt fish overnight before you cook it; is it true that you sing benna[a] in Sunday School?; always eat your food in such a way that it won't turn someone else's stomach; on Sundays try to walk like a lady and not like the slut you are so bent on becoming; don't sing benna in Sunday school; you mustn't speak to wharf-rat boys, not even to give directions; don't eat fruit on the street—flies will follow you; *but I don't sing benna on Sundays at all and never in Sunday school*; this is how to sew on a button; this is how to make a button-hole for the button that you have just sewed on; this is how to hem a dress when you see the hem coming down and so to prevent yourself from looking like the slut I know you are so bent on becoming; this is how you iron your father's khaki shirt so that it doesn't have a crease; this is how you grow okra—far from the house, because okra trees harbor red ants; when you are growing dasheen[b], make sure it gets plenty of water or else it makes your throat itch when you are eating it; this is how you sweep a corner; this is how you sweep a whole house; this is how you sweep a yard; this is how you smile to someone you don't like too much; this is how you smile to someone you like completely; this is how you set a table for tea; this is how you set a table

---

[a]*benna:* popular music, like American rock 'n roll

[b]*dasheen:* tropical starchy tuberous root, typically prepared like a potato

for dinner; this is how you set a table for an important guest; this is how you set a table for lunch; this is how you set a table for breakfast; this is how to behave in the presence of men who don't know you very well, and this way they won't recognize immediately the slut I have warned you against becoming; be sure to wash every day, even if it is with your own spit; don't squat down to play marbles—you are not a boy, you know; don't pick people's flowers—you might catch something; don't throw stones at blackbirds, because it might not be a blackbird at all; this is how to make a bread pudding; this is how to make doukona[c]; this is how to make pepper pot; this is how to make a good medicine for the cold; this is how to make a good medicine to throw away a child before it even becomes a child; this is how to catch a fish; this is how to throw back a fish you don't like, and that way something bad won't fall on you; this is how to bully a man; this is how a man bullies you; this is how to love a man, and if this doesn't work there are other ways, and if they don't work don't feel too bad about giving up; this is how to spit up in the air if you feel like it, and this is how to move quick so that it doesn't fall on you; this is how to make ends meet; always squeeze bread to make sure it's fresh; *but what if the baker won't let me squeeze the bread?*; you mean to say that after all you are really going to be the kind of woman who the baker won't let near the bread?

---

[c]*doukona* a spicy Caribbean dish

Discussion Questions

1. What do you think is the narrator's relationship to the girl? What makes you think this?

2. The narrator gives a variety of advice to the girl. Take the advice and categorize each piece. Do you see any patterns? If so, what are they?

3. Does the narrator cover all the major areas of advice a girl needs? Are there any areas you would add? Why or why not?

4. "Girl" was written in 1983. Do you think the advice given is still applicable to girls of today? Explain your answer.

5. On first read, the narrator seems harsh in her tone and language. Reread the selection and find the playfulness in the exchange. Write your answers and share them with your classmates.

6. How does the advice given here compare to the advice given to Laertes on page 83 of this text and the young man on page 85?

HARRISON BERGERON

KURT VONNEGUT

American author **Kurt Vonnegut** *(1922-2008) was the author of fourteen novels, including* The Sirens of Titan *(1959),* Mother Night *(1961),* Cat's Cradle *(1963),* Slaughterhouse Five *(1969),* Breakfast of Champions *(1973),* Hocus Pocus *(1990), and* Timequake *(1994), as well numerous short stories and books of nonfiction. "Harrison Bergeron" originally appeared in Vonnegut's collection of short stories,* Welcome to the Monkey House *(1970).*

[1]THE YEAR WAS 2081, and everybody was finally equal. They weren't only equal before God and the law. They were equal every which way. Nobody was smarter than anybody else. Nobody was better looking than anybody else. Nobody was stronger or quicker than anybody else. All this equality was due to the 211th, 212th, and 213th Amendments to the Constitution, and to the unceasing vigilance of agents of the United States Handicapper General.

[2]Some things about living still weren't quite right, though. April, for instance, still drove people crazy by not being springtime. And it was in that clammy month that the H-G men took George and Hazel Bergeron's fourteen-year-old son, Harrison, away.

[3]It was tragic, all right, but George and Hazel couldn't think about it very hard. Hazel had a perfectly average intelligence, which meant she couldn't think about anything except in short bursts. And George, while his intelligence was way above normal, had a little mental handicap radio in his ear. He was required by law to wear it at all times. It was tuned to a government transmitter. Every twenty seconds or so, the transmitter would send out some sharp noise to keep people like George from taking unfair advantage of their brains.

[4]George and Hazel were watching television. There were tears on Hazel's cheeks, but she'd forgotten for the moment what they were about.

[5]On the television screen were ballerinas.

[6]A buzzer sounded in George's head. His thoughts fled in panic, like bandits from a burglar alarm.

[7]"That was a real pretty dance, that dance they just did," said Hazel.

[8]"Huh?" said George.

[9]"That dance—it was nice," said Hazel.

[10]"Yup," said George. He tried to think a little about the ballerinas. They weren't really very good—no better than anybody else would have been, anyway. They were burdened with sash-weights and bags of birdshot, and their

faces were masked, so that no one, seeing a free and graceful gesture or a pretty face, would feel like something the cat drug in. George was toying with the vague notion that maybe dancers shouldn't be handicapped. But he didn't get very far with it before another noise in his ear radio scattered his thoughts.

[11]George winced. So did two out of the eight ballerinas. Hazel saw him wince. Having no mental handicap herself, she had to ask George what the latest sound had been. "Sounded like somebody hitting a milk bottle with a ball peen hammer," said George.

[12]"I'd think it would be real interesting, hearing all the different sounds," said Hazel, a little envious. "All the things they think up."

[13]"Um," said George.

[14]"Only, if I was Handicapper General, you know what I would do?" said Hazel. Hazel, as a matter of fact, bore a strong resemblance to the Handicapper General, a woman named Diana Moon Glampers. "If I was Diana Moon Glampers," said Hazel, "I'd have chimes on Sunday. Just chimes. Kind of in honor of religion."

[15]"I could think, if it was just chimes," said George.

[16]"Well—maybe make 'em real loud," said Hazel. "I think I'd make a good Handicapper General."

[17]"Good as anybody else," said George.

[18]"Who knows better'n I do what normal is?" said Hazel.

[19]"Right," said George. He began to think glimmeringly about his abnormal son who was now in jail, about Harrison, but a twenty-one-gun salute in his head stopped that.

[20]"Boy!" said Hazel, "that was a doozy, wasn't it?"

[21]It was such a doozy that George was white and trembling, and tears stood on the rims of his red eyes. Two of the eight ballerinas had collapsed to the studio floor and were holding their temples.

[22]"All of a sudden you look so tired," said Hazel. "Why don't you stretch out on the sofa, so's you can rest your handicap bag on the pillows, honey-bunch." She was referring to the forty-seven pounds of birdshot in a canvas bag, which was padlocked around George's neck. "Go on and rest the bag for a little while," she said. "I don't care if you're not equal to me for a while."

[23]George weighed the bag with his hands. "I don't mind it," he said. "I don't notice it any more. It's just a part of me."

[24]"You been so tired lately—kind of wore out," said Hazel. "If there was just some way we could make a little hole in the bottom of the bag, and just take out a few of them lead balls. Just a few."

[25]"Two years in prison and two thousand dollars fine for every ball I took out," said George. "I don't call that a bargain."

[26]"If you could just take a few out when you came home from work," said Hazel. "I mean—you don't compete with anybody around here. You just set around."

27"If I tried to get away with it," said George, "then other people'd get away with it—and pretty soon we'd be right back to the dark ages again, with everybody competing against everybody else. You wouldn't like that, would you?"

28"I'd hate it," said Hazel.

29"There you are," said George. "The minute people start cheating on laws, what do you think happens to society?"

30If Hazel hadn't been able to come up with an answer to this question, George couldn't have supplied one. A siren was going off in his head.

31"Reckon it'd fall all apart," said Hazel.

32"What would?" said George blankly.

33"Society," said Hazel uncertainly. "Wasn't that what you just said?"

34"Who knows?" said George.

35The television program was suddenly interrupted for a news bulletin. It wasn't clear at first as to what the bulletin was about, since the announcer, like all announcers, had a serious speech impediment. For about half a minute, and in a state of high excitement, the announcer tried to say, "Ladies and gentlemen—"

36He finally gave up, handed the bulletin to a ballerina to read.

37"That's all right," Hazel said of the announcer, "he tried. That's the big thing. He tried to do the best he could with what God gave him. He should get a nice raise for trying so hard."

38"Ladies and gentlemen—" said the ballerina, reading the bulletin. She must have been extraordinarily beautiful because the mask she wore was hideous. And it was easy to see that she was the strongest and most graceful of all the dancers, for her handicap bags were as big as those worn by two-hundred-pound men.

39And she had to apologize at once for her voice, which was a very unfair voice for a woman to use. Her voice was a warm, luminous, timeless melody. "Excuse me—" she said, and she began again, making her voice absolutely uncompetitive.

40"Harrison Bergeron, age fourteen," she said in a grackle squawk, "has just escaped from jail, where he was held on suspicion of plotting to overthrow the government. He is a genius and an athlete, is under-handicapped, and should be regarded as extremely dangerous."

41A police photograph of Harrison Bergeron was flashed on the screen—upside down, then sideways, upside down again, then right side up. The picture showed the full length of Harrison against a background calibrated in feet and inches. He was exactly seven feet tall.

42The rest of Harrison's appearance was Halloween and hardware. Nobody had ever borne heavier handicaps. He had outgrown hindrances faster than the H-G men could think them up. Instead of a little ear radio for a mental handicap, he wore a tremendous pair of earphones, and spectacles with thick wavy lenses. The spectacles were intended to make him not only half blind, but to give him whanging headaches besides.

[43]Scrap metal was hung all over him. Ordinarily, there was a certain symmetry, a military neatness to the handicaps issued to strong people, but Harrison looked like a walking junkyard. In the race of life, Harrison carried three hundred pounds.

[44]And to offset his good looks, the H-G men required that he wear at all times a red rubber ball for a nose, keep his eyebrows shaved off, and cover his even white teeth with black caps at snaggle-tooth random.

[45]"If you see this boy," said the ballerina, "do not—I repeat, do not—try to reason with him."

[46]There was the shriek of a door being torn from its hinges. Screams and barking cries of consternation came from the television set. The photograph of Harrison Bergeron on the screen jumped again and again, as though dancing to the tune of an earthquake.

[47]George Bergeron correctly identified the earthquake, and well he might have—for many was the time his own home had danced to the same crashing tune. "My God—" said George, "that must be Harrison!"

[48]The realization was blasted from his mind instantly by the sound of an automobile collision in his head.

[49]When George could open his eyes again, the photograph of Harrison was gone. A living, breathing Harrison filled the screen.

[50]Clanking, clownish, and huge, Harrison stood in the center of the studio. The knob of the uprooted studio door was still in his hand. Ballerinas, technicians, musicians, and announcers cowered on their knees before him, expecting to die.

[51]"I am the Emperor!" cried Harrison. "Do you hear? I am the Emperor! Everybody must do what I say at once!" He stamped his foot and the studio shook.

[52]"Even as I stand here—" he bellowed, "crippled, hobbled, sickened—I am a greater ruler than any man who ever lived! Now watch me become what I can become!"

[53]Harrison tore the straps of his handicap harness like wet tissue paper, tore straps guaranteed to support five thousand pounds.

[54]Harrison's scrap-iron handicaps crashed to the floor. Harrison thrust his thumbs under the bar of the padlock that secured his head harness. The bar snapped like celery. Harrison smashed his headphones and spectacles against the wall. He flung away his rubber-ball nose, revealing a man that would have awed Thor, the god of thunder.

[55]"I shall now select my Empress!" he said, looking down on the cowering people. "Let the first woman who dares rise to her feet claim her mate and her throne!"

[56]A moment passed, and then a ballerina arose, swaying like a willow.

[57]Harrison plucked the mental handicap from her ear, snapped off her physical handicaps with marvelous delicacy. Last of all, he removed her mask.

[58]She was blindingly beautiful.

[59]"Now—" said Harrison, taking her hand, "shall we show the people the meaning of the word dance? Music!" he commanded.

[60]The musicians scrambled back into their chairs, and Harrison stripped them of their handicaps, too. "Play your best," he told them, "and I'll make you barons and dukes and earls."

[61]The music began. It was normal at first—cheap, silly, false. But Harrison snatched two musicians from their chairs and waved them like batons as he sang the music as he wanted it played. He slammed them back into their chairs.

[62]The music began again and was much improved. Harrison and his Empress merely listened to the music for a while—listened gravely, as though synchronizing their heartbeats with it.

[63]They shifted their weights to their toes.

[64]Harrison placed his big hands on the girl's tiny waist, letting her sense the weightlessness that would soon be hers. And then, in an explosion of joy and grace, into the air they sprang!

[65]Not only were the laws of the land abandoned, but the law of gravity and the laws of motion as well.

[66]They reeled, whirled, swiveled, flounced, capered, gamboled, and spun.

[67]They leaped like deer on the moon.

[68]The studio ceiling was thirty feet high, but each leap brought the dancers nearer to it.

[69]It became their obvious intention to kiss the ceiling. They kissed it.

[70]And then, neutralizing gravity with love and pure will, they remained suspended in air, inches below the ceiling, and kissed each other for a long, long time.

[71]It was then that Diana Moon Glampers, the Handicapper General, came into the studio with a double-barreled ten-gauge shotgun. She fired twice, and the Emperor and the Empress were dead before they hit the floor.

[72]Diana Moon Glampers loaded the gun again. She aimed it at the musicians and told them they had ten seconds to get their handicaps back on.

[73]It was then that the Bergerons' television tube burned out.

[74]Hazel turned to comment about the blackout to George. But George had gone out into the kitchen for a can of beer. George came back in with the beer, paused while a handicap signal shook him up. And then he sat down again.

[75]"You been crying?" he said to Hazel.

[76]"Yup," she said.

[77]"What about?" he said.

[78]"I forget," she said. "Something real sad on television."

[79]"What was it?" he said.

[80]"It's all kind of mixed up in my mind," said Hazel.

[81]"Forget sad things," said George.

[82]"I always do," said Hazel.

[83]"That's my girl," said George. He winced. There was the sound of a rivetting gun in his head.

[84]"Gee—I could tell that one was a doozy," said Hazel.

[85]"You could say that again," said George.

[86]"Gee—" said Hazel, "I could tell that one was a doozy."

Vocabulary

[1]vigilance	[19]glimmeringly	[41]calibrated	[66]flounced
[10]sash-weights	[35]impediment	[42]hindrances	[66]capered
[10]birdshot	[39]luminous	[50]cowered	[66]gamboled
[11]wince	[40]grackle	[62]gravely	

Discussion Questions

1. How are George and Hazel Bergeron described? What sort of life do they lead? What is Vonnegut parodying here?

2. What does the story warn against? To what extent do television, radio, and the mass media generally function like George's mental handicap radio?

3. In the story, to achieve "sameness" what sacrifices are made? Are these sacrifices justifiable? Are they equal in worth to what is gained?

4. How old is Harrison Bergeron? How has he been "handicapped"? Why is he considered to be such a threat to society?

5. What is the meaning of Harrison's and the ballerina's flight-like dance and kissing? What is meant by the statement, "not only were the laws of the land abandoned, but the law of gravity and the laws of motion as well"?

6. Are there any truly heroic or great people in "Harrison Bergeron"? Explain.

7. Think about the emphases on both diversity and sameness in our own society. Compare this to the society in "Harrison Bergeron." Which society seems to be more "utopian"? Why?

8. What point do you think Vonnegut is making? Give examples from the story to support your view.

9. What do you think Karl Marx would think of this society? Ayn Rand?

FROM HIV/AIDS:
THE DEMOGRAPHIC IMPACT

UNITED NATIONS, DEPARTMENT OF ECONOMIC AND SOCIAL AFFAIRS, POPULATION DIVISION

*The **United Nations** officially came into existence in October of 1945 at the conclusion of World War II. Among its objectives, the UN works to promote human rights, protect the environment, fight disease, reduce poverty and promote economic development, especially in the less-developed regions of the world.*

[1]Since 1981, when the first cases of AIDS were diagnosed, the world has been facing the deadliest epidemic in modern history. Nearly 30 years after the start of the epidemic, mortality caused by AIDS has attained orders of magnitude comparable to those associated with other historic visitations of pestilence. In Europe alone, it is estimated that in a five-year period, from 1347 to 1351, over 20 million people died as a result of the Black Death.[a] In contrast, the human immunodeficiency virus (HIV) is a slow killer. However, the Joint United Nations Programme on HIV/AIDS estimates that by the end of 2007, 33 million people were living with HIV/AIDS and that an additional 25 million people had already lost their lives to AIDS.

[2]In spite of the progress made in treating people infected with HIV, in particular in the more developed countries,[b] AIDS remains an incurable and usually fatal disease, especially when coupled with malnutrition in the less-developed regions[c] of the world. UNAIDS estimates that 21.4 million of the 33 million persons infected with HIV were living in sub-Saharan Africa (the area of Africa south of the Sahara Desert), 6 million in South and Southeast Asia and 2 million in Latin America and the Caribbean.

[3]Sub-Saharan Africa is by far the area in the world affected the worst by the AIDS epidemic. The region has just over 10% of the world's population, but

---

[a]The Black Death was a pandemic believed to be bubonic plague that was spread to humans by fleas feeding on infected rats. During the five-year period cited here, the plague killed off approximately 1/3 of Europe's population.

[b]The more-developed regions: all regions of Europe plus Northern America, Australia/New Zealand and Japan.

[c]The less-developed regions: all regions of Africa, Asia (excluding Japan), Latin America and the Caribbean plus Melanesia, Micronesia and Polynesia

is home to 67% of all people living with HIV. An estimated 1.9 million adults and children became infected with HIV during 2007. This brought the total number of people living with HIV/AIDS in the region to just under 22 million by the end of the year. HIV prevalence, expressed as a percentage of the total population of a country infected by HIV/AIDS, varies considerably across this region, ranging from less than 1% in Madagascar to over 20% in Botswana, Lesotho, Zimbabwe and Swaziland (TABLE 1).

TABLE 1: The Prevalence of HIV/AIDS by Percent of Population Affected in Selected Countries

	Country	Prevalence (% of population infected) in Adults (ages 15-49)
AFRICA		
	Botswana	23.9 %
	Ethiopia	6.5 %
	Lesotho	21.6 %
	Liberia	6.5 %
	South Africa	19.4 %
	Swaziland	26.1 %
	Zimbabwe	24.5 %
ASIA		
	Cambodia	1.0 %
	India	0.3%
	Myanmar	0.5 %
EUROPE		
	Russia	1.1 %
	Ukraine	1.6 %
LATIN AMERICA and CARIBBEAN		
	Bahamas	3.0 %
	Haiti	2.2 %
	Trinidad/ Tobago	1.5 %
NORTHERN AMERICA		
	United States	0.7 %

Source: UNAIDS: The Joint United Nations Programme on HIV/AIDS, *AIDS Epidemic Update, 2007*

[4]Since people infected with HIV remain healthy for long periods before showing obvious signs of immunodeficiency, the first stages of the HIV epidemic are difficult to detect. However, social scientists and epidemiologists modeling the impact of the epidemic have long known that its cumulative impact can be serious. In *World Population Prospects: The 2002 Revision,* the United Nations Department of Economic and Social Affairs Population Division incorporated the impact of AIDS into the estimates and projections of the populations of 53 countries. In most of those countries, HIV prevalence is estimated to be 2 per cent or more among the adult population aged 15-49. In addition, a few populous countries with lower prevalence levels, such as India (0.3%), Russia (1.1%) and the United States (0.7%), were included owing to the large number of persons living with HIV (more than one million persons). Of the 53 countries, 38 are in Africa, five are in Asia, eight are in Latin America and the Caribbean and one each is in Europe and Northern America. Of the 33 million adults in the world infected by HIV by 2007, 30.6 million, or 93 per cent, resided in the 53 countries.

[5]In most of the countries that are severely affected by the epidemic, HIV/ AIDS is responsible for stopping or even reversing the long-term health and mortality improvements that had been registered until recently. The spread of HIV has thus compromised the first stage of the epidemiological transition in developing countries—that is, the passage from high to low mortality as infectious diseases are brought under control and are no longer the major cause of death. Indeed, with the emergence of HIV/AIDS, several countries of sub-Saharan Africa, which already lagged behind in the epidemiological transition, have experienced a major setback in terms of combating infectious disease and avoiding premature death. Furthermore, the interaction of HIV with other infectious agents exacerbates its detrimental impact on longevity. The increasing incidence and lethality of tuberculosis in a number of developing countries is one instance of such interaction. In rural Malawi the incidence of tuberculosis doubled between 1986 and 1994, largely because HIV-positive persons are seven times more likely to develop tuberculosis than those who are not infected by HIV.

[6]In many of the countries in Table 1, the prevalence of HIV appeared to be in decline in 2007. Projections now assume that HIV prevalence will peak sometime during the period 2010-2020. In about half of the 53 countries most severely affected by the epidemic, the peak prevalence is estimated to have occurred already, between 1993 and 2001. However, in some of those cases the evidence remains weak that prevalence has indeed passed its peak. Only in Burundi, the Congo, Côte d'Ivoire, Uganda, the United Republic of Tanzania and Zambia is HIV prevalence estimated to have declined by 1.0 percentage points or more from the peak level reached, and only in Thailand and Uganda has prevalence declined by at least one quarter of its peak value. Even in those

populations where prevention efforts have succeeded in lowering HIV prevalence, HIV infection is projected to remain a serious risk for the foreseeable future.

[7]Current estimates indicate that the AIDS epidemic has already had a major impact on life expectancies (TABLE 2). In the seven countries with an adult HIV prevalence of 20 per cent and above, more than 20 years of life expectancy at birth have already been lost to the epidemic, and this effect is expected to intensify in the future. In Zimbabwe, for example, which has one of the highest AIDS-prevalence rates in Africa, average life expectancy dropped from 56.6 years in 1990 to a low of 33.9 years in 2002 (it had come back up to 40.0 in 2005).[d]

TABLE 2: Effect of HIV/AIDS On Life Expectancies in Selected Countries, Both Sexes Combined

Period	Zimbabwe	Swaziland	Lesotho	Botswana	South Africa
1970-1975	55.6	49.6	49.8	56.0	51.0
1975-1980	57.7	52.5	52.2	59.3	55.5
1980-1985	60.4	55.6	55.1	61.5	58.2
1985-1990	56.6	57.7	57.2	63.6	60.8
1990-1995	50.4	58.5	59.7	62.7	61.9
1995-2000	46.8	54.3	55.6	52.6	60.2
2000-2005	40.0	43.9	44.6	46.6	53.4
2005-2010	43.5	39.6	42.6	50.7	49.3
2010-2015	47.4	40.1	44.8	52.0	50.0

Source: *AIDS Epidemic Update, 2007,* UNAIDS: The Joint United Nations Programme on HIV/AIDS; and *UN World Population Prospects, the 2007 Revision,* United Nations Department of Economic and Social Affairs, Population Division

[8]HIV/AIDS is the deadliest epidemic of our time. Over 22 million people have already lost their lives, and more than 42 million are currently living with HIV/AIDS. Even if a vaccine for HIV were discovered today, over 40 million people would still die prematurely as a result of AIDS. In many countries, especially in Africa and the hardest-hit countries such as Botswana, Swaziland and Zimbabwe, the AIDS epidemic has spread rapidly, leaving illness, death, poverty and misery in its wake. In other countries, the disease is still in its early stages. Notably, HIV/AIDS has now taken hold in the largest countries of the world: the number of people infected with HIV has reached one million in China and six million in India, and the destructive effects of the epidemic are

---

[d]In contrast, life expectancies in the Northern America region, both sexes combined, are currently 76.5 and are projected to rise to 82.4 by 2045.

already being felt in those countries.

[9]The epidemic affects every aspect of human life, with devastating consequences. It has imposed heavy burdens on individuals, families, communities and nations. In many countries, the epidemic is undermining personal aspirations, family well-being and national development.

[10]The impact of AIDS is already strikingly apparent in the countries with the highest prevalence rates. In those countries, the impact on mortality and on population size and growth is already substantial. In the most severe case, Botswana, where currently almost one in four adults is HIV positive, the population is expected to decline within the next few years because of the death rate caused by the disease.

[11]HIV/AIDS is not just a demographic disaster; the epidemic has consequences for every sector of society. The epidemic has wide-ranging societal impacts on individuals, families and households; on agricultural sustainability; on business; on the health sector; on education; and on national economic growth.

[12]The burdens of the disease on families and households are staggering. Typically, a family where the disease is present loses an adult in the prime of life, leaving behind not only a bereft family, but also an HIV-infected spouse and orphaned children. During the long period of illness, the loss of income and the cost of caring for family members may bring ruin to the household. The stigma of the disease will be endured not only by those who are ill but also by family members, and, even after death, the stigma will be felt by the survivors. Adult deaths, especially of parents, often cause households to be dissolved and children sent to live with relatives or even abandoned to the streets.

[13]In the agricultural sector, the loss of farm workers to HIV/AIDS has ramifications for food security. A survey in Zimbabwe found that agricultural output declined by nearly 50 per cent among households affected by AIDS. The Food and Agriculture Organization of the United Nations has estimated that the ten most severely affected African countries will lose between 10 and 26 per cent of their agricultural labor force by 2020.

[14]Business enterprises in both the agricultural and non-agricultural sectors are also affected by the disease, as the most productive workers in the labor force become too ill to work and eventually die. Ill workers are less productive, as are those workers who must care for ill family members. The costs of health and death benefits and replacing experienced workers have serious financial implications for businesses and may cause them to become less competitive and eventually close down.

[15]AIDS also reduces the means and the incentives to invest in human capital. The next generation will be less healthy and less well educated than the previous one. In particular, HIV/AIDS seriously threatens the education of the next generation. In households affected by HIV/AIDS, children are often

taken out of school to help at home with care-giving or income-generating activities. AIDS orphans suffer long-term disadvantages when their education is interrupted. Experienced teachers are also dying of AIDS, eroding the quality of education.

[16]Health-care systems were already inadequate in many of the countries even before HIV/AIDS struck. The additional demand for treatment of AIDS and the opportunistic infections that are common in people with compromised immune systems have strained resources, burdened programs and threatened the viability of the entire health-care system in a growing number of countries.

[17]In order to conquer HIV/AIDS, considerably greater efforts and resources will be required. As the Secretary-General concludes in his report, "To finance the global response, ...annual funding for HIV/AIDS programs must increase and fivefold by 2010."

[18]The course of the HIV/AIDS epidemic is by no means predetermined. The eventual course of the disease depends on how individuals, communities, nations and the world respond to the HIV/AIDS threat, today and tomorrow.

Vocabulary

[1]magnitude	[5]exacerbates	[5]lethality	[12]stigma
[1]pestilence	[5]longevity	[9]aspirations	[13]ramifications
[4]epidemiologist	[5]incidence	[12]bereft	[16]viability
[5]mortality			

Discussion Questions

1. In paragraph 1 the authors of this report compare the AIDS epidemic to "The Black Death." What are the similarities and differences of the two?

2. Which area of the world has been hit hardest by the AIDS epidemic? Explain the significance of the statistics 10% and 67% in paragraph 3.

3. In paragraph 5 the report points out an effect of HIV/AIDS that "exacerbates its detrimental impact on longevity." What is the effect?

4. How would you define the overall tone of paragraph 6—optimistic or pessimistic?

5. The text of the report says in paragraph 1 that the first cases of HIV/AIDS were diagnosed in 1981. Looking at the data in Table 2, which of the countries listed there demonstrated an immediate effect on its life expectancy rate after the virus was discovered? Which of the countries saw its life expectancy rate drop to the lowest of the five countries?

6. According to the data in Table 2, which of the five countries currently has the greatest spread between its life expectancy rate and Northern America's? How much is the difference in years?

7. Find the article entitled "United Nations World Population Prospects 2006" elsewhere in this text and explain how the data in Table 2 of that report relates to Botswana's projected decline in population within the next few years as indicated in paragraph 10 of this report.

8. Look at the structure of this report. It begins by putting this epidemic into a historical context and then, in the middle, gives the reader statistical evidence to support a point. What is that point? How would you characterize the information in the concluding section—paragraphs 11-16?

9. Which of the paragraphs in this report do you think most effectively "puts a human face" on this epidemic? Explain why.

FROM HIV/AIDS SURVEILLANCE REPORT
Cases of HIV Infection and AIDS in the United States and Dependent Areas, 2006

CENTERS FOR DISEASE CONTROL AND PREVENTION

*The **United States Centers for Disease Control and Prevention (CDC)** come under the Department of Health and Human Services. CDC surveillance reports are a part of an ongoing, systematic collection, analysis, interpretation, and dissemination of data regarding a health-related event. HIV/AIDS surveillance observes, records and disseminates reports about new cases of HIV and AIDS as well as other diseases.*

Commentary

[1]HIV/AIDS was first recognized in the United States in 1981. The AIDS epidemic has since spread to all of the states and U.S. dependent areas. Since the beginning of the epidemic, all states and U.S. dependent areas have conducted AIDS surveillance by using a standardized, confidential name-based reporting system. However, only 33 states and five dependent areas use a similar uniform system to report HIV infections.

[2]Since many people live for years with HIV before developing AIDS, looking at AIDS statistics alone does not give a full picture of the scope of the problem in the U.S. Surveillance data on HIV infections and a combined category of HIV/AIDS, not just data on AIDS cases alone, provide a more complete picture of the epidemic and the need for prevention and care services.

[3]In recent years, the use of antiretroviral therapy has slowed the progression of HIV in many infected persons and hence contributed to a decline in new cases of AIDS incidence. At the same time, people with AIDS are surviving longer, thus contributing to a steady increase in the number of people living with AIDS. This trend will continue as long as the number of new diagnoses exceeds the number of people dying each year.

[4]Based upon the number of reported AIDS cases, the 33 states in the HIV/AIDS reporting system represent approximately 63% of the epidemic in the 50 states and the District of Columbia. From 2003 through 2006, the total number of new cases of HIV remained stable in the 33 states; however, HIV/AIDS prevalence (i.e., the number of persons living with HIV/AIDS) increased steadily; by the end of 2006, an estimated 491,727 persons in the 33 states were living with HIV/AIDS.

[5]During 2006, an estimated 36,817 new diagnoses of HIV infection were reported from the 38 areas with a history of confidential name-based reporting,

a number that has remained relatively stable since 2001. Of these cases, 73% were among adult or adolescent males, 26% were among adult or adolescent females, and less than 1% were among children under 13 years of age.

[6]It is estimated that around 56,300 Americans became newly infected with HIV in 2006. The number of new infections peaked in 1984-85 at around 130,000 per year, fell to a low of around 49,000 in the early 1990s, peaked again at around 58,000 in the late 1990s, and then declined slightly to its current level. Within this overall pattern are considerable variations among exposure groups: among men who have sex with men, for example, there has been a steady rise in new infections since the early 1990s.

Prevalence rates of HIV infection

[7]At the end of 2006, in the 38 areas with confidential name-based HIV infection reporting since at least 2003, the prevalence rate of HIV infection among adults and adolescents was estimated at 143.7 per 100,000 (1.43 percent of the U.S. population). The rate for adults and adolescents living with HIV infection that had not yet progressed to AIDS ranged from an estimated 4.9 per 100,000 (.049 percent) in American Samoa to an estimated 261.7 per 100,000 (2.6 percent) in New York.

[8]Over time, HIV infection may progress to AIDS and be reported to surveillance. Persons with HIV infection (not AIDS) who are later reported as having AIDS are deleted from the HIV only tables and added to the AIDS tables. Persons with HIV infection may be tested at any point on the clinical spectrum of disease; therefore, the time between diagnosis of HIV infection and diagnosis of AIDS differs. In addition, because surveillance practices differ, the reporting and updating of persons' clinical and vital status differ among states. The completeness of reporting of HIV infection (not AIDS) is estimated at more than 80%.

Cases of HIV/AIDS

[9]From 2003 through 2006, the estimated number of HIV/AIDS cases (cases of HIV infection, regardless whether they have progressed to AIDS) in the 33 states with confidential name-based HIV infection reporting remained stable (Table 1). At the end of 2006, the CDC estimates there were 509,681 people living with HIV/AIDS in the 38 areas that have a history of confidential name-based HIV reporting, based on reported diagnoses and deaths. However, because these figures represent only the 33 reporting states, the total number of people living in the USA with HIV/AIDS is estimated to be around 1.1 million. In 2006, the estimated rate of HIV/AIDS cases in the 33 states was 18.5 per 100,000 population (.185 percent).

TABLE 1: Estimated numbers of cases of HIV/AIDS by age and year of diagnosis

	2003	2004	2005	2006
Age at Diagnosis				
Under 13	211	183	169	135
13-14	53	36	40	41
15-19	993	993	1126	1332
20-24	3163	3368	3592	3886
25-29	4023	4057	4236	4603
30-34	5189	4820	4676	4466
35-39	6369	5807	5535	5442
40-44	5786	5429	5529	5718
45-49	4028	3877	4028	4204
50-54	2451	2401	2547	2718
55-59	1279	1363	1455	1438
60-64	655	702	692	714
65 and over	570	624	613	618

[10]Highlights:

•**Age group**: In 2006, the largest number of HIV/AIDS cases occurred among persons aged 40–44 years, who accounted for 16% of all HIV/AIDS cases diagnosed during the year (Table 1).

•**Race/ethnicity:** In 2006, rates of HIV/AIDS cases were 67.7 per 100,000 in the black population, 25.5 per 100,000 in the Hispanic population, 8.8 per 100,000 in the American Indian/Alaska Native population, 8.2 per 100,000 in the white population, and 6.7 per 100,000 in the Asian/Pacific Islander population (Table 2).

TABLE 2: Estimated numbers of cases of HIV/AIDS by race/ethnicity, 2003-206

Race/Ethnicity	2003	2004	2005	2006
White, not Hispanic	10,033	10,181	10,528	10,758
Black, not Hispanic	17,668	16,718	16,629	17,356
Hispanic	6355	6010	6217	6481
Asian/Pacific Islander	338	339	373	397
American Indian/Alaska Native	179	171	182	166

•**Sex:** In 2006, males accounted for 74% of all HIV/AIDS cases among adults and adolescents.

•**Transmission category:** Among men who have sex with men (MSM), there has been a steady rise in new infections since the early 1990s. From 2003 through 2006, the estimated number of HIV/AIDS cases continued to increase among the MSM population and remained stable among adults and adolescents with HIV infection attributed to high-risk heterosexual contact (heterosexual contact with a person known to have, or to be at high risk for, HIV infection) (Table 3). The estimated number of HIV/AIDS cases decreased among injection drug users (IDUs), MSM who were also IDUs, and among children. MSM (49%) and persons exposed through high-risk heterosexual contact (33%) accounted for 82% of all HIV/AIDS cases diagnosed in 2006.

TABLE 3: Estimated numbers of cases of HIV/AIDS by transmission category, 2003-2006

	2003	2004	2005	2006
Male Adult or Adolescent				
Male-to-Male Sexual Contact (MSM)	15,409	15,880	16,833	17,465
Injection Drug Use (IDU)	3514	3083	2978	3016
MSM and IDU	1349	1299	1247	1180
High-risk Heterosexual Contact	4269	3959	3871	4152
Other (e.g., blood transfusions)	125	110	107	114
Subtotal	24,666	24,331	25,036	25,928
Female Adult or Adolescent				
Injection Drug Use	2027	1856	1720	1712
High-risk Heterosexual Contact	7731	7182	7216	7432
Other	134	107	97	109
Subtotal	9892	9145	9033	9252

[11]Of all HIV infections diagnosed in 2005 in the 33 states with confidential name-based HIV reporting, 38% progressed to AIDS within 12 months after HIV infection was diagnosed. AIDS was diagnosed within 12 months after the diagnosis of HIV infection for larger proportions of persons aged 13–14 years and 35 years and older, for Hispanics, for IDUs, and for males with HIV infection attributed to high-risk heterosexual contact (Table 2).

Cases of AIDS

[12]Through 2006, a total of 992,865 persons in the United States had been reported as having AIDS. Since the beginning of the epidemic in 1981, an estimated 565,927 people with AIDS have died in the U.S.

[13]Three states (California, Florida, and New York) reported 43% of the cumulative AIDS cases and 37% of AIDS cases reported to CDC in 2006. In the United States, the rate of reported AIDS cases in 2006 was 12.9 per 100,000 population. When the U.S. dependent areas were included, the rate of reported AIDS cases ranged from zero per 100,000 (American Samoa, Guam, and the Northern Mariana Islands) to 146.7 per 100,000 (District of Columbia).

[14]AIDS prevalence increased steadily from 2002 through 2006. At the end of 2006, an estimated 436,693 persons in the 50 states and the District of Columbia were living with AIDS.

•In 2006, males accounted for 73% and females for 27% of 38,916 reported AIDS cases among adults and adolescents.

•By age group, most (22%) were aged 40–44 years.

•By race/ethnicity, 44% were black, 35% white, 19% Hispanic, 1% Asian/Pacific Islander, and less than 1% were American Indian/Alaska Native (Figure 1).

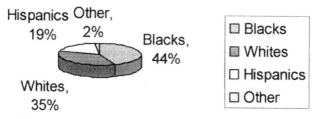

FIGURE 1: Cases of AIDS by Race/Ethnicity

•By sex, 77% of adults and adolescents living with AIDS were male.

•Of the estimated 333,244 male adults and adolescents living with AIDS, 60% had been exposed through male-to-male sexual contact, 19% had been exposed through injection drug use, 12% had been exposed through high-risk heterosexual contact, and 8% had been exposed through both male-to-male sexual contact and injection drug use. Of the estimated 99,671 female adults and adolescents living with AIDS, 66% had been exposed through high-risk heterosexual contact, and 32% had been exposed through injection drug use.

•By region, 41% resided in the South, 29% in the Northeast, 20% in the West, and 11% in the Midwest.

Vocabulary

[3]antiretroviral   [4]prevalence   [10]heterosexual

Discussion Questions

1. What is the distinction between HIV and AIDS ?

2. Explain the differences in the reporting of HIV and AIDS in the United States. Which of the two reporting systems has the more accurate statistics?

3. Explain why this sentence is true (end of paragraph 2): "Surveillance data on HIV infections, compared with data on AIDS, provide a more complete picture of the epidemic and the need for prevention and care services."

4. Based upon the content of this article and outside research, why is ". . .

HIV/AIDS prevalence (i.e., the number of persons living with HIV/AIDS) increas[ing] steadily" in the United States?

5. In the HIV/AIDS surveillance of ten years ago, the CDC reported the highest incidence of HIV infections among late adolescence and early twenties. According to Table 1, what is the age group with the highest incidence of HIV/AIDS in 2006? Why do you suppose this is?

6. Which three states combine to have the highest rate of newly reported AIDS cases? Why do you think this is true of these particular states?

7. Look at the content of paragraph 13. What does the number of AIDS cases per 100,000 population in American compared to the number of AIDS cases per 100,000 in Washington D.C. say about living conditions for residents of our nation's capital?

8. Roughly how many people have died of AIDS in the United States since the beginning of the epidemic? Use an outside source to find out approximately how many people have died worldwide since the beginning of the epidemic (also called a "pandemic").

9. According to Figure 1, blacks account for 44 percent of the total number of AIDS cases reported in the United States. Why is this figure of concern?

10. What would you say are the four or five most significant points contained in the article?

FROM THE INTERNATIONAL DEVELOPMENT AGENDA AND THE CLIMATE CHANGE CHALLENGE

THE COMMITTEE FOR DEVELOPMENT POLICY, UNITED NATIONS OFFICE OF ECONOMIC AND SOCIAL AFFAIRS

*The **United Nations** officially came into existence in October of 1945 at the conclusion of World War II. Among its objectives, the UN works to promote human rights, protect the environment, fight disease, reduce poverty and promote economic development, especially in the less-developed regions of the world.*

FOREWARD

[1]The United Nations Secretary-General has described climate change as a "defining issue of our era." The present Policy Note of the Committee for Development Policy (CDP) examines the severity of the problem and its implications for the international economic development agenda. The report elaborates further on the background and the main findings that were presented by the Committee in its official report to the Economic and Social Council of the United Nations in November, 2007.

[2]The urgency of the challenge posed by climate change is now widely acknowledged, and an agenda for internationally concerted action is being developed. A high-level conference on climate change was convened by the Secretary-General at the United Nations on 24 September 2007 to map out how the world can move forward to address climate change and still promote sustainable economic development. The present Policy Note represents an important input to these international discussions.

INTRODUCTION

[3]Can the world's international economic development goals still be achieved at a time when international, regional and national actions must be taken to confront the challenge of climate change? The present Policy Note of the Committee for Development Policy (CDP) argues that combating climate change and achieving internationally agreed-upon development goals can no longer be placed in separate boxes, but efforts to pursue both objectives should be coherent and mutually reinforcing.

[4]Climate change is the most serious emerging threat that, if not confronted properly, may soon disrupt life on this planet. Climate change, manifested

in the rise of the earth's mean temperature, is already taking its toll in the form of widespread melting glaciers, sea-level rise, extreme weather patterns and other adverse phenomena, as documented by the recent report of the United Nations Intergovernmental Panel on Climate Change (IPCC, 2007). The IPCC report also confirmed that concentrations of greenhouse gases have increased markedly as a result of human activity, with global increases in carbon dioxide (CO_2)—the main greenhouse gas—being primarily the result of fossil fuel use and land use change.

[5]There is no way to stop the process of climate change other than to undertake deep cuts in greenhouse gas emissions. The main initiative in stopping climate change has to come from developed countries, which have been largely responsible for the increase in the greenhouse gas concentration in the earth's atmosphere over the last 200 years since the beginning of the Industrial Revolution. The Industrial Revolution started the present process of unprecedented economic growth and improved living standards, but a massive increase in energy power was needed to support this process. The main sources of energy over the past two centuries have been fossil (carbon-based) fuels, primarily coal and petroleum. The burning of coal and petroleum discharged gases into the atmosphere which could not be absorbed, thus contributing to the emergence of the greenhouse phenomenon and its impact on climate.

[6]The earth can absorb about 5 billion metric tons of carbon dioxide equivalent (CO_2e) each year. However, annual global emissions of CO_2 from fossil fuel combustion alone are now over 27 billion tons. Climate change is not a zero-sum game in which some regions will benefit in the long run while others will lose: the atmosphere is probably our most important "global public good," and eventually all regions will be adversely affected by its deterioration. To implement the deep cuts in greenhouse gas emissions required to stop the process of climate change, the industrialized countries will have to fundamentally rethink their production and consumption patterns and lifestyles.

[7]While the main responsibility for cutting emissions lies with developed countries, developing countries also have a vital interest in climate change. The adverse effects of climate change will continue to prove particularly severe for developing countries because of their 1) geographical location; 2) reliance on climate-related economic activities (such as agriculture); and 3) weak coping capability.

[8]The recommendations of the Committee for Development Policy in this Policy Note are intended to suggest ways to make worldwide economic development sustainable in the face of the challenges posed by climate change and to encourage examination of the roles that both developing and developed countries have to play in this regard. The Committee also points to the necessity to develop further and better integrate climate change mitigation and adaptation

policies into the international economic development agenda; and the need to promote a reduced-carbon pattern of economic development worldwide while, at the same time, meeting countries' goals of improved standards of living and welfare for their populations.

THE GREENHOUSE CHALLENGE

[9]According to IPCC (2007), the earth's temperature is rising because of human activity, and further temperature increases contain the threat of catastrophic consequences. The scientific community has long considered an increase of 2° C above the pre-industrial level as a threshold beyond which dramatic changes are likely to occur. Yet, the danger is that the mutually reinforcing effects of global warming may take the world to a temperature increase of 3° C or higher very soon.

[10]A temperature increase of 3° C or more may lead to, among other adverse consequences, melting of the Greenland ice sheet, which in turn may cause the sea level to rise by up to 7 meters (23 feet), inundating many low-lying densely populated countries and large coastal cities all over the world. The impact will be hardest on developing countries, and particularly on the small island developing states, many of which would—in the case of temperature rises of 3 degrees or more—run the risk of being completely submerged.

[11]Within developing countries, the most affected by any level of climate change will be the poor, who have to rely more on climate-related activities for their livelihood, who are more exposed to the elements of nature, and who have the least resources to cope. Climate change will thus inflict damage precisely on those nations and people who are the least responsible for its cause and the least prepared to deal with its consequences.

GREENHOUSE GASES AND THEIR IMPACT

[12]The most important greenhouse gas is CO_2 (currently constituting 77 percent of the climate change potential). According to the Stern Review conducted for the British government by Sir Nicholas Stern, current levels of greenhouse gases in the atmosphere are 430 parts per million (ppm) of CO_2e as compared to 280 ppm before the Industrial Revolution. These concentrations have already caused the world to warm by more than half a degree Celsius and will lead to at least a further half a degree of warming over the next few decades because of the inertia in the climate system.

[13]Yet, even if the annual flow of emissions were not to increase beyond today's rate, the stock of greenhouse gases in the atmosphere would reach double the pre-industrial levels by 2050, that is to say, 550 ppm CO_2e. At the current rate of increase in the annual flow of emissions, however, this level of 550 ppm CO_2e could be reached as early as 2035. There is a very high likelihood—with a probability of 77 to 99 percent, depending on the climate model used—that, with this flow of emissions, the global average temperature will rise by more

than $2°C$. This demonstrates the urgency of initiating action to sharply reduce greenhouse gas emissions.

[14]Ongoing research indicates that the problem is more serious and more urgent than previously thought. For instance, a study undertaken by the University of East Anglia, United Kingdom, and the Max Planck Institute for Biogeochemistry in Jena, Germany, found that the increase in winds over the Southern Ocean, caused by man-made climate change and ozone depletion, had led to the release of stored carbon dioxide in the ocean into the atmosphere, which in turn is preventing the further absorption of greenhouse gases. Thus a carbon "sink"— a means of absorbing carbon dioxide from the atmosphere, such as a wooded area—will prove less effective than anticipated. In addition, the release of the carbon dioxide is itself contributing to the acidification of the Southern Ocean.

THE CURRENT LEVEL OF GREENHOUSE GAS EMISSIONS

[15]Despite the targets established by the Kyoto Protocol, greenhouse gas emissions have continued to increase. Global CO_2 emissions increased 17 percent between 1990 and 2003 (from 22 to 26 Gigatons CO_2). All regions contributed to the increase in emissions, with the exception of the countries of the former Soviet Union and other Eastern European countries, where there had been a decline owing to their severe economic recession and the closing down of many of their worst polluting industries following the transition from centrally planned to market economies. Emissions in North America increased by 16 per cent (from 5.5 to 6.4 $GtCO_2$); in Western Europe by 4.5 per cent (from 3.5 to 3.6 $GtCO_2$); in Asia and the Pacific by 53 per cent (from 6.3 to 9.7 $GtCO_2$); in Africa by 47 per cent (from 0.6 to 0.9 $GtCO_2$); and in Latin America and the Caribbean by 24 per cent (from 1.0 to 1.3 $GtCO_2$) (see Table 1).

Table 1: Emissions, Population, GDP and Energy Supply by Region, 1990 and 2003

Regions	CO_2 Emissions (Billions of Metric Tons)		Population (millions)		CO2 emissions per capita (metric tons)		Gross Domestic Product (constant, $2000)		Energy supply per $1000 GDP (PPP) (kilogram oil	
	1990	2003	1990	2003	1990	2003	1990	2003	1990	2003
Africa	0.6	0.9	637	881	1.0	1.1	425	645	299	299
Asia & the Pacific	6.4	9.7	3,054	3,674	2.1	2.6	6,119	9,154	271	207
China	—	—	1,155	1,304	—	—	551	1,732	485	220
India	—	—	860	1,099	—	—	288	554	253	191
Europe	8.2	6.8	800	824	10.3	8.3	7,814	9,904	256	203
Eastern Europe	3.3	—	231	223	14.3	—	496	376	557	513
Western Europe	3.5	3.6	381	403	9.1	9.0	6,795	8,842	173	154
Latin America/ Caribbean	1.1	1.3	444	544	2.4	2.4	1,458	2,066	169	165
North America	5.5	6.4	284	325	19.3	19.8	7,591	11,097	277	228
Global	22.2	26.0	5,295	6,359	4.2	4.1	23,671	33,305	261	213

[16]The absolute levels of emissions are thus moving the world away from the Kyoto targets with respect to emission reductions by 2012. In order to move towards these targets (and especially those of the United Nations Framework Convention on Climate Change) without jeopardizing the economic growth needed for achieving developmental goals, there will have to be a significant *decoupling* or *delinking* of GHG emissions from economic growth. The main initiative in cutting carbon emissions will have to come from developed countries because of both their historical responsibility and their continued high current volumes of emissions.

THE CHALLENGE OF STABILIZATION

[17]The magnitude of the challenge facing mankind can be appreciated by looking at the projections for the year 2100 under the IPCC baseline scenario IS92a. According to this scenario, the world population will increase from 6.42 billion in 2005 to 11.3 billion by 2100, world Gross Domestic Product (GDP) will increase eightfold, and energy use will triple from current levels, even though the fraction of energy supplied from fossil fuels will drop from over 80 percent to under 60 percent and the energy intensity of production will fall. Thus, notwithstanding improvements in energy efficiency and reduction in dependence on fossil fuels, CO_2 emissions would reach 75 $GtCO_2$ by 2100 (and atmospheric CO_2 concentration would amount to over 700 ppm).

[18]A reduction in carbon emissions requires a reduction in one or more of the following:

- **Population:** A decline in population growth would bring about a proportional reduction in emissions, without any change in affluence, energy efficiency or carbon intensity.
- **Income:** A slowdown in growth of per capita income (although not considered desirable by most analyses) would similarly reduce emissions proportionately.
- **Energy and carbon intensity:** By investing in energy-efficient production, fuel switching, land-use changes, carbon storage and sequestration, and by improving the efficiency of the conversion of fossil fuels into energy, the volume of emissions would be reduced for a given quantum of energy use and, ultimately, production. Where feasible and appropriate, less energy-and carbon-intensive PCPs would reconcile economic growth and GHG emissions.

[19]As Table 2 illustrates, there is some scope for action with respect to each of these three factors that determine carbon emissions.

[20]Regarding population growth, for example, efforts could be made to bring the global population more in line with the carrying capacity of the earth.

Table 2. Projections of Key Factors in Climate Change 2005-2100

	Population (Billions)	GDP per capita (Constant US $)	Energy intensity (MJ/$)	CO_2 emissions (GtCO₂)
2005 actual data	6.42	$6, 541	12.1	27.5
2100 projection	11.30	$29,730	4.5	75.0
Measures needed for limiting atmospheric CO_2 concentration to 450 ppm	Little change possible, but final figure could be between 9 and 11 billion.	Higher income considered desirable, but quality of growth would need to be improved.	Major potential for change is in this area. Technologies for low-and non-carbon generation of energy are promising.	With no improvements in energy-production efficiency, emissions would be slightly over two times higher (165 GtCO₂).

Yet, population change can take place only gradually, especially as many people born at the present time can expect to live an average of 80 years. At the same time, fertility rates are falling in many countries, a factor which, together with increased longevity, is posing socio-economic challenges.

[21]In any case, changes in the overall size of the world's population cannot be expected to take place within the required time frame—the next three decades—on a sufficient scale to have a major effect on mitigating climate change.

[22]Regarding GDP growth, developed countries would need to focus much more on the quality of growth rather than just the quantity. Alternative settlement and consumption patterns in these countries can probably lead to a more satisfying life even at current or somewhat reduced income levels. Changes in patterns of consumption and production (PCPs) may be needed to help reduce the energy intensity of income. Progress is already being seen in this direction: for example, with the enactment of tighter emission standards for vehicles, charges for bringing vehicles into the most congested parts of major cities (thereby also reducing pollution and traffic jams, and encouraging the use of public transport), stricter building codes, and the use of more fuel-efficient light bulbs. These can only be seen as modest and preliminary steps, and no doubt additional measures will be needed to reduce energy consumption.

[23]The most promising area of action relates to CO_2 intensity of energy, which, under the IS92 scenario, is expected to show only a modest decline from 54.3 to 49.2 $KgCO_2/GJ$ (kilograms of CO_2 per gigajoule of energy). Fortunately, many technologies for low- and non-carbon energy generation are already available in developed countries and further progress can be made through vigorous research .

[24]Wind and solar power could provide sources of carbon-free energy in countries with the right conditions. Wave power is at an early stage of development. Nuclear and hydropower are also alternatives, but both are problematic: nuclear, because of both the dangers of a plant malfunctioning and problems with the disposal of the radioactive waste; and hydroelectricity, because of the

effects of climate change in reducing the flow of water into glacier-fed rivers, as is occurring in the Andes.

[25]Biomass technology is also advancing, but there are considerable disputes as to whether the production of some fuels, such as ethanol, is really cost and energy efficient and whether a surge in the production of biofuels from corn, wheat and soybeans would push up food prices, as already appears to be happening. Moreover, if forested land were cleared to make way for biofuel production, this could have a negative effect on climate change by reducing the size of carbon sinks. At present, subsidies are often used to encourage the construction of facilities for generating clean power, and these might be needed for some time to come. However, recent calculations for Denmark have indicated that wind power actually saves consumers money, as the benefits resulting from lower power prices outweigh the falling costs of the subsidy.

[26]As evidence accumulates on the damaging effects of climate change and the impossibility, as illustrated above, of "business as usual," the question that must be addressed is, have the steps taken so far been adequate—and, in particular, were the goals realistic and have they been actually attained? If the answer is in the negative, the need for even more drastic action than presently contemplated is reinforced.

CONCLUSIONS AND RECOMMENDATIONS

[27]• The response to the climate change threat so far has been inadequate, and there is an urgent need for raising the mitigation and adaptation efforts to an entirely different level. Any post-Kyoto arrangement has to go far beyond the present Protocol in order to reflect properly the enormity and the urgency of the problem.

[28]• While the Kyoto Protocol followed a one-track approach focusing on (marginal) reduction of emissions by developed countries and treating developing countries largely as onlookers, post-Kyoto arrangements have to adopt a simultaneous two-track approach. The first track would aim at very deep cuts in emissions by developed countries; the second would provide a more central role to developing countries by enabling them to both grow faster and make their growth as less-carbonized and decarbonized as possible through the successful adoption and implementation of appropriate climate-friendly development strategies with the necessary technological and financial cooperation from developed countries.

[29]• The United Nations should further contribute to the post-Kyoto process, and the Economic and Social Council could provide a platform for an overarching and sustained policy dialogue about the relationship between climate and development. This policy dialogue should also lead to a process of future revision of the Millennium Development Goals so that the danger of climate change and its overshadowing impact on all other development issues find appropriate reflection.

Vocabulary

[4]adverse	[9]catastrophic	[15]protocol	[18]feasible
[4]phenomena	[10]inundating	[18]affluence	[20]longevity
[5]emissions	[12]inertia	[18]per capita	[26]contemplated
[8]mitigation	[14]ozone	[18]sequestration	[28]implementation
[8]adaptation	[14]depletion	[18]quantum	[29]overarching

Discussion Questions

1. Based upon what you read in the first few paragraphs of this document, what do you think is the primary responsibility of the Committee for Development Policy? How does the problem of climate change affect this responsibility?

2. What does the Committee say about the role of the "developed nations" in the climate change problem in paragraph 5?

3. Not everyone agrees with the first sentence in paragraph 5. Do you agree or do you think there may be other ways of dealing with this issue?

4. The Committee says in paragraph 6, "to stop the process of climate change, the industrialized countries will have to fundamentally rethink their production and consumption patterns and lifestyles." What does Thorstein Veblen say starting on page 208 of this text about the consumption patterns of Americans?

5. What is your view of the quote in question four above? Do you think that Americans need to change their consumption patterns and lifestyles?

6. In paragraph 10, the Committee mentions the effects of the melting Greenland ice sheet. What would a rise in ocean sea level of 23 feet mean to the United States? To New York and New Jersey?

7. What is a "carbon sink"? (paragraph 14) Based upon your knowledge of biological processes, explain how it works.

8. What is the "Kyoto Protocol" mentioned in paragraph 15? What was the response of the United States to Kyoto during the George W. Bush administration? What is the view or policy of the present administration toward Kyoto and subsequent international efforts in this area?

9. Look at Table 1. What was the only region to show a decline in CO_2 emissions? Why did this happen? What does this tell us about the type of economy prevalent in this region in the 20th century?

10. Note in Table 1 that there are no figures for China and India. Why do you think this is so? What do you think the figures would show if they had been included?

11. What does the Committee mean in paragraph 16 when it says that there must be a "delinking" between requirements for cutting CO_2 emissions and economic initiatives of developing economies? Do you think this is the right thing to do? Why or why not?

12. Explain this sentence from paragraph 17 in your own words: ". . . the fraction of energy supplied from fossil fuels will drop from over 80 percent to under 60 percent and the energy intensity of production will fall."

13. What is "biomass technology" discussed in paragraph 25? What are some examples and what are its drawbacks?

14. Which of the Key Factors in climate change listed in Table 2 has the greatest potential for improving the situation? Why?

THE INTERNATIONAL STATUS OF THE SLAVE-TRADE, 1783-1862
FROM *THE SUPPRESSION OF THE SLAVE TRADE*

W.E.B. DUBOIS

W.E.B. DuBois (1868-1963) was the first black to earn a doctorate of philosophy from Harvard University. DuBois founded the Niagara Movement, a group of black leaders committed to racial equality, and was a key member of the NAACP. He wrote The Philadelphia Negro *(1899), the first sociological study of black Americans, and* The Souls of Black Folk *(1903), a treatise against Booker T. Washington's policy of accommodation. Later, DuBois became a communist and moved to Ghana, Africa, where he lived the rest of his life.*

66. The Rise of the Movement Against the Slave-Trade, 1788-1807

[1]At the beginning of the nineteenth century, England held 800,000 slaves in her colonies; France, 250,000; Denmark, 27,000; Spain and Portugal, 600,000; Holland, 50,000; Sweden, 600; there were also about 2,000,000 slaves in Brazil, and about 900,000 in the United States.[a]

[2]This was the powerful basis of the demand for the slave-trade; and against the economic forces which these four and a half millions of enforced laborers represented, the battle for freedom had to be fought.

[3]Denmark first responded to the denunciatory cries of the eighteenth century against slavery and the slave-trade. In 1792, by royal order, this traffic was prohibited in the Danish possessions after 1802. The principles of the French Revolution logically called for the extinction of the slave system by France. This was, however, accomplished more precipitately than the Convention anticipated; and in a whirl of enthusiasm engendered by the appearance of the Dominican deputies, slavery and the slave-trade were abolished in all French colonies February 4, 1794.[b]

[4]This abolition was short-lived, for at the command of the First Consul, slavery and the slave-trade was restored in 1799.[c] The trade was finally abolished by Napoleon during the Hundred Days by a decree, March 29, 1815, which briefly declared: "*A dater de la publication du présent Décret, la Traite des Noirs est abolie.*"[d] The Treaty of Paris eventually confirmed this law.[e]

[5]In England, a bill regulating the trade, which passed in July of 1788, was the last English measure countenancing the traffic. On a motion by Pitt in 1788, the House of Commons had resolved to take up at the next session the question

of the abolition of the trade.[f] It was, accordingly, called up by Wilberforce, and a remarkable parliamentary battle ensued, which lasted continuously until 1805.

[6]This ministry first prohibited the trade with colonies England had acquired by conquest during the Napoleonic Wars; then, in 1806, they prohibited the foreign slave-trade; and finally, on March 25, 1807, enacted the total abolition of the traffic.[g]

67. Concerted Action of the Powers, 1783-1814.

[7]During the peace negotiations between the United States and Great Britain following the end of the American Revolution in 1783, it was proposed by John Jay that there be a proviso inserted as follows: "Provided that the subjects of his Britannic Majesty shall not have any right or claim under the convention, to carry or import into the said States any slaves from any part of the world; it being the intention of the said States entirely to prohibit the importation thereof."[h]

[8]Fox promptly replied: "If that be their policy, it never can be competent to us to dispute with them their own regulations."[i]

[9]In another treaty, signed in London on December 31, 1806, Article 24 provided that "The contracting parties engage to communicate to each other, without delay, all such laws as have been enacted by their respective Legislatures, as also all measures which shall be taken for the abolition or limitation of the African slave trade; and they further agree to use their best endeavors to procure the cooperation of other Powers for the final and complete abolition of a trade so repugnant to the principles of justice and humanity."[j]

[10]This marks the beginning of a long series of treaties between England and other countries looking toward the prohibition of the traffic by international agreement. During the years 1810-1814, England signed treaties relating to the subject with Portugal, Denmark, and Sweden. On May 30, 1814, an additional article to the Treaty of Paris between France and Great Britain engaged these powers "to decree the abolition of the slave-trade so that the said Trade shall cease universally, as it shall cease definitively, under any circumstances, on the part of the French Government, in the course of five years."[k]

[11]In addition to this, the next day a circular letter was dispatched by Lord Castlereagh to Austria, Russia, and Prussia, expressing the hope "that the Powers of Europe, when restoring Peace to Europe will crown this great work by interposing their benign offices in favour of those Regions of the Globe, which yet continue to be desolated by this unnatural and inhuman traffic."[l]

68. Action of the Powers from 1814 to 1820.

[12]In the Treaty of Ghent between Great Britain and the United States, ratified February 17, 1815, Article 10, proposed by Great Britain, declared that, "Whereas the traffic in slaves is irreconcilable with the principles of humanity

and justice," the two countries agreed to use their best endeavors in abolishing the trade.[m]

[13]The final overthrow of Napoleon was marked by a second declaration of the powers, who, "desiring to give effect to the complete and universal abolition of the Slave Trade, and having prohibited without restriction their Colonies and Subjects from taking any part whatever in this Traffic, engage to renew measures for the entire and definitive abolition of a Commerce so odious, and so strongly condemned by the laws of religion and of nature."[n]

69. The Struggle for an International Right of Search, 1820-1840.

[14]Whatever England's motives were, it is certain that only a limited international Right of Visit on the high seas could suppress or greatly limit the slave-trade. Her diplomacy was therefore henceforth directed to this end.

[15]On the other hand, the maritime supremacy of England, so successfully asserted during the Napoleonic wars, would, in case a Right of Search were granted, virtually make England the policeman of the seas; and if nations like the United States had already had just cause to complain of violations by England of their rights on the seas, might not any extension of rights by international agreement be dangerous? These considerations for many years brought the two powers to a deadlock in their efforts to suppress the slave-trade.

[16]The slave-trade was again a subject of international consideration at the Congress of Verona in 1822. Austria, France, Great Britain, Russia, and Prussia were represented. The English delegates declared that, although only Portugal and Brazil allowed the trade, yet the traffic was at that moment carried on to a greater extent than ever before. They said that in seven months of the year 1821 no fewer than 21,000 slaves were abducted, and three hundred and fifty-two vessels entered African ports north of the equator.

[17]"It is obvious," the British said, "that this crime is committed in contravention of the Laws of every Country of Europe, and of America, excepting only of one, and that it requires something more than the ordinary operation of Law to prevent it."[o]

70. Negotiations of 1823-1825.

[18]England did not lose hope of gaining some concession from the United States. A House of Representatives committee in 1822 reported that the only method of suppressing the trade was by granting a Right of Search.[p] The full House agreed on February 28, 1823, to request the President to enter into negotiations with the maritime powers of Europe to denounce the slave-trade as piracy; an amendment "that we agree to a qualified right of search" was, however, defeated.

[19]Another treaty was brought before the Senate April 30, 1824, but was not acted upon until May 21. The same day, President Monroe sent a special

message to the Senate, giving at length the reasons for signing the treaty, and saying that "should this treaty be adopted, there is every reason to believe that it will be the commencement of a system destined to accomplish the entire Abolition of the Slave Trade."

[20]It was, however, a time of great political pot-boiling, and a systematic attack, led by Johnson of Louisiana, was made on all the vital provisions of the treaty. The waters of America were excepted from its application, and the provision which, perhaps, aimed the deadliest blow at American slave-trade interests was likewise struck out; namely, the application of the Right of Search to citizens chartering the vessels of a third nation.[q]

[21]The treaty thus mutilated was not signed by England, who demanded as the least concession the application of the Right of Search to American waters. In the meantime, the United States had invited nearly all nations to denounce the trade as piracy; and the President, the Secretary of the Navy, and a House committee had urgently favored the granting of the Right of Search. The bad faith of the Congress, however, broke off for a time further negotiations with England.

71. The Attitude of the United States and the State of the Slave-Trade.

[22]Congressman Mercer sought repeatedly in the House to have negotiations reopened with England, but without success. Indeed, the chances of success were now for many years imperiled by the recurrence of deliberate searches of American vessels by the British.[r] In the majority of cases, the vessels proved to be slavers, and some of them fraudulently flew the American flag; nevertheless, their molestation by British cruisers created much bad feeling and hindered all steps toward an understanding: the United States was loath to have her criminal negligence in enforcing her own laws thus exposed to foreigners.

[23]Other international questions connected with the trade also strained the relations of the two countries: three different vessels engaged in the domestic slave-trade, driven by the stress of weather, or, in the *Creole* case, captured by Negroes on board, landed slaves in British possessions; England freed them and refused to pay for such as were landed after emancipation had been proclaimed in the West Indies.[s]

[24]The case of the slaver *L'Amistad* also raised difficulties with Spain. This Spanish vessel, after the Negroes on board had mutinied and killed their owners, was seized by a United States vessel and brought into port for adjudication. The court, however, freed the Negroes on the ground that under Spanish law they were not legally slaves; and although the Senate repeatedly tried to compensate the owners, the project did not succeed.[t]

[25]Such proceedings well illustrate the new tendency of the pro-slavery party to neglect the enforcement of the slave-trade laws. Consequently, when, after the treaty of 1831, France and England joined in urging the accession of the United States to it, the British minister said, in December, 1833, "The Executive

at Washington appears to shrink from bringing forward, in any shape, a question, upon which depends the utter and universal Abolition of the Slave Trade—from an apprehension of alarming the Southern States."[u]

[26]Estimates as to the extent of the slave-trade agree that the traffic to North and South America in 1820 was considerable, certainly not much less than 40,000 slaves annually. From that time to about 1825 it declined somewhat, but afterward increased enormously, so that by 1837 the American importation was estimated as high as 200,000 Negroes annually.

[27]The total abolition of the African trade by American countries then brought the traffic down to perhaps 30,000 in 1842. A large and rapid increase of illicit traffic followed so that by 1847 the importation amounted to perhaps 100,000 annually. One province of Brazil is said to have received 173,000 in the years 1846-1849. In the decade 1850-1860 this activity in slave-trading continued and reached very large proportions.

[28]By 1845, a large part of the slave-trade was under the stars and stripes; by 1850 fully one-half the trade, and in the decade 1850-1860 nearly all the traffic found the American flag its best protection.[v]

72. The Quintuple Treaty, 1839-1842.

[29]In 1839 Pope Gregory XVI stigmatized the slave-trade "as utterly unworthy of Christian name," and at the same time, although proscribed by the laws of every civilized State, the trade was flourishing with pristine vigor. Great advantage was given the traffic by the fact that the United States, for two decades after the abortive attempt of 1824, refused to cooperate with the rest of the civilized world, and allowed her flag to shelter and protect the slave-trade.

[30]The United States had invited the world to join her in denouncing the slave-trade as piracy, yet, when such a pirate was waylaid by an English vessel, the United States complained or demanded reparation. The only answer which this country for years returned to the long-continued exposures of American slave-traders and of the fraudulent use of the American flag, was recital of cases where Great Britain had gone beyond her legal powers in her attempt to suppress the slave-trade.[w]

73. Final Concerted Measures, 1842-1862.

[31]England continued to urge the granting of a Right of Search, claiming that the stand of the United States really amounted to the protection of pirates under her flag.[x] The United States answered by alleging that even the Treaty of 1842 had been misconstrued by England,[y] whereupon there was much warm debate in Congress, and several attempts were made to abrogate the slave-trade article of the treaty. The pro-slavery party had become more and more suspicious of England's motives, since they had seen her abolition of the slave-trade blossom into abolition of the system itself, and they seized every opportunity to prevent cooperation with her.

[32]The increase of the slave traffic was so great in the decade 1850-1860 that Lord John Russell proposed to the governments of the United States, France, Spain, Portugal, and Brazil, that they instruct their ministers to meet at London in May or June, 1860 to consider measures for the final abolition of the trade. He stated: "It is ascertained, by repeated instances, that the practice is for vessels to sail under the American flag and no British cruiser can touch them. If no slaves are on board, even though the equipment, the fittings, the water-casks, and other circumstances prove that the ship is on a Slave Trade venture, no American cruiser can touch them."[z]

[33]Continued representations of this kind were made to the paralyzed United States government. Indeed, the slave-trade of the world seemed now to float securely under her flag.

[34]On the outbreak of the Civil War, the Lincoln administration, through

The table below gives the dates of the abolition of the slave-trade by the various nations:

Friends' Exposition of the Slave Trade, 1840-50; Annual Reports of the American and Foreign Anti-Slavery Society

Date	Slave-trade Abolished by	Right of Search Treaty with Great Britain made by	Arrangement for Joint Cruising with Great Britain made by
1802	Denmark		
1807	Great Britain; United States		
1813	Sweden		
1814	Netherlands		
1815	Portugal (north of the equator)		
1817	Spain (north of the equator)	Portugal, Spain	
1818	France	Netherlands	
1820	Spain		
1824		Sweden	
1829	Brazil (?)		
1830	Portugal		
1831-33		France	
1833-39		Denmark	
1841		Austria, Russia, Prussia	
1842			United States
1844		Texas	
1845		Belgium	France
1862		United States	

Secretary Seward, immediately expressed a willingness to do all in its power to suppress the slave-trade.[aa]

[35]Accordingly, on June 7, 1862, a treaty was signed with Great Britain granting a mutual limited Right of Search, and establishing mixed courts for the trial of offenders at the Cape of Good Hope, Sierra Leone, and New York. The efforts of a half-century of diplomacy were finally crowned; Seward wrote to Adams, "Had such a treaty been made in 1808, there would now have been no sedition here."[bb]

Notes and References

[a]Cf. Augustine Cochin, in Lalor, *Cyclopedia*, III. 723.

[b]By a law of Aug. 11, 1792, the encouragement formerly given to the trade was stopped. Cf. *Choix de rapports, opinions et discours prononcés à la tribune nationale depuis 1789* (Paris, 1821), XIV. 425; quoted in Cochin, *The Results of Emancipation* (Booth's translation, 1863), pp. 33, 35-8.

[c]Cochin, *The Results of Emancipation*, (Booth's translation, 1863), pp. 42-7.

[d]*British and Foreign State Papers*, 1815-6, p. 196.

[e]*Ibid.*, pp. 195-9, 292-3; 1816-7, p. 755. It was eventually confirmed by royal ordinance, and the law of April 15, 1818.

[f]For the history of the Parliamentary struggle, cf. Clarkson's and Copley's histories.

[g]*Statute 46 George III.*, ch. 52, 119; *47 George III.*, sess. I. ch. 36.

[h]Sparks, *Diplomatic Correspondence*, X. 154.

[i]Fox to Hartley, June 10, 1783; quoted in Bancroft, *History of the Constitution of the United States*, I. 61.

[j]*American State Papers, Foreign*, III. No. 214, p. 151.

[k]*Ibid.*, pp. 890-1.

[l]*British and Foreign State Papers*, 1815-6, p. 887. Russia, Austria and Prussia returned favorable replies.

[m]*American State Papers, Foreign*, III. No. 271, pp. 735-48; *U.S. Treaties and Conventions* (ed. 1889), p. 405.

[n]This was inserted in the Treaty of Paris, Nov. 20, 1815: *British and Foreign State Papers*, 1815-6. P.

[o]*British and Foreign State Papers*, 1822-3. pp. 94-110.

[p]*House Journal*, 17th Congress, 2nd session, pp. 212, 280.

[q]*Ibid.*, pp. 360-2.

[r]Cf. *House Documents*, 26th Congress, 2nd session. V. No. 115, pp. 35-6.

[s]These were the celebrated cases of the *Encomium, Enterprize*, and *Comet*.

[t]*Senate Documents*, 24th Congress, 2nd Session. II. No. 174.

[u]*British and Foreign State Papers*, 1834-5, p. 136.

[v]*Parliamentary Papers*, 1823, XVIII., *Slave Trade*.

[w]Cf. *British and Foreign State Papers*, from 1836 to 1842.

[x]*House Documents*, 27th Congress, 2nd Session V. No. 192, p. 4.

[y]*House Journal*, 27th Congress, 3rd Session, pp. 485-8.

[z] *British and Foreign State Papers*, 1859-60, pp. 902-3.

[aa]*Senate Executive Documents*, 37th Congress, 2nd Session V. No. 57.

[bb]*Diplomatic Correspondence*, 1862, pp. 64-5/

Vocabulary

[3]denunciatory	[15]maritime	[23]emancipation	[29]vigor
[3] precipitately	[16]abducted	[24]adjudication	[31]waylaid
[5]countenancing	[17]contravention	[25]accession	[31]reparation
[7]proviso	[18]concession	[27]illicit	[32]misconstrued
[9]repugnant	[20]chartering	[29]stigmatized	[32]abrogate
[10]decree	[21]denounce	[29]proscribed	[33]ascertained
[11]interposing	[22]imperiled	[29]pristine	[36]sedition
[11]benign	[22]fraudulently		
[12]irreconcilable	[22]loath		

Discussion Questions

1. Based upon what DuBois says in the first paragraph of this excerpt, how many slaves would you estimate were located in Europe at the beginning of the nineteenth century? How does this compare to the number of slaves in the United States during the same period? Explain your answer.

2. What was the reason that the slave trade flourished in the 18th and early 19th century? Cite an example of where slaves were used and for what purpose.

3. Give a brief summary of what happened to the worldwide slave trade in the last few decades of the 18th century and the beginning of the 19th century. What was happening politically in the United States during this period?

4. Explain the Right of Search or Right of Visit and the role it played in the slave trade in the first half of the 19th century. Where did America stand on this issue?

5. Why did America lag so far behind the rest of the world in the curtailing of the slave trade in the first half of the 19th century?

6. What was the attitude of the American government toward letting British ships stop ships flying the American flag at sea? Why was this a sensitive issue for American lawmakers?

7. Explain what happened in the *L'Amistad* case. Why was this a significant event in the evolution of American laws concerning the slave trade?

8. Using the table, *Friends' Exposition of the Slave Trade, 1840-50* on page 309, explain the significance of the date cited for the abolishing of the slave trade by the United States and the date upon which the U.S. entered into a Right of Search treaty with Great Britain.

9. Overall, what is DuBois' attitude toward the role of the United States in the international slave trade during the period upon which he is focusing?

IS SCIENCE A RELIGION?

RICHARD DAWKINS

Richard Dawkins (1941-   ) was born in Nairobi, Kenya. After earning a doctorate in zoology at Oxford University in 1966, Dawkins taught briefly at the University if California, Berkeley, and then returned to Oxford as a faculty member, retiring as Charles Simonyi Professor of the Public Understanding of Science in 2008. A professed atheist, Dawkins is a prominent critic of creationism—the belief that the universe and life on Earth were created by a deity. His books include The Selfish Gene, The Blind Watchmaker, River Out of Eden, *and, most recently,* Climbing Mount Improbable. *This article is adapted from his acceptance speech of the 1996 Humanist of the Year Award from the American Humanist Association.*

[1]It is fashionable to wax apocalyptic about the threat to humanity posed by the AIDS virus, "mad cow" disease, and many others, but I think a case can be made that *faith* is one of the world's great evils, comparable to the smallpox virus but harder to eradicate.

[2]Faith, being belief that isn't based on evidence, is the principal vice of any religion. And who, looking at Northern Ireland or the Middle East, can be confident that the brain virus of faith is not exceedingly dangerous? One of the stories told to the young Muslim suicide bombers is that martyrdom is the quickest way to heaven—and not just heaven but a special part of heaven where they will receive their special reward of 72 virgin brides. It occurs to me that our best hope may be to provide a kind of "spiritual arms control": send in specially trained theologians to deescalate the going rate in virgins.

[3]Given the dangers of faith—and considering the accomplishments of reason and observation in the activity called science—I find it ironic that, whenever I lecture publicly, there always seems to be someone who comes forward and says, "Of course, your science is just a religion like ours. Fundamentally, science just comes down to faith, doesn't it?"

[4]Well, science is not religion and it doesn't just come down to faith. Although it has many of religion's virtues, it has none of its vices. Science is based upon verifiable evidence. Religious faith not only lacks evidence, its independence from evidence is its pride and joy, shouted from the rooftops. Why else would Christians wax critical of doubting Thomas? The other apostles are held up to us as exemplars of virtue because faith was enough for them. Doubting Thomas, on the other hand, required evidence. Perhaps he should be the patron saint of scientists.

[5]One reason I receive the comment about science being a religion is because I believe in the fact of evolution. I even believe in it with passionate conviction. To some, this may superficially look like faith. But the evidence that makes me believe in evolution is not only overwhelmingly strong; it is freely available to anyone who takes the trouble to read up on it. Anyone can study the same evidence that I have and presumably come to the same conclusion. But if you have a belief that is based solely on faith, I can't examine your reasons. You can retreat behind the private wall of faith where I can't reach you.

[6]Now in practice, of course, individual scientists do sometimes slip back into the vice of faith, and a few may believe so single-mindedly in a favorite theory that they occasionally falsify evidence. However, the fact that this sometimes happens doesn't alter the principle that, when they do so, they do it with shame and not with pride. The method of science is so designed that it usually finds them out in the end.

[7]Science is actually one of the most moral, one of the most honest disciplines around—because science would completely collapse if it weren't for a scrupulous adherence to honesty in the reporting of evidence. (As James Randi[a] has pointed out, this is one reason why scientists are so often fooled by paranormal tricksters and why the debunking role is better played by professional conjurors; scientists just don't anticipate deliberate dishonesty as well.) There are other professions (no need to mention lawyers specifically) in which falsifying evidence, or at least twisting it, is precisely what people are paid for and get brownie points for doing.

[8]Science, then, is free of the main vice of religion, which is faith. But, as I pointed out, science does have some of religion's virtues. Religion may aspire to provide its followers with various benefits—among them explanation, consolation, and uplift. Science, too, has something to offer in these areas.

[9]Humans have a great hunger for explanation. It may be one of the main reasons why humanity so universally has religion, since religions do aspire to provide explanations. We come to our individual consciousness in a mysterious universe and long to understand it. Most religions offer a cosmology and a biology, a theory of life, a theory of origins, and reasons for existence. In doing so, they demonstrate that religion is, in a sense, science; it's just bad science. Don't fall for the argument that religion and science operate on separate dimensions and are concerned with quite separate sorts of questions. Religions have historically always attempted to answer the questions that properly belong to science. Thus religions should not be allowed now to retreat away from the

---

[a]James Randi (Randall James Zwinge; stage name, The Great Randi) is a retired professional stage magician known for challenging claims of paranormal and supernatural phenomena. An organization he founded, the James Randi Educational Foundation, sponsors "The Million-Dollar Challenge," a prize of $1,000,000 for anyone who can demonstrate conclusive evidence of a paranormal, supernatural or occult power or event.

ground upon which they have traditionally attempted to fight. They do offer both a cosmology and a biology; however, in both cases it is false.

[10]Consolation is harder for science to provide. Unlike religion, science cannot offer the bereaved a glorious reunion with their loved ones in the hereafter. Those wronged on this earth cannot, on a scientific view, anticipate a sweet comeuppance for their tormentors in a life to come. It could be argued that, if the idea of an afterlife is an illusion (as I believe it is), the consolation it offers is hollow. But that's not necessarily so; a false belief can be just as comforting as a true one, provided the believer never discovers its falsity. But if consolation comes that cheap, science can weigh in with other cheap palliatives, such as pain-killing drugs, whose comfort may or may not be illusory, but they do work.

[11]Uplift, however, is where science really comes into its own. All the great religions have a place for awe, for ecstatic transport at the wonder and beauty of creation. And it's exactly this feeling of spine-shivering, breath-catching awe—almost worship—this flooding of the chest with ecstatic wonder, that modern science can provide. And it does so beyond the wildest dreams of saints and mystics. The fact that the supernatural has no place in our explanations, in our understanding of so much about the universe and life, doesn't diminish the awe. Quite the contrary. The merest glance through a microscope at the brain of an ant or through a telescope at a long-ago galaxy of a billion worlds is enough to render poky and parochial the very psalms of praise.

[12]Now, as I say, when it is put to me that science or some particular part of science, like evolutionary theory, is just a religion like any other, I usually deny it with indignation. But I've begun to wonder whether perhaps that's the wrong tactic. Perhaps the right tactic is to accept the charge gratefully and demand equal time for science in religious education classes. And the more I think about it, the more I realize that an excellent case could be made for this. So I want to talk a little bit about religious education and the place that science might play in it.

[13]I do feel very strongly about the way children are brought up. I'm not entirely familiar with the way things are in the United States, and what I say may have more relevance to the United Kingdom, where there is state-obliged, legally-enforced religious instruction for all children. That's unconstitutional in the United States, but I presume that children are nevertheless given religious instruction in whatever particular religion their parents deem suitable.

[14]Which brings me to my point about mental child abuse. In a 1995 issue of the *Independent*, one of London's leading newspapers, there was a photograph of a rather sweet and touching scene. It was Christmas time, and the picture showed three children dressed up as the three wise men for a nativity play. The accompanying story described one child as a Muslim, one as a Hindu, and one as a Christian. The supposedly sweet and touching point of the story

was that they were all taking part in this nativity play.

[15]What is not sweet and touching is that these children were all four years old. How can you possibly describe a child of four as a Muslim or a Christian or a Hindu or a Jew? Would you talk about a four-year-old economic monetarist? Would you talk about a four-year-old neo-isolationist or a four-year-old liberal Republican? There are opinions about the cosmos and the world that children, once grown, will presumably be in a position to evaluate for themselves. Religion is the one field in our culture about which it is absolutely accepted, without question—without even noticing how bizarre it is—that parents have a total and absolute say in what their children are going to be, how their children are going to be raised, what opinions their children are going to have about the cosmos, about life, about existence. Do you see what I mean about mental child abuse?

[16]Looking now at the various things that religious education might be expected to accomplish, one of its aims could be to encourage children to reflect upon the deep questions of existence, to invite them to rise above the humdrum preoccupations of ordinary life and think *sub specie aeternitatis*.[b]

[17]Science can offer a vision of life and the universe which, as I've already remarked, for humbling poetic inspiration far outclasses any of the mutually contradictory faiths and disappointingly recent traditions of the world's religions.

[18]For example, how could children in religious education classes fail to be inspired if we could get across to them some inkling of the age of the universe? Suppose that, at the moment of Christ's death, the news of it had started traveling at the maximum possible speed around the universe outwards from the earth. How far would the terrible tidings have traveled by now? Following the theory of special relativity,[c] the answer is that the news could not, under any circumstances whatever, have reached more than one-fiftieth of the way across one galaxy—not one- thousandth of the way to our nearest neighboring galaxy in the 100-million-galaxy-strong universe. The universe at large couldn't possibly be anything other than indifferent to Christ, his birth, his passion, and his death. Even such momentous news as the origin of life on Earth could have traveled only across our little local cluster of galaxies. Yet so ancient was that event on our earthly time-scale that, if you span its age with your open arms, the whole of human history, the whole of human culture, would fall in the dust from your fingertip at a single stroke of a nail file.

---

[b]*sub specie aeternitatis*: in its essential or universal form or nature; that which is eternally and universally true. Dawkins says children should be encouraged to step back from everyday life and think about the "big questions," such as when and how did the universe begin?

[c]"special relativity" refers to Albert Einstein's theory of special relativity, which, among other observations, deals with the constancy of the speed of light

[19]The argument from design, an important part of the history of religion, wouldn't be ignored in my religious education classes, needless to say. The children would look at the spellbinding wonders of the living kingdoms and would consider Darwinism alongside the creationist alternatives and make up their own minds. I think the children would have no difficulty in making up their minds the right way if presented with the evidence. What worries me is not the question of equal time but that, as far as I can see, children in the United Kingdom and the United States are essentially given *no* time with evolution yet are taught creationism (whether at school, in church, or at home).

[20]It would also be interesting to teach more than one theory of creation. The dominant one in this culture happens to be the Jewish creation myth, which is taken over from the Babylonian creation myth. There are, of course, lots and lots of others, and perhaps they should all be given equal time (except that wouldn't leave much time for studying anything else). I understand that there are Hindus who believe that the world was created in a cosmic butter churn and Nigerian peoples who believe that the world was created by God from the excrement of ants. Surely these stories have as much right to equal time as the Judeo-Christian myth of Adam and Eve.

[21]So much for Genesis; now let's move on to the prophets. Halley's Comet will return without fail in the year 2062. Biblical or Delphic prophecies don't begin to aspire to such accuracy; astrologers and Nostradamians dare not commit themselves to factual prognostications but, rather, disguise their charlatanry in a smokescreen of vagueness. When comets have appeared in the past, they've often been taken as portents of disaster. Astrology has played an important part in various religious traditions, including Hinduism. The three wise men I mentioned earlier were said to have been led to the cradle of Jesus by a star. We might ask the children by what physical route do they imagine the alleged stellar influence on human affairs could travel.

[22]Incidentally, there was a shocking program on the BBC radio around Christmas 1995 featuring an astronomer, a bishop, and a journalist who were sent off on an assignment to retrace the steps of the three wise men. Well, you could understand the participation of the bishop and the journalist (who happened to be a religious writer), but the astronomer was a supposedly respectable astronomy writer, and yet she went along with this! All along the route, she talked about the portents of when Saturn and Jupiter were in the ascendant up Uranus or whatever it was. She doesn't actually believe in astrology, but one of the problems is that our culture has been taught to become tolerant of it, vaguely amused by it—so much so that even scientific people who don't believe in astrology sort of think it's a bit of harmless fun. I take astrology very seriously indeed: I think it's deeply pernicious because it undermines rationality, and I should like to see campaigns against it.

[23]When the religious education class turns to ethics, I don't think science

actually has a lot to say, and I would replace it with rational moral philosophy. Do the children think there are absolute standards of right and wrong? And if so, where do they come from? Can you make up good working principles of right and wrong, like "do as you would be done by" and "the greatest good for the greatest number" (whatever that is supposed to mean)? It's a rewarding question, whatever your personal morality, to ask as an evolutionist where morals come from; by what route has the human brain gained its tendency to have ethics and morals, a feeling of right and wrong?

[24]Should we value human life above all other life? Is there a rigid wall to be built around the species *Homo sapiens*, or should we talk about whether there are other species which are entitled to our humanistic sympathies? Should we, for example, follow the right-to-life lobby, which is wholly preoccupied with *human* life, and value the life of a human fetus with the faculties of a worm over the life of a thinking and feeling chimpanzee? What is the basis of this fence that we erect around *Homo sapiens*—even around a small piece of fetal tissue? (Not a very sound evolutionary idea when you think about it.) When, in our evolutionary descent from our common ancestor with chimpanzees, did the fence suddenly rear itself up?

[25]Well, moving on, then, from morals to last things, to eschatology, we know from the second law of thermodynamics that all complexity, all life, all laughter, all sorrow, is hell bent on leveling itself out into cold nothingness in the end. They—and we—can never be more than temporary, local buckings of the great universal slide into the abyss of uniformity.

[26]We know that the universe is expanding and will probably expand forever, although it's possible it may contract again. We know that, whatever happens to the universe, the sun will engulf the earth in about 60 million centuries from now.

[27]Time itself began at a certain moment, and time may end at a certain moment—or it may not. Time may come locally to an end in miniature crunches called black holes. The laws of the universe seem to be true all over the universe. Why is this? Might the laws change in these crunches? To be really speculative, time could begin again with new laws of physics, new physical constants. And it has even been suggested that there could be many universes, each one isolated so completely that, for it, the others don't exist. Then again, there might be a Darwinian selection among universes.

[28]So science could give a good account of itself in religious education. But it wouldn't be enough. I believe that some familiarity with the King James version of the Bible is important for anyone wanting to understand the allusions that appear in English literature. Together with the Book of Common Prayer, the Bible gets 58 pages in the *Oxford Dictionary of Quotations*. Only Shakespeare has more. I do think that not having any kind of biblical education is unfortunate if children want to read English literature and understand the

provenance of phrases like "through a glass darkly," "all flesh is as grass," "the race is not to the swift," "crying in the wilderness," "reaping the whirlwind," "amid the alien corn," "Eyeless in Gaza," "Job's comforters," and "the widow's mite."

[29]I want to return now to the charge that science is just a faith. The more extreme version of that charge—and one that I often encounter as both a scientist and a rationalist—is an accusation of zealotry and bigotry in scientists themselves as great as that found in religious people. Sometimes there may be a little bit of justice in this accusation; but as zealous bigots, we scientists are mere amateurs at the game. We're content to *argue* with those who disagree with us. We don't kill them.

[30]But I would want to deny even the lesser charge of purely verbal zealotry. There is a very, very important difference between feeling strongly, even passionately, about something because we have thought about and examined the evidence for it on the one hand, and feeling strongly about something because it has been internally revealed to us, or internally revealed to somebody else in history and subsequently hallowed by tradition. There's all the difference in the world between a belief that one is prepared to defend by quoting evidence and logic and a belief that is supported by nothing more than tradition, authority, or revelation.

Published in the *Humanist*, January/February 1997

Vocabulary

[1]wax	[7]paranormal	[15]nativity	[23]ethics
[1]apocalyptic	[7]debunking	[19]inkling	[24]*Homo sapiens*
[1]eradicate	[7]conjurors	[19]indifferent	[24]fetus
[2]vice	[9]cosmology	[20]Babylonian	[25]eschatology
[2]martyrdom	[10]bereaved	[20]excrement	[25]thermodynamics
[2]theologians	[10]comeuppance	[21]Genesis	[25]abyss
[2]deescalate	[10]palliatives	[21]Delphic	[28]engulf
[3]ironic	[10]ecstatic	[21]astrologers	[28]speculative
[4]verifiable	[10]mystics	[21]Nostradamians	[28]provenance
[4]doubting Thomas	[10]parochial	[21]prognostications	[28]Gaza
[4]apostles	[10]psalms	[21]charlatanry	[29]zealotry
[4]exemplars	[10]illusory	[21]portents	[29]bigotry
[7]scrupulous	[14]monetarist	[21]stellar	[30]revelation
[7]adherence	[15]nativity	[22]pernicious	

Discussion Questions

1. What does Dawkins believe is a chief threat to humanity? List four of the reasons that he gives for this belief.

2. What is the "martyrdom" that Dawkins mentions in paragraph 2? What do you infer is Dawkins's attitude toward martyrdom?

3. Does Dawkins believe that science is a religion? Where did you find this evidence?

4. Do you agree with Dawkins's assertion in paragraph 19?

5. Dawkins discusses types of reasons and logic. Summarize his argument.

6. What can religion offer that science cannot? What can science offer that religion cannot? Why does Dawkins bring these up in his essay?

7. What does Dawkins say is the difference between science and faith? Do you agree with his assessment? Explain.

8. In his recent book, *The Evolution of God*, Robert Wright compares God to an electron, saying scientists know the electron is there because scientific experiments show its effects, but the scientists don't know what an electron looks like or what its properties are. How does Wright's analogy relate to Dawkins's argument?

9. Based upon your own experience, do you agree with Dawkins' assertion in paragraph 19 that ". . . children in the . . . United States are essentially given no time with evolution yet are taught creationism (whether at school, in church, or at home)"?

10. Read the note on page 339 of this text and compare what Dawkins says in paragraph 24 to Peter Singer's position. What is your position on this issue?

11. Read H. Allen Orr's essay, "Devolution," beginning on page 234 of this text. Compare Orr's position on the role of science to Dawkins's view.

FROM *THE JUNGLE*

UPTON SINCLAIR

*Novelist, essayist, playwright, short story writer and children's book writer, **Upton Beall Sinclair** (1878-1968) is best known for his novel* The Jungle *(1906), which led to the implementation of the Pure Food and Drug Act in 1906. The author of over 100 novels, Sinclair won the Pulitzer Prize for fiction in 1942 for* Dragon's Teeth, *a novel about Germany's descent into Nazism from 1930 to 1934.*

¹Jurgis pointed out the place where the cattle were driven to be weighed upon a great scale that would weigh a hundred thousand pounds at once and record it automatically. It was near to the east entrance that they stood, and all along this east side of the yards ran the railroad tracks into which the cars were run, loaded with cattle. All night long this had been going on, and now the pens were full; by tonight they would all be empty, and the same thing would be done again.

²"And what will become of all these creatures?" cried Teta Elzbieta.

³"By tonight," Jurgis answered, "they will all be killed and cut up; and over there on the other side of the packing houses are more railroad tracks, where the cars come to take them away."

⁴Jurgis said they brought in about ten thousand head of cattle every day, and as many hogs, and half as many sheep—which meant some eight to ten million live creatures turned into food every year.

⁵As they watched, groups of cattle were driven into chutes, a continuous stream of animals. It was uncanny to watch them, pressing on to their fate, all unsuspicious—a very river of death.

⁶Our friends were not poetical, and the sight suggested to them no metaphors of human destiny; they thought only of the wonderful efficiency of it all. The chutes into which the hogs went climbed high up—to the very top of the distant buildings; and Jurgis explained that the hogs went up by the power of their own legs, and then their weight carried them back through all the processes necessary to make them into pork.

⁷Here was where they made Brown's Imperial Hams and Bacon, Brown's Dressed Beef, Brown's Excelsior Sausages! Here was the headquarters of Durham's Leaf Lard, of Durham's Breakfast Bacon, Durham's Canned Beef, Potted Ham, Deviled Chicken, Peerless Fertilizer!

⁸Entering one of the Durham buildings, they found a number of other visitors waiting, and before long there came a guide to escort them through the place. They make a great feature of showing strangers through the packing-

plants, for it is a good advertisement. But Jurgis whispered maliciously that the visitors did not see any more than the packers wanted them to.

[9]The visitors climbed a long series of stairways outside of the building to the top of its five or six stories. Here was the top of the chute, with its river of hogs, all patiently toiling upward; there was a place for them to rest to cool off, and then through another passageway they went into a room from which there is no returning for hogs.

[10]It was a long, narrow room, with a gallery along it for visitors. At the head there was a great iron wheel, about twenty feet in circumference, with rings here and there along its edge. Upon both sides of this wheel there was a narrow space, into which came the hogs at the end of their journey; in the midst of them stood a great burly Negro, bare-armed and bare-chested. He was resting for the moment, for the wheel had stopped while men were cleaning up.

[11]In a minute or two, however, it began slowly to revolve, and then the men upon each side of it sprang to work. They had chains which they fastened about the leg of the nearest hog, and the other end of the chain they hooked into one of the rings upon the wheel. So, as the wheel turned, a hog was suddenly jerked off his feet and borne aloft.

[12]At the same instant the ear was assailed by a most terrifying shriek; the visitors started in alarm, the women turned pale and shrank back. The shriek was followed by another, louder and more agonizing for once started upon that journey, the hog never came back; at the top of the wheel he was shunted off upon a trolley and went sailing down the room.

[13]In the meantime, another was swung up, and then another, and another, until there was a double line of them, each dangling by a foot and kicking in frenzy—and squealing. The uproar was appalling, perilous to the ear-drums; one feared there was too much sound for the room to hold—that the walls must give way or the ceiling crack. There were high squeals and low squeals, grunts, and wails of agony; there would come a momentary lull, and then a fresh out-burst, louder than ever, surging up to a deafening climax. It was too much for some of the visitors—the men would look at each other, laughing nervously, and the women would stand with hands clenched and the blood rushing to their faces, and the tears starting in their eyes.

[14]Heedless of all these things, the men upon the floor were going about their work. Neither squeals of hogs nor tears of visitors made any difference to them; one by one then, hooked up the hogs, and one by one with a swift stroke they slit their throats. There was a long line of hogs, with squeals and life-blood ebbing away together; until at last each vanished with a splash into a huge vat of boiling water.

[15]It was all so very businesslike that one watched it fascinated. It was pork-making by machinery, pork-making by applied mathematics. And yet somehow the most matter-of-fact person could not help thinking of the hogs;

they were so innocent, they came so very trustingly; and they were so very human in their protests—and so perfectly within their rights! They had done nothing to deserve it; and it was adding insult to injury, as the thing was done here, swinging them up in this cold-blooded, impersonal way, without a pretense at apology, without the homage of a tear. Now and then a visitor wept, to be sure; but this slaughtering-machine ran on, visitors or no visitors. It was like some horrible crime committed in a dungeon, all unseen and unheeded, buried out of sight and of memory.

[16]The carcass hog was scooped out of the vat by machinery, and then it fell to the second floor, passing on the way through a wonderful machine with numerous scrapers, which adjusted themselves to the size and shape of the animal, and sent it out at the other end with nearly all of its bristles removed. It was then again strung up by machinery and sent upon another trolley ride, this time passing between two lines of men, who sat upon a raised platform, each doing a certain single thing to the carcass as it came to him.

[17]One scraped the outside of a leg; another scraped the inside of the same leg. One, with a swift stroke, cut the throat; another with two swift strokes severed the head, which fell to the floor and vanished through a hole. Another made a slit down the body; a second opened the body wider; a third with a saw cut the breast-bone, a fourth loosened the entrails; a fifth pulled them out—and they also slid through a hole in the floor. There were men to scrape each side and men to scrape the back; there were men to clean the carcass inside, to trim it and wash it.

[18]Looking down this room, one saw, creeping slowly, a line of dangling hogs a hundred yards in length; and for every yard there was a man, working as if a demon were after him. At the end of this hog's progress every inch of the carcass had been gone over several times; and then it was rolled into the chilling-room, where it stayed for twenty-four hours, and where a stranger might lose himself in a forest of freezing hogs.

[19]Before the carcass was admitted here, however, it had to pass a government inspector, who sat in the doorway and felt of the glands in the neck for tuberculosis. This government inspector did not have the manner of a man who was worked to death; he was apparently not haunted by a fear that the hog might get by him before he had finished his testing. If you were a sociable person, he was quite willing to enter into conversation with you, and to explain to you the deadly nature of the ptomaines which are found in tubercular pork; and while he was talking with you, you could hardly be so ungrateful as to notice that a dozen carcasses were passing him untouched.

[20]The party descended to the next floor, where the various waste materials were treated. Here came the entrails, to be scraped and washed clean for sausage-casings; men and women worked here in the midst of a sickening stench, which caused the visitors to hasten by, gasping. To another room came

all the scraps to be "tanked," which meant boiling and pumping off the grease to make soap and lard; below they took out the refuse, and this, too, was a region in which the visitors did not linger.

[21]There was scarcely a thing needed in the business that Durham and Company did not make. There was a building to which the grease was piped and made into soap and lard. There was a building in which the bristles were cleaned and dried, for the making of hair cushions and such things; there was a building where the skins were dried and tanned, there was another where heads and feet were made into glue, and another where bones were made into fertilizer.

[22]No tiniest particle of organic matter was wasted in Durham's. Out of the horns of the cattle they made combs, buttons, hair-pins, and imitation ivory; out of the shin bones and other big bones they cut knife and toothbrush handles, and mouthpieces for pipes; out of the hoofs they cut hair-pins and buttons, before they made the rest into glue. From such things as feet, knuckles, hide clippings, and sinews came such strange and unlikely products as gelatin, phosphorus, and shoe-blacking. They had a "wool-pullery" for the sheep skins; they made pepsin from the stomachs of the pigs and violin strings from the ill-smelling entrails. When there was nothing else to be done with a thing, they first put it into a tank and got out of it all the tallow and grease, and then they made it into fertilizer.

[23]All these industries were gathered into buildings near by, connected by galleries and railroads with the main establishment; and it was estimated that they had handled nearly a quarter of a billion of animals since the founding of the plant. It was, so Jurgis informed them, the greatest aggregation of labor and capital ever gathered in one place. It employed thirty thousand men, women and children; it supported directly two hundred and fifty thousand people in its neighborhood, and indirectly it supported half a million. It sent its products to every country in the civilized world, and it furnished the food for no fewer than thirty million people!

****

[24]The longer Jurgis worked at Durham's, the more he began to hear things, little by little, in the gossip of those who were obliged to perpetrate them. It seemed as if every time he met a person from a new department, he heard of new swindles and new crimes. There was, for instance, a Lithuanian who was a cattle butcher for the plant where Marija had worked, which killed meat for canning only; and to hear this man describe the animals which came to his place would have been worthwhile for a Dante or a Zola.

[25]It seemed that they must have agencies all over the country to hunt out old and crippled and diseased cattle to be canned. There were cattle which

had been fed on "whiskey-malt," the refuse of the breweries, and had become what the men called "steerly"—which means covered with boils. It was a nasty job killing these, for when you plunged your knife into them, they would burst and splash foul-smelling stuff into your face; and when a man's sleeves were smeared with blood, and his hands steeped in it, how was he ever to wipe his face, or to clear his eyes so that he could see?

[26]It was stuff such as this that made the "embalmed beef" that had killed several times as many United States soldiers as all the bullets of the Spaniards; only the army beef, besides, was not fresh canned, it was old stuff that had been lying for years in the cellars.

[27]Then one Sunday evening, Jurgis sat puffing his pipe by the kitchen stove and talking with an old fellow whom Jonas had introduced, and who worked in the canning rooms at Durham's; and so Jurgis learned a few things about the great and only Durham canned goods, which had become a national institution. They were regular alchemists at Durham's, said the old man. They advertised "potted chicken,"—perhaps they had a secret process for making chickens chemically—who knows? said Jurgis's friend; the things that went into the mixture were tripe, and the fat of pork, and beef suet, and hearts of beef, and finally the waste ends of veal, when they had any. They put these up in several grades, and sold them at several prices; but the contents of the cans all came out of the same hopper.

[28]Anybody who could invent a new imitation had been sure of a fortune from old Durham, said Jurgis's informant; but it was hard to think of anything new in a place where so many sharp wits had been at work for so long; where the owners welcomed tuberculosis in the cattle they were feeding because it made them fatten more quickly; and where they bought up all the old rancid butter left over in the grocery stores of a continent, and "oxidized" it by a forced-air process to take away the odor, rechurned it with skimmed-milk, and sold it in bricks in the cities!

[29]Up to a year or two ago it had been the custom to kill horses in the yards—ostensibly for fertilizer; but after long agitation the newspapers had been able to make the public realize that the horses were being canned. Now it was against the law to kill horses in Packingtown, and the law was really complied with—for the present, at any rate.

[30]There was another interesting set of statistics that a person might have gathered in Packingtown—those of the various afflictions of the workers. When Jurgis had first inspected the packing plants with Szedvilas, he had marveled while he listened to the tale of all the things that were made out of the carcasses of animals, and of all the lesser industries that were maintained there; now he found that each one of these lesser industries was a separate little inferno, in its way as horrible as the killing-beds, the source and fountain of them all. The workers in each of them had their own peculiar diseases. And the wandering

visitor might be skeptical about all the swindles, but he could not be skeptical about these, for the workers bore the evidence of them on their bodies—generally they had only to hold out their hands.

[31]There were the men in the pickle-rooms, for instance, where old Antanas had gotten his death; scarce one of these had not some spot of horror on his person. Let a man so much as scrape his finger pushing a truck in the pickle-rooms, and he might have a sore that would put him out of the world; all the joints in his fingers might be eaten by the acid, one by one.

[32]Of the butchers, beef-boners and trimmers, and all those who used knives, you could scarcely find a person who had the use of his thumb; time and time again the base of it had been slashed, till it was a mere lump of flesh against which the man pressed the knife to hold it. The hands of these men would be crisscrossed with cuts until you could no longer pretend to count them or to trace them. They would have no nails; they had worn them off pulling hides; their knuckles were swollen so that their fingers spread out like a fan.

[33]Then there were men who worked in the cooking-rooms, in the midst of steam and sickening odors, by artificial light; in these rooms the germs of tuberculosis might live for two years, but the supply was renewed every hour. There were the beef-luggers, who carried two-hundred-pound quarters into the refrigerator-cars—a fearful kind of work that began at four o'clock in the morning and that wore out the most powerful men in a few years.

[34]There were those who worked in the chilling-rooms, and whose special disease was rheumatism; the time-limit that a man could work in the chilling-rooms was said to be five years. There were the wool pluckers, whose hands went to pieces even sooner than the hands of the pickle-men; for the pelts of the sheep had to be painted with acid to loosen the wool, and then the pluckers had to pull out this wool with their bare hands, till the acid had eaten their fingers off. There were those who made the tins for the canned meat; and their hands, too, were a maze of cuts, and each cut represented a chance for blood poisoning. Some worked at the stamping machines, and it was very seldom that one could work long there at the pace that was set and not give out and forget himself, and have a part of his hand chopped off.

[35]There were the "hoisters," as they were called, whose task it was to press the lever which lifted the dead cattle off the floor. They ran along upon a rafter, peering down through the damp and the steam; and as old Durham's architects had not built the killing-room for the convenience of the hoisters, at every few feet they would have to stoop under a beam, say four feet above the one they ran on; which got them into the habit of stooping, so that in a few years they would be walking like chimpanzees.

[36]Worst of any, however, were the fertilizer-men, and those who served in the cooking-rooms. These people could not be shown to the visitor, for the odor of a fertilizer-man would scare any ordinary visitor at a hundred yards,

and as for the other men, who worked in tank-rooms full of steam, and in some of which there were open vats near the level of the floor, their peculiar trouble was that they fell into the vats; and when they were fished out, there was never enough of them left to be worth exhibiting. Sometimes they would be overlooked for days, till all but the bones of them had gone out to the world as Durham's Pure Leaf Lard!

****

[37]The more Jurgis saw, and heard, at Durham's the more involved he got in the union. And the boardinghouse where he lived was a regular hotbed of socialist radicalism! The proprietor, Tommy Hinds, would get into a discussion with someone in the lobby, and as the conversation grew animated, others would gather about to listen, until finally everyone in the place would be crowded into a group, and a regular debate would be underway.

[38]This went on every night—when Tommy Hinds was not there to do it, his clerk did it; and when his clerk was away campaigning, the assistant attended to it, while Mrs. Hinds sat behind the desk and did the work. The clerk was an old crony of the proprietor's, an awkward, raw-boned giant of a man, with a lean, sallow face, a broad mouth, and whiskers under his chin, the very type and body of a prairie farmer. He had been that all his life—he had fought the railroads in Kansas for fifty years, a Granger, a Farmers' Alliance man, a "middle-of-the-road" Populist.

[39]Contrary to what one would have expected, all this radicalism did not hurt the boardinghouse business; the radicals flocked to it, and the commercial travelers all found it diverting. These fellows were just "meat" for Tommy Hinds—he would get a dozen of them around him and paint little pictures of "the System." Then he would set them up for Jurgis's story.

[40]"See here," he would say, in the middle of an argument, "I've got a fellow right here in my place who's worked in the meat-packing plant and has seen every bit of it!"

[41]And then Jurgis would come over, and Tommy would say, "Comrade Jurgis, just tell these gentlemen what you saw on the killing-beds."

[42]At first this request caused poor Jurgis the most acute agony, and it was like pulling teeth to get him to talk; but gradually he found out what was wanted, and in the end he learned to stand up and speak his piece with enthusiasm. Tommy would sit by and encourage him with exclamations and shakes of the head; when Jurgis would give the formula for "potted ham," or tell about the diseased hogs that were dropped into the "destructors" at the top and immediately taken out again at the bottom, to be shipped into another state and made into lard, Tommy Hinds would bang his knee and cry, "Do you think a man could make up a thing like that out of his head?"

[43]And then the hotel-keeper would go on to show how the Socialists had the only real remedy for such evils, how they alone "meant business" with the Beef Trust. And when, in answer to this, the listener would say that the whole country was getting stirred up, that the newspapers were full of denunciations of it, and the government taking action against it, Tommy Hinds had a knock-out blow all ready.

[44]"Yes," he would say, "all that is true—but what do you suppose is the reason for it? Are you foolish enough to believe that it's done for the public? There are other trusts in the country just as illegal and extortionate as the Beef Trust; there's the Coal Trust that freezes the poor in winter—there is the Steel Trust that doubles the price of every nail in your shoes—there is the Oil Trust that keeps you from reading at night—and why do you suppose it is that the fury of the press and the government is directed against the Beef Trust?"

[45]And when to this the victim would reply that there was clamor enough over the Oil Trust, Tommy would continue. "Ten years ago Henry D. Lloyd told all the truth about the Standard Oil Company in his *Wealth versus Commonwealth*, and the book was allowed to die, and you hardly every hear of it. And now at last, two magazines have the courage to tackle Standard Oil again and what happens? The newspapers ridicule the authors, the churches defend the criminals and the government does nothing. And now, why is it all different with the Beef Trust?"

[46]"If you were a Socialist," Tommy Hinds would say, "you would understand that the power which really governs the United States today is the Railroad Trust. It is the Railroad Trust that runs your state government, wherever you live, and that runs the United States Senate. And all of the trusts that I have named are in with the Railroad Trust—save only the Beef Trust! The Beef Trust has defied the railroads—it is plundering them day by day by owning its own freight cars, and so the public is roused to fury and the newspapers clamor for action, and the government goes on the warpath! And you poor common people watch and applaud the job, and think it's all done for you and never dream that it is really the grand climax of the century-long battle of commercial competitions—the final death grapple between the chiefs of the Beef Trust and Standard Oil for the prize of the mastery and ownership of the United States of America!"

****

[47]It was all so painfully obvious to Jurgis! It was so incomprehensible how people could fail to see it! Here were all the opportunities of America— the land, and the buildings upon the land, the railroads, the mines, the factories, and the stores, all in the hands of a few private individuals, called capitalists, for whom the people were obliged to work for wages. The whole balance of what the people produced went to heap up the fortunes of these capitalists, to

heap, and heap again, and yet again—and that in spite of the fact that they, and every one about them, lived in unthinkable luxury!

[48]And was it not plain that if the people cut off the share of those who merely "owned," that the share of those who worked would be much greater? That was as plain as two and two makes four; and it was the whole of it, absolutely the whole of it; and yet there were people who could not see it, who would argue about everything else in the world. They would tell you that governments could not manage things as economically as private individuals; they would repeat and repeat that, and think they were saying something!

[49]They could not see that "economical" management by masters meant simply that they, the people, were worked harder and ground closer and paid less! They were wage earners and servants, at the mercy of exploiters whose one thought was to get as much out of them as possible; and they were taking an interest in the process, were anxious lest it should not be done thoroughly enough! Was it not honestly a trial to listen to an argument such as that?

[50]And yet there were things even worse. Jurgis would begin talking to some poor devil who had worked in one shop for the last thirty years, and had never been able to save a penny; who left home every morning at six o'clock to go and tend a machine and come back at night too tired to take his clothes off; who had never had a week's vacation in his life, had never traveled, never had an adventure, never learned anything, never hoped anything—and when Jurgis started to tell him about Socialism, he would sniff and say, "I'm not interested in that stuff—I'm an individualist!"

[51]And then he would go on to tell you that Socialism was "Paternalism," and that if it ever had its way, the world would stop progressing. It was enough to make a mule laugh, to hear arguments like that; and yet it was no laughing matter, as you found out—for how many millions of such poor deluded wretches there were, whose lives had been so stunted by Capitalism that they no longer knew what freedom was!

[52]And they really thought that it was "Individualism" for tens of thousands of them to herd together and obey the orders of a steel magnate, and produce hundreds of millions of dollars of wealth for him, and then let him give them libraries; while for them to take the industry, and run it to suit themselves, and build their own libraries—that would have been "Paternalism"!

[53]Sometimes the agony of such things as this was almost more than Jurgis could bear; yet there was no way of escape from it, there was nothing to do but to dig away at the base of this mountain of ignorance and prejudice. He must keep at the poor fellow; he must hold his temper, and argue with him, and watch for his chance to stick an idea or two into his head. And the rest of the time he must sharpen up his weapons—he must think out new replies to the fellow's objections and provide himself with new facts to prove to the man the folly of his ways.

[54]And Jurgis knew that soon would begin the rush that would never be checked, the tide that would never turn till it has reached its flood—that would be irresistible, overwhelming—the rallying of the outraged workers of America to the socialist standard! And they would be organized, and they would be drilled and they would be marshaled for victory! The opposition would be overcome, it would be swept before the tide and victory would at last be ours!

Vocabulary

[5]uncanny	[24]Dante	[29]ostensibly	[49]exploiters
[15]pretense	[24]Zola	[37]socialist	[51]paternalism
[15]homage	[25]boils	[38]sallow	[51]deluded
[17]entrails	[27]tripe	[38]crony	[51]wretches
[19]carcass	[27]suet	[38]Populist	[51]stunted
[19]ptomaines	[27]hopper	[39]diverting	[52]magnate
[22]pepsin	[28]rancid	[43]denunciations	[53]folly
[22]tallow	[30]affliction	[47]incomprehensible	[54]marshaled

Discussion Questions

1. What do the visitors to Durham's find? Summarize the information using your own words. What are some of the physical effects on the workers of working at Durham's?

2. Reread paragraph 46 and restate the point in your own words. Do you think this is possible in America today?

3. Define socialism. Discuss why the workers might be interested in learning about it.

4. Define capitalism. Discuss why the workers might be interested in this system.

5. *The Jungle* led, among other legislation, to the implementation of the Pure Food and Drug Act. What is the Pure Food and Drug Act? How does it affect us today? Where did you find this information?

6. If you were the owner of a meat processing operation like Durham's, would you be in favor of legislation like the Pure Food and Drug Act? Why or why not?

7. How does legislation like the Pure Food and Drug Act come into existence? How is legislation like this related to capitalism and socialism?

8. Read the excerpt from *The Manifesto of the Communist Party* beginning on page 392 of this text. How are socialism and communism similar? How are they different?

9. Look at "Monster Monopoly' on page 338. How does this political cartoon relate to Sinclair's novel?

10. Look at the "Visitor's Bulletin" from Swift & Company that follows this excerpt. Discuss how it relates to what Sinclair wrote in *The Jungle*.

VISITORS' BULLETIN

SWIFT AND COMPANY

Herewith is a brief description of the many manufacturing operations along the visitors' route at Swift & Company's Chicago plant.

Read it as you make the trip and save it so that you may refresh your memory later.

Swift & Company
U.S.A.

Bird's-eye View of Union Stock Yards Today

From the windows of the Reception Room a good view of the stock yards may be had.

Years ago, when every butcher did his own slaughtering, the expense of preparing meat was high. Today there are between 300 and 400 buyers in the Chicago livestock market every day. Competition is keen, and cattle, hogs, sheep, and calves are dressed by the thousands instead of one or two at a time. Modern mechanical contrivances reduce handling and each worker does that in which he is most expert. This skill in production is the result of scientific management.

2

Visitors' Reception Room

Swift & Company welcomes you to its Chicago plant and hopes that your trip over the visitors' route will be an interesting one. The large number of persons who visit this plant annually is an indication of a gratifying interest in the preparation of the public's meats.

Reception Room

1

1. *Observation Roof:*

(a) Across the street to the right is the five-story General Office building of Swift & Company.

Swift & Company's service in production and distribution of meat and allied products is so extensive that it requires nearly 1,800 persons to handle the office work of the Chicago plant and the general administrative work of the company. The comfort and efficiency of the employes are aided by a ventilating system providing pure air at uniform temperatures throughout all

General Office

3

seasons, insulated ceilings to minimize noise, and conveniences such as restaurant, cafeteria, library, barber shop, club room, and rest rooms.

(b) On the roof of the building to the right you will note a number of chimneys, some of which are smoking. The smoke comes from the wood fires used in smoking Swift's Premium Ham and Bacon, *Ovenized.*

2. Hog Dressing:

(Our visitors' route is arranged so that visitors may avoid seeing the killing. Make your wishes known to the guide.)

Dressing operations begin by suspending the hogs from overhead rails by means of a revolving hoisting wheel. The suspension expedites the process so that 750 hogs an hour can be handled. In a few minutes the animals are ready for the water vats, which soften the hair and bristles. They are then passed through the dehairing machine.

3. Hog Dressing:

The hogs come from the dehairing machine smoothly shaven—an attractive pink and white. They are now placed on a slowly moving overhead traveling chain.

4

Hog Dressing

Workmen stationed along this chain are thus enabled to do their specific tasks with ease. The dressed hogs receive three separate inspections by U. S. Government Inspectors: First, the throat glands and head glands; second, the viscera (these parts being kept with the carcass until after the inspections); third, the spine. Animals not passed for food are disposed of under control of the Federal inspectors.

4. Sliced Bacon:

Below you observe one of the most modernly equipped food-packing departments, the Sliced Bacon Department. Here

5

Sliced Bacon

Swift's Premium Bacon is sliced and about 100 girls are busy packing it into half-pound and one-pound convenient, sanitary packages.

Note that the slices are not touched by hand. As a further aid in sanitation, the room is cooled with air that has been washed. The packing and wrapping machines handle about 50 packages per minute.

5. Pork Cutting:

Dressed hogs are placed in the cooling rooms for 36 to 48 hours until thoroughly

6

chilled so that the flesh is firm enough to cut into the parts demanded by the trade.

(a) The first divisions convert the sides into hams, shoulders, and center cuts. These gravitate directly to the trimming department tables in the room below.

(b) The hams, shoulders, and center cuts produced in the room above are received here. The center cuts are separated into two parts; from one part is drawn the pork loin (from which come the pork chops), and from the other cut the sheet of bones known as spareribs is removed. The piece from which the ribs have been removed is

Pork Cutting

7

the bacon. Hams, shoulders, and bacon are trimmed and prepared for the curing process. The trimmed portions are used in making sausage or lard.

6 (a). Smoked Meat:

We now come to the Smoked Meat Department. Swift's Premium Hams and Bacon, *Ovenized*, are cured in sugar and salt; hams from 30 to 90 days and bacon from 12 to 30 days. The time varies according to size. Swift's Premium Hams and Bacon then receive the final processing that has much to do with their delicious goodness—they are *ovenized*.

Interior of Smoke-oven

8

promptly in pleasant surroundings. Seating capacity is about 700.

Note the prices on the menu board.

8. (a) Experimental Laundry Unit:
(b) Home Economics Kitchen:
(c) Sausage Products Kitchen:
(d) Experimental Bakery:

To the right are situated four additions in experimental equipment. In these divisions scientific studies are made of various products, under the direction of the Swift Research Laboratories, to insure the highest possible degree of quality.

The Swift laboratories, which occupy the two top floors of this building, employ nearly one hundred expert chemists in analytical and research work. Constant effort is being made to better the foods Swift & Company prepares and to find new uses for products manufactured.

9. Loading Platform:

On the right is one of a number of platforms where refrigerator cars are loaded for shipment to distant markets. Meat

Ovenized sums up in one word the present perfection in smoking Swift's Premium Hams and Bacon. It also tells of the skill and accuracy with which they are handled in modern "smoke-ovens."

You will notice each Premium Ham and Bacon is stamped "Swift" on the outer edge with a vegetable marking approved by the government. This mark is the means of identification that assures you that you are getting genuine Premium.

It is not necessary to parboil Swift's Premium Hams, *Ovenized*.

The smoke-ovens are five stories high, and that number of tiers of meat are smoked at one time. The smoking is done over wood fires.

6 (b).

Here we see the method of assembling boxes in which meat is packed for shipment to distant points.

7. Plant Cafeteria:

This is the plant cafeteria, where employes may purchase noon-day luncheons at cost, obtaining warm meals, well prepared, abundant in quantity, and served

9

products are highly perishable and must be kept at cool temperatures at all times. This necessitates the use of about 7,000 refrigerator cars. A refrigerator car is really an "ice-box on wheels."

Shipments from all plants of Swift & Company approximate 200,000 carloads annually.

10. Lamb and Veal Cooling Room:

The "Small Stock" cooler, which has a capacity of 3,000 sheep and lambs and 1,500 calves, is continuously under a temperature of 36° to 38° F. (slightly above freezing). This temperature is maintained in all coolers by mechanical refrigeration operating continuously and controlled by hourly observations day and night. In most cases meats remain in the coolers less than 72 hours.

11 (a). Beef Cooling Room:

This is one of a number of coolers reserved for beef. With beef to the right of you and beef to the left of you, you can imagine yourself in a canyon of beefsteak.

The average steer weighs about 1,000 pounds alive, but in dressed form, as you

Beef Cooler

see it here, the weight amounts to only about 550 pounds. Out of the other 450 pounds are obtained about 150 pounds of by-products. The balance represents shrinkage. There are many grades and weights of beef to suit the needs of every class of trade. The capacity of this room is 3,000 sides of beef. Swift & Company is branding the better grades of beef "Swift's Premium," "Swift's Select," and "Swift's," so that dealers and consumers may now obtain assured quality by brand name.

12

11 (b). Sausage:

Swift & Company manufactures more than 200 different kinds of sausage products. The meats used may be either cured or fresh, depending on the variety of sausage to be made. Careful blending with proper spices produces sausage for all tastes. Some sausage is smoked, some is cured, some is air-dried; all are delightful meat foods.

12. Wholesale Market:

This section is a wholesale market, where nearby retail meat dealers purchase their supplies. Swift & Company has a number of similar establishments in various parts of the Chicago territory, and over 400 in the leading cities throughout the country. In all of these markets the same high standards of sanitation are maintained.

13. Plant Assembly:

The Chicago plant of Swift & Company is divided into 29 divisions; each division elects one of its workers as representative to the Assembly. The 29 elected members and 29 others representing the man-

13

Typical Branch House

agement meet regularly each month or in special sessions when necessary and take up all matters pertaining to working conditions, such as wages, safety, protection, sanitation, service records, vacations, etc. The assembly plan has proved itself to be of great value in bringing about a better understanding on the part of both management and employes concerning their mutual relations.

14. Soap:

We are passing a display of Quick Arrow

14

Soap Flakes and New Sunbrite Cleanser—two of the many fine soap products made by Swift & Company. Quick Arrow is noted for its quick, long-lasting suds. New Sunbrite Cleanser, of course, you have seen advertised many times in leading magazines, and so you know that women everywhere prefer it because it cleans easier, works faster, and won't scratch.

15 (a). Refrigerator Car Exhibit:

At this point at the left is displayed the model of a refrigerator car. This model was originally exhibited at the Paris Exposition in 1900. It affords an opportunity to observe the manner in which products are loaded in refrigerator cars.

Meat is highly perishable and must be kept under refrigeration from the time it is dressed in the packing house until it is in the hands of the cook.

15 (b). Historical Exhibit:

Directly ahead is a relic of olden days that deserves mention in the history of Swift & Company. It is the original hoisting wheel used in dressing cattle by

15

G. F. Swift, the founder of the company, at Barnstable, Mass., 1861-1869. The mechanical methods now in use, when compared with the hand-power methods of the early period, are typical of the great progress that has been made in the industry.

16. Sheep and Lamb Dressing:

(Our visitors' route is arranged so that visitors may avoid seeing the killing. Make your wishes known to the guide.)

The Sheep and Lamb Dressing Department has a capacity of 400 per hour. Another unit equal to this brings the capacity of this plant up to 800 per hour. All work in the dressing process is com-

Dressing Sheep

16

pleted in about 26 minutes. Be sure to notice the careful U. S. Government Inspection, which insures the consumer wholesome meat.

17 (a). Vigoro:

Swift & Company's famous Vigoro is a plant food for lawns, flowers, shrubbery, vegetables, trees, and ferns; in fact, everything grown around the house. It is a complete, balanced plant food. You can sow it like grass seed. Vigoro is on sale in every part of the United States in most stores handling lawn and garden supplies.

17 (b). Pard:

Pard, displayed at your left, is a balanced meat-base food for dogs and cats of all breeds and ages. It is packed under U. S. Government Meat Inspection regulations, which means that it is made from ingredients approved for human consumption.

Pard, a beef ration, is the natural meat food for dogs; pets thrive on it.

18. Margarine:

In the Margarine Factory, two general types of margarine are produced: Mar-

17

garine which is white in color and is made of oleo oil from select beef fats and neutral (from pork leaf fats), combined with vegetable oils and churned in milk. Swift's Premium Margarine comes under this classification. The other margarine is also white in color and is made from vegetable oils only, such as cocoanut oil and peanut oil. It is called Nut Margarine and is churned in milk in the same way as Swift's Premium Margarine. Gem-Nut is our leading brand of this type. Both of these products are wholesome spreads for bread, uniform in quality, and highly nutritious.

19. Cheese Display:

Swift's Brookfield Cheese processing is a succession of carefully performed operations. The raw product is graded, and just the right percentages of aged and current cheese are blended. After pasteurization, the cheese is not touched by hand. From the pasteurizer, the cheese goes into a hopper from which the 5-pound boxes and ½-pound cartons are filled. A close inspection is made of the finished product, and the cheese is taken to the cooler, where it ages before being shipped.

18

20. Packaging Margarine:

On these long tables, each equipped with an endless belt, the margarine, after being molded into uniform prints in the machine at the end of the table, travels to the packaging machine, where it is enclosed in a wrapper and placed in a carton and where the cartons are boxed for shipping.

21. Beef Dressing:

This is the Beef Dressing Department, with a capacity of 180 cattle per hour. Here we see the importance and value of specialization. It would be impossible to train a sufficient number of men to do all of

Dressing Beef

19

the work necessary to dress a steer and do each task expertly. Complete operations now require about 35 minutes.

U. S. Government inspectors examine the glands and vital organs and pass for food purposes only the meat from healthy animals.

Final U. S. Inspection

20

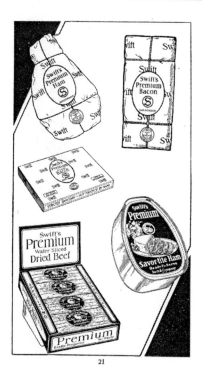

21

22

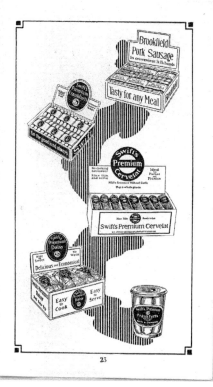

23

24

25

26

27

Probably your parents can remember a time when people bought all their meat from local butchers who killed and dressed such cattle and hogs as they were able to buy from nearby farmers. There were certain days in the week and seasons of the year when the butcher had little or nothing to sell, and he never had any great variety of meats on hand at one time.

What changes have taken place since those days! The demand of people for a constant supply of meats of all kinds, for high quality at the lowest possible prices, and for reliable service has resulted in the vast meat packing business that is so necessary to our nation today.

In running its business, Swift & Company has to please many different kinds of people. There are hundreds of thousands of men raising cattle, sheep, and hogs who must be able to sell their livestock at a good price. Then there are millions of families who want to buy their meat from their meat markets at as low a price as possible. Besides these, there are about 53,000 persons who work for Swift & Company who must be paid, and there are over 50,000 others who have money invested in the business and must get some return from its use.

Swift & Company has always made a point of striving to give all these people a fair deal. This fair dealing, together with a system that wastes nothing, has enabled Swift & Company to reach its present size and position in the business world.

Bird's-eye View of Chicago Plant

In addition to this Chicago establishment, there are large plants at Kansas City, Omaha, St. Paul, East St. Louis, St. Joseph, Fort Worth, Denver, and Portland. Combined, these Swift plants cover over 250 acres of land. These and other establishments of Swift & Company give employment to over 50,000 persons.

Think of the tremendous production handled by the plants! Their annual dressing capacity is over 3,000,000 cattle, 8,000,000 hogs, 5,000,000 sheep, and 1,000,000 calves—or over 57,000 animals every working day, 120 every working minute.

Swift & Company
U.S.A.

Discussion Questions

1. How would you describe the tone of this brochure copy?

2. On page 2 of the brochure is this sentence: "Years ago, when every butcher did his own slaughtering, the expense of preparing meat was high." The brochure then goes on to explain how modern methods have greatly increased efficiency and cut costs of production. What would Karl Marx say about this "progress"? Upton Sinclair?

3. Cite three or more specific elements in the brochure that fit with Upton Sinclair's description of the meat-packing industry.

4. Cite three or more specific elements in the brochure that seem to contradict Sinclair's description of conditions in the meat-packing industry.

5. Observe the language used to describe the gender of the workers in the bacon packaging department in Section 4 on pages 5 and 6 of the brochure. How does this language compare to that used to describe the workers in Section 21 on pages 19 and 20 of the brochure? How do you account for the difference?

6. *The Jungle* was published in 1906 and this brochure in 1933. What conclusions do you draw from this?

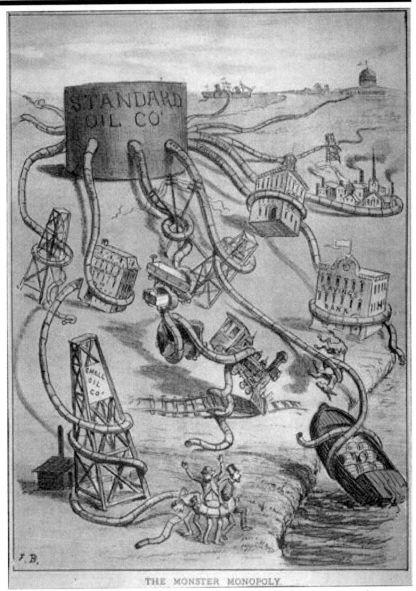

THE MONSTER MONOPOLY

At the turn of the twentieth century Theodore Roosevelt characterized a group of investigative reporters and magazine writers, including Upton Sinclair, as "muckrakers." These writers exposed monopolies, trusts and abusive business practices in a number of industries including meat packing (Sinclair), railroads (Frank Norris), coal mining (Ray Stannard Baker) and patent medicines (Samuel Hopkins Adams), among others. One reporter in particular, Ida Tarbell, helped bring about unprecedented government oversight and regulation of industry because of the illegal and damaging practices (pictured here) detailed in The History of Standard Oil, *her exposé of John D. Rockefeller's powerful oil company,*

JUSTIFYING INFANTICIDE AND NON-VOLUNTARY EUTHANASIA
FROM *Practical Ethics*

PETER SINGER

Peter Albert David Singer (1946-   ), who has been called "one of the leading and most controversial thinkers of our time," was born in Melbourne, Australia. He graduated from the University of Melbourne and attended graduate school at Oxford University, studying moral and political philosophy. While at Oxford, Singer became a vegetarian and animal rights advocate. Singer's appointment to a visiting professor position at Princeton University in 1999 caused a flurry of protests and controversy, primarily because of some of his views that are presented in the excerpt below. Professor Singer, now a permanent resident of the United States, is the Ira W. DeCamp Professor of Bioethics at Princeton and laureate professor at the Centre for Applied Philosophy and Public Ethics at the   University of Melbourne.

NOTE

[1]Peter Singer's philosophy is heavily influenced by the utilitarianism of 19th century philosopher Jeremy Bentham, which holds that all ethical decisions should be based upon the "greatest good for the greatest number." Singer, in his 1974 book, *Animal Rights*, crafted a carefully constructed argument that the right to a happy and satisfying life should not be limited to human beings simply because they happen to be the earth's dominant species. If one accepts that it is wrong for one human to totally dominate another based upon race, gender, IQ, disability or any other arbitrary consideration, then it is wrong for humans to totally dominate animals, to the point of killing and eating them, because they happen to be of another species.

[2]The excerpt below is taken from Chapter 7 of *Practical Ethics*. In earlier chapters, Singer explored the concept of "equal consideration of interests." He says in Chapter 1, "I am accepting that my own interests cannot, simply because they are my interests, count more than the interests of anyone else. Thus my very natural concern that my own interests be looked after must, when I think ethically, be extended to the interests of others." Singer then goes on to build a case for considering that all humans have equal rights, and he then extends those rights to animals.

[3]Then, in Chapter 3, Singer defines "conscious life," saying, "There are many beings who are sentient and capable of experiencing pleasure and pain, but are not rational and self-conscious and so not persons. I shall refer to these beings as conscious beings. Many non-human animals almost certainly fall into this

category; so must newborn infants and some intellectually disabled humans."

[4]This argument lays the foundation for the most controversial part of his philosophy, as excerpted below.

FROM **Chapter 7 Taking Life: Humans**

[5]As we have seen [in earlier chapters], euthanasia is non-voluntary when the subject has never had the capacity to choose to live or die. This is the situation of the severely disabled infant or the older human being who has been intellectually disabled since birth. Euthanasia or other forms of killing are also non-voluntary[a] when the subject is not now but once was capable of making the crucial choice, and did not then express any preference relevant to her present condition.

[6]The case of someone who has never been capable of choosing to live or die is a little more straightforward than that of a person who had, but has now lost, the capacity to make such a decision. We shall, once again, separate the two cases and take the more straightforward one first. For simplicity, I shall concentrate on infants, although everything I say about them would apply to older children or adults whose mental age is and has always been that of an infant.

Life and Death Decisions for Disabled Infants

[7]If we were to approach the issue of life or death for a seriously disabled human infant without any prior discussion of the ethics of killing in general, we might be unable to resolve the conflict between the widely accepted obligation to protect the sanctity of human life and the goal of reducing suffering.[b] Some say that such decisions are "subjective," or that life and death questions must be left to God and Nature. Our previous discussions have, however, prepared the ground, and the principles established and applied in the preceding three chapters make the issue much less baffling than most take it to be.

---

[a]Singer earlier cited two examples of non-voluntary euthanasia that "reached the courts and the popular press":

Louis Repouille had a son who was described as 'incurably imbecile,' had been bed-ridden since infancy and blind for five years. According to Repouille, 'He was just like dead all the time.... He couldn't walk, he couldn't talk, he couldn't do anything.' Repouille killed his son with chloroform.

In 1988 a case arose that well illustrates the way in which modern medical technology forces us to make life and death decisions. Samuel Linares, an infant, swallowed a small object that stuck in his windpipe, causing a loss of oxygen to the brain. He was admitted to a Chicago hospital in a coma and placed on a respirator. Eight months later he was still comatose, still on the respirator, and the hospital was planning to move Samuel to a long-term care unit. Shortly before the move, Samuel's parents visited him in the hospital. His mother left the room while his father produced a pistol and told the nurse to keep away. He then disconnected Samuel from the respirator and cradled the baby in his arms until he died. When he was sure Samuel was dead, he gave up his pistol and surrendered to police. He was charged with murder, but the grand jury refused to issue a homicide indictment, and he subsequently received a suspended sentence on a minor charge arising from the use of the pistol.

[8]In Chapter 4 we saw that the fact that a being is a human being, in the sense of a member of the species Homo sapiens, is not relevant to the wrongness of killing it; it is, rather, characteristics like rationality, autonomy, and self-consciousness that make a difference. Infants lack these characteristics. Killing them, therefore, cannot be equated with killing normal human beings or any other self-conscious beings. This conclusion is not limited to infants who, because of irreversible intellectual disabilities, will never be rational, self-conscious beings. We saw in our discussion of abortion that the potential of a fetus to become a rational, self-conscious being cannot count against killing it at a stage when it lacks these characteristics—not, that is, unless we are also prepared to count the value of rational self-conscious life as a reason against contraception and celibacy. No infant—disabled or not—has as strong a claim to life as beings capable of seeing themselves as distinct entities, existing over time.[c]

[9]The difference between killing disabled and normal infants lies not in any supposed right to life that the latter has and the former lacks, but in other considerations about killing. Most obviously there is the difference that often exists in the attitudes of the parents. The birth of a child is usually a happy event for the parents. They have, nowadays, often planned for the child. The mother has carried it for nine months. From birth, a natural affection begins to bind the parents to it. So one important reason why it is normally a terrible thing to kill an infant is the effect the killing will have on its parents.

[10]It is different when the infant is born with a serious disability. Birth abnormalities vary, of course. Some are trivial and have little effect on the child or its parents; but others turn the normally joyful event of birth into a threat to the happiness of the parents, and any other children they may have.

[11]Parents may, with good reason, regret that a disabled child was ever born. In that event the effect that the death of the child will have on its parents

---

[b]A primary tenet of the philosophical concept of utilitarianism, as expressed by Jeremy Bentham as "the greatest good for the greatest number," is applied by Singer as "the total version" of utilitarianism. In this view, one must look at the sum total of good to be gained by an action weighed against the total bad—or in this specific context, the total amount of suffering experienced by a human being and his/her family weighed against the elimination of suffering. That is, if a severely deformed child is brought into the world to lead a miserable existence, thus bringing pain both to child and to the parents, would it not be better not to have the child, thus eliminating a great deal of misery and suffering and presumably opening the way for the parents to have another child, one without defects.

[c]Singer says in Chapter 4 (entitled "What's Wrong With Killing?"), "A self-conscious being is aware of itself as a distinct entity with a past and a future. (This, remember, was [John] Locke's criterion for being a person.) A being aware of itself in this way will be capable of having desires about its own future."

can be a reason for, rather than against, killing it. Some parents want even the most gravely disabled infant to live as long as possible, and this desire would then be a reason against killing the infant. But what if this is not the case? In the discussion that follows, I shall assume that the parents do not want the disabled child to live. I shall also assume that the disability is so serious that—again in contrast to the situation of an unwanted but normal child today—there are no other couples keen to adopt the infant. This is a realistic assumption even in a society in which there is a long waiting list of couples wishing to adopt normal babies. It is true that from time to time cases of infants who are severely disabled and are being allowed to die have reached the courts in a glare of publicity, and this has led to couples offering to adopt the child. Unfortunately, such offers are the product of the highly publicized dramatic life-and-death situation, and do not extend to the less-publicized but far more common situations in which parents feel themselves unable to look after a severely disabled child, and the child then languishes in an institution.

[12]Infants are sentient beings who are neither rational nor self-conscious.[d] So if we turn to consider the infants in themselves, independently of the attitudes of their parents, since their species is not relevant to their moral status, the principles that govern the wrongness of killing non-human animals who are sentient but not rational or self-conscious must apply here too. As we saw, the most plausible arguments for attributing a right to life to a being apply only if there is some awareness of oneself as a being existing over time, or as a continuing mental self. Nor can respect for autonomy apply where there is no capacity for autonomy. The remaining principles identified in Chapter 4 are utilitarian. Hence the quality of life that the infant can be expected to have is important.

[13]One relatively common birth disability is a faulty development of the spine known as spina bifida. Its prevalence varies in different countries, but it can affect as many as one in five hundred live births. In the more severe cases, the child will be permanently paralyzed from the waist down and lack control of bowels or bladder. Often excess fluid accumulates in the brain, a condition known as hydrocephalus, which can result in intellectual disabilities. Though some forms of treatment exist, if the child is badly affected at birth, the paralysis, incontinence, and intellectual disability cannot be overcome.

[14]Some doctors closely connected with children suffering from severe spina bifida believe that the lives of the worst affected children are so miserable that it is wrong to resort to surgery to keep them alive. Published descriptions of the lives of these children support the judgment that these worst-affected children will have lives filled with pain and discomfort. They need repeated

---

[d]Singer means that while infants have the power of feeling and perception, they have not yet developed a sense of conscious being.

major surgery to prevent curvature of the spine due to the paralysis and to correct other abnormalities. Some children with spina bifida have had forty major operations before they reach their teenage years.

[15]When the life of an infant will be so miserable as not to be worth living, from the internal perspective of the being who will lead that life, both the "prior existence"[e] and the "total" version of utilitarianism entail that, if there are no "intrinsic" reasons for keeping the infant alive—like the feelings of the parents—it is better that the child should be helped to die without further suffering. A more difficult problem arises—and the convergence between the two views ends—when we consider disabilities that make the child's life prospects significantly less promising than those of a normal child, but not so bleak as to make the child's life not worth living. Hemophilia is probably in this category. The hemophiliac lacks the element in normal blood that makes it clot and thus risks prolonged bleeding, especially internal bleeding, from the slightest injury; if allowed to continue, this bleeding leads to permanent crippling and eventually death. The bleeding is very painful and although improved treatments have eliminated the need for constant blood transfusions, hemophiliacs still have to spend a lot of time in hospital. They are unable to play most sports and live constantly on the edge of crisis. Nevertheless, hemophiliacs do not appear to spend their time wondering whether to end it all; most find life definitely worth living, despite the difficulties they face.

[16]Given these facts, suppose that a newborn baby is diagnosed as a hemophiliac. The parents, daunted by the prospect of bringing up a child with this condition, are not anxious for him to live. Could euthanasia be defended here? Our first reaction may well be a firm "no," for the infant can be expected to have a life that is worth living, even if not quite as good as that of a normal baby. The "prior existence" version of utilitarianism supports this judgment. The infant exists. His life can be expected to contain a positive balance of happiness over misery. To kill him would deprive him of this positive balance of happiness. Therefore it would be wrong.

[17]On the "total" version of utilitarianism, however, we cannot reach a decision on the basis of this information alone. The total view makes it necessary to ask whether the death of the hemophiliac infant would lead to the creation of another being who would not otherwise have existed. In other words, if the hemophiliac child is killed, will his parents have another child whom they would not have if the hemophiliac child lives? If they would, is the second child likely

---

[e]The "prior existence" view of utilitarianism applies to those beings who already exist as opposed to those who have not yet been conceived or born. Singer is not comfortable with this viewpoint because, he says, if strictly followed it would not discourage a couple from having a child even though they know that it will inherit a genetic defect, will lead a miserable existence and will almost certainly die before its second birthday.

to have a better life than the one killed?

[18]Often it will be possible to answer both these questions affirmatively. A woman may plan to have two children. If one dies while she is of child-bearing age, she may conceive another in its place. Suppose a woman planning to have two children has one normal child, and then gives birth to a hemophiliac child. The burden of caring for that child may make it impossible for her to cope with a third child; but if the disabled child were to die, she would have another. It is also plausible to suppose that the prospects of a happy life are better for a normal child than for a hemophiliac.

[19]When the death of a disabled infant will lead to the birth of another infant with better prospects of a happy life, the total amount of happiness will be greater if the disabled infant is killed. The loss of happy life for the first infant is outweighed by the gain of a happier life for the second. Therefore, if killing the hemophiliac infant has no adverse effect on others, it would, according to the total view, be right to kill him.

[20]The total view treats infants as replaceable, in much the same way as it treats non-self-conscious animals. Many will think that the replaceability argument cannot be applied to human infants.[f] The direct killing of even the most hopelessly disabled infant is still officially regarded as murder; how then could the killing of infants with far less serious problems, like hemophilia, be accepted? Yet on further reflection, the implications of the replaceability argument do not seem quite so bizarre. For there are disabled members of our species whom we now deal with exactly as the argument suggests we should. These cases closely resemble the ones we have been discussing. There is only one difference, and that is a difference of timing—the timing of the discovery of the problem, and the consequent killing of the disabled being.

[21]Prenatal diagnosis is now a routine procedure for pregnant women. There are various medical techniques for obtaining information about the fetus during the early months of pregnancy. At one stage in the development of these procedures, it was possible to discover the sex of the fetus, but not whether the fetus would suffer from hemophilia. Hemophilia is a sex- linked genetic defect from which only males suffer; females can carry the gene and pass it on to their male offspring without themselves being affected. So a woman who knew that she carried the gene for hemophilia could, at that stage, avoid giving birth to a hemophiliac child only by finding out the sex of the fetus and aborting all male fetuses. Statistically, only half of these male children of women who carried

---

[f]The "replaceability argument" refers to situations such as the killing of an animal to use it for food (e.g., beef cattle) and then breeding another like animal to replace the one that was killed. This can also apply to humans when a woman chooses to abort a fetus known to have severe disabilities and replacing it with another fetus by becoming pregnant again.

the defective gene would have suffered from hemophilia, but there was then no way to find out to which half a particular fetus belonged. Therefore twice as many fetuses were being killed as necessary in order to avoid the birth of children with hemophilia. This practice was widespread in many countries, and yet did not cause any great outcry. Now that we have techniques for identifying hemophilia before birth, we can be more selective, but the principle is the same: women are offered, and usually accept, abortions in order to avoid giving birth to children with hemophilia.

[22]The same can be said about some other conditions that can be detected before birth. Down's syndrome, formerly known as mongolism, is one of these. Children with this condition have intellectual disabilities and most will never be able to live independently, but their lives, like those of small children, can be joyful. The risk of having a Down's syndrome child increases sharply with the age of the mother, and for this reason prenatal diagnosis is routinely offered to pregnant women over 35. Again, undergoing the procedure implies that if the test for Down's syndrome is positive, the woman will consider aborting the fetus and, if she still wishes to have another child, will start another pregnancy, which has a good chance of being normal.

[23]Prenatal diagnosis, followed by abortion in selected cases, is common practice in countries with liberal abortion laws and advanced medical techniques. I think this is as it should be. As the arguments of Chapter 6 indicate, I believe that abortion can be justified. Note, however, that neither hemophilia nor Down's syndrome is so crippling as to make life not worth living from the inner perspective of the person with the condition. To abort a fetus with one of these disabilities, intending to have another child who will not be disabled, is to treat fetuses as interchangeable or replaceable. If the mother has previously decided to have a certain number of children, say two, then what she is doing, in effect, is rejecting one potential child in favor of another. She could, in defense of her actions, say the loss of life of the aborted fetus is outweighed by the gain of a better life for the normal child who will be conceived only if the disabled one dies.

[24]When death occurs before birth, replaceability does not conflict with generally accepted moral convictions. That a fetus is known to be disabled is widely accepted as a ground for abortion. Yet in discussing abortion, we saw that birth does not mark a morally significant dividing line. I cannot see how one could defend the view that fetuses may be "replaced" before birth, but newborn infants may not be. Nor is there any other point, such as viability, that does a better job of dividing the fetus from the infant. Self-consciousness, which could provide a basis for holding that it is wrong to kill one being and replace it with another, is not to be found in either the fetus or the newborn infant. Neither the fetus nor the newborn infant is an individual capable of regarding itself as a distinct entity with a life of its own to lead, and it is only for newborn

infants, or for still earlier stages of human life, that replaceability should be considered to be an ethically acceptable option.

[25]It may still be objected that to replace either a fetus or a newborn infant is wrong because it suggests to disabled people living today that their lives are less worth living than the lives of people who are not disabled. Yet it is surely flying in the face of reality to deny that, on average, this is so. That is the only way to make sense of actions that we all take for granted. Recall thalidomide: this drug, when taken by pregnant women, caused many children to be born without arms or legs. Once the cause of the abnormal births was discovered, the drug was taken off the market, and the company responsible had to pay compensation. If we really believed that there is no reason to think of the life of a disabled person as likely to be any worse than that of a normal person, we would not have regarded this as a tragedy. No compensation would have been sought, or awarded by the courts. The children would merely have been "different." We could even have left the drug on the market so that women who found it a useful sleeping pill during pregnancy could continue to take it. If this sounds grotesque, that is only because we are all in no doubt at all that it is better to be born with limbs than without them. To believe this involves no disrespect at all for those who are lacking limbs; it simply recognizes the reality of the difficulties they face.

[26]In any case, the position taken here does not imply that it would be better that no people born with severe disabilities should survive; it implies only that the parents of such infants should be able to make this decision. Nor does this imply lack of respect or equal consideration for people with disabilities who are now living their own lives in accordance with their own wishes. As we saw at the end of Chapter 2, the principle of equal consideration of interests rejects any discounting of the interests of people on grounds of disability.

[27]Even those who reject abortion and the idea that the fetus is replaceable are likely to regard possible people as replaceable. Recall the second woman in Parfit's case of the two women, described in Chapter 5. She was told by her doctor that if she went ahead with her plan to become pregnant immediately, her child would have a disability (it could have been hemophilia); but if she waited three months her child would not have the disability.[g] If we think she would do wrong not to wait, it can only be because we are comparing the two possible

---

[g]In this hypothetical case discussed in Chapter 5, a woman who has stopped using birth control is told to wait three months before becoming pregnant or her child will have a birth defect. The woman chooses not to wait, her child is born with a birth defect, like hemophilia, and the child later complains that the mother should have waited. The woman tells the child that if she had waited, he/she would never have been born as a new egg and new sperm would have created a different child. In other words, the living child would have been "replaced" and would not have had the opportunity for life at all, albeit with a disability.

lives and judging one to have better prospects than the other. Of course, at this stage no life has begun; but the question is, when does a life, in the morally significant sense, really begin? In Chapters 4 and 5 we saw several reasons for saying that life only begins in the morally significant sense when there is awareness of one's existence over time. The metaphor of life as a journey also provides a reason for holding that in infancy, life's voyage has scarcely begun.

[28]Regarding newborn infants as replaceable, as we now regard fetuses, would have considerable advantages over prenatal diagnosis followed by abortion. Prenatal diagnosis still cannot detect all major disabilities. Some disabilities, in fact, are not present before birth; they may be the result of extremely premature birth, or of something going wrong in the birth process itself. At present, parents can choose to keep or destroy their disabled offspring only if the disability happens to be detected during pregnancy. There is no logical basis for restricting parents' choice to these particular disabilities. If disabled newborn infants were not regarded as having a right to life until, say, a week or a month after birth it would allow parents, in consultation with their doctors, to choose on the basis of far greater knowledge of the infant's condition than is possible before birth.

[29]All these remarks have been concerned with the rightness or wrongness of ending the life of the infant, considered in itself rather than for its effects on others. When we take effects on others into account, the picture may alter. Obviously, to go through the whole of pregnancy and labor, only to give birth to a child who one decides should not live, would be a difficult, perhaps heartbreaking, experience. For this reason many women would prefer prenatal diagnosis and abortion rather than live birth with the possibility of infanticide; but if the latter is not morally worse than the former, this would seem to be a choice that the woman herself should be allowed to make.

[30]Another factor to take into account is the possibility of adoption. When there are more couples wishing to adopt than normal children available for adoption, a childless couple may be prepared to adopt a hemophiliac. This would relieve the mother of the burden of bringing up a hemophiliac child and enable her to have another child if she wished. Then the replaceability argument could not justify infanticide, for bringing the other child into existence would not be dependent on the death of the hemophiliac. The death of the hemophiliac would then be a straightforward loss of a life of positive quality, not outweighed by the creation of another being with a better life.

[31]So the issue of ending life for disabled newborn infants is not without complications, which we do not have the space to discuss adequately. Nevertheless the main point is clear: killing a disabled infant is not morally equivalent to killing a person. Very often it is not wrong at all.

Vocabulary

[1]ethics	[8]rationality	[11]languishes	[16]daunted
[2]excerpt	[8]autonomy	[12]plausible	[21]prenatal
[3]sentient	[8]equated	[12]attributing	[24]viability
[4]euthanasia	[8]celibacy	[13] incontinence	[24]entity
[7] sanctity	[11]keen	[15]intrinsic	[29]infanticide

Discussion Questions

1. Research the terms "ethic of reciprocity" and "the golden rule" and explain how they relate to Singer's "equal consideration of interests" as explained in paragraph 2.

2. Note Singer's mention in paragraph 6 of "older children or adults whose mental age is and has always been that of an infant." What point does he make about them here?

3. In paragraph 8, Singer says that the decision to abort a fetus (in Singer's terms, an entity lacking "rationality, autonomy, and self-consciousness") is essentially the same as making a decision to remain celibate or to practice birth control. Do you agree with this position? If not, why not?

4. In paragraph 11 Singer says that in the discussion to follow he is making an assumption about the wishes of the parents. What is this assumption?

5. What does Singer mean in paragraph 12 when he says, ". . . their species is not relevant to their moral status . . ."?

6. Do you agree or disagree with a woman's decision to abort all male fetuses based on the 50-50 chance that they will be born with hemophilia? Why?

7. How does what Singer says in paragraph 19 fit with his philosophy of total utilitarianism? Do you agree with his point of view here?

8. Explain replaceability. Do you think it's OK to apply this concept to animals? To humans? Explain the reasons for your answers.

9. Singer says in paragraph 24, "That a fetus is known to be disabled is widely accepted as a ground for abortion." Do you agree that this a true statement? Do you agree or disagree that abortion is justifiable in these cases? Why?

10. How does what Singer says in paragraphs 25 and 26 fit with what Harriet McBryde Johnson says in "Unspeakable Conversations" beginning on page 555 in this text? Do you think that Johnson has carefully considered Singer's viewpoint or is she "shooting from the hip" based upon what she has heard about his moral philosophy?

11. Having read both Singer and Johnson, which writer's position fits most closely with your own? Why?

12. Look at Jonathan Swift's argument in his essay, "A Modest Proposal," beginning on page 399 of this text. Do you think that Singer's argument here is an updated version of Swift's work? Explain your answer.

KEW GARDENS

VIRGINIA WOOLF

Virginia Woolf (1882-1941), a founder of Modernism and a central figure in the Bloomsbury Group, is considered by many critics to be one of the most important women writers in English. Her "stream-of-consciousness" essays and novels provide insight into her own life experiences and those of women at the beginning of the twentieth century. She is best known for the novels Jacob's Room *(1922),* Mrs. Dalloway *(1925),* To the Lighthouse *(1927), and* The Waves *(1931). After struggling with depression and mental illness, she committed suicide in 1941. This work appeared originally in a collection of eight short stories entitled* Monday or Tuesday, *published in 1921.*

[1]From the oval-shaped flower-bed there rose perhaps a hundred stalks spreading into heart-shaped or tongue-shaped leaves half way up and unfurling at the tip red or blue or yellow petals marked with spots of colour raised upon the surface; and from the red, blue or yellow gloom of the throat emerged a straight bar, rough with gold dust and slightly clubbed at the end. The petals were voluminous enough to be stirred by the summer breeze, and when they moved, the red, blue and yellow lights passed one over the other, staining an inch of the brown earth beneath with a spot of the most intricate colour. The light fell either upon the smooth, grey back of a pebble, or the shell of a snail with its brown, circular veins, or falling into a raindrop, it expanded the thin walls of water with such intensity of red, blue and yellow that one expected them to burst and disappear. Instead, the drop was left in a second silver grey once more, and the light now settled upon the flesh of a leaf, revealing the branching thread of fibre beneath the surface, and again it moved on and spread its illumination in the vast green spaces beneath the dome of the heart-shaped and tongue-shaped leaves. Then the breeze stirred rather more briskly overhead and the colour was flashed into the air above, into the eyes of the men and women who walk in Kew Gardens in July.

[2]The figures of these men and women straggled past the flower-bed with a curiously irregular movement not unlike that of the white and blue butterflies who crossed the turf in zig-zag flights from bed to bed. The man was about six inches in front of the woman, strolling carelessly, while she bore on with greater purpose, only turning her head now and then to see that the children were not too far behind. The man kept this distance in front of the woman purposely, though perhaps unconsciously, for he wished to go on with his thoughts.

[3]"Fifteen years ago I came here with Lily," he thought. "We sat somewhere over there by a lake and I begged her to marry me all through the hot afternoon. How the dragonfly kept circling round us: how clearly I see the dragonfly and her shoe with the square silver buckle at the toe. All the time I spoke I saw her shoe and when it moved impatiently, I knew without looking up what she was going to say: the whole of her seemed to be in her shoe. And my love, my desire, were in the dragonfly; for some reason I thought that if it settled there, on that leaf, the broad one with the red flower in the middle of it, if the dragonfly settled on the leaf she would say 'Yes' at once. But the dragonfly went round and round: it never settled anywhere, of course not, happily not, or I shouldn't be walking here with Eleanor and the children—Tell me, Eleanor. D'you ever think of the past?"

[4]"Why do you ask, Simon?"

[5]"Because I've been thinking of the past. I've been thinking of Lily, the woman I might have married. . . . Well, why are you silent? Do you mind my thinking of the past?"

[6]"Why should I mind, Simon? Doesn't one always think of the past, in a garden with men and women lying under the trees? Aren't they one's past, all that remains of it, those men and women, those ghosts lying under the trees, . . . one's happiness, one's reality?"

[7]"For me, a square silver shoe buckle and a dragonfly—"

[8]"For me, a kiss. Imagine six little girls sitting before their easels twenty years ago, down by the side of a lake, painting the water—lilies, the first red water-lilies I'd ever seen. And suddenly a kiss, there on the back of my neck. And my hand shook all the afternoon so that I couldn't paint. I took out my watch and marked the hour when I would allow myself to think of the kiss for five minutes only—it was so precious—the kiss of an old grey-haired woman with a wart on her nose, the mother of all my kisses all my life. Come, Caroline, come, Hubert."

[9]They walked on the past the flower-bed, now walking four abreast, and soon diminished in size among the trees and looked half transparent as the sunlight and shade swam over their backs in large trembling irregular patches.

[10]In the oval flower bed the snail, whose shell had been stained red, blue, and yellow for the space of two minutes or so, now appeared to be moving very slightly in its shell, and next began to labour over the crumbs of loose earth which broke away and rolled down as it passed over them. It appeared to have a definite goal in front of it, differing in this respect from the singular high-stepping angular green insect who attempted to cross in front of it, and waited for a second with its antennæ trembling as if in deliberation, and then stepped off as rapidly and strangely in the opposite direction. Brown cliffs with deep green lakes in the hollows, flat, blade-like trees that waved from root to tip, round boulders of grey stone, vast crumpled surfaces of a thin crackling texture—all

these objects lay across the snail's progress between one stalk and another to his goal. Before he had decided whether to circumvent the arched tent of a dead leaf or to breast it, there came past the bed the feet of other human beings.

[11]This time they were both men. The younger of the two wore an expression of perhaps unnatural calm; he raised his eyes and fixed them very steadily in front of him while his companion spoke, and directly his companion had done speaking he looked on the ground again and sometimes opened his lips only after a long pause and sometimes did not open them at all. The elder man had a curiously uneven and shaky method of walking, jerking his hand forward and throwing up his head abruptly, rather in the manner of an impatient carriage horse tired of waiting outside a house; but in the man these gestures were irresolute and pointless. He talked almost incessantly; he smiled to himself and again began to talk, as if the smile had been an answer. He was talking about spirits—the spirits of the dead, who, according to him, were even now telling him all sorts of odd things about their experiences in Heaven.

[12]"Heaven was known to the ancients as Thessaly, William, and now, with this war, the spirit matter is rolling between the hills like thunder." He paused, seemed to listen, smiled, jerked his head and continued:—

[13]"You have a small electric battery and a piece of rubber to insulate the wire—isolate?—insulate?—well, we'll skip the details, no good going into details that wouldn't be understood— and in short the little machine stands in any convenient position by the head of the bed, we will say, on a neat mahogany stand. All arrangements being properly fixed by workmen under my direction, the widow applies her ear and summons the spirit by sign as agreed. Women! Widows! Women in black—"

[14]Here he seemed to have caught sight of a woman's dress in the distance, which in the shade looked a purple black. He took off his hat, placed his hand upon his heart, and hurried towards her muttering and gesticulating feverishly. But William caught him by the sleeve and touched a flower with the tip of his walking-stick in order to divert the old man's attention. After looking at it for a moment in some confusion the old man bent his ear to it and seemed to answer a voice speaking from it, for he began talking about the forests of Uruguay which he had visited hundreds of years ago in company with the most beautiful young woman in Europe. He could be heard murmuring about forests of Uruguay blanketed with the wax petals of tropical roses, nightingales, sea beaches, mermaids, and women drowned at sea, as allowed himself to be moved on by William, upon whose face the look of stoical patience grew slowly deeper and deeper.

[15]Following his steps so closely as to be slightly puzzled by his gestures came two elderly women of the lower middle class, one stout and ponderous, the other rosy cheeked and nimble. Like most people of their station they were

frankly fascinated by any signs of eccentricity indicating a disordered brain, especially in the well-to-do; but they were too far off to be certain whether the gestures were merely eccentric or genuinely mad. After they had scrutinized the old man's back in silence for a moment and given each other a queer, sly look, they went on energetically piecing together their very complicated dialogue:

[16]"Nell, Bert, Lot, Cess, Phil, Pa, he says, I says, she says, I says, I says, I says—"

"My Bert, Sis, Bill, Grandad, the old man, sugar,

Sugar, flour, kippers, greens,

Sugar, sugar, sugar."

[17]The ponderous woman looked through the pattern of falling words at the flowers standing cool, firm, and upright in the earth, with a curious expression. She saw them as a sleeper waking from a heavy sleep sees a brass candlestick reflecting the light in an unfamiliar way, and closes his eyes and opens them, and seeing the brass candlestick again, finally starts broad awake and stares at the candlestick with all his powers. So the heavy woman came to a standstill opposite the oval-shaped flower bed, and ceased even to pretend to listen to what the other woman was saying. She stood there letting the words fall over her, swaying the top part of her body slowly backwards and forwards, looking at the flowers. Then she suggested that they should find a seat and have their tea.

[18]The snail had now considered every possible method of reaching his goal without going round the dead leaf or climbing over it. Let alone the effort needed for climbing a leaf, he was doubtful whether the thin texture which vibrated with such an alarming crackle when touched even by the tip of his horns would bear his weight; and this determined him finally to creep beneath it, for there was a point where the leaf curved high enough from the ground to admit him. He had just inserted his head in the opening and was taking stock of the high brown roof and was getting used to the cool brown light when two other people came past outside on the turf. This time they were both young, a young man and a young woman. They were both in the prime of youth, or even in that season which precedes the prime of youth, the season before the smooth pink folds of the flower have burst their gummy case, when the wings of the butterfly, though fully grown, are motionless in the sun.

[19]"Lucky it isn't Friday," he observed.

[20]"Why? D'you believe in luck?"

[22]"They make you pay sixpence on Friday."

[23]"What's sixpence anyway? Isn't it worth sixpence?"

[24]"What's 'it'—what do you mean by 'it'?"

[25]"O, anything—I mean—you know what I mean."

[26]Long pauses came between each of these remarks; they were uttered in toneless and monotonous voices. The couple stood still on the edge of the

flower bed, and together pressed the end of her parasol deep down into the soft earth. The action and the fact that his hand rested on the top of hers expressed their feelings in a strange way, as these short insignificant words also expressed something, words with short wings for their heavy body of meaning, inadequate to carry them far and thus alighting awkwardly upon the very common objects that surrounded them, and were to their inexperienced touch so massive; but who knows (so they thought as they pressed the parasol into the earth) what precipices aren't concealed in them, or what slopes of ice don't shine in the sun on the other side? Who knows? Who has ever seen this before? Even when she wondered what sort of tea they gave you at Kew, he felt that something loomed up behind her words and stood vast and solid behind them; and the mist very slowly rose and uncovered—O, Heavens, what were those shapes?—little white tables, and waitresses who looked first at her and then at him; and there was a bill that he would pay with a real two-shilling piece, and it was real, all real, he assured himself, fingering the coin in his pocket, real to everyone except to him and to her; even to him it began to seem real; and then—but it was too exciting to stand and think any longer, and he pulled the parasol out of the earth with a jerk and was impatient to find the place where one had tea with other people, like other people.

27"Come along, Trissie; it's time we had our tea."

28"Wherever does one have one's tea?" she asked with the oddest thrill of excitement in her voice, looking vaguely round and letting herself be drawn on down the grass path, trailing her parasol, turning her head this way and that way, forgetting her tea, wishing to go down there and then down there, remembering orchids and cranes among wild flowers, a Chinese pagoda and a crimson crested bird; but he bore her on.

29Thus one couple after another with much the same irregular and aimless movement passed the flower-bed and were enveloped in layer after layer of green blue vapour, in which at first their bodies had substance and a dash of colour, but later both substance and colour dissolved in the green-blue atmosphere. How hot it was! So hot that even the thrush chose to hop, like a mechanical bird, in the shadow of the flowers, with long pauses between one movement and the next; instead of rambling vaguely, the white butterflies danced one above another, making with their white shifting flakes the outline of a shattered marble column above the tallest flowers; the glass roofs of the palm house shone as if a whole market full of shiny green umbrellas had opened in the sun; and in the drone of the aeroplane the voice of the summer sky murmured its fierce soul. Yellow and black, pink and snow white, shapes of all these colours, men, women, and children were spotted for a second upon the horizon, and then, seeing the breadth of yellow that lay upon the grass, they wavered and sought shade beneath the trees, dissolving like drops of water in the yellow and green atmosphere, staining it faintly with red and blue. It seemed as if all gross and heavy bodies had sunk down in the heat motionless and lay huddled upon the ground, but their voices went wavering from them as if they were flames lolling from the thick waxen bodies of candles. Voices. Yes, voices. Wordless voices, breaking the silence suddenly with such depth of contentment, such passion of desire, or, in the voices of children, such freshness of surprise; breaking the silence? But there was no silence; all the time the motor omnibuses were turning their wheels and changing their gear; like a vast nest of Chinese boxes all of wrought steel turning ceaselessly one within another the city murmured; on the top of which the voices cried aloud and the petals of myriads of flowers flashed their colours into the air.

Vocabulary

[1]unfurling	[11]irresolute	[15]ponderous	[29] lolling
[1]voluminous	[11]incessantly	[15]scrutinized	[29] myriads
[10]antennae	[14]gesticulating	[26] parasol	
[10]circumvent	[14]stoical	[26] precipices	

Discussion Questions

1. Where and what are the Kew Gardens that Wolf uses for the setting of the story?

2. The introductory notes indicate that Virginia Woolf was noted for her use of the "stream-of-consciousness" technique in her writing. Research what this term means and then pick out two places in the story where the technique is used.

3. Some literary critics have likened "Kew Gardens" to "an Impressionist canvas." Do you agree with this assessment? Why or why not?

4. What simile does Woolf use that incorporates "zig-zag flights"? Why do you think she included this in the story?

5. Woolf employs an omniscient point of view in which the reader can see into the minds of the characters. Point out four different places in the story where this occurs.

6. When thinking of the past, what does Simon think about? What does Eleanor remember? What do you think Woolf is saying about the differences between men and women?

7. Paragraph 28 consists of one sentence. What does that sentence tell us about the difference between Trissie and her companion?

8. Compare Tissie's relaltionship with her companion to George's relationship with his wife in Ernest Hemingway's "Cat in the Rain" on page 202 of this text.

9. What are some of the themes of the story?

10. Compare the snail's purpose (goal) to the humans' purpose. What do you think Woolf is saying here?

KOREMATSU V. UNITED STATES
(ABRIDGED)

UNITED STATES SUPREME COURT

In February of 1942, just over two months after the attack by Japanese forces on U.S. military bases at Pearl Harbor, Hawaii, President Franklin D. Roosevelt issued Executive Order Number 9066 authorizing a series of military orders designed to prevent any acts of espionage or sabotage in support of Japan that might arise out of the substantial Japanese-American community on the U.S. West Coast. Despite their many positive contributions to the life and economies of the western section of the U.S., especially in California, Japanese-Americans were viewed with suspicion and outright hostility by Americans who feared an imminent attack on the West Coast by Japanese forces.

*Ultimately, more than 100,000 Japanese nationals and Japanese-Americans were shipped to "War Relocation Camps" away from the coast. One U.S. citizen, **Toyosuboro (Fred) Korematsu**, who was arrested for not complying with one of the military orders, appealed his conviction all the way to the U.S. Supreme Court—and lost. For forty years, Korematsu fought to clear his name. In 1984 a federal court acknowledged that Korematsu had been unjustly treated and reversed his conviction. In that case, the court said, "It was uncontroverted at the time of conviction that petitioner was loyal to the United States and had no dual allegiance to Japan. He had never left the United States. He was registered for the draft and willing to bear arms for the United States." (Korematsu had been rejected for military service for health reasons and was working as a welder in the defense industry when he was arrested and sent to a relocation camp.)*

In the 1984 case, the government acknowledged that General J.L. DeWitt, who had issued "Civilian Exclusion Order Number 34" authorizing the relocations in 1942, had "misrepresented the facts" when he told the Defense Department there had been "illegal radio transmitters and shore-to-ship signaling by persons of Japanese ancestry" on the West Coast. In fact, both the Federal Communications Commission and the Federal Bureau of Investigation "categorically denied" General DeWitt's allegations and the U.S. Justice Department said they were "demonstrably false," but DeWitt did not make this information known at the time of Korematsu's original trial.

In vacating Korematsu's conviction, the court in 1984 said, "Korematsu remains on the pages of our legal and political history. As a legal precedent it is now recognized as having very limited application. As historical precedent it stands as a constant caution that in times of war or declared military necessity our institutions must be vigilant in protecting constitutional guarantees. It stands as a caution that in times of distress the shield of military necessity and national security must not be used to protect governmental actions from close scrutiny and accountability. It stands as a caution that in times of international hostility and antagonisms our institutions, legislative, executive and judicial, must be prepared to exercise their authority to protect all citizens from the petty fears and prejudices that are so easily aroused."

Fred Korematsu died in March of 2005.

KOREMATSU v. UNITED STATES
CERTIORARI TO THE CIRCUIT COURT OF APPEALS FOR THE
NINTH CIRCUIT

Argued: October 11, 12, 1944 — Decided: December 18, 1944

Rehearing Denied Feb. 12, 1945
Mr. Justice BLACK delivered the opinion of the Court.

[1]The petitioner, an American citizen of Japanese descent, was convicted in a federal district court for remaining in San Leandro, California, a "Military Area," contrary to Civilian Exclusion Order No. 34 of the Commanding General of the Western Command, U.S. Army, which directed that after May 9, 1942, all persons of Japanese ancestry should be excluded from that area. No question was raised as to petitioner's loyalty to the United States. The Circuit Court of Appeals affirmed Mr. Korematsu's conviction on the charges, and the importance of the constitutional question involved caused us to consent to hear the case.

[2]It should be noted to begin with that all legal restrictions which curtail the civil rights of a single racial group are immediately suspect. That is not to say that all such restrictions are unconstitutional. It is to say that courts must subject them to the most rigid scrutiny. Pressing public necessity may sometimes justify the existence of such restrictions; racial antagonism never can.

[3]In this case, prosecution of Mr. Korematsu was begun by charges of violation of an Act of Congress, of March 21, 1942, which provides that

> ... whoever shall enter, remain in, leave, or commit any act in any military area or military zone prescribed, under the authority of an Executive order of the President, by the Secretary of War, or by any military commander designated by the Secretary of War, contrary to the restrictions applicable to any such area or zone or contrary to the order of the Secretary of War or any such military commander, shall, if it appears that he knew or should have known of the existence and extent of the restrictions or order and that his act was in violation thereof, be guilty of a misdemeanor and upon conviction shall be liable to a fine not to exceed $5,000 or to imprisonment for not more than one year, or both, for each offense.

[4]Exclusion Order No. 34, which the petitioner knowingly and admittedly violated, was one of a number of military orders and proclamations, all of which were substantially based upon Executive Order No. 9066. That order, issued after we were at war with Japan, declared that "the successful prosecution of the

war requires every possible protection against espionage and against sabotage to national-defense material, national-defense premises, and national-defense utilities . . ."

[5]One of the series of orders and proclamations, a curfew order, which like the exclusion order here, was issued pursuant to Executive Order 9066 and subjected all persons of Japanese ancestry in prescribed West Coast military areas to remain in their residences from 8 p.m. to 6 a.m. as a "protection against espionage and against sabotage." In Kiyoshi Hirabayashi v. United States, we sustained a conviction obtained for violation of the curfew order.

[6]In the light of the principles we announced in the Hirabayashi case, we are unable to conclude that it was beyond the war power of Congress and the Executive to exclude those of Japanese ancestry from the West Coast war area and that to apply the curfew and exclusion order against none but citizens of Japanese ancestry amounted to a constitutionally prohibited discrimination solely on account of race.

[7]Like curfew, exclusion of those of Japanese origin was deemed necessary because of the presence of an unascertained number of disloyal members of the group, most of whom we have no doubt were loyal to this country. It was because we could not reject the finding of the military authorities that it was impossible to bring about an immediate segregation of the disloyal from the loyal that we sustained the validity of the curfew order as applying to the whole group. That there were members of the group who retained loyalties to Japan has been confirmed by investigations made subsequent to the exclusion. Approximately five thousand American citizens of Japanese ancestry refused to swear unqualified allegiance to the United States and to renounce allegiance to the Japanese Emperor, and several thousand evacuees requested repatriation to Japan.

[8]We uphold the exclusion order as of the time it was made and when the petitioner violated it. In doing so, we are not unmindful of the hardships imposed by it upon a large group of American citizens. But hardships are part of war, and war is an aggregation of hardships. All citizens alike, both in and out of uniform, feel the impact of war in greater or lesser measure. Citizenship has its responsibilities as well as its privileges, and in time of war the burden is always heavier. Compulsory exclusion of large groups of citizens from their homes, except under circumstances of direst emergency and peril, is inconsistent with our basic governmental institutions. But when under conditions of modern warfare our shores are threatened by hostile forces, the power to protect must be commensurate with the threatened danger.

[9]It is argued that on May 30, 1942, the date the petitioner was charged with remaining in the prohibited area, there were conflicting orders outstanding, forbidding him both to leave the area and to remain there. Of course, a person cannot be convicted for doing the very thing which it is a crime to fail to do. But

the outstanding orders here contained no such contradictory commands. There was an order issued March 27, 1942, which prohibited petitioner and others of Japanese ancestry from leaving the area, but this order was subsequently superseded by the order of May 3, 1942 excluding from the area all persons of Japanese ancestry before 12 o'clock noon, May 9. Further, the May 3 order contained a warning that all such persons found in the prohibited area would be liable to punishment under the March 21, 1942 Act of Congress. Petitioner stipulated in his trial that he knew of the order and violated it.

[10]On May 9, the effective date of the exclusion order, the military authorities had determined that the evacuation should be effected by assembling and placing under guard at central points designated as "assembly centers" all those of Japanese ancestry "to insure the orderly evacuation and resettlement of Japanese voluntarily migrating from military area No. 1." Civilian Restrictive Order No. 1 provided for detention of those of Japanese ancestry in assembly or relocation centers. After May 3, 1942, the date of Exclusion Order No. 34, Korematsu was under compulsion to leave the area not as he would choose but via an Assembly Center. The Assembly Center was conceived as a part of the machinery for group evacuation. The power to exclude includes the power to do it by force if necessary. And any forcible measure must necessarily entail some degree of detention or restraint whatever method of removal is selected. But whichever view is taken, it results in holding that the order under which petitioner was convicted was valid.

[11]It is said that we are dealing here with the case of imprisonment of a citizen in a concentration camp solely because of his ancestry, without evidence or inquiry concerning his loyalty and good disposition towards the United States. Our task would be simple, our duty clear, were this a case involving the imprisonment of a loyal citizen in a concentration camp because of racial prejudice. Regardless of the true nature of the assembly and relocation centers—and we deem it unjustifiable to call them concentration camps with all the ugly connotations that term implies—we are dealing specifically with nothing but an exclusion order. To cast this case into outlines of racial prejudice, without reference to the real military dangers which were presented, merely confuses the issue. Korematsu was not excluded from the Military Area because of hostility to him or his race. He was excluded because we are at war with the Japanese Empire; because the properly constituted military authorities feared an invasion of our West Coast and felt constrained to take proper security measures; because they decided that the military urgency of the situation demanded that all citizens of Japanese ancestry be segregated from the West Coast temporarily; and finally, because Congress, reposing its confidence in this time of war in our military leaders—as inevitably it must—determined that they should have the power to do just this. There was evidence of disloyalty on the part of some, the military

authorities considered that the need for action was great, and time was short. We cannot—by availing ourselves of the calm perspective of hindsight—now say that at that time these actions were unjustified.

AFFIRMED 6-3.

Mr. Justice FRANKFURTER, concurring.

[12]According to my reading of Civilian Exclusion Order No. 34, it was an offense for Korematsu to be found in Military Area No. 1, the territory wherein he was previously living, except within the bounds of the established Assembly Center of that area. Even though the various orders issued by General DeWitt be deemed a comprehensive code of instructions, their tenor is clear and not contradictory. They put upon Korematsu the obligation to leave Military Area No. 1, but only by the method prescribed in the instructions, i.e., by reporting to the Assembly Center. I am unable to see how the legal considerations that led to the decision in Kiyoshi Hirabayashi v. United States fail to sustain the military order which made the conduct now in controversy a crime. And so I join in the opinion of the Court, but should like to add a few words of my own.

[13]The provisions of the Constitution which confer on the Congress and the President powers to enable this country to wage war are as much part of the Constitution as provisions looking to a nation at peace. And we have had recent occasion to quote approvingly the statement of former Chief Justice Hughes that the war power of the Government is "the power to wage war successfully." Therefore, the validity of action under the war power must be judged wholly in the context of war.

[14]If a military order such as that under review does not transcend the means appropriate for conducting war, such action by the military is as constitutional as would be any authorized action by the Interstate Commerce Commission within the limits of the constitutional power to regulate commerce. And being an exercise of the war power explicitly granted by the Constitution for safeguarding the national life by prosecuting war effectively, I find nothing in the Constitution which denies to Congress the power to enforce such a valid military order by making its violation an offense triable in the civil courts.

[15]To find that the Constitution does not forbid the military measures now complained of does not carry with it approval of that which Congress and the Executive did. That is their business, not ours.

Mr. Justice ROBERTS, dissenting.

[16]I dissent because I think the indisputable facts exhibit a clear violation of Constitutional rights.

[17]This is not a case of keeping people off the streets at night as was Kiyoshi Hirabayashi v. United States, nor a case of temporary exclusion of a

citizen from an area for his own safety or that of the community, nor a case of offering him an opportunity to go temporarily out of an area where his presence might cause danger to himself or to his fellows. On the contrary, it is the case of convicting a citizen as a punishment for not submitting to imprisonment in a concentration camp based on his ancestry, and solely because of his ancestry, without evidence or inquiry concerning his loyalty and good disposition towards the United States. If this be a correct statement of the facts disclosed by this record, and facts of which we take judicial notice, I need hardly labor the conclusion that Constitutional rights have been violated.

[18]The petitioner, a resident of San Leandro, Alameda County, California, is a native of the United States of Japanese ancestry who, according to the uncontradicted evidence, is a loyal citizen of the nation.

[19]A chronological recitation of events will make it plain that the petitioner's supposed offense did not, in truth, consist in his refusal voluntarily to leave the area which included his home in obedience to the order excluding him therefrom. Critical attention must be given to the dates and sequence of events.

[20]December 8, 1941, the United States declared war on Japan.

[21]February 19, 1942, the President issued Executive Order No. 9066, which provided that certain Military Commanders might, in their discretion, "prescribe military areas" and define their extent, "from which any or all persons may be excluded, and with respect to which, the right of any person to enter, remain in, or leave shall be subject to whatever restrictions the Military Commander may impose in his discretion."

[22]February 20, 1942, Lieutenant General DeWitt was designated Military Commander of the Western Defense Command embracing the westernmost states of the Union, about one-fourth of the total area of the nation.

[23]March 2, 1942, General DeWitt issued Public Proclamation No. 1, which says the entire Pacific Coast is "particularly subject to attack, to attempted invasion ... and, in connection therewith, is subject to espionage and acts of sabotage." It establishes "as a matter of military necessity" military areas and zones known as Military Areas Nos. 1 and 2. Included in such areas and zones are all of California, Washington, Oregon, Idaho, Montana, Nevada and Utah, and the southern portion of Arizona. The orders required that if any person of Japanese, German or Italian ancestry residing in Area No. 1 desired to change his habitual residence, he must execute and deliver to the authorities a Change of Residence Notice.

[24]March 21, 1942, Congress enacted that anyone who knowingly "shall enter, remain in, leave, or commit any act in any military area or military zone prescribed ... by any military commander ... contrary to the restrictions applicable to any such area or zone or contrary to the order of ... any such military commander" shall be guilty of a misdemeanor. This is the Act under which the

petitioner was charged.

[25]March 24, 1942, General DeWitt instituted the curfew for certain areas within his command.

[26]March 24, 1942, General DeWitt began to issue a series of exclusion orders relating to specified areas.

[27]March 27, 1942, the General issued Proclamation No. 4 which ordered that, as of March 29, 1942, "all alien Japanese and persons of Japanese ancestry who are within the limits of Military Area No. 1 are hereby prohibited from leaving that area for any purpose until and to the extent that a future proclamation or order of this headquarters shall so permit or direct."

[28]May 3, 1942, General DeWitt issued Civilian Exclusion Order No. 34 providing that, after 12 o'clock May 8, 1942, all persons of Japanese ancestry, both alien and non-alien, were to be excluded from a described portion of Military Area No. 1, which included the County of Alameda, California, the site of the home of the petitioner. The order required a responsible member of each family and each individual living alone to report, at a time set, at a Civil Control Station for instructions to go to an Assembly Center, and added that any person failing to comply with the provisions of the order who was found in the described area after the date set would be liable to prosecution under the Act of March 21, 1942

[29]The obvious purpose of the orders, taken together, was to drive all citizens of Japanese ancestry into Assembly Centers within the zones of their residence, under pain of criminal prosecution. In the dilemma that he dare not remain in his home, or voluntarily leave the area without incurring criminal penalties, and that the only way he could avoid punishment was to go to an Assembly Center and submit himself to military imprisonment, the petitioner did nothing.

[30]June 12, 1942, an Information was filed in the District Court for Northern California charging a violation of the Act of March 21, 1942, in that petitioner had knowingly remained within the area covered by Exclusion Order No. 34. The petitioner was tried under a plea of not guilty and convicted. Sentence was suspended and he was placed on probation for five years. He was at once taken into military custody and lodged in an Assembly Center.

[31]The liberty of every American citizen freely to come and to go must frequently, in the face of sudden danger, be temporarily limited or suspended. The civil authorities must often resort to the expedient of excluding citizens temporarily from a locality such as the drawing of fire lines in the case of a conflagration or the removal of persons from the area where a pestilence has broken out. But the facts above recited show that the exclusion was simply a part of an over-all plan for forcible detention.

[32]We cannot shut our eyes to the fact that had the petitioner attempted to violate Proclamation No. 4 and leave the military area in which he lived, he

would have been arrested and tried and convicted for violation of Proclamation No. 4. The two conflicting orders, one which commanded him to stay and the other which commanded him to go, were nothing but a cleverly devised trap to accomplish the real purpose of the military authority, which was to lock him up in a concentration camp. The only course by which the petitioner could avoid arrest and prosecution was to go to that camp according to instructions to be given him when he reported at a Civil Control Center.

[33]These stark realities are met by the suggestion that it is lawful to compel an American citizen to submit to illegal imprisonment on the assumption that he might, after going to the Assembly Center, apply for his discharge by suing out a writ of habeas corpus

[34]I would reverse the judgment of conviction.

Mr. Justice MURPHY, dissenting.

[35]This exclusion of all persons of Japanese ancestry from the Pacific Coast area on a plea of military necessity in the absence of martial law ought not to be approved. Such exclusion goes over the very brink of constitutional power and falls into the ugly abyss of racism.

[36]In dealing with matters relating to the prosecution and progress of a war, we must accord great respect and consideration to the judgments of the military authorities who are on the scene and who have full knowledge of the military facts. The scope of their discretion must, as a matter of necessity and common sense, be wide. And their judgments ought not to be overruled lightly by those whose training and duties ill-equip them to deal intelligently with matters so vital to the physical security of the nation.

[37]At the same time, however, it is essential that there be definite limits to military discretion, especially where martial law has not been declared. Individuals must not be left impoverished of their constitutional rights on a plea of military necessity that has neither substance nor support. Thus, like other claims conflicting with the asserted constitutional rights of the individual, the military claim must subject itself to the judicial process of having its reasonableness determined and its conflicts with other interests reconciled.

[38]The judicial test of whether the Government, on a plea of military necessity, can validly deprive an individual of any of his constitutional rights is whether the deprivation is reasonably related to a public danger that is so "immediate, imminent, and impending" as not to admit of delay and not to permit the intervention of ordinary constitutional processes to alleviate the danger. Civilian Exclusion Order No. 34, banishing from a prescribed area of the Pacific Coast "all persons of Japanese ancestry, both alien and non-alien," clearly does not meet that test. Being an obvious racial discrimination, the order deprives all those within its scope of the equal protection of the laws as guaranteed by the Fifth Amendment.

[39]It must be conceded that the military and naval situation in the spring of 1942 was such as to generate a very real fear of invasion of the Pacific Coast, accompanied by fears of sabotage and espionage in that area. The military command was therefore justified in adopting all reasonable means necessary to combat these dangers. In adjudging the military action taken in light of the then-apparent dangers, we must not erect too high or too meticulous standards; it is necessary only that the action have some reasonable relation to the removal of the dangers of invasion, sabotage and espionage. But the exclusion, either temporarily or permanently, of all persons with Japanese blood in their veins has no such reasonable relation. And that relation is lacking because the exclusion order necessarily must rely for its reasonableness upon the assumption that all persons of Japanese ancestry may have a dangerous tendency to commit sabotage and espionage and to aid our Japanese enemy in other ways. It is difficult to believe that reason, logic or experience could be marshaled in support of such an assumption.

[40]In support of this blanket condemnation of all persons of Japanese descent, however, no reliable evidence is cited to show that such individuals were generally disloyal or had generally so conducted themselves in this area as to constitute a special menace to defense installations or war industries, or had otherwise by their behavior furnished reasonable ground for their exclusion as a group.

[41]Justification for the exclusion is sought, instead, mainly upon questionable racial and sociological grounds not ordinarily within the realm of expert military judgment, supplemented by certain semi-military conclusions drawn from an unwarranted use of circumstantial evidence. Individuals of Japanese ancestry are condemned because they are said to be "a large, unassimilated, tightly knit racial group, bound to an enemy nation by strong ties of race, culture, custom and religion." They are claimed to be given to "emperor-worshipping ceremonies" and to "dual citizenship." And, it is intimated, though not directly charged or proved, that persons of Japanese ancestry were responsible for three minor isolated shellings and bombings of the Pacific Coast area as well as for unidentified radio transmissions and night signaling.

[42]No one denies, of course, that there were some disloyal persons of Japanese descent on the Pacific Coast who did all in their power to aid their ancestral land. Similar disloyal activities have been engaged in by many persons of German, Italian and even more pioneer stock in our country. But to infer that examples of individual disloyalty prove group disloyalty and justify discriminatory action against the entire group is to deny that under our system of law individual guilt is the sole basis for deprivation of rights. Moreover, this inference, which is at the very heart of the evacuation orders, has been used in support of the abhorrent and despicable treatment of minority groups by the dictatorial tyrannies which this nation is now pledged to destroy. To give

constitutional sanction to that inference in this case, however well- intentioned may have been the military command on the Pacific Coast, is to adopt one of the cruelest of the rationales used by our enemies to destroy the dignity of the individual and to encourage and open the door to discriminatory actions against other minority groups.

[43]I dissent, therefore, from this legalization of racism. Racial discrimination in any form and in any degree has no justifiable part whatever in our democratic way of life. It is unattractive in any setting but it is utterly revolting among a free people who have embraced the principles set forth in the Constitution of the United States. All residents of this nation are kin in some way by blood or culture to a foreign land. Yet they are primarily and necessarily a part of the new and distinct civilization of the United States. They must accordingly be treated at all times as the heirs of the American experiment and as entitled to all the rights and freedoms guaranteed by the Constitution.

Mr. Justice JACKSON, dissenting.

[44]Korematsu was born on our soil of parents born in Japan. The Constitution makes him a citizen of the United States by nativity and a citizen of California by residence. No claim is made that he is not loyal to this country. There is no suggestion that apart from the matter involved here he is not law-abiding and well disposed. Korematsu, however, has been convicted of an act not commonly a crime. It consists merely of being present in the state whereof he is a citizen, near the place where he was born, and where all his life he has lived.

[45]Even more unusual is the series of military orders which made this conduct a crime. They forbid such a one to remain, and they also forbid him to leave. They were so drawn that the only way Korematsu could avoid violation was to give himself up to the military authority. This meant submission to custody, examination, and transportation out of the territory, to be followed by indeterminate confinement in detention camps.

[46]A citizen's presence in the locality, however, was made a crime only if his parents were of Japanese birth. Now, if any fundamental assumption underlies our system, it is that guilt is personal and not inheritable. But here is an attempt to make an otherwise innocent act a crime merely because this prisoner is the son of parents as to whom he had no choice, and belongs to a race from which there is no way to resign. If Congress in peace-time legislation should enact such a criminal law, I should suppose this Court would refuse to enforce it.

[47]But the "law" which this prisoner is convicted of disregarding is not found in an act of Congress, but in a military order. Neither the Act of Congress nor the Executive Order of the President, nor both together, would afford a basis for this conviction. It rests on the orders of General DeWitt. And it is

said that if the military commander had reasonable military grounds for issuing the orders, they are constitutional and become law, and the Court is required to enforce them. I cannot subscribe to this doctrine.

[48]I cannot say, from any evidence before me, that the orders of General DeWitt were not reasonably expedient military precautions, nor could I say that they were. But even if they were permissible military procedures, I deny that it follows that they are constitutional. If, as the Court holds, it does follow, then we may as well say that any military order will be constitutional and have done with it.

[49]The limitations under which courts always will labor in examining the necessity for a military order are illustrated by this case. How does the Court know that these orders have a reasonable basis in necessity? No evidence whatever on that subject has been taken by this or any other court. There is sharp controversy as to the credibility of the DeWitt report. So the Court, having no real evidence before it, has no choice but to accept General DeWitt's own unsworn, self-serving statement, untested by any cross-examination, that what he did was reasonable. And thus it will always be when courts try to look into the reasonableness of a military order.

[50]Much is said of the danger to liberty from the Army program for deporting and detaining these citizens of Japanese extraction. But a judicial construction of the due process clause that will sustain this order is a far more subtle blow to liberty than the promulgation of the order itself. A military order, however unconstitutional, is not apt to last longer than the military emergency. Even during that period a succeeding commander may revoke it all. But once a judicial opinion rationalizes such an order to show that it conforms to the Constitution, or rather rationalizes the Constitution to show that the Constitution sanctions such an order, the Court for all time has validated the principle of racial discrimination in criminal procedure and of transplanting American citizens. The principle then lies about like a loaded weapon ready for the hand of any authority that can bring forward a plausible claim of an urgent need. Every repetition imbeds that principle more deeply in our law and thinking and expands it to new purposes. A military commander may overstep the bounds of constitutionality, and it is an incident. But if we review and approve, that passing incident becomes the doctrine of the Constitution.

[51]My duties as a justice as I see them do not require me to make a military judgment as to whether General DeWitt's evacuation and detention program was a reasonable military necessity. I do not suggest that the courts should have attempted to interfere with the Army in carrying out its task. But I do not think they may be asked to execute a military expedient that has no place in law under the Constitution. I would reverse the judgment and discharge the prisoner.

Vocabulary

[2]curtail	[11]constituted	[31]pestilence	[42]infer
[2]scrutiny	[11]constrained	[32]devised	[42] abhorrent
[3]misdemeanor	[11]hindsight	[33]writ	[42]despicable
[4]prosecution	[12]tenor	[33]habeas corpus	[42]sanction
[4]espionage	[13]confer	[35]abyss	[42]rationale
[5]pursuant	[13]validity	[37]martial law	[43]heir
[7]repatriation	[14]transcend	[37]impoverished	[45]indeterminate
[8]compulsory	[16]dissent	[39]meticulous	[48]expedient
[8]dire	[16]judicial	[39]marshaled	[49]credibility
[8]comensurate	[19]recitation	[40]condemnation	[50]promulgation
[9]superseded	[21]discretion	[41]circumstantial evidence	[50]plausible
[10]effected	[31]expedient	[41]unassimilated	
[10]entail	[31]conflagration	[41]intimated	

Discussion Questions

1. What reason does Justice Black cite in paragraph 7 as justification for up-holding Korematsu's conviction?

2. In what ways do Justice Black's language and tone in paragraph 8 echo General W. T. Sherman's in "Capture of Atlanta" beginning on page 189 of this text?

3. Paragraph 9 presents a key argument in support of overturning Korematsu's conviction and then refutes it. What is Justice Black's (along with the majority of the Court) counter-argument?

4. What term does Justice Roberts use in paragraph 32 to describe the military orders that Justice Black refers to in paragraph 9? Which of the justices do you agree with? Why?

5. In paragraph 11, why does Justice Black object to the use of the term "con-centration camp" instead of " assembly and relocation center"?

6. In same paragraph, Justice Black refers to "the real military dangers" that were present at the time of Korematsu's arrest and detention. Using your research skills, find sources (and be prepared to discuss them) that describe the atmosphere on the West Coast of the United States in the months im-mediately following the bombing of Pearl Harbor.

7. Justice Frankfurter indicates that he agrees with the majority decision of the Court. The tone of his last paragraph (15), however, seems to indicate something about his attitude toward the government's actions. What do you think he is saying in that paragraph?

8. Justice Roberts says in paragraph 31, "The liberty of every American citizen freely to come and to go must frequently, in the face of sudden danger, be

temporarily limited or suspended." Do you agree? If so, under what circumstances?

9. Following the 9/11/2001 attacks on the World Trade Center the internet buzzed with stories of the U.S. Government's plans to construct "relocation camps" for American Muslims. What is your analysis of such stories?

10. What is "habeas corpus" and how is it related to the situation described in this case?

11. Justice Murphy acknowledges in paragraph 42 that some "disloyal persons of Japanese descent on the Pacific Coast . . . did all in their power to aid their ancestral land." He further says "Similar disloyal activities have been engaged in by many persons of German, Italian . . . stock . . . ," yet no camps were set up for them. Why do you think this is so?

12. John Okada's story, "No No Boy" beginning on page 430 of this text puts a human face on the legal case cited here. Cite some of the effects of the relocations that Okada describes.

13. In urging President Roosevelt to sign Executive Order 9066 (see following pages), one of his advisors said, "After all, we don't want another Black Tom." Using your research skills, find and briefly explain what the advisor meant by that statement.

EXECUTIVE ORDER NO. 9066

The President
Executive Order Authorizing the Secretary of War to Prescribe Military Areas

Whereas the successful prosecution of the war requires every possible protection against espionage and against sabotage to national-defense material, national-defense premises, and national-defense utilities as defined in Section 4, Act of April 20, 1918, 40 Stat. 533, as amended by the Act of November 30, 1940, 54 Stat. 1220, and the Act of August 21, 1941, 55 Stat. 655 (U.S.C., Title 50, Sec. 104);

Now, therefore, by virtue of the authority vested in me as President of the United States, and Commander in Chief of the Army and Navy, I hereby authorize and direct the Secretary of War, and the Military Commanders whom he may from time to time designate, whenever he or any designated Commander deems such action necessary or desirable, to prescribe military areas in such places and of such extent as he or the appropriate Military Commander may determine, from which any or all persons may be excluded, and with respect to which, the right of any person to enter, remain in, or leave shall be subject to whatever restrictions the Secretary of War or the appropriate Military Commander may impose in his discretion. The Secretary of War is hereby authorized to provide for residents of any such area who are excluded therefrom, such transportation, food, shelter, and other accommodations as may be necessary, in the judgment of the Secretary of War or the said Military Commander, and until other arrangements are made, to accomplish the purpose of this order. The designation of military areas in any region or locality shall supersede designations of prohibited and restricted areas by the Attorney General under the Proclamations of December 7 and 8, 1941, and shall supersede the responsibility and authority of the Attorney General under the said Proclamations in respect of such prohibited and restricted areas.

I hereby further authorize and direct the Secretary of War and the said Military Commanders to take such other steps as he or the appropriate Military Commander may deem advisable to enforce compliance with the restrictions applicable to each Military area hereinabove authorized to be designated, including the use of Federal troops and other Federal Agencies, with authority to accept assistance of state and local agencies.

I hereby further authorize and direct all Executive Departments, independent establishments and other Federal Agencies, to assist the Secretary of War or the said Military Commanders in carrying out this Executive Order, including the furnishing of medical aid, hospitalization, food, clothing, transportation, use of land, shelter, and other supplies, equipment, utilities, facilities, and services.

This order shall not be construed as modifying or limiting in any way the authority heretofore granted under Executive Order No. 8972, dated December 12, 1941, nor shall it be construed as limiting or modifying the duty and responsibility of the Federal Bureau of Investigation, with respect to the investigation of alleged acts of sabotage or the duty and responsibility of the Attorney General and the Department of Justice under the Proclamations of December 7 and 8, 1941, prescribing regulations for the conduct and control of alien enemies, except as such duty and responsibility is superseded by the designation of military areas hereunder.

Franklin D. Roosevelt
The White House,
February 19, 1942

CIVILIAN EXCLUSION ORDER NO. 34

To All Persons of Japanese Ancestry:

Western Defense Command and Fourth Army Wartime Civil Control Administration, Presidio of San Francisco, California

May 3, 1942

Instructions to All Persons of Japanese Ancestry Living in the Following Area:

All of that portion of the County of Alameda, State of California, within the boundary beginning at the point where the southerly limits of the City of Oakland meet San Francisco Bay; thence easterly and following the southerly limits of said city to U.S. Highway No. 50; thence southerly and easterly on said Highway No. 50 to its intersection with California State Highway No. 21; thence southerly on said Highway No. 21 to its intersection, at or near Warm Springs, with California State Highway No. 17; thence southerly on said Highway No. 17 to the Alameda-Santa Clara County line; thence westerly and following said county line to San Francisco Bay; thence northerly, and following the shoreline of San Francisco Bay to the point of Beginning.

Pursuant to the provisions of Civilian Exclusion Order No. 34, this Headquarters, dated May 3, 1942, all persons of Japanese ancestry, both alien and non-alien, will be evacuated from the above area by 12 o'clock noon, P. W. T., Sunday, May 9, 1942.

No Japanese person living in the above area will be permitted to change residence after 12 o'clock noon, P. W. T., Sunday, May 3, 1942, without obtaining special permission from the representative of the Commanding General, Northern California Sector, at the Civil Control Station located at:

920 "C" Street,
Hayward, California.

Such permits will only be granted for the purpose of uniting members of a family, or in cases of grave emergency.

The Civil Control Station is equipped to assist the Japanese population affected by this evacuation in the following ways:

1. Give advice and instructions on the evacuation.

2. Provide services with respect to the management, leasing, sale, storage or other disposition of most kinds of property, such as real estate, business and professional equipment, household goods, boats, automobiles and livestock.

3. Provide temporary residence elsewhere for all Japanese in family groups.

4. Transport persons and a limited amount of clothing and equipment to their new residence.

The Following Instructions Must Be Observed:

1. A responsible member of each family, preferably the head of the family, or the person in whose name most of the property is held, and each individual living alone, will report to the Civil Control Station to receive further instructions. This must be done between 8:00 A. M. and 5:00 P. M. on Monday, May 4, 1942, or between 9:00 A. M. and 5:00 P. M. on Tuesday, May 5, 1942.

2. Evacuees must carry with them on departure for the Assembly Center, the following property:
(a) Bedding and linens (no mattress) for each member of the family;
(b) Toilet articles for each member of the family;
(c) Extra clothing for each member of the family;
(d) Sufficient knives, forks, spoons, plates, bowls and cups for each member of the family;
(e) Essential personal effects for each member of the family.
All items carried will be securely packaged, tied and plainly marked with the name of the owner and numbered in accordance with instructions obtained at the Civil Control Station. The size and number of packages is limited to that which can be carried by the individual or family group.

3. No pets of any kind will be permitted.

4. No personal items and no household goods will be shipped to the Assembly Center.

5. The United States Government through its agencies will provide for the storage, at the sole risk of the owner, of the more substantial household items, such as iceboxes, washing machines, pianos and other heavy furniture. Cooking utensils and other small items will be accepted for storage if crated, packed and plainly marked with the name and address of the owner. Only one name and address will be used by a given family.

6. Each family, and individual living alone, will be furnished transportation to the Assembly Center or will be authorized to travel by private automobile in a supervised group. All instructions pertaining to the movement will be obtained at the Civil Control Station.

Go to the Civil Control Station between the hours of 8:00 A. M. and 5:00 P. M., Monday, May 4, 1942, or between the hours of 8:00 A.M. and 5:00 P. M., Tuesday, May 5, 1942, to receive further instructions.

J. L. DeWITT
Lieutenant General, U.S. Army
Commanding

LEAVING
FROM *EXILED MEMORIES: A CUBAN CHILDHOOD*

PABLO MEDINA

Pablo Medina (1948-) is a poet, novelist, and memoirist. He has taught at Mercer County Community College, the University of Florida, the New School in New York City and is presently a visiting professor at Emerson College in Boston. His novels are The Return of Felix Nogara: A Novel *(2000) and* The Marks of Birth *(1994); his books of poetry are* The Floating Island *(1999) and* Arching into the Afterlife *(1994); his memoir of his Cuban childhood is* Exiled Memories: A Cuban Childhood *(1990).*

[1] 5 A.M., JANUARY 1, 1959, my father rushed into my grandmother's bedroom where I had stayed the night. At first, still in the grip of dreams, I saw him through a haze, his face flushed, eyes round and open. He waved his arms and his mouth was moving, but I couldn't, at that instant between sleep and wakedom, make out what he was saying. In a few seconds, his words had broken through my slumber. *"¡Cayó Batista!"* "Batista fell!"

[2] I jumped out of bed and rushed out to the backyard where someone, I think my great-aunt Lolita, embraced me and pointed out my state of undress. When I came back out, the whole family was cheering and dancing, giving thanks to God that the tyrant had, at long last, been deposed. It was a day of rejoicing, of reveling in a collective hope shared by most that things would be good now that peace had come and corruption had been eradicated. Such feelings I have never since experienced: a bit like drunkenness, yet lighter than that and clearer, like the warm air of that beautiful day, shared by all.

[3] Eventually we found ourselves in Mamamia's living room watching TV and listening on the radio to the latest news reports. The men drank, the women gabbed, the phone rang incessantly with the news everyone knew already, as if it needed repeating over and over to make it real. The craziness spilled over onto the following week and no one bothered to go to work. The whole city was engulfed in the celebration. Patriotic banners appeared everywhere. People smiled. At times one would hear a shout coming from a car driving by or from a stranger across the street: *"¡Viva Fidel! ¡Viva Cuba Libre!"* Throughout the week we awaited the arrival of the rebels into the capital.

[4] Not all were glad of the change. Some were *batistianos*—Batista supporters who believed the man had accomplished many good things for the nation and had given order and prosperity to a people who sorely needed them, no matter that he was corrupt and despotic. Others did not trust this young man, this Fidel Castro. It was difficult to know what he stood for; he was a bit too

fond of slogans like *"Armas, ¿para qué?"*[a] and of dim terms, such as *freedom* and *democracy*; he also seemed inebriated by the adulation he met as he traveled westward in his victory march. "He postures too much as a messiah," "The people are too enamored of him," they would say. Above all, these skeptics were very much troubled by the rumors that Castro was a Marxist and that he would lead the country directly to Russia's door. Finally, there was the group of those who had profited directly through their association with Batista: lawyers, politicians, architects, military men, whose lives and fortunes were suddenly endangered. They plotted ways of leaving the country and taking their wealth. Most embittered, they saw only their losses, closed doors and windows, and planned their escape. The disenchanted ones, however, were in the minority for now. Their voices were drowned out in the quasi-Dionysian chaos of the following weeks. They sat in dark corners and grumbled.

[5]Fidel Castro arrived in Havana on January 8 at the head of a column of *barbudos,*or bearded ones. With him were el Che,[b] his brother Raúl, Camilo Cienfuegos, and all the mythic figures who had fought in the Sierra Maestra. For a boy like myself, whose dreams fed on the feats of warriors struggling against evil, the appearance of the triumphant bearded ones on the streets of my city was the ultimate confirmation that heroes existed beyond the pages of adventure novels.

[6]The whole city turned out to greet them. Women and children crowded round to kiss, to touch, to embrace them. Seeing a rebel on the street was enough to make the heart jump, for they were viewed with an awe bordering on the reverence reserved for saints. These were, after all, our young liberators and they looked the part. Their long hair tied in pony tails, their black berets, their olive green uniforms, and their gun belts were to set the style for many a "revolutionary" of the future. Around their necks hung rosaries, religious medals, scapulae, and other mementos given to them by thankful citizens on their march to Havana. These were the wild men who had redeemed us and in their eyes glowed the future with an intensity evident only among those who have struggled with history.

[7]Along with the revolutionary fervor, and perhaps a direct result of it, there arose in Havana a cult of things military. People started collecting relics of the Revolution—souvenirs of battles they had never witnessed, of a life

---

[a]Literally "Weapons, for whom?" was a slogan used after the revolution to encourage the Castro militia and the Cuban people to trade their weapons for civilian implements such as books and pencils and farming and manufacturing tools.

[b]El Che is Che Guevera, Castro's most famous commandante, who was killed in 1968 attempting to import the Marxist revolution into Bolivia. Raul is Castro's brother; he replaced Fidel as president in 2008. Camilo Cienfuegos was another key Castro commandante during the revolution; he died in a plane crash in 1959.

they had never lived. The most prized of these were the ones given away by the *barbudos*—berets, gun belts, bullets, and even live grenades. Next best was to purchase the wares from street vendors who had astutely put away their costume jewelry and cheap toys and now dealt in war objects. Buying them, however, was akin to cheating—for all one knew one was buying goods made in Japan. I myself was the object of envy of many friends because I had collected three bullets from three different *barbudos*. One in particular, which I kept swaddled in thick cotton and exhibited with great ceremony, piqued their awe—a live .50-caliber still capable of taking any one of our young heads off.

[8]Within days of Fidel's arrival, the first of what was to become a series of ominous and revelatory signs appeared. Although many of Batista's men had escaped on the days immediately preceding and following the fall, many others not high enough in the hierarchy to be aware of the situation remained behind and were subsequently captured by the revolutionary forces. On these men—police captains, army colonels, and a few members of the political bureaucracy—fell the weight of the new "justice."

[9]Of the many military tribunals that were televised during this period I remember only one distinctly, that of Colonel Sosa Blanco. Sosa Blanco's main crime, the tragic flaw that was to lead ineluctably to his end, was that, as colonel in the Cuban army, he had pursued and engaged the rebel forces in the mountains. He was charged with acts of torture, cold-blooded assassinations of innocent peasants, and other crimes against the Cuban people. In spite of the several dozen witnesses that testified before the court and the TV cameras, no charge was ever substantiated. In addition, the colonel was not allowed a lawyer, nor was he given the opportunity to speak in his own defense. He stood, I recall, before the judges, and behind him the rabble packing the gallery interrupted the proceedings with the latest slogans and with the refrain, *Pa-re-dón, Pa-re-dón* (Firing squad! Firing squad!).

[10]At first the colonel stood proudly, facing, no, challenging his captors. As the trial progressed, as more and more of the witnesses brought new charges and as the audience's lust for his death grew, the colonel drooped. Where once his face was raised in arrogance, now it looked shadowy and troubled. Slowly I saw it soften, go from disdain to anger to befuddlement. Then for an instant the light of discovery graced it, but the light was flooded over by the swift realization that he was a condemned man and that his sentence had been passed the moment he'd been captured. He was not on trial here; he was on display. In the end his eyes turned into ashen pits, contorted, twitching, almost like a child's who knows no mercy will come his way.

[11]I did not know whether the charges were true. All the adults around me were dismayed, and so I concurred, giving the man the benefit of my outrage. Sosa Blanco was hardly an honorable man, I found that out later, but what greater punishment did a man deserve than this public humiliation, this

dragging of his character in the mud of collective hatred and vengeance? The colonel was executed a few days after the trial, and that too was aired on TV, but I did not watch. I had had enough. I believed the Revolution to be white and a darkness was creeping in with which I was incapable of coping.

[12]Television, the great filler of my time, was beginning to change. Before Castro it had been solely an entertainment medium; now, along with the trials, aired for the most part during the first three months of the Revolution, there were Fidel's epic policy speeches, and soap operas laden with revolutionary and Marxist motifs.

[13]In the mornings there were children's shows that appeared at first to be little different from pre-revolution ones. As before, a teacher figure talked, sang, and played with a group of youngsters. The emcees in the new programs, however, were quite young and serious minded. They wore army fatigues or militia uniforms and never smiled except when extolling the new system. Then a beatific look came over their faces as if they had personally witnessed what History had prepared for those who loved the Revolution. Besides discussing agrarian reform, the distribution of private property, and other topics that I could only label as profoundly boring, these paramilitary teachers, whose humor had been gobbled up by their zeal (the Revolution allowed fun no quarter), often went on violent tirades against *the yanquis.*

[14]It appeared that the emcees found in that term a synonym for evil. In one such show, the host, a young uniformed woman with hair tied back in a ponytail *a la barbudo,* was involved in an extended tirade against imperialist oppression when a boy in the group spoke up, wanting her to clarify a point she was making. She looked indignantly at the boy and said, "Don't ever speak without raising your hand. You don't want to be like the yanquis, do you?" The boy's lower lip quivered and his face darkened with shame. He had been labeled before the world and his peers: *Yanqui! Outcast! Pariah!*

[15]It took a long while before the shadows of television and what they represented deterred my euphoria. That medium is flat and as such distancing, tingeing real events with unreality. Fantasy is much more powerful, and my fantasy colored everything I saw. The heroes were still glorious: Fidel, strong and determined; Che, with the fierce eyes and soft, convincing smile; Raúl, the quiet one, waiting in the wings. There were also the great projects on hand and dreams that spread beyond the island to all of America.

[16]After a time the novelty passed. Daily life went on for me not much differently than before. I went to school, swam on the beach, read, dreamed, felt lonely, bored, excited. But the cracks in the shining globe of the Revolution multiplied and widened. Newspapers were expropriated; the opposition, afraid of the consequences of speaking up, left the island; all private schools were taken over by a bureaucracy more intent on indoctrinating than educating.

[17]All about me people talked in whispers. My parents looked glum and

asked about school and what we were taught. Friends started leaving, to Miami, Mexico, Spain. Soon family reunions stopped. They were too risky. Freedom had been given and taken away again. This was no dream. The future was the past, except less carefree, less warm, heavier with doctrine and dim visions of a society modeled too far away from our shores: a different sort of yoke. I, like the rest of my family, turned my back on the Revolution. Little did I know that in doing so I would forfeit the place of my birth.

[18]We left on one of the last regularly scheduled flights from Havana. There were tears and embraces with those we left behind. The bitter apple I had swallowed left a lump in my throat that made it difficult to breathe. As we were boarding, my great-uncle Luis took a photograph of us on the boarding ladder, which I still have in my possession. The four of us are smiling and waving. We expected to return in a few months. The months turned to years and our hope was blown away.

[19]The gray snow of disenchantment began to fall over my city and my childhood. The past was fixed in place; fate had conspired to cut me off from it. Suddenly I was surrounded by ice, and I jumped into the white mounds with all the enthusiasm I could muster. I renounced allegiance to the country of my birth when I became an American citizen, yet the blood still pulled and memory called. Thus it was that I became two persons, one a creature of warmth, the other the snow swimmer. The first would be forever a child dancing to the beat of the waves; the second was the adult, striving to emerge from the river of cold—invigorated, wise, at peace with life.

[20]The truism that no one can ever go home again becomes a special predicament for the young exile: my childhood lies inside the bowl of distance and politics, unapproachable and disconnected from my adulthood. The two revolve around each other like twin stars, pulling and tugging, without hope of reconciliation. Everywhere I see Fate smiling the smile of the Sphynx. I could bemoan my state at the hands of the indifferent creature and thus belie a need for control of my life, which is illusion. Instead, I remember the family, their craziness, their resilience, their collective tongue wagging wildly at despair, and I too smile.

Vocabulary

[2]reveling
[2]eradicated
[3]incessantly
[4]despotic
[4]inebriated
[4]adulation
[4]messiah
[4]enamored
[4]Marxist
[4]disenchanted
[4]quasi-Dionysian
[6]scapulae

[7]fervor
[7]astutely
[7]akin
[7]piqued
[8]ominous
[8]revelatory
[8]hierarchy
[9]tribunals
[9]ineluctably
[9]substantiated
[9]rabble
[10]disdain

[10]befuddlement
[10]contorted
[11]concurred
[12]motifs
[13]extolling
[13]beatific
[13]agrarian
[13]paramilitary
[13]zeal
[13]tirades
[13]*yanquis*

[14]imperialist
[14]pariah
[15]deterred
[15]euphoria
[16]expropriated
[16]indoctrinating
[17]yoke
[19]invigorated
[20]truism
[20]belie
[20]resilience

Discussion Questions

1. Who is Batista? Who is Castro? Using you research skills, compile some details of what happened between these two men and give a short synopsis to the class.

2. Discuss Medina's family's initial reaction to the news of Batista's fall. Why might they have reacted that way?

3. What were the concerns of those not happy about the overthrow of Batista and the takeover by Castro? Were they justified?

4. Explain what Medina means when he writes in paragraph 11, "I believed the Revolution to be white and a darkness was creeping in with which I was incapable of coping." Be sure to discuss the symbolism.

5. In paragraph 12 Medina says that the television soap operas were "laden with revolutionary and Marxist motifs." What does he mean by this?

6. How would you describe Medina's view of Marxism as expressed in this excerpt?

7. Discuss Medina's reflection on his family's relocation to the United States.

8. Medina has not returned to Cuba. Discuss how you might feel and react if you were unable to return to the home of your youth.

LEVITICUS
FROM THE TORAH

The Torah comprises the five books of Moses, a central text of the Jewish religion and a significant portion of the Christian Old Testament. Many of the laws governing Jews are found in Leviticus.

19

¹The LORD spoke to Moses, saying:

²Speak to the whole Israelite community and say to them: You shall be holy, for I, the LORD your God, am holy.

³You shall each revere his mother and his father, and keep My sabbaths: I the LORD am your God.

⁴Do not turn to idols or make molten gods for yourselves: I the LORD am your God.

⁵When you sacrifice an offering of well-being to the LORD, sacrifice it so that it may be accepted on your behalf. ⁶It shall be eaten on the day you sacrifice it, or on the day following; but what is left by the third day must be consumed in fire. ⁷If it should be eaten on the third day, it is an offensive thing, it will not be acceptable. ⁸And he who eats of it shall bear his guilt, for he has profaned what is sacred to the LORD; that person shall be cut off from his kin.

⁹When you reap the harvest of your land, you shall not reap all the way to the edges of your field, or gather the gleanings of your harvest. ¹⁰You shall not pick your vineyard bare, or gather the fallen fruit of your vineyard; you shall leave them for the poor and the stranger: I the LORD am your God.

¹¹You shall not steal; you shall not deal deceitfully or falsely with one another. ¹²You shall not swear falsely by My name, profaning the name of your God: I am the LORD.

¹³You shall not defraud your neighbor. You shall not commit robbery. The wages of a laborer shall not remain with you until morning.

¹⁴You shall not insult the deaf, or place a stumbling block before the blind. You shall fear your God: I am the LORD.

¹⁵You shall not render an unfair decision: do not favor the poor or show deference to the rich; judge your neighbor fairly. ¹⁶Do not deal basely with your fellows. Do not profit by the blood of your neighbor: I am the LORD.

¹⁷You shall not hate your kinsman in your heart. Reprove your neigh-

bor, but incur no guilt because of him. [18]You shall not take vengeance or bear a grudge against your kinsfolk. Love your neighbor as yourself. I am the LORD.

[19]You shall observe My laws.

[20]You shall not let your cattle mate with a different kind; you shall not sow your field with two kinds of seed; you shall not put on cloth from a mixture of two kinds of material.

[21]If a man has carnal relations with a woman who is a slave and has been designated for another man, but has not been redeemed or given her freedom, there shall be an indemnity; they shall not, however, be put to death, since she has not been freed. [22] But he must bring to the entrance of the Tent of Meeting, as his guilt offering to the LORD, a ram of guilt offering. [23]With the ram of guilt offering the priest shall make expiation for him before the LORD for the sin that he committed; and the sin that he committed will be forgiven him.

[24]When you enter the land and plant any tree for food, you shall regard its fruit as forbidden. Three years it shall be forbidden for you, not to be eaten. [25]In the fourth year all its fruit shall be set aside for jubilation before the LORD; [26]and only in the fifth year may you use its fruit—that its yield to you may be increased: I the LORD am your God.

[27]You shall not eat anything with its blood. You shall not practice divination or soothsaying. [28]You shall not round off the side-growth on your head, or destroy the side-growth of your beard. [29]You shall not make gashes in your flesh for the dead, or incise any marks on yourselves: I am the LORD.

[30]Do not degrade your daughter and make her a harlot, lest the land fall into harlotry and the land be filled with depravity. [31]You shall keep My sabbaths and venerate My sanctuary: I am the LORD.

[32]Do not turn to ghosts and do not inquire of familiar spirits, to be defiled by them: I the LORD am your God.

[33]You shall rise before the aged and show deference to the old; you shall fear your God: I am the LORD.

[34]When a stranger resides with you in your land, you shall not wrong him.

[35]The stranger who resides with you shall be to you as one of your citizens; you shall love him as yourself, for you were strangers in the land of Egypt: I the LORD am your God.

[36]You shall not falsify measures of length, weight, or capacity. You shall have an honest balance, honest weights, an honest *ephah*[a] and an honest *hin*.[b]

[37]I the LORD am your God who freed you from the land of Egypt. [38]You shall faithfully observe all My laws and all My rules: I am the LORD.

---

[a]measure of grain

[b]weight

Vocabulary

[3]revere

[3]sabbaths

[4]idols

[8]profaned

[8]kin

[9]gleanings

[10]vineyard

[15]deference

[16]basely

[17]reprove

[21]carnal

[21]indemnity

[23]expiation

[27]divination

[27]soothsaying

[29]incise

[30]harlot

[30]depravity

[31]venerate

[32]defiled

Discussion Questions

1. Leviticus contains many of the laws governing Jews. What do you think is the function of these laws for a society?

2. Do you see these laws as rules or advice? Give a brief explanation.

3. Have you heard of any of the laws contained in Leviticus? If so, which ones? Did you know they came from this source?

4. Why do you think the words "I the LORD am your God" are repeated throughout the reading?

5. Do you think any of the laws are applicable to our society? Which ones? Which laws do you think are no longer applicable?

6. Look at Chapter 12 of the Bhagavad Gita beginning on page 144 of this text, the Eightfold Path beginning on page 178, Sura 2 of the Holy Qur'an beginning on page 457, and the Sermon on the Mount on page 489. Compare these works to Leviticus and explain what they all have in common.

LOVING V. COMMONWEALTH OF VIRGINIA

UNITED STATES SUPREME COURT

In 1958, Mildred Delores Jeter, a woman of African and Rappahannock Native American descent, and Richard Perry Loving, a white man, left their native Virginia to get married in the neighboring District of Columbia. This was a violation of Virginia's Racial Integrity Act, a state law banning marriage between any white person and any non-white person. A few weeks after their return to their home in Central Point, Virginia, the Caroline County sheriff and two deputies burst into their bedroom at 2 a.m. and charged the couple with having interracial sexual relations, also a violation of Virginia law.

In their defense, Mrs. Loving pointed to a marriage certificate on the wall in their bedroom. That document, instead of defending them, became the evidence the police needed for a criminal charge since it showed they had been married in another state. Specifically, they were charged under the Virginia Criminal Code, which prohibited interracial couples from being married out of state and then returning to Virginia, and which classified "miscegenation" as a felony punishable by a prison sentence of between one and five years. They pleaded guilty and were sentenced to one year in jail, to be suspended for 25 years with the stipulation they move out of Virginia. They were arrested again for traveling together as a couple when when they came back to Virginia to visit family and friends. In 1963, as the civil rights movement gained momentum, the Lovings, wishing to return to Virginia to live, asked U.S. Attorney General Robert F. Kennedy for help in getting their sentences overturned. With the aid of the American Civil Liberties Union (ACLU), the Lovings were able to get their case heard by the United States Supreme Court. The decision in this case overturned anti-misegenation laws in 16 states.

LOVING V. COMMONWEALTH OF VIRGINIA

APPEAL FROM THE SUPREME COURT OF APPEALS OF VIRGINIA

Argued: April 10, 1967 -- Decided: June 12, 1967

[1]**Abstract:** Proceeding on motion to vacate sentences for violating state ban on interracial marriages. The Circuit Court of Caroline County, Virginia, denied motion, and writ of error was granted. The Virginia Supreme Court of Appeals affirmed the convictions, and probable jurisdiction was noted. The United States Supreme Court, Mr. Chief Justice Warren, held that miscegenation statutes adopted by Virginia to prevent marriages between persons solely on basis of racial classification violate equal protection and due process clauses

of the Fourteenth Amendment. [**The text of the Fourteenth Amendment to the Constitution is included here following the Discussion Questions.**]

[2]Philip J. Hirschkop, Bernard S. Cohen, Alexandria, Va., for appellants.

[3]R. D. McIlwaine, III, Richmond, Va., for appellee.

[4]William M. Marutani, Philadelphia, Pa., for Japanese American Citizens League, as amicus curiae, by special leave of Court.

[5]Mr. Chief Justice WARREN delivered the opinion of the Court:

[6]This case presents a constitutional question never addressed by this Court: whether a statutory scheme adopted by the State of Virginia to prevent marriages between persons solely on the basis of racial classifications violates the Equal Protection and Due Process Clauses of the Fourteenth Amendment. For reasons which seem to us to reflect the central meaning of those constitutional commands, we conclude that these statutes cannot stand consistently with the Fourteenth Amendment.

[7]Section 1 of the Fourteenth Amendment provides:

> All persons born or naturalized in the United States and subject to the jurisdiction thereof, are citizens of the United States and of the State wherein they reside. No State shall make or enforce any law which shall abridge the privileges or immunities of citizens of the United States; nor shall any State deprive any person of life, liberty, or property, without due process of law; nor deny to any person within its jurisdiction the equal protection of the laws.

[8]In June 1958, two residents of Virginia, Mildred Jeter, a Negro woman, and Richard Loving, a white man, were married in the District of Columbia pursuant to its laws. Shortly after their marriage, the Lovings returned to Virginia and established their marital abode in Caroline County. At the October Term, 1958, of the Circuit Court of Caroline County, a grand jury issued an indictment charging the Lovings with violating Virginia's ban on interracial marriages. On January 6, 1959, the Lovings pleaded guilty to the charge and were sentenced to one year in jail; however, the trial judge suspended the sentence for a period of 25 years on the condition that the Lovings leave the State and not return to Virginia together for 25 years. He stated in an opinion that:

> [9]Almighty God created the races white, black, yellow, malay and red, and he placed them on separate continents. And but for the interference

with his arrangement there would be no cause for such marriages. The fact that he separated the races shows that he did not intend for the races to mix.

[10]After their convictions, the Lovings took up residence in the District of Columbia. On November 6, 1963, they filed a motion in the state trial court to vacate the judgment and set aside the sentence on the ground that the statutes which they had violated were repugnant to the Fourteenth Amendment. The motion not having been decided by October 28, 1964, the Lovings instituted a class action in the United States District Court for the Eastern District of Virginia requesting that a three-judge court be convened to declare the Virginia anti-miscegenation statutes unconstitutional and to enjoin state officials from enforcing their convictions. On January 22, 1965, the state trial judge denied the motion to vacate the sentences, and the Lovings perfected an appeal to the Supreme Court of Appeals of Virginia. On February 11, 1965, the three-judge District Court continued the case to allow the Lovings to present their constitutional claims to the highest state court.

[11]The Virginia Supreme Court of Appeals upheld the constitutionality of the anti-miscegenation statutes and, after modifying the sentence, affirmed the convictions. The Lovings appealed this decision, and we noted probable jurisdiction on December 12, 1966.

[12]The two statutes under which appellants were convicted and sentenced are part of a comprehensive statutory scheme aimed at prohibiting and punishing interracial marriages. The Lovings were convicted of violating sections 20-58 of the Virginia Code:

[13]Leaving State to evade law: If any white person and colored person shall go out of this State, for the purpose of being married, and with the intention of returning, and be married out of it, and afterwards return to and reside in it, cohabiting as man and wife, they shall be punished as provided in s 20--59, and the marriage shall be governed by the same law as if it had been solemnized in this State. The fact of their cohabitation here as man and wife shall be evidence of their marriage.

[14]Section 20--59, which defines the penalty for miscegenation, provides:

Punishment for marriage: If any white person intermarry with a colored person, or any colored person intermarry with a white person, he shall be guilty of a felony and shall be punished by confinement in the penitentiary for not less than one nor more than five years.

[15]Other central provisions in the Virginia statutory scheme are sections

20-57, which automatically void all marriages between "a white person and a colored person" without any judicial proceeding, and sections 20-54 and 1-14 which, respectively, define "white persons" and "colored persons and Indians" for purposes of the statutory prohibitions. The Lovings have never disputed in the course of this litigation that Mrs. Loving is a "colored person" or that Mr. Loving is a "white person" within the meanings given those terms by the Virginia statutes.

[16]Section 20-57 of the Virginia Code provides:

Marriages void without decree—All marriages between a white person and a colored person shall be absolutely void without any decree of divorce or other legal process.

[17]Section 20-54 of the Virginia Code provides:

Intermarriage prohibited; meaning of term 'white persons'—It shall hereafter be unlawful for any white person in this State to marry any save a white person, or a person with no other admixture of blood than white and American Indian. For the purpose of this chapter, the term 'white person' shall apply only to such person as has no trace whatever of any blood other than Caucasian; but persons who have one-sixteenth or less of the blood of the American Indian and have no other non-Caucasic blood shall be deemed to be white persons. All laws heretofore passed and now in effect regarding the intermarriage of white and colored persons shall apply to marriages prohibited by this chapter.

[18]The exception for persons with less than one-sixteenth "of the blood of the American Indian" is apparently accounted for, in the words of a tract issued by the Registrar of the State Bureau of Vital Statistics, by "the desire of all to recognize as an integral and honored part of the white race the descendants of John Rolfe and Pocahontas."

[19]Section 1-14 of the Virginia Code provides:

Colored persons and Indians defined—Every person in whom there is ascertainable any Negro blood shall be deemed and taken to be a colored person, and every person not a colored person having one fourth or more of American Indian blood shall be deemed an American Indian; except that members of Indian tribes existing in this Commonwealth having one fourth or more of Indian blood and less than one sixteenth of Negro blood shall be deemed tribal Indians.

[20]Virginia is now one of 16 States which prohibit and punish marriages

on the basis of racial classifications. Penalties for miscegenation arose as an incident to slavery and have been common in Virginia since the colonial period. The present statutory scheme dates from the adoption of the Racial Integrity Act of 1924, passed during the period of extreme nativism which followed the end of the First World War. The central features of this Act, and current Virginia law are the absolute prohibition of a "white person" marrying other than another "white person," a prohibition against issuing marriage licenses until the issuing official is satisfied that the applicants' statements as to their race are correct, certificates of "racial composition" to be kept by both local and state registrars, and the carrying forward of earlier prohibitions against racial intermarriage.

[21]After the initiation of this litigation, Maryland repealed its prohibitions against interracial marriage, leaving Virginia and 15 other States with statutes outlawing interracial marriage.

[22]Over the past 15 years, 14 States have repealed laws outlawing interracial marriages: Arizona, California, Colorado, Idaho, Indiana, Maryland, Montana, Nebraska, Nevada, North Dakota, Oregon, South Dakota, Utah, and Wyoming.

[23]The first state court to recognize that miscegenation statutes violate the Equal Protection Clause was the Supreme Court of California.

[24]In upholding the constitutionality of these provisions in the decision below, the Supreme Court of Appeals of Virginia referred to its 1955 decision in Naim v. Naim, as stating the reasons supporting the validity of these laws. In Naim, the state court concluded that the State's legitimate purposes were "to preserve the racial integrity of its citizens," and to prevent "the corruption of blood," "a mongrel breed of citizens," and "the obliteration of racial pride," obviously an endorsement of the doctrine of White Supremacy. The court also reasoned that marriage has traditionally been subject to state regulation without federal intervention, and, consequently, the regulation of marriage should be left to exclusive state control by the Tenth Amendment.

[25]While the state court is no doubt correct in asserting that marriage is a social relation subject to the State's police power, the State does not contend in its argument before this Court that its powers to regulate marriage are unlimited notwithstanding the commands of the Fourteenth Amendment. Nor could it do so in light of Meyer v. State of Nebraska (1923), and Skinner v. State of Oklahoma (1942). Instead, the State argues that the meaning of the Equal Protection Clause, as illuminated by the statements of the Framers,[a] is only that state penal laws containing an interracial element as part of the definition of the offense must apply equally to whites and Negroes in the sense that members of each

---

[a]"Framers" refers to the members of the Constitutional Convention who wrote and adopted the Constitution in 1787; they are often referred to as the "Framers of the Constitution." Here, however, Warren is referring to the framers of the Fourteenth Amendment, that is, the members of the 39th congress.

race are punished to the same degree. Thus, the State contends that, because its miscegenation statutes punish equally both the white and the Negro participants in an interracial marriage, these statutes, despite their reliance on racial classifications, do not constitute an invidious discrimination based upon race.

[26]The second argument advanced by the State assumes the validity of its equal application theory. The argument is that, if the Equal Protection Clause does not outlaw miscegenation statutes because of their reliance on racial classifications, the question of constitutionality would thus become whether there was any rational basis for a State to treat interracial marriages differently from other marriages. On this question, the State argues, the scientific evidence is substantially in doubt and, consequently, this Court should defer to the wisdom of the state legislature in adopting its policy of discouraging interracial marriages.

[27]Because we reject the notion that the mere "equal application" of a statute containing racial classifications is enough to remove the classifications from the Fourteenth Amendment's proscription of all invidious racial discriminations, we do not accept the State's contention that these statutes should be upheld if there is any possible basis for concluding that they serve a rational purpose. The mere fact of equal application does not mean that our analysis of these statutes should follow the approach we have taken in cases involving no racial discrimination where the Equal Protection Clause has been arrayed against a statute discriminating between the kinds of advertising which may be displayed on trucks in New York City, Railway Express Agency, Inc. v. People of State of New York, 336 U.S. 106, 69 S.Ct. 463, 93 L.Ed. 533 (1949), or an exemption in Ohio's ad valorem tax for merchandise owned by a non-resident in a storage warehouse, Allied Stores of Ohio, Inc. v. Bowers, (1959). In these cases, involving distinctions not drawn according to race, the Court has merely asked whether there is any rational foundation for the discriminations, and has deferred to the wisdom of the state legislatures. In the case at bar, however, we deal with statutes containing racial classifications, and the fact of equal application does not immunize the statute from the very heavy burden of justification which the Fourteenth Amendment has traditionally required of state statutes drawn according to race.

[28]The State argues that statements in the Thirty-ninth Congress about the time of the passage of the Fourteenth Amendment indicate that the Framers did not intend the Amendment to make unconstitutional state miscegenation laws. Many of the statements alluded to by the State concern the debates over the Freedmen's Bureau Bill, which President Andrew Johnson vetoed, and the Civil Rights Act of 1866, enacted over his veto. While these statements have some relevance to the intention of Congress in submitting the Fourteenth Amendment, it must be understood that they pertained to the passage of specific statutes and not to the broader, organic purpose of a constitutional amendment. As for the various statements directly concerning the Fourteenth Amendment,

we have said in connection with a related problem that although these historical sources "cast some light" they are not sufficient to resolve the problem; at
best, they are inconclusive. The most avid proponents of the post-War Amendments undoubtedly intended them to remove all legal distinctions among "all
persons born or naturalized in the United States." Their opponents, just as
certainly, were antagonistic to both the letter and the spirit of the Amendments
and wished them to have the most limited effect.

[29]We have rejected the proposition that the debates in the Thirty-ninth Congress or in the state legislatures which ratified the Fourteenth Amendment supported the theory advanced by the State, that the requirement of equal protection of the
laws is satisfied by penal laws defining offenses based on racial classifications so
long as white and Negro participants in the offense were similarly punished.

[30]The State finds support for its "equal application" theory in the decision
of the Court in Pace v. State of Alabama, (1883). In that case, the Court upheld a
conviction under an Alabama statute forbidding adultery or fornication between
a white person and a Negro which imposed a greater penalty than that of a statute
proscribing similar conduct by members of the same race. The Court reasoned
that the statute could not be said to discriminate against Negroes because the punishment for each participant in the offense was the same. However, as recently as
the 1964 Term, in rejecting the reasoning of that case, we stated "Pace represents
a limited view of the Equal Protection Clause which has not withstood analysis
in the subsequent decisions of this Court." As we there demonstrated, the Equal
Protection Clause requires the consideration of whether the classifications drawn
by any statute constitutes an arbitrary and invidious discrimination. The clear and
central purpose of the Fourteenth Amendment was to eliminate all official state
sources of invidious racial discrimination in the States.

[31]There can be no question but that Virginia's miscegenation statutes rest
solely upon distinctions drawn according to race. The statutes proscribe generally accepted conduct if engaged in by members of different races. Over
the years, this Court has consistently repudiated "distinctions between citizens
solely because of their ancestry" as being "odious to a free people whose institutions are founded upon the doctrine of equality." At the very least, the
Equal Protection Clause demands that racial classifications, especially suspect
in criminal statutes, be subjected to the "most rigid scrutiny," and, if they are
ever to be upheld, they must be shown to be necessary to the accomplishment
of some permissible State objective, independent of the racial discrimination
which it was the object of the Fourteenth Amendment to eliminate. Indeed, two
members of this Court have already stated that they "cannot conceive of a valid
legislative purpose which makes the color of a person's skin the test of whether
his conduct is a criminal offense."

[32]There is patently no legitimate overriding purpose independent of invidious racial discrimination which justifies this classification. The fact that Virginia

prohibits only interracial marriages involving white persons demonstrates that the racial classifications must stand on their own justification, as measures designed to maintain White Supremacy. We have consistently denied the constitutionality of measures which restrict the rights of citizens on account of race. There can be no doubt that restricting the freedom to marry solely because of racial classifications violates the central meaning of the Equal Protection Clause.

[33]Appellants point out that the State's concern in these statutes, as expressed in the words of the 1924 Act's title, "An Act to Preserve Racial Integrity," extends only to the integrity of the white race. While Virginia prohibits whites from marrying any nonwhite (subject to the exception for the descendants of Pocahontas), Negroes, Orientals, and any other racial class may intermarry without statutory interference. Appellants contend that this distinction renders Virginia's miscegenation statutes arbitrary and unreasonable, even assuming the constitutional validity of an official purpose to preserve "racial integrity." We need not reach this contention because we find the racial classifications in these statutes repugnant to the Fourteenth Amendment, even assuming an even-handed State purpose to protect the "integrity" of all races.

[34]These statutes also deprive the Lovings of liberty without due process of law in violation of the Due Process Clause of the Fourteenth Amendment. The freedom to marry has long been recognized as one of the vital personal rights essential to the orderly pursuit of happiness by free men.

[35]Marriage is one of the "basic civil rights of man," fundamental to our very existence and survival. Skinner v. State of Oklahoma, (1942) and Maynard v. Hill, (1888). To deny this fundamental freedom on so unsupportable a basis as the racial classifications embodied in these statutes, classifications so directly subversive of the principle of equality at the heart of the Fourteenth Amendment, is surely to deprive all the State's citizens of liberty without due process of law. The Fourteenth Amendment requires that the freedom of choice to marry not be restricted by invidious racial discriminations. Under our Constitution, the freedom to marry or not marry, a person of another race resides with the individual and cannot be infringed by the State.

These convictions must be reversed. It is so ordered.

Reversed.

Mr. Justice STEWART, concurring:

[36]I have previously expressed the belief that "it is simply not possible for a state law to be valid under our Constitution which makes the criminality of an act depend upon the race of the actor." McLaughlin v. State of Florida, (concurring opinion). Because I adhere to that belief, I concur in the judgment of the Court.

Vocabulary

[1]writ	[8]abode	[24]mongrel	[30]fornication
[1]jurisdiction	[8]indictment	[24]obliteration	[31]repudiated
[2]appellant	[10]repugnant	[25]assert	[31]odious
[3]appellee	[10]enjoin	[25]invidious	[32]patently
[4]amicus curiae	[13]cohabiting	[27]proscription	[35]infringed
[6]statutory	[15]litigation	[27]contention	[36]adhere
[8]pursuant	[19]ascertainable	[28]alllude	
[8]marital	[20]nativism	[28]avid	

Discussion Questions

1. Why do you think William M. Marutani was involved in this case?

2. In paragraph 6 how does Chief Justice Warren characterize the question that is the primary element of this case?

3. What reason did the trial judge use to justify the Virginia statute that was at issue in this case?

4. Cite two reasons why the Lovings decided to try to appeal their case in 1963.

5. How much "Indian blood" did the Virginia statute allow a white person to have and still be categorized as white? Do the math and figure out how many generations back that goes.

6. What does Warren cite in paragraph 18 as the Virginia legislature's reason for allowing their white citizens to have some Indian blood in them and still be considered white? What do you think Chief Justice Warren's tone is in this paragraph?

7. What does Chief Justice Warren cite as Virginia's reasons for upholding its anti-miscegenation statutes in the Naim v Naim case? How does Warren characterize these reasons? Do you agree or disagree with Warren?

8. Chief Justice Warren cites two arguments by the Commonwealth of Virginia (paragraphs 25 and 26) in support of its position. What are the two arguments?

9. In paragraph 30, Warren cites a Supreme Court decision. Pace v. State of Alabama, that Virginia used in support of its argument. What does Warren say about the Pace decision?

10. In paragraph 32 Warren discusses statutes designed to preserve "racial integrity." What does he say about them?

11. What does Warren say about the institution of marriage at the end of this decision? Do you agree?

12. This decision, based primarily on the "equal protection" clause of the Fourteenth Amendment to the Constitution, applied to the marriage of people of different races 40 years ago. What impact do you think this decision has had on American society? Do you see other areas in American society today where the arguments used here might apply?

AMENDMENT XIV

Passed by Congress June 13, 1866. Ratified July 9, 1868.

The Fourteenth Amendment to the United States Constitution was passed by the 39th Congress in July of 1866 in the aftermath of the Civil War.

In the months following Lee's surrender at Appomattox, southern legislatures had begun enacting "black codes" aimed at undermining President Lincoln's Emancipation Proclamation and curtailing the freedom and rights of the South's freed slaves. The codes varied from state to state but common provisions included requiring blacks to enter into annual labor contracts with severe penalties for violations imposed on black "employees" but not on white employers; forcing black children into apprenticeships with masters having the right to use corporal punishment; and giving local sheriffs the right to round up unemployed blacks and sell them into private service if they couldn't pay heavy fines for vagrancy.

In Washington, meanwhile, the House and Senate had voted to refuse to seat Southerners sent from the conquered Confederacy thus giving a group of "Radical Republicans" the power to push through legislation that punished the South. These Republican initiatives to give full rights of citizenship to the South's freed blacks gained widespread support in the North. As a part of this effort, the Congress passed the Thirteenth, Fourteenth and Fifteenth Amendments to the Constitution, which required approval from two-thirds of the states. (The Thirteenth Amendment made slavery illegal in the United States and the Fifteenth Amendment said, "The rights of citizens of the United States to vote shall not be denied or abridged by the United States or any state on account of race, color or previous condition of servitude.")

Knowing full well that the existing legislatures of the Confederate states, whose votes were needed for ratification, would never approve the three amendments, the Congress passed the Reconstruction Act of 1867, dissolving existing Southern legislatures and establishing instead five military districts. The only way the former Confederate states could remove themselves from military rule and regain full statehood was to establish a civil government that would swear an oath of allegiance to the United States; to give full voting rights to black men; and to ratify the Thirteenth, Fourteenth and Fifteenth Amendments. To this day, some state legislatures view the ratification of the far-reaching Fourteenth Amendment as resting on shaky legal ground because the Southern states were coerced into approving it.

Note: Article I, section 2, of the Constitution was modified by section 2 of the 14th amendment.

Section 1.

All persons born or naturalized in the United States, and subject to the jurisdiction thereof, are citizens of the United States and of the State wherein they reside.[a] No State shall make or enforce any law which shall abridge the privileges or immunities of citizens of the United States; nor shall any State deprive any person of life, liberty, or property, without due process of law; nor deny to any person within its jurisdiction the equal protection of the laws.

Section 2.

Representatives shall be apportioned among the several States according to their respective numbers, counting the whole number of persons in each State, excluding Indians not taxed.[b] But when the right to vote at any election for the choice of electors for President and Vice-President of the United States, Representatives in Congress, the Executive and Judicial officers of a State, or the members of the Legislature thereof, is denied to any of the male inhabitants of such State, being twenty-one years of age,* and citizens of the United States, or in any way abridged, exceptfor participation in rebellion, or other crime, the basis of representation therein shall be reduced in the proportion which the number of such male citizens shall bear to the whole number of male citizens twenty-one years of age in such State.
Changed by section 1 of the 26th amendment.

Section 3.

No person shall be a Senator or Representative in Congress, or elector of President and Vice-President, or hold any office, civil or military, under the United States, or under any State, who, having previously taken an oath, as a member of Congress, or as an officer of the United States, or as a member of any State legislature, or as an executive or judicial officer of any State, to support the Constitution of the United States, shall have engaged in insurrection or rebellion against the same, or given aid or comfort to the enemies thereof. But Congress may by a vote of two-thirds of each House, remove such disability.

Section 4.

The validity of the public debt of the United States, authorized by law, including debts incurred for payment of pensions and bounties for services in suppressing insurrection or rebellion, shall not be questioned. But neither the United

---

[a] The Supreme Court has never addressed the issue of whether children born of illegal aliens in the United States are entitled to U.S. citizenship though the language of the Fourteenth Amendment seems to indicate they are.

[b] "Indians not taxed" is a phrase used in many documents to refer to American Indians living on reservations in the United States. At the time of this amendment neither women of any race nor Indians could vote. The Fifteenth Amendment (1870) gave the vote to black men only. All women were granted the right to vote through the Nineteenth Amendment, ratified in 1920. Native Americans were given full citizenship and the right to vote through an act of Congress in 1924.

States nor any State shall assume or pay any debt or obligation incurred in aid of insurrection or rebellion against the United States, or any claim for the loss or emancipation of any slave; but all such debts, obligations and claims shall be held illegal and void.

Section 5.
The Congress shall have the power to enforce, by appropriate legislation, the provisions of this article.

COMMENTARY ON THE SECTIONS OF THE FOURTEENTH AMENDMENT:

Section 1 formally defines citizenship and protects the civil rights of citizens from infringement by the states. This section limited somewhat the power of state legislatures and reversed the Supreme Court's Dred Scott decision that had denied citizenship to blacks. The second sentence of this section contains two important concepts: "due process" and "equal protection." The intent was to protect newly freed slaves by giving them citizenship and assuring that, as citizens, the states could not deprive them of any of the rights of citizenship unless"due process" of law was applied. "Equal protection" meant that the states had to apply their laws as well as the laws of the United States to all their citizens equally regardless of race. The courts have applied these concepts to a wide variety of cases over the years, including contracts, labor relations and education.

Section 2 contains a threat to punish the states of the Confederacy if they refused to allow black men to vote by reducing the number of representatives in Congress from those states in proportion to the number of blacks prevented from voting. This was a club held over the heads of the Southern states until the Fifteenth Amendment could be passed and ratified (1870).

Section 3 was intended to prevent certain office holders/leaders of the Confederate States from holding state or national office as punishment for participating in the rebellion.

Section 4 said that neither the United States nor any individual states would bear responsibility for paying off the debts of the rebellious Southern states, affecting some European countries that had loaned money to the Confederacy.

FROM *THE MANIFESTO OF THE COMMUNIST PARTY*

KARL MARX AND FRIEDRICH ENGELS

Karl Marx (1818-1883) was the founder of international Communism. He studied law at Bonn and Berlin as well as history and Hegelian philosophy. While in Brussels with Frederich Engels, he organized the Communist League. In 1848, along with Engels, he wrote The Communist Manifesto, *attacking the state as the instrument of oppression, and religion and culture as the ideologies of the capitalist class. In 1867, he wrote the first volume of* Das Kapital. *His philosophies changed world history.*

Chapter I, Bourgeois and Proletarians

[1]The history of all existing societies is the history of class struggles.

[2]In ancient times society was divided into various orders that reflected social rank: in ancient Rome, patricians, knights, plebeians, slaves; in the Middle Ages, feudal lords, vassals, guild-masters journeymen, apprentices, serfs.

[3]We now live in the age of the bourgeoisie, an era with one outstanding characteristic: it has clarified and simplified class conflicts. Society has evolved into two opposing classes, two huge and hostile camps directly facing one other—the bourgeoisie and the proletariat.

[4]In the Middle Ages a few of the serfs managed to better themselves and become the chartered burghers of the earliest towns. These burgesses became the foundations of the emerging bourgeoisie.

[5]Eventually, however, the feudal system of industry, in which industrial production was monopolized by closed guilds, could no longer meet the needs of new and growing markets. The manufacturing system took its place. The guild-masters, the artisans who hand-crafted goods like furniture, clocks, glass bottles and guns, were pushed aside by the manufacturing middle class. The traditional division of labour between the different corporate guilds disappeared, replaced by the division of labour within each workshop.

[6]Modern industry established the world market, for which the discovery of America paved the way. This ever-expanding market has immensely developed commerce, navigation and all forms of communication. And in proportion as industry, commerce, navigation, transportation and communication systems extended, in the same proportion the bourgeoisie developed, increased its capital, and pushed into the background the traditional classes handed down from the Middle Ages.

[7]Wherever the bourgeoisie has gotten the upper hand, it has put an end to all feudal, patriarchal, idyllic relations. It has ruthlessly destroyed the old feudal ties that bound people to their "natural superiors" and has left no other bond between human beings than naked self-interest, than callous "cash payment."

[8]The bourgeoisie has drowned the most heavenly ecstasies of religious fervour, of chivalrous enthusiasm, of philistine sentimentalism, in the icy water of egotistical calculation. It has resolved personal worth into exchange value, and in place of mankind's unalienable chartered freedoms has set up that single, unconscionable freedom—Free Trade. In other words, for exploitation that was once hidden by religious and political illusions, the bourgeoisie has substituted naked, shameless, direct, brutal exploitation.

[9]The bourgeoisie has ripped sentimentalism away from the family and has reduced traditional family ties to mere monetary relationships.

[10]The need of a constantly expanding market for its products chases the bourgeoisie over the whole surface of the globe. It must nestle everywhere, settle everywhere, establish connections everywhere.

[11]The bourgeoisie has subjected the once-bucolic countryside to the rule of the town. It has created enormous cities and has shifted a considerable portion of the population from rural to urban life. Just as it has made the country dependent on the towns, so it has made undeveloped and semi-developed countries dependent on the industrialized, developed ones—nations of peasants dependent on nations of bourgeois, the East on the West.

[12]The bourgeoisie increasingly does away with the scattered state of the population, of the means of production, and of property. It has geographically condensed the population, centralized the means of production, and concentrated property in a few hands. The inevitable result of this is political centralization. In Europe, historically independent provinces with separate interests, laws, governments and systems of taxation, have become single nations, with one government, one code of laws, one national class interest, one frontier and one customs tariff.

[13]At a certain stage in the development of the feudal organization of agriculture and manufacturing, the feudal relations of property became no longer compatible with the developing productive forces; the traditional views of property became so many fetters. They had to be burst asunder; they *were* burst asunder.

[14]Into their place stepped free competition accompanied by a social and political constitution adapted to it, and by the economic and political sway of the bourgeois class.

[15]But now, the weapons with which the bourgeoisie felled feudalism to the ground are being turned against the bourgeoisie itself.

[16]Not only has the bourgeoisie forged the weapons that bring death to itself, but it has also called into existence the people who are to wield those

weapons—the modern working class, the proletarians.

[17]In proportion as the bourgeoisie, i.e., capital, is developed, in the same proportion is the proletariat, the modern working class, developed—a class of labourers, who live only so long as they find work, and who find work only so long as their labour increases capital. These labourers, who must sell themselves piecemeal, are a commodity like every other article of commerce and are consequently exposed to all the uncertainties of competition, to all of the fluctuations of the market.

[18]Due to the extensive use of machinery and the division of labour, the work of the proletarians has lost all individual character and pride of workmanship. Workers have become appendages of their machines, and it is only the most simple, most monotonous, most repetitive and most easily acquired skill that is required of them.

[19]Modern industry has converted the little workshop of the master craftsman into the great factory of the industrial capitalist. Masses of labourers, crowded into the factory, are treated like slaves. Not only are they slaves of the bourgeois class and the bourgeois state, they are daily and hourly enslaved by the machine, by the overseer and by the bourgeois boss himself.

[20]The more modern industry develops, the more is the labour of men superseded by that of women. Differences of age and sex no longer have any distinctive social validity for the working class. All are instruments of labour, more or less expensive to use, according to their age and sex.

[21]No sooner have the labourers received their wages in cash, for the moment escaping exploitation by the manufacturer, than they are set upon by the other portions of the bourgeoisie—the landlord, the tavern keeper, the store owner, the money lender, etc.

[22]Thus the workers begin to form combinations (trade unions) against the bourgeoisie; they club together to keep up the rate of wages; they found permanent associations to prepare beforehand for occasional revolts. Here and there the contest breaks out into riots.

[23]Now and then the workers are victorious, but only for a short time. The real fruit of their battles lies not in the immediate result but in the ever-expanding solidarity of the workers. This solidarity is furthered by the improved means of communication created by modern industry that place workers of different localities in contact with one another.

[24]All previous historical movements were movements of minorities, or in the interest of minorities. The proletarian movement is the self-conscious, independent movement of the immense majority, in the interest of the immense majority. Of all the classes that stand face-to-face with the bourgeoisie, the proletariat is the only truly revolutionary class. The proletariat, presently the lowest layer of our society, cannot stir, cannot raise itself up, without the upper levels of society being blasted into the air.

Chapter II, Proletarians and Communists

[25]The Communists are distinguished from other working-class parties by this only: 1) in the national struggles of the proletarians of the different countries, the Communists point out and bring to the forefront the common interests of the entire proletariat, independent of all nationality; 2) the Communists always and everywhere represent the working class as a whole.

[26]The immediate aim of the Communists is the same as that of all the other proletarian parties: the formation of the proletariat into a class, the overthrow of bourgeois supremacy, the conquest of political power by the proletariat.

[27]You are horrified at our intending to do away with private property. But in your existing society, private property is already done away with for nine-tenths of the population; its existence for the few is solely due to its non-existence in the hands of those nine-tenths. You reproach us, therefore, with intending to do away with a form of property, the necessary condition for whose existence is the non-existence of any property for the immense majority of society.

[28]In a word, you reproach us with intending to do away with your property. Precisely so; that is just what we intend.

[29]From the moment when labour can no longer be converted into capital, money or rent—into a social power capable of being monopolised—i.e., from the moment when individual property can no longer be transformed into bourgeois property, into capital, from that moment, you say, individuality vanishes.

[30]You must, therefore, confess that by "individual" you mean no other person than the bourgeois, than the middle class owner of property. This person must, indeed, be swept out of the way and made impossible.

[31]It has been objected that upon the abolition of private property all work will cease and universal laziness will overtake us.

[32]According to this, bourgeois society ought long ago to have gone to the dogs through sheer idleness; for those of its members who work acquire nothing, and those who acquire anything do not work.

[33]The bourgeois claptrap abut the family and education, about the hallowed co-relation of parent and child, becomes all the more disgusting by the action of modern industry; capitalism destroys all family ties among the proletarians, and their children are transformed into simple articles of commerce and instruments of labour.

[34]"But you Communists would introduce a community of working women!" screams the whole bourgeoisie in chorus.

[35]The bourgeois male sees in his wife a mere instrument of production. He believes that all instruments of production are to be exploited in common, and naturally he can come to no other conclusion than women should be used just like all other means of production.

[36]Nothing is more ridiculous than the virtuous indignation of our bour-

geois at the idea of a community of women, which, they pretend, is to be openly and officially established by the Communists. The Communists have no need to introduce a community of women; it has existed almost from time immemorial.

[37]Our bourgeois, not content with having the wives and daughters of their proletarians at their disposal, not to speak of common prostitutes, take the greatest pleasure in seducing each other's wives.

[38]Bourgeois marriage is in reality a system of wives in common and thus at the most what the Communists might possibly be reproached for is that they desire to introduce, in substitution for a hypocritically concealed, an openly legalized, community of women. It is self-evident that the abolition of the present system of production must bring with it the abolition of the community of women springing from that system, i.e., of prostitution both public and private.

[39]The Communists are further reproached with desiring to abolish countries and nationalities. The workers have no country. We cannot take from them what they do not have. National differences and antagonisms are disappearing daily due to the freedom of commerce and the development of the world market. The supremacy of the proletariat will cause national differences to disappear even faster. United action of the working class in the leading civilized countries is one of the first conditions for the emancipation of the proletariat.

[40]The Communist revolution is the most radical rupture with traditional property relations to be proposed in modern times; no wonder that its development involves the most radical break with traditional ideas.

[41]But let us have done with the bourgeois objections to Communism.

[42]We have seen that the first step in the revolution by the working class is to raise the proletariat to the position of ruling class, to establish true democracy.

[43]The proletariat will use its political supremacy to wrest by degrees all capital from the bourgeoisie; to centralize all instruments of production in the hands of the state, i.e., of the   proletariat organized as the ruling class; and to increase the total of productive forces as rapidly as possible.

[44]Of course, in the beginning this cannot be effected except by means of despotic inroads on the rights of property and on the conditions of bourgeois production; by means of measures, therefore, which appear economically insufficient and untenable, but which, in the course of the movement outstrip themselves, necessitate further inroads upon the old social order, and are unavoidable as a means of entirely revolutionizing the mode of production.

[45]These measures will, of course, be different in different countries, but in the most advanced countries the following will be generally applicable:

1. Abolition of property in land and application of all rents of land to public purposes.

2. A heavy progressive or graduated income tax.
3. Abolition of all rights of inheritance.
4. Confiscation of the property of all emigrants and rebels.
5. Centralization of credit in the hands of the state by means of a national bank with state capital and an exclusive monopoly.
6. Centralization of the means of communication and transport in the hands of the state.
7. Extension of factories and instruments of production owned by the state; the bringing into cultivation of waste lands, and the improvement of the soil generally in accordance with a common plan.
8. Equal obligation of all to work. Establishment of industrial armies, especially for agriculture.
9. Combination of agriculture with manufacturing industries; gradual abolition of the distinction between town and country by a more equitable distribution of the population over the country.
10. Free education for all children in public schools. Abolition of child factory labour in its present form. Combination of education with industrial production.

[46]When class distinctions have disappeared and all production has been concentrated in the hands of the working class, public power will lose its political character. Political power is merely the organized power of one class for oppressing another. If the proletariat during its contest with the bourgeoisie is compelled by the force of circumstances to organize itself as a class; if by means of a revolution it makes itself the ruling class and, as such, sweeps away by force the old conditions of production, then it will, along with these conditions, have swept away the conditions for the existence of class antagonisms and of classes generally, and will thereby have abolished its own supremacy as a class.

[47]In place of the old bourgeois society, with its classes and class antagonisms, we shall have an association in which the free development of each is the condition for the free development of all.

* * * * * * *

[48]From each according to his abilities, to each according to his needs.

Vocabulary

[2]patricians	[7]idyllic	[13]fetters	[33]hallowed
[2]plebeians	[7]callous	[17]piecemeal	[39]emancipation
[2]feudal	[8]chivalrous	[20]superseded	[43]wrest
[2]vassals	[8]fervor	[27]reproach	[44]despotic
[2]serfs	[8]philistine	[31]abolition	[44]untenable
[3]bourgeoisie	[11]bucolic	[33]claptrap	[45]emigrants
[7]patriarchal			

Discussion Questions

1. Look up the meaning of "manifesto." How does this reading fulfill that definition?

2. Look up and copy the meaning of "bourgeois" and "proletarian." Do you think there are "bourgeois" and "proletarians" today? If so, who would they be?

3. Discuss Marx and Engels's description of the bourgeois.

4. Discuss Marx and Engels's description of the role of bourgeois women. Do you think their description is accurate?

5. Explain the meaning of "From each according to his abilities, to each according to his needs" in terms of the reading.

6. Marx and Engels state, "National differences and antagonisms are disappearing daily due to the freedom of commerce and the development of the world market." Do you find this to be true today? Give examples and discuss your answers with your classmates.

7. Marx and Engels say, "We have seen that the first step in the revolution by the working class is to raise the proletariat to the position of ruling class, to establish true democracy." What do they mean by "true democracy"? How would this work?

8. Marx and Engels also state, "This person [the middle class property owner] must, indeed, be swept out of the way and made impossible." What, exactly, does this mean? Historically, how was this implemented in Marxist regimes?

9. What adjective(s) would you use to describe the tone of this piece?

10. Read "Money" by Ayn Rand on page 409 of this text. Discuss the two views of economics represented by "Money" and "The Manifesto of the Communist Party."

11. Comment on what Pablo Medina says about Fidel Castro's brand of Marxism in "Leaving" beginning on page 371 of this text.

A MODEST PROPOSAL
FOR PREVENTING THE CHILDREN OF POOR PEOPLE IN IRELAND
FROM BEING A BURDEN TO THEIR PARENTS OR COUNTRY, AND
FOR MAKING THEM BENEFICIAL TO THE PUBLIC

JONATHAN SWIFT

Jonathan Swift (1667-1745), born of English parents in Dublin, Ireland, is considered by most critics to be the foremost prose satirist in the English language. Writing in support of Irish causes, Swift produced his most memorable works: "Proposal for Universal Use of Irish Manufacture" (1720), "The Drapier's Letters" (1724), Gulliver's Travels (1726), and "A Modest Proposal"(1728). Swift published his works pseudonymously since several of his publications resulted in a price being placed on his head although he was never arrested nor brought to trial.

[1]It is a melancholy object to those who walk through this great town[a] or travel in the country, when they see the streets, the roads, and cabin doors, crowded with beggars of the female sex, followed by three, four, or six children, all in rags and importuning every passenger for an alms. These mothers, instead of being able to work for their honest livelihood, are forced to employ all their time in strolling to beg sustenance for their helpless infants, who, as they grow up, either turn thieves for want of work, or leave their dear native country to fight for the Pretender in Spain,[b] or sell themselves to the Barbadoes.[c]

[2]I think it is agreed by all parties that this prodigious number of children in the arms, or on the backs, or at the heels of their mothers, and frequently of their fathers, is in the present deplorable state of the kingdom a very great additional grievance; and, therefore, whoever could find out a fair, cheap, and easy method of making these children sound, useful members of the commonwealth, would deserve so well of the public as to have his statue set up for a preserver of the nation.

[3]But my intention is very far from being confined to provide only for the children of professed beggars; it is of a much greater extent, and shall take in

---

[a]Dublin, Ireland

[b]A reference to James Stuart of England, a Roman Catholic, who tried unsuccessfully to claim the British throne in the 18th century—thus, the "pretender" to the throne.

[c]Many poor Irish were forced by economics into a contract of indentured servitude in exchange for passage to the West Indies, to seek a better life in the "New World."

the whole number of infants at a certain age who are born of parents in effect as little able to support them as those who demand our charity in the streets.

[4]As to my own part, having turned my thoughts for many years upon this important subject, and maturely weighed the several schemes of other projectors,[d] I have always found them grossly mistaken in the computation. It is true, a child just dropped from its dam[e] may be supported by her milk for a solar year, with little other nourishment; at most not above the value of 2s.,[f] which the mother may certainly get, or the value in scraps, by her lawful occupation of begging; and it is exactly at one year old that I propose to provide for them in such a manner as instead of being a charge upon their parents or the parish,[g] or wanting food and raiment for the rest of their lives, they shall on the contrary contribute to the feeding, and partly to the clothing, of many thousands.

[5]There is likewise another great advantage in my scheme, that it will prevent those voluntary abortions, and that horrid practice of women murdering their bastard children, alas! too frequent among us! sacrificing the poor innocent babes I doubt more to avoid the expense than the shame, which would move tears and pity in the most savage and inhuman breast.

[6]The number of souls in this kingdom being usually reckoned one million and a half, of these I calculate there may be about two hundred thousand couple whose wives are breeders; from which number I subtract thirty thousand couples who are able to maintain their own children, although I apprehend there cannot be so many, under the present distresses of the kingdom; but this being granted, there will remain an hundred and seventy thousand breeders. I again subtract fifty thousand for those women who miscarry, or whose children die by accident or disease within the year. There only remains one hundred and twenty thousand children of poor parents annually born. The question therefore is, how this number shall be reared and provided for, which, as I have already said, under the present situation of affairs, is utterly impossible by all the methods hitherto proposed. For we can neither employ them in handicraft or agriculture; we neither build houses (I mean in the country) nor cultivate land: they can very seldom pick up a livelihood by stealing, till they arrive at six years old, except where they are of towardly[h] parts, although I confess they learn the rudiments

---

[d]ones who devise plans or schemes

[e]"Dame," or woman, in this context a mother with an infant.

[f]2s—two shillings (British coins) equal to about $.25

[g]Parishes were responsible for the support of their unemployed.

[h]well-made; in this reference, mature or advanced for their age

much earlier, during which time, they can however be properly looked upon only as probationers, as I have been informed by a principal gentleman in the county of Cavan, who protested to me that he never knew above one or two instances under the age of six, even in a part of the kingdom so renowned for the quickest proficiency in that art.

[7]I am assured by our merchants that a boy or a girl before twelve years old is no salable commodity; and even when they come to this age they will not yield above three pounds, or three pounds and half-a-crown[i] at most on the exchange; which cannot turn to account either to the parents or kingdom, the charge of nutriment and rags having been at least four times that value.

[8]I shall now therefore humbly propose my own thoughts, which I hope will not be liable to the least objection.

[9]I have been assured by a very knowing American of my acquaintance in London, that a young healthy child well nursed is at a year old a most delicious, nourishing, and wholesome food, whether stewed, roasted, baked, or boiled; and I make no doubt that it will equally serve in a fricassee or a ragout.

[10]I do therefore humbly offer it to public consideration that of the hundred and twenty thousand children already computed, twenty thousand may be reserved for breed, whereof only one-fourth part to be males; which is more than we allow to sheep, black cattle or swine; and my reason is, that these children are seldom the fruits of marriage, a circumstance not much regarded by our savages, therefore one male will be sufficient to serve four females. That the remaining hundred thousand may, at a year old, be offered in the sale to the persons of quality[j] and fortune through the kingdom; always advising the mother to let them suck plentifully in the last month, so as to render them plump and fat for a good table. A child will make two dishes at an entertainment for friends; and when the family dines alone, the fore or hind quarter will make a reasonable dish, and seasoned with a little pepper or salt will be very good boiled on the fourth day, especially in winter.

[11]I have reckoned upon a medium that a child just born will weigh 12 pounds, and in a solar year, if tolerably nursed, increaseth to 28 pounds.

[12]I grant this food will be somewhat dear,[k] and therefore very proper for landlords, who, as they have already devoured most of the parents, seem to have the best title to the children.

[13]Infants' flesh will be in season throughout the year, but more plentiful

---

[i]British monetary units. A pound was worth about 4 to 5 American dollars; a half-crown was about $.30.

[j]superiority of birth or rank

[k]expensive

in March, and a little before and after; for we are told by a grave author, an eminent French physician, that fish being a prolific diet, there are more children born in Roman Catholic countries about nine months after Lent than at any other season; therefore, reckoning a year after Lent, the markets will be more glutted than usual, because the number of popish[l] infants is at least three to one in this kingdom: and therefore it will have one other collateral advantage, by lessening the number of papists[m] among us.

[14]I have already computed the charge of nursing a beggar's child (in which list I reckon all cottagers, laborers, and four-fifths of the farmers) to be about two shillings per annum, rags included; and I believe no gentleman would repine to give ten shillings for the carcass of a good fat child, which, as I have said, will make four dishes of excellent nutritive meat, when he hath only some particular friend or his own family to dine with him. Thus the squire will learn to be a good landlord,[n] and grow popular among his tenants; the mother will have eight shillings net profit, and be fit for work till she produces another child.

[15]Those who are more thrifty (as I must confess the times require) may flay the carcass; the skin of which artificially dressed will make admirable gloves for ladies, and summer boots for fine gentlemen.

[16]As to our city of Dublin, shambles[o] may be appointed for this purpose in the most convenient parts of it, and butchers we may be assured will not be wanting; although I rather recommend buying the children alive, and dressing them hot from the knife, as we do roasting pigs.

[17]A very worthy person, a true lover of his country, and whose virtues I highly esteem, was lately pleased in discoursing on this matter to offer a refinement upon my scheme. He said that many gentlemen of this kingdom, having of late destroyed their deer, he conceived that the want of venison might be well supplied by the bodies of young lads and maidens, not exceeding fourteen years of age nor under twelve; so great a number of both sexes in every country being now ready to starve for want of work and service; and these to be disposed of by their parents, if alive, or otherwise by their nearest relations. But with due deference to so excellent a friend and so deserving a patriot, I cannot be altogether in his sentiments; for as to the males, my American acquaintance assured me, from frequent experience, that their flesh was generally tough and lean, like

---

[l]referring or realting to the Roman Catholic church (of the pope)

[m]a disparaging term for a Roman Catholic

[n]British landlords were to blame for much of the misery imposed upon the Irish.

[o]meat markets in town where animals are slaughtered and butchered

that of our schoolboys by continual exercise, and their taste disagreeable; and to fatten them would not answer the charge. Then as to the females, it would, I think, with humble submission be a loss to the public, because they soon would become breeders themselves; and besides, it is not improbable that some scrupulous people might be apt to censure such a practice (although indeed very unjustly), as a little bordering upon cruelty; which, I confess, hath always been with me the strongest objection against any project, however so well intended.

[18]But in order to justify my friend, he confessed that this expedient was put into his head by the famous Psalmanazar,[p] a native of the island Formosa, who came from thence to London above twenty years ago, and in conversation told my friend, that in his country when any young person happened to be put to death, the executioner sold the carcass to persons of quality as a prime dainty; and that in his time the body of a plump girl of fifteen, who was crucified for an attempt to poison the emperor, was sold to his imperial majesty's prime minister of state, and other great mandarins of the court, in joints from the gibbet, at four hundred crowns. Neither indeed can I deny, that if the same use were made of several plump young girls in this town, who without one single groat[q] to their fortunes cannot stir abroad without a chair,[r] and appear at playhouse and assemblies in foreign fineries which they never will pay for, the kingdom would not be the worse.

[19]Some persons of a desponding spirit are in great concern about that vast number of poor people, who are aged, diseased, or maimed, and I have been desired to employ my thoughts what course may be taken to ease the nation of so grievous an encumbrance. But I am not in the least pain upon that matter, because it is very well known that they are every day dying and rotting by cold and famine, and filth and vermin, as fast as can be reasonably expected. And as to the young laborers, they are now in as hopeful a condition; they cannot get work, and consequently pine away for want of nourishment, to a degree that if at any time they are accidentally hired to common labor, they have not strength to perform it; and thus the country and themselves are happily delivered from the evils to come.

[20]I have too long digressed, and therefore shall return to my subject. I think the advantages by the proposal which I have made are obvious and many, as well as of the highest importance.

[21]For first, As I have already observed, it would greatly lessen the num-

---

[p]an 18th century English literary imposter who passed himself off as a native of Formosa.

[q]an English silver coin worth four pence, used from the 14th to the 17th century

[r]can't go anywhere unless they are carried by their servants in a sedan chair

ber of papists, with whom we are yearly overrun, being the principal breeders of the nation as well as our most dangerous enemies; and who stay at home on purpose with a design to deliver the kingdom to the Pretender, hoping to take their advantage by the absence of so many good protestants, who have chosen rather to leave their country than stay at home and pay tithes against their conscience to an episcopal curate.

[22]Secondly, The poorer tenants will have something valuable of their own, which by law may be made liable to distress and help to pay their landlord's rent, their corn and cattle being already seized, and money a thing unknown.

[23]Thirdly, Whereas the maintenance of an hundred thousand children, from two years old and upward, cannot be computed at less than ten shillings apiece per annum, the nation's stock will be thereby increased fifty thousand pounds per annum, beside the profit of a new dish introduced to the tables of all gentlemen of fortune in the kingdom who have any refinement in taste. And the money will circulate among ourselves, the goods being entirely of our own growth and manufacture.

[24]Fourthly, The constant breeders, beside the gain of eight shillings sterling per annum by the sale of their children, will be rid of the charge of maintaining them after the first year.

[25]Fifthly, This food would likewise bring great custom to taverns; where the vintners will certainly be so prudent as to procure the best receipts for dressing it to perfection, and consequently have their houses frequented by all the fine gentlemen, who justly value themselves upon their knowledge in good eating: and a skilful cook, who understands how to oblige his guests, will contrive to make it as expensive as they please.

[26]Sixthly, This would be a great inducement to marriage, which all wise nations have either encouraged by rewards or enforced by laws and penalties. It would increase the care and tenderness of mothers toward their children, when they were sure of a settlement for life to the poor babes, provided in some sort by the public, to their annual profit instead of expense. We should see an honest emulation among the married women, which of them could bring the fattest child to the market. Men would become as fond of their wives during the time of their pregnancy as they are now of their mares in foal, their cows in calf, their sows when they are ready to farrow; nor offer to beat or kick them (as is too frequent a practice) for fear of a miscarriage.

[27]Many other advantages might be enumerated. For instance, the addition of some thousand carcasses in our exportation of barreled beef, the propagation of swine's flesh, and improvement in the art of making good bacon, so much wanted among us by the great destruction of pigs, too frequent at our tables; which are no way comparable in taste or magnificence to a well-grown, fat, yearling child, which roasted whole will make a considerable figure at a lord mayor's feast or any other public entertainment. But this and many others I omit, being studious of brevity.

[28]Supposing that one thousand families in this city would be constant customers for infants' flesh, besides others who might have it at merry meetings, pariculary weddings and christenings, I compute that Dublin would take off[s] annually about twenty thousand carcasses, and the rest of the kingdom (where probably they will be sold somewhat cheaper) the remaining eighty thousand.

[29]I can think of no one objection that will possibly be raised against this proposal, unless it should be urged that the number of people will be hereby much lessened in the kingdom. This I freely own, and it was indeed one principal design in offering it to the world. I desire the reader will observe, that I calulate my remedy for this one individual kingdom of Ireland and for no other that ever was, is, or I think ever can be upon earth. Therefore let no man talk to me of other expedients: of taxing our absentees at five shillings a pound:[t] of using neither clothes nor household funiture except what is of our own growth and manufacture: of utterly rejecting the materials and instruments that promote foreign luxury: of curing the expensiveness of pride, vanity, idleness, and gaming in our women: of introducing a vein of parsimony, prudence, and temperance: of learning to love our country, in the want of which we differ even from Laplanders and the inhabitants of Topinamboo:[u] of quitting our animosities and factions, nor acting any longer like the Jews, who were murdering one another at the very moment their city was taken:[v] of being a little cautious not to sell our country and conscience for nothing: of teaching landlords to have at least one degree of mercy toward their tenants: lastly, of putting a spirit of honesty, industry and skill into our shokeepers; who, if resolution could now be taken to buy only our native goods, would immediately unite to cheat and exact upon us in the price, the measure, and the goodness, nor could ever yet be brought to make one fair proposal of just dealing, though often and earnestly invited to it.

[30]But as to myself, having been wearied out for many years with offering in vain, idle, visionary thoughts, and at length utterly despairing of success, I fortunately fell upon this proposal, which as it is wholly new, so it hath something sold and real, of no expense and little trouble, full in our own power, and

---

[s]eat, consume

[t]taxing wealthy people who emigrate to ensure that some of their wealth remains in the country

[u]Lapland (northern portion of Norway, Sweden and Finland) and Topinamboo (part of Brazil) are distant, supposedly uncivilized and wild places, whose inhabitants still love their homelands more, Swift asserts, than the Irish love Ireland.

[v]In 70 AD, Romans captured the Jewish city of Jerusalem while the defenders fought among themselves.

whereby we can incur no danger in disobliging England.[w] For this kind of commodity will not bear exportation, the flesh being of too tender a consistence to admit a long continuance in salt, although perhaps I could name a country which would be glad to eat up our whole nation with it.[x]

[31]After all, I am not so violently bent upon my own opinion as to reject any offer proposed by wise men, which shall be found equally innocent, cheap, easy, and effectual. But before something of that kind shall be advanced in contradiction to my scheme, and offering a better, I desire the author or authors will be pleased maturely to consider two points. First, as things now stand, how they will be able to find food and raiment for an hundred thousand useless mouths and backs. And secondly, there being a round million of creatures in human figure throughout this kingdom, whose whole subsistence put into a common stock would leave them in debt two millions of pounds sterling, adding those who are beggars by profession to the bulk of farmers, cottagers, and laborers, with their wives and children who are beggars in effect: I desire those politicians who dislike my overture, and may perhaps be so bold as to attempt an answer, that they will first ask the parents of these mortals, whether they would not at this day think it a great happiness to have been sold for food, at a year old in the manner I prescribe, and thereby have avoided such a perpetual scene of misfortunes as they have since gone through by the oppression of landlords, the impossibility of paying rent without money or trade, the want of common sustenance, with neither house nor clothes to cover them from the inclemencies of the weather, and the most inevitable prospect of entailing the like or greater miseries upon their breed for ever.

[32]I profess, in the sincerity of my heart, that I have not the least personal interest in endeavoring to promote this necessary work, having no other motive than the public good of my country, by advancing our trade, providing for infants, relieving the poor, and giving some pleasure to the rich. I have no children by which I can propose to get a single penny; the youngest being nine years old, and my wife past child-bearing.

****

Some background information: Swift published the Modest Proposal in 1729 as a pamphlet (a kind of essay in an unbound booklet). From the 12th century onward, Ireland had been a colony of its stronger and richer neighbor, England, and at times its people had been brutally repressed. Most of the native-born Irish were Roman

---

[w]inconveniencing or offending England. In this and the following sentence, Swift is suggesting that, since the meat of Irish children could not be preserved well enough to be exported to England, this new Irish meat would have no disruptive effect on meat production or markets in England.

[x]Swift insinuates that England would be glad "to eat up" Ireland, even without any salt.

Catholics and were employed as agricultural laborers or tenant farmers on the land of English Protestant landowners. The landowners were paid from the produce of the land at rates which the workers could rarely afford, and thus large numbers of the Irish were kept in an ongoing condition of virtual slavery. In times of drought or plant disease, starvation was as common as in the Third World today.

A Brief Irish History to 1729

390-461	St. Patrick brings Christianity to Ireland
795-1014	Vikings begin a series of invasions
1169	Following the Norman invasion of England in 1066, long-term British involvement in Ireland begins
1541	Henry VIII of England, a Protestant, declares himself King of Ireland
1649	Oliver Cromwell crushes Irish opposition.
1703,	Protestants own 90% of the country's land.
1695-1728	Penal Laws: English parliamentary acts against Catholics, these restrict Catholics from

- bearing arms and owning horses worth over five pounds
- obtaining an education
- buying land
- serving in the army, holding public office, entering the legal profession or voting

Vocabulary

[1]melancholy   [13]collateral   [18]expedient   [25]oblige
[1]importuning   [13]papists   [18]mandarins   [25]contrive
[1]sustenance   [14]cottagers   [18]gibbet   [26]inducement
[2]prodigious   [14]per annum   [18]groat   [26]emulation
[2]deplorable   [14]repine   [18]fineries   [26]farrow
[2]commonwealth   [14]carcass   [19]encumbrance   [27]enumerated
[3]professed   [15]flay   [19]vermin   [28]propagation
[5]apprehend   [15]dressed   [19]pine away   [27]comparable
[6]hitherto   [16]shambles   [20]digressed   [27]yearling
[6]rudiments   [17]virtues   [21]tithes   [27]brevity
[6]renowned   [17]esteem   [21]episcopal   [28]bent
[9]fricassee   [17]discoursing   [21]curate   [28]effectual
[9]ragout   [17]venison   [25]vintners   [28]subsistence
[12]dear   [17]deference   [25]prudent   [28]overture
[13]prolific   [17]scrupulous   [25]procure   [28]sustenance
[13]glutted   [17]censure   [25]frequented   [29]profess

Discussion Questions

1. Define satire and irony. In what ways is this essay satirical? Ironic?

2. Discuss the importance of the title. Why does Swift use the term "modest"?

3. For what problem does Swift propose his solution?

4. Without making value judgments, briefly summarize Swift's argument. What evidence does he use to support his argument? How well does he make his case?

5. Whom does Swift blame for Ireland's problems? (Hint: There's more than one.)

6. At the end of the essay, Swift suggests a number of alternatives. Are we the readers meant to take them seriously or consider them to be ironic?

7. What is the purpose of the last paragraph?

8. How or in what ways is "A Modest Proposal" relevant to our society today?

9. Read Peter Singer's "Justifying Infanticide" beginning on page 339 of this text. Is Singer's work an updated version of "Modest Proposal"? Support your answer.

MONEY
FROM *ATLAS SHRUGGED*

AYN RAND

Alissa Rosenbaum, Ayn Rand (1905-1982), was a novelist, essayist and philosopher born in St. Petersburg, Russia. She witnessed the Russian Revolution, from which she learned to hate the concept of "Collectivism." She immigrated to the United States in 1926, never to return to Russia. In her novels The Fountainhead *(1943) and* Atlas Shrugged *(1957) Rand dramatized the major elements of her philosophy of "reason, individualism, and capitalism," which she called "Objectivism."*

[1]"So you think that money is the root of all evil?" said Francisco d'Anconia. "Have you ever asked what is the root of money? Money is a tool of exchange, which can't exist unless there are goods produced and men able to produce them. Money is the material shape of the principle that men who wish to deal with one another must deal by trade and give value for value. Money is not the tool of the moochers, who claim your product by tears, or of the looters, who take it from you by force. Money is made possible only by the men who produce. Is this what you consider evil?

[2]"When you accept money in payment for your effort, you do so only on the conviction that you will exchange it for the product of the effort of others. It is not the moochers or the looters who give value to money. Not an ocean of tears, not all the guns in the world can transform those pieces of paper in your wallet into the bread you will need to survive tomorrow. Those pieces of paper, which should have been gold, are a token of honor—your claim upon the energy of the men who produce. Your wallet is your statement of hope that somewhere in the world around you there are men who will not default on that moral principle which is the root of money. Is this what you consider evil?

[3]"Have you ever looked for the root of production? Take a look at an electric generator and dare tell yourself that it was created by the muscular effort of unthinking brutes. Try to grow a seed of wheat without the knowledge left to you by men who had to discover it for the first time. Try to obtain your food by means of nothing but physical motions—and you'll learn that man's mind is the root of all the goods produced and of all the wealth that has ever existed on earth.

[4]"But you say that money is made by the strong at the expense of the weak? What strength do you mean? It is not the strength of guns or muscles.

Wealth is the product of man's capacity to think. Then is money made by the man who invents a motor at the expense of those who did not invent it? Is money made by the intelligent at the expense of the fools? By the able at the expense of the incompetent? By the ambitious at the expense of the lazy? Money is made—before it can be looted or mooched—made by the effort of every honest man, each to the extent of his ability. An honest man is one who knows that he can't consume more than he has produced.

5"To trade by means of money is the code of the men of good will. Money rests on the axiom that every man is the owner of his mind and his effort. Money allows no power to prescribe the value of your effort except the voluntary choice of the man who is willing to trade you his effort in return. Money permits you to obtain for your goods and your labor that which they are worth to the men who buy them, but no more. Money permits no deals except those to mutual benefit by the unforced judgment of the traders. Money demands of you the recognition that men must work for their own benefit, not for their own injury, for their gain, not their loss—the recognition that they are not beasts of burden, born to carry the weight of your misery—that you must offer them values, not wounds—that the common bond among men is not the exchange of suffering, but the exchange of goods. Money demands that you sell, not your weakness to men's stupidity, but your talent to their reason; it demands that you buy, not the shoddiest they offer, but the best that your money can find. And when men live by trade—with reason, not force, as their final arbiter—it is the best product that wins, the best performance, the man of best judgment and highest ability—and the degree of a man's productiveness is the degree of his reward. This is the code of existence whose tool and symbol is money. Is this what you consider evil?

6"But money is only a tool. It will take you wherever you wish, but it will not replace you as the driver. It will give you the means for the satisfaction of your desires, but it will not provide you with desires. Money is the scourge of the men who attempt to reverse the law of causality—the men who seek to replace the mind by seizing the products of the mind.

7"Money will not purchase happiness for the man who has no concept of what he wants; money will not give him a code of values, if he's evaded the knowledge of what to value, and it will not provide him with a purpose, if he's evaded the choice of what to seek. Money will not buy intelligence for the fool, or admiration for the coward, or respect for the incompetent. The man who attempts to purchase the brains of his superiors to serve him, with his money replacing his judgment, ends up by becoming the victim of his inferiors. The men of intelligence desert him, but the cheats and the frauds come flocking to him, drawn by a law which he has not discovered: that no man may be smaller than his money. Is this the reason why you call it evil?

8"Only the man who does not need it is fit to inherit wealth—the man who would make his own fortune no matter where he started. If an heir is equal to his money, it serves him; if not, it destroys him. But you look on and you cry that money corrupted him. Did it? Or did he corrupt his money? Do not envy a worthless heir; his wealth is not yours and you would have done no better with it. Do not think that it should have been distributed among you; loading the world with fifty parasites instead of one would not bring back the dead virtue which was the fortune. Money is a living power that dies without its root. Money will not serve the mind that cannot match it. Is this the reason why you call it evil?

⁹"Money is your means of survival. The verdict you pronounce upon the source of your livelihood is the verdict you pronounce upon your life. If the source is corrupt, you have damned your own existence. Did you get your money by fraud? By pandering to men's vices or men's stupidity? By catering to fools, in the hope of getting more than your ability deserves? By lowering your standards? By doing work you despise for purchasers you scorn? If so, then your money will not give you a moment's or a penny's worth of joy. Then all the things you buy will become, not a tribute to you, but a reproach; not an achievement, but a reminder of shame. Then you'll scream that money is evil. Evil, because it would not pinch-hit for your self-respect? Evil, because it would not let you enjoy your depravity? Is this the root of your hatred of money?

¹⁰"Money will always remain an effect and refuse to replace you as the cause. Money is the product of virtue, but it will not give you virtue and it will not redeem your vices. Money will not give you the unearned, neither in matter nor in spirit. Is this the root of your hatred of money?

¹¹"Or did you say it's the love of money that's the root of all evil? To love a thing is to know and love its nature. To love money is to know and love the fact that money is the creation of the best power within you, and your pass-key to trade your effort for the effort of the best among men. It's the person who would sell his soul for a nickel, who is loudest in proclaiming his hatred of money—and he has good reason to hate it. The lovers of money are willing to work for it. They know they are able to deserve it.

¹²"Let me give you a tip on a clue to men's characters: the man who damns money has obtained it dishonorably; the man who respects it has earned it.

¹³"Run for your life from any man who tells you that money is evil. That sentence is the leper's bell of an approaching looter. So long as men live together on earth and need means to deal with one another—their only substitute, if they abandon money, is the muzzle of a gun.

¹⁴"But money demands of you the highest virtues, if you wish to make it or to keep it. Men who have no courage, pride or self-esteem, men who have no moral sense of their right to their money and are not willing to defend it as they defend their life, men who apologize for being rich—will not remain rich for

long. They are the natural bait for the swarms of looters that stay under rocks for centuries, but come crawling out at the first smell of a man who begs to be forgiven for the guilt of owning wealth. They will hasten to relieve him of the guilt—and of his life, as he deserves.

[15]"Then you will see the rise of the men of the double standard—the men who live by force, yet count on those who live by trade to create the value of their looted money—the men who are the hitchhikers of virtue. In a moral society, these are the criminals, and the statutes are written to protect you against them. But when a society establishes criminals-by-right and looters-by-law—men who use force to seize the wealth of disarmed victims—then money becomes its creators' avenger. Such looters believe it safe to rob defenseless men, once they've passed a law to disarm them. But their loot becomes the magnet for other looters, who get it from them as they got it. Then the race goes, not to the ablest at production, but to those most ruthless at brutality. When force is the standard, the murderer wins over the pickpocket. And then that society vanishes in a spread of ruins and slaughter.

[16]"Do you wish to know whether that day is coming? Watch money. Money is the barometer of a society's virtue. When you see that trading is done not by consent but by compulsion—when you see that in order to produce, you need to obtain permission from men who produce nothing—when you see that money is flowing to those who deal, not in goods, but in favors—when you see that men get richer by graft and by pull than by work, and your laws don't protect you against them, but protect them against you—when you see corruption being rewarded and honesty becoming a self-sacrifice—you may know that your society is doomed. Money is so noble a medium that it does not compete with guns and it does not make terms with brutality. It will not permit a country to survive as half-property, half-loot.

[17]"Whenever destroyers appear among men, they start by destroying money, for money is men's protection and the base of a moral existence. Destroyers seize gold and leave to its owners a counterfeit pile of paper. This kills all objective standards and delivers men into the arbitrary power of an arbitrary setter of values. Gold was an objective value, an equivalent of wealth produced. Paper is a mortgage on wealth that does not exist, backed by a gun aimed at those who are expected to produce it. Paper is a check drawn by legal looters upon an account which is not theirs: upon the virtue of the victims. Watch for the day when it bounces, marked, 'Account overdrawn.'

[18]"When you have made evil the means of survival, do not expect men to remain good. Do not expect them to stay moral and lose their lives for the purpose of becoming the fodder of the immoral. Do not expect them to produce, when production is punished and looting rewarded. Do not ask, 'Who is destroying the world?' You are.

[19]"You stand in the midst of the greatest achievements of the greatest

productive civilization and you wonder why it's crumbling around you, while you're damning its life-blood—money. You look upon money as the savages did before you, and you wonder why the jungle is creeping back to the edge of your cities. Throughout men's history, money was always seized by looters of one brand or another, whose names changed, but whose method remained the same: to seize wealth by force and to keep the producers bound, demeaned, defamed, deprived of honor. That phrase about the evil of money, which you mouth with such righteous recklessness, comes from a time when wealth was produced by the labor of slaves—slaves who repeated the motions once discovered by somebody's mind and left unimproved for centuries. So long as production was ruled by force, and wealth was obtained by conquest, there was little to conquer, yet through all the centuries of stagnation and starvation, men exalted the looters as aristocrats of the sword, as aristocrats of birth, as aristocrats of the bureau, and despised the producers, as slaves, as traders, as shopkeepers—as industrialists.

[20]"To the glory of mankind, there was, for the first and only time in history a country of money—and I have no higher, more reverent tribute to pay to America, for this means a country of reason, justice, freedom, production, achievement. For the first time, man's mind and money were set free, and there were no fortunes-by-conquest, but only fortunes-by-work, and instead of swordsmen and slaves, there appeared the real maker of wealth, the greatest worker, the highest type of human being—the self-made man—the American industrialist.

[21]"If you ask me to name the proudest distinction of Americans, I would choose—because it contains all the others—the fact that they were the people who created the phrase 'to make money.' No other language or nation had ever used these words before; men had always thought of wealth as a static quantity—to be seized, begged, inherited, shared, looted or obtained as a favor. Americans were the first to understand that wealth has to be created. The words 'to make money' hold the essence of human morality.

[22]"Yet these were the words for which Americans were denounced by the rotted cultures of the looters' continents. Now the looters' credo has brought you to regard your proudest achievements as a hallmark of shame, your prosperity as guilt, your greatest men, the industrialists, as blackguards, and your magnificent factories as the product and property of muscular labor, the labor of whip-driven slaves, like the pyramids of Egypt. The rotter who simpers that he sees no difference between the power of the dollar and the power of the whip, ought to learn the difference on his own hide— as, I think, he will.

[23]"Until and unless you discover that money is the root of all good, you ask for your own destruction. When money ceases to be the tool by which men deal with one another, then men become the tools of men. Blood, whips and guns—or dollars. Take your choice—there is no other—and your time is running out."

Vocabulary

[1]moochers	[8]parasite	[15]statutes	[19]exalted
[5]axiom	[9]pander	[16]graft	[21]static
[5]shoddiest	[9]vice	[18]fodder	[22]credo
[5]arbiter	[9]tribute	[19]demeaned	[22]blackguard
[6]scourge	[9]reproach	[19]defamed	[22]rotter
[6]causality	[13]leper's bell	[19]stagnation	

Discussion Questions

1. What is Francisco d'Anconia's view of money?

2. He gives numerous examples of this view in this excerpt. Pick out the two or three that you think are the strongest arguments for his view.

3. In paragraph 4 d'Anconia says, "But you say that money is made by the strong at the expense of the weak?" He then goes on to define two different types of strength. What are they and which does he support?

4. What does d'Anconia mean in paragraph 16 when he says, "Money is the barometer of a society's virtue"?

5. What is d'Anconia talking about in paragraph 17 when he talks about "gold" and "paper"?

6. Do you agree with d'Anconia's assessment of money? Explain.

7. *Atlas Shrugged* was written in 1957, post World War II, during the Cold War with the then USSR. Do you think Rand's views, as portrayed through d'Anconia, are valid today?

8. What do you think Karl Marx would make of d'Anconia's philosophy of money in this excerpt?

MOONLIGHT SONATA

ALEXANDER WOOLLCOTT

*A New Jersey native, **Alexander Woollcott** (1887-1943) was an author, drama critic and actor. Known for his sardonic wit, Woollcott wrote for The New York* Times, New York Herald, *New York* World, *and* The New Yorker. *His books include* Two Gentlemen and a Lady *(1928) and* While Rome Burns *(1934).*

[1]If this report were to be published in its own England, I would have to cross my fingers in a little foreword explaining that all the characters were fictitious which stern requirement of the British libel law would embarrass me slightly because none of the characters is fictitious, and the story told to Katharine Cornell by Clemence Dane and by Katharine Cornell told to me — chronicles what, to the best of my knowledge and belief, actually befell a young English physician whom I shall call Alvan Barach, because that does not happen to be his name. It is an account of a hitherto unreported adventure he had two years ago when he went down into Kent to visit an old friend — let us call *him* Ellery Cazalet — who spent most of his days on the links and most of his nights wondering how he would ever pay the death duties on the collapsing family manor-house to which he had indignantly fallen heir.

[2]This house was a shabby little cousin to Compton Wynyates, with roof-tiles of Tudor red making it cozy in the noonday sun, and a hoarse bell which, from the clock tower, had been contemptuously scattering the hours like coins ever since Henry VIII was a rosy stripling. Within, Cazalet could afford only a doddering couple to fend for him, and the once sumptuous gardens did much as they pleased under the care of a single gardener. I think I must risk giving the gardener's real name, for none I could invent would have so appropriate a flavor. It was John Scripture, and he was assisted, from time to time, by an aged and lunatic father, who, in his lucid intervals, would be let out from his captivity under the eaves of the lodge to putter amid the lewd topiarian extravagance of the hedges.

[3]The doctor was to come down when he could, with a promise of some good golf, long nights of exquisite silence, and a ghost or two thrown in if his fancy ran that way. It was characteristic of his rather ponderous humor that, in writing to fix a day, he addressed Cazalet at "The Creeps, Seven-oaks, Kent." When he arrived, it was to find his host away from home and not due back until all hours. Barach was to dine alone with a reproachful setter for a companion, and not wait up. His bedroom on the ground floor was beautifully paneled

from footboard to ceiling, but some misguided housekeeper under the fourth George had fallen upon the lovely woodwork with a can of black varnish. The dowry brought by a Cazalet bride of the mauve decade had been invested in a few vintage bathrooms, and one of these had replaced a prayer closet that once opened into this bedroom. There was only a candle to read by, but the light of full moon came waveringly through the wind-stirred vines that half curtained the mullioned windows.

[4]In this museum, Barach dropped off to sleep. He did not know how long he had slept when he found himself awake again, and conscious that something was astir in the room. It took him a moment to place the movement, but at last, in a patch of moonlight, he made out a hunched figure that seemed to be sitting with bent, engrossed head in the chair by the door. It was the hand, or rather the whole arm, that was moving, tracing a recurrent if irregular course in the air. At first the gesture was teasingly half-familiar, and then Barach recognized it as the one a woman makes when embroidering. There would be a hesitation as if the needle were being thrust through some taut, resistant material, and then, each time, the long swift, sure pull of the thread.

[5]To the startled guest, this seemed the least menacing activity he had ever heard ascribed to a ghost, but just the same he had only one idea, and that was to get out of that room with all possible dispatch. His mind made a hasty reconnaissance. The door into the hall was out of the question, for madness lay that way. At least he would have to pass right by that weaving arm. Nor did he relish a blind plunge into the thorny shrubbery beneath his window, and a barefoot scamper across the frosty turf. Of course, there was the bathroom, but that was small comfort if he could not get out of it by another door. In a spasm of concentration, he remembered that he *had* seen another door. Just at the moment of this realization, he heard the comfortingly actual sound of a car coming up the drive, and guessed that it was his host returning. In one magnificent movement, he leaped to the floor, bounded into the bathroom, and bolted its door behind him. The floor of the room beyond was quilted with moonlight. Wading through that, he arrived breathless, but unmolested, in the corridor. Further along he could see the lamp left burning in the entrance hall and hear the clatter of his host closing the front door.

[6]As Barach came hurrying out of the darkness to greet him, Cazalet boomed his delight at such affability, and famished by his long, cold ride, proposed an immediate raid on the larder. The doctor, already sheepish at his recent panic, said nothing about it, and was all for food at once. With lighted candles held high, the foraging party descended on the offices, and mein host was descanting on the merits of cold roast beef, Cheddar cheese, and milk as a light midnight snack, when he stumbled over a bundle on the floor. With a cheerful curse at the old goody of the kitchen who was always leaving something about, he bent to see what it was this time, and let out a whistle of surprise.

Then, by two candles held low, he and the doctor saw something they will not forget while they live. It was the body of the cook. Just the body. The head was gone. On the floor alongside lay a bloody cleaver.

⁷"Old Scripture, by God!" Cazalet cried out, and in a flash, Barach guessed. Still clutching a candle in one hand, he dragged his companion back through the interminable house to the room from which he had fled, motioning him to be silent, tiptoeing the final steps. That precaution was wasted, for a regiment could not have disturbed the rapt contentment of the ceremony still in progress within. The old lunatic had not left his seat by the door. Between his knees he still held the head of the woman he had killed. Scrupulously, happily, crooning at his work, he was plucking out the gray hairs one by one.

Vocabulary

¹Katharine Cornell	²lucid	³mullioned	⁶affability
¹Clemence Dane	²lewd	⁴engrossed	⁶larder
¹links	²topiarian	⁴recurrent	⁶foraging
²Tudor	³reproachful	⁴taut	⁶descanting
²contemptuously	³dowry	⁵ascribed	⁷interminable
²Henry VIII	³mauve	⁵dispatch	⁷rapt
²stripling	³vintage	⁵relish	⁷crooning
²lunatic			

Discussion Questions

1. In paragraph 1 Woollcott says, "If this report were to be published in its own England . . ." What does this mean? Where do you think it was first published? How do you know?

2. Who was Katharine Cornell? What does the use of her name indicate to us as readers of this story?

3. Who is described as "an aged and lunatic father"? What is the root of "lunatic"? What does it mean?

4. How many times is "moonlight" mentioned in the story? In what context?

5. What is "Moonlight Sonata"? Who created it? How does it relate to this story?

MUSIC

ALLAN BLOOM

*Political scientist and writer, **Allan Bloom** (1930-1992) was educated at the University of Chicago; he joined their liberal arts faculty in 1955, moved on to Cornell and the University of Toronto, and returned to Chicago to teach political philosophy. At the time of his death, Bloom was co-director of the John M. Olin Center for Inquiry into the Theory and Practice of Democracy, a forum for reconsideration and anlaysis of the fundamental principles and current practices of American politics and society. Among his books is the bestseller* Closing of the American Mind *(1987), a damning critique of U.S. higher education.*

[1]Civilization or, to say the same thing, education, is the taming or domestication of the soul's raw passions—not suppressing or excising them, which would deprive the soul of its energy—but forming and informing them as art. The goal of harmonizing the enthusiastic part of the soul with what develops later, the rational part, is perhaps impossible to attain. But without it, one can never be whole. Music, or poetry, which is what music becomes as reason emerges, always involves a delicate balance between passion and reason, and even in its highest and most developed forms—religious, warlike and erotic— that balance is always tipped, if ever so slightly, toward the passionate. Music, as everyone experiences, provides an unquestionable justification and a fulfilling pleasure for the activities it accompanies: the soldier who hears the marching band is enthralled and reassured; the religious person is exalted in prayer by the sound of the organ in the church; and the lover is carried away and his conscience stilled by the romantic guitar. Armed with music, man can damn rational doubt. Out of the music emerge the gods that suit it, and they educate us by their example and their commandments.

[2]Plato's Socrates disciplines the ecstasies and thereby provides little consolation or hope to humanity. According to the Socratic formula, the lyrics— speech and, hence, reason—must determine the music—harmony and rhythm. Pure music can never endure this constraint. Students are not in a position to know the pleasures of reason; they can only see it as a disciplinary and repressive parent. But they do see, in the case of Plato, that that parent has figured out what they are up to. Plato teaches that, in order to take the spiritual temperature of an individual or a society, one must "mark the music." To Plato and Nietzsche, the history of music is a series of attempts to give form and beauty to the dark, chaotic, premonitory forces in the soul— to make them serve a higher

purpose, an ideal, to give our human duties a fullness. Bach's religious intentions and Beethoven's revolutionary and humane ones are clear enough examples. Such cultivation of the soul uses the passions and satisfies them while sublimating them and giving them an artistic unity. Those of us whose noblest activities are accompanied by a music that expresses them while providing a pleasure extending from the lowest bodily to the highest spiritual, is whole, and there is no tension in us between the pleasant and the good. By contrast those whose business life is prosaic and unmusical and whose leisure is made up of coarse, intense entertainments, is divided, and each side of their existence is undermined by the other.

[3]Hence, for those who are interested in psychological health, music is at the center of education, both for giving the passions their due and for preparing the soul for the unhampered use of reason. The centrality of such education was recognized by all the ancient educators. It is hardly noticed today that in Aristotle's *Politics* the most important passages about the best regime concern musical education, or that the *Poetics* is an appendix to the *Politics*. Classical philosophy did not censor the singers. It persuaded them. And it gave them a goal, one that was understood by them, until only yesterday. But those who do not notice the role of music in Aristotle and despise it in Plato went to school with Hobbes, Locke and Smith, where such considerations have become unnecessary.

[4]The triumphant Enlightenment rationalism thought that it had discovered other ways to deal with the irrational part of the soul, and that reason needed less support from it. Only in those great critics of Enlightenment and rationalism, Rousseau and Nietzsche, does music return, and they were the most musical of philosophers. Both thought that the passions—and along with them their ministerial arts—had become thin under the rule of reason and that, therefore, people themselves and what they see in the world have become correspondingly thin. Rousseau and Nietzsche wanted to cultivate the enthusiastic states of the soul and to re-experience the Corybantic possession deemed a pathology by Plato. Nietzsche, particularly, sought to tap again the irrational sources of vitality, to replenish our dried-up stream from barbaric sources and thus encouage the Dionysian and the music derivative from it.

[5]This is the significance of rock music. I do not suggest that it has any high intellectual sources. But it has risen to its current heights in the education of the young on the ashes of classical music, and in an atmosphere in which there is no intellectual resistance to attempts to tap the rawest passions. Modern-day rationalists, such as economists, are indifferent to it and what it represents. The irrationalists are all for it. There is no need to fear that "the blond beasts" are going to come forth from the bland souls of our adolescents. But rock music has one appeal only, a barbaric appeal, to sexual desire—not

love, not eros, but sexual desire undeveloped and untutored. It acknowledges the first emanations of children's emerging sensuality and addresses them seriously, eliciting them and legitimating them, not as little sprouts that must be carefully tended in order to grow into gorgeous flowers, but as the real thing. Rock gives children, on a silver platter, with all the public authority of the entertainment industry, everything their parents always used to tell them they had to wait for until they grew up and would understand later.

[6]Young people know that rock has the beat of sexual intercourse. That is why Ravel's *Bolero* is the one piece of classical music that is commonly known and liked by them. In alliance with some real art and a lot of pseudo-art, an enormous industry cultivates the taste for the orgiastic state of feeling connected with sex, providing a constant flood of fresh material for voracious appetites. Never was there an art form directed so exclusively to children.

[7]Ministering to and according with the arousing and cathartic music, the lyrics celebrate puppy love as well as polymorphous attractions, and fortify them against traditional ridicule and shame. The words implicitly and explicitly describe bodily acts that satisfy sexual desire and treat them as its only natural and routine culmination for children who do not yet have the slightest imagination of love, marriage or family. This has a much more powerful effect than does pornography on youngsters, who have no need to watch others do grossly what they can so easily do themselves. Voyeurism is for old perverts; active sexual relations are for the young. All they need is encouragement.

[8]The inevitable corollary of such sexual interest is rebellion against the parental authority that represses it. Selfishness thus becomes indignation and then transforms itself into morality. The sexual revolution must overthrow all forces of domination, the enemies of nature and happiness. From love comes hate, masquerading as social reform. A worldview is balanced on the sexual fulcrum. What were once unconscious or half-conscious childish resentments become the new Scripture. And then comes the longing for the classless, prejudice-free, conflictless, universal society that necessarily results from liberated consciousness—"We Are the World," a pubescent version of *Alle Menschen weerden Bruder*, the fulfillment of which has been inhibited by the political equivalents of Mom and Dad.

[9]These are the three great lyrical themes: sex, hate and a smarmy, hypocritical version of brotherly love. Such polluted sources issue a muddy stream where only monsters can swim. A glance at the videos that project images on the wall of Plato's cave since MTV took it over suffices to prove this. Hitler's image recurs frequently enough in exciting contexts to give none pause. Nothing noble, sublime, profound, delicate, tasteful or even decent can find a place in such tableaux. There is room only for the intense, changing, crude and immediate, which Tocqueville warned us would be the character of democratic art, combined with a pervasiveness, importance and content beyond Tocqueville's wildest imagination.

¹⁰Picture a thirteen-year-old boy sitting in the living room of his family home doing his math assignment while wearing his Walkman headphones or watching MTV. He enjoys the liberties hard won over centuries by the alliance of philosophic genius and political heroism, consecrated by the blood of martyrs; he is provided with comfort and leisure by the most productive economy ever known to mankind; science has penetrated the secrets of nature in order to provide him with the marvelous, lifelike electronic sound and image reproduction he is enjoying. And in what does progress culminate? A pubescent child whose body throbs with orgasmic rhythms; whose feelings are made articulate in hymns to the joys of onanism or the killing of parents; whose ambition is to win fame and wealth in imitating the drag-queen who makes the music. In short, life is made into a nonstop, commercially prepackaged masturbational fantasy.

¹¹This description may seem exaggerated, but only because some would prefer to regard it as such. The continuing exposure to rock music is a reality, not one confined to a particular class or type of child. One need only ask first-year university students what music they listen to, how much of it and what it means to them, in order to discover that the phenomenon is universal in America, that it begins in adolescence or a bit before and continues through the college years. It is the youth culture and, as I have so often insisted, there is now no other countervailing nourishment for the spirit.

¹²Some of this culture's power comes from the fact that it is so loud. It makes conversation impossible, so that much of friendship must be without the shared speech that Aristotle asserts is the essence of friendship and the only true common ground. With rock, illusions of shared feelings, bodily contact and grunted formulas, which are supposed to contain so much meaning beyond speech, are the basis of association. None of this contradicts going about the business of life, attending classes and doing the assignments for them. But the meaningful inner life is with the music.

Vocabulary

¹excising	³Aristotle	⁵eliciting	⁷voyeurism
¹exalted	³Hobbes	⁶Ravel	⁸corollary
¹enthralled	³Locke	⁶pseudo	⁸fulcrum
²Plato	⁴Rousseau	⁶pseudo-art	⁹tableaux
²Socrates	⁴Nietzsche	⁶orgiastic	⁹Tocqueville
²constraint	⁴Corybantic	⁷cathartic	¹⁰consecrated
²chaotic	⁴pathology	⁷polymorphous	¹⁰pubescent
²premonitory	⁴Dionysian	⁷eros	¹⁰onanism
²sublimating	⁵bland	⁷culmination	¹¹countervailling
³regime	⁵emanations		

Discussion Questions

1. Bloom starts this article discussing the dichotomy of passion and reason. Explain his point in your own words.

2. Bloom states that "for those of us who are interested in psychological health, music is at the center of education, both for giving the passions their due and for preparing the soul for the unhampered use of reason." Do you agree or disagree? Explain your answer.

3. Bloom makes references to Plato, Socrates, Ravel's *Bolero*, Rousseau, Locke, Toqueville, Hobbes and *Alle Menschen weerden Bruder*. Briefly explain who or what each of these is.

4. The second part of Bloom's article discusses the role of rock music in society. Summarize Bloom's points in your own words. Do you agree or disagree with Bloom's assessment of rock and roll? Explain your answer.

5. Bloom states, "These are the three great lyrical themes [of rock and roll]: sex, hate, and a smarmy hypocritical version of brotherly love." If you agree with Bloom on this point, find a rock and roll song for each category and explain how it fits that category. If you disagree, create your own categories and explain your choices.

6. Bloom says that rock and roll makes life "into a nonstop, commercially prepackaged masturbational fantasy." Do you think Bloom has effectively supported his assertion? Explain your answer.

THE MYTH OF THE LATIN WOMAN: I JUST MET A GIRL NAMED MARIA
JUDITH ORTIZ COFER

Judith Ortiz Cofer (1952-   ) was born in Hormigueros, Puerto Rico and moved at the age of four with her family to Paterson, NJ. She earned a BA in English from Augusta (Georgia) College in 1974 and an MA in English, from Florida Atlantic University in 1977. A poet and author of fiction and nonfiction, Ms. Cofer is currently Regents' and Franklin Professor of English and Creative Writing at the University of Georgia in Athens, GA.

[1]On a bus trip to London from Oxford University where I was earning some graduate credits one summer, a young man, obviously fresh from a pub, spotted me and as if struck by inspiration went down on his knees in the aisle. With both hands over his heart he broke into an Irish tenor's rendition of "Maria" from *West Side Story*. My politely amused fellow passengers gave his lovely voice the round of gentle applause it deserved. Though I was not quite as amused, I managed my version of an English smile: no show of teeth, no extreme contortions of the facial muscles—I was at this time of my life practicing reserve and cool. Oh, that British control, how I coveted it. But Maria had followed me to London, reminding me of a prime fact of my life: you can leave the Island, master the English language, and travel as far as you can, but if you are a Latina, especially one like me who so obviously belongs to Rita Moreno's[a] gene pool, the Island travels with you.

[2]This is sometimes a very good thing—it may win you that extra minute of someone's attention. But with some people, the same things can make you an island—not so much a tropical paradise as an Alcatraz,[b] a place nobody wants to visit. As a Puerto Rican girl growing up in the United States and wanting like most children to "belong," I resented the stereotype that my Hispanic appearance called forth from many people I met.

[3]Our family lived in a large urban center in New Jersey during the sixties, where life was designed as a microcosm of my parents' casas[c] on the island. We

---

[a]Rita Moreno (1931-   ) is an actress of Puerto Rican heritage who won an Oscar as Best Supporting Actress for her portrayal of Anita, a sexy Hispanic "spitfire," in *West Side Story*.

[b]Alcatraz is a former federal prison, now a tourist attraction, located on an isolated island in San Francisco Bay.

[c]*casa*: house

spoke in Spanish, we ate Puerto Rican food bought at the bodega,[d] and we practiced strict Catholicism complete with Saturday confession and Sunday mass at a church where our parents were accommodated into a one-hour Spanish mass slot, performed by a Chinese priest trained as a missionary for Latin America.

[4]As a girl I was kept under strict surveillance, since virtue and modesty were, by cultural equation, the same as family honor. As a teenager I was instructed on how to behave as a proper senorita. But it was a conflicting message girls got, since the Puerto Rican mothers also encouraged their daughters to look and act like women and to dress in clothes our Anglo friends and their mothers found too "mature" for our age. It was, and is, cultural, yet I often felt humiliated when I appeared at an American friend's party wearing a dress more suitable to a semiformal than to a playroom birthday celebration. At Puerto Rican festivities, neither the music nor the colors we wore could be too loud. I still experience a vague sense of letdown when I'm invited to a "party" and it turns out to be a marathon conversation in hushed tones rather than a fiesta with salsa, laughter, and dancing—the kind of celebration I remember from my childhood.

[5]I remember Career Day in our high school, when teachers told us to come dressed as if for a job interview. It quickly became obvious that to the barrio[e] girls, "dressing up" sometimes meant wearing ornate jewelry and clothing that would be more appropriate (by mainstream standards) for the company Christmas party than as daily office attire. That morning I had agonized in front of my closet, trying to figure out what a "career girl" would wear because, essentially, except for Marlo Thomas[f] on TV, I had no models on which to base my decision. I knew how to dress for school: at the Catholic school I attended we all wore uniforms; I knew how to dress for Sunday mass, and I knew what dresses to wear for parties at my relatives' homes. Though I do not recall the precise details of my Career Day outfit, it must have been a composite of the above choices. But I remember a comment my friend (an Italian-American) made in later years that coalesced my impressions of that day. She said that at the business school she was attending the Puerto Rican girls always stood out for wearing "everything at once." She meant, of course, too much jewelry, too many accessories. On that day at school, we were simply made the negative models by the nuns who were themselves not credible fashion experts to any of

---

[d]*bodega*: small grocery store

[e]*barrio*: neighborhood

[f]Marlo Thomas (1937-   ) is an actress who starred in a late 1960's TV sitcom, *That Girl*, about an aspiring actress from a small town who lived in New York City and somehow managed to dress in the latest fashions while working in temp jobs.

us. But it was painfully obvious to me that to the others, in their tailored skirts and silk blouses, we must have seemed "hopeless" and "vulgar." Though I now know that most adolescents feel out of step much of the time, I also know that for the Puerto Rican girls of my generation that sense was intensified. The way our teachers and classmates looked at us that day in school was just a taste of the culture clash that awaited us in the real world, where prospective employers and men on the street would often misinterpret our tight skirts and jingling bracelets as a come-on.

[6]Mixed cultural signals have perpetuated certain stereotypes—for example, that of the Hispanic woman as the "Hot Tamale" or sexual firebrand. It is a one-dimensional view that the media have found easy to promote. In their special vocabulary, advertisers have designated "sizzling" and "smoldering" as the adjectives of choice for describing not only the foods but also the women of Latin America. From conversations in my house I recall hearing about the harassment that Puerto Rican women endured in factories where the "boss men" talked to them as if sexual innuendo was all they understood and, worse, often gave them the choice of submitting to advances or being fired. It is custom, however, not chromosomes, that leads us to choose scarlet over pale pink. As young girls, we were influenced in our decisions about clothes and colors by the women—older sisters and mothers who had grown up on a tropical island where the natural environment was a riot of primary colors, where showing your skin was one way to keep cool as well as to look sexy. Most important of all, on the island, women perhaps felt freer to dress and move more provocatively, since, in most cases, they were protected by the traditions, mores, and laws of a Spanish/Catholic system of morality and machismo whose main rule was: *You may look at my sister, but if you touch her I will kill you.* The extended family and church structure could provide a young woman with a circle of safety in her small pueblo[g] on the island; if a man "wronged" a girl, everyone would close in to save her family honor.

[7]This is what I have gleaned from my discussions as an adult with older Puerto Rican women. They have told me about dressing in their best party clothes on Saturday nights and going to the town's plaza to promenade with their girlfriends in front of the boys they liked. The males were thus given an opportunity to admire the women and to express their admiration in the form of *piropos:* erotically charged street poems they composed on the spot. I have been subjected to a few *piropos* while visiting the Island, and they can be outrageous, although custom dictates that they must never cross into obscenity. This ritual, as I understand it, also entails a show of studied indifference on the woman's part; if she is "decent," she must not acknowledge the man's impassioned words. So I do understand how things can be lost in translation. When

---

[g]community

a Puerto Rican girl dressed in her idea of what is attractive meets a man from the mainstream culture who has been trained to react to certaintypes of clothing as a sexual signal, a clash is likely to take place. The line I first heard based on this aspect of the myth happened when the boy who took me to my first formal dance leaned over to plant a sloppy overeager kiss painfully on my mouth, and when I didn't respond with sufficient passion said in a resentful tone: "I thought you Latin girls were supposed to mature early"—my first instance of being thought of as a fruit or vegetable—I was supposed to *ripen,* not just grow into Womanhood like other girls.

[8]It is surprising to some of my professional friends that some people, including those who should know better, still put others "in their place." Though rarer, these incidents are still commonplace in my life. It happened to me most recently during a stay at a very classy metropolitan hotel favored by young professional couples for their weddings. Late one evening after the theater, as I walked toward my room with my new colleague (a woman with whom I was coordinating an arts program), a middle-aged man in a tuxedo, a young girl in satin and lace on his arm, stepped directly into our path. With his champagne glass extended toward me, he exclaimed, "Evita!"[h]

[9]Our way blocked, my companion and I listened as the man half-recited, half-bellowed, "Don't Cry for Me, Argentina." When he finished, the young girl said: "How about a round of applause for my daddy?" We complied, hoping this would bring the silly spectacle to a close. I was becoming aware that our little group was attracting the attention of the other guests. "Daddy" must have perceived this too, and he once more barred the way as we tried to walk past him. He began to shout-sing a ditty to the tune of "La Bamba"—except the lyrics were about a girl named Maria whose exploits all rhymed with her name and gonorrhea. The girl kept saying "Oh, Daddy" and looking at me with pleading eyes. She wanted me to laugh along with the others. My companion and I stood silently waiting for the man to end his offensive song. When he finished, I looked not at him but at his daughter. I advised her calmly never to ask her father what he had done in the army. Then I walked between them and to my room. My friend complimented me on my cool handling of the situation. I confessed to her that I really had wanted to push the jerk into the swimming pool. I knew that this same man—probably a corporate executive, well educated, even worldly by most standards—would not have been likely to regale a white woman with a dirty song in public. He would perhaps have checked his impulse by assuming that she could be somebody's wife or mother, or at least

---

[h]Evita is a reference to Eva Peron (1919-1952), the second wife of Argentinian President Juan Peron. She became an immensely popular and powerful political figure with widespread support among labor unions and poor, unskilled workers. Her life is the subject of the popular musical *Evita.*

somebody who might take offense. But to him, I was just an Evita or a Maria: merely a character in his cartoon-populated universe.

[10]Because of my education and my proficiency with the English language, I have acquired many mechanisms for dealing with the anger I experience. This was not true for my parents, nor is it true for the many Latin women working at menial jobs who must put up with stereotypes about our ethnic group such as: "They make good domestics." This is another facet of the myth of the Latin woman in the United States. Its origin is simple to deduce. Work as domestics, waitressing, and factory jobs are all that's available to women with little English and few skills. The myth of the Hispanic menial has been sustained by the same media phenomenon that made "Mammy" from *Gone with the Wind* America's idea of the black woman for generations; Maria, the housemaid or counter girl, is now indelibly etched into the national psyche. The big and the little screens have presented us with the picture of the funny Hispanic maid, mispronouncing words and cooking up a spicy storm in a shiny California kitchen.

[11]This media-engendered image of the Latina in the United States has been documented by feminist Hispanic scholars, who claim that such portrayals are partially responsible for the denial of opportunities for upward mobility among Latinas in the professions. I have a Chicana friend working on a Ph.D. in philosophy at a major university. She says her doctor still shakes his head in puzzled amazement at all the "big words" she uses. Since I do not wear my diplomas around my neck for all to see, I too have on occasion been sent to that "kitchen," where some think I obviously belong.

[12]One such incident that has stayed with me, though I recognize it as a minor offense, happened on the day of my first public poetry reading. It took place in Miami in a boat-restaurant where we were having lunch before the event. I was nervous and excited as I walked in with my notebook in my hand. An older woman motioned me to her table. Thinking (foolish me) that she wanted me to autograph a copy of my brand new slender volume of verse, I went over. She ordered a cup of coffee from me, assuming that I was the waitress. Easy enough to mistake my poems for menus, I suppose. I know that it wasn't an intentional act of cruelty, yet of all the good things that happened that day, I remember that scene most clearly, because it reminded me of what I had to overcome before anyone would take me seriously. In retrospect I understand that my anger gave my reading fire, that I have almost always taken doubts in my abilities as a challenge—and that the result is, most times, a feeling of satisfaction at having won a convert when I see the cold, appraising eyes warm to my words, the body language change, the smile that indicates that I have opened some avenue for communication. That day I read to that woman and her lowered eyes told me that she was embarrassed at her little faux pas, and when I willed her to look up at me, it was my victory, and she graciously allowed me to punish her with my full attention. We shook hands at the end of

the reading, and I never saw her again. She has probably forgotten the whole thing but maybe not.

[13]Yet I am one of the lucky ones. My parents made it possible for me to acquire a stronger footing in the mainstream culture by giving me the chance at an education. And books and art have saved me from the harsher forms of ethnic and racial prejudice that many of my Hispanic *companeras* have had to endure. I travel a lot around the United States, reading from my books of poetry and my novel, and the reception I most often receive is one of positive interest by people who want to know more about my culture. There are, however, thousands of Latinas without the privilege of an education or the entree into society that I have. For them life is a struggle against the misconceptions perpetuated by the myth of the Latina as whore, domestic, or criminal. We cannot change this by legislating the way people look at us. The transformation, as I see it, has to occur at a much more individual level. My personal goal in my public life is to try to replace the old pervasive stereotypes and myths about Latinas with a much more interesting set of realities. Every time I give a reading, I hope the stories I tell, the dreams and fears I examine in my work, can achieve some universal truth which will get my audience past the particulars of my skin color, my accent, or my clothes.

[14]I once wrote a poem in which I called us Latinas "God's brown daughters." This poem is really a prayer of sorts, offered upward, but also, through the human-to-human channel of art, outward. It is a prayer for communication, and for respect. In it, Latin women pray "in Spanish to an Anglo God/with a Jewish heritage," and they are "fervently hoping/that if not omnipotent/at least He be bilingual."

Vocabulary

[1]covet	[6]innuendo	[10]menial	[12]convert
[3]microcosm	[6]mores	[10]deduce	[12]faux pas
[5]coalesced	[6]machismo	[10] psyche	[13]entree
[5]credible	[7]gleaned	[11]engendered	[13]pervasive
[6]perpetuated	[9] regale	[12]retrospect	

Discussion Questions

1. In paragraph 2 Professor Cofer uses the metaphor of Alcatraz prison located on an island in San Francisco Bay, "a place nobody wants to visit." What are some further implications of this metaphor?

2. Paragraph 3, consisting of only two sentences, is rich in detail. Expand upon some of the ideas expressed in this paragraph.

3. What is the "conflicting message" that Cofer describes in paragraph 4?

How does describing this here and in the following paragraph set the stage for a description of the problems she will encounter later as a grownup?

4. What other cultural influences from her place of birth contribute to problems she later faces in her adopted country?

5. What stereotypes of Latina women does Cofer describe that affect them in the workplace? This essay first appeared nearly 20 years ago. Do you think her observations are still accurate?

6. What does Cofer indicate is the single most important factor in her ability to rise above the stereotypical role imposed upon Latina women in America?

from **NO-NO BOY**

JOHN OKADA

John Okada (1923-1970) attended the University of Washington and Columbia University. He served in the U.S. Army in World War II. No-No Boy, *originally published in 1957, is his only published novel. He died in obscurity believing that Asian-Americans had rejected his work. Parts of* No-No-Boy *are now frequently used in many anthologies.*

¹December the Seventh of the year 1941 was the day when the Japanese bombs fell on Pearl Harbor.

²As of that moment, the Japanese in the United States became, by virtue of their ineradicable brownness and the slant eyes which, upon close inspection, will seldom appear slanty, animals of a different breed. The moment the impact of the words solemnly being transmitted over the several million radios of the nation struck home, everything Japanese and everyone Japanese became despicable.

³The college professor, finding it suddenly impossible to meet squarely the gaze of his polite, serious, but now too Japanese-ish star pupil, coughed on his pipe and assured the lad that things were a mess. Conviction lacking, he failed at his attempt to be worldly and assuring. He mumbled something about things turning out one way or the other sooner or later and sighed with relief when the little fellow, who hardly ever smiled and, now, probably never would, stood up and left the room.

⁴In a tavern, a drunk, irrigating the sponge in his belly, let it be known to the world that he never thought much about the sneaky Japs and that this proved he was right. It did not matter that he owed his Japanese landlord three-weeks' rent, nor that industrious Japanese had often picked him off the sidewalk and deposited him on his bed. Someone set up a round of beer for the boys in the place and, further fortified, he announced with patriotic tremor in his alcoholic tones that he would be first in line at the recruiting office the very next morning. That night the Japanese landlord picked him off the sidewalk and put him to bed.

⁵Jackie was a whore and the news made her unhappy because she got two bucks a head and the Japanese boys were clean and considerate and hot and fast. Aside from her professional interest in them, she really liked them. She was sorry and, in her sorrow, she suffered a little with them.

⁶A truck and a keen sense of horse-trading had provided a good living for Herman Fine. He bought from and sold primarily to Japanese hotel-keep-

ers and grocers. No transaction was made without considerable haggling and clever maneuvering, for the Japanese could be and often were a shifty lot whose solemn promises frequently turned out to be groundwork for more extended and complex stratagems to cheat him out of his rightful profit. Herman Fine listened to the radio and cried without tears for the Japanese, who, in an instant of time that was not even a speck on the big calendar, had taken their place beside the Jew. The Jew was used to suffering. The writing for them was etched in caked and dried blood over countless generations upon countless generations. The Japanese did not know. They were proud, too proud, and they were ambitious, too ambitious. Bombs had fallen and, in less time than it takes a Japanese farmer's wife in California to run from the fields into the house and give birth to a child, the writing was scrawled for them. The Jap-Jew would look in the mirror this Sunday night and see a Jap-Jew.

[7]The indignation, the hatred, the patriotism of the American people shifted into full-throated condemnation of the Japanese who blotted their land. The Japanese who were born Americans and remained Japanese because biology does not know the meaning of patriotism no longer worried about whether they were Japanese-Americans or American-Japanese. They were Japanese, just as were their Japanese mothers and Japanese fathers and Japanese brothers and sisters. The radio had said as much.

[8]First, the real Japanese-Japanese were rounded up. These real Japanese-Japanese were Japanese nationals who had the misfortune to be diplomats and businessmen and visiting professors. They were put on a boat and sent back to Japan.

[9]Then the alien Japanese, the ones who had been in America for two, three, or even four decades, were screened, and those found to be too actively Japanese were transported to the hinterlands and put in a camp.

[10]The security screen was sifted once more and, this time, the lesser lights were similarly plucked and deposited. An old man, too old, too feeble, and too scared, was caught in the net. In his pocket was a little, black book. He had been a collector for the Japan-Help-the-Poor-and-Starving-and-Flooded-Out-and-Homeless-and-Crippled-and-What-Have-You Fund. "Yamada-san, 50 American cents; Okada-san, two American dollars; Watanabe-san, 24 American cents; Takizakisan, skip this month because boy broke leg"; and so on down the page. Yamada-san, Okada-san, Watanabe-san, Takizaki-san, and so on down the page were whisked away from their homes while weeping families wept until the tears must surely have been wept dry, and then wept some more.

[11]By now, the snowball was big enough to wipe out the rising sun. The big rising sun would take a little more time, but the little rising sun which was the Japanese in countless Japanese communities in the coastal states of Washington, Oregon, and California presented no problem. The whisking and transporting of Japanese and the construction of camps with barbed wire and

ominous towers supporting fully armed soldiers in places like Idaho and Wyoming and Arizona, places which even Hollywood scorned for background, had become skills which demanded the utmost of America's great organizing ability.

[12]And so, a few months after the seventh day of December of the year nineteen forty-one, the only Japanese left on the west coast of the United States was Matsusaburo Inabukuro who, while it has been forgotten whether he was Japanese-American or American-Japanese, picked up an "I am Chinese" –not American or American-Chinese or Chinese-American but "I am Chinese" – button and got a job in a California shipyard.

[13]Two years later a good Japanese-American who had volunteered for the army sat smoking in the belly of a B-24 on his way back to Guam from a reconnaissance flight to Japan. His job was to listen through his earphones, which were attached to a high-frequency set, and jot down air-ground messages spoken by Japanese-Japanese in Japanese planes and in Japanese radio shacks.

[14]The lieutenant who operated the radar-detection equipment was a blond giant from Nebraska.

[15]The Lieutenant from Nebraska said: "Where you from?"

[16]The Japanese-American who was an American soldier answered: "No place in particular."

[17]"You got folks?

[18]"Yeah, I got folks."

[19]"Where at?"

[20]"Wyoming, out in the desert."

[21]"Farmers, huh?"

[22]"Not quite."

[23]"What's that mean?

[24]"Well, it's this way...." And then the Japanese-American whose folks were still Japanese-Japanese, or else they would not be in a camp with barbed wire and watchtowers with soldiers holding rifles, told the blond giant from Nebraska about the removal of the Japanese from the Coast, which was called the evacuation, and about the concentration camps, which were called relocation centers.

[25]The lieutenant listened and he didn't believe it. He said: "That's funny. Now, tell me again."

[26]The Japanese-American soldier of the American army told it again and didn't change a word.

[27]The lieutenant believed him this time. "Hell's bells," he exclaimed, "if they'd done that to me, I wouldn't be sitting in the belly of a broken-down B-24 going back to Guam from a reconnaissance mission to Japan."

[28]"I got reasons," said the Japanese-American soldier soberly.

[29]"They could kiss my ass," said the Lieutenant from Nebraska.

[30]"I got reasons," said the Japanese-American soldier soberly, and he was

thinking about a lot of things but mostly about his friend who didn't volunteer for the army because his father had been picked up in the second screening and was in a different camp from the one he and his mother and two sisters were in. Later on, the army tried to draft his friend out of the relocation camp into the army and the friend had stood before the judge and said let my father out of that other camp and come back to my mother who is an old woman but misses him enough to want to sleep with him and I'll try on the uniform. The judge said he couldn't do that and the friend said he wouldn't be drafted and they sent him to the federal prison where he now was.

[31]"What the hell are we fighting for?" said the lieutenant from Nebraska.

[32]"I got reasons," said the Japanese-American soldier soberly and thought some more about his friend who was in another kind of uniform because they wouldn't let his father go to the same camp with his mother and sisters.

Vocabulary

[2]ineradicable   [9]hinterlands   [11]ominous   [13]reconnaissance
[6]stratagems

Discussion Questions

1. John Okada starts this excerpt with the various reactions of Americans to the Japanese bombing of Pearl Harbor. Summarize these reactions. Do any of these reactions surprise you? Discuss why or why not.

2. The novel *No-No Boy* is filled with irony. Look up the meaning of irony and find at least three examples in this excerpt. Discuss what makes each ironic.

3. The Japanese-American soldier tells the Lieutenant from Nebraska that "I got reasons" for being in the army. What do you think are his reasons? Do you agree with them?

4. Most of the characters are described by their occupation, for example, "the college professor" and "the Japanese landlord." Why do you think Okada didn't name these characters but rather gave them titles?

5. What is your view of the resettlement of the Nisei (Japanese-Americans) that was carried out by the U.S. government during this period? Why did the government adopt this policy? Do you think it was the right thing to do at the time?

6. Do you think the Japanese-American soldier in the story has choices? If so, what are they? If not, why not?

7. Read Executive Order No. 9066 and Civilian Exclusion Order No. 34 on pages 367 and 369 of this text. Do you think Okada's depiction of the Japanese-American internments in his novel exaggerates the actual event? Explain the reason for your answer.

FROM *THE ORIGIN OF SPECIES* AND *THE DESCENT OF MAN*

CHARLES DARWIN

Charles Darwin (1809-1882) received his divinity degree from Cambridge University after studying medicine at Edinburgh University. He accepted an invitation to serve as an unpaid naturalist for a five-year expedition to South America's Pacific Coast on the H.M.S. Beagle. *Darwin's research from this journey formed the basis of his famous book* On The Origin of Species by Means of Natural Selection. *Published in 1859, his theory of evolution, which challenged beliefs about the creation of life, caused a storm of controversy.*

The Origin of Species
The Struggle for Existence

[1]All organic beings are exposed to severe competition. Nothing is easier than to admit in words the truth of the universal struggle for life, or more difficult—at least I have found it so—than constantly to bear this conclusion in mind. We behold the face of nature bright with gladness; we often see superabundance of food. We do not see—or we forget—that the birds which are beautifully singing around us live mostly on insects or seeds and are thus constantly destroying life. Or we forget how largely these songsters, or their eggs or nestlings, are destroyed by birds and beasts of prey. We do not always bear in mind that, although food may now be plentiful, it is not so at all seasons of each recurring year.

[2]A struggle for existence inevitably follows from the high rate at which all organic beings tend to increase. Every being, which during its natural lifetime produces several eggs or seed, must suffer destruction during some period of its life and during some season or occasional year. Otherwise, on the principle of geometrical increase, its numbers would quickly become so inordinately great that no country could support the product. Hence, as more individuals are produced than can possibly survive, there must in every case be a struggle for existence, either one individual with another of the same species or with the individuals of distinct species or with the physical conditions of life. It is the doctrine of Malthus applied with manifold force to the whole animal and vegetable kingdoms.

[3]There is no exception to the rule that every organic being naturally increases at so high a rate that, if not destroyed, the earth would soon be covered

by the progeny of a single pair. Even slow-breeding man has doubled in twenty-five years, and at this rate, in less than a thousand years, there would literally not be standing room for his progeny.

[4]In a state of nature there are very few animals which do not mate at least annually. Hence we may confidently assert that all animals are tending to increase at a geometrical ratio so that all would rapidly stock any area in which they could anyhow exist—and that this geometrical tendency to increase must be checked by destruction at some period of life.

[5]Our familiarity with the larger domestic animals tends, I think, to mislead us: we see no great destruction falling on them, but we do not keep in mind that thousands are annually slaughtered for food, and that in a state of nature an equal number would have somehow to be disposed of.

[6]In looking at Nature, it is most necessary to keep the foregoing considerations always in mind—never to forget that every single organic being may be said to be striving to the utmost to increase in numbers; that each lives by a struggle at some period of its life; that heavy destruction falls either on the young or old, during each generation or at recurrent intervals. Lighten any check, mitigate the destruction ever so little, and the number of the species will almost instantaneously increase to any amount.

Natural Selection or Survival of the Fittest

[7]Can it be thought improbable, seeing that variations useful to man have undoubtedly occurred, that other variations useful in some way to each being in the great and complex battle of life, should occur in the course of many successive generations? If such do occur, can we doubt (remembering that many more individuals are born than can possibly survive) that individuals having any advantage, however slight, over others, would have the best chance of surviving and of procreating their kind?

[8]On the other hand, we may feel sure that any variation in the least degree injurious would be rigidly destroyed. This preservation of favorable individual difference and variation and the destruction of those which are injurious, I have called Natural Selection, or the Survival of the Fittest.

[9]We shall best understand the probable course of natural selection by taking the case of a country undergoing some slight physical change, for instance, of climate. The proportional numbers of its inhabitants will almost immediately undergo a change, and some will probably become extinct.

[10]It may metaphorically be said that Natural Selection is daily and hourly scrutinizing, throughout the world, the slightest variation; rejecting those that are bad, preserving and adding up all that are good; silently and insensibly working, *whenever and wherever opportunity offers,* at the improvement of each organic being in relation to its organic and inorganic conditions of life. We see nothing of these slow changes in progress until the hand of time has marked

the lapse of ages, and so imperfect is our view into long-past geological ages that we see only that the forms of life are now different from what they formerly were.

[11]It has been asserted that of the best short-beaked tumbler-pigeons a greater number perish in the egg than are able to get out of it; so that fanciers assist in the act of hatching. Now if nature had to make the beak of a full-grown pigeon very short for the bird's own advantage, the process of modification would be very slow, and there would be simultaneously the most rigorous selection of all the young birds within the egg, which had the most powerful and hardest beaks, for all with weak beaks would inevitably perish; or, more delicate and more easily broken shells might be selected, the thickness of the shell being known to vary like every other structure.

[12]It may be well here to remark that with all beings there must be much fortuitous destruction, which can have little or no influence on the course of natural selection. For instance, a vast number of eggs or seeds are annually devoured, and these could be modified through natural selection only if they varied in some manner which protected them from their enemies. Yet many of these eggs or seeds would perhaps, if not destroyed, have yielded individuals better adapted to their conditions of life than any of those which happened to survive.

[13]So again a vast number of mature animals and plants, whether or not they be the best adapted to their conditions, must be annually destroyed by accidental causes, which would not be in the least degree mitigated by certain changes of structure or constitution which would in other ways be beneficial to the species.

Illustrations of the Action of Natural Selection, or, The Survival of the Fittest

[14]In order to make it clear how, I believe, natural selection acts, I must beg permission to give one or two illustrations. Let us take the case of a wolf, which preys on various animals, securing some by craft, some by strength and some by fleetness; and let us suppose that the fleetest prey, a deer for instance, had from any change in the country, increased in numbers or that other prey had decreased in numbers during that season of the year when the wolf was hardest pressed for food. Under such circumstances the swiftest and slimmest wolves would have the best chance of surviving and so be preserved or selected—provided always that they retained the strength to master their prey at this or some other period of the year when they were compelled to prey on other animals.

[15]I can see no more reason to doubt that this would be the result, than that a breeder should be able to improve the fleetness of greyhounds by careful and methodical selection, or by that kind of unconscious selection which follows from each owner tying to keep the best dogs without any thought of modifying the breed.

[16]I may add that according to Mr. Pierce, there are two varieties of the wolf inhabiting the Catskill Mountains, in the United States, one with a light greyhound-like form, which pursues deer, and the other bulky, with shorter legs, which more frequently attacks the shepherd's flocks.

Sexual Selection

[17]This leads me to say a few words on what I have called Sexual Selection. This form of selection depends not on a struggle for existence in relation to other organic beings or to external conditions, but on a struggle between the individuals of one sex, generally the males, for the possession of the other sex.

[18]The result is not death to the unsuccessful competitor, but few or no offspring. Sexual selection is, therefore, less rigorous than natural selection. Generally, the most vigorous males, those which are best fitted for their places in nature, will leave most progeny. But in many cases, victory depends not so much on general vigor, as on having special weapons, confined to the male sex. A hornless stag or spurless rooster would have poor chance of leaving numerous offspring. Sexual selection, by always allowing the victor to breed, might surely give indomitable courage, length to the spur, and strength to the wing to strike in the spurred leg, in nearly the same manner as does the brutal cockfighter by the careful selection of his best roosters.

[19]How low in the scale of nature the law of battle descends I know not; male alligators have been described as fighting, bellowing, and whirling round, like Indians in a war dance, for the possession of the females; male salmons have been observed fighting all day long; male stag-beetles sometimes bear wounds from the huge mandibles of other males; the males of certain four-winged insects have been frequently seen fighting for a particular female who sits by, an apparently unconcerned beholder of the struggle, and then retires with the conqueror.

Conclusion

[20]I formerly spoke to very many naturalists on the subject of evolution and never once met with any sympathetic agreement. It is probable that some did then believe in evolution, but they were either silent or expressed themselves so ambiguously that it was not easy to understand their meaning. Since the first edition of the present work appeared, however, things are wholly changed and almost every naturalist admits the great principle of evolution.

[21]Analogy would lead me to the belief that all animals and plants are descended from some one prototype. With all organic beings excepting perhaps some of the very lowest, sexual production seems to be essentially similar. With all, as far as is at present known, the germinal vesicle is the same so that all organisms start from a common origin.

[22]If we look even to the two main divisions—namely, to the animal and

vegetable kingdoms—certain low forms are so far intermediate in character that naturalists have disputed to which kingdom they should be referred. As Professor Asa Gray has remarked, "the spores and other reproductive bodies of many of the lower algae may claim to have first a characteristically animal and then an unequivocally vegetable existence." Therefore, on the principle of natural selection with divergence of character, it does not seem incredible that, from such low and intermediate form, both animals and plants may have been developed; and if we admit this we must likewise admit that all the organic beings which have ever lived on this earth may be descended from some one primordial form.

[23]Judging from the past, we safely infer that not one living species will transmit its unaltered likeness to a distant futurity. And of the species now living very few will transmit progeny of any kind to a far distant futurity; for the manner in which all organic beings are grouped, shows that the greater number of species in each genus, and all the species in many genera, have left no descendants but have become utterly extinct.

[24]We can so far take a prophetic glance into futurity as to foretell that it will be the common and widely spread species, belonging to the larger and dominant groups within each class, which will ultimately prevail and procreate new and dominant species. As all the living forms of life are the lineal descendants of those which lived long before the Cambrian epoch, we may feel certain that the ordinary succession by generation has never once been broken and that no cataclysm has desolated the whole world. Hence, we may look with some confidence to a secure future of great length. And as natural selection works solely by and for the good of each being, all corporal and mental endowments will tend to progress toward perfection.

* * * * * * * *

The Descent of Man

[25]It seems worthwhile to see how far the principle of evolution would throw light on some of the more complex problems in the natural history of man. False facts are highly injurious to the progress of science, for they often endure long; but false views, if supported by some evidence, do little harm, for everyone takes pleasure in trying to prove their falseness; and when this is done, one path towards error is closed and the road to truth is often at the same time opened.

[26]The main conclusion here arrived at, and now held by many naturalists who are well competent to form a sound judgment, is that man is descended from some less highly organized form. The grounds upon which this conclusion rests will never be shaken, for the close similarity between man and the lower animals in embryonic development, as well as in innumerable points of

structure and construction, both of high and of the most trifling importance—the rudiments which he retains and the abnormal reversions to which he is occasionally liable—are facts which cannot be disputed.

[27]The great principle of evolution stands up clear and firm when these groups of facts are considered in connection with others, such as the mutual affinities of the members of the same group, their geographical distribution in past and present times, and their geological succession. It is incredible that all these facts should speak falsely.

[28]He who is not content to look at the phenomena of nature as disconnected cannot any longer believe that man is the work of a separate act of creation. He will be forced to admit that the close resemblance of the embryo of man to that, for instance, of a dog—the construction of his skull, limbs and whole frame on the same plan with that of other mammals, independently of the use to which the parts may be put—the occasional reappearance of various structures, for instance of several muscles, which man does not normally possess but which are common to the Quadrumana—and a crowd of analogous facts—all point in the plainest manner to the conclusion that man is the co-descendent with other mammals of a common progenitor.

[29]Through the means just specified, aided perhaps by others as yet undiscovered, man has been raised to his present state. But since he attained to the rank of manhood, he has diverged into distinct races, or as they may more fitly be called, sub-species. Some of these, such as the Negro and European, are so distinct that, if specimens had been brought to a naturalist without any further information, they would undoubtedly have been considered by him as good and true species. Nevertheless all the races agree in so many unimportant details of structure and in so many mental peculiarities that these can be accounted for only by inheritance from a common progenitor and a progenitor thus characterized would probably deserve to rank as man.

[30]By considering the embryological structure of man—the homologies which he presents with the lower animals—the rudiments which he retains—and the reversions to which he is liable, we can partly recall in imagination the former condition of our early progenitors and can approximately place them in their proper place in the zoological series. We thus learn that man is descended from a hairy, tailed quadruped, probably arboreal in its habits, and an inhabitant of the Old World.

[31]This creature, if its whole structure had been examined by a naturalist, would have been classed amongst the Quadrumana, as surely as the still more ancient progenitor of the Old and New World monkeys. The Quadrumana and all the higher mammals are probably derived from an ancient marsupial animal and this through a long series of diversified forms, from some amphibian-like creature and this again from some fish-like animal.

[32]In the dim obscurity of the past we can see that the early progenitor

of all the Vertebrata must have been an aquatic animal provided with brachiae, with the two sexes united in the same individual, and with the most important organs of the body (such as the brain and heart) imperfectly or not at all developed. This animal seems to have been more like the larvae of the existing marine Ascidians than any other known form.

[33]The high standard of our intellectual powers and moral disposition is the greatest difficulty which presents itself after we have been driven to this conclusion on the origin of man. But everyone who admits the principle of evolution must see that the mental powers of the higher animals, which are same in kind with those of man, though so different in degree, are capable of advancement.

[34]Thus, the interval between the mental powers of one of the higher apes and of a fish is immense; yet, their development does not offer any special difficulty, for with our domesticated animals the mental faculties are certainly variable, and the variations are inherited. No one doubts that they are of the utmost importance to animals in a state of nature. Therefore, the conditions are favorable for their development through natural selection. The same conclusion may be extended to man; the intellect must have been all-important to him, even at a very remote period, as enabling him to invent and use language, to make weapons, tools, traps, etc., where with the aid of his social habits, he long ago became the most dominant of all living creatures.

[35]A great stride in the development of the intellect will have followed as soon as the half-art and half-instinct of language came into use, for the continued use of language will have reacted on the brain and produced an inherited effect; and this again will have reacted on the improvement of language. As Mr. Chancey Wright has well remarked, the largeness of the brain in man relative to his body, compared with the lower animals, may be attributed in chief part to the early use of some simple form of language—that wonderful engine which affixes signs to all sorts of objects and qualities and excites trains of thought which would never arise from the mere impression of the senses, or they did arise, could not be followed out.

[36]The belief in God has often been advanced as not only the greatest but the most complete of all the distinctions between man and the lower animals. It is, however, impossible to maintain that this belief is innate or instinctive in man. On the other hand, a belief in all-pervading spiritual agencies seems to be universal and apparently follows from a considerable advance in man's reason and from a still greater advance in his faculties of imagination, curiosity and wonder. I am aware that the assumed instinctive belief in God has been used by many persons as an argument for His existence. But this is a rash argument, as we should then be compelled to believe in the existence of many cruel and malignant spirits only a little more powerful than man, for the belief in them is far more general that in a beneficent Deity. The idea of a universal and beneficent

Creator does not seem to arise in the mind of man until he has been elevated by long-continued culture.

[37]I am aware that the conclusions arrived at in this work will be denounced by some as highly irreligious, but those who denounce them need to show why it is more irreligious to explain the origin of man as a distinct species by descent from some lower form, through the laws of variation and natural selection, than to explain the birth of the individual through the laws of ordinary reproduction. The birth both of the species and of the individual are equally parts of the grand sequence of events, which our minds refuse to accept as the result of blind chance.

* * * * * * * *

[38]Sexual selection has been treated at great length in this work, for, as I have attempted to show, it has played an important part in the history of the organic world. In the several great classes of the animal kingdom—in mammals, birds, reptiles, fishes, insects, and even crustaceans—the differences between the sexes follow nearly the same rules. The males are almost always the wooers, and they alone are armed with special weapons for fighting with their rivals. They are generally larger and stronger than the females and are endowed with the requisite qualities of courage and pugnacity. They are provided, either exclusively or in a much higher degree than the females, with organs for vocal or instrumental music, and with odoriferous glands. They are ornamental with infinitely diversified appendages, and with the most brilliant or conspicuous colors, often arranged in elegant patterns, while the females are unadorned. When the sexes differ in more important structures, it is the male which is provided with special sense-organs for discovering the female, with locomotive organs for reaching her, and often with prehensile organs for holding her.

[39]The males (passing over a few exceptional cases) are the more active in courtship; they are the better armed, and are rendered the more attractive in various ways. It is to be especially observed that the males display their attractions with elaborate care in the presence of the females; and that they rarely or never display them excepting during the season of love. It is incredible that all this should be purposeless.

[40]Bearing in mind these facts, and the marked results of man's unconscious selection, when applied to domesticated animals and cultivated plants, it seems to me almost certain that if the individuals of one sex were, during a long series of generations, to prefer pairing with certain individuals of the other sex, characterized in one peculiar manner, the offspring would slowly but surely become modified in this same manner. I have not attempted to conceal that, excepting when the males are more numerous than the females, or when polygamy prevails, it is doubtful how the more attractive males succeed in leav-

ing a large number of offspring to inherit their superiority in ornaments or other charms than the less attractive males; but I have shown that this would probably follow from the females—especially the more vigorous ones, which would be the first to breed—preferring not only the more attractive but at the same time the more vigorous and victorious males.

[41]Everyone who admits the principle of evolution, and yet faces great difficulty in admitting that female mammals, birds, reptiles, and fish, could have acquired the high taste implied by the beauty of the males, and which generally coincides with our own standard, should reflect that the nerve-cells of the brain in the highest as well as in the lowest members of the Vertebrate series, are derived from those of the common progenitor of this great Kingdom. For we can thus see how it has come to pass that certain mental faculties, in various and widely distinct groups of animals, have been developed in nearly the same manner and to nearly the same degree.

* * * * * * * *

[42]Man scans with scrupulous care the character and pedigree of his horses, cattle, and dogs before he matches them; but when he comes to his own marriage he rarely, or never, takes any such care. He is impelled by nearly the same motives as the lower animals, when they are left to their own free choice, though he is so far superior to them that he highly values mental charms and virtues. On the other hand he is strongly attracted by mere wealth or rank. Yet he might by selection do something not only for the bodily constitution and frame of his offspring, but for their intellectual and moral qualities. Both sexes ought to refrain from marriage if they are in any marked degree inferior in body or mind; but such hopes are Utopian and will never be even partially realized until the laws of inheritance are thoroughly known. Everyone does good service, who aids toward this end. When the principles of breeding and inheritance are better understood, we shall not hear ignorant members of our legislature rejecting with scorn a plan for ascertaining whether or not consanguineous marriages are injurious to man.

[43]The advancement of the welfare of mankind is a most intricate problem: all ought to refrain from marriage who cannot avoid abject poverty for their children; for poverty is not only a great evil, but tends to its own increase by leading to recklessness in marriage. On the other hand, as Mr. Galton has remarked, if the prudent avoid marriage, while the reckless marry, the inferior members tend to supplant the better members of society. Man, like every other animal, has no doubt advanced to his present high condition through a struggle for existence consequent on his rapid multiplication; and if he is to advance still higher, it is to be feared that he must remain subject to a severe struggle. Otherwise he would sink into indolence, and the more gifted men would not

be more successful in the battle of life than the less gifted. Hence our natural rate of increase, though leading to many and obvious evils, must not be greatly diminished by any means. There should be open competition for all men; and the most able should not be prevented by laws or customs from succeeding best and rearing the largest number of offspring.

* * * * * * * *

[44]The main conclusion arrived at in this work, namely, that man is descended from some lowly organized form, will, I regret to think, be highly distasteful to many. But there can hardly be a doubt that we are descended from barbarians. The astonishment which I felt on first seeing a party of Fuegians on a wild and broken shore will never be forgotten by me, for the reflection at once rushed into my mind—such were our ancestors. These men were absolutely naked and bedaubed with paint, their long hair was tangled, their mouths, frothed with excitement, and their expression was wild, startled, and distrustful. They possessed hardly any arts, and like wild animals lived on what they could catch; they had no government and were merciless to every one not of their own small tribe. He who has seen a savage in his native land will not feel much shame if forced to acknowledge that the blood of some more humble creature flows in his veins. For my own part I would as soon be descended from that heroic little monkey who braved his dreaded enemy in order to save the life of his keeper, or from that old baboon, who descending from the mountains, carried away in triumph his young comrade from a crowd of astonished dogs, as from a savage who delights to torture his enemies, offers up bloody sacrifices, practices infanticide without remorse, treats his wives like slaves, knows no decency, and is haunted by the grossest superstitions.

[45]Man may be excused for feeling some pride at having risen, though not through his own exertions, to the very summit of the organic scale; and the fact of his having thus risen, instead of having been aboriginally placed there, may give him hope for a still higher destiny in the distant future. But we are not here concerned with hopes or fears, only with the truth as far as our reason permits us to discover it; and I have given the evidence to the best of my ability. We must, however, acknowledge, as it seems to me, that man with all his noble qualities, with sympathy which feels for the most debased, with benevolence which extends not only to other men but to the humblest living creature, with his godlike intellect which has penetrated into the movements and constitution of the solar system—with all these exalted powers—man still bears in his bodily frame the indelible stamp of his lowly origin.

Vocabulary

[1]organic	[21]vesicle	[28]phenomena	[38]pugnacity
[1]recurring	[22]divergence	[28]quadrumanna	[38]appendages
[2]inordinately	[22]primordial	[30]homologies	[38]prehensile
[2]Malthus	[23]infer	[31]marsupial	[40]polygamy
[3]progeny	[23]genus	[32]Vertebrata	[42]impelled
[6]mitigate	[23]genera	[32]brachiae	[42]Utopian
[7]procreating	[24]prophetic	[32]larvae	[42]ascertaining
[10]metaphorically	[24]lineal	[32]marine	[42]consanguineous
[10]inorganic	[24]Cambrian	[32]ascidians	[43]abject
[10]scrutinizing	[24]epoch	[36]innate	[42]indolence
[11]rigorous	[24]cataclysm	[36]pervading	[44]bedaubed
[12]fortuitous	[24]corporal	[36]faculties	[44]frothed
[18]indomitable	[24]endowments	[36]beneficent	[44]infanticide
[19]mandibles	[26]embryonic	[36]deity	[45]aboriginally
[20]ambiguously	[26]rudiments	[37]irreligious	[45]debased
[22]analogy	[26]reversions	[38]crustaceans	[45]exalted
[21]prototype	[27]affinities	[38]wooers	[45]indelible
[21]germinal			

Discussion Questions

Origin of Species

1. Darwin states, "All organic beings are exposed to severe competition." Quote the example Darwin gives and then give one of your own.

2. Darwin also states, "A struggle for existence inevitably follows from the high rate at which all organic beings tend to increase." In your own words, explain what this means.

3. Who is Malthus (paragraph 2)? Why would Darwin mention him?

4. Explain Darwin's reason for some individuals' survival over others, in other words how Natural Selection, or Survival of the Fittest, works.

5. Explain the difference between Natural Selection and Sexual Selection.

6. What kind of prey does the bulky, short-legged Catskill Mountain wolf go after? Why?

7. Darwin concludes this section with "And as natural selection works solely for the good of each being, all corporal and mental endowments will tend to progress toward perfection." What does this mean? Do you agree? Why? Why not?

8. Read "Rats: Who's Racing Whom?" by Des Kennedy beginning on page 464 of this text. What connections do you see between Darwin's assertions and the rats' behavior?

The Descent of Man

1. Upon what evidence does Darwin base his conclusion that "man is descended from some less highly organized form"?

2. Sketch Darwin's evolutionary ladder leading to man, starting from the "larvae of the existing marine Ascidians."

3. What does Darwin say is the single most important factor in making man the "most dominant of all living creatures"?

4. Related to 3 above, how does Darwin explain the "largeness of the brain in man relative to his body"?

5. In your opinion, do Darwin's comments concerning the male role in sexual selection hold true for *Homo sapiens*?

6. What does Darwin say about the role of the female in sexual selection in regard to the passing on of desirable traits?

7. Darwin says, "Both sexes ought to refrain from marriage if they are in any marked degree inferior in body or mind; but such hopes are Utopian . . ." What does this mean? What is the meaning of the term "eugenics"?

8. Look at the front page of the July 22, 1925 edition of the New York *Times* on the next page. How does the lead story ("Scopes Guilty") relate to this excerpt from *The Origin of Species/Descent of Man*?

9. Read "Devolution" by H. Allen Orr beginning on page 234 of this text. How does his essay relate to this selection and the New York *Times* article on the next page?

o York Times.

THE WEATHER
Showers today and tomorrow; fresh south and southwest winds.
Temperature yesterday—Max., 73; min., 66.
☞ For weather report see Page 22.

ORK, WEDNESDAY, JULY 22, 1925.

TWO CENTS New York | THREE CENTS Within 200 Miles | FOUR CENTS Elsewhere in the U. S.

SCOPES GUILTY, FINED $100, SCORES LAW; BENEDICTION ENDS TRIAL, APPEAL STARTS; DARROW ANSWERS NINE BRYAN QUESTIONS

Both Sides Speed Procedure for Scopes Appeal; Defense Cost $25,000, With Lawyers Serving Free

Special to The New York Times.

KNOXVILLE, Tenn., July 21.—With the conviction of John Thomas Scopes, attorneys for the defense at Dayton began at once to formulate their plans for the appeal. The case will come before the Supreme Court when that tribunal sits in Knoxville in September. Attorneys for both sides today agreed to expedite the appeal procedure in order to assure a hearing of the issues at that session.

Clarence Darrow, chief of the defense staff, is expected to argue the case before the Supreme Court here. Frank Spurlock, prominent attorney of Chattanooga, assisting the defense, will also plead for Mr. Scopes, being well versed in the peculiarities of Tennessee law. John R. Neal of Knoxville also is expected to take an important part in the appeal proceedings.

For the State, Attorney General Stewart and Ben G. McKenzie doubtless will carry the burden.

The defense's appeal will consist of two main points: First, that the Anti-Evolution law is unconstitutional; second, that even though the law were valid, Mr. Scopes did not violate it, and that the defense was prohibited from proving this at the Dayton trial.

DAYTON, Tenn., July 21 (AP).—A misdemeanor case carrying as a penalty to the guilty offender a fine of $100 and costs of the trial brought an expenditure to the defenders of John Thomas Scopes of about $25,000.

The actual court costs are estimated at well over $300, or more than treble the fine assessed.

The greatest expense of the trial was the cost of bringing expert witnesses, who were not allowed to testify. Defense counsel estimated that cost to be $20,000 to $25,000.

Attorneys on both sides bore their own expenses and served without fees.

In addition several hundred dollars was paid out by the county in preparing the Court House for the trial.

FINAL SCENES DRAMATIC

Defense Suddenly Decides to Make No Plea and Accept Conviction.

BRYAN IS DISAPPOINTED

Loses Chance to Examine Darrow and His Long-Prepared Speech is Undelivered.

HIS EVIDENCE IS EXPUNGED

Differences Forgotten in the End as All Concerned Exchange Felicitations.

Special to The New York Times.

DAYTON, Tenn., July 21.—The trial of John Thomas Scopes for teaching evolution in Tennessee, which Clarence Darrow characterized today as "the first case of its kind since we stopped trying people for witchcraft," is over. Mr. Scopes was found guilty and fined $100, and his counsel will appeal to the Supreme Court of Tennessee for reversal of the verdict. The scene will then be shifted from Dayton to Knoxville, where the case will probably come up on the first Monday in September.

But the end of the trial did not end its battle on evolution, for not long after its conclusion William Jennings Bryan opened fire on Clarence Darrow with a strong statement and a list of nine questions on the basic principles of the Christian religion. To these Mr. Darrow replied and added a statement explaining Mr. Bryan's "rabies." Dudley Field Malone also contributed a statement predicting ultimate victory for evolution and repeating that Mr. Bryan ran away from the fight.

The end of the trial came as unexpectedly as everything else in this trial, in which nothing has happened according to schedule except the opening of court each morning with prayer. It was reached practically by agreement between counsel in an effort to end the case forever, although all the testimony offered before the jury took only two hours.

Young Scopes, in his shirt sleeves, his collar open at the neck, his parrot-colored hair brushed back, stood up before the bar with a gold epauletted policeman beside him, and Judge Raulston had pronounced sentence before his counsel could suggest that Mr. Scopes might have something to say.

HYLAN REFUSES BAIT TO GO ON BENCH AND QUIT MAYOR'S RACE

Foes Realize Need for Keeping Him on Ticket to Block Third-Party Plan.

McCOOEY CALLS LEADERS

Brooklyn Chief Confers With Olvany, but Both Refuse to Tell What Was Said.

HEARST EMISSARY ACTIVE

Meeting of Borough Leaders on Mayoralty Situation is Put Off Until Next Week.

In a final attempt to avert an open break and keep him in line for the ticket, Democrats who do not believe Mayor Hylan could make a winning fight for a third term, yesterday sent friendly emissaries to the Mayor, who now are bringing all their persuasive powers to bear with a view to inducing him to quit the Mayoralty race and accept a nomination for the Supreme Court in the Second Judicial District.

Up to last night these envoys of the anti-Hylan forces had not been able to budge Mayor Hylan from his determination to make a fight for the Mayoralty again. It was stated, however, that the pressure would continue, and that when the Mayor awakened to a realization of his loss of popularity with the voters there was hope, that he would yield to their representations.

In the meantime the anti-Hylan forces are sparring for time. It was announced yesterday that the conferences of the five Democratic borough leaders, at which the Democratic city slate is to be decided upon, would be deferred until next week. This announcement was made after John H. McCooey, the Democratic leader in Brooklyn, which is Mayor Hylan's home borough, had met George W. Olvany, the Tammany chieftain, at the Hotel Vanderbilt, where they discussed the tangled Mayoralty situation for an hour or more over their representations.

Neither Mr. Olvany nor Mr. McCooey would disclose any part of their conversation, except to say that it had been wholly informal and that naturally no decision of any kind had been reached. Prior to meeting Mr. Olvany, the Democratic leader in Brooklyn had talked for almost an hour with James F. Sinnott, one of his district leaders and a high spokesman for Mayor Hylan himself.

Confer in McCooey's Office.

This conference was held in Mr. McCooey's office at the Hall of Records in Brooklyn. What they talked about can only be surmised, for there was no announcement after their meeting. It was presumed, however, that the sole topic was Mayor Hylan's chances to get a renomination for Mayor.

G. G. HAVEN A SUICIDE DUE TO ILL HEALTH

Banker and Opera Patron Shoots Himself After Vain Struggle to Recover.

FRIEND DISCOVERS BODY

Dr. E. Eliot Finds Him Dead in His Room While Wife is Away Shopping.

George Griswold Haven, senior member of the banking firm of Strong, Sturgis & Co. at 11 Wall Street and President of the Metropolitan-Opera and Real Estate Company, which controls the Metropolitan Opera House, committed suicide by shooting himself through the head with a revolver at his residence, 4 East Fifty-third Street, yesterday morning.

Mr. Haven, who was 48 years old, had

BONAPARTE GIVES PROPERTY TO WIFE

Great-Grandnephew of the Emperor Signs Away All but $5,000 a Year.

AGREEMENT ENDS HER SUIT

Referee Files Report and Recommends That Leon Jacobs, Lawyer, Get $5,000 Fee.

The details of the settlement of the suit brought by Jerome Napoleon Bonaparte, great-grandnephew of the Emperor, against his wife, Blanche Bonaparte, to set aside an agreement transferring all of his property to her, became known in the Supreme Court yesterday, when a report was filed by Emanuel B. Cohen, appointed referee to determine the amount of the fee to be paid to Leon R. Jacobs, who acted

---

...ewer of 40 Lives, ...onors on Tablet

...the Battery Dock, saved more than on drowning off the ...ry Park, will be the ... to have his name tablet to be placed Dock Commissioner announced yesterday.

...be a memorial to ...F. Murphy, who Commissioner from will be presented by by, a nephew of the ... Annually a Dock new Man" will have ... on the tablet. be presented with a ...ers of the department may have more than ...ls for saving life.

KE THREAT TO HOOVER

il Warns of Gen-Over West Virginia Fight.

KEFELLER AID

ults by Armed racite Conferees le Headway.

New York Times.
.Y., N. J., July 21.—racite operators and afternoon in fruitless new wage agreement, the bituminous coal drew up plans for sign against soft coal thern West Virginia, chief representative of Workers in that territorial telegram to Secretary Hoover and Secretary denouncing the Anthracite, a subsidiary of teel Corporation, and Coal Company for ation of the Jackson. He declared that "undone to prevent this the agreement it of the miners of the Virginia to join with Workers of America of ... in a general strike," time Mr. Bittner, after the Hotel Ambassador Townsend, chief counsel Northern West Virginia to John D. Rockesmuel Untermyer, allegproceedings have been hundreds of miners and nd that armed guards others. Mr. Untermyer because of his large interdisheen Steel Corporation of the Bethlehem Mines Rockefeller is supposed in the Consolidation.

THE OVAL PORTRAIT

EDGAR ALLAN POE

Edgar Allan Poe (1809-1849) transformed the short story from amusing little stories to art. He created the detective story and perfected the psychological thriller. As a writer of a novel, short stories, poetry and essays, he was a success, but he couldn't hold a job as an editor, mainly because of his drinking. Some of his more famous and influential works are "MS Found in a Bottle" (1833), "The Narrative of Arthur Gordon Pym" (1837), "The Fall of the House of Usher" (1839), "The Murders in the Rue Morgue" (1841), "The Raven" (1845), and "The Bells" (1849).

¹The chateau in which my valet had ventured to make forcible entrance, rather than permit me, in my desperately wounded condition, to pass a night in the open air, was one of those piles of commingled gloom and grandeur which have so long frowned among the Apennines, not less in fact than in the fancy of Mrs. Radcliffe. To all appearance it had been temporarily and very lately abandoned.

²We established ourselves in one of the smallest and least amply furnished apartments. It lay in a remote turret of the building. Its decorations were rich, yet tattered and antique. Its walls were hung with tapestry and bedecked with manifold and multiform armorial trophies, together with an unusually great number of very spirited modern paintings in frames of rich, golden arabesque. In these paintings, which depended from the walls not only in their main surfaces, but in very many nooks which the bizarre architecture of the chateau rendered necessary—in these paintings my incipient delirium, perhaps, had caused me to take deep interest; so that I bade Pedro to close the heavy shutters of the room, since it was already night, to light the tongues of a tall candelabrum which stood by the head of the bed, and to throw open far and wide the fringed curtains of black velvet which enveloped the bed itself. I wished all this done that I might resign myself, if not to sleep, at least alternately to the contemplation of these pictures, and the perusal of a small volume which had been found upon the pillow, and which purported to criticize and explain them.

³Long, long I read—and devoutly, devotedly I gazed. Rapidly and gloriously the hours flew by and the deep midnight came. The position of the candelabrum displeased me, and out-reaching my hand with difficulty, rather than disturb my slumbering valet, I placed it so as to throw its rays more fully upon the book.

[4]But the action produced an effect altogether unanticipated. The rays of the numerous candles (for there were many) now fell within a niche of the room which had hitherto been thrown into deep shade by one of the bed-posts. I thus saw in vivid light a picture all unnoticed before. It was the portrait of a young girl just ripening into womanhood. I glanced at the painting hurriedly, and then closed my eyes. Why I did this was not at first apparent even to my own perception. But while my lids remained thus shut, I ran over in my mind my reason for so shutting them. It was an impulsive movement to gain time for thought, to make sure that my vision had not deceived me, to calm and subdue my fancy for a more sober and more certain gaze. In a very few moments I again looked fixedly at the painting.

[5]That I now saw aright I could not and would not doubt; for the first flashing of the candles upon that canvas hall seemed to dissipate the dreamy stupor which was stealing over my senses, and to startle me at once into waking life. The portrait, as I have already said, was that of a young girl. It was a mere head and shoulders done in what is technically termed a vignette manner, much in the style of the favorite heads of Sully. The arms, the bosom, and even the ends of the enchanted hair melted imperceptibly into the vague yet deep shadow which formed the background of the whole. The frame was oval, richly gilded and filigreed in Moresque. As a thing of art nothing could be more admirable than the painting itself. But it could have been neither the execution of the work, nor the immortal beauty of the countenance, which had so suddenly and so vehemently moved me. Least of all, could it have been that my fancy, shaken from its half slumber, had mistaken the head for that of a living person. I saw at once that the peculiarities of the design, of the vignetting, and of the frame, must have instantly dispelled such an idea—must have prevented even its momentary entertainment. Thinking earnestly upon these points, I remained, for an hour perhaps, half sitting, half reclining, with my vision riveted upon the portrait. At length, satisfied with the true secret of its effect, I fell back within the bed. I had found the spell of the picture in an absolute *life-likeness* of expression, which, at first, finally confounded, subdued, and appalled me. With deep and reverent awe I replaced the candelabrum in its former position. The cause of my deep agitation being thus shut from view, I sought eagerly the volume which discussed the paintings and their histories. Turning to the number which designated the oval portrait, I there read the vague and quaint words which follow:

> [6]She was a maiden of rarest beauty, and not more lovely than full of glee. And evil was the hour when she saw, and loved, and wedded the painter. He, passionate, studious, austere, and having already a bride in his Art: she a maiden of rarest beauty, and not more lovely than full of glee; all light and smiles, and frolicsome as the young fawn; loving and cherishing all things; hating only the Art which was her rival; dreading only the

palette and brushes and other untoward instruments which deprived her of the countenance of her lover. It was thus a terrible thing for this lady to hear the painter speak of his desire to portray even his young bride. But she was humble and obedient, and sat meekly for many weeks in the dark high turret-chamber where the light dripped upon the pale canvas only from overhead. But he, the painter, took glory in his work, which went on from hour to hour, and from day to day. And he was a passionate and wild, and moody man, who became lost in reveries; so that he *would* not see the light which fell so ghastly in that lone turret withered the health and the spirits of his bride, who pined visibly to all but him. Yet she smiled on and still on, uncomplainingly, because she saw that the painter (who had high renown) took a fervid and burning pleasure in his task, and wrought day and night to depict her who so loved him, yet who grew daily more dispirited and weak. And in sooth some who beheld the portrait spoke of its resemblance in low words, as of a mighty marvel, and a proof not less of the power of the painter than of his deep love for her whom he depicted so surpassingly well. But at length, as the labor drew nearer to its conclusion, there were admitted none into the turret; for the painter had grown wild with the ardor of his work, and turned his eyes from the canvas rarely, even to regard the countenance of his wife. And he *would* not see that the tints which he spread upon the canvas were drawn from the cheeks of her who sat beside him. And when many weeks had passed, and but little remained to do, save one brush upon the mouth and one tint upon the eye, the spirit of the lady again flickered up as the flame within the socket of the lamp. And then the brush was given, and then the tint was placed; and for one moment, the painter stood entranced before the work which he had wrought; but in the next, while he yet gazed, he grew tremulous and very pallid, and aghast, and crying with a loud voice, "This is indeed *Life* itself!" turned suddenly to regard his beloved—*She was dead.*

Vocabulary

[1]chateau	[2]arabesque	[5]vignette	[6]austere
[1]valet	[2]incipient	[5]imperceptibly	[6]reveries
[1]commingled	[2]candelabrum	[5]gilded	[6]pined
[1]grandeur	[2]perusal	[5]Sully	[6]renown
[1]Apennines	[2]purported	[5]filigreed	[6]fervid
[1]Mrs. Radcliffe	[4]niche	[5]countenance	[6]tremulous
[2]bedecked	[4]perception	[5]vehemently	[6]pallid
[2]manifold	[5]dissipate	[5]confounded	[6]aghast
[2]armorial	[5]stupor	[5]appalled	

Discussion Questions

1. The opening sentence has 58 words, quite long by modern standards. Explain in your own words what information is being given in this sentence.

2. Who is Mrs. Radcliffe? Why does Poe mention her? What effect is this supposed to have on a reader in the 1840's? How does this add to the atmosphere of the story?

3. What is wrong with the narrator? What do you surmise happened to him based upon his description of where he is?

4. From what source does the narrator glean the "story within the story"? How does finding this move the Poe story along?

5. What is the narrator's impression of the portrait? Be specific.

6. If we were to look at the last sentence of this story in a religious context, of what sin would the painter be guilty?

7. What is the natural, as opposed to the supernatural, reason for the death of the maiden?

8. Research *The Picture of Dorian Gray* by Oscar Wilde and explain how it relates to this story.

FROM THE QUR'AN AS CONVEYED TO THE PROPHET MUHAMMAD
TRANSLATION BY
MOHAMMED MARMADUKE PICKTHALL (1875-1936)

The Qur'an (also known as the Koran) is accepted by Muslims worldwide as a message conveyed directly from the Almighty Himself (Allah) to humanity. According to the religion of Islam, the Qur'an was transmitted to believers from Allah through the angel Gabriel to the **Prophet Muhammad** *in fragments over a period of approximately 23 years from 610 AD to Muhammad's death in 632 AD. Muhammad was 40 years old when Allah began to reveal the words of the Qur'an to him, and he was 63 when the revelation was completed.*

The message was given to Muhammad in Arabic and over the centuries has been translated into numerous other languages. Followers of the Islamic faith, however, maintain there can be no direct translation of the text; to be fully understood and appreciated, the message must be read in its original Arabic. The Qur'an contains many references to earlier prophets Moses and Jesus Christ in the Judeo-Christian tradition; the majority of Muslims in the world view Muhammad as the final, and thus the most enlightened, messenger of Allah to humanity.

The Qur'an comprises 114 chapters (suras) each containing a number of verses on a variety of subjects. One difficulty for Westerners in reading the Qur'an is the order in which familiar Judeo-Christian narratives appear in the work. Note in the following excerpts, for example, that the references to Cain and Abel appear in Sura (chapter) 5 while the story of Adam appears in Sura 7. References to familiar personalities from the Torah and Holy Bible, such as Abraham, Noah, Moses, Mary and Jesus, are interspersed throughout the Qur'an in instructions and admonitions to the faithful to live their lives in a way that pleases Allah. The excerpts from Sura 2 are intended to illustrate how the Qur'an serves as a guide for living a righteous life.

Sura 7: al-A`raf

1 Alif. Lam. Mim. Sad.[a]

2 This is a Scripture that is revealed unto thee (Muhammad)—so let there be no heaviness in thy heart therefrom—that thou mayst warn thereby, and let this be a Reminder unto believers.

3 (Saying): Follow that which is sent down unto you from your Lord, and follow no protecting friends beside Him. Little do ye recollect!

---

[a]These are English words that describe Arabic letters found at the beginning of many of the *suras*. The significance of the letters is a matter of conjecture, with the most commonly held belief that they convey the divine mystery contained in the Qur'an.

4 How many a township have We destroyed! As a raid by night, or while they slept at noon, Our terror came unto them.

5 No plea had they, when Our terror came unto them, save that they said: Lo! We were wrong-doers.

6 Then verily We shall question those unto whom Our message hath been sent, and verily We shall question the messengers.

7 Then verily We shall narrate unto them the event with knowledge, for We were not absent when it came to pass.

8 The weighing on that day is the true weighing. As for those whose scale is heavy, they are the successful.

9 And as for those whose scale is light: those are they who lose their souls because they used to wrong Our revelations.

10 And We have given you (mankind) power in the earth, and appointed for you therein livelihoods. Little give ye thanks!

11 And We created you, then fashioned you, then told the angels: Fall ye prostrate before Adam! And they fell prostrate, all save Iblis, who was not of those who make prostration.

12 He said: What hindered thee that thou didst not fall prostrate when I bade thee? Iblis[b] said: I am better than him. Thou created me of fire while him Thou didst create of mud.

13 He said: Then go down hence! It is not for thee to show pride here, so go forth! Lo! thou art of those degraded.

14 He said: Reprieve me till the day when they are raised from the dead.

15 He said: Lo! thou art of those reprieved.

16 He said: Now, because Thou hast sent me astray, verily I shall lurk in ambush for them on Thy Right Path.

17 Then I shall come upon them from before them and from behind them and from their right hands and from their left hands, and Thou wilt not find most of them beholden unto Thee.

18 He said: Go forth from hence, degraded, banished. As for such of them as follow thee, surely I will fill hell with all of you.

19 And unto man: O Adam! Dwell thou and thy wife in the Garden and eat from whence ye will, but come not nigh this tree lest ye become wrong-doers.

20 Then Satan whispered to them that he might manifest unto them that which was hidden from them of their shame, and he said: Your Lord forbade you from this tree only lest ye should become angels or become of the immortals.

21 And he swore unto them saying: Lo! I am a sincere adviser unto you.

22 Thus did he lead them on with guile. And when they tasted of the tree their shame was manifest to them and they began to hide by heaping on themselves some of the leaves of the Garden. And their Lord called them, say-

---

[b]Iblis is the primary evil spirit (Shaitan or Satan) in Islam.

ing: Did I not forbid you from that tree and tell you: Lo! Satan is an open enemy to you?

23 They said: Our Lord! We have wronged ourselves. If thou forgive us not and have not mercy on us, surely we are of the lost!

24 He said: Go down from hence, one of you a foe unto the other. There will be for you on earth a habitation and provision for a while.

25 He said: There shall ye live, and there shall ye die, and thence shall ye be brought forth.

26 O Children of Adam! We have revealed unto you raiment to conceal your shame, and splendid vesture, but the raiment of restraint from evil, that is best. This is of the revelations of Allah, that they may remember.

27 O Children of Adam! Let not Satan seduce you as he caused your first parents to go forth from the Garden and tore off from them their robe of innocence that he might manifest their shame to them. Lo! he seeth you, he and his tribe, from whence ye see him not. Lo! We have made the devils protecting friends for those who believe not.

28 And when they do some lewdness they say: We found our fathers doing it and Allah hath enjoined it on us. Say: Allah, verily, enjoineth not lewdness. Tell ye concerning Allah that which ye know not?

29 Say: My Lord enjoineth justice. And set your faces upright toward Him at every place of worship and call upon Him, making religion pure for Him only. As He brought you into being, so return ye unto Him.

30 A party hath He led aright, while error hath just hold over another party, for lo! they choose the devils for protecting supporters instead of Allah and deem that they are rightly guided.

31 O Children of Adam! Look to your adornment at every place of worship, and eat and drink, but be not prodigal. Lo! He loveth not the prodigals.

32 Say: Who hath forbidden the adornment of Allah which He hath brought forth for His bondmen, and the good things of His providing? Say: Such, on the Day of Resurrection, will be only for those who believed during the life of the world. Thus do we detail Our revelations for people who have knowledge.

****

40 Lo! they who deny Our revelations and scorn them, for them the gates of heaven will not be opened nor will they enter the Garden until the camel goeth through the needle's eye. Thus do We requite the guilty.

41 Theirs will be a bed of hell, and over them coverings of hell. Thus do We requite wrong-doers.

42 But as for those who believe and do good works—We tax not any soul beyond its scope—Such are rightful owners of the Garden. They abide therein.

43 And We remove whatever rancor may be in their hearts. Rivers flow beneath them. And they say: The praise to Allah, Who hath guided us to this. We could not truly have been led aright if Allah had not guided us. Verily the messengers of our Lord did bring the Truth. And it is cried unto them: This is the Garden. Ye inherit it for what ye used to do.

44 And the dwellers of the Garden cry unto the dwellers of the Fire: We have found that which our Lord promised us to be the Truth. Have ye too found that which your Lord promised the Truth? They say: Yea, verily. And a crier in between them crieth: The curse of Allah is on evil-doers,

45 Who debar men from the path of Allah and would have it crooked, and who are disbelievers in the Last Day.

46 Between them is a veil. And on the Heights are men who know them all by their marks. And they call unto the dwellers of the Garden: Peace be unto you! They enter it not although they hope to enter.

47 And when their eyes are turned toward the dwellers of the Fire, they say: Our Lord! Place us not with the wrong-doing folk.

48 And the dwellers on the Heights call unto men whom they know by their marks, saying: What did your multitude and that in which ye took your pride avail you?

49 Are these they of whom ye swore that Allah would not show them mercy? Unto them it hath been said: Enter the Garden. No fear shall come upon you nor is it ye who will grieve.

50 And the dwellers of the Fire cry out unto the dwellers of the Garden: Pour on us some water or some wherewith Allah hath provided you. They say: Lo! Allah hath forbidden both to disbelievers in His guidance.

51 Who took their religion for a sport and pastime, and whom the life of the world beguiled, so this day We have forgotten them even as they forgot the meeting of this their Day and as they used to deny Our tokens.

52 Verily We have brought them a Scripture which We expounded with knowledge, a guidance and a mercy for a people who believe.

53 Await they aught save the fulfillment thereof? On the day when the fulfillment thereof cometh, those who were before forgetful thereof will say: The messengers of our Lord did bring the Truth! Have we any intercessors, that they may intercede for us? Or can we be returned to life on earth, that we may act otherwise than we used to act? They have lost their souls, and that which they devised hath failed them.

54 Lo! your Lord is Allah Who created the heavens and the earth in six Days, then mounted He the Throne. He covereth the night with the day, which is in haste to follow it, and hath made the sun and the moon and the stars subservient by His command. His verily is all creation and commandment. Blessed be Allah, the Lord of the Worlds!

****

Sura 5: al-Ma'idah

27 But recite unto them with truth the tale of the two sons of Adam, how they offered each a sacrifice, and it was accepted from the one of them and it was not accepted from the other. The one said: I will surely kill thee. The other answered: Allah accepteth only from those who ward off evil.

28 Even if thou stretch out thy hand against me to kill me, I shall not stretch out my hand against thee to kill thee, lo! I fear Allah, the Lord of the Worlds.

29 Lo! I would rather thou shouldst bear the punishment of the sin against me and thine own sin and become one of the owners of the fire. That is the reward of evil-doers.

30 But the other's mind imposed on him the killing of his brother, so he slew him and became one of the losers.

31 Then Allah sent a raven scratching up the ground to show him how to hide his brother's naked corpse. He said: Woe unto me! Am I not able to be as this raven and so hide my brother's naked corpse ? And he became repentant.

32 For that cause We decreed for the Children of Israel that whosoever killeth a human being for other than manslaughter or corruption in the earth, it shall be as if he had killed all mankind, and whoso saveth the life of one, it shall be as if he had saved the life of all mankind. Our messengers came unto them of old with clear proofs of Allah's Sovereignty, but afterwards lo! many of them became prodigals in the earth.

33 The only reward of those who make war upon Allah and His messenger and strive after corruption in the land will be that they will be killed or crucified, or have their hands and feet on alternate sides cut off, or will be expelled out of the land. Such will be their degradation in the world, and in the Hereafter theirs will be an awful doom;

34 Save those who repent before ye overpower them. For know that Allah is Forgiving, Merciful.

unto you, and know from Allah that which ye know not.

Sura 11: Hud

25 And We sent Noah unto his folk and he said: Lo! I am a plain warner unto you.

26 That ye serve none, save Allah. Lo! I fear for you the retribution of a painful Day.

27 The chieftains of his folk, who disbelieved, said: We see thee but a mortal like us, and we see not that any follow thee save the most abject among us, without reflection. We behold in you no merit above us—nay, we deem you liars.

28 He said: O my people! Bethink you, if I rely on a clear proof from my Lord and there hath come unto me a mercy from His presence, and it hath been made obscure to you, can we compel you to accept it when ye are averse thereto ?

29 And O my people! I ask of you no wealth therefor. My reward is the concern only of Allah, and I am not going to thrust away those who believe—Lo! they have to meet their Lord!—but I see you a folk that are ignorant.

30 And, O my people! who would deliver me from Allah if I thrust them away? Will ye not then reflect ?

31 I say not unto you: I have the treasures of Allah nor I have knowledge of the Unseen, nor say I: Lo! I am an angel! Nor say I unto those whom your eyes scorn that Allah will not give them good—Allah knoweth best what is in their hearts—Lo! then indeed I should be of the wrong-doers.

32 They said: O Noah! Thou hast disputed with us and multiplied disputation with us; now bring upon us that wherewith thou threatenest us, if thou art of the truthful.

33 He said: Only Allah will bring it upon you if He will, and ye can by no means escape.

34 My counsel will not profit you if I were minded to advise you, if Allah's will is to keep you astray. He is your Lord and unto Him ye will be brought back.

35 And say they again: He hath invented it? Say: If I have invented it, upon me be my crimes, but I am innocent of all that ye commit.

36 And it was inspired in Noah, saying: No-one of thy folk will believe save him who hath believed already. Be not distressed because of what they do.

37 Build the ship under Our eyes and by Our inspiration, and speak not unto Me on behalf of those who do wrong. Lo! they will be drowned.

38 And he was building the ship, and every time that chieftains of his people passed him, they made mock of him. He said: Though ye make mock of Us, yet We mock at you even as ye mock;

39 And ye shall know to whom a punishment that will confound him cometh, and upon whom a lasting doom will fall.

40 Thus it was till, when Our commandment came to pass and the sky gushed forth water, We said: Load therein two of every kind, a pair (the male and female), and thy household, save him against whom the word hath gone forth already, and those who believe. And but a few were they who believed with him.

41 And he said: Embark therein! In the name of Allah be its course and its mooring. Lo! my Lord is Forgiving, Merciful.

42 And it sailed with them amid waves like mountains, and Noah cried unto his son—and he was standing aloof—O my son! Come ride with us, and be not with the disbelievers.

43 He said: I shall betake me to some mountain that will save me from the water. Noah said: This day there is none that saveth from the commandment of Allah save him on whom He hath had mercy. And the wave came in between them, so he was among the drowned.

44 And it was said: O earth! Swallow thy water and, O sky! be cleared of clouds! And the water was made to subside. And the commandment was fulfilled. And the ship came to rest upon the mount Al-Judi and it was said: A far removal for wrongdoing folk!

45 And Noah cried unto his Lord and said: My Lord! Lo! my son is of my household! Surely Thy promise is the truth and Thou are the Most Just of Judges.

46 He said: O Noah! Lo! he is not of thy household; lo! he is of evil conduct, so ask not of Me that whereof thou hast no knowledge. I admonish thee lest thou be among the ignorant.

47 He said: My Lord! Lo! in Thee do I seek refuge from sin that I should ask of Thee that whereof I have no knowledge. Unless Thou forgive me and have mercy on me I shall be among the lost.

48 It was said unto him: O Noah! Go thou down from the mountain with peace from Us and blessings upon thee and some nations that will spring from those with thee. There will be other nations unto whom We shall give enjoyment a long while and then a painful doom from Us will overtake them.

49 This is of the tidings of the Unseen which We inspire in thee. Thou thyself knewest it not, nor did thy folk know it before this. Then have patience. Lo! the sequel is for those who ward off evil.

****

Sura 2: al-Baqarah

185 The month of Ramadan in which was revealed the Qur'an, a guidance for mankind, and clear proofs of the guidance, and the Criterion of right and wrong. And whosoever of you is present, let him fast the month, and whosoever of you is sick or on a journey, let him fast the same number of other days. Allah desireth for you ease; He desireth not hardship for you; and He desireth that ye should complete the period, and that ye should magnify Allah for having guided you, and that ye may be thankful.

186 And when My servants question thee concerning Me, then surely I am nigh. I answer the prayer of the suppliant when he crieth unto Me. So let them hear My call and let them trust in Me, in order that they may be led aright.

187 It is made lawful for you to go in unto your wives on the night of the fast. They are raiment for you and ye are raiment for them. Allah is aware that

ye were deceiving yourselves in this respect and He hath turned in mercy toward you and relieved you. So hold intercourse with them and seek that which Allah hath ordained for you, and eat and drink until the white thread becometh distinct to you from the black thread of the dawn. Then strictly observe the fast till nightfall and touch them not, but be at your devotions in the mosques. These are the limits imposed by Allah, so approach them not. Thus Allah expoundeth His revelation to mankind that they may ward off evil.

188 And eat not up your property among yourselves in vanity, nor seek by it to gain the hearing of the judges that ye may knowingly devour a portion of the property of others wrongfully.

189 They ask thee, O Muhammad, of new moons, say: They are fixed seasons for mankind and for the pilgrimage. It is not righteousness that ye go to houses by the backs thereof (as do the idolaters at certain seasons), but the righteous man is he who wardeth off evil. So go to houses by the gates thereof, and observe your duty to Allah, that ye may be successful.

190 Fight in the way of Allah against those who fight against you, but begin not hostilities. Lo! Allah loveth not aggressors.

191 And slay them wherever ye find them, and drive them out of the places whence they drove you out, for persecution is worse than slaughter. And fight not with them at the Inviolable Place of Worship until they first attack you there, but if they attack you there then slay them. Such is the reward of disbelievers.

192 But if they desist, then lo! Allah is Forgiving, Merciful.

193 And fight them until persecution is no more, and religion is for Allah. But if they desist, then let there be no hostility except against wrong-doers.

194 This is the forbidden month for forbidden hostility and forbidden things in retaliation. And one who attacketh you, attack him in like manner as he attacked you. Observe your duty to Allah, and know that Allah is with those who ward off evil.

195 Spend your wealth for the cause of Allah, and be not cast by your own hands to ruin; and do good. Lo! Allah loveth the beneficent.

196 Perform the pilgrimage and the visit to Mecca[c] for Allah. And if ye are prevented, then send such gifts as can be obtained with ease, and shave not your heads until the gifts have reached their destination. And whoever among you is sick or hath an ailment of the head must pay a ransom of fasting or almsgiving or offering. And if ye are in safety, then whosoever contenteth himself with the visit for the pilgrimage shall give such gifts as

---

[c]Mecca (also spelled Makkah) is located in modern Saudi Arabia and is the holiest site in Islam with two to three million Muslim pilgrims visiting the city of 1,700,000 annually.

can be had with ease. And whosoever cannot find such gifts, then a fast of three days while on the pilgrimage, and of seven when ye have returned; that is, ten in all. That is for him whoso folk are not present at the Inviolable Place of Worship. Observe your duty to Allah, and know that Allah is severe in punishment.

****

217 They question thee (O Muhammad) with regard to warfare in the sacred month. Say: Warfare therein is a great transgression, but to turn men from the way of Allah, and to disbelieve in Him and in the Inviolable Place of Worship, and to expel His people thence, is a greater wrong with Allah; for persecution is worse than killing. And they will not cease from fighting against you till they have made you renegades from your religion, if they can. And whoso becometh a renegade and dieth in his disbelief: such are they whose works have fallen both in the world and the Hereafter. Such are rightful owners of the Fire: they will abide therein.

218 Lo! those who believe, and those who emigrate to escape the persecution and strive in the way of Allah, these have hope of Allah's mercy. Allah is Forgiving, Merciful.

219 They question thee about strong drink and games of chance. Say: In both is great sin, and some utility for men; but the sin of them is greater than their usefulness. And they ask thee what they ought to spend. Say: that which is superfluous. Thus Allah maketh plain to you His revelations, that haply ye may reflect upon the world and the Hereafter.

220 And they question thee concerning orphans. Say: To improve their lot is best. And if ye mingle your affairs with theirs, then they are your brothers. Allah knoweth him who spoileth from him who improveth. Had Allah willed He could have overburdened you. Allah is Mighty and Wise.

221 Wed not idolatresses till they believe; for lo! a believing bondwoman[d] is better than an idolatress though she please you; and give not your daughters in marriage to idolaters till they believe, for lo! a believing slave is better than an idolater though he please you. These invite unto the Fire, and Allah inviteth unto the Garden, and unto forgiveness by His grace, and expoundeth His revelations to mankind that haply they may remember.

222 They question thee, O Muhammad, concerning menstruation. Say: It is an illness, so let women alone at such times and go not in unto them till they are cleansed. And when they have purified themselves, then go in unto them as Allah hath enjoined upon you. Truly Allah loveth those who turn

---

[d]Bondwoman is a woman in bondage, a slave.

unto Him, and loveth those who have a care for cleanness.

223 Your women are a tilth for you to cultivate, so go to your tilth as ye will, and send good deeds before you for your souls, and fear Allah, and know that ye will one day meet Him. Give glad tidings to believers, O Muhammad.

224 And make not Allah, by your oaths, a hindrance to your being righteous and observing your duty unto Him and making peace among mankind. Allah is Hearer, Knower.

225 Allah will not take you to task for that which is unintentional in your oaths. But He will take you to task for that which your hearts have garnered. Allah is Forgiving, Clement.

226 Those who forswear their wives must wait four months; then, if they change their mind, lo! Allah is Forgiving, Merciful.

227 And if they decide upon divorce let them remember that Allah is Hearer, Knower.

228 Women who are divorced shall wait, keeping themselves apart, three monthly courses. And it is not lawful for them that they should conceal that which Allah hath created in their wombs if they are believers in Allah and the Last Day. And their husbands would do better to take them back in that case if they desire a reconciliation. And they (women) have rights similar to those of men over them in kindness, and men are a degree above them. Allah is Mighty and Wise.

229 Divorce must be pronounced twice and then a woman must be retained in honor or released in kindness. And it is not lawful for you that ye take from women aught of that which ye have given them; except in the case when both fear that they may not be able to keep within the limits imposed by Allah. And if ye fear that they may not be able to keep the limits of Allah, in that case it is no sin for either of them if the woman ransom herself. These are the limits imposed by Allah. Transgress them not. For whoso transgresseth Allah's limits: such are wrong-doers.

230 And if he hath divorced her the third time, then she is not lawful unto him thereafter until she hath wedded another husband. Then if he (the other husband) divorce her it is no sin for both of them that they come together again if they consider that they are able to observe the limits of Allah. These are the limits of Allah. He manifesteth them for people who have knowledge.

231 When ye have divorced women, and they have reached their term, then retain them in kindness or release them in kindness. Retain them not to their hurt so that ye transgress the limits. He who doeth that hath wronged his soul. Make not the revelations of Allah a laughing-stock by your behavior, but remember Allah's grace upon you and that which He hath revealed unto you of the Scripture and of wisdom, whereby He doth exhort you. Observe your duty to Allah and know that Allah is Aware of all things.

232 And when ye have divorced women and they reach their term, place not difficulties in the way of their marrying their husbands if it is agreed between them in kindness. This is an admonition for him among you who believeth in Allah and the Last Day. That is more virtuous for you, and cleaner. Allah knoweth; ye know not.

233 Mothers shall suckle their children for two whole years; that is for those who wish to complete the suckling. The duty of feeding and clothing nursing mothers in a seemly manner is upon the father of the child. No-one should be charged beyond his capacity. A mother should not be made to suffer because of her child, nor should he to whom the child is born be made to suffer because of his child. And on the father's heir is incumbent the like of that which was incumbent on the father. If they desire to wean the child by mutual consent and after consultation, it is no sin for them; and if ye wish to give your children out to nurse, it is no sin for you, provided that ye pay what is due from you in kindness. Observe your duty to Allah, and know that Allah is Seer of what ye do.

234 Such of you as die and leave behind them wives, they (the wives) shall wait, keeping themselves apart, four months and ten days. And when they reach the term prescribed for them, then there is no sin for you in aught that they may do with themselves in decency. Allah is informed of what ye do.

235 There is no sin for you in that which ye proclaim or hide in your minds concerning your troth with women. Allah knoweth that ye will remember them. But plight not your troth with women except by uttering a recognized form of words. And do not consummate the marriage until the term prescribed is run. Know that Allah knoweth what is in your minds, so beware of Him; and know that Allah is Forgiving, Clement.

236 It is no sin for you if ye divorce women while yet ye have not touched them, nor appointed unto them a portion. Provide for them, the rich according to his means, and the straitened according to his means, a fair provision. This is a bounden duty for those who do good.

237 If ye divorce them before ye have touched them and ye have appointed unto them a portion, then pay the half of that which ye appointed, unless they (the women) agree to forgo it. To forgo is nearer to piety. And forget not kindness among yourselves. Allah is Seer of what ye do.

238 Be guardians of your prayers, and of the midmost prayer, and stand up with devotion to Allah.

239 And if ye go in fear, then pray standing or on horseback. And when ye are again in safety, remember Allah, as He hath taught you that which heretofore ye knew not.

240 In the case of those of you who are about to die and leave behind them wives, they should bequeath unto their wives a provision for the year without turning them out, but if they go out of their own accord, there is no sin

for you in that which they do of themselves within their rights. Allah is Mighty and Wise.

241 For divorced women a provision in kindness: a duty for those who ward off evil.

242 Thus Allah expoundeth unto you His revelations so that ye may understand.

****

Vocabulary

Sura 7

6 verily	31 prodigal
11 prostrate	40 requite
12 bade	43 rancor
17 beholden	45 debar
19 whence	48 avail
19 nigh	51 beguiled
20 manifest	52 expounded
22 guile	53 aught
24 hence	53 intercessors
25 thence	54 subservient
26 raiment	
26 vesture	**Sura 5**
28 lewdness	30 slew
28 enjoined	31 repentant

Sura 11

25 retribution	225 garnered
27 abject	225 clement
28 averse	231 exhort
42 aloof	232 admonition
	233 incumbent
Sura 2	233 wean
186 suppliant	235 troth
195 beneficent	235 plight (v)
196 inviolable	235 consummate
217 transgression	236 straitened
218 emigrate	237 piety
219 superfluous	240 bequeath
221 idolatresses	
223 tilth	

Discussion Questions

1. Note the changing point of view throughout the suras. Sura 7 begins with Allah speaking to Muhammad in the first person. At what point (verse number) does the point of view shift? Can you find where it shifts back to Allah speaking in first person again?

2. What are the similarities, differences between the version of the Garden of Eden story contained here in Sura 7 and the one presented in Genesis in the Torah?

3. In verses 44 and 45 of Sura 7, Allah speaks of "the Garden," "the dwellers of the Fire" and "the Last Day." Based upon your own background knowledge, or research, explain what these references correspond to in Judeo-Christian tradition. The "dwellers on the Heights"?

4. In verse 53 of Sura 7, the sinners ask, "Or can we be returned to life on

earth, that we may act otherwise than we used to act?" What is Allah's answer? Based upon your own background knowledge, or research, explain how a follower of Hinduism or Buddhism might respond to that question. A follower of Jewish or Christian tradition?

5. What are the similarities and differences between the story in Sura 5, verses 27-34 and the story of Cain and Abel in the Torah?

6. What are the similarities and differences in the story of Noah contained in Sura 11 and the one found in Genesis?

7. In Sura 2, Chapter 187, Muhammad speaks of Ramadan and tells his followers, ". . . on the night of the fast . . . . They are raiment for you and ye are raiment for them." What do you think is meant by this?

8. In this sura, what does Allah say is worse than killing during the forbidden month? (See verses 190, 191, 193, 217.) Some political and religious leaders in the western world have pointed to verses such as these as encouraging religious extremism. Do you agree or disagree with this assessment. Why?

9. Note the different tone and purpose of the content of Sura 2. Would you say this is more like Genesis or Levitticus in the Hebrew Torah? Explain your answer.

10. Look at Chapter 12 of the Bhagavad Gita beginning on page 146 of this text, the Eightfold Path beginning on page 178, Leviticus beginning on page 377 and the Sermon on the Mount on page 489. Compare these works to Sura 2 of the Qur'an and explain what they all have in common.

RATS: WHO'S RACING WHOM?
FROM *CREATURES WE LOVE TO HATE*

DES KENNEDY

Des Kennedy, a writer living in Canada, writes about environmental issues, gardening, and rural living. His articles have appeared in Harrowsmith, Fine Gardening, Probe Post *and* Canadian Geographic. *His book,* Creatures We Love to Hate *(1992), contains a series of articles on animals and plants of ill repute.*

[1]"Eating rats can open up a new supply of meat, turning a harm into a benefit." This was the upbeat assessment of China's official *Economic Information Daily* in early 1991. The paper was trying to stimulate interest in rodent meat, available in Chinese markets for twenty-five *yuan* ($5.75) per kilogram. Besides the traditional preparation by roasting, stewing, smoking, stir- or deep-frying, the paper was urging its readers to widen the horizons of their rodent cuisine with dishes such as rat steamed with lotus leaves with chestnuts and bamboo shoots. Or fried with asparagus. How about a hearty bowl of rat soup?

[2]Some would see all this as a delicious bit of table-turning on the rats, which have been freeloading off human food supplies for far too long. And who better than the Chinese to initiate such a campaign? For it was China which likely gave the world its worst and most prolific rat. The "Year of the Rat," 1984 got a lot of coverage in the Chinese calendar, but in the previous year Beijing hosted one of history's biggest rat kills. With rodents running out of control in the city, officials launched a counter-attack which saw over 2 million rats dispatched. Residents hunted them ruthlessly, killing over 76,000 per day. One neighborhood group was credited with, "wiping out more than 7,000 rats by baiting and beating." Reports said soldiers clubbed about 400,000 rats to death, while construction workers clobbered them in the depths of the city's labyrinthine sewer system. By the time the slaughter had stopped, the rat population was supposed to have been cut by as much as 95 per cent in some districts.

[3]The rat has been called the most successful biological opponent of humans on earth. We've trapped it, poisoned it, bred dogs and kept snakes to kill

it, studied it obsessively, done everything we can think of to defeat it—and failed! There are about 4 billion rats on earth—roughly one of them for every one of us—according to the World Health Organization. Very much our mirror image, they're smart, organized into strictly disciplined social units, clannish, tremendously adaptable, ferocious in combat. In short, like ourselves, they're survivors. It's not without reason that we call the daily grind of our lives "the rat race."

[4]We hate them as competitors and speak of them with disgust. When we smell a rat, we sense there's treachery afoot. To rat on someone is to squeal, to become the lowest sort of informer. Strikebreakers used to be called rats the way they're now called scabs. "You dirty rat!" we snarl at adversaries. Inextricable entanglements become a rat's nest. Desperation forces one to fight like a cornered rat, while hopeless dejection makes one look like a drowned rat. Final failure and defeat leads you to exclaim, like Charlie Brown, a simple and pathetic "Rats!"

[5]But what rats are we talking about? There are hundreds of species worldwide—pack rats, rabbit, rice and rock rats. There are water rats and African swamp rats and a giant Sumatran bamboo rat. We lump them all together, equally odious, equally beneath contempt—without just cause, of course. Take, for example, our native wood rat *(Neotoma cinara)*. This bushytailed character goes quietly about its business, feeding on the roots, stems, leaves and seeds of plants, perhaps eating a few insects, and generally doing no more harm than pilfering the odd shiny trinket with which to adorn its nest. We call it the "trade rat" or "pack rat." *Walker's Animals of the World* says pack rats are, "neat and solitary animals and make pleasing pets if their extreme timidity can be overcome."

[6]Pack rats have nothing to do with rat packs or with the bad rap rats have gotten. The rats which swarm in packs through our cities and which have been called "humanity's most formidable foe," are Old World rats, imports of the genus *Rattus*. Originating in Eastern Asia, they've become communal species, living in or near our buildings and feeding off our food, following us wherever we've settled. Commonly they're called the house rat, earth rat or alley rat, the barn or dump rat, the water, sewer, river or wharf rat. There are just two main problem species: one is the black rat *(R. rattus)* which is also called the roof or house rat. The second, and by far the worst, is the brown rat *(R. norvegicus)* known as the Norway rat.

[7]The roof rat is a large, slim specimen with a long, naked and scaly tail, large ears and a pointed snout. A skilled climber—it can run along a strand of thin-diameter wire—it reached coastal North America in sailing ships and settled in port cities, living in the upper stories of buildings. On the west coast it has established wild populations near the forest fringe and on small islands, where it has eliminated smaller native rodents. Less aggressive than the Nor-

way rat, the roof rat is also far less of a pest and has been largely displaced by its burly brown cousin.

[8]The Norway rat is bigger, fiercer and more adaptable than the roof rat. A ground dweller, it's thought to have originated along stream banks in southeast Asia and gradually become communal, spreading with the development of canals and rice paddies. An aggressive colonizer, it's now found throughout the world, living in underground tunnels or in cellars, basements or the lower floors of buildings, in garbage dumps and sewers. Blunt-nosed and thick-bodied, it can nevertheless wriggle through holes less than five centimeters wide. True to its streamside heritage, it dives and swims well. In 1987, "huge and vicious" Norwegian sewer rats were reported swimming up drain pipes and into toilets of homes in Honolulu.

[9]I know the feeling of dread that invading rats can inspire. When first married, my new bride, Sandy, and I rented a cute little tumble-down cottage in Richmond, just south of Vancouver. Lacking storm sewers, the area was crisscrossed with many kilometers of deep ditches running along the roadsides, and we'd sometimes spot rats swimming in the ditches. We slept on a mattress on the floor in those days, and one night I was jolted awake by Sandy. "There was a rat in your hair!" she gasped. "Nonsense," I replied, "a nightmare, go back to sleep," Then we both saw it: on the other side of the little bedroom, a large rat slunk out of the closet and disappeared into the kitchen. Disgust and fright shook me.

[10]But do wild rats really merit such alarm and revulsion, or have we pictured them as vicious, dirty and despicable for reasons that have more to do with ourselves than with them? As carriers of the plague, rats became synonymous with death and disease, but the real villain of that piece was the flea, which victimized rats the same way it did humans or any other host. Chipmunks, ground squirrels, Marmots and voles can all be infected, yet none of these suffer our revulsion.

[11]There's no question that rats spread disease. Food contaminated with their droppings can cause salmonella or food poisoning as well as leptospiral jaundice. Murine typhus fever is spread by fleas from infected rats. A bite from an infected animal can cause "rat-bite fever." One research project that involved trapping over a thousand rats in Baltimore found that two-thirds of them were infected with the virus that causes haemorrhagic fever. A serious and sometimes fatal disease in Asia, the virus can cause chronic kidney disease and even kidney failure in humans.

[12]Besides contaminating food with their urine, feces and hair, rats steal millions of tons of food every year. The World Health Organization has estimated that they consume 30 million tons of food annually, much of that in the world's starvation areas. In other words, rats make off with enough food to feed 150 million starving people every year. In the United States alone, annual

losses caused directly by rats are now estimated to approximate one billion dollars.

[13]Commensal rats are omnivorous, eating a range of plant and animal matter. They'll eat everything humans do and more—including things like beeswax, paper, soap and leather. One 1975 study found the Norway rat prefers animal matter, including bird eggs, fish, mice, poultry, and young lambs and pigs. Under stress or hunger, they'll eat just about anything, and a pack will attack larger animals, even humans. *Walker's Mammals of the World* claims that "rats make direct attacks on about fourteen thousand persons annually in the United States, and occasionally inflict mortal wounds."

[14]Like mice, rats prefer to live close to their food supply. For such world travelers they're real stay-at-homes, often occupying a range no more than forty-five meters in diameter. Favorite haunts for urban brown rats are the alleys behind restaurants and supermarkets, where food is scattered around. In residential areas, they'll excavate burrows near homes where garbage, compost heaps, pet dishes and bird feeders provide regular and easy pickings. Hidden under shrubbery or beneath piles of bricks or boards, the burrows have numerous escape tunnels.

[15]In mild climates rats may remain outdoors all year, but in colder zones they'll move into nearby buildings for the winter, occupying barns, silos, warehouses, homes and other structures. Studies in Maryland found that an average city block is home to between 25 and 150 Norway rats, while in the countryside a farm might have between 75 and 300 of them. An old rule of thumb says that you find about the same number of rats as humans in a city. Not that you'll see them; highly secretive, rats are seldom seen in their true numbers. Another old rule says that for every rat you do spot, there will be nineteen more that you don't.

[16]Life within the rat pack has proven an endless source of fascination for biologists and behavioral psychologists. A rat colony is a strictly organized social hierarchy in which dominance and submission determine who lives where, who eats what and who gets to reproduce. Researchers have reported several different forms of social structure for the Norway rat. One U.S. Public Health Service study conducted by J. B. Calhoun demonstrated how two parallel social systems functioned in an artificial colony. In one part of the experimental enclosure, dominant males established individual territories around burrows containing a number of families. These high-ranking males excluded other males and they alone mated with females in their territory. When resident females were reproductively active, they excluded all other rats, including juveniles, from the burrow. Reproduction was regular and successful. Females collectively raised and nursed the young. In short, the territorial burrows were the essence of efficiency, discipline and harmony.

[17]By contrast, Calhoun reported, within the same enclosure there existed

a disorganized underclass in which no territories were established and whose members were condemned to a permanent submissive status. Subordinate rats, primarily males, raised in the territorial burrows were eventually forced into the disorganized area and never allowed to return to the privileged enclave. Large packs of rats formed in this disorganized area, where females in heat would be followed by dozens of males and mounted hundreds of times in one night. The stress of such mating behavior, combined with poorly organized burrows and badly maintained nests, resulted in reproductive failure within the rat "ghetto," thus regulating the overall population in the enclosure.

[18]Under favorable conditions, rats are prolific breeders. The breeding season lasts all year, with spring and autumn peaks. Gestation takes three weeks, and a dominant female averages five litters a year, but may raise as many as twelve. Litters average about nine naked and blind babies, but may have up to twenty-two. The young mature in about fifty-two days. Somebody has calculated that if all the offspring of a single pair of brown rats survived and bred, they could total 359 million in a year!

[19]But the figure is meaningless, since rats are far more efficient than humans in controlling their own populations. When overcrowding occurs within a colony, weak members may be killed, denied food or forced out of the colony. Rat fights and rat cannibalism contribute to an average life expectancy of only three months, with less than 10 per cent of rats surviving more than a year.

[20]Much has been made of the rat's capacity to kill other rats, and back-porch philosophers can be counted upon to mention that of all the mammals only humans and rats kill members of their own species. "In their behavior towards members of their own community," wrote Konrad Lorenz in *On Aggression,* rats are "the model of social virtue; but they change into horrible brutes as soon as they encounter members of any other society of their own species." As evidence, he described experiments in which researchers placed a mix of wild rats in an enclosure.

[21]"Bloody tragedies" ensued, until a dominant pair had managed to kill off all potential competitors.

[22]Equally bloody results came from inserting a strange rat into an established colony. "What rats do when a member of a strange rat clan enters their territory or is put there by a human experimenter is one of the most horrible and repulsive things which can be observed in animals." As soon as a resident rat scents the stranger, "the information is transmitted like an electric shock through the resident rat, and at once the whole colony is alarmed by a process of mood transmission which is communicated in the brown rat by expression movements but in the house rat by a sharp, shrill, satanic cry which is taken up by all members of the tribe within earshot." Then, "with their eyes bulging from their sockets, their hair standing on end, the rats set out on the rat hunt." The strange rat is slowly torn to pieces by the residents. "Only rarely does one

see an animal in such desperation and panic, so conscious of the inevitability of a terrible death, as a rat which is about to be slain by rats. It ceases to defend itself." This, observed Lorenz, is totally at odds with how a cornered rat will fight against any other foe, where even in the face of certain death it will attack, springing at the enemy, "with the shrill war cry of its species."

[23]Not long ago the *New York Times* reported that, "scientists studying the rat express nothing but admiration for the rat's instincts, ingenuity and tenacity." The article quoted Dr. James Childs of Johns Hopkins Medical Center: "They are genuine survivors; they can live under a remarkably wide range of conditions." We get an inkling of just how wide that range can be from the 1980 discovery of a rat colony thriving on the island of Runit in the South Pacific atoll of Enewetok. During the forties and fifties, a total of forty-three atomic bomb tests had totally contaminated the island with radioactivity, rendering it unsafe for human habitation for twenty-five thousand years. Yet there were the rats.

[24]Their capacity for survival is the stuff of legend. Rats are said to leave a house which is about to fall, and sailors have an age-old superstition that rats will desert a ship before she sets sail on a voyage that will end in her loss.

[25]One of the keys to the rat's survival, writes Lorenz, is "a conservation and traditional passing-on of acquired experience." So, if a rat finds some food with which the pack is unfamiliar, it will describe to the others whether or not it should be eaten. If the food is shunned by a couple of members, no other rat will touch it. Sometimes they'll even sprinkle a poisoned bait with urine or feces. Says Lorenz, "the most astonishing fact is that knowledge of the danger of a certain bait is transmitted from generation to generation and the knowledge long outlives those individuals which first made the experience." The difficulty of successfully combating, the brown rat, he concludes, "lies chiefly in the fact that the rat operates basically with the same methods as those of man, by traditional transmission of experience and its dissemination within the close community."

[26]Ratacake, Krumkill and Rat-Nip are three of the many rodent poisons on the market. Of the roughly two dozen registered rodenticides, one of the most popular is Warfarin, an anti-coagulant that works by reducing the animal's blood-clotting ability, resulting in death from hemorrhaging. It's touted as being less hazardous to other organisms than are the fast-acting single-dose rodenticides, which can also poison children, pets and birds. A rat has to eat Warfarin for a week or more for it to take effect. Two drawbacks: rats can learn not to accept the bait, and resistant strains of rats have evolved—the so-called "Super Rats, " which are immune to the poison. In grain-handling and storage facilities, powerful fumigants are used to control rats. Traps are recommended for control of small populations, though here again a pack can learn to avoid a baited trap after it has caught one or two members.

[27]Good sanitation is the real key to effective rat control, which means denying the rats nesting sites and food supplies. All food should be in sealed containers, garbage cans tightly lidded and compost heaps made rodent-proof. Piles of lumber or other old building supplies may cover rat burrows and should be cleared away. Beatrice Trilm Hunter notes a slightly more esoteric approach: "In Vermont, a man troubled with rats succeeded in capturing the king rat and placed it in an empty milk can. The squeals scared away the remainder of the pack. The man made a recording of the distress call and played it to keep the rats away."

[28]Let's face it: rats aren't all bad. The common laboratory rat, which is a white mutant form of the Norway rat, has contributed tremendously to medical research. Konrad Lorenz, having catalogued the savageries of rat warfare, writes: "One would hardly expect to see the development of the society which is soon built by the victorious murderers. The tolerance, the tenderness which characterizes the relation of mammal mothers to their children, extends in the case of the rats not only to the fathers but to all grandparents, uncles, aunts, cousins, and so on."

[29]Serious conflict simply doesn't occur, even when the colony numbers many dozens of animals. Food is readily shared, with smaller rats being able to push forward and take food away from larger ones with impunity. "The ceremony of friendly contact is the so-called 'creeping under,' which is performed particularly by young animals while larger animals show their sympathy for smaller ones by creeping over them."

[30]Most of the world's rat species, *Walker's Animals of the World* points out, occupy natural habitats and have nothing to do with humans, neither entering buildings nor pillaging agricultural areas. "Many of these species have relatively restricted ranges and habitat tolerances and some may be threatened with extinction." For example, one native species has disappeared completely from parts of Australia, apparently the victim of excessive livestock grazing. *Walker's* maintains that "the activities of a few commensal and pest species of *Rattus* have adversely affected the reputation of the entire genus and, indeed, of all mammals that contain the term rat in their vernacular names." Perhaps it could be said that, rather than humans participating in "the rat race," rats that have learned to live with us have become frantic co-participants in "the human race."

Vocabulary

[2]prolific	[10]despicable	[17]enclave	[26]fumigants
[2]labyrinthine	[11]jaundice	[18]gestation	[27]esoteric
[4]inextricable	[11]murine	[23]ingenuity	[29]impunity
[5]odious	[11]typhus	[23]tenacity	[30]pillaging
[6]communal	[13]commensal	[25]disemmination	[30]vernacular
[10]revulsion	[13]omnivorous	[26]anti-coagulant	

Discussion Questions

1. What type of lead-in does Kennedy use for the introduction? Was it effective in catching your attention? Explain your answer.

2. Including its physical appearance and habitat, paraphrase the description of the Norway rat.

3. Explain the ways in which Kennedy points out that rats are a health menace.

4. Discuss the "class system" in the rat world. Do you see any parallels to the human world? Discuss them.

5. Darwin, in *The Origin of Species*, beginning on page 434 of this text, discusses survival of the fittest. In what ways do rats exhibit a capacity for survival?

6. Kennedy cites many sources in his article. Find at least three places where Kennedy has used sources in quotations and paraphrases. Why do you think he chose to use outside sources?

7. How does Kennedy's description of the process rats use to choose a mate either support or contradict Darwin's theory of sexual selection (page 437)?

ROE V. WADE (ABRIDGED)

UNITED STATES SUPREME COURT

Roe v. Wade ranks among the most controversial and po-litically polarizing cases ever decided by the United States Supreme Court. According to the Roe decision in 1973, most state laws against abortion violated a woman's right to privacy under the Due Process Clause of the Fourteenth Amendment to the United States Constitution. The Roe decision overturned all state and federal laws that were inconsistent with the justices' findings.

    Roe v Wade started a national contoversy that contiues today and may have generated more bitterness on both sides (pro-choice v. pro-life) than any issue since the question of slavery. The "Jane Roe" of the lawsuit was actually Norma Leah McCorvey who claimed she had been a victim of rape and was thus seeking an abortion. Unable to obtain a legal abortion, McCorvey gave birth to a baby girl and put the infant up for adoption. In later years, McCorvey worked in an abortion clinic, recanted the rape allegation, converted to Roman Catholicism and became active in the pro-life movement.

ROE v. WADE, DISTRICT ATTORNEY OF DALLAS COUNTY
APPEAL FROM THE UNITED STATES DISTRICT COURT FOR THE
NORTHERN DISTRICT OF TEXAS

Argued December 13, 1971 — Decided January 22, 1973

MR. JUSTICE BLACKMUN delivered the opinion of the Court.

MR. JUSTICE REHNQUIST, dissenting.

MR. JUSTICE STEWART, concurring.

I

    [1]A pregnant single woman (Roe) brought a class action suit challeng-ing the constitutionality of the Texas criminal abortion laws, which proscribe procuring or attempting an abortion except on medical advice for the purpose of saving the mother's life. A three-judge District Court held that Roe and members of her class had standing to sue and presented a justiciable[a] contro-versy. Ruling that declaratory, though not injunctive, relief was warranted, the court declared the abortion statutes void as vague and overbroadly infringing the plaintiffs' Ninth and Fourteenth Amendment rights. Appellants directly

---

[a]Justiciable is a legal term meaning that an issue under consideration can be settled by law or through the action of a court.

appealed to this Court on the injunctive[b] rulings, and appellee cross-appealed from the District Court's grant of declaratory[c] relief to Roe.

Held:

[2]1. Roe has standing to sue.

[3]2. Contrary to appellee's contention, the natural termination of Roe's pregnancy did not moot her suit. Litigation involving pregnancy, which is "capable of repetition, yet evading review," is an exception to the usual federal rule that an actual controversy must exist at review stages and not simply when the action is initiated.

[4]3. State criminal abortion laws, like those involved here, that except from criminality only a life-saving procedure on the mother's behalf without regard to the stage of her pregnancy and other interests involved, violate the Due Process Clause of the Fourteenth Amendment, which protects against State action the right to privacy,

[6](b) For the stage subsequent to approximately the end of the first trimester, the State, in promoting its interest in the health of the mother, may, if it chooses, regulate the abortion procedure in ways that are reasonably related to maternal health.

[7](c) For the stage subsequent to viability the State, in promoting its interest in the potentiality of human life, may, if it chooses, regulate, and even proscribe, abortion except where necessary, in appropriate medical judgment, for the preservation of the life or health of the mother.

[8]4. The State may define the term "physician" to mean only a physician currently licensed by the State, and may proscribe any abortion by a person who is not a physician as so defined.

[9]5. It is unnecessary to decide the injunctive relief issue since the Texas authorities will doubtless fully recognize the Court's ruling that the Texas criminal abortion statutes are unconstitutional.

MR. JUSTICE BLACKMUN delivered the opinion of the Court.

[10]This Texas federal appeal presents constitutional challenges to state criminal abortion legislation. The Texas statutes under attack here are typical of those that have been in effect in many states for approximately a century. The

---

[b]Injunctive in this context means that Roe asked the lower federal appeals court to issue an injunction stopping the State of Texas from prosecuting women for obtaining an abortion. The appeals court granted "declaratory" relief to Roe (see below) but refused to order the injunction. She's appealing to get the injunction

[c]Declaratory relief means that the district court agreed with Roe on the facts of the case and held that the Texas anti-abortion law was unconstitutional. The district attorney is appealing that decision.

Georgia statutes, in contrast, have a modern cast and are a legislative product that, to an extent at least, obviously reflects the influences of recent attitudinal change, of advancing medical knowledge and techniques, and of new thinking about an old issue.

[11]We forthwith acknowledge our awareness of the sensitive and emotional nature of the abortion controversy, of the vigorous opposing views, even among physicians, and of the deep and seemingly absolute convictions that the subject inspires. One's philosophy, one's experiences, one's exposure to the raw edges of human existence, one's religious training, one's attitudes toward life and family and their values, and the moral standards one establishes and seeks to observe, are all likely to influence and to color one's thinking and conclusions about abortion.

[12]Our task, of course, is to resolve the issue by constitutional measurement, free of emotion and of predilection. We seek earnestly to do this, and, because we do, we have inquired into, and in this opinion place some emphasis upon, medical and medical-legal history and what that history reveals about man's attitudes toward the abortion procedure over the centuries. We bear in mind, too, Mr. Justice Holmes' admonition in his now-vindicated dissent in Lochner v. New York, (1905).[d]

> [The Constitution] is made for people of fundamentally differing views, and the accident of our finding certain opinions natural and familiar or novel and even shocking ought not to cloud our judgment upon the question whether statutes embodying them conflict with the Constitution of the United States.

[13]The Texas statutes that concern us here make it a crime to "procure an abortion," as therein defined, or to attempt one, except with respect to "an abortion procured or attempted by medical advice for the purpose of saving the life of the mother." Similar statutes are in existence in a majority of the states.

[14]Texas first enacted a criminal abortion statute in 1854. This was soon modified into language that has remained substantially unchanged to the present time. The final article in each of these compilations provided the same exception, as does the present Article 1196, for an abortion by "medical advice for the purpose of saving the life of the mother."

---

[d]The essence of this case was whether New York State had the right to limit the work week to 60 hours (six days per week, 10 hours per day) to, in the State's view, protect the health and welfare of its workers or whether this law interfered with the constitutional right of employers to enter into a contract with their employees so long as both sides agreed to the terms of the contract. The U.S. Supreme Court upheld the latter view, with Justice Oliver Wendell Holmes, and others, dissenting in a 5-4 decision. The dissenters held that the State had the constitutional right to protect its citizens in the workplace, a view that later became widely accepted.

II

[15]Jane Roe, a single woman who was residing in Dallas County, Texas, instituted this federal action in March 1970 against the District Attorney of the county. She sought a declaratory judgment that the Texas criminal abortion statutes were unconstitutional on their face and an injunction restraining the defendant from enforcing the statutes.

[16]Roe alleged that she was unmarried and pregnant; that she wished to terminate her pregnancy by an abortion "performed by a competent, licensed physician, under safe, clinical conditions"; that she was unable to get a "legal" abortion in Texas because her life did not appear to be threatened by the continuation of her pregnancy; and that she could not afford to travel to another jurisdiction in order to secure a legal abortion under safe conditions. She claimed that the Texas statutes were unconstitutionally vague and that they abridged her right of personal privacy, protected by the First, Fourth, Fifth, Ninth, and Fourteenth Amendments. By an amendment to her complaint, Roe purported to sue "on behalf of herself and all other women" similarly situated.

[17]On the merits, the District Court held that the "fundamental right of single women and married persons to choose whether to have children is protected by the Ninth Amendment, through the Fourteenth Amendment," and that the Texas criminal abortion statutes were void on their face because they were both unconstitutionally vague and constituted an overbroad infringement of the plaintiffs' Ninth Amendment rights. The court then held that abstention was warranted with respect to the requests for an injunction and dismissed the application for injunctive relief.

[18]Plaintiff Roe (appellant) has appealed to this Court from that part of the District Court's judgment denying the injunction. The defendant District Attorney (appellee) has cross-appealed, pursuant to the same statute, from the court's grant of declaratory relief to Roe.

III

[19]On the issue of justiciability, despite the use of the pseudonym, no suggestion is made that Roe is a fictitious person. For purposes of her case, we accept as true, and as established, her existence; her pregnant state, as of the inception of her suit in March 1970 and as late as May 21 of that year when she filed an alias affidavit with the District Court; and her inability to obtain a legal abortion in Texas.

[20]The District Attorney notes that the record does not disclose that Roe was pregnant at the time of the District Court hearing on May 22, 1970, or on the following June 17 when the court's opinion and judgment were filed. And he suggests that Roe's case must now be moot because she and all other members of her class are no longer subject to any 1970 pregnancy.

[21]The usual rule in federal cases is that an actual controversy must exist

at stages of appellate review and not simply at the date the action is initiated. But when, as here, pregnancy is a significant fact in the litigation, the normal 266-day human gestation period is so short that the pregnancy will come to term before the usual appellate process is complete. If that termination makes a case moot, pregnancy litigation seldom will survive much beyond the trial stage, and appellate review will be effectively denied. Our law should not be that rigid.

[22]We, therefore, agree with the District Court that Jane Roe had standing to undertake this litigation, that she presented a justiciable controversy, and that the natural termination of her 1970 pregnancy has not rendered her case moot.

IV

[23]The principal thrust of appellant's attack on the Texas statutes is that they improperly invade a right, said to be possessed by the pregnant woman, to choose to terminate her pregnancy. Appellant Roe claims this right in the concept of personal "liberty" embodied in the Fourteenth Amendment's Due Process Clause; or in personal, marital, familial, and sexual privacy said to be protected by the Bill of Rights; or among those rights reserved to the people by the Ninth Amendment. Before addressing this claim, we feel it desirable briefly to survey, in several aspects, the history of abortion, for such insight as that history may afford us, and then to examine the State purposes and interests behind the criminal abortion laws.

V

[24]It is perhaps not generally appreciated that the restrictive criminal abortion laws in effect in a majority of states today are of relatively recent vintage. Those laws, generally proscribing abortion or its attempt at any time during pregnancy except when necessary to preserve the pregnant woman's life, are not of ancient or even of common-law origin. Instead, they derive from statutory changes effected, for the most part, in the latter half of the 19th century.

[A lengthy discussion of the history of abortion, starting back in Greek and Roman times and the common law of European counties, primarily England, through the Middle Ages, follows here in the original text of the decision and is summarized here.]

[25]1. The common law: It is undisputed that at common law, abortion performed before "quickening"—the first recognizable movement of the fetus in utero, appearing usually from the 16th to the 18th week of pregnancy—was not an indictable offense. The absence of a common-law crime for pre-quickening abortion appears to have developed from earlier philosophical, theological, and civil and canon law concepts of when life begins. These disciplines variously

approached the question in terms of the point at which the embryo or fetus became "formed" or recognizably human, or in terms of when a "person" came into being, that is, infused with a "soul" or "animated." Christian theology and the canon law came to fix the point of animation at 40 days for a male and 80 days for a female, a view that persisted until the 19th century. There was agreement that prior to the 40 or 80-day point the fetus was to be regarded as part of the mother, and its destruction, therefore, was not homicide. Due perhaps to Aquinas' definition of movement as one of the two first principles of life, Bracton[e] focused upon quickening as the critical point. The significance of quickening was echoed by later common-law scholars and found its way into the received common law in this country.

[26]Whether abortion of a quick fetus was a felony at common law, or even a lesser crime, is still disputed. Bracton, writing early in the 13th century, thought it homicide. A recent review of the common-law precedents argues, however, that even post-quickening abortion was never established as a common-law crime. This is of some importance because while most American courts ruled that abortion of an unquickened fetus was not criminal under their received common law, others held that abortion of a quick fetus was a "misprision," a term they translated to mean "misdemeanor." Review of all the reported cases makes it now appear doubtful that abortion was ever firmly established as a common-law crime even with respect to the destruction of a quick fetus.

[27]2. English statutory law: England's first criminal abortion statute came in 1803. It made abortion of a quick fetus a capital crime, but provided lesser penalties for the felony of abortion before quickening, and thus preserved the "quickening" distinction. This contrast was continued in the general revision of 1828. It disappeared, however, together with the death penalty, in 1837 and did not reappear in the Offenses Against the Person Act of 1861 that formed the core of English anti-abortion law until the liberalizing reforms of 1967.

[28]In 1929, the Infant Life (Preservation) Act came into being. Its emphasis was upon the destruction of "the life of a child capable of being born alive." It made a willful act performed with the necessary intent a felony "unless the act which caused the death of the child was done in good faith for the purpose only of preserving the life of the mother."

[29]The Abortion Act of 1967 permits a licensed physician to perform an abortion where two other licensed physicians agree (a) "that the continuance of the pregnancy would involve risk to the life of the pregnant woman, or of injury to the physical or mental health of the pregnant woman or any existing children

---

[e]Henry of Bracton (circa 1210-1268) was an English lawyer and judge whose book *On the Laws and Customs of England* helped establish the early British legal code, partially based upon categories used in ancient Roman law.

of her family, greater than if the pregnancy were terminated," or (b) "that there is a substantial risk that if the child were born it would suffer from such physical or mental abnormalities as to be seriously handicapped." The Act also provides that, in making this determination, "account may be taken of the pregnant woman's actual or reasonably foreseeable environment." It also permits a physician, without the concurrence of others, to terminate a pregnancy where he is of the good-faith opinion that the abortion "is immediately necessary to save the life or to prevent grave permanent injury to the physical or mental health of the pregnant woman."

[30]3. The American law: In this country, the law in effect in all but a few states until mid-19th century was the pre-existing English common law. Connecticut, the first state to enact abortion legislation, adopted in 1821 that part of Lord Ellenborough's Act[f] that related to a woman "quick with child." The death penalty was not imposed. Abortion before quickening was made a crime in that state only in 1860.

[31]In 1828, New York enacted legislation that, in two respects, was to serve as a model for early anti-abortion statutes. First, while barring destruction of an unquickened fetus as well as a quick fetus, it made the former only a misdemeanor, but the latter second-degree manslaughter. Second, it incorporated a concept of therapeutic abortion by providing that an abortion was excused if it "shall have been necessary to preserve the life of such mother, or shall have been advised by two physicians to be necessary for such purpose."

[32]By 1840, when Texas had received the common law, only eight American states had statutes dealing with abortion. It was not until after the War Between the States that legislation began generally to replace the common law. Most of these initial statutes dealt severely with abortion after quickening but were lenient with it before quickening.

[33]Gradually, in the middle and late 19th century the quickening distinction disappeared from the statutory law of most states and the degree of the offense and the penalties were increased. By the end of the 1950's, a large majority of the jurisdictions banned abortion, whenever and however performed, unless done to save or preserve the life of the mother. The exceptions, Alabama and the District of Columbia, permitted abortion to preserve the mother's health. Three states permitted abortions that were not "unlawfully" performed or that were not "without lawful justification," leaving interpretation of those standards to the courts. In the past several years, however, a trend toward liberalization of abortion statutes has resulted in adoption, by about one-third of the

---

[f]Lord Ellenborough's Act, officially known as the "Malicious Shooting or Stabbing Act," was introduced in the English Parliament by Edward Law (Lord Ellenborough) and contained a section that clarified abortion law in England and Ireland.

states, of less stringent laws, most of them patterned after the ALI Model Penal Code.[g]

[34]It is thus apparent that at the time of the adoption of our Constitution, and throughout the major portion of the 19th century, abortion was viewed with less disfavor than under most American statutes currently in effect. Phrasing it another way, a woman enjoyed a substantially broader right to terminate a pregnancy than she does in most states today. At least with respect to the early stage of pregnancy, and very possibly without such a limitation, the opportunity to make this choice was present in this country well into the 19th century.

[35]4. The position of the American Medical Association: The anti-abortion mood prevalent in this country in the late 19th century was shared by the medical profession. Indeed, the attitude of the profession may have played a significant role in the enactment of stringent criminal abortion legislation during that period.

[36]An AMA Committee on Criminal Abortion was appointed in May 1857. It presented its report to the Twelfth Annual Meeting in 1859. That report observed that the Committee had been appointed to investigate criminal abortion "with a view to its general suppression." It deplored abortion and its frequency.

[37]The Committee then offered, and the Association adopted, resolutions protesting "against such unwarrantable destruction of human life," calling upon state legislatures to revise their abortion laws and requesting the cooperation of state medical societies "in pressing the subject."

[38]In 1871 a long and vivid report was submitted by the Committee on Criminal Abortion recommending, among other things, that it "be unlawful and unprofessional for any physician to induce abortion or premature labor without the concurrent opinion of at least one respectable consulting physician, and then always with a view to the safety of the child—if that be possible," and calling "the attention of the clergy of all denominations to the perverted views of morality entertained by a large class of females—aye, and men also, on this important question."

[39]Except for periodic condemnation of the criminal abortionist, no further formal AMA action took place until 1967 when the Committee on Human Reproduction urged the adoption of a stated policy of opposition to induced abortion, except when there is "documented medical evidence" of a threat to the health or life of the mother, or that the child "may be born with incapacitating

---

[g]The ALI (American Law Institute) Model Penal Code (MPC) was adopted by that body in 1962 and last updated in 1981. The purpose of the MPC was to help state legislatures update and standardize penal laws to bring about more uniformity across all of the fifty states.

physical deformity or mental deficiency," or that a pregnancy "resulting from legally established statutory or forcible rape or incest may constitute a threat to the mental or physical health of the patient," two other physicians "chosen because of their recognized professional competence have examined the patient and have concurred in writing, " and the procedure "is performed in a hospital accredited by the Joint Commission on Accreditation of Hospitals."

[40]In 1970, after the introduction of a variety of proposed resolutions, and of a report from its Board of Trustees, a reference committee noted "polarization of the medical profession on this controversial issue"; division among those who had testified; a difference of opinion among AMA councils and committees; "the remarkable shift in testimony" in six months, felt to be influenced "by the rapid changes in state laws and by the judicial decisions which tend to make abortion more freely available;" and a feeling "that this trend will continue." On June 25, 1970, the House of Delegates adopted preambles and resolutions asserting that abortion is a medical procedure that should be performed by a licensed physician in an accredited hospital only after consultation with two other physicians and in conformity with state law, and that no party to the procedure should be required to violate personally held moral principles.

[41]5. The position of the American Bar Association: At its meeting in February 1972 the ABA House of Delegates approved, with 17 opposing votes, the Uniform Abortion Act that had been drafted and approved the preceding August by the Conference of Commissioners on Uniform State Laws.[h]

VI

[42]Three reasons have been advanced to explain historically the enactment of criminal abortion laws in the 19th century and to justify their continued existence.

[43]It has been argued occasionally that these laws were the product of a Victorian social concern to discourage illicit sexual conduct. Texas, how-

---

[h]The ABA Uniform Abortion Act of 1972 created a model for the states to follow should they so chose. It simply said that abortions should be performed only by qualified physicians and only within 20 weeks of the commencement of the pregnancy or after 20 weeks "only if the physician has reasonable cause to believe (i) there is a substantial risk that continuance of the pregnancy would endanger the life of the mother or would gravely impair the physical or mental health of the mother, (ii) that the child would be born with grave physical or mental defect, or (iii) that the pregnancy resulted from rape or incest, or illicit intercourse with a girl under the age of 16 years."

The ABA also included this explanatory note: "This Act is based largely upon the New York abortion act following a review of the more recent laws on abortion in several states and upon recognition of a more liberal trend in laws on this subject. Recognition was given also to the several decisions in state and federal courts which show a further trend toward liberalization of abortion laws, especially during the first trimester of pregnancy."

ever, does not advance this justification in the present case, and it appears that no court or commentator has taken the argument seriously. The appellants and amici contend, moreover, that this is not a proper State purpose at all and suggest that, if it were, the Texas statutes are overbroad in protecting it since the law fails to distinguish between married and unwed mothers.

[44]A second reason is concerned with abortion as a medical procedure. When most criminal abortion laws were first enacted, the procedure was a hazardous one for the woman. This was particularly true prior to the development of antisepsis. Antiseptic techniques, of course, were based on discoveries by Lister, Pasteur, and others first announced in 1867, but were not generally accepted and employed until about the turn of the century. Abortion mortality was high. Even after 1900, and perhaps until as late as the development of antibiotics in the 1940's, standard modern techniques such as dilation and curettage were not nearly so safe as they are today. Thus, it has been argued that a state's real concern in enacting a criminal abortion law was to protect the pregnant woman, that is, to restrain her from submitting to a procedure that placed her life in serious jeopardy.

[45]Modern medical techniques have altered this situation. Appellants and various amici refer to medical data indicating that abortion in early pregnancy, that is, prior to the end of the first trimester, although not without its risk, is now relatively safe. Mortality rates for women undergoing early abortions, where the procedure is legal, appear to be as low as or lower than the rates for normal childbirth. Consequently, any interest of the State in protecting the woman from an inherently hazardous procedure, except when it would be equally dangerous for her to forgo it, has largely disappeared. The prevalence of high mortality rates at illegal "abortion mills" strengthens, rather than weakens, the State's interest in regulating the conditions under which abortions are performed. Moreover, the risk to the woman increases as her pregnancy continues. Thus, the State retains a definite interest in protecting the woman's own health and safety when an abortion is proposed at a late stage of pregnancy.

[46]The third reason is the State's interest—some phrase it in terms of duty—in protecting prenatal life. Some of the argument for this justification rests on the theory that a new human life is present from the moment of conception. The State's interest and general obligation to protect life then extends, it is argued, to prenatal life. Only when the life of the pregnant mother herself is at stake, balanced against the life she carries within her, should the interest of the embryo or fetus not prevail.

[47]Parties challenging state abortion laws have sharply disputed in some courts the contention that a purpose of these laws, when enacted, was to protect prenatal life. Pointing to the absence of legislative history to support the contention, they claim that most state laws were designed solely to protect the woman. Because medical advances have lessened this concern, at least with

respect to abortion in early pregnancy, they argue that with respect to such abortions the laws can no longer be justified by any State interest. There is some scholarly support for this view of original purpose. The few state courts called upon to interpret their laws in the late 19th and early 20th centuries did focus on the State's interest in protecting the woman's health rather than in preserving the embryo and fetus.

[48]It is with these interests, and the weight to be attached to them, that this case is concerned.

VII

[49]The Constitution does not explicitly mention any right of privacy. In a line of decisions, however, going back perhaps as far as Union Pacific R. Co. v. Botsford, (1891), the Court has recognized that a right of personal privacy, or a guarantee of certain areas or zones of privacy, does exist under the Constitution. In varying contexts, the Court or individual Justices have, indeed, found at least the roots of that right in the First Amendment; in the Fourth and Fifth Amendments; in the Ninth Amendment; or in the concept of liberty guaranteed by the first section of the Fourteenth Amendment. These decisions make it clear that only personal rights that can be deemed "fundamental" or "implicit in the concept of ordered liberty," Palko v. Connecticut, (1937), are included in this guarantee of personal privacy. They also make it clear that the right has some extension to activities relating to marriage, Loving v. Virginia,
(1967); to procreation, Skinner v. Oklahoma, (1942); contraception, Eisenstadt v. Baird (1972); family relationships, Prince v. Massachusetts, (1944); and to child rearing and education, Pierce v. Society of Sisters, (1925).

[50]This right of privacy, whether it be founded in the Fourteenth Amendment's concept of personal liberty and restrictions upon State action, as we feel it is, or, as the District Court determined, in the Ninth Amendment's reservation of rights to the people, is broad enough to encompass a woman's decision whether or not to terminate her pregnancy. The detriment that the State would impose upon the pregnant woman by denying this choice altogether is apparent. Specific and direct harm medically diagnosable even in early pregnancy may be involved. Maternity, or additional offspring, may force upon the woman a distressful life and future. Psychological harm may be imminent. Mental and physical health may be taxed by child care. There is also the distress, for all concerned, associated with the unwanted child, and there is the problem of bringing a child into a family already unable, psychologically and otherwise, to care for it. In other cases, as in this one, the additional difficulties and continuing stigma of unwed motherhood may be involved. All these are factors the woman and her responsible physician necessarily will consider in consultation.

[51]On the basis of elements such as these, appellant and some amici argue that the woman's right is absolute and that she is entitled to terminate her preg-

nancy at whatever time, in whatever way, and for whatever reason she alone chooses. With this we do not agree. Appellant's arguments that Texas either has no valid interest at all in regulating the abortion decision, or no interest strong enough to support any limitation upon the woman's sole determination, are unpersuasive. The Court's decisions recognizing a right of privacy also acknowledge that some State regulation in areas protected by that right is appropriate. As noted above, a state may properly assert important interests in safeguarding health (e.g. requiring vaccination), in maintaining medical standards, and in protecting potential life. At some point in pregnancy, these respective interests become sufficiently compelling to sustain regulation of the factors that govern the abortion decision. The privacy right involved, therefore, cannot be said to be absolute.

[52]We, therefore, conclude that the right of personal privacy includes the abortion decision, but that this right is not unqualified and must be considered against important State interests in regulation.

VIII

[53]The District Court held that the appellee failed to meet his burden of demonstrating that the Texas statute's infringement upon Roe's rights was necessary to support a compelling State interest, and that, although the appellee presented "several compelling justifications for State presence in the area of abortions," the statutes outstripped these justifications and swept "far beyond any areas of compelling State interest." Appellant and appellee both contest that holding. Appellant, as has been indicated, claims an absolute right that bars any State imposition of criminal penalties in the area. Appellee argues that the State's determination to recognize and protect prenatal life from and after conception constitutes a compelling State interest. As noted above, we do not agree fully with either formulation.

[54]A. The appellee and certain amici argue that the fetus is a "person" within the language and meaning of the Fourteenth Amendment. In support of this, they outline at length and in detail the well-known facts of fetal development. If this suggestion of personhood is established, the appellant's case, of course, collapses, for the fetus' right to life would then be guaranteed specifically by the Amendment. The appellant conceded as much on reargument. On the other hand, the appellee conceded on reargument that no case could be cited that holds that a fetus is a person within the meaning of the Fourteenth Amendment.

[55]Our observation above that throughout the major portion of the 19th century prevailing legal abortion practices were far freer than they are today, persuades us that the word "person," as used in the Fourteenth Amendment, does not include the unborn. This is in accord with the results reached in those

few cases where the issue has been squarely presented.

[56]This conclusion, however, does not of itself fully answer the contentions raised by Texas, and we pass on to other considerations.

[57]B. The pregnant woman cannot be isolated in her privacy. She carries an embryo and, later, a fetus, if one accepts the medical definitions of the developing young in the human uterus. The situation therefore is inherently different from marital intimacy, or bedroom possession of obscene material, or marriage, or procreation, or education, with which Eisenstadt and Griswold, Stanley, Loving, Skinner, and Pierce were respectively concerned. As we have intimated above, it is reasonable and appropriate for a state to decide that at some point in time another interest, that of health of the mother or that of potential human life, becomes significantly involved. The woman's privacy is no longer sole, and any right of privacy she possesses must be measured accordingly.

[58]Texas urges that, apart from the Fourteenth Amendment, life begins at conception and is present throughout pregnancy, and that, therefore, the State has a compelling interest in protecting that life from and after conception. We need not resolve the difficult question of when life begins. When those trained in the respective disciplines of medicine, philosophy, and theology are unable to arrive at any consensus, the judiciary, at this point in the development of man's knowledge, is not in a position to speculate as to the answer.

[59]It should be sufficient to note briefly the wide divergence of thinking on this most sensitive and difficult question. As we have noted, the common law found greater significance in quickening. Physicians and their scientific colleagues have regarded that event with less interest and have tended to focus either upon conception, upon live birth, or upon the interim point at which the fetus becomes "viable," that is, potentially able to live outside the mother's womb, albeit with artificial aid. Viability is usually placed at about seven months (28 weeks) but may occur earlier, even at 24 weeks.

[60]In areas other than criminal abortion, the law has been reluctant to endorse any theory that life, as we recognize it, begins before live birth or to accord legal rights to the unborn except in narrowly defined situations and except when the rights are contingent upon live birth. Some states permit the parents of a stillborn child to maintain an action for wrongful death because of prenatal injuries. Such an action, however, would appear to be one to vindicate the parents' interest and is thus consistent with the view that the fetus, at most, represents only the potentiality of life. In short, the unborn have never been recognized in the law as persons in the whole sense.

IX

[61]In view of all this, we do not agree that, by adopting one theory of life, Texas may override the rights of the pregnant woman that are at stake. We

repeat, however, that the State does have an important and legitimate interest in preserving and protecting the health of the pregnant woman, whether she be a resident of the state or a nonresident who seeks medical consultation and treatment there, and that it has still another important and legitimate interest in protecting the potentiality of human life. These interests are separate and distinct. Each grows in substantiality as the woman approaches term and, at a point during pregnancy, each becomes "compelling."

[62]With respect to the State's important and legitimate interest in the health of the mother, the "compelling" point, in the light of present medical knowledge, is at approximately the end of the first trimester. This is so because of the now-established medical fact, referred to above, that until the end of the first trimester mortality in abortion may be less than mortality in normal childbirth. It follows that, from and after this point, a state may regulate the abortion procedure to the extent that the regulation reasonably relates to the preservation and protection of maternal health. Examples of permissible State regulation in this area are requirements as to the qualifications of the person who is to perform the abortion; as to the licensure of that person; as to the facility in which the procedure is to be performed, that is, whether it must be a hospital or may be a clinic or some other place of less-than-hospital status; as to the licensing of the facility; and the like.

[63]This means, on the other hand, that, for the period of pregnancy prior to this "compelling" point, the attending physician, in consultation with his patient, is free to determine, without regulation by the State, that, in his medical judgment, the patient's pregnancy should be terminated. If that decision is reached, the judgment may be effectuated by an abortion free of interference by the State.

[64]With respect to the State's important and legitimate interest in potential life, the "compelling" point is at viability. This is so because the fetus then presumably has the capability of meaningful life outside the mother's womb. State regulation protective of fetal life after viability thus has both logical and biological justifications. If the State is interested in protecting fetal life after viability, it may go so far as to proscribe abortion during that period, except when it is necessary to preserve the life or health of the mother.

[65]Measured against these standards, Article 1196 of the Texas Penal Code, in restricting legal abortions to those "procured or attempted by medical advice for the purpose of saving the life of the mother," sweeps too broadly. The statute makes no distinction between abortions performed early in pregnancy and those performed later, and it limits to a single reason, "saving the mother's life," the legal justification for the procedure. The statute, therefore, cannot survive the constitutional attack made upon it here.

X

To summarize and to repeat:

[66]1. A state criminal abortion statute of the current Texas type, that excepts from criminality only a lifesaving procedure on behalf of the mother, without regard to pregnancy stage and without recognition of the other interests involved, violates the Due Process Clause of the Fourteenth Amendment.

(a) For the stage prior to approximately the end of the first trimester, the abortion decision and its effectuation must be left to the medical judgment of the pregnant woman's attending physician.

(b) For the stage subsequent to approximately the end of the first trimester, the State, in promoting its interest in the health of the mother, may, if it chooses, regulate the abortion procedure in ways that are reasonably related to maternal health.

(c) For the stage subsequent to viability, the State in promoting its interest in the potentiality of human life may, if it chooses, regulate, and even proscribe, abortion except where it is necessary, in appropriate medical judgment, for the preservation of the life or health of the mother.

[67]2. The State may define the term "physician," as it has been employed in the preceding paragraphs of this Part X of this opinion, to mean only a physician currently licensed by the State, and may proscribe any abortion by a person who is not a physician as so defined.

[68]This holding, we feel, is consistent with the relative weights of the respective interests involved, with the lessons and examples of medical and legal history, with the intent of the common law, and with the demands of the profound problems of the present day. The decision leaves the State free to place increasing restrictions on abortion as the period of pregnancy lengthens, so long as those restrictions are tailored to the recognized State interests. The decision vindicates the right of physicians to administer medical treatment according to their professional judgment up to the points where important State interests provide compelling justifications for intervention. Up to those points, the abortion decision in all its aspects is inherently, and primarily, a medical decision, and basic responsibility for it must rest with the physician. If an individual practitioner abuses the privilege of exercising proper medical judgment, the usual remedies, judicial and intra-professional, are available.

XI

[69]Our conclusion that Article 1196 is unconstitutional means, of course, that the Texas abortion statutes, as a unit, must fall.

[70]Although the District Court granted appellant Roe declaratory relief, it stopped short of issuing an injunction against enforcement of the Texas statutes. The Court has recognized that different considerations enter into a federal court's decision as to declaratory relief, on the one hand, and injunctive relief, on the other.

[71]We find it unnecessary to decide whether the District Court erred in withholding injunctive relief, for we assume the Texas prosecutorial authorities will give full credence to this decision that the present criminal abortion statutes of that state are unconstitutional.

[72]In all other respects, the judgment of the District Court is affirmed. Costs are allowed to the appellee.

It is so ordered.

Vocabulary

[1]proscribe	[17]infringement	[27]felony	[50]encompass
[1]procuring	[17]abstention	[29]concurrence	[50]detriment
[1]infringing	[18]pursuant	[33]stringent	[50]imminent
[1]plaintiff	[19]pseudonym	[36]deplored	[50]stigma
[1]appellant	[19]inception	[37]unwarrantable	[51]compelling
[1]appellee	[19]affadavit	[40]polarization	[51]absolute
[3]moot	[21]gestation	[43]Victorian	[52]infringement
[3]litigation	[23]marital	[43]illicit	[57]intimated
[6]trimester	[23]familial	[43]amici (amicus	[58]speculate
[6]maternal	[24]vintage	curiae)	[59]divergence
[7]subsequent	[25]common law	[44]antisepsis	[59]albeit
[7]viability	[25]in utero	[44]dilation	[60]contingent
[10]statutes	[25]indictable	[44]curettage	(upon)
[12]predilection	[25]theological	[45]mortality rate	[63]effectuated
[12]admonition	[25]canon law	[45]inherently	[71]erred
[12]vindicated	[26]fetus	[45]prevalence	[71]credence
[14]compilation	[25]infused	[46]prenatal	
[16]abridged	[26]precedent	[47]contention	
[16]purported	[26]misdemeanor	[49]explicitly	

Discussion Questions

1. Legal briefs and court decisions such as this one are high-level forms of argument. This decision is long and complex. Create an outline of the structure of the Court's argument in this case.

2. Explain why Roe is suing the State of Texas and why the Dallas County district attorney is counter-suing.

3. Explain how the tone of the language in paragraph 9 indicates the perceived power and status of the United States Supreme Court.

4. Summarize the facts of Roe's case and the essential point of her argument.

5. What is the main point of the district attorney's counter-argument?

6. Read paragraph 20 carefully. What is the Dallas County district attorney seeking here and what is the Supreme Court's response?

7. What is the significance of the terms "quick" and "quickening" and why does the Court keep referring to them?

8. What are English "common law" and "statutory law," (paragraphs 25-29) and why do the justices devote so much discussion to them?

9. Look at the language used in paragraph 29 section (a). What words have been added here that gave British doctors much more latitude in deciding whether to recommend abortion?

10. In the 1950's most states in America banned abortion unless it was necessary "to preserve the life of the mother." What was the difference in the language of the Alabama and District of Columbia laws compared to the rest of the states?

11. Look at the language of the American Medical Association recommendation in paragraph 39. Compare this to the British Law of 1967 discussed in paragraph 29. What new language appears in the AMA recommendation that adds a whole new dimension to the discussion?

12. We frequently hear references to Americans' "constitutional right to privacy." Is this language accurate? Explain.

13. Read paragraph 50 carefully and explain how "Amendment XIV" beginning on page 389 of this text and "Justifying Infanticide" beginning on page 339 relate to this paragraph.

14. When all was said and done, did Roe get the abortion?

THE SERMON ON THE MOUNT
FROM THE HOLY BIBLE, KING JAMES VERSION

NEW TESTAMENT, MATTHEW CHAPTER 5

Followers of the Christian religion refer to the second major section of The Holy Bible as The New Testament and the much longer first section (which is the same basic text as the Tanakh or Hebrew Bible in Judaism) as The Old Testament. The Book of Matthew tells the story of the birth, life and death by crucifixion of Jesus of Nazareth, the Christ (from the Greek Khristos—"the messiah" or "the anointed.") In the Sermon on the Mount Jesus Christ tells his disciples how to live their lives on earth and how to achieve a state of grace that will bring them into everlasting life in the Kingdom of Heaven after their death.

¹And seeing the multitudes, he[a] went up into a mountain: and when he was set, his disciples came unto him:

²And he opened his mouth, and taught them, saying,

³Blessed are the poor in spirit: for theirs is the kingdom of heaven.

⁴Blessed are they that mourn: for they shall be comforted.

⁵Blessed are the meek: for they shall inherit the earth.

⁶Blessed are they which do hunger and thirst after righteousness: for they shall be filled.

⁷Blessed are the merciful: for they shall obtain mercy.

⁸Blessed are the pure in heart: for they shall see God.

⁹Blessed are the peacemakers: for they shall be called the children of God.

¹⁰Blessed are they which are persecuted for righteousness' sake: for theirs is the kingdom of heaven.

¹¹Blessed are ye, when men shall revile you, and persecute you, and shall say all manner of evil against you falsely, for my sake.

¹²Rejoice, and be exceeding glad: for great is your reward in heaven: for so persecuted they the prophets which were before you.

¹³Ye are the salt of the earth: but if the salt have lost its savor, wherewith shall it be salted? It is thenceforth good for nothing, but to be cast out, and to be trodden under foot of men.

¹⁴Ye are the light of the world. A city that is set on an hill cannot be hid.

---

[a]"He" is Jesus in this narrative told to us by the Apostle Matthew.

[15]Neither do men light a candle, and put it under a bushel, but on a candlestick; and it giveth light unto all that are in the house.

[16]Let your light so shine before men, that they may see your good works, and glorify your Father which is in heaven.

[17]Think not that I am come to destroy the law, or the prophets: I am not come to destroy, but to fulfill.

[18]For verily I say unto you, Till heaven and earth pass, one jot or one tittle shall in no wise pass from the law, till all be fulfilled.

[19]Whosoever therefore shall break one of these least commandments, and shall teach men so, he shall be called the least in the kingdom of heaven: but whosoever shall do and teach them, the same shall be called great in the kingdom of heaven.

[20]For I say unto you, That except your righteousness shall exceed the righteousness of the scribes and Pharisees, ye shall in no case enter into the kingdom of heaven.

[21]Ye have heard that it was said of them of old time, Thou shalt not kill; and whosoever shall kill shall be in danger of the judgment:

[22]But I say unto you, That whosoever is angry with his brother without a cause shall be in danger of the judgment: and whosoever shall say to his brother, Raca,[b] shall be in danger of the council: but whosoever shall say, Thou fool, shall be in danger of hell fire.

[23]Therefore if thou bring thy gift to the altar, and there rememberest that thy brother hath ought[c] against thee;

[24]Leave there thy gift before the altar, and go thy way; first be reconciled to thy brother, and then come and offer thy gift.

[25]Agree with thine adversary quickly, while thou art in the way with him; lest at any time the adversary deliver thee to the judge, and the judge deliver thee to the officer, and thou be cast into prison.

[26]Verily I say unto thee, Thou shalt by no means come out thence, till thou hast paid the uttermost farthing.

[27]Ye have heard that it was said by them of old time, Thou shalt not commit adultery:

[28]But I say unto you, That whosoever looketh on a woman to lust after her hath committed adultery with her already in his heart.

[29]And if thy right eye offend thee, pluck it out, and cast it from thee: for it is profitable for thee that one of thy members should perish, and not that thy whole body should be cast into hell.

---

[b]"Raca" is an Aramaic word (an ancient Semitic language that Jesus spoke) that means "empty-headed." These lines have generated much discussion among New Testament scholars with the broad consensus seeming to be, "Don't lash out against your brother" (perhaps literally your sibling but more likely in the broader sense of any person) or you will be guilty of "murder in your heart" and will put yourself in danger of going to hell.

[30]And if thy right hand offend thee, cut it off, and cast it from thee: for it is profitable for thee that one of thy members should perish, and not that thy whole body should be cast into hell.

[31]It hath been said, Whosoever shall put away his wife, let him give her a writing of divorcement:

[32]But I say unto you, That whosoever shall put away his wife, saving for the cause of fornication, causeth her to commit adultery: and whosoever shall marry her that is divorced committeth adultery.

[33]Again, ye have heard that it hath been said by them of old time, Thou shalt not forswear thyself, but shalt perform unto the Lord thine oaths:

[34]But I say unto you, Swear not at all; neither by heaven; for it is God's throne:

[35]Nor by the earth; for it is his footstool: neither by Jerusalem; for it is the city of the great King.

[36]Neither shalt thou swear by thy head, because thou canst not make one hair white or black.

[37]But let your communication be, Yea, yea; Nay, nay: for whatsoever is more than these cometh of evil.

[38]Ye have heard that it hath been said, An eye for an eye, and a tooth for a tooth:

[39]But I say unto you, That ye resist not evil: but whosoever shall smite thee on thy right cheek, turn to him the other also.

[40]And if any man will sue thee at the law, and take away thy coat, let him have thy cloak also.

[41]And whosoever shall compel thee to go a mile, go with him twain.

[42]Give to him that asketh thee, and from him that would borrow of thee turn not thou away.

[43]Ye have heard that it hath been said, Thou shalt love thy neighbour, and hate thine enemy.

[44]But I say unto you, Love your enemies, bless them that curse you, do good to them that hate you, and pray for them which despitefully use you, and persecute you;

[45]That ye may be the children of your Father which is in heaven: for he maketh his sun to rise on the evil and on the good, and sendeth rain on the just and on the unjust.

[46]For if ye love them which love you, what reward have ye? do not even the publicans the same?

[47]And if ye salute your brethren only, what do ye more than others? do not even the publicans so?

[48]Be ye therefore perfect, even as your Father which is in heaven is perfect.

Vocabulary

[1]disciple	[20]Pharisees	[26]uttermost	[46]publican
[12]prophet	[10]persecuted	[26]farthing	[47]brethren
[18]tittle	[25]adversary	[32]fornication	
[20]scribe	[26]verily	[41]twain	

Discussion Questions

1. Who is speaking in lines 1 and 2?

2. Who 'opened his mouth" in line 2?

3. Lines 3 through 11 are commonly known as "the beatitudes." What is the meaning of this term?

4. Several phrases from this work, such as "the meek shall inherit the earth" are common sayings in American culture. Working with a classmate, see how many more common phrases you can find.

5. In line 21 Jesus says, ". . . it was said of them of old time, Thou shalt not kill; and whosoever shall kill shall be in danger of the judgment." Based upon your knowledge of Judeo-Christian tradition or from research, explain where this reference came from.

6. At what point in this text (which line number) does Jesus switch from describing to prescribing; that is, where does he begin telling his listeners what they need to do to achieve salvation?

7. Do you agree with the advice Jesus gives his disciples in lines 39-44?

8. Look at verses 226-232 in Sura 2 of the Qur'an on page 460 in this text. What are the similarities/differences between those verses and lines 31 and 32 here?

9. Look at Chapter 12 of the Bhagavad Gita beginning on page 146 of this text, the Eightfold Path beginning on page 178, Leviticus beginning on page 377 and Sura 2 of the Qur'an on page 457. Compare these works to the Sermon on the Mount and explain what they all have in common.

SEX

EDWARD O. WILSON

Edward O. Wilson (1929-   ) is the author of two Pulitzer Prize-winning books, On Human Nature *(1978) and* The Ants *(1990). He has also been awarded numerous fellowships, honors, and awards, including the National Medal of Science (1977), the Gold Medal of the Worldwide Fund for Nature (1990), the International Prize for Biology from Japan (1993), and the Audubon Medal of the National Audubon Society (1995).*

[1]Sex is central to human biology and a protean phenomenon that permeates every aspect of our existence and takes new forms through each step in the life cycle. Its complexity and ambiguity are due to the fact that sex is not designed primarily for reproduction. Evolution has devised much more efficient ways for creatures to multiply than the complicated procedures of mating and fertilization. Bacteria simply divide in two (in many species, every twenty minutes), fungi shed immense numbers of spores, and hydras bud offspring directly from their trunks. Each fragment of a shattered sponge grows into an entire new organism. If multiplication were the only purpose of reproductive behavior, our mammalian ancestors could have evolved without sex. Every human being might be asexual and sprout new offspring from the surface cells of a neutered womb. Even now, a swift, bacterium-like method of asexual reproduction occurs on the rare occasions when identical twins are created by a single division of an already fertilized egg.

[2]Nor is the primary function of sex the giving and receiving of pleasure. The vast majority of animal species perform the sexual act mechanically and with minimal foreplay. Pairs of bacteria and protozoans form sexual unions without the benefit of a nervous system, while corals, clams, and many other invertebrate animals simply shed their sex cells into the surrounding water—literally without giving the matter a thought, since they lack a proper brain. Pleasure is at best an enabling device for animals that copulate, a means for inducing creatures with versatile nervous systems to make the heavy investment of time and energy required for courtship, sexual intercourse, and parenting.

[3]Moreover, sex is in every sense a gratuitously consuming and risky activity. The reproductive organs of human beings are anatomically complex in ways that make them subject to lethal malfunctions, such as ectopic pregnancy and venereal disease. Courtship activities are prolonged beyond the minimal needs of signaling. They are energetically expensive, and even dangerous, to

the degree that the more ardent are put at greater risk of being killed by rivals or predators. At the microscopic level, the genetic devices by which sex is determined are finely tuned and easily disturbed. In human beings one sex chromosome too few or too many, or a subtle shift in the hormone balance of a developing fetus, creates abnormalities in physiology and behavior.

[4]Thus sex by itself lends no straightforward Darwinian advantage. Moreover, sexual reproduction automatically imposes a genetic deficit. If an organism multiplies without sex, all of its offspring will be identical to itself. If, on the other hand, an organism accepts sexual partnership with another, unrelated individual, half the genes in each of its offspring will be of alien origin. With each generation thereafter, the investment in genes per descendant will be cut in half.

[5]So there are good reasons for reproduction to be nonsexual. It can be made private, direct, safe, energetically cheap, and selfish. Why, then, has sex evolved?

[6]The principal answer is that sex creates diversity. And diversity is the way a parent hedges its bets against an unpredictably changing environment. Imagine a case of two animal species, both of which consist entirely of individuals carrying two genes. Let us arbitrarily label one gene A and the other a. For instance, these genes might be for brown (A) versus blue (a) eye color, or right-handedness (A) versus left-handedness (a). Each individual is Aa because it possesses both genes. Suppose that one species reproduces without sex. Then all the offspring of every parent will be Aa.

[7]The other population uses sex for reproduction; it produces sex cells, each of which contains only one of the genes, A or a. When two individuals mate they combine their sex cells, and since each adult contributes sex cells bearing either A or a, three kinds of offspring are possible: AA, Aa, and aa. So, from a starting population of Aa individuals, asexual parents can produce only Aa offspring, while sexual parents can produce AA, Aa, and aa offspring. Now let the environment change—say a hard winter, a flood, or the invasion of a dangerous predator—so that aa individuals are favored. In the next generation, the sexually reproducing population will have the advantage and will consist predominantly of aa organisms until conditions change to favor, perhaps, AA or Aa individuals.

[8]Diversity, and thus adaptability, explains why so many kinds of organisms bother with sexual reproduction. They vastly outnumber the species that rely on the direct and simple but, in the long run, less prudent modes of sexless multiplication.

[9]Then why are there usually just two sexes? It is theoretically possible to evolve a sexual system based on one sex—anatomically uniform individuals who produce identically shaped reproductive cells and combine them indiscriminately. Some lower plants do just that. It is also possible to have hundreds

of sexes, which is the mode among some fungi. But a two-sex system prevails through most of the living world. This system appears to permit the most efficient possible division of labor.

[10]The quintessential female is an individual specialized for making eggs. The large size of the egg enables it to resist drying, to survive adverse periods by consuming stored yolk, to be moved to safety by the parent, and to divide at least a few times after fertilization before needing to ingest nutrients from the outside. The male is defined as the manufacturer of the sperm, the little gamete. A sperm is a minimum cellular unit, stripped down to a head packed with DNA and powered by a tail containing just enough stored energy to carry the vehicle to the egg.

[11]When the two gametes unite in fertilization they create an instant mixture of genes surrounded by the durable housing of the egg. By cooperating to create zygotes, the female and male make it more likely that at least some of their offspring will survive in the event of a changing environment. A fertilized egg differs from an asexually reproducing cell in one fundamental respect: it contains a newly assembled mixture of genes.

[12]The anatomical difference between the two kinds of sex cell is often extreme. In particular, the human egg is eighty-five thousand times larger than the human sperm. The consequences of this gametic dimorphism ramify throughout the biology and psychology of human sex. The most important immediate result is that the female places a greater investment in each of her sex cells. A woman can expect to produce only about four hundred eggs in her lifetime. Of these a maximum of about twenty can be converted into healthy infants. The costs of bringing an infant to term and caring for it afterward are relatively enormous. In contrast, a man releases 100 million sperm with each ejaculation. Once he has achieved fertilization, his purely physical commitment has ended. His genes will benefit equally with those of the female, but the investment will be far less than hers unless she can induce him to contribute to the care of the offspring. If a man were given total freedom to act, he could theoretically inseminate thousands of women in his lifetime.

[13]The resulting conflict of interest between the sexes is a property of not only human beings but also the majority of animal species Males are characteristically aggressive, especially toward one another and most intensely during the breeding season. In most species, assertiveness is the most profitable male strategy. During the full period of time it takes to bring a fetus to term, from the fertilization of the egg to the birth of the infant, one male can fertilize many females but a female can be fertilized by only one male. Thus if males are able to court one female after another, some will be big winners and others will be absolute losers, while virtually all healthy females will succeed in being fertilized. It pays males to be aggressive, hasty, fickle, and undiscriminating.

In theory it is more profitable for females to be coy, to hold back until they can identify males with the best genes. In species that rear young, it is also important for the females to select males who are more likely to stay with them after insemination.

[14]Human beings obey this biological principle faithfully. It is true that the thousands of existing societies are enormously variable in the details of their sexual mores and the division of labor between the sexes. This variation is based on culture. Societies mold their customs to the requirements of the environment and in so doing duplicate in totality a large fraction of the arrangements encountered throughout the remainder of the animal kingdom: from strict monogamy to extreme forms of polygamy, and from a close approach to unisex to extreme differences between men and women in behavior and dress. People change their attitudes consciously and at will; the reigning fashion of a society can shift within a generation. Nevertheless, this flexibility is not endless, and beneath it all lie general features that conform closely to the expectations from evolutionary theory. So let us concentrate initially on the biologically significant generalities and defer, for the moment, consideration of the undeniably important plasticity controlled by culture.

[15]We are, first of all, moderately polygynous, with males initiating most of the changes in sexual partnership. About three-fourths of all human societies permit the taking of multiple wives, and most of them encourage the practice by law and custom. In contrast, marriage to multiple husbands is sanctioned in less than one percent of societies. The remaining monogamous societies usually fit that category in a legal sense only, with concubinage and other extramarital stratagems being added to allow *de facto* polygyny.

[16]Because women are commonly treated by men as a limited resource and hence as valued property, they are the beneficiaries of hypergamy, the practice of marrying upward in social position. Polygyny and hypergamy are essentially complementary strategies. In diverse cultures men pursue and acquire, while women are protected and bartered. Sons sow wild oats and daughters risk being ruined. When sex is sold, men are usually the buyers. It is to be expected that prostitutes are the despised members of society; they have abandoned their valuable reproductive investment to strangers. In the twelfth century, Maimonides[a] neatly expressed this biological logic as follows:

[17]For fraternal sentiments and mutual love and mutual help can be found in their perfect form only among those who are related by their ancestry. Accordingly a single tribe that is united through a common ancestor—even if he is remote—because of this, love one another, help one another, and have pity on one another; and the attainment of these things is the greatest purpose of the

---

[a]Twelfth-century rabbi and philosopher

Law. Hence harlots are prohibited because through them lines of ancestry are destroyed. For a child born of them is a stranger to the people; no one knows to what family group he belongs, and no one in his family group knows him; and this is the worst of conditions for him and his father.

[18]Anatomy bears the imprint of the sexual division of labor. Men are on the average 20 to 30 percent heavier than women. Pound for pound, they are stronger and quicker in most categories of sport. The proportion of their limbs, their skeletal torsion, and the density of their muscles are particularly suited for running and throwing, the archaic specialties of the ancestral hunter-gatherer males. The world track records reflect the disparity. Male champions are always between 5 and 20 percent faster than women champions: in 1974 the difference was 8 percent in the 100 meters, 11 percent in the 400 meters, 15 percent in the mile, 10 percent in the 10,000 meters, and so on through every distance. Even in the marathon, where size and brute strength count least, the difference was 13 percent. Women marathoners have comparable endurance, but men are faster—their champions run twenty-six five-minute miles one after another. The gap cannot be attributed to a lack of incentive and training. The great women runners of East Germany and the Soviet Union are the products of nationwide recruitment and scientifically planned training programs. Yet their champions, who consistently set Olympic and world records, could not place in an average men's regional track meet. The overlap in performances between all men and women is of course great; the best women athletes are better than most male athletes, and women's track and field is an exciting competitive world of its own. But there is a substantial difference between average and best performances. The leading woman marathon runner in the United States in 1975, for example, would have ranked 752nd in the national men's listing. Size is not the determinant. The smaller male runners, at 125 to 130 pounds, perform as well relative to women as do their taller and heavier competitors.

[19]It is of equal importance that women match or surpass men in a few other sports, and these are among the ones furthest removed from the primitive techniques of hunting and aggression: long-distance swimming, the more acrobatic events of gymnastics, precision (but not distance) archery, and small-bore rifle shooting. As sports and sport-like activities evolve into more sophisticated channels dependent on skill and agility, the overall achievements of men and women can be expected to converge more closely.

[20]The average temperamental differences between the human sexes are also consistent with the generalities of mammalian biology. Women as a group are less assertive and physically aggressive. The magnitude of the distinction depends on the culture. It ranges from a tenuous, merely statistical difference in egalitarian settings to the virtual enslavement of women

in some extreme polygynous societies. But the variation in degree is not nearly so important as the fact that women differ consistently in this qualitative manner regardless of the degree. The fundamental average difference in personality traits is seldom if ever transposed.

[21]The physical and temperamental differences between men and women have been amplified by culture into universal male dominance. History records not a single society in which women have controlled the political and economic lives of men. Even when queens and empresses ruled, their intermediaries remained primarily male. At the present writing not a single country has a woman as head of state, although Golda Meir of Israel and Indira Gandhi of India were, until recently, assertive, charismatic leaders of their countries. In about 75 percent of societies studied by anthropologists, the bride is expected to move from the location of her own family to that of her husband, while only 10 percent require the reverse exchange. Lineage is reckoned exclusively through the male line at least five times more frequently than it is through the female line. Men have traditionally assumed the positions of chieftains, shamans, judges, and warriors. Their modern technocratic counterparts rule the industrial states and head the corporations and churches.

[22]These differences are a simple matter of record—but what is significance for the future? How easily can they be altered?

[23]It is obviously of vital social importance to try to make a free assessment of the relative contributions of heredity and environment to the differentiation of behavioral roles between the sexes. Here is what I believe the evidence shows: modest genetic differences exist between the sexes; the behavioral genes interact with virtually all existing environments to create a noticeable divergence in early psychological development; and the divergence is almost always widened in later psychological development by cultural sanctions and training. Societies can probably cancel the modest genetic differences entirely by careful planning and training, but the convergence will require a conscious decision based on fuller and more exact knowledge than is now available.

[24]The evidence for genetic difference in behavior is varied and substantial. In general, girls are more predisposed to be more intimately sociable and less physically venturesome. From the time of birth, for example, they smile more than boys. This trait may be especially revealing, since the infant smile, of all human behaviors, is most fully innate in that its form and function are virtually invariant. Several independent studies have shown that newborn females respond more frequently than males with eyes-closed, reflexive smiling. The habit is soon replaced by deliberate communicative smiling that persists into the second year of life. Frequent smiling then becomes one of the more persistent of female traits and endures through

adolescence and maturity. By the age of six months, girls also pay closer attention to sights and sounds used in communication than they do to nonsocial stimuli. Boys of the same age make no such distinction. The ontogeny then precedes as follows: one-year-old girls react with greater fright and inhibition to clay faces, and they are more reluctant to leave their mothers' sides in novel situations. Older girls remain more affiliative and less physically venturesome than boys of the same age.

[25]In her study of the !Kung San, Patricia Draper found no difference in the way young boys and girls are reared. All are supervised closely but unobtrusively and are seldom given any work. Yet boys wander out of view and earshot more frequently than girls, and older boys appear to be slightly more prone to join the men hunters than are the girls to join the women gatherers. In still closer studies, N. G. Blurton Jones and Melvin J. Konner found that boys also engage more frequently in rough-and-tumble play and overt aggression. They also associate less with adults than do girls. From these subtle differences the characteristic strong sexual division of labor in !Kung encampments emerges by small steps.

[26]In Western cultures boys are also more venturesome than girls and more physically aggressive on the average. Eleanor Maccoby and Carol Jacklin, in their review *The Psychology of Sex Differences,* concluded that this male trait is deeply rooted and could have a genetic origin. From the earliest moments of social play, at age 2 to 2 1/2 years, boys are more aggressive in both words and actions. They have a larger number of hostile fantasies and engage more often in mock fighting, overt threats, and physical attacks, which are directed preferentially at other boys during efforts to acquire dominance status. Other studies, summarized by Ronald P. Rohner, indicate that the differences exist in many cultures.

[27]The skeptic favoring a totally environmental explanation might still argue that the early divergence in role playing has no biological component but is merely a response to biased training practices during very early childhood. If it occurs, the training would have to be subtle, at least partly unconscious in application, and practiced by parents around the world. The hypothesis of total environmentalism is made more improbable by recent evidence concerning the biology of hermaphrodites, who are genetically female but acquire varying degrees of masculine anatomy during the early stages of fetal development. The anomaly occurs in one of two ways.

[28]The first is a rare hereditary condition caused by a change in a single gene site and known as the female adrenogenital syndrome. In either sex, possession of two of the altered genes—hence a complete lack of the normal gene in each cell of the body—prevents the adrenal glands from manufacturing their proper hormone, cortisol. In its place the adrenal glands secrete a precursor substance which has an action similar to that of the male sex

hormone. If the individual is genetically male, the hormonal boost has no significant effect on sexual development. If the fetus is female, the abnormal level of male hormone alters the external genitalia in the direction of maleness. Sometimes the clitoris of such an individual is enlarged to resemble a small penis, and the labia majora are closed. In extreme cases a full penis and empty scrotum are developed.

[29]The second means of producing the effect is by artificial hormone treatment. During the 1950s women were often given progestins, a class of artificial substances that act like progesterone, the normal hormone of pregnancy, to help them prevent miscarriages. It was discovered that in a few cases progestins, by exerting a masculinizing effect on female fetuses, transformed them into hermaphrodites of the same kind caused by the female adrenogenital syndrome.

[30]By sheer accident the hormone-induced hermaphrodites approach a properly controlled scientific experiment designed to estimate the influence of heredity on sex differences. The experiment is not perfect, but it is as good as any other we are likely to encounter. The hermaphrodites are genetically female, and their internal sexual organs are fully female. In most of the cases studied in the United States, the external genitalia were altered surgically to an entirely female condition during infancy, and the individuals were then reared as girls. These children were subjected during fetal development to male hormones or to substances that mimic them but then "trained" to be ordinary girls until maturity. In such cases it is possible to dissect the effects of learning from the effects of deeper biological alterations, which in some cases stem directly from known gene mutation. Behavioral maleness would almost certainly have to be ascribed to the effect of the hormones on development of the brain.

[31]Did the girls show behavioral changes connected with their hormonal and anatomical masculinization? As John Money and Anke Ehrhardt discovered, the changes were both quite marked and correlated with the physical changes. Compared with unaffected girls of otherwise similar social backgrounds, the hormonally altered girls were more commonly regarded as tomboys while they were growing up. They had a greater interest in athletic skills, were readier to play with boys, preferred slacks to dresses and toy guns to dolls. The group with the adrenogenital syndrome was more likely to show dissatisfaction with being assigned to a female role. The evaluation of this latter group is flawed by the fact that cortisone had to be administered to the girls to offset their genetic defect. It is possible that hormone treatment alone could somehow have biased the girls toward masculine behavior. If the effect occurred, it was still biological in nature, although not as deep as fetal masculinization. And of course, the effect could not have occurred in the progestin-altered girls.

[32]So at birth the twig is already bent a little bit—what are we to make of that? It suggests that the universal existence of sexual division of labor is not entirely an accident of cultural evolution. But it also supports the conventional view that the enormous variation among societies in the degree of that division is due to cultural evolution. Demonstrating a slight biological component delineates the options that future societies may consciously select. Here the second dilemma of human nature presents itself. In full recognition of the struggle for women's rights that is now spreading throughout the world, each society must make one or the other of the three following choices:

[33]*Condition its members so as to exaggerate sexual differences in behavior.* This is the pattern in almost all cultures. It results more often than not in domination of women by men and exclusion of women from many professions and activities. But this need not be the case. In theory at least, a carefully designed society with strong sexual divisions could be richer in spirit, more diversified, and even more productive than a unisex society. Such a society might safeguard human rights even while channeling men and women into different occupations. Still, some amount of social injustice would be inevitable, and it could easily expand to disastrous proportions.

[34]*Train its members so as to eliminate all sexual differences in behavior.* By the use of quotas and sex-biased education it should be possible to create a society in which men and women as *groups* share equally in all professions, cultural activities, and even, to take the absurd extreme, athletic competition. Although the early predispositions that characterize sex would have to be blunted, the biological differences are not so large as to make the undertaking impossible. Such control would offer the great advantage of eliminating even the hint of group prejudice (in addition to individual prejudice) based on sex. It could result in a much more harmonious and productive society. Yet the amount of regulation required would certainly place some personal freedoms in jeopardy, and at least a few individuals would not be allowed to reach their full potential.

[35]*Provide equal opportunities and access but take no further action.* To make no choice at all is of course the third choice open to all cultures. *Laissez-faire*[b] on first thought might seem to be the course most congenial to personal liberty and development, but this is not necessarily true. Even with identical education for men and women and equal access to all professions, men are likely to maintain disproportionate representation in political life, business, and science. Many would fail to participate fully in the equally important, formative aspects of child rearing. The result might be legitimately viewed as restrictive on the complete emotional development

---

[b]Nonintervention; no restrictions

of individuals. Just such a divergence and restriction has occurred in the Israeli *kibbutzim*, which represent one of the most powerful experiments in egalitarianism conducted in modern times.

[36]From the time of the greatest upsurge of the *kibbutz* movement, in the 1940s and 1950s, its leaders promoted a policy of complete sexual equality, of encouraging women to enter roles previously reserved for men. In the early years it almost worked. The first generation of women were ideologically committed, and they shifted in large numbers to politics, management, and labor. But they and their daughters have regressed somewhat toward traditional roles, despite being trained from birth in the new culture. Furthermore, the daughters have gone further than the mothers. They now demand and receive a longer period of time each day with their children, time significantly entitled "the hour of love." Some of the most gifted have resisted recruitment into the higher levels of commercial and political leadership so that the representation in these roles is far below that enjoyed by the same generation of men. It has been argued that this reversion merely represents the influence of the strong patriarchal tradition that persists in the remainder Israeli society, even though the role division is now greater inside the *kibbutzim* than outside. The Israeli experience shows how difficult it is to predict the consequences and assess the meaning of changes in behavior based on either heredity or ideology.

[37]From this troubling ambiguity concerning sex roles one firm conclusion can be drawn: the evidences of biological constraint alone cannot prescribe an ideal course of action. However, they can help us to define the options and to assess the price of each. The price to be measured in the added energy required for education and reinforcement and in the attrition of individual freedom and potential. And let us face the real issue squarely: since every option has a cost, and concrete ethical principles will rarely find universal acceptance: the choice cannot be made easily. In such cases we could do well to consider the wise counsel of Hans Morgenthau: "In the combination of political wisdom, moral courage and moral judgment, man reconciles his political nature with his moral destiny. That this conciliation is nothing more than a *modus vivendi*,[c] uneasy, precarious, and even paradoxical, can disappoint only those who prefer to gloss over and to distort the tragic contradictions of human existence with the soothing logic of a specious concord." I am suggesting that the contradictions are rooted in the surviving relics of our prior genetic history, and that one of the most inconvenient and senseless, but nevertheless unavoidable of these residues is the modest predisposition toward sex role differences.

---

[c]In this context, way of living; compromise.

Vocabulary

[1]protean
[1]phenomenon
[1]permeates
[1]ambiguity
[1]fungi
[1]spores
[1]hydras
[1]organism
[1]asexual
[1]neutered
[1]womb
[2]protozoans
[2]invertebrate
[2]copulate
[2]inducing
[3]gratuitously
[3]ectopic
[3]venereal
[3]ardent
[6]diversity
[6]hedges
[6]arbitrarily
[8]adaptability
[8]prudent
[8]anatomically

[10]quintessential
[10]ingest
[10]gamete
[10]DNA
[11]zygotes
[12]dimorphism
[12]ramify
[12]ejaculation
[12]induce
[12]inseminate
[13]assertiveness
[13]fickle
[13]coy
[13]insemination
[14]mores
[14]monogamy
[14]polygamy
[14]reigning
[14]plasticity
[15]polygynous
[15]monogamous
[15]concubinage
[16]bartered
[17]harlot
[18]torsion

[18]disparity
[19]converge
[20]magnitude
[20]tenuous
[21]amplified
[21]assertive
[21]charismatic
[21]anthropologists
[21]lineage
[21]shamans
[21]technocratic
[23]differentiation
[23]divergence
[24]predisposed
[24]venturesome
[24]innate
[24]invariant
[24]stimuli
[24]ontogeny
[24]novel
[24]affiliative
[25]unobtrusively
[25]earshot
[25]overt
[25]encampments

[28]adrenal glands
[28]precursor
[28]genitalia
[28]clitoris
[28]labia majora
[28]scrotum
[30]ascribed
[31]marked
[31]correlated
[32]delineates
[34]predispositions
[35]congenial
[35]*kibbutzim*
[36]ideologically
[36]regressed
[36]reversion
[36]patriarchal
[37]attrition
[37]precarious
[37]paradoxical
[37]specious
[37]concord
[37]residues
[37]predisposition

Discussion Questions

1. Wilson states that "sex is not designed primarily for reproduction" nor is it for "giving and receiving of pleasure," and it is a "gratuitously consuming and risky activity." What reasons does Wilson give to support these statements?

2. What, according to Wilson, is the reason for sex? What advantages does sex afford for reproduction?

3. What are the consequences of the female's egg being substantially larger than the male sperm?

4. Who has the greater investment in the developing fetus — the female or the male? Why?

5. Define *polygyny* and *hypergamy*.

6. What social, physical and temperamental differences does Wilson attribute to human males and females?

7. What differences from normal development did the females with adreno-genital syndrome exhibit?

8. What three choices do societies have in socializing males and females in terms of cultural evolution?

9. What does the Israeli *kibbutz* movement show us about changes in behavior?

10. Summarize Wilson's conclusion. What does he want us to think about in terms of cost versus benefit?

THE SNIPER

LIAM O'FLAHERTY

Liam O'Flaherty (1896-1984) was a leading Irish novel-ist of the early twentieth century. He studied at several colleges, and he served in the Irish Guards during World War I. Among his works are Spring Sowing *(1924),* Mr. Gilhooley *(1926),* Short Stories *(1937),* Land *(1946), and* The Peddler's Revenge *(1976).*

¹The long June twilight faded into night. Dublin lay enveloped in dark-ness but for the dim light of the moon that shone through fleecy clouds, casting a pale light as of approaching dawn over the streets and the dark waters of the Liffey. Around the beleaguered Four Courts the heavy guns roared. Here and there through the city, machine-guns and rifles broke the silence of the night, spasmodically, like dogs barking on lone farms. Republicans and Free Staters were waging civil war.

²On a roof-top near O'Connell Bridge, a Republican sniper lay watching. Beside him lay his rifle and over his shoulders were slung a pair of field glasses. His face was the face of a student, thin and ascetic, but his eyes had the cold gleam of the fanatic. They were deep and thoughtful, the eyes of a man who is used to looking at death.

³He was eating a sandwich hungrily. He had eaten nothing since morn-ing. He had been too excited to eat. He finished the sandwich, and, taking a flask of whiskey from his pocket, he took a short draught. Then he returned the flask to his pocket. He paused for a moment, considering whether he should risk a smoke. It was dangerous. The flash might be seen in the darkness and there were enemies watching. He decided to take the risk.

⁴Placing a cigarette between his lips, he struck a match. There was a flash and a bullet whizzed over his head. He dropped immediately. He had seen the flash. It came from the opposite side of the street.

⁵He rolled over the roof to a chimney stack in the rear, and slowly drew himself up behind it, until his eyes were level with the top of the parapet. There was nothing to be seen—just the dim outline of the opposite housetop against the blue sky. His enemy was under cover.

⁶Just then an armored car came across the bridge and advanced slowly up the street. It stopped on the opposite side of the street, fifty yards ahead. The sniper could hear the dull panting of the motor. His heart beat faster. It was an enemy car. He wanted to fire, but he knew it was useless. His bullets would never pierce the steel that covered the gray monster.

⁷Then round the corner of a side street came an old woman, her head covered by a tattered shawl. She began to talk to the man in the turret of the car. She was pointing to the roof where the sniper lay. An informer.

⁸The turret opened. A man's head and shoulders appeared, looking toward the sniper. The sniper raised his rifle and fired. The head fell heavily on the turret wall. The woman darted toward the side street. The sniper fired again. The woman whirled round and fell with a shriek into the gutter.

⁹Suddenly from the opposite roof a shot rang out and the sniper dropped his rifle with a curse. The rifle clattered to the roof. The sniper thought the noise would wake the dead. He stopped to pick the rifle up. He couldn't lift it. His forearm was dead.

¹⁰"Christ," he muttered, "I'm hit." Dropping flat onto the roof, he crawled back to the parapet. With his left hand he felt the injured right forearm. There was no pain—just a deadened sensation, as if the arm had been cut off.

¹¹Quickly he drew his knife from his pocket, opened it on the breast-work of the parapet, and ripped open the sleeve. There was a small hole where the bullet had entered. On the other side there was no hole. The bullet had lodged in the bone. It must have fractured it. He bent the arm below the wound. The arm bent back easily. He ground his teeth to overcome the pain.

¹²Then taking out the field dressing, he ripped open the packet with his knife. He broke the neck of the iodine bottle and let the bitter fluid drip into the wound. A paroxysm of pain swept through him. He placed the cotton wadding over the wound and wrapped the dressing over it. He tied the ends with his teeth.

¹³Then he lay against the parapet, and, closing his eyes, he made an effort of will to overcome the pain.

¹⁴In the street beneath all was still. The armored car had retired speedily over the bridge, with the machine-gunner's head hanging lifelessly over the turret. The woman's corpse lay still in the gutter.

¹⁵The sniper lay still for a long time nursing his wounded arm and planning escape. Morning must not find him wounded on the roof. The enemy on the opposite roof covered his escape. He must kill that enemy and he could not use his rifle. He had only a revolver to do it. Then he thought of a plan.

¹⁶Taking off his cap, he placed it over the muzzle of his rifle. Then he pushed the rifle slowly over the parapet, until the cap was visible from the opposite side of the street. Almost immediately there was a report, and a bullet pierced the center of the cap. The sniper slanted the rifle forward. The cap slipped down into the street. Then catching the rifle in the middle, the sniper dropped his left hand over the roof and let it hang, lifelessly. After a few moments he let the rifle drop to the street. Then he sank to the roof, dragging his hand with him.

¹⁷Crawling quickly to the left, he peered up at the corner of the roof. His

ruse had succeeded. The other sniper, seeing the cap and rifle fall, thought he had killed his man. He was now standing before a row of chimney pots, looking across, with his head clearly silhouetted against the western sky.

[18]The Republican sniper smiled and lifted his revolver above the edge of the parapet. The distance was about fifty yards—a hard shot in the dim light, and his right arm was paining him like a thousand devils. He took a steady aim. His hand trembled with eagerness. Pressing his lips together, he took a deep breath through his nostrils and fired. He was almost deafened with the report and his arm shook with the recoil.

[19]Then when the smoke cleared he peered across and uttered a cry of joy. His enemy had been hit. He was reeling over the parapet in his death agony. He struggled to keep his feet, but he was slowly falling forward, as if in a dream. The rifle fell from his grasp, hit the parapet, fell over, bounded off the pole of a barber's shop beneath and then clattered on the pavement

[20]Then the dying man on the roof crumpled up and fell forward. The body turned over and over in space and hit the ground with a dull thud. Then it lay still.

[21]The sniper looked at his enemy falling and he shuddered. The lust of battle died in him. He became bitten by remorse. The sweat stood out in beads on his forehead. Weakened by his wound and the long summer day of fasting and watching on the roof, he revolted from the sight of the shattered mass of his dead enemy. His teeth chattered; he began to gibber to himself, cursing the war, cursing himself, cursing everybody.

[22]He looked at the smoking revolver in his hand, and with an oath he hurled it to the roof at his feet. The revolver went off with the concussion and the bullet whizzed past the sniper's head. He was frightened back to his senses by the shock. His nerves steadied. The cloud of fear scattered from his mind and he laughed.

[23]Taking the whiskey flask from his pocket, he emptied it at a draught. He felt reckless under the influence of the spirit. He decided to leave the roof now and look for his company commander, to report. Everywhere around was quiet. There was not much danger in going through the streets. He picked up his revolver and put it in his pocket. Then he crawled down through the sky-light to the house underneath.

[24]When the sniper reached the laneway on the street level, he felt a sudden curiosity as to the identity of the enemy sniper whom he had killed. He decided that he was a good shot, whoever he was. He wondered did he know him. Perhaps he had been in his own company before the split in the army. He decided to risk going over to have a look at him. He peered round the corner into O'Connell Street. In the upper part of the street there was heavy firing, but around here all was quiet.

[25]The sniper darted across the street. A machine-gun tore up the ground

around him with a hail of bullets, but he escaped. He threw himself face down-ward beside the corpse. The machine-gun stopped.

²⁶Then the sniper turned over the dead body and looked into his brother's face.

Vocabulary

¹beleaguered	³draught	⁸turret	¹⁷ruse
¹spasmodically	⁵parapet	¹²paroxysm	²¹gibber
²ascetic			

Discussion Questions

1. Describe the setting of the story. Discuss how O'Flaherty's description of the setting establishes the tone for the story.

2. This story is an example of historical fiction. What historical event is being described here? What is the background to this conflict? Have the problems been resolved in today's Ireland?

3. Describe the sniper physically and emotionally. Look especially carefully at O'Flaherty's description. How much do we learn about the sniper? For example, how old is he approximately? What has his life been like to this point? What does he look like?

4. Note the way O'Flaherty uses language. For example, he says the man's head fell "heavily" on the turret wall. What does the author's use of that adverb tell us about the sniper? Find one or two other uses of descriptive langauage that you think are effective.

5. Note again how O'Flaherty uses the word "darted" when describing the woman's attempt to escape. Why didn't he simply say she "ran"?

6. Why did O'Flaherty make the informer an old woman? Why not a middle-aged man? Or a young woman?

7. Does the sniper change during the story? If so, how does he change?

8. What is the irony of this story?

9. O'Flaherty ends the story rather abruptly. Why do you think he ends the story in this way? Discuss your answer with your classmates.

10. Look at the front page of the June 30, 1922, edition of the New York *Times* on the next page. In what ways does the content of the newspaper relate to this piece of creative fiction?

11. Alone or with a writing group, continue the story.

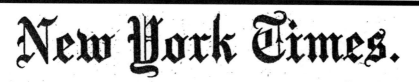

New York Times.

NEW YORK, FRIDAY, JUNE 30, 1922.　　　TWO CENTS | In Greater New York | THREE CENTS Within 200 Miles | FOUR CENTS Elsewhere

PART OF DUBLIN FOUR COURTS CAPTURED; STORMED BY FREE STATERS, 33 MEN TAKEN; O'CONNOR IS AT BAY IN SMALL BUILDING

WHOLE CITY IS TERRORIZED

Irregular Troops Take Up Sniping Posts In Many Buildings.

PEOPLE RUSH TO SUBURBS

Fear Extension of Fighting Zone and Invasion of Dublin by More Rebels.

BARRICADES ARE SET UP

Business at a Standstill and Railroad Communication Practically Cut Off.

Copyright, 1922, by The New York Times Company.
Special Cable to THE NEW YORK TIMES.

DUBLIN, June 30.—The Free State troops' victory late at night followed a day of intense fighting by the regular forces. The irregulars seized many buildings throughout the city, which they fortified and used as sniping posts to harass the Free State troops and to terrorize the city. Similar methods were employed by I. W. W. sympathizers.

Corner buildings commanding important streets are specially favored for this work and it is not too much to say that Dublin bristles with rebel forts.

Several more ambushes were reported, and these added to the casualties, which are now known to exceed fifty, mostly civilians.

Dublin City is almost completely isolated from the rest of the country, and people are flocking to the suburbs. Roads from the city are trenched and otherwise blocked. The railroads are at a standstill, bridges in some cases being blown up. The telephones and telegraphs are taken over by the Government, which is also enforcing a rigid censorship on the newspapers.

In these circumstances there is little news from the South and West, and there is much apprehension in Dublin as to what is happening throughout the country. Reports that have come from Cork indicate that the Republicans are seizing Post Offices, those at Limerick, Waterford and Butlevant having already been taken. It is also reported

Rebels Cut London Cable to Southern Ireland; Post Offices Shut Down in the Disturbed Regions

Copyright, 1922, by The New York Times Company
Special Cable to THE NEW YORK TIMES.

LONDON, June 29.—The Irish rebels have cut the cable between Dublin and this country.

There are two submarine cables to Ireland, the second one being that which goes to Belfast. That one is in order and communication with Ireland is being kept up through Belfast.

The telephones to Dublin were all stopped on Wednesday, and since that time there has been no telephone communication with that city. News received in London tonight says that post offices throughout the South and West of Ireland are steadily shutting down and the staffs leaving, but the Dublin Post Office was still open at 7 o'clock this evening.

LONDON, June 29 (Associated Press).—The Postmaster General announces that the cable between Anglesey, Wales, and Kingstown has been cut and that telegraphic communication between Great Britain and southern Ireland has therefore ceased. The cable to Belfast, however, is working and is the only means of communication with Ireland. It is also improbable that letters can be delivered anywhere in southern Ireland.

A Cork dispatch reporting the cessation of rail and telegraphic services says that the lines between Limerick Junction and Dundrum and between Limerick and Tipperary have been torn up and that the railway bridge between Limerick Junction and Emly has been destroyed.

FREE STATE TROOPS DECLINE BRITISH AID

Churchill Tells Commons That in Rejecting Assistance the Irish Are Well Advised.

A MOVE TO RESTORE ORDER

Secretary Deprecates Any Hint That Provisional Regime Is Not Trying to Back Treaty.

Copyright, 1922, by The New York Times Company.
Special Cable to THE NEW YORK TIMES.

LONDON, June 29.—Winston Churchill made the following statement in Parliament today on the situation in Dublin:

"I am afraid I have very little to add to the full and continuous reports which reach this country through the medium of the press.

REPORTER'S DASH WITH DUBLIN NEWS

Cable Cut, He Uses Mail Boat's Wireless, Then Telephone From Holyhead to London.

DESCRIBES HEAVY FIGHTING

Battle Spreading Over Wide Area, a Grave Threat to Free State Troops.

The rebels having cut the submarine cable between Dublin and England, Frederic B. Harvey, one of THE NEW YORK TIMES special correspondents in Dublin, left last night by the mail boat Hibernia and by means of wireless from the ship and the use of telephone at Holyhead sent the following message to the London office of THE TIMES:

By FREDERIC B. HARVEY.

SURRENDER IS DEMANDED

Renewal of Firing at 3:45 A. M. Indicates O'Connor Holds Out.

CASUALTIES ARE SLIGHT

Splendid Charge After Eight-Hour Bombardment Carries Main Building.

ARMS AND MINES SEIZED

Barry, Rebel Chief of Staff, Is Taken Posing as Nurse Seeking to Enter Four Courts.

Copyright, 1922, by The New York Times Company
Special Cable to THE NEW YORK TIMES.

DUBLIN, Friday, June 30—4:00 A. M. — The Free State forces stormed the Four Courts at midnight and captured the two main parts of it, with thirty-three prisoners, including Commandant Thomas Barry.

Rory O'Connor, the rebel leader, Liam Mellowes and the remainder of the garrison were driven to a smaller building, where their surrender is demanded.

The Four Courts was entered by the Free Staters through a breach which was made after the building had been bombarded continuously for eight and a half hours.

They are now working their way through the whole building.

The following official communiqué was issued from the Free State Headquarters at 2 A. M.:

After considerable fighting during the course of yesterday evening our troops succeeded in dislodging the irregulars from the greater part of the Four Courts.

THE STORM

KATE CHOPIN

*A widow with six children, **Kate Chopin** (1851-1904) began writing after returning to her native St. Louis from Louisiana. Her writings include* At Fault *(1890);* Bayou Folk *(1894); and her most well-known work,* The Awakening *(1899), about a young woman's discontentment with her life, leading to adultery and suicide. Although the novel was praised for its literary merit, its theme raised a scandal, causing Chopin to lose her confidence and stop writing.*

I

¹The leaves were so still that even Bibi thought it was going to rain. Bobinôt, who was accustomed to converse on terms of perfect equality with his little son, called the child's attention to certain somber clouds that were rolling with sinister intention from the west, accompanied by a sullen, threatening roar. They were at Friedheimer's store and decided to remain there till the storm had passed. They sat within the door on two empty kegs. Bibi was four years old and looked very wise.

²"Mama'll be 'fraid, yes," he suggested with blinking eyes.

³"She'll shut the house. Maybe she got Sylvie helpin' her this evenin'," Bobinôt responded reassuringly.

⁴"No; she ent got Sylvie. Sylvie was helpin' her yistiday," piped Bibi.

Bobinôt arose and going across to the counter purchased a can of shrimps, of which Calixta was very fond. Then he returned to his perch on the keg and sat stolidly holding the can of shrimps while the storm burst. It shook the wooden store and seemed to be ripping great furrows in the distant field. Bibi laid his little hand on his father's knee and was not afraid.

II

⁵Calixta, at home, felt no uneasiness for their safety. She sat at a side window sewing furiously on a sewing machine. She was greatly occupied and did not notice the approaching storm. But she felt very warm and often stopped to mop her face on which the perspiration gathered in beads. She unfastened her white sacque[a] at the throat. It began to grow dark, and suddenly realizing the situation she got up hurriedly and went about closing windows and doors.

⁶Out on the small front gallery she had hung Bobinôt's Sunday clothes to dry and she hastened out to gather them before the rain fell. As she stepped

---

[a]*sacque:* free-falling, pleated lady's gown; a "sack-dress"

outside, Alcée Laballière rode in at the gate. She had not seen him very often since her marriage, and never alone. She stood there with Bobinôt's coat in her hands, and the big rain drops began to fall. Alcée rode his horse under the shelter of a side projection where the chickens had huddled and there were plows and a harrow piled up in the corner.

[7]"May I come and wait on your gallery till the storm is over, Calixta?" he asked.

[8]"Come 'long in, M'sieur Alcée."

[9]His voice and her own startled her as if from a trance, and she seized Bobinôt's vest. Alcée, mounting to the porch, grabbed the trousers and snatched Bibi's braided jacket that was about to be carried away by a sudden gust of wind. He expressed an intention to remain outside, but it was soon apparent that he might as well have been out in the open: the water beat in upon the boards in driving sheets, and he went inside, closing the door after him. It was even necessary to put something beneath the door to keep the water out.

[10]"My! what a rain! It's good two years since it rain' like that," exclaimed Calixta as she rolled up a piece of bagging and Alcée helped her to thrust it beneath the crack. She was a little fuller of figure than five years before when she married; but she had lost nothing of her vivacity. Her blue eyes still retained their melting quality; and her yellow hair, dishevelled by the wind and rain, kinked more stubbornly than ever about her ears and temples.

[11]The rain beat upon the low, shingled roof with a force and clatter that threatened to break an entrance and deluge them there. They were in the dining room—the sitting room—the general utility room. Adjoining was her bedroom, with Bibi's couch alongside her own. The door stood open, and the room with its white, monumental bed, its closed shutters, looked dim and mysterious.

[12]Alcée flung himself into a rocker and Calixta nervously began to gather up from the floor the lengths of a cotton sheet which she had been sewing.

[13]"If this keeps up, Dieu sait[b] if the levee's goin' to stan it!" she exclaimed.

[14]"What have you got to do with the levees?"

[15]"I got enough to do! An' there's Bobinôt with Bibi out in that storm—if he only didn' left Friedheimer's!"

[16]"Let us hope, Calixta, that Bobinôt's got sense enough to come in out of a cyclone." She went and stood at the window with a greatly disturbed look on her face. She wiped the frame that was clouded with moisture. It was stiflingly hot. Alcée got up and joined her at the window, looking over her shoulder. The rain was coming down in sheets obscuring the view of far-off cabins and enveloping the distant wood in a gray mist. The playing of the lightning was incessant. A bolt struck a tall chinaberry tree at the edge of the field. It filled

[b]*dieu sait*: God knows

all visible space with a blinding glare and the crash seemed to invade the very boards they stood upon. Calixta put her hands to her eyes, and with a cry, staggered backward. Alcée's arm encircled her, and for an instant he drew her close and spasmodically to him.

[17]"Bonté!"[c] she cried, releasing herself from his encircling arm and retreating from the window, "the house'll go next! If I only knew w'ere Bibi was!" She would not compose herself; she would not be seated. Alcée clasped her shoulders and looked into her face. The contact of her warm, palpitating body when he had unthinkingly drawn her into his arms, had aroused all the old-time infatuation and desire for her flesh.

[18]"Calixta," he said, "don't be frightened. Nothing can happen. The house is too low to be struck, with so many tall trees standing about. There! aren't you going to be quiet? say, aren't you?" He pushed her hair back from her face that was warm and steaming. Her lips were as red and moist as pomegranate seed. Her white neck and a glimpse of her full, firm bosom disturbed him powerfully. As she glanced up at him, the fear in her liquid blue eyes had given place to a drowsy gleam that unconsciously betrayed a sensuous desire. He looked down into her eyes and there was nothing for him to do but to gather her lips in a kiss. It reminded him of Assumption.

[19]"Do you remember—in Assumption, Calixta?" he asked in a low voice broken by passion. Oh! she remembered; for in Assumption he had kissed her and kissed and kissed her; until his senses would well nigh fail, and to save her he would resort to a desperate flight. If she was not an immaculate dove in those days, she was still inviolate; a passionate creature whose very defenselessness had made her defense, against which his honor forbade him to prevail. Now— well, now—her lips seemed in a manner free to be tasted, as well as her round, white throat and her whiter breasts.

[20]They did not heed the crashing torrents, and the roar of the elements made her laugh as she lay in his arms. She was a revelation in that dim, mysterious chamber; as white as the couch she lay upon. Her firm, elastic flesh that was knowing for the first time its birthright, was like a creamy lily that the sun invites to contribute its breath and perfume to the undying life of the world.

[21]The generous abundance of her passion, without guile or trickery, was like a white flame which penetrated and found response in depths of his own sensuous nature that had never yet been reached.

[22]When he touched her breasts they gave themselves up in quivering ecstasy, inviting his lips. Her mouth was a fountain of delight. And when he possessed her, they seemed to swoon together at the very borderland of life's mystery.

[23]He stayed cushioned upon her, breathless, dazed, enervated, with his

---

[c] *bonté* : My goodness !

heart beating like a hammer upon her. With one hand she clasped his head, her lips lightly touching his forehead. The other hand stroked with a soothing rhythm his muscular shoulders.

[24]The growl of the thunder was distant and passing away. The rain beat softly upon the shingles, inviting them to drowsiness and sleep. But they dared not yield.

III

[25]The rain was over; and the sun was turning the glistening green world into a palace of gems. Calixta, on the gallery, watched Alcée ride away. He turned and smiled at her with a beaming face; and she lifted her pretty chin in the air and laughed aloud.

[26]Bobinôt and Bibi, trudging home, stopped without at the cistern to make themselves presentable.

[27]"My! Bibi, w'at will yo' mama say! You ought to be ashame'. You oughta' put on those good pants. Look at 'em! An' that mud on yo' collar! How you got that mud on yo' collar, Bibi? I never saw such a boy!" Bibi was the picture of pathetic resignation. Bobinôt was the embodiment of serious solicitude as he strove to remove from his own person and his son's the signs of their tramp over heavy roads and through wet fields. He scraped the mud off Bibi's bare legs and feet with a stick and carefully removed all traces from his heavy brogans. Then, prepared for the worst—the meeting with an over-scrupulous housewife, they entered cautiously at the back door.

[28]Calixta was preparing supper. She had set the table and was dripping coffee at the hearth. She sprang up as they came in.

[29]"Oh, Bobinôt! You back! My! but I was uneasy. W'ere you been during the rain? An' Bibi? he ain't wet? he ain't hurt?" She had clasped Bibi and was kissing him effusively. Bobinôt's explanations and apologies which he had been composing all along the way, died on his lips as Calixta felt him to see if he were dry, and seemed to express nothing but satisfaction at their safe return.

[30]"I brought you some shrimps, Calixta," offered Bobinôt, hauling the can from his ample side pocket and laying it on the table.

[31]"Shrimps! Oh, Bobinôt! you too good fo' anything!" and she gave him a smacking kiss on the cheek that resounded, "J'vous réponds,[d] we'll have a feas' to-night! umph-umph!"

[32]Bobinôt and Bibi began to relax and enjoy themselves, and when the three seated themselves at table they laughed much and so loud that anyone might have heard them as far away as Laballière's.

---

[d] *J' vous responds*: I tell you

IV

[33]Alcée Laballière wrote to his wife, Clarisse, that night. It was a loving letter, full of tender solicitude. He told her not to hurry back, but if she and the babies liked it at Biloxi, to stay a month longer. He was getting on nicely; and though he missed them, he was willing to bear the separation a while longer—realizing that their health and pleasure were the first things to be considered.

V

[34]As for Clarisse, she was charmed upon receiving her husband's letter. She and the babies were doing well. The society was agreeable; many of her old friends and acquaintances were at the bay. And the first free breath since her marriage seemed to restore the pleasant liberty of her maiden days. Devoted as she was to her husband, their intimate conjugal life was something which she was more than willing to forego for a while.

[35]So the storm passed and everyone was happy.

Vocabulary

[1]somber	[9]disheveled	[17]pomegranate	[25]cistern
[1]sinister	[10]deluge	[18]immaculate	[26]embodiment
[1]sullen	[11]levee	[18]inviolate	[26]solicitude
[4]stolidly	[15]incessant	[20]guile	[26]brogans
[4]furrows	[15]spasmodically	[21]swoon	[27]effusively
[5]harrow	[16]palpitating	[22]enervated	[32]conjugal
[9]vivacity			

Discussion Questions

1. What is the specified time and place in the story?

2. Discuss the significance of the title.

3. Discuss one symbol in the story. Explain the symbol and what it means. Refer to the text and explain which character(s) is understood better through the symbol.

4. What is the irony in the story?

5. Explain the significance of the last line of the story: "So the storm passed and everyone was happy."

6. This story was not published in Chopin's lifetime; it was found later in her papers. What do you think it says about her feelings on the sexual mores of the time period?

THE STORY OF AN HOUR

KATE CHOPIN

*A widow with six children, **Kate Chopin** (1851-1904) began writing after returning to her native St. Louis from Louisiana. Her writings include* At Fault *(1890);* Bayou Folk *(1894); and her most well-known work,* The Awakening *(1899), about a young woman's discontentment with her life, leading to adultery and suicide. Although the novel was praised for its literary merit, its theme raised a scandal, causing Chopin to lose her confidence and stop writing.*

[1]Knowing that Mrs. Mallard was afflicted with a heart trouble, great care was taken to break to her as gently as possible the news of her husband's death.

[2]It was her sister Josephine who told her, in broken sentences; veiled hints that revealed in half concealing. Her husband's friend Richards was there, too, near her. It was he who had been in the newspaper office when intelligence of the railroad disaster was received, with Brently Mallard's name leading the list of "killed." He had only taken the time to assure himself of its truth by a second telegram, and had hastened to forestall any less careful, less tender friend in bearing the sad message.

[3]She did not hear the story as many women have heard the same, with a paralyzed inability to accept its significance. She wept at once, with sudden, wild abandonment, in her sister's arms. When the storm of grief had spent itself she went away to her room alone. She would have no one follow her.

[4]There stood, facing the open window, a comfortable, roomy armchair. Into this she sank, pressed down by a physical exhaustion that haunted her body and seemed to reach into her soul.

[5]She could see in the open square before her house the tops of trees that were all aquiver with the new spring life. The delicious breath of rain was in the air. In the street below a peddler was crying his wares. The notes of a distant song which some one was singing reached her faintly, and countless sparrows were twittering in the eaves.

[6]There were patches of blue sky showing here and there through the clouds that had met and piled one above the other in the west facing her window.

[7]She sat with her head thrown back upon the cushion of the chair, quite motionless, except when a sob came up into her throat and shook her, as a child who has cried itself to sleep continues to sob in its dreams.

[8]She was young, with a fair, calm face, whose lines bespoke repression and even a certain strength. But now there was a dull stare in her eyes, whose gaze was fixed away off yonder on one of those patches of blue sky. It was not a glance of reflection, but rather indicated a suspension of intelligent thought.

[9]There was something coming to her and she was waiting for it, fearfully. What was it? She did not know; it was too subtle and elusive to name. But she felt it, creeping out of the sky, reaching toward her through the sounds, the scents, the color that filled the air.

[10]Now her bosom rose and fell tumultuously. She was beginning to recognize this thing that was approaching to possess her, and she was striving to beat it back with her will—as powerless as her two white slender hands would have been.

[11]When she abandoned herself a little whispered word escaped her slightly parted lips. She said it over and over under her breath: "free, free, free!" The vacant stare and the look of terror that had followed it went from her eyes. They stayed keen and bright. Her pulses beat fast, and the coursing blood warmed and relaxed every inch of her body.

[12]She did not stop to ask if it were or were not a monstrous joy that held her. A clear and exalted perception enabled her to dismiss the suggestion as trivial.

[13]She knew that she would weep again when she saw the kind, tender hands folded in death; the face that had never looked save with love upon her, fixed and gray and dead. But she saw beyond that bitter moment a long procession of years to come that would belong to her absolutely. And she opened and spread her arms out to them in welcome.

[14]There would be no one to live for during those coming years; she would live for herself. There would be no powerful will bending hers in that blind persistence with which men and women believe they have a right to impose a private will upon a fellow creature. A kind intention or a cruel intention made the act seem no less a crime as she looked upon it in that brief moment of illumination.

[15]And yet she had loved him—sometimes. Often she had not. What did it matter! What could love, the unsolved mystery, count for in face of this possession of self-assertion which she suddenly recognized as the strongest impulse of her being!

[16]"Free! Body and soul free!" she kept whispering.

[17]Josephine was kneeling before the closed door with her lips to the keyhold, imploring for admission. "Louise, open the door! I beg you; open the door—you will make yourself ill. What are you doing, Louise? For heaven's sake open the door."

[18]"Go away. I am not making myself ill." No; she was drinking in a very elixir of life through that open window.

[19]Her fancy was running riot along those days ahead of her. Spring days, and summer days, and all sorts of days that would be her own. She breathed a quick prayer that life might be long. It was only yesterday she had thought with a shudder that life might be long.

[20]She arose at length and opened the door to her sister's importunities. There was a feverish triumph in her eyes, and she carried herself unwittingly like a goddess of Victory. She clasped her sister's waist, and together they descended the stairs. Richards stood waiting for them at the bottom.

[21]Someone was opening the front door with a latchkey. It was Brently Mallard who entered, a little travel-stained, composedly carrying his grip-sack and umbrella. He had been far from the scene of the accident and did not even know there had been one. He stood amazed at Josephine's piercing cry; at Richards' quick motion to screen him from the view of his wife.

[22]But Richards was too late.

[23]When the doctors came they said she had died of heart disease—of joy that kills.

Vocabulary

[2]veiled
[5]wares
[8]bespoke
[10]tumultuously
[12]exalted
[12]perception
[14]persistence
[18]elixir
[19]fancy
[20]importunities

Discussion Questions

1. What is Mrs. Mallard's health problem? Where is this information? Why is knowing this important to the story?

2. Discuss Mrs. Mallard's changing attitude towards the news of her husband's death.

3. How does the narrator explain Mrs. Mallard's change of attitude?

4. Discuss the symbolism of the setting as described in paragraphs 5 and 6.

5. In paragraph 14, Mrs. Mallard thinks: "There would be no powerful will bending hers in that blind persistence with which men and women believe they have the right to impose a private view upon a fellow creature. A kind intention or a cruel intention made the act seem no less a crime...." Explain the meaning of these thoughts.

6. Chopin takes the reader through Mrs. Mallard's thought processes about her husband's death to a climactic point toward the end of the story. Quote

the line where Mrs. Mallard comes to the full, powerful realization of the significance of her husband's death.

7. What do we learn about Brently Mallard throughout the story? How does knowing this information shape your opinion of Mrs. Mallard?

8. The story ends ironically in two distinct ways. What are the two ironies?

9. What was the role of women in American culture during the late Victorian period? What laws directly affected them? Where did you find this information? In what ways are these roles the same or different from women's roles in society today?

TO BUILD A FIRE

JACK LONDON

*The works of **Jack London** (1876-1916), prolific American novelist and short story writer, often examined the theme of the overwhelming power of nature and the struggle for survival. In his lifetime, London was one of America's most popular authors. His first novel,* The Son Of The Wolf, *appeared in 1900. His Alaska stories,* The Call Of The Wild *(1903),* White Fang *(1906) and* Burning Daylight *(1910) gained a large reading public. Among his other works are* The Sea-Wolf *(1904) and* The Road, *a collection of short stories. "To Build A Fire" was first published in* The Century Magazine, *August, 1908.*

[1]Day had broken cold and gray, exceedingly cold and gray, when the man turned aside from the main Yukon trail and climbed the high earth-bank, where a dim and little-traveled trail led eastward through the fat spruce timberland. It was a steep bank, and he paused for breath at the top, excusing the act to himself by looking at his watch. It was nine o'clock. There was no sun nor hint of sun, though there was not a cloud in the sky. It was a clear day, and yet there seemed an intangible pall over the face of things, a subtle gloom that made the day dark, and that was due to the absence of sun. This fact did not worry the man. He was used to the lack of sun. It had been days since he had seen the sun, and he knew that a few more days must pass before that cheerful orb, due south, would just peep above the sky-line and dip immediately from view.

[2]The man flung a look back along the way he had come. The Yukon lay a mile wide and hidden under three feet of ice. On top of this ice were as many feet of snow. It was all pure white, rolling in gentle undulations where the ice-jams of the freeze-up had formed. North and south, as far as his eye could see, it was unbroken white, save for a dark hair-line that curved and twisted from around the spruce-covered island to the south, and that curved and twisted away into the north, where it disappeared behind another spruce-covered island. This dark hair-line was the trail—the main trail—that led south five hundred miles to the Chilcoot Pass, Dyea, and salt water; and that led north seventy miles to Dawson, and still on to the north a thousand miles to Nulato, and finally to St. Michael on the Bering Sea, a thousand miles and half a thousand more.

[3]But all this—the mysterious, far-reaching hair-line trail, the absence of sun from the sky, the tremendous cold, and the strangeness and weirdness of it all—made no impression on the man. It was not because he was long used to it. He was a newcomer in the land, a *chechaquo*, and this was his first winter. The

trouble with him was that he was without imagination. He was quick and alert in the things of life, but only in the things and not in the significances. Fifty degrees below zero meant eighty-odd degrees of frost. Such fact impressed him as being cold and uncomfortable, and that was all. It did not lead him to meditate upon his frailty as a creature of temperature, and upon man's frailty in general, able only to live within certain narrow limits of heat and cold; and from there on it did not lead him to the conjectural field of immortality and man's place in the universe. Fifty degrees below zero stood for a bite of frost that hurt and that must be guarded against by the use of mittens, ear-flaps, warm moccasins, and thick socks. Fifty degrees below zero was to him just precisely fifty degrees below zero. That there should be anything more to it than that was a thought that never entered his head.

[4]As he turned to go on, he spat speculatively. There was a sharp, explosive crackle that startled him. He spat again. And again, in the air, before it could fall to the snow, the spittle crackled. He knew that at fifty below spittle crackled on the snow, but this spittle had crackled in the air. Undoubtedly it was colder than fifty below—how much colder he did not know. But the temperature did not matter. He was bound for the old claim on the left fork of Henderson Creek, where the boys were already. They had come over across the divide from the Indian Creek country, while he had come the roundabout way to take a look at the possibilities of getting out logs in the spring from the islands in the Yukon. He would be in to camp by six o'clock, a bit after dark, it was true, but the boys would be there, a fire would be going, and a hot supper would be ready. As for lunch, he pressed his hand against the protruding bundle under his jacket. It was also under his shirt, wrapped up in a handkerchief and lying against the naked skin. It was the only way to keep the biscuits from freezing. He smiled agreeably to himself as he thought of those biscuits, each cut open and sopped in bacon grease, and each enclosing a generous slice of fried bacon.

[5]He plunged in among the big spruce trees. The trail was faint. A foot of snow had fallen since the last sled had passed over, and he was glad he was without a sled, light. In fact, he carried nothing but the lunch wrapped in the handkerchief. He was surprised, however, at the cold. It certainly was cold, he concluded, as he rubbed his numb nose and cheek-bones with his mittened hand. He was a warm-whiskered man, but the hair on his face did not protect the high cheek-bones and the eager nose that thrust itself aggressively into the frosty air.

[6]At the man's heels trotted a dog, a big native husky, the proper wolf-dog, gray-coated and without any visible or temperamental difference from its brother, the wild wolf. The animal was depressed by the tremendous cold. It knew that it was no time for traveling. Its instinct told it a truer tale than was told to the man by the man's judgment. In reality, it was not merely colder than fifty below zero; it was colder than sixty below, than seventy below. It was

seventy-five below zero. Since the freezing-point is thirty-two above zero, it meant that one hundred and seven degrees of frost obtained. The dog did not know anything about thermometers. Possibly in its brain there was no sharp consciousness of a condition of very cold such as was in the man's brain. But the brute had its instinct. It experienced a vague but menacing apprehension that subdued it and made it slink along at the man's heels, and that made it question eagerly every unwonted movement of the man as if expecting him to go into camp or to seek shelter somewhere and build a fire. The dog had learned fire, and it wanted fire, or else to burrow under the snow and cuddle its warmth away from the air.

⁷The frozen moisture of its breathing had settled on its fur in a fine powder of frost, and especially were its jowls, muzzle, and eyelashes whitened by its crystalled breath. The man's red beard and mustache were likewise frosted, but more solidly, the deposit taking the form of ice and increasing with every warm, moist breath he exhaled. Also, the man was chewing tobacco, and the muzzle of ice held his lips so rigidly that he was unable to clear his chin when he expelled the juice. The result was that a crystal beard of the color and solidity of amber was increasing its length on his chin. If he fell down it would shatter itself, like glass, into brittle fragments. But he did not mind the appendage. It was the penalty all tobacco-chewers paid in that country, and he had been out before in two cold snaps. They had not been so cold as this, he knew, but by the spirit thermometer at Sixty Mile he knew they had been registered at fifty below and at fifty-five.

⁸He held on through the level stretch of woods for several miles, crossed a wide flat of niggerheads, and dropped down a bank to the frozen bed of a small stream. This was Henderson Creek, and he knew he was ten miles from the forks. He looked at his watch. It was ten o'clock. He was making four miles an hour, and he calculated that he would arrive at the forks at half-past twelve. He decided to celebrate that event by eating his lunch there.

⁹The dog dropped in again at his heels, with a tail drooping discouragement, as the man swung along the creek-bed. The furrow of the old sled-trail was plainly visible, but a dozen inches of snow covered the marks of the last runners. In a month no man had come up or down that silent creek. The man held steadily on. He was not much given to thinking, and just then particularly he had nothing to think about save that he would eat lunch at the forks and that at six o'clock he would be in camp with the boys. There was nobody to talk to; and, had there been, speech would have been impossible because of the ice-muzzle on his mouth. So he continued monotonously to chew tobacco and to increase the length of his amber beard.

¹⁰Once in a while the thought reiterated itself that it was very cold and that he had never experienced such cold. As he walked along he rubbed his cheek-bones and nose with the back of his mittened hand. He did this auto-

matically, now and again changing hands. But rub as he would, the instant he stopped, his cheek-bones went numb, and the following instant the end of his nose went numb. He was sure to frost his cheeks; he knew that, and experienced a pang of regret that he had not devised a nose-strap of the sort Bud wore in cold snaps. Such a strap passed across the cheeks, as well, and saved them. But it didn't matter much, after all. What were frosted cheeks? A bit painful, that was all; they were never serious.

[11]Empty as the man's mind was of thoughts, he was keenly observant, and he noticed the changes in the creek, the curves and bends and timber-jams, and always he sharply noted where he placed his feet. Once, coming around a bend, he shied abruptly, like a startled horse, curved away from the place where he had been walking, and retreated several paces back along the trail. The creek he knew was frozen clear to the bottom—no creek could contain water in that arctic winter,—but he knew also that there were springs that bubbled out from the hillsides and ran along under the snow and on top the ice of the creek. He knew that the coldest snaps never froze these springs, and he knew likewise their danger. They were traps. They hid pools of water under the snow that might be three inches deep, or three feet. Sometimes a skin of ice half an inch thick covered them, and in turn was covered by the snow. Sometimes there were alternate layers of water and ice-skin, so that when one broke through he kept on breaking through for a while, sometimes wetting himself to the waist.

[12]That was why he had shied in such panic. He had felt the give under his feet and heard the crackle of a snow-hidden ice-skin. And to get his feet wet in such a temperature meant trouble and danger. At the very least it meant delay, for he would be forced to stop and build a fire, and under its protection to bare his feet while he dried his socks and moccasins. He stood and studied the creek-bed and its banks, and decided that the flow of water came from the right. He reflected awhile, rubbing his nose and cheeks, then skirted to the left, stepping gingerly and testing the footing for each step. Once clear of the danger, he took a fresh chew of tobacco and swung along at his four-mile gait. In the course of the next two hours he came upon several similar traps. Usually the snow above the hidden pools had a sunken, candied appearance that advertised the danger. Once again, however, he had a close call; and once, suspecting danger, he compelled the dog to go on in front. The dog did not want to go. It hung back until the man shoved it forward, and then it went quickly across the white, unbroken surface. Suddenly it broke through, floundered to one side, and got away to firmer footing. It had wet its forefeet and legs, and almost immediately the water that clung to it turned to ice. It made quick efforts to lick the ice off its legs, then dropped down in the snow and began to bite out the ice that had formed between the toes. This was a matter of instinct. To permit the ice to remain would mean sore feet. It did not know this. It merely obeyed the mysterious prompting that arose from the deep crypts of its being. But the man

knew, having achieved a judgment on the subject, and he removed the mitten from his right hand and helped tear out the ice-particles. He did not expose his fingers more than a minute, and was astonished at the swift numbness that smote them. It certainly was cold. He pulled on the mitten hastily, and beat the hand savagely across his chest.

[13]At twelve o'clock the day was at its brightest. Yet the sun was too far south on its winter journey to clear the horizon. The bulge of the earth intervened between it and Henderson Creek, where the man walked under a clear sky at noon and cast no shadow. At half-past twelve, to the minute, he arrived at the forks of the creek. He was pleased at the speed he had made. If he kept it up, he would certainly be with the boys by six. He unbuttoned his jacket and shirt and drew forth his lunch. The action consumed no more than a quarter of a minute, yet in that brief moment the numbness laid hold of the exposed fingers. He did not put the mitten on, but, instead, struck the fingers a dozen sharp smashes against his leg. Then he sat down on a snow-covered log to eat. The sting that followed upon the striking of his fingers against his leg ceased so quickly that he was startled. He had had no chance to take a bite of biscuit. He struck the fingers repeatedly and returned them to the mitten, baring the other hand for the purpose of eating. He tried to take a mouthful, but the ice-muzzle prevented. He had forgotten to build a fire and thaw out. He chuckled at his foolishness, and as he chuckled he noted the numbness creeping into the exposed fingers. Also, he noted that the stinging which had first come to his toes when he sat down was already passing away. He wondered whether the toes were warm or numb. He moved them inside the moccasins and decided that they were numb.

[14]He pulled the mitten on hurriedly and stood up. He was a bit frightened. He stamped up and down until the stinging returned into the feet. It certainly was cold, was his thought. That man from Sulphur Creek had spoken the truth when telling how cold it sometimes got in the country. And he had laughed at him at the time! That showed one must not be too sure of things. There was no mistake about it, it *was* cold. He strode up and down, stamping his feet and threshing his arms, until reassured by the returning warmth. Then he got out matches and proceeded to make a fire. From the undergrowth, where high water of the previous spring had lodged a supply of seasoned twigs, he got his firewood. Working carefully from a small beginning, he soon had a roaring fire, over which he thawed the ice from his face and in the protection of which he ate his biscuits. For the moment the cold of space was outwitted. The dog took satisfaction in the fire, stretching out close enough for warmth and far enough away to escape being singed.

[15]When the man had finished, he filled his pipe and took his comfortable time over a smoke. Then he pulled on his mittens, settled the ear-flaps of his cap firmly about his ears, and took the creek trail up the left fork. The dog was disappointed and yearned back toward the fire. This man did not know cold.

Possibly all the generations of his ancestry had been ignorant of cold, of real cold, of cold one hundred and seven degrees below freezing-point. But the dog knew; all its ancestry knew, and it had inherited the knowledge. And it knew that it was not good to walk abroad in such fearful cold. It was the time to lie snug in a hole in the snow and wait for a curtain of cloud to be drawn across the face of outer space whence this cold came. On the other hand, there was no keen intimacy between the dog and the man. The one was the toil-slave of the other, and the only caresses it had ever received were the caresses of the whip-lash and of harsh and menacing throat-sounds that threatened the whip-lash. So the dog made no effort to communicate its apprehension to the man. It was not concerned in the welfare of the man; it was for its own sake that it yearned back toward the fire. But the man whistled and spoke to it with the sound of whip-lashes, and the dog swung in at the man's heels and followed after.

[16]The man took a chew of tobacco and proceeded to start a new amber beard. Also, his moist breath quickly powdered with white his mustache, eyebrows, and lashes. There did not seem to be so many springs on the left fork of the Henderson, and for half an hour the man saw no signs of any. And then it happened. At a place where there were no signs, where the soft, unbroken snow seemed to advertise solidity beneath, the man broke through. It was not deep. He wet himself halfway to the knees before he floundered out to the firm crust.

[17]He was angry and cursed his luck aloud. He had hoped to get into camp with the boys at six o'clock, and this would delay him an hour, for he would have to build a fire and dry out his foot-gear. This was imperative at that low temperature—he knew that much; and he turned aside to the bank, which he climbed. On top, tangled in the underbrush about the trunks of several small spruce trees, was a high-water deposit of dry fire-wood—sticks and twigs, principally, but also larger portions of seasoned branches and fine, dry, last-year's grasses. He threw down several large pieces on top of the snow. This served for a foundation and prevented the young flame from drowning itself in the snow it otherwise would melt. The flame he got by touching a match to a small shred of birch-bark that he took from his pocket. This burned even more readily than paper. Placing it on the foundation, he fed the young flame with wisps of dry grass and with the tiniest dry twigs.

[18]He worked slowly and carefully, keenly aware of his danger. Gradually, as the flame grew stronger, he increased the size of the twigs with which he fed it. He squatted in the snow, pulling the twigs out from their entanglement in the brush and feeding directly to the flame. He knew there must be no failure. When it is seventy-five below zero, a man must not fail in his first attempt to build a fire—that is, if his feet are wet. If his feet are dry, and he fails, he can run along the trail for half a mile and restore his circulation. But the circulation of wet and freezing feet cannot be restored by running when it is seventy-five below. No

matter how fast he runs, the wet feet will freeze the harder.

[19]All this the man knew. The old-timer on Sulphur Creek had told him about it the previous fall, and now he was appreciating the advice. Already all sensation had gone out of his feet. To build the fire he had been forced to remove his mittens, and the fingers had quickly gone numb. His pace of four miles an hour had kept his heart pumping blood to the surface of his body and to all the extremities. But the instant he stopped, the action of the pump eased down. The cold of space smote the unprotected tip of the planet, and he, being on that unprotected tip, received the full force of the blow. The blood of his body recoiled before it. The blood was alive, like the dog, and like the dog it wanted to hide away and cover itself up from the fearful cold. So long as he walked four miles an hour, he pumped that blood, willy-nilly, to the surface; but now it ebbed away and sank down into the recesses of his body. The extremities were the first to feel its absence. His wet feet froze the faster, and his exposed fingers numbed the faster, though they had not yet begun to freeze. Nose and cheeks were already freezing, while the skin of all his body chilled as it lost its blood.

[20]But he was safe. Toes and nose and cheeks would be only touched by the frost, for the fire was beginning to burn with strength. He was feeding it with twigs the size of his finger. In another minute he would be able to feed it with branches the size of his wrist, and then he could remove his wet foot-gear, and, while it dried, he could keep his naked feet warm by the fire, rubbing them at first, of course, with snow. The fire was a success. He was safe. He remembered the advice of the old-timer on Sulphur Creek, and smiled. The old-timer had been very serious in laying down the law that no man must travel alone in the Klondike after fifty below. Well, here he was; he had had the accident; he was alone; and he had saved himself. Those old-timers were rather womanish, some of them, he thought. All a man had to do was to keep his head, and he was all right. Any man who was a man could travel alone. But it was surprising, the rapidity with which his cheeks and nose were freezing. And he had not thought his fingers could go lifeless in so short a time. Lifeless they were, for he could scarcely make them move together to grip a twig, and they seemed remote from his body and from him. When he touched a twig, he had to look and see whether or not he had hold of it. The wires were pretty well down between him and his finger-ends.

[21]All of which counted for little. There was the fire, snapping and crackling and promising life with every dancing flame. He started to untie his moccasins. They were coated with ice; the thick German socks were like sheaths of iron halfway to the knees; and the moccasin strings were like rods of steel all twisted and knotted as by some conflagration. For a moment he tugged with his numb fingers, then, realizing the folly of it, he drew his sheath-knife.

[22]But before he could cut the strings, it happened. It was his own fault

or, rather, his mistake. He should not have built the fire under the spruce tree. He should have built it in the open. But it had been easier to pull the twigs from the brush and drop them directly on the fire. Now the tree under which he had done this carried a weight of snow on its boughs. No wind had blown for weeks, and each bough was fully freighted. Each time he had pulled a twig he had communicated a slight agitation to the tree—an imperceptible agitation, so far as he was concerned, but an agitation sufficient to bring about the disaster. High up in the tree one bough capsized its load of snow. This fell on the boughs beneath, capsizing them. This process continued, spreading out and involving the whole tree. It grew like an avalanche, and it descended without warning upon the man and the fire, and the fire was blotted out! Where it had burned was a mantle of fresh and disordered snow.

[23]The man was shocked. It was as though he had just heard his own sentence of death. For a moment he sat and stared at the spot where the fire had been. Then he grew very calm. Perhaps the old-timer on Sulphur Creek was right. If he had only had a trail-mate he would have been in no danger now. The trail-mate could have built the fire. Well, it was up to him to build the fire over again, and this second time there must be no failure. Even if he succeeded, he would most likely lose some toes. His feet must be badly frozen by now, and there would be some time before the second fire was ready.

[24]Such were his thoughts, but he did not sit and think them. He was busy all the time they were passing through his mind. He made a new foundation for a fire, this time in the open, where no treacherous tree could blot it out. Next, he gathered dry grasses and tiny twigs from the high-water flotsam. He could not bring his fingers together to pull them out, but he was able to gather them by the handful. In this way he got many rotten twigs and bits of green moss that were undesirable, but it was the best he could do. He worked methodically, even collecting an armful of the larger branches to be used later when the fire gathered strength. And all the while the dog sat and watched him, a certain yearning wistfulness in its eyes, for it looked upon him as the fire-provider, and the fire was slow in coming.

[25]When all was ready, the man reached in his pocket for a second piece of birch-bark. He knew the bark was there, and, though he could not feel it with his fingers, he could hear its crisp rustling as he fumbled for it. Try as he would, he could not clutch hold of it. And all the time, in his consciousness, was the knowledge that each instant his feet were freezing. This thought tended to put him in a panic, but he fought against it and kept calm. He pulled on his mittens with his teeth, and threshed his arms back and forth, beating his hands with all his might against his sides. He did this sitting down, and he stood up to do it; and all the while the dog sat in the snow, its wolf-brush of a tail curled around warmly over its forefeet, its sharp wolf-ears pricked forward intently as it watched the man. And the man, as he beat and threshed with his arms and

hands, felt a great surge of envy as he regarded the creature that was warm and secure in its natural covering.

[26]After a time he was aware of the first faraway signals of sensation in his beaten fingers. The faint tingling grew stronger till it evolved into a stinging ache that was excruciating, but which the man hailed with satisfaction. He stripped the mitten from his right hand and fetched forth the birch-bark. The exposed fingers were quickly going numb again. Next he brought out his bunch of sulphur matches. But the tremendous cold had already driven the life out of his fingers. In his effort to separate one match from the others, the whole bunch fell in the snow. He tried to pick it out of the snow, but failed. The dead fingers could neither touch nor clutch. He was very careful. He drove the thought of his freezing feet, and nose, and cheeks, out of his mind, devoting his whole soul to the matches. He watched, using the sense of vision in place of that of touch, and when he saw his fingers on each side of the bunch, he closed them—that is, he willed to close them, for the wires were down, and the fingers did not obey. He pulled the mitten on the right hand and beat it fiercely against his knee. Then, with both mittened hands, he scooped the bunch of matches, along with much snow, into his lap. Yet he was no better off.

[27]After some manipulation he managed to get the bunch between the heels of his mittened hands. In this fashion he carried it to his mouth. The ice crackled and snapped when by a violent effort he opened his mouth. He drew the lower jaw in, curled the upper lip out of the way, and scraped the bunch with his upper teeth in order to separate a match. He succeeded in getting one, which he dropped on his lap. He was no better off. He could not pick it up. Then he devised a way. He picked it up in his teeth and scratched it on his leg. Twenty times he scratched before he succeeded in lighting it. As it flamed he held it with his teeth to the birch-bark. But the burning brimstone went up his nostrils and into his lungs, causing him to cough spasmodically. The match fell into the snow and went out.

[28]The old-timer on Sulphur Creek was right, he thought in the moment of controlled despair that ensued: after fifty below, a man should travel with a partner. He beat his hands, but failed in exciting any sensation. Suddenly he bared both hands, removing the mittens with his teeth. He caught the whole bunch between the heels of his hands. His arm-muscles not being frozen enabled him to press the hand-heels tightly against the matches. Then he scratched the bunch along his leg. It flared into flame, seventy sulphur matches at once! There was no wind to blow them out. He kept his head to one side to escape the strangling fumes, and held the blazing bunch to the birch-bark. As he so held it, he became aware of sensation in his hand. His flesh was burning. He could smell it. Deep down below the surface he could feel it. The sensation developed into pain that grew acute. And still he endured it, holding the flame of the matches clumsily to the bark that would not light readily because his own burning hands were in the way, absorbing most of the flame.

²⁹At last, when he could endure no more, he jerked his hands apart. The blazing matches fell sizzling into the snow, but the birch-bark was alight. He began laying dry grasses and the tiniest twigs on the flame. He could not pick and choose, for he had to lift the fuel between the heels of his hands. Small pieces of rotten wood and green moss clung to the twigs, and he bit them off as well as he could with his teeth. He cherished the flame carefully and awkwardly. It meant life, and it must not perish. The withdrawal of blood from the surface of his body now made him begin to shiver, and he grew more awkward. A large piece of green moss fell squarely on the little fire. He tried to poke it out with his fingers, but his shivering frame made him poke too far, and he disrupted the nucleus of the little fire, the burning grasses and tiny twigs separating and scattering. He tried to poke them together again, but in spite of the tenseness of the effort, his shivering got away with him, and the twigs were hopelessly scattered. Each twig gushed a puff of smoke and went out. The fire-provider had failed. As he looked apathetically about him, his eyes chanced on the dog, sitting across the ruins of the fire from him, in the snow, making restless, hunching movements, slightly lifting one forefoot and then the other, shifting its weight back and forth on them with wistful eagerness.

³⁰The sight of the dog put a wild idea into his head. He remembered the tale of the man, caught in a blizzard, who killed a steer and crawled inside the carcass, and so was saved. He would kill the dog and bury his hands in the warm body until the numbness went out of them. Then he could build another fire. He spoke to the dog, calling it to him; but in his voice was a strange note of fear that frightened the animal, who had never known the man to speak in such way before. Something was the matter, and its suspicious nature sensed danger—it knew not what danger, but somewhere, somehow, in its brain arose an apprehension of the man. It flattened its ears down at the sound of the man's voice, and its restless, hunching movements and the liftings and shiftings of its forefeet became more pronounced; but it would not come to the man. He got on his hands and knees and crawled toward the dog. This unusual posture again excited suspicion, and the animal sidled mincingly away.

³¹The man sat up in the snow for a moment and struggled for calmness. Then he pulled on his mittens, by means of his teeth, and got upon his feet. He glanced down at first in order to assure himself that he was really standing up, for the absence of sensation in his feet left him unrelated to the earth. His erect position in itself started to drive the webs of suspicion from the dog's mind; and when he spoke peremptorily, with the sound of whip-lashes in his voice, the dog rendered its customary allegiance and came to him. As it came within reaching distance, the man lost his control. His arms flashed out to the dog, and he experienced genuine surprise when he discovered that his hands could not clutch, that there was neither bend nor feeling in the fingers. He had forgotten for the moment that they were frozen and that they were freezing more and more. All

this happened quickly, and before the animal could get away, he encircled its body with his arms. He sat down in the snow, and in this fashion held the dog, while it snarled and whined and struggled.

[32]But it was all he could do, hold its body encircled in his arms and sit there. He realized that he could not kill the dog. There was no way to do it. With his helpless hands he could neither draw nor hold his sheath-knife nor throttle the animal. He released it, and it plunged wildly away, with tail between its legs, and still snarling. It halted forty feet away and surveyed him curiously, with ears sharply pricked forward. The man looked down at his hands in order to locate them, and found them hanging on the ends of his arms. It struck him as curious that one should have to use his eyes in order to find out where his hands were. He began threshing his arms back and forth, beating the mittened hands against his sides. He did this for five minutes, violently, and his heart pumped enough blood up to the surface to put a stop to his shivering. But no sensation was aroused in the hands. He had an impression that they hung like weights on the ends of his arms, but when he tried to run the impression down, he could not find it.

[33]A certain fear of death, dull and oppressive, came to him. This fear quickly became poignant as he realized that it was no longer a mere matter of freezing his fingers and toes, or of losing his hands and feet, but that it was a matter of life and death with the chances against him. This threw him into a panic, and he turned and ran up the creek-bed along the old, dim trail. The dog joined in behind and kept up with him. He ran blindly, without intention, in fear such as he had never known in his life. Slowly, as he ploughed and floundered through the snow, he began to see things again—the banks of the creek, the old timber-jams, the leafless aspens, and the sky. The running made him feel better. He did not shiver. Maybe, if he ran on, his feet would thaw out; and, anyway, if he ran far enough, he would reach camp and the boys. Without doubt he would lose some fingers and toes and some of his face; but the boys would take care of him, and save the rest of him when he got there. And at the same time there was another thought in his mind that said he would never get to the camp and the boys; that it was too many miles away, that the freezing had too great a start on him, and that he would soon be stiff and dead. This thought he kept in the background and refused to consider. Sometimes it pushed itself forward and demanded to be heard, but he thrust it back and strove to think of other things.

[34]It struck him as curious that he could run at all on feet so frozen that he could not feel them when they struck the earth and took the weight of his body. He seemed to himself to skim along above the surface, and to have no connection with the earth. Somewhere he had once seen a winged Mercury, and he wondered if Mercury felt as he felt when skimming over the earth.

[35]His theory of running until he reached camp and the boys had one flaw in it: he lacked the endurance. Several times he stumbled, and finally he tot-

tered, crumpled up, and fell. When he tried to rise, he failed. He must sit and rest, he decided, and next time he would merely walk and keep on going. As he sat and regained his breath, he noted that he was feeling quite warm and comfortable. He was not shivering, and it even seemed that a warm glow had come to his chest and trunk. And yet, when he touched his nose or cheeks, there was no sensation. Running would not thaw them out. Nor would it thaw out his hands and feet. Then the thought came to him that the frozen portions of his body must be extending. He tried to keep this thought down, to forget it, to think of something else; he was aware of the panicky feeling that it caused, and he was afraid of the panic. But the thought asserted itself, and persisted, until it produced a vision of his body totally frozen. This was too much, and he made another wild run along the trail. Once he slowed down to a walk, but the thought of the freezing extending itself made him run again.

³⁶And all the time the dog ran with him, at his heels. When he fell down a second time, it curled its tail over its forefeet and sat in front of him, facing him, curiously eager and intent. The warmth and security of the animal angered him, and he cursed it till it flattened down its ears appeasingly. This time the shivering came more quickly upon the man. He was losing in his battle with the frost. It was creeping into his body from all sides. The thought of it drove him on, but he ran no more than a hundred feet, when he staggered and pitched headlong. It was his last panic. When he had recovered his breath and control, he sat up and entertained in his mind the conception of meeting death with dignity. However, the conception did not come to him in such terms. His idea of it was that he had been making a fool of himself, running around like a chicken with its head cut off—such was the simile that occurred to him. Well, he was bound to freeze anyway, and he might as well take it decently. With this new-found peace of mind came the first glimmerings of drowsiness. A good idea, he thought, to sleep off to death. It was like taking an anaesthetic. Freezing was not so bad as people thought. There were lots worse ways to die.

³⁷He pictured the boys finding his body next day. Suddenly he found himself with them, coming along the trail and looking for himself. And, still with them, he came around a turn in the trail and found himself lying in the snow. He did not belong with himself any more, for even then he was out of himself, standing with the boys and looking at himself in the snow. It certainly was cold, was his thought. When he got back to the States he could tell the folks what real cold was. He drifted on from this to a vision of the old-timer on Sulphur Creek. He could see him quite clearly, warm and comfortable, and smoking a pipe.

³⁸"You were right, old hoss; you were right," the man mumbled to the old-timer of Sulphur Creek. Then the man drowsed off into what seemed to him the most comfortable and satisfying sleep he had ever known. The dog sat facing him and waiting. The brief day drew to a close in a long, slow twilight. There were no signs of a fire to be made, and, besides, never in the dog's ex-

perience had it known a man to sit like that in the snow and make no fire. As the twilight drew on, its eager yearning for the fire mastered it, and with a great lifting and shifting of forefeet, it whined softly, then flattened its ears down in anticipation of being chidden by the man. But the man remained silent. Later, the dog whined loudly. And still later it crept close to the man and caught the scent of death. This made the animal bristle and back away. A little longer it delayed, howling under the stars that leaped and danced and shone brightly in the cold sky. Then it turned and trotted up the trail in the direction of the camp it knew, where were the other food-providers and fire-providers.

Vocabulary

[1]intangible	[7]appendage	[17]imperative	[27]spasmodically
[1]pall	[9]furrow	[19]extremities	[28]ensued
[1]orb	[10]reiterated	[21]conflagration	[30]sidled
[2]undulation	[12]gingerly	[21]folly	[30]mincingly
[3]conjectural	[12]compelled	[22]imperceptible	[31]peremptorily
[4]speculatively	[12]floundered	[22]mantle	[33]poignant
[6]unwonted	[12]crypts	[24]flotsam	[38]chidden
[7]jowls	[12]smote	[24]wistfulness	

Discussion Questions

1. At the beginning of the story, what is the difference between the dog's reaction to the cold and the man's?

2. Where is the plot established? At what point in the story did you develop a sense of the conflict that was developing?

3. At what point did you begin to suspect what the man's ultimate fate would be?

4. Why doesn't the author give the main character in the story a name?

5. Why does London include the scene where the man tries to kill the dog to survive? What statement is he making?

6. What purpose does the dog serve in the story? What role does "the old timer" play?

7. What does the man represent? The dog? What is London saying about man's intellect versus the dog's instincts?

8. Does this story validate or refute Darwin's theory of survival of the fittest? Explain your answer.

THE TROUBLE WITH TALENT: ARE WE BORN SMART OR DO WE GET SMART?

KATHY SEAL

Kathy Seal *is a journalist and author who has written about education and psychology since 1985 for such publications as* The New York *Times,* Family Circle, *and* Parents. *Seal attended Barnard College, where she graduated magna cum laude. She is the author of two books:* Riches and Fame and the Pleasures of Sense *(1971) and* Motivated Minds: Raising Children to Love Learning *(2001). "The Trouble with Talent" appeared in the July, 1993 issue of* Lear's *magazine.*

[1]Jim Stigler was in an awkward position. Fascinated by the fact that Asian students routinely do better than American kids at elementary math, the UCLA psychologist wanted to test whether persistence might be the key factor. So he designed and administered an experiment in which he gave the same insolvable math problem to separate small groups of Japanese and American children.

[2]Sure enough, most American kids attacked the problem, struggled briefly—then gave up. The Japanese kids, however, worked on and on and on. Eventually, Stigler stopped the experiment when it began to feel inhumane: If the Japanese kids were uninterrupted, they seemed willing to plow on indefinitely.

[3]"The Japanese kids assumed that if they kept working, they'd eventually get it," Stigler recalls. "The Americans thought, 'Either you get it or you don't.'"

[4]Stigler's work, detailed in his 1992 book *The Learning Gap* (Summit, Books/Simon & Schuster), shatters our stereotypical notion that Asian education relies on rote and drill. In fact, Japanese and Chinese elementary schoolteachers believe that their chief task is to stimulate thinking. They tell their students that anyone who thinks long enough about a problem can move toward its solution.

[5]Stigler concludes that the Asian belief in hard work as the key to success is one reason why Asians outperform us academically. Americans are persuaded that success in school requires inborn talent. "If you believe that achievement is mostly caused by ability," Stigler says, "at some fundamental level you don't believe in education. You believe education is sorting kids, and that kids in some categories can't learn. The Japanese believe *everybody* can master the curriculum if you give them the time."

[6]Stigler and his coauthor, Harold W. Stevenson of the University of Michigan, are among a growing number of educational psychologists who

argue that the American fixation on innate ability causes us to waste the potential of many of our children. He says that this national focus on the importance of natural talent is producing kids who give up easily and artful dodgers who would rather look smart than actually learn something.

[7]Cross-cultural achievement tests show how wide the gap is: In a series of studies spanning a ten-year period, Stigler and Stevenson compared math test scores at more than 75 elementary schools in Sendai, Japan; T'aipei, Taiwan; Beijing, China; Minneapolis; and Chicago. In each study, the scores of fifth graders in the best-performing American school were lower than the scores of their counterparts in the worst-performing Asian school. In other studies, Stigler and Stevenson found significant gaps in reading tests as well.

[8]Respect for hard work pervades Asian culture. Many folk tales make the point that diligence can achieve any goal—for example, the poet Li Po's story of the woman who grinds a piece of iron into a needle, and Mao Tse-tung's recounting of an old man who removes a mountain with just a hoe. The accent on academic effort in Asian countries demonstrates how expectations for children are both higher and more democratic there than in America. "If learning is gradual and proceeds step by step," says Stigler, "anyone can gain knowledge."

[9]To illustrate this emphasis, Stigler videotaped a Japanese teacher at work. The first image on screen is that of a young woman standing in front of a class of fifth graders. She bows quickly. "Today," she says, "we will be studying triangles:" The teacher reminds the children that they already know how to find the area of a rectangle. Then she distributes a quantity of large paper triangles—some equilateral, others right or isosceles—and asks the class to think about "the best way to find the area of a triangle:" For the next 141/2 minutes, 44 children cut, paste, fold, draw, and talk to each other. Eventually nine kids come to the blackboard and take turns explaining how they have arranged the triangles into shapes for which they can find the areas. Finally, the teacher helps the children to see that all nine solutions boil down to the same formula: $a = (b \times h) \div 2$ (the area equals the product of the base multiplied by the height, divided by two).

[10]Stigler says that the snail-like pace of the lesson—60 minutes from start to finish—allows the brighter students enough time to understand the concept in depth, as they think through nine different ways to find the areas of the three kinds of triangles. Meanwhile, slower students—even learning-disabled students—benefit from hearing one concept explained in many different ways. Thus children of varied abilities have the same learning opportunity, and the result is that a large number of Japanese children advance relatively far in math.

[11]Americans, on the other hand, group children by ability throughout their school careers. Assigning students to curricular tracks according to abil-

ity is common, but it happens even in schools where formal tracking is not practiced.

[12]So kids always know who the teacher thinks is "very smart, sorta smart, and kinda dumb," says social psychologist Jeff Howard, president of the Efficacy Institute, a nonprofit consulting firm in Lexington, Massachusetts, that specializes in education issues. "The idea of genetic intellectual inferiority is rampant in [American] society, especially as applied to African-American kids:"

[13]A consequence is that many kids face lower expectations and a watered-down curriculum. "A student who is bright is expected just to 'get it,'" Stigler says. "Duller kids are assumed to lack the necessary ability for ever learning certain material."

[14]Our national mania for positive self-esteem too often leads us to puff up kids' confidence, and we may forget to tell them that genius is 98 percent perspiration. In fact, our reverence for innate intelligence has gone so far that many Americans believe people who work hard in school must lack ability. "Our idealization of a gifted person is someone so smart they don't have to try" says Sandra Graham of UCLA's Graduate School of Education.

[15]Columbia University psychologist Carol Dweck has conducted a fascinating series of studies over the past decade documenting the dangers of believing that geniuses are born rather than made. In one study, Dweck and UCLA researcher Ualanne Henderson asked 229 seventh graders whether people are "born smart" or "get smart" by working hard. Then they compared the students' sixth and seventh grade achievement scores. The scores of kids with the get-smart beliefs stayed high or improved, and those of the kids subscribing to the born-smart assumption stayed low or declined. Surprisingly, even kids who believed in working hard but who had low confidence in their abilities did very well. And the kids whose scores dropped the most were the born-smart believers with high confidence.

[16]Dweck's conclusion: "If we want our kids to succeed, we should emphasize effort and steer away from praising or blaming intelligence per se."

[17]Psychologist Ellen Leggett, a former student of Dweck's at Harvard, has found that bright girls are more likely than boys to believe that people are born smart. That finding could help to explain why many American girls stop taking high school math and science before boys do.

[18]Seeing intelligence as an inborn trait also turns children into quitters, says Dweck. "Kids who believe you're born smart or not are always worried about their intelligence, so they're afraid to take risks," Dweck explains. "But kids who think you can get smart aren't threatened by a difficult task or by failures and find it kind of exciting to figure out what went wrong and to keep at it." Or, in Jeff Howard's words, "If I know I'm too stupid to learn, why should I bang my head against the wall trying to learn?"

[19]Getting Americans to give up their worship of natural ability and to replace it with the Asian belief in effort seems a mammoth undertaking. But Dweck maintains that it's possible to train kids to believe in hard work. The key to bringing kids around, says Dweck, is for the adults close to them to talk and act upon a conviction that effort is what counts.

[20]The Efficacy Institute is working on exactly that. The institute's work is based on theories that Howard developed as a doctoral candidate at Harvard as he investigated why black students weren't performing in school as well as whites and Asians. Using the slogan, "Think you can; work hard; get smart," the institute conducts a seminar for teachers that weans them from the born-smart belief system.

[21]"We tell teachers to talk to kids with the presumption that they can all get A's in their tests," explains project specialist Kim Taylor. Most kids respond immediately to their teachers' changed expectations, Howard says. As proof, he cites achievement-test scores of 137 third grade students from six Detroit public schools who were enrolled in the Efficacy Institute program during 1989 and 1990. The students' scores rose 2.4 grade levels (from 2.8 to 5.2) in one year, compared with a control group of peers whose scores only went up by less than half a grade level.

[22]Institute trainers now work in approximately 55 school districts, from Baltimore to St. Louis to Sacramento. In five cities, they're working to train every teacher and administrator in the school district.

[23]While current efforts for change are modest, no less a force than the Clinton administration is weaving this new thinking into its education agenda. During a talk this past spring to the California Teachers Association, U.S. Secretary of Education Richard Riley pledged to work on setting national standards in education. "These standards," he says, "must be for all of our young people, regardless of their economic background. We must convince people that children aren't born smart. They get smart."

Vocabulary

[2]inhumane	[6]innate	[12]rampant	[19]mammoth
[4]stereotypical	[6]artful dodgers	[14]mania	[20]weans
[4]rote	[8]pervades	[16]per se	[21]presumption
[6]fixation	[8]diligence		

Discussion Questions

1. What type of introduction does Seal use? Do you find it effective?
2. What difference concerning insolvable problems did Stigler find between

the American and Japanese students? Why is this information important to understanding the thesis?

3. What cultural difference between the Japanese and American students did the researchers find?

4. What is the difference between the Japanese and American method of teaching? What example(s) does Seal provide to support this?

5. Summarize the researchers' thoughts on intelligence and effort.

6. How does the conclusion tie-up the essay? Do you find it effective? Explain.

7. What is Seal's thesis and what evidence does she provide to support it?

TRUE AMERICANISM

THEODORE ROOSEVELT

Theodore Roosevelt (1858-1919) became America's youngest president at age 42 upon the assassination of William McKinley in 1901. Roosevelt was noted for his remarkable energy and achieved success as a writer, soldier, explorer, hunter, historian and naturalist. As president, Roosevelt was known as a progressive reformer. He believed in American capitalism but also believed that government must regulate business and protect the public from abuses. The Pure Food and Drug Act was passed during his administration and 40 monopolistic trusts were dissolved. Roosevelt was an unapologetic "jingoist," an extremely patriotic believer in "my country, right or wrong." This essay was originally published in The Forum *magazine in April of 1894.*

[1]PATRIOTISM was once defined as "the last refuge of a scoundrel"; and somebody has recently remarked that when Dr. Johnson[a] gave this definition, he was ignorant of the infinite possibilities contained in the word "reform."[b] Of course, both gibes were quite justifiable in so far as they were aimed at people who use noble names to camouflage dishonorable purposes. Equally, of course, anyone who fails to see that love of country is one of the elemental virtues shows little wisdom and a low sense of duty, even though scoundrels play upon that love for their own selfish ends.

[2]What is true of patriotism and reform is true also of Americanism. There are always plenty of scoundrels ready to belittle reform movements or to bolster existing evil in the name of Americanism; but this does not alter the fact that the people who can do most in this country are and must be those whose Americanism is most sincere and intense. Those who do iniquity in the name of patriotism, of reform, of Americanism, are merely one small division of the class that has always existed and will always exist—the class of hypocrites and demagogues, the class that is out to steal and use the principles of righteousness in the interests of evil-doing.

---

[a]Dr, Samuel Johnson (1709-1784) was an English essayist, biographer, novelist, poet, dramatist and literary critic. His most notable contribution to literary scholarship was his *Dictionary of the English Language*, which stood as the most authoritative work of its kind for well over 100 years.

[b]"Reform" was a key element of Theodore Roosevelt's eight years as president, especially in the area of the regulation of big business and an insistence that corporations take responsibility for their actions.

[3]The sturdiest and truest Americans are the very people who have the least sympathy with those who invoke the spirit of Americanism to support what is vicious in our government or to throw obstacles in the way of those who strive to reform it. To appeal to national prejudice against a given reform movement is in every way unworthy and silly. It is as childish to denounce free trade because England has adopted it as it is to advocate it for the same reason. It is eminently proper, in dealing with the tariff, to consider the effect in times past of tariff legislation upon other nations as well as the effect upon our own; but in drawing conclusions it is in the highest degree foolish to try to promote prejudice against one system because it is used in some given country, or to argue in its favor because the economists of that country have found that it was suited to their own particular needs.

[4]For example, in attempting to solve our difficult problem of municipal government, it is silly to refuse to benefit by whatever is good in the examples of Manchester and Berlin because these cities are foreign, exactly as it is foolish to blindly copy their examples without reference to our own totally different conditions. As for the absurdity of declaiming against civil-service reform, for instance, as "Chinese" because written examinations have been used in China, it would be just as unreasonable to declaim against gunpowder because it was first utilized by the same people. In short, those who, whether from simple ignorance or from an active interest in misgovernment, try to appeal to American prejudice against things foreign to induce Americans to oppose any measure for good should be looked upon by their fellow Americans with the heartiest contempt.

[5]We Americans have many grave problems to solve, many threatening evils to fight, and many deeds to do, if, as we hope and believe, we have the wisdom, the strength, the courage, and the virtue to do them. But we must face facts as they are. We must neither surrender ourselves to a foolish optimism, nor succumb to a timid and ignoble pessimism. Our nation is that one among all the nations of the earth which holds in its hands the fate of the coming years. We enjoy exceptional advantages while at the same time being menaced by exceptional dangers; and all signs indicate that we shall either fail greatly or succeed greatly. I firmly believe that we shall succeed; but we must not foolishly ignore the dangers by which we are threatened, for that is the way to fail.

[6]On the contrary, we must soberly set to work to find out all we can about the existence and extent of every evil, must acknowledge it to be such, and must then attack it with unyielding resolution. There are many such evils, and each must be fought after a fashion; yet there is one quality which we must bring to the solution of every problem—that is, an intense and passionate Americanism. We shall never be successful over the dangers that confront us; we shall never achieve true greatness, nor reach the lofty ideal which the founders and preservers of our mighty Federal Republic have set before us, unless we are

Americans in heart and soul, in spirit and purpose, keenly alive to the responsibility implied in the very name of "American," and proud beyond measure of the glorious privilege of bearing it.

[7]There are two or three sides to the question of Americanism, and two or three senses in which the word "Americanism" can be used to express the antithesis of what is unwholesome and undesirable. In the first place we wish to be broadly American and national, as opposed to being local or sectional. We do not wish, in politics, in literature, or in art, to develop that unwholesome parochial spirit, that over-exaltation of the little community at the expense of the great nation, which produces what has been described as the patriotism of the village, the patriotism of the belfry. Politically, the indulgence of this spirit was the chief cause of the calamities which befell the ancient republics of Greece, the medieval republics of Italy, and the petty States of Germany as it was in the last century. It is this spirit of provincial patriotism, this inability to take a view of broad adhesion to the whole nation that has been chief among the causes producing such anarchy in the South American States, and has resulted in presenting to us not one great Spanish-American federal nation stretching from the Rio Grande to Cape Horn, but a squabbling multitude of revolution-ridden States, not one of which stands even in the second rank as a power.

[8]For us a nation, however, politically this question of American nationality has been settled once and for all. We are no longer in danger of repeating in our history the shameful and contemptible disasters that have befallen the Spanish possessions on this continent since they threw off the yoke of Spain. Indeed, there is, all through our life, very much less of this parochial spirit than there was formerly. Still, there is an occasional outcropping here and there; and it is just as well that we should keep steadily in mind the futility of talking of a Northern literature or a Southern literature, an Eastern or a Western school of art or science. Joel Chandler Harris is emphatically a national writer; so is Mark Twain.[c] They do not write merely for Georgia or Missouri or California any more than for Illinois or Connecticut; they write as Americans and for all people who can read English. St. Gaudens[d] lives in New York; but his work is just as distinctive of Boston or Chicago. It is of very great consequence that we should have a full and ripe literary development in the United States, but it is not of the least consequence whether New York, or Boston, or Chicago, or San Francisco becomes the literary or artistic centre of the United States.

---

[c]Joel Chandler Harris wrote the "Uncle Remus" stories and was viewed in his time as a "southern" writer. Likewise, Mark Twain's stories based upon his experiences, including a stint as a silver miner, in the American west and then his later stories, (*Tom Sawyer, Huckleberry Finn*) set along the Mississippi River, caused some critics to characterize him as a "regionalist" writer.

[d]Louis St. Gaudens was an American-born sculptor who studied briefly in France and came back to America to do a number of notable pieces found on public buildings. He changed the spelling of his name to distinguish himself from his more famous older brother, also a sculptor, Augustus Saint Gaudens. Both are representative of the "American Renaissance" in the fine arts.

[9]There is a second side to this question of a broad Americanism, however. The patriotism of the village or the belfry is bad, but the lack of all patriotism is even worse. There are philosophers who assure us that, in the future, patriotism will be regarded not as a virtue at all, but merely as a mental stage in the journey toward a state of feeling when our patriotism will include the whole human race and all the world. This may be so; but the age of which these philosophers speak is still several eons distant. In fact, philosophers of this type are so very advanced that they are of no practical service to the present generation. It may be, that in ages so remote that we cannot now understand any of the feelings of those who will dwell in them, patriotism will no longer be regarded as a virtue, exactly as it may be that in those remote ages people will look down upon and disregard monogamic marriage; but as things now are and have been for two or three thousand years past, and are likely to be for two or three thousand years to come, the words "home" and "country" mean a great deal. Nor do they show any tendency to lose their significance. At present, treason, like adultery, ranks as one of the worst of all possible crimes.

[10]One may fall very far short of treason and yet be an undesirable citizen in the community. Those American citizens who, for example, become Europeanized, who lose their power of doing good work on this side of the water, and who lose their love for their native land, are not traitors; but they are silly and undesirable citizens. They are emphatically noxious element in our body politic as are the people who come here from abroad and yet remain foreigners. Nothing will more quickly or more surely disqualify someone from doing good work in the world than the acquisition of that flabby habit of mind which its possessors style "cosmopolitanism."

[11]It is not only necessary to Americanize the immigrants of foreign birth who settle among us, but it is even more necessary for those among us who are by birth and descent already Americans not to throw away our birthright, and, with incredible and contemptible foolishness, to wander back to bow down before the alien gods whom our forefathers forsook. It is hard to believe that there is any necessity to warn Americans that, when they seek to model themselves on the lines of other civilizations, they make themselves the object of scorn of all right-thinking people; and yet the necessity certainly exists to give this warning to many of our citizens who pride themselves on their standing in the world of art and letters, or, perhaps, on what they would style their social leadership in the community. It is always better to be an original than an imitation, even when the imitation is of something better than the original; but what shall we say of the fool who is content to be an imitation of something worse? Even if the weaklings who seek to be other than Americans were right in deeming other nations to be better than their own, the fact yet remains that to be a first-class American is fifty-fold better than to be a second-class imitation of a Frenchman or Englishman. As a matter of fact, however, those of our countrymen who do

believe in American inferiority are always individuals who, however cultivated, have some organic weakness in their moral or mental make-up; and the great mass of our people, who are robustly patriotic, and who have sound, healthy minds, are justified in regarding these feeble renegades with a half- impatient and half-amused scorn.

[12]We believe in waging relentless war on political evils of all kinds, and it makes no difference to us if they happen to be of purely native growth. We grasp at any good, no matter where it comes from. We do not accept the evil that springs from another system of government as an adequate excuse for imposing it upon our own. But it remains true that, in spite of all our faults and shortcomings, no other land offers such glorious possibilities to those able to take advantage of them as does ours; it remains true that none of our people can do any work really worth doing unless they do it primarily as an American. It is because certain classes of our people still retain their spirit of colonial dependence on, and exaggerated deference to, European opinion, that they fail to accomplish what they ought to.

[13]It is precisely along the lines where we have worked most independently that we have accomplished the greatest results; and it is in those professions where there has been no servility to, but merely a wise profiting by foreign experience, that we have produced our greatest leaders. Our soldiers and statesmen and orators; our explorers, our wilderness-winners and commonwealth-builders; the people who have made our laws and seen that they were executed; and the other people whose energy and ingenuity have created our marvelous material prosperity—all these have been those who have drawn wisdom from the experience of every age and nation, but who have nevertheless thought, and worked, and conquered, and lived, and died, purely as Americans; and on the whole they have done better work than has been done in any other country during the short period of our national life.

[14]On the other hand, it is in those professions where our people have striven hardest to mold themselves in conventional European forms that they have succeeded least; and this holds true to the present day, the failure being of course most conspicuous where someone takes up residence in Europe and becomes a second-rate European, because he is over-civilized, over-sensitive, over-refined, and has lost the hardihood and manly courage by which alone he can conquer in the keen struggle of our national life. Be it remembered, too, that this same being does not really become a European; he only ceases being an American, and becomes nothing. He throws away a great prize for the sake of a lesser one, and does not even get the lesser one. The painter who goes to Paris, not merely to get two or three years' thorough training in his art, but with the deliberate purpose of living there permanently, and with the intention of following in the ruts worn deep by ten thousand earlier travelers, instead of striking off to rise or fall on a new line, thereby forfeits all chance of doing the best

work. He must content himself with aiming at that kind of mediocrity which consists in doing fairly well what has already been done better; and he usually never even sees the grandeur and picturesqueness lying open before the eyes of everyone who can read the book of America's past and the book of America's present.

[15]Thus it is also with the undersized man of letters, who flees his country because he, with his delicate, effeminate sensitiveness, finds the conditions of life on this side of the water crude and raw; in other words, because he finds that he cannot play a man's part among men, and so goes where he will be sheltered from the winds that harden stouter souls. This emigre may write graceful and pretty verses, essays, novels; but he will never do work to compare with that of his brother, who is strong enough to stand on his own feet, and do his work as an American. Thus it is with the scientists who spend their youth in German universities and can thenceforth work only in the fields already fifty times furrowed by the German plows. Thus it is with that most foolish of parents who send their children to be educated abroad, not knowing what every clear-sighted American knows, that the Americans who are to make their way in America should be brought up among fellow Americans.

[16]It is among the people who like to consider themselves, and, indeed, to a large extent are, the leaders of the so-called social world, especially in some of the northeastern cities, that this colonial habit of thought, this thoroughly provincial spirit of admiration for things foreign and inability to stand on one's own feet becomes most evident and most despicable. We believe in every kind of honest and lawful pleasure, so long as getting it is not made a person's chief business; and we believe heartily in the good that can be done by men and women of leisure who work hard in their leisure, whether at politics or philanthropy, literature or art. But a leisure class whose leisure simply means idleness is a curse to the community, and in so far as its members distinguish themselves chiefly by aping the worst traits of similar people across the water, they become both comic and noxious elements of the body politic.

[17]The third sense in which the word "Americanism" may be employed is with reference to the Americanizing of the newcomers to our shores. We must Americanize them in every way, in speech, in political ideas and principles, and in their way of looking at the relations between Church and State. We welcome the German or the Irishman who becomes an American. We have no use for the German or Irishman who remains such. We do not wish German-Americans and Irish- Americans who figure as such in our social and political life; we want only Americans, and, provided they are such, we do not care whether they are of native or of Irish or of German ancestry. We have no room in any healthy American community for a German-American vote or an Irish-American vote, and it is contemptible to put planks into any party platform with the purpose of catching such a vote. We have no room for any people who do not act and vote

simply as Americans.

[18]Moreover, we have as little use for people who carry religious prejudices into our politics as for those who carry prejudices of caste or nationality. We stand solidly in favor of the public school system in its entirety. We believe that English, and no other language, is that in which all the school exercises should be conducted. We are against any division of the school fund, and against any appropriation of public money for sectarian purposes. We are against any recognition whatever by the state in any shape or form of state-aided parochial schools. But we are equally opposed to any discrimination against or for an individual because of his or her creed. We demand that all citizens, Protestant and Catholic, Jew and Gentile, shall have fair treatment in every way; that all alike shall have their rights guaranteed them. The very reasons that make us unqualified in our opposition to state-aided sectarian schools make us equally adamant that, in the management of our public schools, the adherents of each creed shall be given exact and equal justice, wholly without regard to their religious affiliations; that trustees, superintendents, teachers, scholars, all alike shall be treated without any reference whatsoever to the creed they profess. We maintain that it is an outrage, in voting for candidates for any position, whether state or national, to take into account their religious faith, provided only they are good Americans. When a secret society does what in some places the American Protective Association[e] seems to have done, and tries to proscribe Catholics both politically and socially, the members of such society show that they themselves are as utterly un-American, as alien to our school of political thought, as the worst immigrants who land on our shores. Their conduct is equally low and contemptible; they are the worst foes of our public school system because they strengthen the hands of the advocates of private and sectarian education; they should receive the hearty condemnation of all Americans who are truly patriotic.

[19]The mighty tide of immigration to our shores has brought in its train much of good and much of evil; and whether the good or the evil shall win out depends mainly on whether these newcomers do or do not throw themselves heartily into our national life, cease to be foreigners, and become Americans like the rest of us. More than a third of the people of the northern United States are of foreign birth or parentage. An immense number of them have become completely Americanized, and these stand on exactly the same plane as the descendants of the Puritans and other early European immigrants among us—and do their full and honorable share of the nation's work.

[20]However, where immigrants, or the children of immigrants, do not heart-

---

[e]The American Protective Association was an anti-Roman Catholic society founded in 1887 that advocated restricting Catholic immigration, making the ability to speak English a requirement for American citizenship, barring Catholics from holding public office and removing Catholic teachers from public schools.

ily and in good faith throw in their lot with us, but cling to the speech, the customs, the ways of life, and the habits of thought of the old world which they have left, they thereby harm both themselves and us. If they remain alien elements, unassimilated, and with interests separate from ours, they are mere obstructions to the current of our national life and, moreover, can get no good from it themselves. In fact, though we ourselves also suffer from their perversity, it is they who really suffer most. It is an immense benefit to immigrants to change them into American citizens. To bear the name of "American" is to bear the most honorable of titles; and whoever does not so believe has no business to bear the name at all, and, if they come from a foreign land, the sooner they go back there the better. Besides, those who do not become Americanized nevertheless fail to remain citizens of their native lands and become nothing at all. The immigrant cannot possibly remain what he or she was, or continue to be a member of the old-world society. If they try to retain their old language, in a few generations it becomes a barbarous babble; if they try to retain their old customs and ways of life, in a few generations they become uncouth boors. They have cut themselves off from the old world and cannot retain their connection with it; and if they wish ever to amount to anything they must throw themselves heart and soul, and without reservation, into the new life to which they have come.

[21]It is urgently necessary to check and regulate our immigration by much more drastic laws than now exist both to keep out laborers who tend to depress the labor market, and to keep out races which do not assimilate readily with our own as well as unworthy individuals of all races—not only criminals, idiots, and paupers, but anarchists [f] of the Most and O'Donovan Rossa[g] type. From their own standpoint, it is beyond all question the wise thing for immigrants to become thoroughly Americanized. Moreover, from our standpoint, we have a right to demand it. We freely extend the hand of welcome and of good-fellowship to all people, regardless of their creed or birthplace, who come here

---

[f]The political philosophy of anarchism, which holds that all forms of compulsory government are repressive and unnecessary, was a significant force in Roosevelt's day. A number of violent acts in America at this time, including bombings and assassinations, were attributed to anarchists, most of them immigrants from Europe. In fact, it would be an avowed anarchist, Leon Czolgosz, who would assassinate President William McKinley in 1901 and put Roosevelt in the White House seven years after this essay was published.

[g]Johann Most was an Austrian-born anarchist whose writings advocated violence to achieve elimination of government. He emigrated to the United States and was jailed three times here, the last in 1902 for writing an editorial celebrating the assassination of McKinley. Jeremiah O'Donovan Rossa was a founder of the Irish Republican Brotherhood who was essentially exiled to the United States by the British. He initiated the first Irish dynamite bombings of English cities to pressure the British government to grant independence to Ireland.

honestly intent on becoming good United States citizens like the rest of us; but we have a right, and it is our duty, to demand that they shall indeed become so and shall not confuse the issues with which we are struggling by introducing among us their old-world quarrels and prejudices. There are certain ideas which they must give up. For instance, they must learn that American life is incompatible with the existence of any form of anarchy, or of any secret society[h] having murder for its aim, whether at home or abroad. They must also learn that we demand full religious toleration and the complete separation of church and state. Moreover, they must not bring in their old-world religious, race and national antipathies, but must merge them into love for our common country, and must take pride in the things which we can all take pride in.

[22]They must revere only our flag; not only must it come first, but no other flag should even come second. They must learn to celebrate Washington's birthday rather than that of the Queen or Kaiser, and the Fourth of July instead of St. Patrick's Day. Our political and social questions must be settled on their own merits and not be complicated by quarrels between England and Ireland, or France and Germany, with which we have nothing to do: it is an outrage to fight an American political campaign with reference to questions of foreign politics.

[23]Above all, the immigrant must learn to talk and think and be United States. The immigrant of today can learn much from the experience of the immigrants of the past who came to America prior to the Revolutionary War. We were then already what we are now—a people of mixed blood. Many of our most illustrious Revolutionary names were borne by men of mixed ancestry: Jay, Sevier, Marion, Laurens. But the Huguenots were, on the whole, the best immigrants we have ever received; sooner than any other, and more completely, they became American in speech, conviction, and thought. The Hollanders took longer than the Huguenots to become completely assimilated; nevertheless, they in the end became so, immensely to their own advantage. One of the leading Revolutionary generals, Schuyler, and one of the Presidents of the United States, Van Buren, were of Dutch blood; but they rose to their positions, the highest in the land, because they had become Americans and had ceased being Hollanders. If they had remained members of an alien body, cut off by their speech and customs and belief from the rest of the American community, Schuyler would have lived his life as a boorish, provincial squire, and Van Buren would have ended his days a small tavern-keeper. So it is with the Germans of Pennsylvania. Those of them who became Americanized have furnished to

---

[h]Roosevelt here refers to loose-knit violent organizations, often started in their homelands and brought to America by some immigrants. These included, among others, the Molly McGuires, an Irish group active in the Pennsylvania coal fields; Chinese "tongs" that started as support groups for Chinese immigrants but evolved into criminal gangs; and the Italian Mafia.

our history a multitude of honorable names from the days of the Muhlenbergs onward; but those who did not become Americanized form to the present day an unimportant body of no significance in American existence. So it is with the Irish, who gave to Revolutionary annals such names as Carroll and Sullivan, and to the Civil War men like Sheridan—men who were Americans and nothing else. The Irish who remain such and busy themselves solely with alien politics can have only an unhealthy influence upon American life and can never rise as do their compatriots who become straightout Americans. Thus it has ever been with all people who have come here, of whatever stock or blood. The same thing is true of the churches. A church which remains foreign in language or spirit is doomed.

[24]But I wish to be distinctly understood on one point. Americanism is a question of spirit, conviction, and purpose, not of creed or birthplace. The politician who bids for the Irish or German vote, or the Irishman or German who votes as an Irishman or German, is despicable, for all citizens of this commonwealth should vote solely as Americans; but they are not one bit less despicable than the voters who vote against a good American, merely because that American happens to have been born in Ireland or Germany. Know-nothingism,[i] in any form is as utterly un-American as foreignism. It is an outrage to oppose a candidate because of his or her religion or birthplace, and all good citizens will hold any such effort in rightfully deserved contempt. Anyone from a foreign land who has really become an American has the right to stand on exactly the same footing as any native-born citizen in the land and is just as much entitled to the friendship and support, social and political, of his or her neighbors. Among those with whom I have been thrown into close personal contact socially and who have been among my most dependable friends and allies politically are many Americans who happen to have been born on the other side of the water; and there could be no better people in the ranks of our native-born citizens.

[25]In closing, I cannot better express the ideal attitude that should be taken by our fellow-citizens of foreign birth than by quoting the words of a representative American, born in Germany, the Honorable Richard Guenther, of Wisconsin. In a speech spoken at the time of the Samoan trouble[j] he said:

> We know as well as any other class of American citizens where our duties belong. We will work for our country in time of peace and fight for it

---

[i]"Know-Nothings" were members of a semi-secret political movement opposed to the immigration of Irish Catholics into the United States in the early 1800's. Members were instructed to say, "I know nothing" when asked about the group's activities.

[j]Roosevelt refers to ongoing conflicts between Germany, Great Britain and the United States as they backed competing sides in a Samoan civil war. Each of the three major naval powers were jockeying for position to get a refueling station in Samoa for their ships.

in time of war, if a time of war should ever come. When I say our country, I mean, of course, our adopted country. I mean the United States of America. After passing through the crucible of naturalization, we are no longer Germans; we are Americans. Our attachment to America cannot be measured by the length of our residence here. We are Americans from the moment we touch the American shore until we are laid in American graves. We will fight for America whenever necessary. America, first, last, and forever. America against Germany, America against the world; America, right or wrong; always America. We are Americans.

²⁶All honor to the man who spoke such words as those; and I believe they express the feelings of the great majority of those among our fellow-American citizens who were born abroad. We Americans can only do our allotted task well if we face it steadily and bravely, seeing but not fearing the dangers. Above all we must stand shoulder to shoulder, not asking as to the ancestry or creed of our comrades but only demanding that they be in very truth Americans and that we all work together, heart, hand, and head, for the honor and the greatness of our common country.

Vocabulary

¹gibes	⁷antithesis	¹³servility	¹⁸Gentile
¹elemental	⁷parochial	¹³ingenuity	¹⁸proscribe
²bolster	⁷exhaltation	¹⁵emigre	²⁰uncouth
²iniquity	⁷adhesion	¹⁵furrowed	²⁰boor
²demagogues	⁷anarchy	¹⁶provincial	²¹antipathies
⁴declaiming	¹⁰noxious	¹⁸caste	²³Huguenots
⁴induce	¹⁰cosmopolitanism	¹⁸creed	²³annals
⁵ignoble	¹²deference	¹⁸sectarian	²⁴despicable

Discussion Questions

1. In the first four paragraphs of this essay, is Roosevelt arguing primarily for or against adapting ideas and policies from countries outside of America?

2. In paragraph 3 Roosevelt mentions "tariff legislation." Tariffs have been an issue throughout American history and continue to cause congressional debate today. Based on some outside research, give a brief explanation of "the tariff" and cite a case of an American industry in recent years that has requested tariff protection.

3. How does what Roosevelt says in paragraph 5 relate to America's place in the world today?

4. Explain in your own words what Roosevelt means in paragraph 7 by an

"unwholesome parochial spirit." Cite an example of where this phenomenon has caused problems somewhere in the world since 1990.

5. In paragraph 8, Roosevelt says that Harris and Twain "write as Americans and for all people who can read English." What do you think Roosevelt's view of bilingual education in some areas of the United States (like California and Arizona) would be? What is your position on this issue?

6. Do you think Roosevelt is right when he says it will be two or three thousand years before the people of the world consider themselves "citizens of the world" rather than of individual countries? Has the shift toward a "global economy" resulted in a moving away from nationalism?

7. In paragraph 11, Roosevelt is concerned about Americans who go abroad and become citizens of other countries. Do you think this is still an issue today? Support your answer.

8. The introductory notes say that Theodore Roosevelt was known as a "jingoist." Look up the word "jingoism." Explain its origin and how it relates to paragraph 13.

9. What is Roosevelt's primary complaint in paragraphs 14-16? Does this still occur today?

10. Roosevelt was sickly as a child and through a lifelong devotion to rigorous exercise, including boxing, he developed great physical stamina and energy. How does this relate to what he says in paragraph 15?

11. What does Roosevelt mean by the "leisure class" in paragraph 16? Cite an example of someone in America today who might be considered a member of this class.

12. Thorstein Veblen also discusses the leisure class beginning on page 208 of this text. What are the similarities and differences of each author's view of the leisure class?

13. In paragraph 20 Roosevelt says, ". . . where immigrants . . . do not heartily and in good faith throw in their lot with us, but cling to the speech, the customs, the ways of life, and the habits of thought of the Old World which they have left, they thereby harm both themselves and us." Research the term "multiculturalism" and explain how it relates to Roosevelt's position.

TRUTH AND CONSEQUENCES
BRENDAN GILL

*Brendan Gill (1914-1997) spent his entire working life—
60 years—on the staff of* The New Yorker *magazine as critic of film, drama and architecture. A champion of architectural preservation and other visual arts, he chaired the
Andy Warhol Foundation for the Visual Arts and authored
15 books, including* Here at The New Yorker.

[1]She had straight blond hair and a red mouth, and she was lame. Every day she played golf and went swimming in the center of a crowd of boys. Charles, sitting with his mother on the hotel porch, watched her and nodded while his mother repeated, "Isn't it extraordinary, a girl like that? I wonder what in the world they see in her." Charles took to walking past the pool during the morning as the girl and boys lay there side by side, laughing. He listened carefully to her voice. It was low, unhurried, forceful. So, he thought, was her language. Every other word seemed to him to be "damn," "hell," and worse. She spoke of God, to whom Charles was preparing to dedicate his life, as if He were a friend in the next block. "I swear to God," the girl said. "I must have told you this one, for God's sake." Charles walked out of range of the jokes that followed. He was eighteen and he was spending this last vacation with his mother before entering a seminary. In eight more summers he would be a priest. The girl's language sent sharp lightnings through him. He had never seen or heard anyone like her before in his life.

[2]"One night after dinner, while his mother was upstairs swallowing a pill, the girl sat down beside him on the hotel porch. Her lips were smiling, her eyes the color of her blue, open blouse. "We ought to know each other," she said. "You ought to join the rest of us at the pool."

[3]"I'm with Mother."

[4]The girl covered his hand with hers. "Well, for God's sake, you're old enough to swim by yourself, aren't you?"

[5]Charles felt that he ought to explain before it was too late, before she said something he could never forget. "I'm going to be a priest," he said.

[6]The girl kept smiling. "A priest? With a turn-around collar and everything?"

[7]He nodded.

[8]"So you can't come swimming with the gang?"

[9]"That has nothing to do with it. I just thought I ought to tell you. I always do tell people."

[10]"You can still come dancing with us if you want to?"

[11]"Certainly."

[12]"Could you take me to a movie if you wanted to?"

[13]"Yes."

[14]"I never met a boy who was going to be a priest. Could you take me out for a ride tonight if you wanted to?"

[15]He said in relief, "We didn't bring our car."

[16]"Oh, hell. I mean in my car. I mean just for example. I didn't say I'd go with you." She stared at him slowly from head to foot. "It would be funny, with a boy who was going to be a priest."

[17]Fortunately, Charles thought, his mother would be coming downstairs at any moment now. She would make short shrift of the girl. "You oughtn't to keep swearing like that," he said.

[18]He expected her to laugh, but she didn't. She ran her hand up and down the bare brown leg that was shorter than the other. "Like what?" she said.

[19]"Like 'for God's sake.' That's taking the name of the Lord in vain. That's one of the Ten Commandments."

[20]"I'm an awful damn fool," the girl said. "I talk like that to keep people from thinking about my leg. But I didn't know you were going to be a priest."

[21]Charles wanted to get rid of her, but he didn't know how. He stood up and said, "I don't think you ought to worry about things like that. I hadn't even noticed.

[22]She stood up beside him. Her eyes shone in the mountain light. "Oh, damn you, please don't lie to me," she said. "Of course you've noticed. But does it bother you? Does it make you want to stay away from me?"

[23]"No," he said. "Oh, no."

[24]She slipped her hand under his arm. "Thanks for saying that so nice and hard. I haven t asked anybody that in a long time."

[25]Without having willed it, stupidly, Charles found himself walking the length of the porch beside the girl. Her blond hair touched the shoulder of his coat. It was difficult to tell, looking down at her, that she was lame. He bent his head to smell her perfume. "Tell me what you do," he said.

[26]"You mean, bang, just like that, what do I do?"

[27]"Not that you have to tell me."

[28]"But I do. It's just that there aren't any surprises in me. I'm not beautiful or tormented—or not much tormented. I don't do anything. I got out of Walker's and I had a party and now I guess I'll be on the loose like this for a couple of years. Finally somebody may ask me to marry him, and quick like a fish I will. I hope I'll have sense enough for that, and I'll be terribly glad when I've done it. I'll try to let him win most of the arguments well have. I'll try to be good about satisfying him, the way all those awful books say, and about having good kids for him, and all that."

[29]Charles felt himself stumbling. She had told him everything about her-

self. She had told him the truth, which he hadn't wanted. They reached the end of the porch and stood facing the valley between the mountains. Two old men were playing croquet in the gathering darkness, the wooden mallets and balls knocking softly together, the white trousers moving like disembodied spirits across the lawn. Charles and the girl could hear, below them in the kitchen, the clatter of dishes being washed and stacked and the high, tired voices of the waitresses.

[30]"Now talk about you," the girl said. "You think you want to be a priest?"

[31]"Why—yes."

[32]"It isn't just a vow your mother made while she was carrying you?"

[33]Charles laughed, and was surprised at how easily he laughed. "Well," he said, "I guess Mother's always wanted me to be a priest, especially after Dad died. We went abroad then, Mother and I. We spent the summer in Rome. We had an audience with the Pope—the old one, a little man with thick glasses and a big ring. We got so we were going to Mass and even to Communion every day. When we came back to this country, I started in at a Catholic school. I liked it. I graduated this year. I'm going down to the seminary in the fall. I guess I'll like that, too."

[34]"But isn't there more to it than that?" the girl said. "I'm not a Catholic—I'm not anything—but don't you have to have some kind of a call, bells ringing, something like that?"

[35]"You mean a vocation. Yes. Well, I guess I have a vocation all right."

[36]"But what is it? How can you be sure?"

[37]Charles gripped the railing of the porch. He had never been able to answer that question. He remembered kneeling beside his mother's bed, month after month, year after year. "Don't you feel it, darling?" his mother had whispered. "Don't you feel how wonderful it will be? Don't you feel how God wants you?" Charles had told himself finally that he was able to answer that question. The next day his mother, dabbing her eyes, had said, "Here's my boy, Father Duffy. I'm giving him to you." And Father Duffy had said, "Ah, you're an example to Irish mothers everywhere. Are you sure you want to come with us, boy?" "Yes, Father, I do," Charles had said, watching his mother. He had spoken an answer, written an answer, lived an answer, but he had never believed it. He had been waiting to believe it. Now he heard himself saying, for the first time, "No, I can't be sure."

[38]The girl said, "Then you're not going to be a priest. You mustn't be. Why are you so damned afraid to face the truth?" Charles saw his mother walking heavily along the porch. He studied her as if she were a stranger. What an enormous old woman she was, and how strong she was, and how she had driven him! He took the girl's hand. It was cool and unmoving. He felt the porch floor trembling under his mother's approach.

Vocabulary

[17]short shrift   [28]tormented   [33]vocation

[22]shone   [29]disembodied

Discussion Questions.

1. Explain the title of the story. What do you think it means?

2. What image of the girl do you get from what Gill tells us in the first paragraph? What impression do you form of Charles?

3. In the first paragraph we also learn "In eight more summers he [Charles] would be a priest." What does this tell you about how Charles counts time?

4. What is so different and distracting to Charles about the girl? How does her disability affect her?

5. What does the girl mean when she says, "I got out of Walker's and then I had a party"?

6. What does the girl mean by "those awful books" in paragraph 28?

7. Why does Charles want to become a priest?

8. What does the author mean in paragraph 29 when he says, "She had told him the truth, which he hadn't wanted"?

9. How does Charles's view of his mother change from the beginning of the story?

10. Why would the porch "tremble" under Charles's mother's approach?

11. What do you think will happen when Charles's mother reaches Charles and the girl?

TWO VIEWS OF THE MISSISSIPPI

MARK TWAIN

Mark Twain, the pseudonym of Samuel Clemens (1835-1910), was a major writer of American literature who gained international fame as an author, lecturer, journalist, satirist, and humorist. Most famous for Huckleberry Finn, *he also wrote* The Adventures of Tom Sawyer, The Prince and the Pauper, Life on the Mississippi, A Connecticut Yankee in King Arthur's Court *and numerous other works. After Twain's death his literary stature further increased, with such writers as Ernest Hemingway and William Faulkner declaring his works, particularly* Huckleberry Finn, *a major influence on 20th-century American fiction.*

[1] Now when I had mastered the language of this water, and had come to know every trifling feature that bordered the great river as familiarly as I knew the letters of the alphabet, I had made a valuable acquisition. But I had lost something, too. I had lost something which could never be restored to me while I lived. All the grace, the beauty, the poetry, had gone out of the majestic river! I still keep in mind a certain wonderful sunset which I witnessed when steamboating was new to me. A broad expanse of the river was turned to blood; in the middle distance the red hue brightened into gold, through which a solitary log came floating black and conspicuous; in one place a long, slanting mark lay sparkling upon the water; in another the surface was broken by boiling, tumbling rings, that were as many-tinted as an opal; where the ruddy flush was faintest, was a smooth spot that was covered with graceful circles and radiating lines ever so delicately traced; the shore on our left was densely wooded, and the somber shadow that fell from this forest was broken in one place by a long, ruffled trail that shone like silver; and high above the forest wall a clean-stemmed dead tree waved a single leafy bough that glowed like a flame in the unobstructed splendor that was flowing from the sun. There were graceful curves, reflected images, woody heights, soft distances; and over the whole scene, far and near, the dissolving lights drifted steadily, enriching it every passing moment with new marvels of coloring.

[2] I stood like one bewitched. I drank it in, in a speechless rapture. The world was new to me, and I had never seen anything like this at home. But as I have said, a day came when I began to cease from noting the glories and the charms which the moon and the sun and the twilight wrought upon the river's face; another day came when I ceased altogether to note them. Then, if that sunset scene had been repeated, I should have looked upon it without rapture,

and should have commented upon it, inwardly, after this fashion: "This sun means that we are going to have wind tomorrow; that floating log means that the river is rising, small thanks to it; that slanting mark on the water refers to a bluff reef which is going to kill somebody's steamboat one of these nights, if it keeps on stretching out like that; those tumbling 'boils' show a dissolving bar and a changing channel there; the lines and circles in the slick water over yonder are a warning that that troublesome place is shoaling up dangerously; that silver streak in the shadow of the forest is the 'break' from a new snag, and he has located himself in the very best place he could have found to fish for steamboats; that tall dead tree, with a single living branch, is not going to last long, and then how is a body ever going to get through this blind place at night without the friendly old landmark?"

   [3]No, the romance and beauty were all gone from the river. All the value and feature of it had for me now was the amount of usefulness it could furnish toward compassing the safe piloting of a steamboat. Since those days, I have pitied doctors from my heart. What does the lovely flush in a beauty's cheek mean to a doctor but a "break" that ripples above some deadly disease? Are not all her visible charms sown thick with what are to him the signs and symbols of hidden decay? Does he ever see her beauty at all, or doesn't he simply view her professionally, and comment upon her unwholesome condition all to himself? And doesn't he sometimes wonder whether he has gained most or lost most by learning his trade?

Vocabulary

[1]trifling	[1]ruddy	[2]rapture	[3]compassing
[1]acquisition	[1]somber	[2]shoal	[3]sown
[1]opal			

Discussion Questions

1. What are Twain's two views of the Mississippi River?

2. What influenced each of these views?

3. Twain says that he both gained and lost something from his mastering the river. What did he gain and lose?

4. What is Twain saying about what we gain and lose when we mature? Do you agree with his position?

5. Compare this essay with Richard Rodriquez's "The Achievement of Desire" on page 76 of this text. What similarities of message do you see?

UNSPEAKABLE CONVERSATIONS
HARRIET MCBRYDE JOHNSON

Harriet McBryde Johnson (1957-2008) was an attorney and outspoken advocate of the rights of the disabled. Severely handicapped by a degenerative neuromuscular disorder, Johnson attained national prominence when she confronted Princeton University bioethics professor Peter Singer at his lecture at the College of Charleston in 2001, leading to a pair of debates between the two at Princeton and extensive media coverage. Johnson graduated from Charleston Southern University in 1978 and earned a master's degree in public administration from the College of Charleston. She graduated from the University of South Carolina School of Law in 1985. She wrote a memoir, Too Late to Die Young, *a novel,* Accidents of Nature, *and numerous magazine and newspaper articles.*

¹He insists he doesn't want to kill me. He simply thinks it would have been better, all things considered, to have given my parents the option of killing the baby I once was, and to let other parents kill similar babies as they come along and thereby avoid the suffering that comes with lives like mine and satisfy the reasonable preferences of parents for a different kind of child. It has nothing to do with me. I should not feel threatened.

²Whenever I try to wrap my head around his tight string of syllogisms, my brain gets so fried it's . . . almost fun. Mercy! It's like "Alice in Wonderland."

³It is a chilly Monday in late March, just less than a year ago. I am at Princeton University. My host is Prof. Peter Singer, often called—and not just by his book publicist—the most influential philosopher of our time. He is the man who wants me dead. No, that's not at all fair. He wants to legalize the killing of certain babies who might come to be like me if allowed to live. He also says he believes that it should be lawful under some circumstances to kill, at any age, individuals with cognitive impairments so severe that he doesn't consider them "persons." What does it take to be a person? Awareness of your own existence in time. The capacity to harbor preferences as to the future, including the preference for continuing to live.

⁴At this stage of my life, he says, I am a person. However, as an infant, I wasn't. I, like all humans, was born without self-awareness. And eventually, assuming my brain finally gets so fried that I fall into that wonderland where self and other and present and past and future blur into one boundless, formless all or nothing, then I'll lose my personhood and therefore my right to life. Then, he says, my family and doctors might put me out of my misery, or out of

my bliss or oblivion, and no one count it murder.

[5]I have agreed to two speaking engagements. In the morning, I talk to 150 undergraduates on selective infanticide. In the evening, it is a convivial discussion, over dinner, of assisted suicide. I am the token cripple with an opposing view.

[6]I had several reasons for accepting Singer's invitation, some grounded in my involvement in the disability rights movement, others entirely personal. For the movement, it seemed an unusual opportunity to experiment with modes of discourse that might work with very tough audiences and bridge the divide between our perceptions and theirs. I didn't expect to straighten out Singer's head, but maybe I could reach a student or two. Among the personal reasons: I was sure it would make a great story, first for telling and then for writing down.

[7]By now I've told it to family and friends and colleagues, over lunches and dinners, on long car trips, in scads of e-mail messages and a couple of formal speeches. But it seems to be a story that just won't settle down. After all these tellings, it still lacks a coherent structure; I'm miles away from a rational argument. I keep getting interrupted by questions—like these:

[8]Q: Was he totally grossed out by your physical appearance?

A: He gave no sign of it. None whatsoever.

Q: How did he handle having to interact with someone like you?

A: He behaved in every way appropriately, treated me as a respected professional acquaintance and was a gracious and accommodating host.

Q: Was it emotionally difficult for you to take part in a public discussion of whether your life should have happened?

A: It was very difficult. And horribly easy.

Q: Did he get that job at Princeton because they like his ideas on killing disabled babies?

A: It apparently didn't hurt, but he's most famous for animal rights. He's the author of "Animal Liberation."'

Q: How can he put so much value on animal life and so little value on human life?

[9]That last question is the only one I avoid. I used to say I don't know; it doesn't make sense. But now I've read some of Singer's writing, and I admit it does make sense—within the conceptual world of Peter Singer. But I don't want to go there. Or at least not for long.

[10]So I will start from those other questions and see where the story goes this time.

[11]That first question, about my physical appearance, needs some explaining. It's not that I'm ugly. It's more that most people don't know how to look at me. The sight of me is routinely discombobulating. The power wheelchair is enough to inspire gawking, but that's the least of it. Much more impressive is

the impact on my body of more than four decades of a muscle-wasting disease. At this stage of my life, I'm Karen Carpenter[a] thin, flesh mostly vanished, a jumble of bones in a floppy bag of skin. When, in childhood, my muscles got too weak to hold up my spine, I tried a brace for a while, but fortunately a skittish anesthesiologist said no to fusion, plates and pins—all the apparatus that might have kept me straight. At 15, I threw away the back brace and let my spine reshape itself into a deep twisty S-curve. Now my right side is two deep canyons. To keep myself upright, I lean forward, rest my rib cage on my lap, plant my elbows beside my knees. Since my backbone found its own natural shape, I've been entirely comfortable in my skin.

[12]I am in the first generation to survive to such decrepitude. Because antibiotics were available, we didn't die from the childhood pneumonias that often come with weakened respiratory systems. I guess it is natural enough that most people don't know what to make of us.

[13]Two or three times in my life—I recall particularly one largely crip, largely lesbian cookout halfway across the continent—I have been looked at as a rare kind of beauty. There is also the bizarre fact that where I live, Charleston, S.C., some people call me Good Luck Lady: they consider it propitious to cross my path when a hurricane is coming and to kiss my head just before voting day. But most often the reactions are decidedly negative. Strangers on the street are moved to comment:

> *I admire you for being out; most people would give up.*
> *God bless you! I'll pray for you.*
> *You don't let the pain hold you back, do you?*
> *If I had to live like you, I think I'd kill myself.*

[14]I used to try to explain that in fact I enjoy my life, that it's a great sensual pleasure to zoom by power chair on these delicious muggy streets, that I have no more reason to kill myself than most people. But it gets tedious. God didn't put me on this street to provide disability awareness training to the likes of them. In fact, no god put anyone anywhere for any reason, if you want to know.

[15]But they don't want to know. They think they know everything there is to know, just by looking at me. That's how stereotypes work. They don't know that they're confused, that they're really expressing the discombobulation that comes in my wake.

---

[a]Karen Anne Carpenter (1950 –1983) with her brother Richard formed a highly successful "All-American" 1970's singing act, The Carpenters. Karen was the first celebrity to suffer from anorexia nervosa, a little-known illness at that time. Her fans and the public were shocked when popular magazines of the era ran photos of her as her condition deteriorated. She died at the age of 32 from heart failure attributed to complications connected to her illness.

[16]So. What stands out when I recall first meeting Peter Singer in the spring of 2001 is his apparent immunity to my looks, his apparent lack of discombobulation, his immediate ability to deal with me as a person with a particular point of view.

[17]Then, 2001. Singer has been invited to the College of Charleston, not two blocks from my house. He is to lecture on "Rethinking Life and Death." I have been dispatched by Not Dead Yet, the national organization leading the disability-rights opposition to legalized assisted suicide and disability-based killing. I am to put out a leaflet and do something during the Q. and A.

[18]On arriving almost an hour early to reconnoiter, I find the scene almost entirely peaceful; even the boisterous display of South Carolina spring is muted by gray wisps of Spanish moss and mottled oak bark.

[19]I roll around the corner of the building and am confronted with the unnerving sight of two people I know sitting on a park bench eating veggie pitas with Singer. Sharon is a veteran activist for human rights. Herb is South Carolina's most famous atheist. Good people, I've always thought—now sharing veggie pitas and conversation with a proponent of genocide. I try to beat a retreat, but Herb and Sharon have seen me. Sharon tosses her trash and comes over. After we exchange the usual courtesies, she asks, "Would you like to meet Professor Singer?"

[20]She doesn't have a clue. She probably likes his book on animal rights. "I'll just talk to him in the Q. and A."

[21]But Herb, with Singer at his side, is fast approaching. They are looking at me, and Herb is talking, no doubt saying nice things about me. He'll be saying that I'm a disability rights lawyer and that I gave a talk against assisted suicide at his secular humanist group a while back. He didn't agree with everything I said, he'll say, but I was brilliant. Singer appears interested, engaged. I sit where I'm parked. Herb makes an introduction. Singer extends his hand.

[22]I hesitate. I shouldn't shake hands with the Evil One. But he is Herb's guest, and I simply can't snub Herb's guest at the college where Herb teaches. Hereabouts, the rule is that if you're not prepared to shoot on sight, you have to be prepared to shake hands. I give Singer the three fingers on my right hand that still work. "Good afternoon, Mr. Singer, I'm here for Not Dead Yet." I want to think he flinches just a little. Not Dead Yet did everything possible to disrupt his first week at Princeton. I sent a check to the fund for the 14 arrestees, who included comrades in power chairs. But if Singer flinches, he instantly recovers. He answers my questions about the lecture format. When he says he looks forward to an interesting exchange, he seems entirely sincere.

[23]It *is* an interesting exchange. In the lecture hall that afternoon, Singer lays it all out. The "illogic" of allowing abortion but not infanticide, of allowing withdrawal of life support but not active killing. Applying the basic assumptions of preference utilitarianism, he spins out his bone-chilling argu-

ment for letting parents kill disabled babies and replace them with nondisabled babies who have a greater chance at happiness. It is all about allowing as many individuals as possible to fulfill as many of their preferences as possible.

[24]As soon as he's done, I get the microphone and say I'd like to discuss selective infanticide. As a lawyer, I disagree with his jurisprudential assumptions. Logical inconsistency is not a sufficient reason to change the law. As an atheist, I object to his using religious terms ("the doctrine of the sanctity of human life") to characterize his critics. Singer takes a note pad out of his pocket and jots down my points, apparently eager to take them on, and I proceed to the heart of my argument: that the presence or absence of a disability doesn't predict quality of life. I question his replacement-baby theory, with its assumption of "other things equal," arguing that people are not fungible. I draw out a comparison of myself and my nondisabled brother Mac (the next-born after me), each of us with a combination of gifts and flaws so peculiar that we can't be measured on the same scale.

[25]He responds to each point with clear and lucid counterarguments. He proceeds with the assumption that I am one of the people who might rightly have been killed at birth. He sticks to his guns, conceding just enough to show himself open-minded and flexible. We go back and forth for 10 long minutes. Even as I am horrified by what he says, and by the fact that I have been sucked into a civil discussion of whether I ought to exist, I can't help being dazzled by his verbal facility. He is so respectful, so free of condescension, so focused on the argument, that by the time the show is over, I'm not exactly angry with him. Yes, I am shaking, furious, enraged—but it's for the big room, 200 of my fellow Charlestonians who have listened with polite interest, when in decency they should have run him out of town on a rail.

[26]My encounter with Peter Singer merits a mention in my annual canned letter that December. I decide to send Singer a copy. In response, he sends me the nicest possible e-mail message. Dear Harriet (if he may) . . . Just back from Australia, where he's from. Agrees with my comments on the world situation. Supports my work against institutionalization. And then some pointed questions to clarify my views on selective infanticide.

[27]I reply. Fine, call me Harriet, and I'll reciprocate in the interest of equality, though I'm accustomed to more formality. Skipping agreeable preambles, I answer his questions on disability-based infanticide and pose some of my own. Answers and more questions come back. Back and forth over several weeks it proceeds, an engaging discussion of baby killing, disability prejudice and related points of law and philosophy. Dear Harriet. Dear Peter.

[28]Singer seems curious to learn how someone who is as good an atheist as he is could disagree with his entirely reasonable views. At the same time, I am trying to plumb his theories. What has him so convinced it would be best to allow parents to kill babies with severe disabilities, and not other kinds of

babies, if no infant is a "person" with a right to life? I learn it is partly that both biological and adoptive parents prefer healthy babies. But I have trouble with basing life-and-death decisions on market considerations when the market is structured by prejudice. I offer a hypothetical comparison: "What about mixed-race babies, especially when the combination is entirely nonwhite, who I believe are just about as unadoptable as babies with disabilities?" Wouldn't a law allowing the killing of these undervalued babies validate race prejudice? Singer agrees there is a problem. "It would be horrible," he says, "to see mixed-race babies being killed because they can't be adopted, whereas white ones could be." What's the difference? Preferences based on race are unreasonable. Preferences based on ability are not. Why? To Singer, it's pretty simple: disability makes a person "worse off."

[29]Are we "worse off"? I don't think so. Not in any meaningful sense. There are too many variables. For those of us with congenital conditions, disability shapes all we are. Those disabled later in life adapt. We take constraints that no one would choose and build rich and satisfying lives within them. We enjoy pleasures other people enjoy, and pleasures peculiarly our own. We have something the world needs.

[30]Pressing me to admit a negative correlation between disability and happiness, Singer presents a situation: imagine a disabled child on the beach, watching the other children play.

[31]It's right out of the telethon.[b] I expected something more sophisticated from a professional thinker. I respond: "As a little girl playing on the beach, I was already aware that some people felt sorry for me, that I wasn't frolicking with the same level of frenzy as other children. This annoyed me, and still does." I take the time to write a detailed description of how I, in fact, had fun playing on the beach, without the need of standing, walking or running. But, really, I've had enough. I suggest to Singer that we have exhausted our topic, and I'll be back in touch when I get around to writing about him.

[32]He responds by inviting me to Princeton. I fire off an immediate maybe.

[33]Of course I'm flattered. Mama will be impressed.

[34]But there are things to consider. Not Dead Yet says—and I completely agree—that we should not legitimate Singer's views by giving them a forum. We should not make disabled lives subject to debate. Moreover, any spokesman chosen by the opposition is by definition a token. But even if I'm a token, I won't have to act like one. And anyway, I'm kind of stuck. If I decline, Singer can make some hay: "I offered them a platform, but they refuse rational discussion." It's an old trick, and I've laid myself wide open.

---

[b]"The telethon" is a reference to the annual Jerry Lewis Telethon for the Muscular Dystrophy Association; Johnson was an outspoken critic of the telethon, accusing supporters of fostering a "charity mentality" and using "pity-based tactics."

[35]My invitation is to have an exchange of views with Singer during his undergraduate course. He also proposes a second "exchange," open to the whole university, later in the day. This sounds a lot like debating my life—and on my opponent's turf, with my opponent moderating, to boot. I offer a counterproposal, to which Singer proves amenable. I will open the class with some comments on infanticide and related issues and then let Singer grill me as hard as he likes before we open it up for the students. Later in the day, I might take part in a discussion of some other disability issue in a neutral forum. Singer suggests a faculty-student discussion group sponsored by his department but with cross-departmental membership. The topic I select is "Assisted Suicide, Disability Discrimination and the Illusion of Choice: A Disability Rights Perspective." I inform a few movement colleagues of this turn of events, and advice starts rolling in. I decide to go with the advisers who counsel me to do the gig, lie low and get out of Dodge.

[36]I ask Singer to refer me to the person who arranges travel at Princeton. I imagine some capable and unflappable woman like my sister, Beth, whose varied job description at a North Carolina university includes handling visiting artists. Singer refers me to his own assistant, who certainly seems capable and unflappable enough. However, almost immediately Singer jumps back in via e-mail. It seems the nearest hotel has only one wheelchair-accessible suite, available with two rooms for $600 per night. What to do? I know I shouldn't be so accommodating, but I say I can make do with an inaccessible room if it has certain features. Other logistical issues come up. We go back and forth. Questions and answers. Do I really need a lift-equipped vehicle at the airport? Can't my assistant assist me into a conventional car? How wide is my wheelchair?

[37]By the time we're done, Singer knows that I am 28 inches wide. I have trouble controlling my wheelchair if my hand gets cold. I am accustomed to driving on rough, irregular surfaces, but I get nervous turning on steep slopes. Even one step is too many. I can swallow purees, soft bread and grapes. I use a bedpan, not a toilet. None of this is a secret; none of it cause for angst. But I do wonder whether Singer is jotting down my specs in his little note pad as evidence of how "bad off" people like me really are.

[38]I realize I must put one more issue on the table: etiquette. I was criticized within the movement when I confessed to shaking Singer's hand in Charleston, and some are appalled that I have agreed to break bread with him in Princeton. I think they have a very good point, but, again, I'm stuck. I'm engaged for a day of discussion, not a picket line. It is not in my power to marginalize Singer at Princeton; nothing would be accomplished by displays of personal disrespect. However, chumminess is clearly inappropriate. I tell Singer that in the lecture hall it can't be Harriet and Peter; it must be Ms. Johnson and Mr. Singer.

[39]He seems genuinely nettled. Shouldn't it be Ms. Johnson and Professor Singer, if I want to be formal? To counter, I invoke the ceremonial low-country

usage, Attorney Johnson and Professor Singer, but point out that Mr./Ms. is the custom in American political debates and might seem more normal in New Jersey. All right, he says. Ms./Mr. it will be.

[40]I describe this awkward social situation to the lawyer in my office who has served as my default lunch partner for the past 14 years. He gives forth a full-body shudder.

[41]"That poor, sorry son of a bitch! He has no idea what he's in for."

[42]Being a disability rights lawyer lecturing at Princeton does confer some cachet at the Newark airport. I need all the cachet I can get. Delta Airlines has torn up my power chair. It is a fairly frequent occurrence for any air traveler on wheels.

[43]When they inform me of the damage in Atlanta, I throw a monumental fit and tell them to have a repair person meet me in Newark with new batteries to replace the ones inexplicably destroyed. Then I am told no new batteries can be had until the morning. It's Sunday night. On arrival in Newark, I'm told of a plan to put me up there for the night and get me repaired and driven to Princeton by 10 a.m.

[44]"That won't work. I'm lecturing at 10. I need to get there tonight, go to sleep and be in my right mind tomorrow."

[45]"What? You're lecturing? They told us it was a conference. We need to get you fixed tonight!"

[46]Carla, the gate agent, relieves me of the need to throw any further fits by undertaking on my behalf the fit of all fits.

[47]Carmen, the personal assistant with whom I'm traveling, pushes me in my disabled chair around the airport in search of a place to use the bedpan. However, instead of diaper-changing tables, which are functional though far from private, we find a flip-down plastic shelf that doesn't look like it would hold my 70 pounds of body weight. It's no big deal; I've restricted my fluids. But Carmen is a little freaked. It is her first adventure in power-chair air travel. I thought I prepared her for the trip, but I guess I neglected to warn her about the probability of wheelchair destruction. I keep forgetting that even people who know me well don't know much about my world.

[48]We reach the hotel at 10:15 p.m., four hours late.

[49]I wake up tired. I slept better than I would have slept in Newark with an unrepaired chair, but any hotel bed is a near guarantee of morning cranki-ness. I tell Carmen to leave the TV off. I don't want to hear the temperature.

[50]I do the morning stretch. Medical people call it passive movement, but it's not really passive. Carmen's hands move my limbs, following my precise instructions, her strength giving effect to my will. Carmen knows the routine, so it is in near silence that we begin easing slowly into the day. I let myself be propped up to eat oatmeal and drink tea. Then there's the bedpan and then bathing and dressing, still in bed. As the caffeine kicks in, silence gives way to

conversation about practical things. Carmen lifts me into my chair and straps a rolled towel under my ribs for comfort and stability. She tugs at my clothes to remove wrinkles that could cause pressure sores. She switches on my motors and gives me the means of moving without anyone's help. They don't call it a power chair for nothing.

[51]I drive to the mirror. I do my hair in one long braid. Even this primal hairdo requires, at this stage of my life, joint effort. I undo yesterday's braid, fix the part and comb the hair in front. Carmen combs where I can't reach. I divide the mass into three long hanks and start the braid just behind my left ear. Section by section, I hand it over to her, and her unimpaired young fingers pull tight, crisscross, until the braid is fully formed.

[52]A big polyester scarf completes my costume. Carmen lays it over my back. I tie it the way I want it, but Carmen starts fussing with it, trying to tuck it down in the back. I tell her that it's fine, and she stops.

[53]On top of the scarf, she wraps the two big shawls that I hope will substitute for an overcoat. I don't own any real winter clothes. I just stay out of the cold, such cold as we get in Charleston.

We review her instructions for the day. Keep me in view and earshot. Be instantly available but not intrusive. Be polite, but don't answer any questions about me. I am glad that she has agreed to come. She's strong, smart, adaptable and very loyal. But now she is digging under the shawls, fussing with that scarf again.

[54]"Carmen. What are you doing?"

[55]"I thought I could hide this furry thing you sit on."

[56]"Leave it. Singer knows lots of people eat meat. Now he'll know some crips sit on sheepskin."

[57]The walk is cold but mercifully short. The hotel is just across the street from Princeton's wrought-iron gate and a few short blocks from the building where Singer's assistant shows us to the elevator. The elevator doubles as the janitor's closet—the cart with the big trash can and all the accouterments is rolled aside so I can get in. Evidently there aren't a lot of wheelchair people using this building.

[58]We ride the broom closet down to the basement and are led down a long passageway to a big lecture hall. As the students drift in, I engage in light badinage with the sound technician. He is squeamish about touching me, but I insist that the cordless lavaliere is my mike of choice. I invite him to clip it to the big polyester scarf.

[59]The students enter from the rear door, way up at ground level, and walk down stairs to their seats. I feel like an animal in the zoo. I hadn't reckoned on the architecture, those tiers of steps that separate me from a human wall of apparent physical and mental perfection, that keep me confined down here in my pit.

[60]It is 5 before 10. Singer is loping down the stairs. I feel like signaling to Carmen to open the door, summon the broom closet and get me out of here. But Singer greets me pleasantly and hands me Princeton's check for $500, the fee he offered with apologies for its inadequacy.

[61]So. On with the show.

[62]My talk to the students is pretty Southern. I've decided to pound them with heart, hammer them with narrative and say "y'all" and "folks." I play with the emotional tone, giving them little peaks and valleys, modulating three times in one 45-second patch. I talk about justice. Even beauty and love. I figure they haven't been getting much of that from Singer.

[63]Of course, I give them some argument too. I mean to honor my contractual obligations. I lead with the hypothetical about mixed-race, nonwhite babies and build the ending around the question of who should have the burden of proof as to the quality of disabled lives. And woven throughout the talk is the presentation of myself as a representative of a minority group that has been rendered invisible by prejudice and oppression, a participant in a discussion that would not occur in a just world.

[64]I let it go a little longer than I should. Their faces show they're going where I'm leading, and I don't look forward to letting them go. But the clock on the wall reminds me of promises I mean to keep, and I stop talking and submit myself to examination and inquiry.

[65]Singer's response is surprisingly soft. Maybe after hearing that this discussion is insulting and painful to me, he doesn't want to exacerbate my discomfort. His reframing of the issues is almost pro forma, abstract, entirely impersonal. Likewise, the students' inquiries are abstract and fairly predictable: anencephaly, permanent unconsciousness, eugenic abortion. I respond to some of them with stories, but mostly I give answers I could have e-mailed in.

[66]I call on a young man near the top of the room.

[67]"Do you eat meat?"

[68]"Yes, I do."

[69]"Then how do you justify—"

[70]"I haven't made any study of animal rights, so anything I could say on the subject wouldn't be worth everyone's time."

[71]The next student wants to work the comparison of disability and race, and Singer joins the discussion until he elicits a comment from me that he can characterize as racist. He scores a point, but that's all right. I've never claimed to be free of prejudice, just struggling with it.

[72]Singer proposes taking me on a walk around campus, unless I think it would be too cold. What the hell? "It's probably warmed up some. Let's go out and see how I do."

[73]He doesn't know how to get out of the building without using the stairs, so this time it is my assistant leading the way. Carmen has learned of another

elevator, which arrives empty. When we get out of the building, she falls behind a couple of paces, like a respectful chaperone.

[74]In the classroom there was a question about keeping alive the unconscious. In response, I told a story about a family I knew as a child, which took loving care of a nonresponsive teenage girl, acting out their unconditional commitment to each other, making all the other children, and me as their visitor, feel safe. This doesn't satisfy Singer. "Let's assume we can prove, absolutely, that the individual is totally unconscious and that we can know, absolutely, that the individual will never regain consciousness."

[75]I see no need to state an objection, with no stenographer present to record it; I'll play the game and let him continue.

[76]"Assuming all that," he says, "don't you think continuing to take care of that individual would be a bit—weird?"

[77]"No. Done right, it could be profoundly beautiful."

[78]"But what about the caregiver, a woman typically, who is forced to provide all this service to a family member, unable to work, unable to have a life of her own?"

[79]"That's not the way it should be. Not the way it has to be. As a society, we should pay workers to provide that care, in the home. In some places, it's been done that way for years. That woman shouldn't be forced to do it, any more than my family should be forced to do my care."

[80]Singer takes me around the architectural smorgasbord that is Princeton University by a route that includes not one step, unramped curb or turn on a slope. Within the strange limits of this strange assignment, it seems Singer is doing all he can to make me comfortable.

[81]He asks what I thought of the students' questions.

[82]"They were fine, about what I expected. I was a little surprised by the question about meat eating."

[83]"I apologize for that. That was out of left field. But—I think what he wanted to know is how you can have such high respect for human life and so little respect for animal life."

[84]"People have lately been asking me the converse, how you can have so much respect for animal life and so little respect for human life."

[85]"And what do you answer?"

[86]"I say I don't know. It doesn't make a lot of sense to me."

[87]"Well, in my view—"

[88]"Look. I have lived in blissful ignorance all these years, and I'm not prepared to give that up today."

[89]"Fair enough," he says and proceeds to recount bits of Princeton history. He stops. "This will be of particular interest to you, I think. This is where your colleagues with Not Dead Yet set up their blockade." I'm grateful for the reminder. My brothers and sisters were here before me and behaved far more

appropriately than I am doing.

[90]A van delivers Carmen and me early for the evening forum. Singer says he hopes I had a pleasant afternoon.

[91]Yes, indeed. I report a pleasant lunch and a very pleasant nap, and I tell him about the Christopher Reeve[c] Suite in the hotel, which has been remodeled to accommodate Reeve, who has family in the area.

[92]"Do you suppose that's the $600 accessible suite they told me about?"

[93]"Without doubt. And if I'd known it was the Christopher Reeve Suite, I would have held out for it."

[94]"Of course you would have!" Singer laughs. "And we'd have had no choice, would we?"

[95]We talk about the disability rights critique of Reeve and various other topics. Singer is easy to talk to, good company. Too bad he sees lives like mine as avoidable mistakes.

[96]I'm looking forward to the soft vegetarian meal that has been arranged; I'm hungry. Assisted suicide, as difficult as it is, doesn't cause the kind of agony I felt discussing disability-based infanticide. In this one, I understand, and to some degree can sympathize with, the opposing point of view—misguided though it is.

[97]My opening sticks to the five-minute time limit. I introduce the issue as framed by academic articles Not Dead Yet recommended for my use. Andrew Batavia[d] argues for assisted suicide based on autonomy, a principle generally held high in the disability rights movement. In general, he says, the movement fights for our right to control our own lives; when we need assistance to effect our choices, assistance should be available to us as a matter of right. If the choice is to end our lives, he says, we should have assistance then as well. But Carol Gill[e] says that it is differential treatment—disability discrimination—to try to prevent most suicides while facilitating the suicides of ill and disabled people. The social-science literature suggests that the public in general, and physicians in particular, tend to underestimate the quality of life of disabled people, compared with our own assessments of our lives. The case for assisted

---

[c]Christopher Reeve (1952-2004), an athletic, solidly built actor who starred in four *Superman* movies, fell from a horse and was paralyzed from the neck down. He was a strong advocate for people with spinal cord injuries and for embryonic stem cell research until has death from cardiac arrest at the age of 52. The Christopher and Dana Reeve Paralysis Act, a bill to advance research and improve quality of life for people with spinal cord injuries, was signed into law by President Barrack Obama March 31, 2009.

[d]Andrew I. Batavia, a quadriplegic as a result of a spinal cord injury, is an attorney and health and disability expert who favors legalization of assisted suicide.

[e]Carol Gill, PhD, is a clinical psychologist and an expert on suicide among people with disabilities and has written and testified extensively in opposition to assisted suicide.

suicide rests on stereotypes that our lives are inherently so bad that it is entirely rational if we want to die.

[98]I side with Gill. What worries me most about the proposals for legalized assisted suicide is their veneer of beneficence—the medical determination that, for a given individual, suicide is reasonable or right. It is not about autonomy but about nondisabled people telling us what's good for us.

[99]In the discussion that follows, I argue that choice is illusory in a context of pervasive inequality. Choices are structured by oppression. We shouldn't offer assistance with suicide until we all have the assistance we need to get out of bed in the morning and live a good life. Common causes of suicidality—dependence, institutional confinement, being a burden—are entirely curable. Singer, seated on my right, participates in the discussion but doesn't dominate it. During the meal, I occasionally ask him to put things within my reach, and he competently complies.

[100]I feel as if I'm getting to a few of them, when a student asks me a question. The words are all familiar, but they're strung together in a way so meaningless that I can't even retain them—it's like a long sentence in Tagalog. I can only admit my limitations. "That question's too abstract for me to deal with. Can you rephrase it?"

[101]He indicates that it is as clear as he can make it, so I move on.

[102]A little while later, my right elbow slips out from under me. This is awkward. Normally I get whoever is on my right to do this sort of thing. Why not now? I gesture to Singer. He leans over, and I whisper, "Grasp this wrist and pull forward one inch, without lifting." He follows my instructions to the letter. He sees that now I can again reach my food with my fork. And he may now understand what I was saying a minute ago, that most of the assistance disabled people need does not demand medical training.

[103]A philosophy professor says, "It appears that your objections to assisted suicide are essentially tactical."

[104]"Excuse me?"

[105]"By that I mean they are grounded in current conditions of political, social and economic inequality. What if we assume that such conditions do not exist?"

[106]"Why would we want to do that?"

[107]"I want to get to the real basis for the position you take."

[108]I feel as if I'm losing caste.[f] It is suddenly very clear that I'm not a philosopher. I'm like one of those old practitioners who used to visit my law school, full of bluster about life in the real world. Such a bore! A once-sharp

---

[f]"Losing caste" is a saying based upon Asian caste systems and is typically used to mean one is doing something, like work, that is beneath one's station in life. In this context, Ms. Johnson is saying she feels like she's "in over her head" or "out of her league" with these philosophy professors.

mind gone muddy! And I'm only 44—not all that old.

[109]The forum is ended, and I've been able to eat very little of my pureed food. I ask Carmen to find the caterer and get me a container. Singer jumps up to take care of it. He returns with a box and obligingly packs my food to go.

[110]When I get home, people are clamoring for the story. The lawyers want the blow-by-blow of my forensic triumph over the formidable foe; when I tell them it wasn't like that, they insist that it was. Within the disability rights community, there is less confidence. It is generally assumed that I handled the substantive discussion well, but people worry that my civility may have given Singer a new kind of legitimacy. I hear from Laura, a beloved movement sister. She is appalled that I let Singer provide even minor physical assistance at the dinner. "Where was your assistant?" she wants to know. How could I put myself in a relationship with Singer that made him appear so human, even kind?

[111]I struggle to explain. I didn't feel disempowered; quite the contrary, it seemed a good thing to make him do some useful work. And then, the hard part: I've come to believe that Singer actually is human, even kind in his way. There ensues a discussion of good and evil and personal assistance and power and philosophy and tactics for which I'm profoundly grateful.

[112]I e-mail Laura again. This time I inform her that I've changed my will. She will inherit a book that Singer gave me, a collection of his writings with a weirdly appropriate inscription: "To Harriet Johnson, So that you will have a better answer to questions about animals. And thanks for coming to Princeton. Peter Singer. March 25, 2002." She responds that she is changing her will, too. I'll get the autographed photo of Jerry Lewis she received as an M.D.A. poster child. We joke that each of us has given the other a "reason to live."

[113]I have had a nice e-mail message from Singer, hoping Carmen and I and the chair got home without injury, relaying positive feedback from my audiences—and taking me to task for a statement that isn't supported by a relevant legal authority, which he looked up. I report that we got home exhausted but unharmed and concede that he has caught me in a generalization that should have been qualified. It's clear that the conversation will continue.

[114]I am soon sucked into the daily demands of law practice, family, community and politics. In the closing days of the state legislative session, I help get a bill passed that I hope will move us one small step toward a world in which killing won't be such an appealing solution to the "problem" of disability. It is good to focus on this kind of work. But the conversations with and about Singer continue. Unable to muster the appropriate moral judgments, I ask myself a tough question: am I in fact a silly little lady whose head is easily turned by a man who gives her a kind of attention she enjoys? I hope not, but I confess that I've never been able to sustain righteous anger for more than about 30 minutes at a time. My view of life tends more toward tragedy.

[115]The tragic view comes closest to describing how I now look at Peter Singer. He is a man of unusual gifts, reaching for the heights. He writes that he is trying to create a system of ethics derived from fact and reason, that largely throws off the perspectives of religion, place, family, tribe, community and maybe even species—to "take the point of view of the universe." His is a grand, heroic undertaking.

[116]But like the protagonist in a classical drama, Singer has his flaw. It is his unexamined assumption that disabled people are inherently "worse off," that we "suffer," that we have lesser "prospects of a happy life." Because of this all-too-common prejudice, and his rare courage in taking it to its logical conclusion, catastrophe looms. Here in the midpoint of the play, I can't look at him without fellow-feeling.

[117]I am regularly confronted by people who tell me that Singer doesn't deserve my human sympathy. I should make him an object of implacable wrath, to be cut off, silenced, destroyed absolutely. And I find myself lacking a logical argument to the contrary.

[118]I am talking to my sister Beth on the phone. "You kind of like the monster, don't you?" she says.

[119]I find myself unable to evade, certainly unwilling to lie. "Yeah, in a way. And he's not exactly a monster."

[120]"You know, Harriet, there were some very pleasant Nazis. They say the SS guards went home and played on the floor with their children every night."

[121]She can tell that I'm chastened; she changes the topic, lets me off the hook. Her harshness has come as a surprise. She isn't inclined to moralizing; in our family, I'm the one who sets people straight.

[122]When I put the phone down, my argumentative nature feels frustrated. In my mind, I replay the conversation, but this time defend my position.

[123]"He's not exactly a monster. He just has some strange ways of looking at things."

[124]"He's advocating genocide."

[125]"That's the thing. In his mind, he isn't. He's only giving parents a choice. He thinks the humans he is talking about aren't people, aren't 'persons.'"

[126]"But that's the way it always works, isn't it? They're always animals or vermin or chattel goods. Objects, not persons. He's repackaging some old ideas. Making them acceptable."

[127]"I think his ideas are new, in a way. It's not old-fashioned hate. It's a twisted, misinformed, warped kind of beneficence. His motive is to do good."

[128]"What do you care about motives?" she asks. "Doesn't this beneficent killing make disabled brothers and sisters just as dead?"

[129]"But he isn't killing anyone. It's just talk."

[130]"Just talk? It's talk with an agenda, talk aimed at forming policy. Talk

that's getting a receptive audience. You of all people know the power of that kind of talk."

[131]"Well, sure, but—"

[132]"If talk didn't matter, would you make it your life's work?"

[133]"But," I say, "his talk won't matter in the end. He won't succeed in reinventing morality. He stirs the pot, brings things out into the open. But ultimately we'll make a world that's fit to live in, a society that has room for all its flawed creatures. History will remember Singer as a curious example of the bizarre things that can happen when paradigms collide."

[134]"What if you're wrong? What if he convinces people that there's no morally significant difference between a fetus and a newborn, and just as disabled fetuses are routinely aborted now, so disabled babies are routinely killed? Might some future generation take it further than Singer wants to go? Might some say there's no morally significant line between a newborn and a 3-year-old?"

[135]"Sure. Singer concedes that a bright line cannot be drawn. But he doesn't propose killing anyone who prefers to live."

[136]"That overarching respect for the individual's preference for life—might some say it's a fiction, a fetish, a quasi-religious belief?"

[137]"Yes," I say. "That's pretty close to what I think. As an atheist, I think all preferences are moot once you kill someone. The injury is entirely to the surviving community."

[138]"So what if that view wins out, but you can't break disability prejudice? What if you wind up in a world where the disabled person's 'irrational' preference to live must yield to society's 'rational' interest in reducing the incidence of disability? Doesn't horror kick in somewhere? Maybe as you watch the door close behind whoever has wheeled you into the gas chamber?"

[139]"That's not going to happen."

[140]"Do you have empirical evidence?" she asks. "A logical argument?"

[141]"Of course not. And I know it's happened before, in what was considered the most progressive medical community in the world. But it won't happen. I have to believe that."

[142]Belief. Is that what it comes down to? Am I a person of faith after all? Or am I clinging to foolish hope that the tragic protagonist, this one time, will shift course before it's too late?

[143]I don't think so. It's less about belief, less about hope, than about a practical need for definitions I can live with.

[144]If I define Singer's kind of disability prejudice as an ultimate evil, and him as a monster, then I must so define all who believe disabled lives are inherently worse off or that a life without a certain kind of consciousness lacks value. That definition would make monsters of many of the people with whom I move on the sidewalks, do business, break bread, swap stories and share the grunt

work of local politics. It would reach some of my family and most of my non-disabled friends, people who show me personal kindness and who sometimes manage to love me through their ignorance. I can't live with a definition of ultimate evil that encompasses all of them. I can't refuse the monster-majority basic respect and human sympathy. It's not in my heart to deny every single one of them, categorically, my affection and my love.

[145]The peculiar drama of my life has placed me in a world that by and large thinks it would be better if people like me did not exist. My fight has been for accommodation, the world to me and me to the world.

[146]As a disability pariah, I must struggle for a place, for kinship, for community, for connection. Because I am still seeking acceptance of my humanity, Singer's call to get past species seems a luxury way beyond my reach. My goal isn't to shed the perspective that comes from my particular experience, but to give voice to it. I want to be engaged in the tribal fury that rages when opposing perspectives are let loose.

[147]As a shield from the terrible purity of Singer's vision, I'll look to the corruption that comes from interconnectedness. To justify my hopes that Singer's theoretical world—and its entirely logical extensions—won't become real, I'll invoke the muck and mess and undeniable reality of disabled lives well lived. That's the best I can do.

Vocabulary

[2] syllogisms
[3] cognitive
[5] infanticide
[5] convivial
[11] discombobulate
[11] gawking
[11] skittish
[11] fusion
[12] decrepitude
[12] propitious
[18] reconnoiter
[18] mottled
[23] infanticide
[23] utilitarianism
[24] jurisprudential

[24] sanctity
[24] fungible
[25] lucid
[25] condescension
[27] preambles
[28] plumb
[28] hypothetical
[29] congenital
[29] constraints
[35] amenable
[36] unflappable
[36] logistical
[37] angst
[38] marginalize
[39] nettled

[42] cachet
[43] inexplicably
[51] hanks
[57] accouterments
[58] badinage
[58] lavaliere
[60] loping
[65] exacerbate
[65] pro forma
[65] anencephaly
[65] eugenic
[71] elicits
[80] smorgasbord
[97] autonomy
[97] inherently

[98] beneficence
[98] illusory
[100] Tagalog
[110] forensic
[116] protagonist
[116] inherently
[17] implacablr
[117] wrath
[121] chastened
[126] chattel
[133] paradigm
[136] fetish
[137] moot
[140] empirical
[146] pariah

Discussion Questions

1. Why do you think Ms. Johnson begins her essay by using the pronoun "he" instead of identifying Peter Singer by name?

2. How would you describe the author's tone in paragraph 2? Why do you think she uses this tone here?

3. What two reasons does Ms. Johnson say were her motivation for accepting Singer's invitation to speak at Princeton? Why do you think she characterizes the Princeton students as a "very tough audience"?

4. Johnson says in response to a question that it was emotionally difficult and yet "horribly easy" to participate in a discussion about whether she should have been allowed to live. What do you think she means by this apparent contradiction?

5. In paragraph 12, Ms. Johnson indicates she is "in the first generation to survive to such decrepitude." What does she mean by this? How might this be related to Charles Darwin's theory of natural selection?

6. What two significant points does Johnson make in paragraph 14?

7. Beginning with paragraph 17, how does Ms. Johnson's essay relate to your answer to question 3?

8. In paragraph 24, Ms. Johnson refers to Singer's "replacement baby theory." Refer to the excerpt from Professor Singer's writings beginning on page 339 of this text and explain what Johnson means by this comment.

9. In the same paragraph, what does the author mean by "people are not fungible"?

10. In paragraph 25, Ms. Johnson says she is enraged at her fellow Charlestonians for not running Singer out of town on a rail. Do you agree with her? Why or why not?

11. What dilemma does Johnson describe in paragraph 34? Do you think she made the right choice in accepting Singer's invitation?

12. Summarize Johnson's strategy as described in paragraph 62. Do you think this is an effective approach for this particular audience? Why or why not?

13. Why do you think Ms. Johnson is more comfortable discussing assisted suicide than disability-based infanticide? What are your views on these two topics?

14. Explain what Johnson is referring to when she says in paragraph 89, "My brothers and sisters were here before me and behaved far more appropriately than I am doing."

15. In the evening debate at Princeton, what argument does Carol Gill make about how disabled people view the qualities of their lives? What points does Johnson make in support of Gill's position?

16. In paragraph 102 Johnson describes asking Singer to help her with a

physical problem. What point about people with disabilities does she hope Singer will get as a result of the incident?

17. Why are some of Johnson's colleagues within the disabilities community upset with the way she interacted with Singer at the forum? What is Johnson feeling emotionally about Singer at this point?

18. What does Johnson say is Singer's "flaw"? Do you agree that this is a prejudice that is commonly held?

19. What is Johnson referring to when she says, "And I know it's happened before, in what was considered the most progressive medical community in the world" in paragraph 141?

20. What are Ms. Johnson's reasons for not wanting to characterize Professor Singer as "an ultimate evil"?

21. Overall, how would you characterize Harriet McBryde Johnson's feelings about Peter Singer after her experiences with him?

VIOLET

NOREEN DUNCAN

Noreen Duncan is a professor of English and former chair of the English Department at Mercer County Community College where she teaches creative writing and serves as an advisor for the college's literary magazines. Professor Duncan was born and educated in Trinidad. Her work, primarily short fiction, has appeared in a number of literary reviews.

[1]So when Violet smartly put out her tan leather gloved right hand and indicated her right hand turning into Newbold Street and into the driveway of number 22 to park her Morris Oxford behind her brother-in-law Basil's Austin Princess, the first to enter Trinidad after the war, the passersby on the pavement stopped respectfully, aware that they were witnessing, if not exactly a regal turn of events, at least a high class right hand turning. For there was no doubt that Violet was high class. She never had to say it, people could smell it, the drop of 4711 on her hankie the more obvious indication, of course.

[2]As she applied the hand brake, she composed her mouth, both to hold in the inevitable *cheups*[a] as she contemplated another wasted evening at home with the Duchess and the Headmaster, her parents, and the unruly nephews, as well as to clearly enunciate the call for the yard boy: "Charles!" He didn't come. He never came when she first called, and she would have to call again, bawl out his name, so improper. The Duchess would accuse her of being improper, even though it was her fault that Charlie wouldn't come on the first call. He was spoiled and a liar. He had told the nephews that he was their cousin, and Superior, the Duchess' *macomere* from St. Vincent, who was really only a servant and a bad cook, but who took over the place like she was some kind of housekeeper, had corroborated the lie. Charlie's mother was a servant, Superior's helper. Fastness! That was why she was so sorry she had ever come back to Trinidad, people were always minding your business and lying and never knew their place. Imagine they said that she had tried to marry Basil before he had married her sister, Hyacinth, the mother of the nephews. Basil put on airs and people thought he had studied in England, but he hadn't even reached seventh standard, and too besides, he was only a civil service clerk, driving the Princess out on Saturdays and Sundays and walking to his office during the week with an umbrella, just like if he was some blasted Englishman. If

---

[a]A sound made by sucking air through teeth: "ffft"

he wasn't married to her sister, she wouldn't even talk to him, and anyhow, he was the one who put love notes under her bedroom door and tried to kiss her the night the Duchess and Headmaster made Hyacinth and him tell people that they were engaged, and then they posted the banns in Trinity Church that next Sunday and almost didn't wait a month for the wedding.

[3]She cheupsed then: "Charles!" He came round the side of the house slowly from the kitchen, and she had to tell him again, every day, to open the car door for her. Like he forgot. Every day. "Open the door, Charles. Here, take my briefcase and those packages in the back seat, and be careful this time how you handle them. You almost broke the bottles yesterday. And when you finish putting them inside, wipe down the car and lock it up." She saw the cut-eye, but she was already too tired to box him, the drive up from Arima was exhausting, and she needed a cup of tea and a bath, to wash the smells of the drug store and those annoying little people buying ointment and carbolic soap all day, out of her skin.

[4]She hated Trinidad and Trinidadians. If it wasn't for her parents running out of money because her lazy rum-drinking brother had failed his medical exams for the third time and the university had expelled him, and he had to go to the States to try to get his medical training there, as the Headmaster was determined that all of his sons would be doctors, especially after his oldest and brightest son, as soon as he qualified had died so unexpectedly of fever in London, she would never have come back to this small-minded place. She could have had her qualifications as a dentist and been married to a university-educated man, but the Headmaster had made her come home from her studies at McGill University, just as she had got Pierre to say that he realised that they belonged together, and she even had this little pearl ring to prove it. And even though she had come back to her parents' house, she had prepared her trousseau, had had her cotton sheets and silk bedspread and linen table cloths and embroidered hand towels and crochet doilies and kitchen towels made. And every month when she got her salary, she had paid something on the silver set at Stetchers. Everything was ready, put away in the little storeroom behind the servants' quarters. Pierre had promised to write, but he had never written; all she had were the little ring and the photos of them in the park in Montreal and of the week that they had run away to New York, and of the headstone of his grave, those she kept under her pillow. She had strictly forbidden anyone in the house, especially Superior, to make her bed or to touch any of her things, but they did anyway, and the Duchess encouraged them.

[5]There he was making noise and causing ruction as usual, Piaf, the little white poodle that she was keeping for her friend Louise who had had to leave Trinidad in a hurry, when *The Trinidad Guardian* ran her picture on the front page smiling demurely, the morning after she had called the friend of a friend at the newspaper and announced that she had married the Premier, although he

was a Roman Catholic and had not been able to get the Pope to annul his marriage to his first wife. Violet missed Louise who wasn't as small-minded as the others, particularly the girls who had been to school with her. They were all unhappily married and producing a string band of children, and they had never even been anywhere, but they were always making style on her, pretending that their silly little husbands who were always trying to make arrangements to meet her somewhere, adored them. She and Louise went to the cinema every Saturday afternoon and then to the Dairies for ice-cream and down the islands most weekends, until the Premier had taken over her life, and Louise had to stay at home and wait for him to telephone or come late at night after her servant had gone to sleep, and it looked like the neighbours on the street had turned off their lights and gone to sleep

[6]Violet braced herself for the long evening with the Duchess, Hyacinth and Superior, none of whom cared about her day, or her long drive, or the small people who bothered her all day, but they would expect her to listen to them regale the smallness of their day at home, the serial stories on Redifussion[b] and the gossip of the street sellers and the beggars who came to the house with the usual daily sameness and dullness and regularity. Basil would be resting from the exertions of his office work, and the Headmaster, never forgetting who he was and lest anyone else should, was giving free private lessons to the nephews and some of the neighbourhood children whose parents were grateful and sent him navel oranges from their trees or *benne* balls[c] from their relatives in Tobago, by way of payment for those lessons.

[7]But today there was excitement going on. The nephews and the other children were loud in the dining room, clearly the Headmaster was not in charge, not wielding his freshly picked cherry whip. Hyacinth and Superior were silent, unusual for those two *mauvais langues*,[d] and the Duchess, herself, was not her usual self, holding court in the front gallery, but sitting on a kitchen bench, drinking a cup of tea in the midst of all the confusion, she also quiet. Only Piaf's behaviour was as normal, and he wasn't normally part of the household. The Headmaster and Basil had their heads together, whispering nervously about something so serious that they neither hushed the loud nephews nor seemed to notice Violet's return home. But as the Headmaster rallied, resuming his usual scholarly demeanour, and lifted the receiver of the telephone, Basil, forgetting his Oxonion[e] tones, bawled out his wife's name, "Hyacind!"

---

[b]A type of directly wired radio, somewhat like today's cable TV except only one station was available

[c]Hard, chewy, round candy made of sesame seeds and molasses

[d]Mean-spirited gossips; literally, "evil-tongues"

[e]A reference to Oxford University

[8]She, Hyacinth, was so startled by this change in her husband that she too forgot herself and ran to the toilet instead of answering the summons, causing Superior to forget herself and run to see what he wanted, or probably to try to find out what he and the Headmaster had been conspiring. That's when everybody else seemed to notice Violet, and the Duchess finally explained the reason for the disorderly household: a thief had stolen the gold bangles right off of the wrists of one of the children, right there in the driveway, just as she was on her way into the house for her private lessons, in broad daylight. The Headmaster had gotten through to the Officer-in-Charge at the Besson Street Police Headquarters and was offering by way of preamble and evidence of his superior citizenry, his credentials: Headmaster, retired, Deacon of Trinity Cathedral, extant, and Father of Dr. So and So, late of London, deceased. He also made some preliminary remarks about the results of the miseducation or undereducation of certain members of the Trinidad population who did not understand their place in the society, all this before he was able to tell, with much editorialising, what had happened in his driveway. The Duchess had retired to her bedroom, later to emerge to be interviewed by the policeman, dispatched from Headquarters, to take a statement from the child who was alone in the driveway during the robbery, but who was not allowed to tell the constable anything as the Headmaster would recount the incident himself, being, in his mind, the only person qualified to speak properly to the authorities.

[9]Only after the policeman had left, and Superior had boiled many kettles of water for tea for all, and Charlie had washed and locked up the car, and the Duchess and the Headmaster had settled themselves on the gallery chairs, and Basil had gone to lie down, tired as usual, and the nephews and the other children had been sent to play in Victoria Park, only then did Hyacinth remember that there had been a letter for Violet, with American stamps, which was none of her business. Violet took her bath, accepted tea and biscuits from Superior, sat in the gallery with her parents to hear the story told again and again, embellished and embroidered and theorised about, until the Headmaster had become part of the saga, recounting the words that he himself said to the thief, and the Duchess remembering that when she awoke that morning, she had said to Superior, ask her if that wasn't true, that she had dreamt something that told her something would go wrong that self same day.

[10]And then it seemed a lifetime later, the nephews had finally stopped jumping on the beds, and their grandfather had had his Epsom salts, and their parents had gone for a drive so that Basil could get some fresh air so that he could get a restful night's sleep so that he could do a good day's work the next day, and the household was quiet. Violet went to her room with a glass of sherry and the letter. She put on her nightie and put Ponds on her face and three curlers in her hair and plucked her eyebrows and turned on her bedside light and gently peeled the flap of the letter. Just as she had hoped and knew, Louise was

in New York. It wasn't a long letter, just that she had arrived safely in New York, she did not explain, but someone who she wouldn't or couldn't name had sent her money for her two week stay in the Park Plaza Hotel, and she was getting a regular allowance, monthly, from Trinidad, so that she had an apartment in Brooklyn, but she was lonely. She missed Piaf, but most of all she missed her friend, not the person who was evidently supporting her in New York, but Violet, the only person in the world who understood her, really. Please come. That was all. Before she fell asleep, Violet's pillow case was wet with perspiration or tears.

[11]The next morning, the Duchess arose earlier than her usual, dressed carefully in her hat, put *eau de toilette* on her hankie and sent one of the nephews to call the mother of the child who had been robbed. While she waited, she had her morning tea and made the daily arrangements with Superior. Basil had read his newspaper, taken his umbrella and strolled off to work. Violet's car was gone. She must have left very early as noone had seen her, even Charlie and the Headmaster who were usually the first up and about, one to feed the chickens and sweep the drains, the other to supervise the work. Hyacinth was not an early riser. The Duchess had spoken authoritatively to the child's mother who was instructed to dress the girl in her Sunday School dress, not in her school uniform, polished shoes, white socks, and ribbons in her hair, please, and called for a taxi to take them to Police Headquarters where she would give another report to the police and inspect some police photographs so that she and perhaps the girl could identify the criminal. When they finished assisting the police with their investigations, it was lunch time and the Duchess would have her noontime meal and lie down, but before that she told the mother of the child she would give her money to replace the gold bracelets, but, she lectured, none of her children had been allowed to wear gold jewelry, even to church, and look how well they had turned out.

[12]Charlie was the first to raise the alarm. Hyacinth and her mother had been looking out in the gallery when Basil came up the street from his office with his furled brolly,[f] and the Headmaster was washing his hands after having finished his afternoon exertions. He had been particularly instructive with the cherry whip, perhaps to make up for the lapse the afternoon before. The nephews were free to play in the park before bedtime, and Piaf was barking his little head off, annoying Superior, who had told him to *marche* more than once. But Charlie, who had no watch, and probably couldn't read the clock, knew that Violet was late, and was so confident that he went boldly into the gallery and informed the Duchess that her younger daughter was late. They didn't panic right away. In fact, it wasn't until it grew dark that the Headmaster conferred with his son-in-law before he rang up the Arima police station, then

---

[f]An umbrella

the San Juan police station, and then the Morvant police station, ordering the respective sergeants-in-charge to look out for Violet's Morris along the Eastern Main Road. Then finally, he had Basil take out the Princess, was Basil to get no rest in that household? For a few minutes, they worried about who would go in the car to look for Violet, but the Headmaster remembered himself and decided that Charlie should go in case the Morris had fallen into a ditch, and it would take two men to hoist it out and anyway, he, the Headmaster, would be the most qualified to manage the telephone, and who would protect the ladies and the children?

[13]But even though Basil drove all the way to Arima and went into the houses near the drugstore and in his beautiful best English, Charlie having to translate for him, enquired about his sister-in-law, nobody had seen her. As a matter of fact, she had not come into the drug store at all at all that day, and when was she coming back, so and so had a boil and a child had had a worm and Senna or sulphur ointment were needed? When he finally drove into the driveway at number 22, it was very late, but all the lights were blazing, only the children had gone to bed, the rest of the household were wide awake, and very worried, Hyacinth seemed to have been crying. The Headmaster had telephoned the police stations a dozen times and demanded that they produce his daughter, and another young constable had been sent to the house, asking a lot of blasted-stupid questions so that the Headmaster had to have a few hard words with him, and then he had had to ring up the station again and register another complaint and threaten to have them all dismissed, they really had no idea who he was. Basil was worried too, but it looked as if nobody was planning to go to bed that night and he would be expected to stay up with them! Charlie and Piaf were the calmest and quietest. Three or four times, Superior had to be reminded to put the kettle on, Hyacinth wept feebly and continuously, seeing an opportunity to rest her head on Basil's somewhat reluctant shoulder, and the Duchess asked her husband every five minutes to ring up the police again.

[14]It wasn't until dawn that Superior and the Duchess thought to check her bedroom, and they discovered then what they should have hours before, but Charlie knew, Violet's clothes were gone and her bed had not been made. The women spent the day crying. The Headmaster put on his bespoke[g] suit and his deceased son's university tie and made Basil drive him to see the Bishop of Trinity Cathedral and then to the chambers of his solicitor, neither of whom had any idea what he could do, but they listened to him and promised to take steps, although they didn't say where or to what end. By the time he and Basil eventually drove into the driveway again, it was late, getting dark almost. The Duchess rang up two or three of Violet's school friends and asked how they were and their little darlings and their better halves, and give her best regards to their dear mamas, but naturally she couldn't come out and ask if anybody knew where Violet was. People were just too fast and talkative.

---

[g]Special, very expensive; bespoke tailors catered to a select clientele

Vocabulary

[1]regal	[3]carbolic	[7]demeanour (demeanor)	[9]saga
[2]contemplated	[4]trousseau	[8]bangles	[10]Epsom salts
[2]unruly	[5]ruction	[8]preamble	[11]*eau de toilette*
[2]enunciate	[5]demurely	[8]extant	[12]furled
[2]bawl	[6]regale	[8]recount	[12]exertions
[2]corroborated	[6]exertions	[9]embellished	[14]solicitor
[2]banns			

Discussion Questions

1. Where does this story take place? When?

2. This story appears to be written in the third-person point of view. Is it really third person? Explain.

3. What is Violet's view of her place in society? Does she work? If so, where?

4. Who is the Headmaster? What is his view of his place in society? What aspirations did he hold for his eldest son? What happened? What effect did this have on Violet's life?

5. Who is Pierre? How did he fit into Violet's life? What happened to him?

6. Who are Superior and Charles? How do they fit into Violet's life? How does she relate to them?

7. Who is the Duchess? What is Violet's attitude toward the Headmaster and the Duchess?

8. Violet says of her school friends, "They were all unhappily married, . . ." but they ". . . were always making style on her. . . ." What does "making style" seem to mean in this context? What does Violet say about the husbands of her school friends?

9. Who are Basil and Hyacinth? How do they fit into Violet's life?

10. How does the author's introduction of the characters early in the story help us to formulate our view of Violet and her view of the world?

11. What incident occurs that causes consternation in the household? How is the Headmaster described in the context of this incident?

12. How does the Headmaster maintain discipline among his pupils?

13. Who is Louise? Describe Violet's relationship with her. How does this fit into the story?

14. What happens to Violet at the end of the story? What is the significance of the closing line, "People were just too fast and talkative"?

A WEDDING WITHOUT MUSICIANS

SHOLOM ALEICHEM

Sholom Aleichem, *the pen name of* ***Solomon Rabinowitz,*** *(1859-1916) is the foremost writer of stories in Yiddish. Aleichem played a major role in creating a great body of Yiddish literature and in promoting it to the world. The play* Fiddler on the Roof *is based on several of his short stories. With over 200,000 participants, his funeral in New York was the largest ever seen up to that time.*

[1]The last time I told you about our Straggler Special, I described the miracle of *Hashono Rabo*. This time I shall tell you about another miracle in which the Straggler Special figured, how thanks to the Straggler Special the town of Heissin was saved from a terrible fate.

[2]This took place during the. days of the Constitution when reprisals against the Jews were going on everywhere. Though I must tell you that we Jews of Heissin have never been afraid of pogroms. Why? Simply because there is no one in our town who can carry out a pogrom. Of course you can imagine that if we looked very hard we could find one or two volunteers who wouldn't deny themselves the pleasure of ventilating us a little, that is, breaking our bones or burning down our houses. For example, when reports of pogroms began drifting in, the few squires, who are enemies of our people, wrote confidential letters to the proper authorities, saying it might be a good idea if "something were done" in Heissin also; but since there was no one here to do it, would they be so kind as to send help, in other words, would they dispatch some "people" as quickly as possible.

[3]And before another twenty-four hours had passed a reply came, also confidentially, that "people" were being sent. From where? From Zhmerinko, from Kazatin, Razdilno, Popelno and other such places that had distinguished themselves in beating up Jews. Do you want to know how we learned of this deep secret? We found it out through our regular source of news, Noah Tonkonoy. Noah Tonkonoy is a man whom God has endowed with a pair of extra-long legs and he uses them to good purpose. He never rests and he is seldom to be found at home. He is always busy with a thousand things and most of these things have to do with other people's business rather than his own. By trade he is a printer, and because he is the only printer in Heissin he knows all the squires and the police and has dealings with officialdom and is in on all their secrets.

[4]Noah Tonkonoy spread the good news all over town. He told the secret

to one person at a time, in strictest confidence, of course, saying, "I am telling this only to you. I wouldn't tell it to anyone else." And that is how the whole town became aware of the fact that a mob of hooligans was on the way, and that a plan for beating up Jews had been worked out. The plan told exactly when they would start, on which day, at which hour and from which point, and by what means—everything to the last detail.

⁵You can imagine what terror this struck in our hearts. Panic spread quickly. And among whom do you think it spread first? Among the poor, of course. It's a peculiar thing about poor people. When a rich man is afraid of a pogrom, you can understand why. He is afraid, poor fellow, that he will be turned into a pauper. But those of you who are already paupers, what are you afraid of? What have you got to lose? But you should have seen how they bundled up their children and packed up their belongings and began running hither and yon, looking for a place to hide. Where can a person hide? This one hides in a friendly peasant's cellar, another in the Notary's attic, a third in the Director's office at the factory. Everyone finds a spot for himself.

⁶I was the only one in town who wasn't anxious to hide. I am not boasting about my bravery. But this is the way I see it: what's the sense of being afraid of a pogrom? I don't say that I am a hero. I might have been willing to hide too, when the hour of reckoning came. But I asked myself first, "How can I be sure that during the slaughter the friendly neighbor in whose cellar I was hiding, or the Notary, or the Director of the factory himself, wouldn't ..." You understand. And all that aside, how can you leave a town wide open like that? It's no trick to run away. You have to see about doing something. But, alas, what can a Jew do? He appeals to a friendly official. And that is just what we did.

⁷In every town there is at least one friendly official you can appeal to. We had one too, the Inspector of Police, a jewel of a fellow, willing to listen to us and willing to accept a gift on occasion. We went to the Inspector with the proper gifts and asked for his protection. He reassured us at once. He told us to go home and sleep in peace. Nothing would happen. Sounds good, doesn't it? But we still had our walking newspaper, Noah, who was broadcasting another secret through the length and breadth of the town. The secret was that a telegram had just arrived. He swore by everything holy that he had seen it himself. What was in that telegram? Only one word—*Yediem*. An ugly word. It means simply, "We are coming."

⁸We ran back to the Inspector. "Your honor," we told him, "it looks bad." "What looks bad?" he asked, and we told him, "A telegram has just arrived." "From where?" We told him. "And what does it say?" We told him, "*Yediem*." At this he burst out laughing. "You are big fools," he said. "Only yesterday I ordered a regiment of Cossacks from Tolchin."

[9]When we heard this, we breathed more easily. When a Jew hears that a Cossack is coming, he takes courage; he can face the world again. The question remained: who would arrive first, the Cossacks from Tolchin, or the hooligans from Zhmerinko? Common sense told us that the hooligans would arrive first because they were coming by train, while the Cossacks were coming on horseback. But we pinned all our hopes on the Straggler Special. God is merciful. He would surely perform a miracle and the Straggler would be at least a few hours late. This wasn't too much to hope for, since it happened nearly every day. But this one time it looked as though the miracle wouldn't take place. The Straggler kept going from station to station as regular as a clock. You can imagine how we felt when we learned, confidentially, of course, through Noah Tonkonoy, that a telegram had arrived from the last station, from Krishtopovka. *Yediem*, it said, and not just *yediem*—but *yediem*, with a *hurrah!* in front of it.

[10]Naturally we took this last bit of news straight to the Inspector. We begged. him not to rely on the Cossacks who might or might not arrive from Tolchin sometime, but to send police to the station, at least for the sake of appearances, so that our enemies wouldn't think that we were completely at their mercy. The Inspector listened to our pleas. He did what we asked, and more. He got himself up in full uniform, with all his orders and medals, and took the whole police force, that is, the gendarme and his assistant, to the station with him to meet the train.

[11]But our enemies weren't asleep either. They also put on their full dress uniforms, complete with ribbons and medals, took a couple of priests along, and also came to meet the train. The Inspector asked them sternly, "What are you doing here?" And they asked him the same question, "What are you doing here?"

[12]They bandied words back and forth, and the Inspector let them know in no uncertain terms that their trouble was for nothing. As long as he was in charge, there would be no pogrom in Heissin. They listened, smiled knowingly, and answered with insolence, "We shall see."

[13]Just then a train whistle was heard from the distance. The sound struck terror to our hearts. We waited for another of whistle to blow and after that for the shouts of "Hurrah!" What would happen after the Hurrah! we knew only too well from hearsay. We waited, but heard nothing more. What had happened? The sort of thing that could only happen to our Straggler Special.

[14]When the Straggler Special drew into the station, the engineer stopped the locomotive, stepped out calmly and made his way toward the buffet. We met him halfway. "Well, my good fellow, and where are the cars?"

[15]"Which cars?"

[16]"Can't you see that you are here with the locomotive and without cars?"

[17]He stared at us. "What do I care about the cars? They are the business of the crew."

[18]"Where's the crew?"

[19]"How should I know where the crew is? The conductor blows the whistle when he is ready and I whistle back to let him know that I am starting, and off we go. I don't have an extra pair of eyes in back of my head to see what's going on behind me."

[20]That was his story and according to that he was right. But right or wrong, there stood the Straggler Special without cars and without passengers. In other words, it was a wedding without musicians.

[21]Later we learned that a band of hooligans had been on the way to Heissin, all of them handpicked youths, armed to the teeth with clubs and knives and other weapons. Their spirits were high and liquor flowed freely. At the last station, Krishtopovka, they invited the crew to join them and treated everybody to drinks—the conductor, the fireman, the gendarmes. But in the midst of this revelry they forgot one little detail—to couple the cars back to the locomotive. And so the locomotive went off at the usual time to Heissin and the rest of the Straggler Special remained standing in Krishtopovka.

[22]Neither the hooligans nor the other passengers nor the crew noticed that they were standing still. They continued to empty bottle after bottle and to make merry, until the station master suddenly noticed that the locomotive had gone off and left the cars behind. He raised the alarm, the crew came tumbling out. A hue and cry was raised. The hooligans blamed the crew, the crew blamed the hooligans, but what good did it do? At last they decided that the only thing to do was to set out for Heissin on foot. They took heart and began marching toward Heissin, singing and shouting as they went.

[23]And so they arrived in their usual good form, singing and yelling and brandishing their clubs. But it was already too late. In the streets of Heissin the Cossacks from Tolchin were riding up and down on horseback with whips in their hands. Within half an hour not one of the hooligans remained in town. They ran off like rats in a famine, they melted like ice in summer.

[24]Now, I ask you, didn't the Straggler Special deserve to be showered with gold, or at least written up?

Vocabulary

[2]pogroms	[8]Cossacks	[12]bandied	[21]gendarmes
[2]squires	[9]hooligans	[12]insolence	[23]brandishing

Discussion Questions

1. What does the author's pen name mean? Where did you find this information?

2. What is the significance of the name of the train in this story? What does the name imply about the "track record" of the train?

3. The subject matter of this story is quite serious—a *pogrom*. What tone does the writer use in the story? Why?

4. How does Noah Tonkonoy's trade fit with his role as the town gossip?

5. Do you agree that the rich have reason to be afraid of a *pogrom* but the poor really don't? Discuss with your classmates.

6. How do the narrator's comments about "the friendly neighbor," the Notary and the Director of the factory relate to what happened to the Jews of Europe in World War II?

7. What is the role of the Cossacks in this story? If something like this were to happen to a minority group in the United States, what group would be in the role of the Cossacks? The hooligans?

8. Why were Jews subjected to *pogroms* in eastern Europe in the 19th and 20th centuries? What reason did Christians use to justify *pogroms*?

9. What is Aleichem's comment about human nature at the end of the story when the engineer tells the people why he arrived without the cars?

WHAT TO THE SLAVE IS THE FOURTH OF JULY?

FREDERICK DOUGLASS

Frederick Douglass (1818-1895) was a major voice in the effort to end slavery in America. Known for his oratory skills, Douglass, a former slave, was engaged by the American Anti-Slavery Society for a tour of lectures that brought him national recognition. In 1845, he published his biography, Narrative of the Life of Frederick Douglass, *which brought him international acclaim. Douglass served as an advisor to Presidents Abraham Lincoln and Andrew Johnson.*

EXTRACT FROM AN ORATION, AT ROCHESTER, JULY 5, 1852.

[1]FELLOW CITIZENS—Pardon me, and allow me to ask, why am I called upon to speak here to-day? What have I, or those I represent, to do with your national independence? Are the great principles of political freedom and of natural justice, embodied in that Declaration of Independence extended to us? And am I therefore, called upon to bring our humble offering to the national altar, and to confess the benefits, and express devout gratitude for the blessings, resulting from your independence to us?

[2]Would to God, both for your sakes and ours, that an affirmative answer could be truthfully returned to these questions! Then would my task be light, and my burden easy and delightful. For who is there so cold that a nation's sympathy could not warm him? Who so obdurate and dead to the claims of gratitude, that would not thankfully acknowledge such priceless benefits? Who so stolid and selfish, that would not give his voice to swell the hallelujahs of a nation's Jubilee, when the chains of servitude had been torn from his limbs? I am not that man. In a case like that, the dumb might eloquently speak, and the "lame man leap as an hart."

[3]But, such is not the state of the case. I say it with a sad sense of the disparity between us. I am not included within the pale of this glorious anniversary! Your high independence only reveals the immeasurable distance between us. The blessings in which you this day rejoice, are not enjoyed in common. The rich inheritance of justice, liberty, prosperity, and independence, bequeathed by your fathers, is shared by you, not by me. The sunlight that brought life and healing to you has brought stripes and death to me. This Fourth of July *you* may rejoice, *I* must mourn. To drag a man in fetters into the grand illuminated temple of liberty, and call upon him to join you in joyous anthems, were inhu-

man mockery and sacrilegious irony. Do you mean, citizens, to mock me, by asking me to speak to-day? If so, there is a parallel to your conduct. And let me warn you that it is dangerous to copy the example of a nation whose crimes, towering up to heaven, were thrown down by the breath of the Almighty, burying that nation in irrecoverable ruin! I can to-day take up the plaintive lament of a peeled and woe-smitten people.

⁴"By the rivers of Babylon, there we sat down. Yea! We wept when we remembered Zion. We hanged our harps upon the willows in the midst thereof. For there, they that carried us away captive, required of us a song; and they who wasted us required of us mirth, saying, 'Sing us one of the songs of Zion.' How can we sing the Lord's song in a strange land? If I forget thee, O Jerusalem, let my right hand forget her cunning. If I do not remember thee, let my tongue cleave to the roof of my mouth."

⁵Fellow-citizens, above your national, tumultuous joy, I hear the mournful wail of millions, whose chains, heavy and grievous yesterday, are to-day rendered more intolerable by the jubilant shouts that reach them. If I do forget, if I do not faithfully remember those bleeding children of sorrow this day, "may my right hand forget her cunning, and may my tongue cleave to the roof of my mouth!" To forget them, to pass lightly over their wrongs, and to chime in with the popular theme, would be treason most scandalous and shocking, and would make me a reproach before God and the world. My subject, then, fellow-citizens, is AMERICAN SLAVERY. I shall see this day and its popular characteristics from the slave's point of view. Standing there, identified with the American bondman, making his wrongs mine, I do not hesitate to declare, with all my soul, that the character and conduct of this nation never looked blacker to me than on this Fourth of July. Whether we turn to the declarations of the past, or to the professions of the present, the conduct of the nation seems equally hideous and revolting. America is false to the past, false to the present, and solemnly binds herself to be false to the future. Standing with God and the crushed and bleeding slave on this occasion, I will, in the name of humanity which is outraged, in the name of liberty which is fettered, in the name of the constitution and the bible, which are disregarded and trampled upon, dare to call in question and to denounce, with all the emphasis I can command, everything that serves to perpetuate slavery—the great sin and shame of America! I will not equivocate; I will not excuse; I will use the severest language I can command; and yet not one word shall escape me that any man, whose judgment is not blinded by prejudice, or who is not at heart a slaveholder, shall not confess to be right and just.

⁶But I fancy I hear some one of my audience say, it is just in this circumstance that you and your brother abolitionists fail to make a favorable impression on the public mind. Would you argue more, and denounce less, would you persuade more and rebuke less, your cause would be much more likely to

succeed. But, I submit, where all is plain there is nothing to be argued. What point in the anti-slavery creed would you have me argue? On what branch of the subject do the people of this country need light? Must I undertake to prove that the slave is a man? That point is conceded already. Nobody doubts it. The slaveholders themselves acknowledge it when they punish disobedience on the part of the slave. There are seventy-two crimes in the state of Virginia, which, if committed by a black man, (no matter how ignorant he be,) subject him to the punishment of death; while only two of these same crimes will subject a white man to the like punishment. What is this but the acknowledgment that the slave is a moral, intellectual, and responsible being.

⁷The manhood of the slave is conceded. It is admitted in the fact that southern statute books are covered with enactments forbidding, under severe fines and penalties, the teaching of the slave to read or write. When you can point to any such laws, in reference to the beasts of the field, then I may consent to argue the manhood of the slave. When the dogs in your streets, when the fowls of the air, when the cattle on your hills, when the fish of the sea, and the reptiles that crawl, shall be unable to distinguish the slave from a brute, then will I argue with you that the slave is a man!

⁸For the present, it is enough to affirm the equal manhood of the negro race. Is it not astonishing that, while we are plowing, planting, and reaping, using all kinds of mechanical tools, erecting houses, constructing bridges, building ships, working in metals of brass, iron, copper, silver, and gold; that, while we are reading, writing, and cyphering, acting as clerks, merchants, and secretaries, having among us lawyers, doctors, ministers, poets, authors, editors, orators, and teachers; that, while we are engaged in all manner of enterprises common to other men—digging gold in California, capturing the whale in the Pacific, feeding sheep and cattle on the hillside, living, moving, acting, thinking, planning, living in families as husbands, wives, and children, and, above all, confessing and worshiping the Christian's God, and looking hopefully for life and immortality beyond the grave,—we are called upon to prove that we are men!

⁹Would you have me argue that man is entitled to liberty? that he is the rightful owner of his own body? You have already declared it. Must I argue the wrongfulness of slavery? Is that a question for republicans? Is it to be settled by the rules of logic and argumentation, as a matter beset with great difficulty, involving a doubtful application of the principle of justice, hard to be understood? How should I look to-day in the presence of Americans, dividing and subdividing a discourse, to show that men have a natural right to freedom, speaking of it relatively and positively, negatively and affirmatively? To do so, would be to make myself ridiculous, and to offer an insult to your understanding. There is not a man beneath the canopy of heaven that does not know that slavery is wrong *for him*.

[10]What! am I to argue that it is wrong to make men brutes, to rob them of their liberty, to work them without wages, to keep them ignorant of their relations to their fellow-men, to beat them with sticks, to flay their flesh with the lash, to load their limbs with irons, to hunt them with dogs, to sell them at auction, to sunder their families, to knock out their teeth, to burn their flesh, to starve them into obedience and submission to their masters? Must I argue that a system, thus marked with blood and stained with pollution, is wrong? No; I will not. I have better employment for my time and strength than such arguments would imply.

[11]What, then, remains to be argued? Is it that slavery is not divine; that God did not establish it; that our doctors of divinity are mistaken? There is blasphemy in the thought. That which is inhuman cannot be divine. Who can reason on such a proposition! They that can, may; I cannot. The time for such argument is past.

[12]At a time like this, scorching irony, not convincing argument, is needed. Oh! had I the ability, and could I reach the nation's ear, I would to-day pour out a fiery stream of biting ridicule, blasting reproach, withering sarcasm, and stern rebuke. For it is not light that is needed, but fire; it is not the gentle shower, but thunder. We need the storm, the whirlwind, and the earthquake. The feeling of the nation must be quickened; the conscience of the nation must be roused; the propriety of the nation must be startled; the hypocrisy of the nation must be exposed; and its crimes against God and man must be proclaimed and denounced.

[13]What to the American slave is your Fourth of July? I answer, a day that reveals to him, more than all other days in the year, the gross injustice and cruelty to which he is the constant victim.

[14]To him, your celebration is a sham; your boasted liberty, an unholy license; your national greatness, swelling vanity; your sounds of rejoicing are empty and heartless; your denunciations of tyrants, brass-fronted impudence; your shouts of liberty and equality, hollow mockery; your prayers and hymns, your sermons and thanksgivings, with all your religious parade and solemnity, are to him mere bombast, fraud, deception, impiety, and hypocrisy—a thin veil to cover up crimes which would disgrace a nation of savages. There is not a nation on the earth guilty of practices more shocking and bloody, than are the people of these United States, at this very hour.

[15]Go where you may, search where you will, roam through all the monarchies and despotisms of the old world, travel through South America, search out every abuse, and when you have found the last, lay your facts by the side of the every-day practices of this nation, and you will say with me, that, for revolting barbarity and shameless hypocrisy, America reigns without a rival.

Vocabulary

[2]obdurate	[3]sacrilegious	[5]tumultuous	[10]sunder
[2]stolid	[3]plaintive	[5]reproach	[11]divinity
[2]dumb	[3]lament	[5]perpetuate	[11]blasphemy
[2]hart	[4]Babylon	[5]equivocate	[14]sham
[3]disparity	[4]Zion	[6]rebuke	[14]impudence
[3]pale	[4]mirth	[6]creed	[14]bombast
[3]bequeathed	[4]cunning	[8]cyphering	[14]impiety
[3]fetters	[4]cleave	[10]flay	[15]despotisms

Discussion Questions

1. Douglass delivered this speech in Rochester, NY. What is the significance of that city in the abolitionist movement? What kind of audience would Douglass have been addressing?

2. What does Douglass mean when he says, "I am not included within the pale of this glorious anniversary"?

3. Douglass frequently resorts to the device of the rhetorical question. Pick out two rhetorical questions from the first three paragraphs of the speech and explain why he used them.

4. What is the source of the fourth paragraph ("By the rivers of Babylon . . .")? What was Douglass' purpose in using this extended quote?

5. Look closely at Douglass' diction in the fifth paragraph ("Fellow-citizens, above your national, tumultuous joy, I hear . . ."). Pick out three phrases that might be likely to offend members of his audience. Do you think they were offended?

6. In the sixth paragraph ("But I fancy I hear . . . "), Douglass constructs an argument. What is he arguing? Cite two of his premises.

7. What, specifically, does Douglass say about the contribution of African-Americans to the building of the United States? Do you think he has a valid point? Why or why not?

8. The last sentence of this portion of the speech uses powerful diction. What does Douglass say about the United States of America in this last sentence? Do you agree or disagree with him?

WILL WOMEN GO CRAZY IN POLITICS?
EDITORIAL, *NEW YORK TIMES*, MARCH 9, 1870

Henry Jarvis Raymond and George Jones began publication of the **New York** **Times** *on September 18, 1851. In 1896, Adolph Ochs, publisher of* The Chatenooga Times, *acquired controlling ownership of the New York* Times; *the newspaper has stayed in the Ochs/Sulzberger family ever since. The New York* Times *company has been awarded 113 Pulitzer Prizes for journalism, more than any other news organization in the United States.*

[1]There is a curious debate going on in England between the *Pall Mall Gazette* and the *Spectator* about what the *Spectator* calls the "Physiology of Political Women," the question being, what will be the probable effect on women's physical health of their participation in politics. The *Pall Mall Gazette* thinks it will break them down through over-excitement; while the *Spectator* is satisfied that we cannot judge what its effects will be from what we see of the results of women's excitement now, inasmuch as the "excitement" to which they are exposed in our day is Society excitement, coupled with late hours, bad air, and unwholesome food.

[2]The excitement of politics, on the whole, it thinks likely to be wholesome and cites the vigorous health of female politicians, like ELIZABETH of England, MARIA THERESA of Austria, and CATHARINE of Russia, in support of its position. The matter seems very interesting in presence of the fact that we are evidently on the verge of seeing female suffrage adopted in several of the States, and that in two of the Territories, Wyoming and Utah, it is already in operation.

[3]But we do not believe it is quite as interesting as it looks. The celebrated female politicians, whose robust health we are called on to admire and draw deductions from, were picked women, who may be said to have made their own position. They sought all the difficulties they had to encounter, and their experience, therefore, is of little or no use to their sisters. Indeed, citing them by way of encouragement to the sex, in general, is very like holding prize fighters up as examples of what men in general are capable of in the way of bodily endurance. Prize fighters select themselves for their work; no one thinks of going into the ring unless in addition to general bodily health and size of muscle, he has thorough confidence in his own powers and is eager to try them.

[4]So also with regard to the possibility, now so much agitated, of giving young men a university education while supporting themselves by manual la-

bor. It is folly to argue that any university can be based on such a plan, or that young men in general could fall in with it, from the fact that some young men have been known to do it in universities already in existence. The young men who have done it have been selected for the ordeal by nature herself. No young man has ever attempted to undergo it, or has ever undergone it successfully, who did not feel himself equal to it and did not desire education almost passionately; and who, moreover, was not prepared to make sacrifices in pursuit of it, which not one in a thousand would be prepared to undergo.

⁵The true reason for believing that political excitement will not prove injurious to women is, in our opinion, to be found in the fact that it is not very injurious to men,—mainly that the great mass of them will keep out of politics and will not get excited about it. There is probably no country in the world in which the interest in politics is so general as it is in this, and yet when we come down to the hard facts of the case, the number of men who pay enough attention to politics to distract their attention from their private affairs or indeed who get in the least degree wrought up about them,—except at great crises such as the late war, which do not come in any country more than once in a couple of centuries,—is exceedingly small.

⁶There is a class who are excited about them and whose nerves the fortunes of political campaigns really shake, but they are the politicians proper, who, like the pugilists, choose this line of occupation because they like it and feel equal to it. The sensitive, nervous men who cannot stand the worry and excitement of the business either never go into it or speedily leave it. So will it be with women. The Anthonys and Stantons will always be found in the arena, and will be none the worse for it as far as their nerves go; the great body of the sex, even if they vote, will keep out of it, and take just that somewhat languid, pleasant interest in politics that their husbands and brothers take, if they take any at all,—but it will always play a very small part in their thoughts or lives.

⁷Indeed, in all the talk one hears about women's participation in politics and the professions, the state of the heath of the sex, is singularly overlooked and the number of women really equal to any work not sedentary is infinitesimally small. As for the labor of the bar, or of medicine or of the counting room, continuous, exhausting, accompanied with great anxiety, considerable exposure to weather and variations of temperature, and full of trials to temper, to self-love, to vanity, to generosity, and faith, as they all are, there is probably not one of our readers who can point to even two women in his acquaintance who are fit for them, or who would, with a full knowledge of what they were, think of encountering them. The number of women, even in easy circumstances, who can keep house without feeling what are called its "cares" overwhelming is alarmingly small. These cares consist simply in the management of servants— three or four all told—and the ordering of breakfast and dinner, and the superintendence of a certain amount of sweeping and scouring, and they have to be

borne, let it be remembered, within the privacy of home, with times and seasons perfectly within the woman's control, and her bed within easy reach. How few, nevertheless, find them so light as to have easy minds or strength left for the proper training of their children or the duties of even a moderate amount of hospitality.

[8]If it be said that though this may be true of married women, it is not true of unmarried ones, and that they would probably bear the wear and tear of business and the professions better, the answer is that girls are the material out of which matrons are made, and that there is no reason in the world either moral or physical, for supposing that they would confront the cares of the bar, or the hospital, or the broker's office a whit more successfully than those of the household. The notion that they would swarm into politics, be found going crazy in great numbers on caucuses and mass meetings, and practically "dividing the time" with strong-lunged males on the stump, we look on, therefore as a veritable hallucination.

[9]We venture to predict that the advocates of female suffrage will be found, as soon as it is achieved, denouncing the female voters for their apathy and indifference, and that the female voters will be found bearing their reproaches with the most complete equanimity. A considerable number of female doctors will always be found, doubtless practicing in the large cities, but the country male doctors, we fancy, will long have a monopoly of their weary rides and infinitesimal fees; and as to women's making much of a figure at the Bar, those who know what prodigious vigor of digestion and what soundness of constitution are necessary, even on the part of males, for success in the practice of the law, will be amused by the mention of the thing. They will not go crazy over the law any more than over politics. No classes or bodies of person voluntarily pursue any calling to which they find their powers generally unequal. They avoid it.

[10]With the suffrage, however, will come certain responsibilities which cannot and ought not to be avoided. Serving on juries is one of them, and we see that a jury of women has been already summoned in Wyoming Territory. Now, anybody who knows what sitting all day in a crowded court room, and giving even tolerably close attention to a case, and trying to understand the evidence, follow the counsel or judge, really means, in the way of physical exhaustion, need not feel much hesitation about anticipating even far greater reluctance amongst women, about serving on juries, than amongst men. In short, whichever way we look at the duties which they are seeking, or others are seeking for them, the question comes up irresistibly, where are they going to get the bodily strength to perform them? At the bottom of the "woman question" lies the question of woman's health, and until the latter is solved we suspect the former will give the public very little trouble in practice, whatever the amount of noise it creates. The female sex in America at this moment can, as a whole,

for physical reasons, no more compete with the male sex in the various callings of life than it can fly; and we say his not by way throwing cold water on any movement for the extension of woman's "sphere," or for giving her a greater variety of occupation, but by way of quieting the apprehensions of those who fancy that when women get the ballot or get the professions thrown open to them, we are going to have a social convulsion.

[11]The work of the world, happily or unhappily, is done under certain laws which neither Legislature nor society can change, and one of these is that to the strong hand and strong head, the capacious lungs and vigorous frame, falls, and will always fall, the heavy burdens, and that where the heavy burdens fall the great prizes fall too. This is not pleasant for the weak, but it is the fact, and will be to the end.

Vocabulary

[1]physiology	[6]pugilist	[8]whit	[9]equanimity
[2]suffrage	[6]languid	[8]caucuses	[10]fancy
[4]folly	[7]sedentary	[8]veritable	[11]capacious
[5]wrought up	[7]infinitesimal	[9]reproaches	

Discussion Questions

1. What is an editorial? Explain how this piece fits the definition of an editorial.

2. What is the main point—thesis—of this editorial? What points does the writer supply for support? Do you find the support convincing? Explain.

3. Do you think the writer of the editorial was a man or a woman? Why?

4. The writer cites some women in history and then uses a prizefighting analogy to make a point about these women. What point is the writer making?

5. What professions does the writer say are beyond the capabilities of women? Are women still effectively barred from these professions today?

6. In paragraph 5 the writer refers to the "late war." To what is the writer referring?

7. In paragraph 6 the writer makes an allusion to two specific women. Who are they and why are they significant?

8. Read the last paragraph of the editorial. What scientific theory would have influenced the writer to make this assertion?

9. Paraphrase the argument of the piece. Write a paragraph agreeing or disagreeing with the argument. Be sure to make reference to the editorial's supporting points.

WORLD POPULATION GROWTH FROM YEAR 0 TO 2050

FROM **1998 REVISION of the UNITED NATIONS OFFICIAL WORLD POPULATION ESTIMATES and PROJECTIONS**

THE UNITED NATIONS DEPARTMENT OF ECONOMIC AND SOCIAL AFFAIRS, POPULATION DIVISION

*The **United Nations** officially came into existence on 24 October 1945. Among its objectives, the UN works to promote human rights, protect the environment, fight disease and reduce poverty.*

[1]The rapid growth of the world population is a recent phenomenon in the history of the world. It is estimated that 2000 years ago the population of the world was about 300 million. For a very long time the world population did not grow significantly, with periods of growth followed by periods of decline. It took more than 1600 years for the world population to double to 600 million.

[2]The world population was estimated at 791 million in 1750, with 64 percent in Asia, 21 per cent in Europe and 13 per cent in Africa. Northern America was still nearly empty. By 1900, 150 years later, the world population had only slightly more than doubled, to 1,650 million. The major growth had been in Europe, whose share had increased to 25 per cent, and in Northern America and in Latin America, whose share had increased to 5 per cent each. Meanwhile the share of Asia had decreased to 57 per cent and that of Africa to 8 per cent. The growth of the world population accelerated after 1900, with 2,520 million in 1950, a 53 per cent increase in 50 years.

[3]The rapid growth of the world population started in 1950, with a sharp reduction in mortality in the less-developed regions, resulting in an estimated population of 6,055 million in the year 2000, nearly two-and-a-half times the population in 1950. With the declines in fertility in most of the world, the global growth rate of population has been decreasing since its peak of 2.0 per cent in 1965-1970. In 1998, the world's population stands at 5.9 billion and is growing at 1.3 per cent per year, or an annual net addition of 78 million people.

World Population Milestones

World Population reached:
1 billion in 1804
2 billion in 1927 (123 years later)
3 billion in 1960 (33 years later)
4 billion in 1974 (14 years later)
5 billion in 1987 (13 years later)

World Population may reach:
6 billion in 1999 (12 years later)
7 billion in 2013 (14 years later)
8 billion in 2028 (15 years later)
9 billion in 2054 (26 years later)

Source: United Nations Population Division, *World Population Prospects: The 1998 Revision.*

[4]According to the medium variant of the 1998 Revision of the official United Nations estimates and projections, by 2050 the world is expected to have 8,909 million people, an increase of slightly less than half from the 2000 population. By then the share of Asia will have stabilized at 59 per cent, that of Africa will have more than doubled, to 20 per cent, and that of Latin America nearly doubled, to 9 per cent. Meanwhile the share of Europe will decline to 7 per cent, less than one third its peak level. While in 1900 the population of Europe was three times that of Africa, in 2050 the population of Africa will be nearly three times that of Europe.

[5]The world population will continue to grow after 2050. Long-range population projections of the United Nations indicate a population growth well into the twenty-second century.

World Population Growth, from Year 0 to 2050

Year	Population (in billions)	Source
0	0.30	Durand
1000	0.31	Durand
1250	0.40	Durand
1500	0.50	Durand
1750	0.79	D & C
1800	0.98	D & C
1850	1.26	D & C
1900	1.65	D & C
1910	1.75	Interp.
1920	1.86	WPP63
1930	2.07	WPP63
1940	2.30	WPP63
1950	2.52	WPP98
1960	3.02	WPP98
1970	3.70	WPP98
1980	4.44	WPP98
1990	5.27	WPP98
1998	5.90	WPP98
2000	6.06	WPP98
2010	6.79	WPP98
2020	7.50	WPP98
2030	8.11	WPP98
2040	8.58	WPP98
2050	8.91	WPP98

Population for World and Major Areas, 1750-2050

A. Population size (millions)

Major area	1750	1800	1850	1900	1950	1998	2050
World	791	978	1262	1650	2521	5901	8909
Africa	106	107	111	133	221	749	1766
Asia	502	635	809	947	1402	3585	5268
Europe	163	203	276	408	547	729	628
Latin America/ Caribbean	16	24	38	74	167	504	809
Northern America	2	7	26	82	172	305	392
Oceania	2	2	2	6	13	30	46

B. Percentage Distribution

Major Area	1750	1800	1850	1900	1950	1998	2050
World	100	100	100	100	100	100	100
Africa	13.4	10.9	8.8	8.1	8.8	12.7	19.8
Asia	63.5	64.9	64.1	57.4	55.6	60.8	59.1
Europe	20.6	20.8	21.9	24.7	21.7	12.4	7.0
Latin America/ Caribbean	2.0	2.5	3.0	4.5	6.6	8.5	9.1
Northern America	0.3	0.7	2.1	5.0	6.8	5.2	4.4
Oceania	0.3	0.2	0.2	0.4	0.5	0.5	0.5

Sources: United Nations, 1973. *The Determinants and Consequences of Population Trends, Vol.1* (United Nations, New York).

Sources: *Durand*—J.D. Durand, 1974. *Historical Estimates of World Population: An Evaluation* (University of Pennsylvania, Population Studies Center, Philadelphia), mimeo.

D & C— United Nations, 1973. *The Determinants and Consequences of Population Trends, Vol.1* (United Nations, New York).

WPP63—United Nations, 1966. *World Population Prospects as Assessed in 1963* (United Nations, New York).

WPP98—United Nations, *World Population Prospects: The 1998 Revision* (United Nations, New York).

Discussion Questions

1. To what does the article attribute the recent rapid growth of the world population starting in 1950?

2. How long did it take for the world's population to double from 2 billion to 4 billion? From 4 billion to 8 billion? Why is this trend significant?

3. Who was Robert Malthus? Where did you find this information? What did he say that relates to population increases like those shown in "World Population Milestones"?

4. This article says that in 1900 the population of Europe was three times that of Africa but that in 2050 the population of Africa will be nearly three times that of Europe. Why? What impact might this have on the world in the 21st century? Do you think this will have any significance to us in the United States?

FROM **WORLD POPULATION PROSPECTS:** **THE 2006 REVISION**
UNITED NATIONS, DEPARTMENT OF ECONOMIC AND SOCIAL AFFAIRS, POPULATION DIVISION

*The **United Nations** officially came into existence in October of 1945 at the conclusion of World War II. Among its objectives, the UN works to promote human rights, protect the environment, fight disease, reduce poverty and promote economic development, especially in the less-developed regions of the world.*

[1]The 2006 Revision is the twentieth round of official United Nations population estimates and projections prepared by the Population Division of the Department of Economic and Social Affairs of the United Nations Secretariat. These estimates and projections are used throughout the United Nations system as the basis for activities requiring population information.

[2]According to the 2006 Revision, the world population will likely increase by 2.5 billion over the next 43 years, passing from the current 6.7 billion to 9.2 billion in 2050. This increase is equivalent to the overall number of people in the world in 1950, and it will be absorbed mostly by the less-developed regions,[a] whose population is projected to rise from 5.4 billion in 2007 to 7.9 billion in 2050 (Table 1). In contrast, the population of the more-developed regions[b] is expected to remain largely unchanged at 1.2 billion and would have declined were it not for the projected net migration from developing to developed countries, which is expected to average 2.3 million persons per year after 2010.

TABLE 1: PROJECTED POPULATION CHANGE BY REGION 2005-2050 (in millions)

Region	2005	2010	2015	2020	2025	2030	2035	2040	2045	2050
World	6 514	6 906	7 295	7 667	8 010	8 317	8 587	8 823	9 025	9 191
Africa	922	1 032	1 149	1 270	1 393	1 518	1 642	1 765	1 884	1 997
Asia	3 938	4 166	4 389	4 596	4 778	4 930	5 051	5 147	5 219	5 265
Europe	731	730	727	722	715	706	697	687	676	664
Latin America and Caribbean	557	593	627	659	688	712	733	749	761	769
Northern America	332	348	364	379	392	405	416	427	436	445

[a]The less-developed regions: all regions of Africa, Asia (excluding Japan), Latin America and the Caribbean plus Melanesia, Micronesia and Polynesia.

[b]The more-developed regions: all regions of Europe plus Northern America, Australia/New Zealand and Japan.

³The 2006 Revision confirms the diversity of demographic dynamics among the different world regions. While the population at the global level is on track to surpass 9 billion by 2050 and hence continues to increase, that of the more-developed regions is hardly changing and will age markedly. Between 2005 and 2050, half of the increase in the world population will be accounted for by a rise in the population aged 60 years or over, whereas the number of children (persons under age 15) will decline slightly. As already noted, virtually all population growth is occurring in the less-developed regions and especially in the group of the 50 least-developed countries, many of which still have relatively youthful populations that are expected to age only moderately over the foreseeable future. Among the rest of the developing countries, rapid population aging is expected.

⁴Underlying these varied patterns of growth and changes in the age structure are distinct trends in fertility[c] and mortality. Below-replacement fertility[d] prevails in the more-developed regions and is expected to continue to 2050. Fertility is still high in most of the least-developed countries and, although it is expected to decline, it will remain higher than in the rest of the world. In the rest of the developing countries, fertility has declined markedly since the late 1960s and is expected to reach below-replacement levels by 2050 in the major-

TABLE 2: TRENDS IN FERTILITY BY REGION, 1975-2050

Years	Africa	Asia	Europe	Latin America And Caribbean	Northern America
1975-1980	6.61	4.19	1.97	4.48	1.78
1980-1985	6.45	3.67	1.89	3.92	1.81
1985-1990	6.13	3.40	1.83	3.41	1.89
1990-1995	5.68	2.97	1.57	3.03	1.99
1995-2000	5.28	2.67	1.40	2.73	1.95
2000-2005	4.98	2.47	1.41	2.52	1.99
2005-2010	4.67	2.34	1.45	2.37	2.00
2010-2015	4.32	2.24	1.48	2.23	1.97
2015-2020	3.95	2.16	1.52	2.12	1.91
2020-2025	3.61	2.08	1.56	2.04	1.85
2025-2030	3.30	2.01	1.61	1.97	1.83
2030-2035	3.04	1.95	1.65	1.92	1.84
2035-2040	2.81	1.93	1.69	1.89	1.84
2040-2045	2.62	1.91	1.73	1.87	1.85
2045-2050	2.46	1.90	1.76	1.86	1.85

[c]Fertility: the average number of live births produced by the women of a defined group (e.g., of a particular country or region) expressed as the number of children per woman

[d]Below-replacement fertility: live births below 2.1 children per woman, the number commonly used to indicate replacement of mother and father in a population.

ity of those countries (Table 2). Mortality[e] in the established market economies of the developed world is low and continues to decline, but it has been stagnant or even increasing in a number of countries with economies in transition, largely as a result of deteriorating social and economic conditions and, in some cases, because of the spread of HIV. Mortality is also decreasing in the majority of developing countries, but in those highly affected by the HIV/AIDS epidemic, mortality has been increasing.

[5]The HIV/AIDS epidemic continues to expand. The number of countries with a significant number of infected people according to the 2006 Revision is 62, up from 60 in the 2004 Revision and 53 in the 2002 Revision. Although HIV prevalence in some countries has been revised downward since 2004 on the basis of newly available nationally representative data, the toll of the disease continues to be high and is expected to remain so, despite projected reductions in the prevalence of HIV infection. In the 2006 Revision, the 62 countries considered to be highly affected by the HIV/AIDS epidemic include 40 located in Africa (Table 3). In projecting the effect of the disease, it is assumed that 31 of the most affected countries will manage to provide by 2015 antiretroviral treatment to 70 per cent or more of the persons who have developed full-blown AIDS.

TABLE 3: NUMBER OF AIDS CASES AS A PERCENTAGE OF POPULATION IN HARDEST-HIT COUNTRIES

Country	Percent of Population with AIDS	Country	Percent of Population with AIDS
Swaziland	26.1 %	South Africa	19.4 %
Zimbabwe	24.5 %	Zambia	16.1 %
Botswana	23.9 %	Malawi	15 %
Lesotho	21.6 %	Kenya	12.9 %
Namimbia	21.3 %	Central African Republic	11.8 %

[6]In the rest of the affected countries, treatment levels are expected to be lower, reaching between 40 per cent and 50 per cent by 2015. It is further assumed that persons receiving treatment survive, on average, 17.5 years instead of the 10 years expected in the absence of treatment. Mainly as a result of these assumptions and owing to the downward revision of the prevalence of HIV infection in countries where nationally representative data on the epidemic have become available, an estimated 32 million fewer deaths are projected to occur during 2005-2020 in the 62 countries most affected by the epidemic according to the 2006 Revision than those projected in the 2004 Revision. These changes

---

[e]Mortality: the number of deaths in a period of time (e.g., one year) expressed as a number per unit of population (typically per 1000 or 100,000 people)

also contribute to make the population projected to 2050 larger according to the 2006 Revision than according to the 2004 Revision (9.2 billion versus 9.1 billion).

[7]Fertility continues to decline in developing countries. According to the 2006 Revision, fertility in the less-developed countries as a whole is expected to drop from 2.75 children per woman in 2005-2010 to 2.05 children per woman in 2045-2050. The reduction expected in the group of 50 least-developed countries is even sharper: from 4.63 children per woman in 2005-2010 to 2.50 children per woman 2045-2050. To achieve such reductions, it is essential that access to family planning expand in the poorest countries of the world. The urgency of realizing the reductions of fertility projected is brought into focus by considering that, if fertility were to remain constant at the levels estimated for 2000-2005, the population of the less-developed regions would increase to 10.6 billion instead of the 7.9 billion projected by assuming that fertility declines. That is, without further reductions of fertility, the world population could increase by twice as many people as those who were alive in 1950.

[8]Other key findings resulting from the comprehensive review of past worldwide demographic trends and future prospects presented in the 2006 Revision are summarized below:

1. In July 2007 the world population will reach 6.7 billion, 547 million more than in 2000 or a gain of 78 million persons annually. Assuming that fertility levels continue to decline, the world population is expected to reach 9.2 billion in 2050 and to be increasing by about 30 million persons annually at that time, according to the medium variant.

2. Because of its low and declining rate of population growth, the population of developed countries as a whole is expected to remain virtually unchanged between 2007 and 2050, at about 1.2 billion, according to the medium variant. In contrast, the population of the 50 least developed countries will likely more than double, passing from 0.8 billion in 2007 to 1.7 billion in 2050. Growth in the rest of the developing world is also projected to be robust, though less rapid, with its population rising from 4.6 billion to 6.2 billion between 2007 and 2050 according to the medium variant.

3. Population growth remains concentrated in the populous countries. During 2005-2050, eight countries are expected to account for half of the world's projected population increase: India, Nigeria, Pakistan, the Democratic Republic of the Congo, Ethiopia, the United States of America, Bangladesh and China, listed according to the size of their contribution to global population growth.

4. Life expectancy remains low on average in the least developed countries, at just 55 years, and although it is projected to reach 67 years in 2045-2050, achieving such an increase is contingent on reducing the spread of HIV and combating successfully other infectious diseases. Similar challenges must be confronted if the projected increase of life expectancy in the rest of the developing countries, from under 68 years today to 76 years by mid-century, is to be achieved. Tables 4 and 5 illustrate the contrast in current life expectancies in a less-developed region, sub-Saharan Africa, vs a more developed region, Northern America.

TABLE 4: LIFE EXPECTANCIES SUB-SAHARAN AFRICA 2000-2050

Period	Both Sexes Combined	Male	Female
2000-2005	48.8	47.6	49.0
2005-2010	50.0	49.0	51.0
2010-2015	51.8	50.9	52.9
2015-2020	53.8	52.8	54.8
2020-2025	55.7	54.6	56.8
2025-2030	57.6	56.3	58.3
2030-2035	59.4	58.1	60.7
2035-2040	61.1	59.7	62.5
2040-2045	62.8	61.4	64.2
2045-2050	64.5	62.9	66.1

TABLE 5: LIFE EXPECTANCIES NORTHERN AMERICA 2000-2050

Period	Both Sexes Combined	Male	Female
2000-2005	77.6	74.9	80.3
2005-2010	78.5	75.9	81.0
2010-2015	79.1	76.5	81.7
2015-2020	79.7	77.1	82.3
2020-2025	80.3	77.7	82.9
2025-2030	80.9	78.2	83.5
2030-2035	81.5	78.8	84.1
2035-2040	82,1	79.4	84.7
2040-2045	82.7	80.0	85.3
2045-2050	83.3	80.7	85.9

5. Among the more developed regions, Eastern Europe has the lowest life expectancy at birth and has had a declining life expectancy since the late 1980s.

In 2005-2010 life expectancy in the region, at 68.6 years, is lower than it was in 1960-1965 (69.3 years). The Russian Federation and Ukraine have experienced serious increases in mortality, partly because of the spread of HIV.

6. Despite the advances made in treating people infected with HIV and in controlling the spread of the epidemic, its impact in terms of mortality and slower population growth continues to be evident in many countries. In Southern Africa, the region with the highest prevalence of the disease, life expectancy has fallen from 62 years in 1990-1995 to 49 years in 2005-2010 and is not expected to regain the level it had in the early 1990s before 2045. As a consequence, the growth rate of the population in the region has plummeted, passing from 2.5 per cent annually in 1990-1995 to 0.6 per cent annually in 2005-2010 and is expected to continue declining for the foreseeable future.

7. The contribution of international migration to population growth in the more developed regions has increased in significance as fertility declines. During 2005-2050, the net number of international migrants to more developed regions is projected to be 103 million, a figure that counterbalances the excess of deaths over births (74 million) projected over the period.

8. In 2005-2010, the contribution of net migration was higher than the contribution of natural increase (births minus deaths) to population growth in eight countries or areas, namely, Belgium, Canada, Hong Kong (China SAR), Luxembourg, Singapore, Spain, Sweden and Switzerland. In a further eight countries or areas, net migration counterbalanced the excess of deaths over births. These countries or areas are Austria, Bosnia and Herzegovina, the Channel Islands, Greece, Italy, Portugal, Slovakia and Slovenia.

9. In terms of annual averages during 2005-2050, the major net receivers of international migrants are projected to be the United States (1.1 million annually), Canada (200,000), Germany (150,000), Italy (139,000), the United Kingdom (130,000), Spain (123,000) and Australia (100,000). The countries with the highest levels of net emigration are projected to be China (-329,000 annually), Mexico (-306,000), India (-241,000), the Philippines (-180,000), Pakistan (-167,000) and Indonesia (-164,000).

10. Under-five mortality, expressed as the probability of dying between birth and the exact age of five, is an important indicator of development and the well-being of children. In 1950-1955, almost a quarter (236 deaths per 1,000 births) of all children born worldwide did not reach their fifth birthday. By 2005-2010, this rate had fallen to 74 deaths per 1,000 births (Table 6). Al-

though child mortality has fallen in all major areas, sub-Saharan Africa has lagged behind in achieving lower levels of child mortality. In the 1950s, sub-Saharan Africa and South-Central Asia had similarly high levels of child mortality and both experienced significant reductions until the 1980s but thereafter, the pace of decline in child mortality in sub-Saharan Africa slowed down. As a result, by 2005-2010, under-five mortality had reached 82 deaths per 1,000 births in South-Central Asia, but it was still a high 155 deaths per 1,000 births in sub-Saharan Africa.

TABLE 6 UNDER-FIVE MORTALITY (per 1,000 live births) BY SELECTED COUNTRIES, 2000-2050

Country Or Area	2000-2005	2005- 2010	2010- 2015	2015- 2020	2020- 2025	2045 2050
World	80.3	73.7	66.7	60.3	54.8	31.9
Afghanistan	252.0	235.4	219.9	203.8	187.4	106.9
Angola	245.9	230.8	213.1	195.0	178.2	102.1
Argentina	17.4	15.5	13.8	12.4	11.2	7.0
Australia	6.0	5.6	5.2	5.1	4.5	3.2
Bangladesh	83.1	69.3	55.6	44.3	35.7	14.9
Canada	6.2	5.9	5.6	5.3	5.1	4.2
China	31.9	29.4	26.1	23.2	20.6	12.3
Cuba	7.7	6.5	5.7	5.0	4.7	2.8
Haiti	82.4	71.5	63.6	61.4	59.2	30.2
India	89.9	78.6	68.6	60.1	53.0	29.7
Iran	43.6	35.5	29.0	23.9	20.2	10.9
Iraq	124.1	105.4	68.5	48.3	36.7	15.7
Italy	6.3	6.1	5.8	5.6	5.3	4.3
Jamaica	18.9	17.2	16.3	15.4	14.6	10.9
Liberia	222.2	205.2	186.4	168.3	151.5	79.1
Mexico	24.7	20.2	16.8	14.2	12.1	7.1
Norway	4.9	4.4	4.3	4.2	4.0	3.2
Pakistan	108.5	95.2	83.7	74.0	65.8	35.5
Puerto Rico	9.7	8.7	7.9	7.3	7.0	5.6
United States	8.4	7.8	7.4	7.0	6.6	5.1

Vocabulary

[3]diversity	[4]stagnant	[8]1 variant	[8]6 plummeted
[3]demographic	[5]prevalence	[8]2 robust	[8]10 sub-Saharan
[3]hence	[5]antiretroviral	[8]4 contingent	

Discussion Questions

1. What was the total population of the world in 1950? How many people will be added to the world population between now and 2050?

2. According to Table 1 which region of the world will have the largest share of the world's population in 2050? Using your research skills find out and identify the two largest countries in this region.

3. In which regions of the world will the aging population (over 60 years of age) increase markedly over the next 40 years? In which regions will the population remain relatively young? What do you think this will mean to the social fabric and economies of these regions?

4. What is the definition of "below-replacement fertility"?

5. Is Northern America currently above or below replacement fertility? By how much?

6. Looking at the fertility projections for Northern America in Table 2, what would you expect to happen to the population in this region between now and 2050?

7. Looking at the population projections in Table 1, what will happen to the population of Northern America between now and 2050?

8. How do you explain the apparent contradiction in the answers to questions 6 and 7 above?

9. Will the greater population growth between 2010 and 2050 occur in the "more-developed" or "less-developed" regions of the world? Why? (Hint: Look at Table 2.)

10. What is the current difference in life expectancies (both sexes combined) between Sub-Saharan Africa and Northern America? What factors discussed in the text of this document help explain this difference?

11. Even though Eastern Europe is considered a part of a "more-developed" region, its life expectancy rate is dropping. Why?

12. Which country indicated in Table 6 currently has the highest mortality rate for children under five years of age? What **percent** of this country's children die before age five? Why do you think this is the case?

13. What percent of children under five die annually in the United States?

14. Which countries have a better record than the United States in under-five mortality?

15. Since the United States is considered to be a world leader in health care, what factors do you think cause those other countries to have a lower under-five mortality rate?

THE YELLOW WALLPAPER
CHARLOTTE PERKINS GILMAN

Charlotte Perkins Gilman (1860-1935) was one of the earliest feminist writers. Her prolific writings supported her views of women's rights and socialism. Among her numerous works are In This Our World *(1893),* Women and Economics *(1898),* The Home: Its Work and Influence *(1903), and* Herland *(1914). In 1900, she married George Gilman, her first cousin, and, in 1935, after battling cancer for several years, she took her own life.*

[1] It is very seldom that mere ordinary people like John and myself secure ancestral halls for the summer.

[2] A colonial mansion, a hereditary estate, I would say a haunted house and reach the height of romantic felicity—but that would be asking too much of fate!

[3] Still I will proudly declare that there is something queer about it. Else, why should it be let so cheaply? And why has it stood so long untenanted?

[4] John laughs at me, of course, but one expects that in marriage. John is practical in the extreme. He has no patience with faith, an intense horror of superstition, and he scoffs openly at any talk of things not to be felt and seen and put down in figures. John is a physician, and perhaps—(I would not say it to a living soul, of course, but this is dead paper and a great relief to my mind)—perhaps that is one reason I do not get well faster.

[5] You see he does not believe I am sick!

[6] And what can one do?

[7] If a physician of high standing, and one's own husband, assures friends and relatives that there is really nothing the matter with one but temporary nervous depression—a slight hysterical tendency—what is one to do?

[8] My brother is also a physician, and also of high standing, and he says the same thing.

[9] So I take phosphates or phosphites—whichever it is, and tonics, and journeys, and air, and exercise, and am absolutely forbidden to "work" until I am well again.

[10] Personally, I disagree with their ideas.

[11] Personally, I believe that congenial work, with excitement and change, would do me good.

[12] But what is one to do?

***

[13]I did write for a while in spite of them; but it does exhaust me a good deal—having to be so sly about it, or else meet with heavy opposition.

[14]I sometimes fancy that in my condition if I had less opposition and more society and stimulus—but John says the very worst thing I can do is to think about my condition, and I confess it always makes me feel bad.

[15]So I will let it alone and talk about the house.

[16]The most beautiful place! It is quite alone, standing well back from the road, quite three miles from the village. It makes me think of English places that you read about, for there are hedges and walls and gates that lock and lots of separate little houses for the gardeners and people. There is a delicious garden! I never saw such a garden—large and shady, full of box-bordered paths, and lined with long grape-covered arbors with seats under them.

[17]There were greenhouses, too, but they are all broken now.

[18]There was some legal trouble, I believe, something about the heirs and coheirs; anyhow, the place has been empty for years.

[19]That spoils my ghostliness, I am afraid, but don't care—there is something strange about the house—I can feel it.

[20]I even said so to John one moonlit evening, but he said what I felt was a draught and shut the window.

[21]I get unreasonably angry with John sometimes. I'm sure I never used to be so sensitive. I think it is due to this nervous condition.

[22]But John says if I feel so, I shall neglect proper self-control; so I take pains to control myself—before him, at least, and that makes me very tired.

[23]I don't like our room a bit. I wanted one downstairs that opened on the piazza and had roses all over the window, and such pretty old-fashioned chintz hangings! but John would not hear of it.

[24]He said there was only one window and not room for two beds, and no near room for him if he took another.

[25]He is very careful and loving and hardly lets me stir without special direction.

[26]I have a scheduled prescription for each hour in the day; he takes all care from me, and so I feel basely ungrateful not to value it more.

[27]He said we came here solely on my account, that I was to have perfect rest and all the air I could get. "Your exercise depends on your strength, my dear," said he, "and your food somewhat on your appetite; but air you can absorb all the time." So we took the nursery at the top of the house.

[28]It is a big, airy room, the whole floor nearly, with windows that look all ways, and air and sunshine galore. It was nursery first and then playroom and gymnasium, I should judge; for the windows are barred for little children, and there are rings and things in the walls.

[29]The paint and paper look as if a boys' school had used it. It is stripped off—the paper in great patches all around the head of my bed, about as far as I

can reach, and in a great place on the other side of the room low down. I never saw a worse paper in my life.

[30]One of those sprawling, flamboyant patterns committing every artistic sin.

[31]It is dull enough to confuse the eye in following, pronounced enough to constantly irritate and provoke study, and when you follow the lame uncertain curves for a little distance they suddenly commit suicide—plunge off at outrageous angles, destroy themselves in unheard of contradictions.

[32]The color is repellent, almost revolting—a smouldering unclean yellow, strangely faded by the slow-turning sunlight.

[33]It is a dull yet lurid orange in some places, a sickly sulphur tint in others.

[34]No wonder the children hated it! I should hate it myself if I had to live in this room long.

[35]There comes John, and I must put this away—he hates to have me write a word.

* * *

[36]We have been here two weeks, and I haven't felt like writing before, since that first day.

[37]I am sitting by the window now, up in this atrocious nursery, and there is nothing to hinder my writing as much as I please, save lack of strength.

[38]John is away all day, and even some nights when his cases are serious.

[39]I am glad my case is not serious!

[40]But these nervous troubles are dreadfully depressing.

[41]John does not know how much I really suffer. He knows there is no reason to suffer, and that satisfies him.

[42]Of course it is only nervousness. It does weigh on me so not to do my duty in any way!

[43]I meant to be such a help to John, such a real rest and comfort, and here I am a comparative burden already!

[44]Nobody would believe what an effort it is to do what little I am able,—to dress and entertain, and order things.

[45]It is fortunate Mary is so good with the baby. Such a dear baby!

[46]And yet I cannot be with him, it makes me so nervous.

[47]I suppose John never was nervous in his life. He laughs at me so about this wallpaper!

[48]At first he meant to repaper the room, but afterwards he said that I was letting it get the better of me, and that nothing was worse for a nervous patient than to give way to such fancies.

[49]He said that after the wallpaper was changed it would be the heavy bedstead, and then the barred windows, and then that gate at the head of the stairs,

and so on.

[50]"You know the place is doing you good," he said, "and really, dear, I don't care to renovate the house just for a three months' rental."

[51]"Then do let us go downstairs," I said, "there are such pretty rooms there."

[52]Then he took me in his arms and called me a blessed little goose, and said he would go down to the cellar, if I wished, and have it whitewashed into the bargain.

[53]But he is right enough about the beds and windows and things.

[54]It is as airy and comfortable a room as any one need wish, and, of course, I would not be so silly as to make him uncomfortable just for a whim.

[55]I'm really getting quite fond of the big room, all but that horrid paper.

[56]Out of one window I can see the garden, those mysterious deep-shaded arbors, the riotous old-fashioned flowers, and bushes and gnarly trees.

[57]Out of another I get a lovely view of the bay and a little private wharf belonging to the estate. There is a beautiful shaded lane that runs down there from the house. I always fancy I see people walking in these numerous paths and arbors, but John has cautioned me not to give way to fancy in the least. He says that with my imaginative power and habit of story-making, a nervous weakness like mine is sure to lead to all manner of excited fancies, and that I ought to use my will and good sense to check the tendency. So I try.

[58]I think sometimes that if I were only well enough to write a little it would relieve the press of ideas and rest me.

[59]But I find I get pretty tired when I try.

[60]It is so discouraging not to have any advice and companionship about my work. When I get really well, John says we will ask Cousin Henry and Julia down for a long visit; but he says he would as soon put fireworks in my pillow-case as to let me have those stimulating people about now.

[61]I wish I could get well faster.

[62]But I must not think about that. This paper looks to me as if it knew what a vicious influence it had! There is a recurrent spot where the pattern lolls like a broken neck and two bulbous eyes stare at me upside down.

[63]I get positively angry with the impertinence of it and the everlasting-ness. Up and down and sideways they crawl, and those absurd, unblinking eyes are everywhere. There is one place where two breadths didn't match, and the eyes go all up and down the line, one a little higher than the other.

[64]I never saw so much expression in an inanimate thing before, and we all know how much expression they have! I used to lie awake as a child and get more entertainment and terror out of blank walls and plain furniture than most children could find in a toy-store.

[65]I remember what a kindly wink the knobs of our big old bureau used to have, and there was one chair that always seemed like a strong friend.

[66]I used to feel that if any of the other things looked too fierce I could always hop into that chair and be safe.

[67]The furniture in this room is no worse than inharmonious, however, for we had to bring it all from downstairs. I suppose when this was used as a playroom they had to take the nursery things out, and no wonder! I never saw such ravages as the children have made here.

[68]The wallpaper, as I said before, is torn off in spots, and it sticketh closer than a brother—they have had perseverance as well as hatred.

[69]Then the floor is scratched and gouged and splintered, the plaster itself is dug out here and there, and this great heavy bed which is all we found in the room, looks as if it had been through the wars.

[70]But I don't mind it a bit—only the paper.

[71]There comes John's sister. Such a dear girl as she is and so careful of me! I must not let her find me writing.

[72]She is a perfect and enthusiastic housekeeper, and hopes for no better profession. I verily believe she thinks it is the writing which made me sick!

[73]But I can write when she is out and see her a long way off from these windows.

[74]There is one that commands the road, a lovely shaded winding road, and one that just looks off over the country. A lovely country, too, full of great elms and velvet meadows.

[75]This wallpaper has a kind of sub-pattern in a different shade, a particularly irritating one, for I can only see it in certain lights, and not clearly then.

[76]But in the places where it isn't faded and where the sun is just so—I can see a strange, provoking, formless sort of figure, that seems to skulk about behind that silly and conspicuous front design.

[77]There's sister on the stairs!

***

[78]Well, the Fourth of July is over! The people are all gone and I am tired out. John thought it might do me good to see a little company, so we just had mother and Nellie and the children down for a week.

[79]Of course I didn't do a thing. Jennie sees to everything now.

[80]But it tired me all the same.

[81]John says if I don't pick up faster he shall send me to Weir Mitchell in the fall.

[82]But I don't want to go there at all. I had a friend who was in his hands once, and she says he is just like John and my brother, only more so!

[83]Besides, it is such an undertaking to go so far.

[84]I don't feel as if it was worthwhile to turn my hand over for anything, and I'm getting dreadfully fretful and querulous.

[85]I cry at nothing, and cry most of the time.

[86]Of course I don't when John is here, or anybody else, but when I am alone.

[87]And I am alone a good deal just now. John is kept in town very often by serious cases, and Jennie is good and lets me alone when I want her to.

[88]So I walk a little in the garden or down that lovely lane, sit on the porch under the roses, and lie down up here a good deal.

[89]I'm getting really fond of the room in spite of the wallpaper. Perhaps because of the wallpaper.

[90]It dwells in my mind so!

[91]I lie here on this great immovable bed—it is nailed down, I believe—and follow that pattern about by the hour. It is as good as gymnastics, I assure you. I start, we'll say, at the bottom, down in the corner over there where it has not been touched, and I determine for the thousandth time that I will follow that pointless pattern to some sort of a conclusion.

[92]I know a little of the principle of design, and I know this thing was not arranged on any laws of radiation, or alternation, or repetition, or symmetry, or anything else that I ever heard of.

[93]It is repeated, of course, by the breadths, but not otherwise. Looked at in one way each breadth stands alone, the bloated curves and flourishes—a kind of "debased Romanesque" with delirium tremens—go waddling up and down in isolated columns of fatuity.

[94]But, on the other hand, they connect diagonally, and the sprawling outlines run off in great slanting waves of optic horror, like a lot of wallowing seaweeds in full chase. .

[95]The whole thing goes horizontally, too, at least it seems so, and I exhaust myself in trying to distinguish the order of its going in that direction. They have used a horizontal breadth for a frieze, and that adds wonderfully to the confusion.

[96]There is one end of the room where it is almost intact, and there, when the crosslights fade and the low sun shines directly upon it, I can almost fancy radiation after all,—the interminable grotesques seem to form around a common centre and rush off in headlong plunges of equal distraction.

[97]It makes me tired to follow it. I will take a nap I guess.

* * *

[98]I don't know why I should write this.

[99]I don't want to.

[100]I don't feel able. And I know John would think it absurd. But I must say what I feel and think in some way—it is such a relief!

[101]But the effort is getting to be greater than the relief.

[102]Half the time now I am awfully lazy and lie down ever so much.

[103]John says I mustn't lose my strength and has me take cod liver oil and lots of tonics and things, to say nothing of ale and wine and rare meat.

[104]Dear John! He loves me very dearly and hates to have me sick. I tried to have a real earnest, reasonable talk with him the other day and tell him how I wish he would let me go and make a visit to Cousin Henry and Julia.

[105]But he said I wasn't able to go, nor able to stand it after I got there; and I did not make out a very good case for myself, for I was crying before I had finished.

[106]It is getting to be a great effort for me to think straight. Just this nervous weakness I suppose.

[107]And dear John gathered me up in his arms and just carried me upstairs and laid me on the bed, and sat by me and read to me till it tired my head.

[108]He said I was his darling and his comfort and all he had, and that I must take care of myself for his sake, and keep well.

[109]He says no one but myself can help me out of it, that I must use my will and self-control and not let any silly fancies run away with me.

[110]There's one comfort—the baby is well and happy, and does not have to occupy this nursery with the horrid wallpaper.

[111]If we had not used it, that blessed child would have! What a fortunate escape! Why, I wouldn't have a child of mine, an impressionable little thing, live in such a room for worlds.

[112]I never thought of it before, but it is lucky that John kept me here after all, for I can stand it so much easier than a baby, you see.

[113]Of course I never mention it to them any more—I am too wise,—but I keep watch of it all the same.

[114]There are things in that paper that nobody knows but me, or ever will.

[115]Behind that outside pattern the dim shapes get clearer every day.

[116]It is always the same shape, only very numerous.

[117]And it is like a woman stooping down and creeping about behind that pattern. I don't like it a bit. I wonder—I begin to think—I wish John would take me away from here!

* * *

[118]It is so hard to talk with John about my case because he is so wise, and because he loves me so.

[119]But I tried it last night.

[120]It was moonlight. The moon shines in all around just as the sun does.

[121]I hate to see it sometimes, it creeps so slowly, and always comes in by one window or another.

[122]John was asleep and I hated to waken him, so I kept still and watched

the moonlight on that undulating wallpaper till I felt creepy.

[123]The faint figure behind seemed to shake the pattern, just as if she wanted to get out.

[124]I got up softly and went to feel and see if the paper did move, and when I came back John was awake.

[125]"What is it, little girl?" he said. "Don't go walking about like that— you'll get cold."

[126]I thought it was a good time to talk, so I told him that I really was not gaining here, and that I wished he would take me away.

[127]"Why darling!" said he, "our lease will be up in three weeks, and I can't see how to leave before.

[128]"The repairs are not done at home, and I cannot possibly leave town just now. Of course, if you were in any danger, I could and would, but you really are better, dear, whether you can see it or not. I am a doctor, dear, and I know. You are gaining flesh and color, your appetite is better, I feel really much easier about you."

[129]"I don't weigh a bit more," said I, "nor as much; and my appetite may be better in the evening when you are here, but it is worse in the morning when you are away!"

[130]"Bless her little heart!" said he with a big hug, "she shall be as sick as she pleases! But now let's improve the shining hours by going to sleep and talk about it in the morning!"

[131]"And you won't go away?" I asked gloomily.

[132]"Why, how can I, dear? It is only three weeks more and then we will take a nice little trip of a few days while Jennie is getting the house ready. Really, dear, you are better!"

[133]"Better in body perhaps—" I began, and stopped short, for he sat up straight and looked at me with such a stern, reproachful look that I could not say another word.

[134]"My darling," said he, "I beg of you, for my sake and for our child's sake, as well as for your own, that you will never for one instant let that idea enter your mind! There is nothing so dangerous, so fascinating, to a temperament like yours. It is a false and foolish fancy. Can you not trust me as a physician when I tell you so?"

[135]So of course I said no more on that score, and we went to sleep before long. He thought I was asleep first, but I wasn't, and lay there for hours trying to decide whether that front pattern and the back pattern really did move together or separately.

* * *

[136]On a pattern like this, by daylight, there is a lack of sequence, a defi-

ance of law, that is a constant irritant to a normal mind.

[137]The color is hideous enough, and unreliable enough, and infuriating enough, but the pattern is torturing.

[138]You think you have mastered it, but just as you get well underway in following, it turns a back somersault and there you are. It slaps you in the face, knocks you down, and tramples upon you. It is like a bad dream.

[139]The outside pattern is a florid arabesque, reminding one of a fungus. If you can imagine a toadstool in joints, an interminable string of toadstools, budding and sprouting in endless convolutions—why, that is something like it.

[140]That is, sometimes!

[141]There is one marked peculiarity about this paper, a thing nobody seems to notice but me, and that is that it changes as the light changes.

[142]When the sun shoots in through the east window—I always watch for that first long, straight ray—it changes so quickly that I never can quite believe it.

[143]That is why I watch it always.

[144]By moonlight—the moon shines in all night when there is a moon—I wouldn't know it was the same paper.

[145]At night in any kind of light, in twilight, candle light, lamplight, and worst of all by moonlight, it becomes bars! The outside pattern I mean, and the woman behind it is as plain as can be.

[146]I didn't realize for a long time what the thing was that showed behind, that dim sub-pattern, but now I am quite sure it is a woman.

[147]By daylight she is subdued, quiet. I fancy it is the pattern that keeps her so still. It is so puzzling. It keeps me quiet by the hour.

[148]I lie down ever so much now. John says it is good for me, and to sleep all I can.

[149]Indeed he started the habit by making me lie down for an hour after each meal.

[150]It is a very bad habit I am convinced, for you see I don't sleep.

[151]And that cultivates deceit, for I don't tell them I'm awake—O no!

[152]The fact is I am getting a little afraid of John.

[153]He seems very queer sometimes, and even Jennie has an inexplicable look.

[154]It strikes me occasionally, just as a scientific hypothesis,—that perhaps it is the paper!

[155]I have watched John when he did not know I was looking, and come into the room suddenly on the most innocent excuses, and I've caught him several times looking at the paper! And Jennie too. I caught Jennie with her hand on it once.

[156]She didn't know I was in the room, and when I asked her in a quiet, a very quiet voice, with the most restrained manner possible, what she was do-ing with the paper—she turned around as if she had been caught stealing, and

looked quite angry—asked me why I should frighten her so!

[157]Then she said that the paper stained everything it touched, that she had found yellow smooches on all my clothes and John's, and she wished we would be more careful!

[158]Did not that sound innocent? But I know she was studying that pattern, and I am determined that nobody shall find it out but me!

* * *

[159]Life is very much more exciting now than it used to be. You see I have something more to expect, to look forward to, to watch. I really do eat better and am more quiet than I was.

[160]John is so pleased to see me improve! He laughed a little the other day, and said I seemed to be flourishing in spite of my wallpaper.

[161]I turned it off with a laugh. I had no intention of telling him it was because of the wallpaper—he would make fun of me. He might even want to take me away.

[162]I don't want to leave now until I have found it out. There is a week more, and I think that will be enough.

* * *

[163]I'm feeling ever so much better! I don't sleep much at night, for it is so interesting to watch developments; but I sleep a good deal in the daytime.

[164]In the daytime it is tiresome and perplexing.

[165]There are always new shoots on the fungus, and new shades of yellow all over it. I cannot keep count of them, though I have tried conscientiously.

[166]It is the strangest yellow, that wall-paper! It makes me think of all the yellow things I ever saw—not beautiful ones like buttercups, but old foul, bad yellow things.

[167]But there is something else about that paper—the smell! I noticed it the moment we came into the room, but with so much air and sun it was not bad. Now we have had a week of fog and rain, and whether the windows are open or not, the smell is here.

[168]It creeps all over the house.

[169]I find it hovering in the dining-room, skulking in the parlor, hiding in the hall, lying in wait for me on the stairs.

[170]It gets into my hair.

[171]Even when I go to ride, if I turn my head suddenly and surprise it— there is that smell!

[172]Such a peculiar odor, too! I have spent hours in trying to analyze it, to find what it smelled like.

¹⁷³It is not bad—at first, and very gentle, but quite the subtlest, most enduring odor I ever met.

¹⁷⁴In this damp weather it is awful. I wake up in the night and find it hanging over me.

¹⁷⁵It used to disturb me at first. I thought seriously of burning the house—to reach the smell.

¹⁷⁶But now I am used to it. The only thing I can think of that it is like is the color of the paper! A yellow smell.

¹⁷⁷There is a very funny mark on this wall, low down, near the mopboard. A streak that runs round the room. It goes behind every piece of furniture, except the bed, a long, straight, even smooch, as if it had been rubbed over and over.

¹⁷⁸I wonder how it was done and who did it, and what they did it for. Round and round and round—round and round and round—it makes me dizzy!

* * *

¹⁷⁹I really have discovered something at last.

¹⁸⁰Through watching so much at night, when it changes so, I have finally found out.

¹⁸¹The front pattern does move—and no wonder! The woman behind shakes it!

¹⁸²Sometimes I think there are a great many women behind, and sometimes only one, and she crawls around fast, and her crawling shakes it all over.

¹⁸³Then in the very bright spots she keeps still, and in the very shady spots she just takes hold of the bars and shakes them hard.

¹⁸⁴And she is all the time trying to climb through. But nobody could climb through that pattern—it strangles so; I think that is why it has so many heads.

¹⁸⁵They get through, and then the pattern strangles them off and turns them upside down, and makes their eyes white!

¹⁸⁶If those heads were covered or taken off it would not be half so bad.

* * *

¹⁸⁷I think that woman gets out in the daytime!

¹⁸⁸And I'll tell you why—privately—I've seen her!

¹⁸⁹I can see her out of every one of my windows!

¹⁹⁰It is the same woman, I know, for she is always creeping, and most women do not creep by daylight.

¹⁹¹I see her on that long road under the trees, creeping along, and when a

carriage comes she hides under the blackberry vines.

[192]I don't blame her a bit. It must be very humiliating to be caught creeping by daylight!

[193]I always lock the door when I creep by daylight. I can't do it at night, for I know John would suspect something at once.

[194]And John is so queer now, that I don't want to irritate him. I wish he would take another room! Besides, I don't want anybody to get that woman out at night but myself.

[195]I often wonder if I could see her out of all the windows at once.

[196]But, turn as fast as I can, I can only see out of one at one time.

[197]And though I always see her, she may be able to creep faster than I can turn!

[198]I have watched her sometimes away off in the open country, creeping as fast as a cloud shadow in a high wind.

* * *

[199]If only that top pattern could be gotten off from the under one! I mean to try it, little by little.

[200]I have found out another funny thing, but I shan't tell it this time! It does not do to trust people too much.

[201]There are only two more days to get this paper off, and I believe John is beginning to notice. I don't like the look in his eyes.

[202]And I heard him ask Jennie a lot of professional questions about me. She had a very good report to give.

[203]She said I slept a good deal in the daytime.

[204]John knows I don't sleep very well at night, for all I'm so quiet!

[205]He asked me all sorts of questions, too, and pretended to be very loving and kind.

[206]As if I couldn't see through him!

[207]Still, I don't wonder he acts so, sleeping under this paper for three months.

[208]It only interests me, but I feel sure John and Jennie are secretly affected by it.

* * *

[209]Hurrah! This is the last day, but it is enough. John is to stay in town overnight and won't be out until this evening.

[210]Jennie wanted to sleep with me—the sly thing! but I told her I should undoubtedly rest better for a night all alone.

²¹¹That was clever, for really I wasn't alone a bit! As soon as it was moonlight and that poor thing began to crawl and shake the pattern, I got up and ran to help her.

²¹²I pulled and she shook, I shook and she pulled, and before morning we had peeled off yards of that paper.

²¹³A strip about as high as my head and half around the room.

²¹⁴And then when the sun came and that awful pattern began to laugh at me, I declared I would finish it today!

²¹⁵We go away tomorrow, and they are moving all my furniture down again to leave things as they were before.

²¹⁶Jennie looked at the wall in amazement, but I told her merrily that I did it out of pure spite at the vicious thing.

²¹⁷She laughed and said she wouldn't mind doing it herself, but I must not get tired.

²¹⁸How she betrayed herself that time!

²¹⁹But I am here, and no person touches this paper but me,—not alive!

²²⁰She tried to get me out of the room—it was too patent! But I said it was so quiet and empty and clean now that I believed I would lie down again and sleep all I could; and not to wake me even for dinner—I would call when I woke.

²²¹So now she is gone, and the servants are gone, and the things are gone, and there is nothing left but that great bedstead nailed down, with the canvas mattress we found on it.

²²²We shall sleep downstairs tonight, and take the boat home tomorrow.

²²³I quite enjoy the room now that it is bare again.

²²⁴How those children did tear about here!

²²⁵This bedstead is fairly gnawed!

²²⁶But I must get to work.

²²⁷I have locked the door and thrown the key down into the front path.

²²⁸I don't want to go out, and I don't want to have anybody come in, till John comes.

²²⁹I want to astonish him.

²³⁰I've got a rope up here that even Jennie did not find. If that woman does get out and tries to get away, I can tie her!

²³¹But I forgot I could not reach far without anything to stand on!

²³²This bed will not move!

²³³I tried to lift and push it until I was lame, and then I got so angry I bit off a little piece at one corner—but it hurt my teeth.

²³⁴Then I peeled off all the paper I could reach standing on the floor. It sticks horribly and the pattern just enjoys it! All those strangled heads and bulbous eyes and waddling fungus growths just shriek with derision!

²³⁵I am getting angry enough to do something desperate. To jump out of

the window would be admirable exercise, but the bars are too strong even to try.

²³⁶Besides I wouldn't do it. Of course not. I know well enough that a step like that is improper and might be misconstrued.

²³⁷I don't like to look out of the windows even—there are so many of those creeping women, and they creep so fast.

²³⁸I wonder if they all come out of that wallpaper as I did?

²³⁹But I am securely fastened now by my well-hidden rope—you don't get me out in the road there!

²⁴⁰I suppose I shall have to get back behind the pattern when it comes night, and that is hard!

²⁴¹It is so pleasant to be out in this great room and creep around as I please!

²⁴²I don't want to go outside. I won't, even if Jennie asks me to.

²⁴³For outside you have to creep on the ground, and everything is green instead of yellow.

²⁴⁴But here I can creep smoothly on the floor, and my shoulder just fits in that long smooch around the wall, so I cannot lose my way.

²⁴⁵Why there's John at the door!

²⁴⁶It is no use, young man, you can't open it!

²⁴⁷How he does call and pound!

²⁴⁸Now he's crying for an axe.

²⁴⁹It would be a shame to break down that beautiful door!

²⁵⁰"John dear!" said I in the gentlest voice, "the key is down by the front steps, under a plantain leaf!"

²⁵¹That silenced him for a few moments.

²⁵²Then he said—very quietly indeed, "Open the door, my darling!"

²⁵³"I can't," said I. "The key is down by the front door under a plantain leaf!"

²⁵⁴And then I said it again, several times, that he had to go and see, and he got it of course, and came in. He stopped short by the door.

²⁵⁵"What is the matter?" he cried. "For God's sake, what are you doing!"

²⁵⁶I kept on creeping just the same, but I looked at him over my shoulder.

²⁵⁷"I've got out at last," said I, "in spite of you and Jane. And I've pulled off most of the paper, so you can't put me back!"

²⁵⁸Now why should that man have fainted? But he did, and right across my path by the wall, so that I had to creep over him every time!

Vocabulary

[2]felicity
[11]congenial
[16]arbors
[20]draught
[23]piazza
[23]chintz
[56]gnarly
[57]wharf
[57]fancy
[62]recurrent

[62]bulbous
[63]impertinence
[64]inanimate
[67]ravages
[68]perseverance
[72]verily
[76]skulk
[84]querulous
[93]debased

[93]Romanesque
[93]delirium tremens
[93]fatuity
[94]wallowing
[95]frieze
[122]undulating
[133]reproachful
[139]florid
[139]arabesque

[139]convolutions
[153]inexplicable
[154]hypothesis
[164]perplexing
[169]skulking
[220]patent
[234]derision
[236]misconstrued
[253]plantain

Discussion Questions

1. The narrator says, paragraph 4, "John laughs at me, of course, but one expects that in marriage." What does this tell the reader about her marriage? What does it tell you about how she perceives herself and how she perceives her role as John's wife?

2. What room does John choose for their bedroom? How is this symbolic of their relationship?

3. What role does the wallpaper play in the narrator's mental disintegration?

4. Who is the woman behind the yellow wallpaper, who looks out through its bars at the narrator as she sleeps? Why does she creep about the yard and garden at night?

5. Why is the narrator given no name? Why is the husband named John? Why is his sister named Jane?

6. Why does Gilman choose to use first-person point of view? How does the style of the story reflect the narrator's mental condition (e.g., the short paragraphs, the repetition)?

7. John is clearly not dealing with his wife's illness in the proper way. Do you think he is malicious toward her? Explain.

8. How does the narrator contribute to the lack of communication in her marriage, and thus to her own illness?

9. The ending of this story has been greatly debated. Do you think the ending is a point where the narrator has triumphed over her husband, the wallpaper, and society, or is the ending a point where the narrator has failed by being driven insane by the paper and not escaping from the room? Be sure to support your answer.

WHY I WROTE
"THE YELLOW WALLPAPER"
CHARLOTTE PERKINS GILMAN

This article first appeared in *The Forerunner* 1913.

[1]Many and many a reader has asked why I wrote "The Yellow Wallpaper." When the story first came out, in the *New England Magazine* about 1891, a Boston physician made protest in *The Transcript*. Such a story ought not to be written, he said; it was enough to drive anyone mad to read it.

[2]Another physician, in Kansas I think, wrote to say that it was the best description of incipient insanity he had ever seen, and—begging my pardon—had I been there?

[3]Now the story of the story is this:

[4]For many years I suffered from a severe and continuous nervous breakdown tending to melancholia—and beyond. During about the third year of this trouble, I went, in devout faith and some faint stir of hope, to a noted specialist in nervous diseases, the best known in the country. This wise man put me to bed and applied the rest cure, to which a still-good physique responded so promptly that he concluded there was nothing much the matter with me and sent me home with solemn advice to "live as domestic a life as far as possible," to "have but two hours' intellectual life a day," and "never to touch pen, brush, or pencil again" as long as I lived. This was in 1887.

[5]I went home and obeyed those directions for some three months and came so near the borderline of utter mental ruin that I could see over it.

[6]Then, using the remnants of intelligence that remained, and helped by a wise friend, I cast the noted specialist's advice to the winds and went to work again—work, the normal life of every human being; work, in which is joy and growth and service, without which one is a pauper and a parasite—ultimately recovering some measure of power.

[7]Being naturally moved to rejoicing by this narrow escape, I wrote "The Yellow Wallpaper," with its embellishments and additions, to carry out the ideal (I never had hallucinations or objections to my mural decorations) and sent a copy to the physician who so nearly drove me mad. He never acknowledged receiving it.

[8]The little book is valued by alienists[a] and as a good specimen of one

---

[a] An "alienist," at the time this was written in the late 1800's, referred to those who treated the mentally ill (a psychiatrist or psychologist today) who were believed to be "alienated" from reality. The archaic term was revived somewhat in 1994 by author Caleb Carr who wrote a best-selling mystery novel entitled *The Alienist*.

kind of literature. It has, to my knowledge, saved one woman from a similar fate—so terrifying her family that they let her out into normal activity and she recovered.

⁹But the best result is this. Many years later I was told that the great specialist had admitted to friends of his that he had altered his treatment of neurasthenia since reading "The Yellow Wallpaper."

¹⁰It was not intended to drive people crazy, but to save people from being driven crazy, and it worked.

Vocabulary

²incipient
⁴melancholia
⁴embellishments
⁹neurasthenia

Discussion Questions

1. What modern term is used for "melancholia" and how is it typically treated today?

2. Explain what Gilman is referring to when she uses the words "pauper" and "parasite" in paragraph 6.

3. What does Gilman mean by "embellishments and additions" in paragraph 7?

4. What comment does Gilman make about the medical science of her time in paragraph 10?

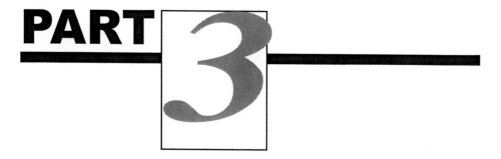

PART 3

GRAMMAR AND MECHANICS

PARTS OF SPEECH

PARTS OF SPEECH: The PARTS OF SPEECH are the basic building blocks of our language.

NOUNS: A NOUN is a word that names a person, place, thing, activity, condition, characteristic or idea. Nouns may be proper (Lucinda, Washington, Hudson) or common (woman, state, river).

- *Sharif* is the best *runner* on the *team*.

VERBS: A VERB is a word that indicates some kind of action or links words or word groups.

- Todd *drove* Samantha's car into a brick wall.
- Samantha and Todd *are* good friends.

ADJECTIVES: An ADJECTIVE modifies (limits or describes) a noun or pronoun and tells us certain things such as how many, what kind or which one:

- Alex saw *three baby* elephants at the circus.

ADVERBS: An ADVERB modifies a verb, adjective or another adverb and usually tells us how, when, where or why.

- James *quickly* dropped the cigarette when he saw his father.

PRONOUNS: A PRONOUN takes the place of a noun.

- *He* arrived earlier than expected.
- *They* were happy to see *her*.

CONJUNCTIONS: A CONJUNCTION joins words, phrases or clauses of equal rank.

The COORDINATING CONJUNCTIONS: for, and, nor, but, or, yet, so (the FANBOYS).

- Bill *and* Bob went to the concert, *but* they forgot their tickets.

The ADVERBIAL CONJUNCTIONS (also known as CONJUNCTIVE ADVERBS): also, however, therefore, thus, moreover, consequently, as a result, for example, for instance, in fact, instead, meanwhile, nevertheless, then, otherwise, furthermore.

Note the punctuation in the examples below. When the adverbial conjunction is placed between two independent clauses, it is preceded by either a semicolon or a period and followed by a comma.

- Bill and Bob went to the concert; *however,* they forgot their tickets.
- Susan went to the Northern Star Mall; *then,* she went to a movie.
- Bill and Bob went to the concert. *However,* they forgot their tickets.
- Susan went to the Northern Star Mall. *Then,* she went to a movie.

If an adverbial conjunction is placed <u>within</u> a sentence rather than <u>between</u> two sentences, it is usually enclosed within commas. (Sometimes, when the adverbial conjunction is placed next to a verb and the commas interrupt the flow of the sentence, they're dropped.)

- Bill and Bob went to the concert. As they approached the front gate, *however,* they realized they had forgotten their tickets.
- Susan went to the Northern Star Mall. She *then* went to a movie. (Here, enclosing *then* in commas would interfere with the flow of the sentence.)

The **SUBORDINATING CONJUNCTIONS**: after, although, as, as if, as long as, as soon as, because, before, even though, even if, if, since, so that, though, unless, until, when, whenever, where, wherever, whether, while.

- *Because* I was late, I didn't go in.
- I didn't go in *because* I was late.
- *Even though* I knew her, I was too shy to say hello.
- I was too shy to say hello *even though* I knew her.

PREPOSITIONS: A **PREPOSITION** shows the relationship of a noun or pronoun to another word or group of words in a sentence.

- Put the mustard *on* the hot dog.
- Lance placed the jack *under* the bumper.

INTERJECTIONS: An **INTERJECTION** usually stands by itself and expresses a strong feeling or emotion.

- *Wow!* Jeff Gordon ran that lap at 184.88 m.p.h.

ARTICLES: An **ARTICLE** is a short word placed before a noun, a noun equivalent, or a word modifying a noun. In English we have only three: *a, an, the.*

- *The* contractors installed *a* new curb in *the* parking lot.

EXERCISE 1   PARTS OF SPEECH: Put the letter of the underlined part of speech in the appropriate numbered blank.

A = Noun	**D** = Adverb	**G** = Conjunction
B = Verb	**E** = Preposition	**H** = Pronoun
C = Adjective	**F** = Article	**I** = Interjection

                  1   2   3

Swimming is my <u>favorite</u> activity; before I go into the <u>pool</u>, however, I <u>put</u> on my goggles and my water wings.

    4   5   6   7

I <u>always</u> love to jump <u>into</u> a pool on a <u>hot</u> day; <u>however</u>, I must admit that I enjoy swimming in the ocean most of all.

  8   9   10   11   12   13

<u>One</u> day I hit <u>my</u> head on <u>the</u> edge of the <u>diving</u> board. <u>Ouch!</u> That <u>really</u> hurt.

           14   15   16   17

My friends Sammy <u>and</u> <u>Maxine</u> took <u>me</u> to the hospital. <u>On</u> the way, we hit a telephone pole.

     18   19   20

That <u>was</u> not one <u>of</u> my <u>better</u> days.

1. _____	5. _____	9. _____	13. _____	17. _____
2. _____	6. _____	10. _____	14. _____	18. _____
3. _____	7. _____	11. _____	15. _____	19. _____
4. _____	8. _____	12. _____	16. _____	20. _____

SUBJECTS AND VERBS

The core of any sentence is the subject/verb (predicate) unit. The **SUBJECT** is the word or group of words that tells who or what the sentence is about. The **PREDICATE** is the word or group of words that tells what the subject is, what it is doing or what is being done to it.

We often use the words *predicate* and *verb* interchangeably, but technically they are not the same. The predicate includes the verb as well as other words or word groups related to the verb. Similarly, the subject is usually a noun or a pronoun along with words that describe or give further information about the noun or pronoun.

Some of the simplest possible sentences in English are

- I am.
- John slept.

These are sentences—they have a subject, predicate (the verb) and a complete thought. They won't take us very far, but they <u>are</u> sentences.

Of course the vast majority of your sentences will consist of considerably more detail than we see in these two-word units. You'll want to add more details in the form of other **PARTS OF SPEECH**, like adjectives and adverbs as well as **PHRASES** and **CLAUSES**.

- My brother John slept for ten hours last night.

My brother John is the <u>complete subject</u> (the noun with its accompanying words) and *slept for ten hours last night* is the <u>complete predicate</u> (the verb with the words and phrases that go along with it).

The <u>simple subject</u> is *John*, and the <u>simple predicate</u> is the verb *slept.*

For a group of words to be considered a sentence, it must have at least one combination of a subject and predicate.

> **NOTE:** When you are trying to figure out if a group of words has a subject and a predicate, be careful. In English we have forms of the verb called *verbals* that look like verbs but really aren't. For a verb unit to be a predicate, it must contain a **finite verb.** Look at the examples below:
>
> - Sidney walking her dog.
>
> *Walking* looks like a verb, but it isn't—it's a verbal (a participle). To make *walking* into a finite verb (a verb that forms a complete sentence), we need to add something to it:
>
> - Sidney **is** walking her dog.
>   **or**
> - Sidney, walking her dog, **was** tired, wet and disgusted.
>
> To be a finite verb, *walking* needs either an **auxiliary verb** (*is* in the first sentence) or another finite verb (*was* in the second sentence) to complete the thought.

EXERCISE 2   SIMPLE SUBJECTS AND PREDICATES:

Underline the simple subject/simple predicate unit in each of the following sentences.

1. Pablo Neruda was born in Parral, Chile on July 12, 1904.
2. The Chilean poet left his village in 1921 to study at the University of Chile in Santiago.
3. At the age of 17, Neruda won first prize in a poetry contest in Santiago.
4. Many critics cite Neruda as the outstanding poet in the Spanish language.
5. In 1971 Neruda won the Nobel Prize in literature.

EXERCISE 3 COMPLETE SUBJECTS AND PREDICATES:

Draw one line under the complete subject and two lines under the complete predicate in each of the following sentences.

1. West Indian author V.S. Naipaul won the Nobel Prize for Literature in 2001.
2. The grandson of a Brahmin from Utar Pradesh, India, Naipaul was born in Caguanas, Trinidad, on August 17, 1932.
3. Naipaul published his most famous work, *A House for Ms. Biswas*, in 1961.

4. In 1950, Naipaul, armed with a scholarship to University College, Oxford, left the West Indies for good and moved to England.

5. V.S. Naipaul now lives in London with his wife and maintains a cottage near Salisbury, where he works on his writing.

PHRASES AND CLAUSES

PHRASES

A **PHRASE** is a group of related words having a single function. A phrase may have a noun or a verb in it, but it won't have a subject-verb unit (otherwise, it would be a clause).

THE PREPOSITIONAL PHRASE (functions as an adjective or an adverb)
- Darryl and James went *to the store*. (used as an adverb, tells where they went)
- They went to the store *on the corner*. (used as an adjective, gives further information about the store)

THE GERUND PHRASE (functions as a noun)
- *Staying out of trouble* became my number one priority. (noun, used as a subject)
- Sheila loves *dancing in the dark*. (noun, used as a direct object)

THE PARTICIPIAL PHRASE (functions as an adjective)
- Alice, *bleeding from a head wound*, was rushed to the hospital. (adjective, gives further information about Alice)

THE INFINITIVE PHRASE (the **INFINITIVE** is formed by the word *to* plus the present tense of a verb [*to run; to go*] and functions as an adjective, adverb or noun)
- I have no desire *to go*. (adjective modifying *desire*)
- I was ready *to go*. (adverb modifying *ready*)
- *To forgive* is divine. (noun as subject of the sentence)

CLAUSES

A **CLAUSE** is a group of related words having a single function and containing **both** a subject and a verb. Clauses may be either **INDEPENDENT** or **DEPENDENT**. An independent clause is, by definition, a complete sentence.

A dependent clause needs an independent clause to complete the thought. Dependent clauses, like phrases, function as "stretched out" parts of speech.

THE NOUN CLAUSE: Like a noun, a <u>NOUN CLAUSE</u> can function as a subject, object or predicate noun. This type of clause usually begins with one of these words: *whoever, whichever, whatever, who, that, what, how, why, when,* or *where.*

- *Whatever you want to do* is all right with me. (used as subject)
- I will do *whatever you tell me to do.* (used as direct object)
- *What you see* is *what you get.* (used as subject and predicate noun)

THE ADJECTIVE CLAUSE: Just as an adjective gives additional information about a noun, the <u>ADJECTIVE CLAUSE</u> modifies a noun or a phrase that comes before it in the sentence. This type of clause begins with one of these relative pronouns: *who, whom, whose, which* or *that.*

- Lateesha is the student *who is running for SGA president.* (modifies <u>student</u>)
- Andrew, *who ran unopposed last year,* has a fight on his hands in this election. (modifies <u>Andrew</u>)
- That's Larry, *whose car you ran into last night.* (modifies <u>Larry</u>)
- Your conduct, *which we have discussed before,* is not acceptable behavior in a college classroom. (modifies <u>conduct</u>)

THE ADVERB CLAUSE: Like a single-word adverb, this type of clause modifies a verb, adjective or adverb. It begins with a subordinating conjunction, such as *after, although, as, as if, as long as, as soon as, because, before, even though, if, since, so that, though, unless, until, when, whenever, where, wherever, whether, while.* Unlike the adjective clause, the adverb clause is moveable and can appear at the beginning or at the end of the sentence. Note that the comma drops out when the adverb clause is at the end of the sentence.

- *When Lance gets here,* we can start the study session. (modifies <u>can start</u>)
- We can start the study session *when Lance gets here.*

EXERCISE 4 PHRASES/CLAUSES: Indicate in the appropriate blanks below whether each of the underlined groups of words is a **A** = a phrase or **B** = a clause.

_____ 1. <u>Fishing from a party boat on a hot summer day</u> is my favorite recreational activity.

_____ 2. Maria is the woman <u>whom we went to see after the movie last night</u>.

_____ 3. The short story that I was reading described a conflict <u>between two brothers</u>.

_____ 4. The Republican sniper fired at <u>whoever was on the roof of the building on the other side of the street</u>.

_____ 5. <u>I went to see her in the hospital</u> because she is my friend.

EXERCISE 5   INDEPENDENT/DEPENDENT CLAUSES:

Indicate in the blanks below whether each of the underlined clauses in the sentences below is **A** = independent or **B** = dependent.

_____ 1. Henry VIII, <u>who was born in 1491</u>, reigned as the King of England from 1509 until 1547.

_____ 2. <u>Because he had six wives and was one of the most powerful rulers in British history</u>, Henry VIII is a well-known figure in world history.

_____ 3. Even though Hollywood has often portrayed Henry as a fat, obnoxious slob with a turkey leg in one hand and rack of ribs in the other, <u>he was actually handsome, athletic, and artistically gifted</u>.

_____ 4. After he became king, <u>Henry married Catherine of Aragón</u>, who was his brother's widow, but she failed to produce a male heir who lived beyond infancy.

_____ 5. Henry began a decade-long battle with the Roman Catholic church <u>that eventually led the king to break with Rome and to establish an English church with him at its head.</u>

_____ 6. The Anglican Church, <u>which is also known as the Church of England</u>, is still the official church of Great Britain.

_____ 7. <u>After Henry officially broke away from the pope and the Roman church</u>, he had his marriage to Catherine annulled and married Anne Boleyn.

_____ 8. For a variety of reasons, <u>Anne and Henry had a serious falling out</u>, and Henry had his wife beheaded.

_____ 9. In 1543 Henry married his sixth wife, Catherine Parr, <u>who survived him</u>.

_____ 10. Catherine was fortunate to escape being executed, <u>which was the fate of two of Henry's wives who preceded her, Anne Boleyn and Catherine Howard</u>.

SENTENCES

SENTENCES

To be a sentence, a group of words must have a subject and verb and express a complete thought.

- Kate Chopin wrote many great short stories.

Kate Chopin is the subject of the sentence, *wrote* is the verb, and the idea that she wrote short fiction with lasting appeal to a wide audience completes the thought.

SENTENCE TYPES

An important consideration for any writer is SENTENCE VARIETY. Varied sentence patterns make your paragraphs interesting to read.

The four patterns are simple, compound, complex and compound-complex.

THE SIMPLE SENTENCE: one independent clause.

- Paul Robeson was born on April 9, 1898, in Princeton, N.J.
- Robeson graduated from Rutgers University in 1919 and earned a law degree from Columbia University in 1923.

THE COMPOUND SENTENCE: two or more independent clauses.

- Paul Robeson worked in a law office for about a year, but he left the legal profession to pursue a career in acting.
- Robeson appeared in many Broadway plays in the early part of the 20th century; he is best known for playing the title role in *Othello*.

THE COMPLEX SENTENCE: one independent clause and one or more dependent clauses (in brackets in the examples below).

- Paul Robeson, [who was also an outstanding singer], performed in a number of musicals, including *Show Boat*. (Adjective clause)
- [When he toured Europe and America as an interpreter of Negro spirituals,] Robeson achieved great success. (Adverb clause)
- [That Paul Robeson was a significant influence in American musical theater] is beyond question. (Noun clause as subject)

THE COMPOUND-COMPLEX SENTENCE: two or more independent clauses and one or more dependent clauses (in brackets in the examples below).

- Paul Robeson was a wonderful actor and singer, but his career in America was badly damaged [when he became interested in communism.]

In the example above, the part of the sentence from *Paul Robeson* to *damaged* is a compound sentence. Adding the dependent *when* clause makes the sentence compound-complex.

A compound-complex sentence may be long:

- When Paul Robeson made his stage debut in *Taboo* with Margaret Wycherly in May of 1922, his performance was widely acclaimed by critics, and he was offered a contract to play the same role in England with Mrs. Patrick Campbell.

Or a compound-complex sentence may be short:

- After *Taboo* closed its run, Robeson starred in *The Emperor Jones*, and once again he received rave reviews.

EXERCISE 6 TYPES OF SENTENCES: Indicate in the appropriate blanks below whether each of the following sentences is **A** = simple; **B** = compound; **C** = complex; **D** = compound-complex

C 1. Marcus Garvey, who was a charismatic and sometimes eccentric black leader, played a significant role in New York City's minority communities in the early part of the 20th century.

B 2. Garvey was born in 1887 in the West Indies; he died in 1940.

B 3. Garvey worked as a printer and editor in Jamaica, and in 1914 he organized the Universal Negro Improvement Association (UNIA).

C 4. When Garvey emigrated to New York City in 1916, he founded a branch of the UNIA and edited the *Negro World*, a weekly newspaper.

A 5. Garvey's UNIA had the broad purpose of promoting brotherhood and unity among black Americans and promoting the development of independent black communities and nations, especially in Africa.

_D._ 6. Garvey, who was a gifted orator, pushed for a "Back to Africa" movement, but he was not widely supported by other black Americans.

_C._ 7. Because he was convinced that black people could not prosper as a minority race in America, Garvey urged American blacks to leave the country.

_B._ 8. As a part of the movement, Garvey started the Black Star Line Steamship Company, but his dream of providing black Americans with service between the United States, Africa and the West Indies never materialized.

_C._ 9. Garvey eventually went back to Jamaica where he was elected several times to the Kingston Council.

_A._ 10. Small groups of Garvey's followers still exist today in a few American cities and in some parts of the Caribbean.

SENTENCE VARIETY

Good writers need to pay some attention to the kinds of sentences they use in their essays. Many times college-level writers stick strictly to what they know and are used to and do not expand their style of writing to include different types of sentences. Look at how repetitive and boring this writing style is:

> Des Kennedy says there are four billion rats on earth. That means roughly one rat for every two humans. Kennedy calls rats "the most successful biological opponent of humans on earth." He also says we have done everything we can think of to defeat them. We have studied them obsessively. We have trapped them. We have poisoned them. We have bred dogs to hunt them and kill them. We have even trained snakes to eradicate them. But rats are smart. They form social groups. They know how to enforce discipline in their groups. They do this mainly by killing outsiders. These outsiders try to enter the group. They also kill members of their own group. These members don't follow the rules. Kennedy says rats are skilled at adapting to new situations. They can quickly adjust to meet threats. He also says they are ferocious in combat. In other words, Kennedy says, rats are a lot like us.

This could have been an interesting, attention-grabbing introductory paragraph in an essay about Des Kennedy's article on rats, but with those elementary-school sentences, who would want to read further? Only your mother would be willing to read a whole essay written like this—and even she might fall asleep in the middle of it.

The average sentence length in a college-level essay is about 20 words. What would you say is the average length of the sentences in the "Rats" paragraph? About nine words? Sentences of this type just don't do the job in college writing.

Several different grammatical patterns of sentence openings can be used to vary the structure and variety of your sentences. You don't have to know the grammatical terminology to use each of these techniques. You should, however, be aware that you shouldn't be using the same patterns (especially simple sentences) over and over again and that you have a number of different ways to vary your sentences to help hold your reader's interest. Let's look at one particular theme: *I need a new car.*

Prepositional Phrase:
- *After work today* I'm going to Peterson's Ford to look at new cars.

Participial Phrase:
- *Bracing myself for the usual battle with the sales person,* I went to look at new cars.

Gerund Phrase:
- *Keeping my old Toyota* is simply not an option.

Infinitive Phrase:
- *To maintain my sanity,* I really must buy a new car.

Noun Clause:
- *Whatever I have to do to get rid of the Toyota* is worth the effort.

Adverb Clause—Time:
- *When the amount of oil I was putting into the Toyota roughly equaled the amount of gas,* I knew it was time to get rid of the car.

Adverb Clause—Cause:
- *Since the Toyota failed inspection,* I can't wait too long.

Adverb Clause—Concession and Contrast:
- *Although I can't really afford it,* I'll find a way to finance it.

Adverb Clause—Condition:
- *If the Toyota starts blowing any more smoke,* I'll need to install fog lights.

In addition to using these techniques for starting your sentences, you have two basic methods for combining short sentences to improve the stylistic quality of your writing: **subordination** or **coordination.**

COMBINING SENTENCES: SUBORDINATION

SUBORDINATION means taking one element of a sentence and giving it less grammatical weight than another part of the sentence. By taking two short, simple ideas and making one of them into a **dependent clause,** and one into an **independent clause,** you form a **complex sentence.**

Let's look back at the "Rats" sample on page 637 and see which sentences can be combined using subordination.

- Des Kennedy says there are four billion rats on earth. That means roughly one rat for every two humans

Combined Des Kennedy says there are four billion rats on earth, which means roughly one rat for every two humans (Make the second sentence into a dependent adjective clause using *which*.)

- They do this mainly by killing outsiders. These outsiders try to enter the group.

Combined They do this mainly by killing outsiders when the outsiders try to enter the group. (Make the second sentence into a dependent adverb clause using *when*.)

- They also kill members of their own group. These members don't follow the rules.

Combined They also kill members of their own group if the members don't follow the rules. (Make the second sentence into a dependent adverb clause using *if*.)

EXERCISE 7 COMBINING SENTENCES USING SUBOR-
DINATION: Combine the following sentences by subordinating one of the sentences to the other. In some cases you may need to eliminate or move certain words. You may also want to switch the order of the clauses.

EXAMPLES:
- Joe DiMaggio missed two of his most productive playing years. This happened because he served in the army during World War II.

Serving in the army during World War II caused Joe Dimaggio to miss two of his most productive playing years.

or

Joe DiMaggio missed two of his most productive playing years because he served in the army during World War II.

1. Joe DiMaggio's father was a fisherman. He thought his eldest son, Joe, was lazy.

_____

_____

2. His father was very strict about money. Young Joe brought home all the money he made as a newsboy in his hometown of San Francisco.

_____

_____

3. At one point Joe's friends thought that he had given up on baseball. This wasn't true.

_____

_____

4. Joe bought a new Cadillac even though he didn't even have a driver's license. He was signed by the Yankees in 1936.

_____

_____

5. All of the newspaper reporters and photographers clamoring to talk to DiMaggio and to take his picture bothered him. Joe was basically a shy person.

_____

_____

COMBINING SENTENCES: COORDINATION

When you use coordination, you take two simple sentences and combine them by making the two elements of equal weight. Since each of the combined elements is an **independent clause** (complete sentence), you have created a **compound sentence.**

Let's look at the "Rats" paragraph as it now reads—after we used _subordination_ to combine some of the sentences—and see if we can use _coordination_ to improve it a little more.

Des Kennedy says there are four billion rats on earth, which means roughly one rat for every two humans. Kennedy calls rats "the most successful biological opponent of humans on earth." He also says we have done everything we can think of to defeat them. We have studied them obsessively. We have trapped them. We have poisoned them. We have bred dogs to hunt them and kill them. We have even trained snakes to eradicate them. But rats are smart. They form social groups. They know how to enforce discipline in their groups. They do this primarily by killing outsiders when the outsiders try to enter the group. They also kill members of their own group if the members don't follow the rules. Kennedy says rats are skilled at adapting to new situations. They can quickly adjust to meet threats. He also says they are ferocious in combat. In other words, Kennedy says, rats are a lot like us.

We can take some of the short sentences and combine them into compound sentences:

- We have trapped them. We have poisoned them. We have bred dogs to hunt them and kill them.
Combined We have trapped and poisoned them, and we have bred dogs to hunt and kill them.

- They form social groups. They know how to enforce discipline in the groups.
Combined They form social groups, and they know how to enforce discipline in the groups

- Kennedy says rats are skilled at adapting to new situations. They can quickly adjust to meet threats.
Combined Kennedy says rats are skilled at adapting to new situations; they can quickly adjust to meet threats.

Here we have used the two most common methods of combining sentences to create a compound sentence: 1) by using a **coordinating conjunction** (the "fanboys": *for, and, nor, but, or, yet, so*) and 2) by using a **semicolon**.

After using the techniques of subordination and coordination, this is how the "Rats" paragraph now reads:

Des Kennedy says there are four billion rats on earth, which means roughly one rat for every two humans. Kennedy calls rats "the most successful biological opponent of humans on earth." He also says we have done everything we can think of to defeat them. We have studied them obsessively. We have trapped and poisoned them, and we have bred dogs to hunt them and kill them. We have even trained snakes to eradicate them. But rats are smart. They form social groups, and they know how to enforce discipline in the groups. They do this primarily by killing outsiders when the outsiders try to enter the group. They also kill members of their own group if the members don't follow the rules. Kennedy says rats are skilled at adapting to new situations; they can quickly adjust to meet threats. He also says they are ferocious in combat. In other words, Kennedy says, rats are a lot like us.

EXERCISE 8   COMBINING SENTENCES USING COOR-DINATION: Using coordination, rewrite the following short sentences, combining them to make them stronger. You may use either the *fanboys*, a semicolon with an adverbial conjunction (see page 653), or just a semicolon. If you use a *fanboys* word, don't forget to put a comma in front of it. If you use an adverbial conjunction, put a comma after it.

EXAMPLES: The sphinx is a figure from Egyptian mythology. We get its name from the Greek verb *sphingein,* meaning "to bind together."

> *The sphinx is a figure from Egyptian mythology, but we get its name from the Greek verb "sphingien," meaning "to bind together."*
>
> **or**
>
> *The sphinx is a figure from Egyptian mythology; however, we get its name from the Greek verb "sphingien," meaning "to bind together."*

1. The body of the sphinx is a lion. The head is that of a woman.

_____

2. Most people are familiar with pictures of the Great Sphinx at Giza in Egypt. When we think of a sphinx, we tend to think of that one.

_____

3. At one time a temple stood in front of the Great Sphinx. It is now almost completely eroded away by the sand.

_____

_____

4. In the second century B.C.E. the Romans wanted to devise a method for keeping sand away from the Great Sphinx. They built walls of brick and stone around the entire area.

_____

_____

5. Sphinxes were generally objects of ancient worship. They were also used as symbolic guardians of entranceways.

_____

_____

EXERCISE 9   COMBINING SENTENCES USING COORDINATION AND SUBORDINATION: Rewrite the following short sentences, combining them into one sentence using the techniques of coordination and subordination, as described previously.

EXAMPLE: Queen Victoria of England was born in London, England. She was born May 24, 1819. She died on January 22, 1901. When Victoria died, she was 81 years old. She died on the Isle of Wight.

Queen Victoria of England was born in London, England on May 24, 1819, and she died at the age of 81 January 22, 1901 on the Isle of Wight.

1. Queen Victoria had a remarkable influence on the world. She was England's longest-reigning monarch. She ruled the British Empire for 63 years, 7 months and 2 days.

_____

_____

2. Victoria was carefully protected. She was not even allowed to walk down the stairs alone This went on until she came to the throne.

_____

_____

3. Victoria became queen in 1837. She was 18 years old. Almost immediately she achieved great popularity.

4. Victoria's mother and uncle wanted Victoria to get married. They introduced her to Prince Albert of Germany. Victoria liked him. She proposed to the handsome prince in October of 1838. She was 19 years old.

5. Victoria was a political liberal. Albert was a conservative. Somehow they managed to achieve a balance in their marriage that had a positive effect on Victoria's governing of England.

EXERCISE 10   COMBINING SENTENCES USING COORDINATION AND SUBORDINATION: Rewrite the following paragraph, using any of the techniques discussed above to combine short sentences where appropriate to make them stronger.

In 1863 Édouard Manet caused a scandal in Parisian art circles. He exhibited a large painting at the Salon des Refusés. The painting was entitled *Déjeuner sur l'herbe*. It depicted two seated, clothed men having a picnic lunch. Sitting with the men was a naked woman. Another nearly nude woman was shown bathing in a lake. The lake was a few feet away from the two men and the naked woman. The subject matter of this painting caused a major controversy in Paris. The painter, Manet, was rebelling against something. He was painting middle-class French life. He wasn't painting traditional Biblical, historical or allegorical subjects. These are subjects that French painters had typically depicted. French painting at this time was dominated by the Ecole des Beaux-Arts. They taught traditional neo-classicist painting techniques. They also stressed traditional subject matter. Manet's painting was intended to shock them. It did. Many young painters joined Manet's circle of artists. They met at the Café Guerbois in Montmartre. Montmartre is a section of Paris. Manet and his fellow artists would soon be recognized as the leaders of a movement. This movement would come to be called "French Impressionism."

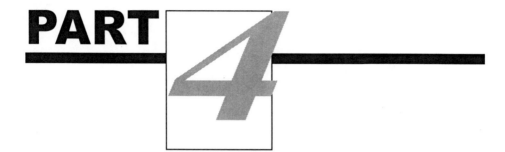

PART 4

IMPROVING SENTENCES

ELIMINATING SENTENCE FRAGMENTS

A <u>**SENTENCE FRAGMENT**</u> occurs when an essential element of the sentence is missing.

A <u>**FRAGMENT**</u> is also known as an <u>**INCOMPLETE SENTENCE**</u>.

- When Doug gave the money to his grandmother. (Dependent clause)

- Who was standing on the corner under a streetlight. (Dependent clause. Note the end punctuation here. If you put a question mark after this clause, it would be a sentence. Written with a period, however, it's a fragment.)

- Smoking a foul-smelling cigar. (Phrase)

MAKING DEPENDENT CLAUSES INTO SENTENCES

Dependent clauses begin with one of these subordinating words: *whoever, whichever, whatever, who, that, what, how, why, when,* or *where* (noun clause)

OR

who, whom, whose, which, that (adjective clause)

OR

after, although, as, as if, as long as, as soon as, because, before, even though, even if, if, since, so that, though, unless, until, when, whenever, where, wherever, whether, while (adverb clause).

Normally, the easiest way to make a dependent clause into a sentence is to connect it to the sentence that precedes or follows it, creating a <u>**COMPLEX SENTENCE.**</u>

Fragment: Because you weren't at the meeting. We decided to elect another chairperson. (Put a comma after the dependent clause and connect it to the independent clause.)

Complex Sentence: Because you weren't at the meeting, we decided to elect another chairperson.

Fragment:	I never received the package. That you said you mailed to me last week.
	(Drop the period and the upper-case T and attach the fragment to the independent clause that precedes it.)
Complex Sentence:	I never received the package that you said you mailed to me last week.

Another method you can use to make a dependent-clause fragment into a sentence is to drop the subordinating word and add a coordinating conjunction, creating a **COMPOUND SENTENCE.**

Fragment:	Because you weren't at the meeting. We decided to elect another chairperson
Compound Sentence:	You weren't at the meeting, so we decided to elect another chairperson.

Fragment:	Bianca hoped she would win the lottery. Although she knew the odds were against her.
~~**Complex Sentence:**~~ *Compound Sentence*	Bianca hoped she would win the lottery, but she knew the odds were against her.

Fragment:	Even though Henry has cheated me out of a lot of money. I still like him.
Compound Sentence:	Henry has cheated me out of a lot of money, yet I still like him.

A third method is to make two **SIMPLE SENTENCES.** If you use this method, however, be sure that you aren't weakening your writing style by overloading your writing with short, simple sentences.

Fragment:	Because you weren't at the meeting. We decided to elect another chairperson.
Simple Sentence:	You weren't at the meeting. We decided to elect another chairperson.

EXERCISE 1 ELIMINATING DEPENDENT-CLAUSE
FRAGMENTS: Complete each of the following dependent-clause fragments by adding an independent clause. Remember to use a comma at the end of the clause if the adverb clause comes at the beginning of the sentence and to drop the comma if the adverb clause is at the end.

EXAMPLE: If you get a chance, *please send me an e-mail and let me know when you will be arriving.*

1.   Whenever I listen to classical music.

   _____

2.   Because overpopulation is a worldwide concern.

   _____

3.   The story "Girl" that Jamaica Kincaid wrote.

   _____

4.   After we read Hanley's short story "The Butterfly."

   _____

5.   The woman who spoke to our criminal justice class yesterday.

   _____

ELIMINATING OTHER KINDS OF FRAGMENTS
Word groups other than dependent clauses can also cause fragments. The fragment is underlined.

- Johnny took his mother to her appointment with the doctor. <u>Then waited outside in the car.</u>
- I saw you yesterday. <u>Waiting for your friends at Freehold Raceway Mall</u>.

The same techniques you use to eliminate dependent-clause fragments are used here: either combine the two groups of words into one sentence, or make the fragment into its own sentence.

- Johnny took his mother to her appointment with the doctor and then waited outside in the car. (No comma before the *and* because this is not a compound sentence.)

  OR

- Johnny took his mother to her appointment with the doctor. Then he waited outside in the car.

- I saw you yesterday, waiting for your friends at Freehold Raceway Mall. (Usually, when you have an *ing* fragment, you will put a comma between the *ing* word group and the rest of the sentence.)

A NOTE ON THE "YOU UNDERSTOOD" SENTENCE

One sentence pattern in English that often looks like a fragment but really isn't is called the **imperative mood** or the "you understood" sentence. "Imperative" in this context means to tell someone to do something, to give an order. Look at these examples:

- Don't just stand there.
- Help me!

These are not fragments. They are full, complete sentences with the subject "you" being implied but not stated:

- (You) Don't just stand there.
- (You) Help me!

EXERCISE 2   ELIMINATING FRAGMENTS: Find and correct the five sentence fragments in the following passage.

Thurgood Marshall was named to the United States Supreme Court in

1967 and died in 1997. The first African-American to be named to the highest

court in the land, Marshall was a moderate but steadfast voice in the American

civil-rights movement. Frequently cautioning people that equal rights must be

won by arguments in the courtroom, not violence in the streets. Born in Balti-

more, Maryland in 1908 and graduating with honors from Lincoln University in

Pennsylvania. Marshall was first in his law school class at Howard University. He then returned to Baltimore to practice law. He became chief counsel for the National Association for the Advancement of Colored People (NAACP) and was eventually named special counsel at NAACP headquarters in New York City.

Marshal argued 32 cases before the United States Supreme Court. He won 29 of them, a remarkable record. One of Marshall's important cases concerned the exclusion of African-Americans from juries. The Supreme Court ruling such exclusions illegal under the United States Constitution. Marshall also won decisions overturning laws in the south barring African-Americans from voting in primary elections. As well as invalidating restrictions against minorities that made it virtually impossible for them to buy and own a home.

Marshall's most important victory was Brown vs Topeka Board of Education in 1954, the case that overturned the "separate but equal" doctrine. Prior to the Brown decision, African-Americans in the south and southwest had been forced to attend segregated schools. That were anything but "equal" to those attended by white students. Marshall's accomplishments won him wide recognition, resulting in appointments to federal judgeships and ultimately to the highest court in the land.

AVOIDING RUN-ON SENTENCES AND COMMA SPLICES

RUN-ON SENTENCES

A **RUN-ON SENTENCE** consists of two sentences run together with no punctuation or joining word between them. The run-on sentence is also known as a **FUSED SENTENCE.**

- Gina is a good basketball player she practices for two hours every day. (This "sentence" consists of two independent clauses run together between *player* and *she*. Each of the clauses is a sentence unto itself.)

- Stephanie bought a new car last year she's having difficulty making the payments. (The run-on occurs between *year* and *she's*.)

ELIMINATING RUN-ONS

MAKE TWO SENTENCES
The first and easiest method for eliminating a run-on is to put a period at the end of the first sentence and a capital letter at the beginning of the second. While this is an easy option, it may not be the best choice stylistically. It can make your sentences too short and choppy, giving the reader the impression that your style is immature.

- Gina is a good basketball player she practices for two hours every day.
Revised Gina is a good basketball player. She practices for two hours every day.

- Stephanie bought a new car last year she's having difficulty making the payments.
Revised Stephanie bought a new car last year. She's having difficulty

making the payments.

USE A COMMA AND A COORDINATING CONJUNCTION *for, and, nor, but, or, yet, so* (the FANBOYS)

- Willie doesn't really like Margaret he still dates her because she has money.

    Revised Willie doesn't really like Margaret, *but* he still dates her because she has money.

- Lou parked his motorcycle in the driveway then he went into the house.

    Revised Lou parked his motorcycle in the driveway, *and* then he went into the house.

USE A SEMICOLON

- Jon Stewart hosted *The Tonight Show* last night he was very funny.

    Revised Jon Stewart hosted *The Tonight Show* last night; he was very funny.

- Shahid bought a new BMW last week he loves that car.

    Revised Shahid bought a new BMW last week; he loves that car.

USE A SEMICOLON AND AN ADVERBIAL CONJUNCTION *also, however, therefore, thus, moreover, consequently, as a result, for example, for instance, in fact, instead, meanwhile, nevertheless, then, otherwise, furthermore*

- Hargrove practices his jump shot for two hours every day he now makes nine out of ten.

    Revised Hargrove practices his jump shot for two hours every day; *as a result*, he now makes nine out of ten.

- Lannie's son bought a new computer he can't figure out how to use it.

    Revised Lannie's son bought a new computer; *however*, he can't figure out how to use it.

- Brandi likes to travel she has visited every continent.
Revised Brandi likes to travel; *in fact*, she has visited every continent.

USE A SUBORDINATING WORD *after, although, as, as if, as long as, as soon as, because, before, even though, even if, if, since, so that, though, unless, until, when, whenever, where, wherever, whether, while.*

- David was late for class this morning his car had a flat tire.
Revised David was late for class this morning *because* his car had a flat tire.

- Marcus says he'll work for you tonight he leaves his day job at 4.
Revised Marcus says he'll work for you tonight *after* he leaves his day job at 4.

Note that not all of the methods cited above work equally well with each sentence. Some of the sentences sound better using one alternative rather than another. Part of your responsibility, and talent, as a writer is to choose the alternative that communicates and sounds the best.

EXERCISE 3   ELIMINATING RUN-ONS: Eliminate each of the following run-on sentences using the techniques explained above. Try to use a variety of techniques.

1. Charles A. Lindbergh was born in 1902 in Detroit, Michigan he was the first person to fly alone across the Atlantic Ocean.

2. Lindbergh's father was a member of the U.S. Congress and was often away in Washington young Charles was raised more by his mother, a high school science teacher.

3. Lindbergh graduated from high school in 1918 he spent two years running his family's farm in Minnesota.

4. Lindbergh learned to fly as a teenager after undergoing further training he was commissioned a second lieutenant in the Army Air Service Reserve.

5. On May 21, 1927, Lindbergh flew non-stop from Roosevelt Field on Long Island to Le Bourget airport outside of Paris in 33 hours he won

a $25,000 prize and became an instant hero.

6. Lindbergh met the daughter of the U.S. Ambassador to Mexico, Anne Spencer Morrow, in Mexico City in 1928 they were married in 1929.

7. The first of the Lindberghs' six children, Charles, Jr., was kidnapped from the Lindbergh home in Hopewell, N.J. the baby's body was found in the woods a month later.

8. A sensational trial, with massive media coverage, was held in Flemington the man accused of the crime, Bruno Richard Hauptmann, was convicted.

9. Bruno Richard Hauptmann maintained his innocence to the end he was executed in the electric chair at Trenton State Prison on April 3, 1936.

10. The kidnapping and murder of the Lindbergh baby shocked and angered members of Congress they passed the "Lindbergh Act," a federal law authorizing life imprisonment for anyone who takes a kidnap victim across state lines.

COMMA SPLICES

A COMMA SPLICE is a run-on sentence with a comma inappropriately placed between the two sentences when a semicolon, a period or a joining word is required.

- Frieda is a good DJ, she plays at parties every weekend.

The comma splice occurs between *DJ* and *she*. The writer has recognized that each of the clauses is independent and that something is needed to separate them. The comma, however, is not strong enough. This is still a form of a run-on or fused sentence.

The same techniques used for eliminating run-on sentences are used to eliminate comma splices: make two sentences; use a comma and a coordinating conjunction; use a subordinating word; use a semicolon; or use a semicolon and an adverbial conjunction.

EXERCISE 4 ELIMINATING COMMA SPLICES: Eliminate each of the comma splices using the techniques explained in this section. Use a variety of techniques. Three of the sentences are not comma splices and should be left alone.

1. Lightning is a high-voltage electrical spark, usually a few miles long, it occurs in the earth's atmosphere.

2. The average lightning discharge is about 100 million volts, it produces enough energy to keep a room air conditioner running non-stop for two weeks.

3. In the early days of the earth, lightning may have been responsible for the synthesis of organic chemicals, thus leading to the development of life.

4. Thunderstorms occur when the atmosphere is unstable, they begin to form when moist, warm air near the earth rises.

5. The rising warm air produces many small cumulus clouds, at first, they don't produce rain or electrical discharges.

6. These clouds increase in size and energy, they eventually surge upward to form a much larger cloud that produces rain and lightning.

7. Some of these clouds become huge thunderstorms, producing more than 1,000 flashes of lightning per minute.

8. Special cameras have taken pictures of cloud-to-ground discharges, these cameras show that lightning starts with a phenomenon known as a stepped leader.

9. When the stepped leader gets close to the ground, it triggers a return surge called the return stroke.

10. The return stroke follows the path of the stepped leader upward, this is the bright flash that is seen by the human eye and recorded in photographs.

USING VERBS

Most problems with **VERBS** occur when 1) the subject and the verb don't agree in **NUMBER**; 2) the **PASSIVE VOICE** is used in place of the **ACTIVE VOICE**.

SUBJECT-VERB AGREEMENT

Verbs and their subjects must agree in number—that is, if a subject is singular, the verb must be singular. If the subject is plural, the verb must also be plural. The problem is, a singular verb often has an s on it, making it seem like it's plural. Look at these examples:

- **Mary gives** money to charity. (*Mary* is a singular noun and *gives* is a singular verb.)
- **Rita runs** every day. (*Rita* is a singular subject and *runs* is a singular verb.)

Conversely, a plural verb drops the s. Look at these examples:

- Those **women give** to charity. (*Women* is a plural noun and *give* is a plural verb.)
- Those football **players run** every day. (*Players* is a plural noun and *run* is a plural verb.)

PROBLEMS WITH SUBJECT-VERB AGREEMENT

Words Between the Subject and Verb

Sometimes words that come between a subject and verb (usually a prepositional phrase) will cause a writer to make a mistake in subject-verb agreement.

Incorrect The errors in my last essay was the reason for my low grade. (The subject, *errors*, is plural and the verb, *was*, should be singular; it should be changed to *were*.)

Revised The **errors** in my last essay **were** the reason for my low grade.

Incorrect The counselors in the YMCA summer camp for the exceptional child wants a pay raise for the upcoming season. (The subject, *counselors*, is plural, but the verb, *wants*, should be singular and should be changed to *want*.)

Revised The **counselors** in the YMCA summer camp for the exceptional child **want** a pay raise for the upcoming season.

Compound Subjects

Another instance that can lead to errors in subject-verb agreement is the compound subject when two subjects are joined by *and*.

> **Incorrect**   Jeremy and Roberto, who played the lead parts, was two of the most talented actors we've ever had in our theater program. (The subject consists of two elements, so the verb should be the plural *were*.)
>
> **Revised**   **Jeremy and Roberto,** who played the lead parts, **were** two of the most talented actors we've ever had in our theater program.

Correlatives

When subjects are joined by *either . . . or, neither… nor, not only … but also* or *whether … or,* the verb agrees with the subject closer to the verb.

- Neither spotted owls nor the **snail darter was** included on the endangered species list. (The singular *snail darter* is the subject closest to the verb.)

- Not only the coach in the dugout but also the **player**s on the field **know** when Smitty wants to lay down a bunt. (The plural *players* is the subject closest to the verb.)

Indefinite Pronouns

By far the most difficult problem with subject-verb agreement is in sentences containing **INDEFINITE PRONOUNS**. Some indefinite pronouns are singular, some are plural, and some can be either singular or plural.

Always Singular		Always Plural	Sometimes Singular and Sometimes Plural
anybody	anyone	both	all
everybody	everyone	few	any
nobody	either	others	many
somebody	neither	several	most
anything	each		some
nothing	none		
everything	another		
something	whatever		
one	whichever		
each one	whoever		
no one	someone		

Singular

> **Nobody** *is* right 100 percent of the time.
> **Anyone** who *wants* to go on the trip must be at the gym by 5 p.m.
> **None** of Tchaikovsky's operas *was* successful

Plural

> **Few** *were* willing to put their lives on the line.
> **Both** *want* to go.
> **Several** *are* included on the list.

Sometimes Singular, Sometimes Plural

> **Some** [of the **people** at the party] *want* to leave. (Plural)
> **Some** [of the **ink**] *is* left in the bottle. (Singular)
> **Most** [of the **passengers**] *are* staying on board tonight. (Plural)
> **Most** [of the **food**] *is* still there on the table. (Singular)

EXERCISE 5 ELIMINATING PROBLEMS WITH SUBJECT-VERB AGREEMENT: Eliminate any errors in verb use in the following sentences. Each of the sentences has one error.

1. Neither Alice nor Henry were available to come into work today.

2. Working in a candy factory with all of the heat and sweet smells are attractive to some people.

3. Something about working in a large room with thousands of pieces of sweet little candies make some people happy and others depressed.

4. Yesterday, hundreds of boxes of candy and one empty carton was sitting on the counter next to the conveyor belt.

5. Today, every one of the workers in all sections are taking a break at the same time.

ACTIVE/PASSIVE VOICE

When a verb is in the **ACTIVE VOICE**, the subject is doing the action indicated by the verb. When the verb is in the **PASSIVE VOICE**, the subject is being acted upon.

Voice has nothing to do with **VERB TENSE**; they are altogether different.

Future tense/active voice: The supervisor will fire Joe.
Future tense/passive voice: Joe will be fired by the supervisor.

In the first sentence the word "supervisor" is the subject and <u>is doing an action</u> to Joe. In the second sentence "Joe" is the subject but is <u>being acted upon</u> by the supervisor.

Active Voice
- Carl stuffed the tomatoes.
- Jerome will buy a new Lexus.

Passive Voice
- The tomatoes were stuffed by Carl.
- A new Lexus will be bought by Jerome.

The passive voice is not incorrect; it is useful when you want to emphasize the receiver of an action. For example, look at the "Carl stuffed the tomatoes" sentence. If you want to emphasize the fact that Carl accomplished this task, then you use the active voice. If, on the other hand, you want to emphasize that the tomatoes were stuffed by Carl as opposed to being stuffed by one of his coworkers, then you use the passive voice.

The problem arises when student-writers overuse the passive voice or use it in such a way that it sounds awkward and wordy.

Active: Deepti put the articles of used clothing into the box.
Passive: The articles of used clothing were put into the box by Deepti.

Active: Fiona plays the piano for all of the performances.
Passive: The piano is played by Fiona for all of the performances.

Active: You should put the money on the counter
Passive: The money should be put on the counter by you.

Which sentences sound better? Which are shorter, clearer and to the point? In most of your writing you will want to use the active voice.

EXERCISE 6   ELIMINATING PROBLEMS WITH AC-
TIVE/ PASSIVE VOICE: Rewrite each of the following sentences, changing the passive to the active voice.

1. When you receive the package in the mail, it should be opened immediately.

   _____

2. Yesterday in my math class, six problems were put on the board by the professor.

   _____

3. His new Mercedes will be driven into the garage by Raoul.

   _____

4. Mr. Snodgrass is being evaluated by Mrs. Carpenter later today.

   _____

5. I'll write the names of the employees, but the list of their responsibilities should be compiled by you.

   _____

6. Lanni was driven to work today by Jerome.

   _____

7. The package should be picked up no later than 3 p.m. by Fed Ex.

   _____

8. The invitations are being sent out by Leslie today.

   _____

9. After Tom finishes painting the porch, the brushes and rollers should be cleaned.

   _____

10. Termination notices will be sent out today by Mr. Suarez to everyone in your department.

   _____

APPROPRIATE USE OF PRONOUNS

Like subjects and verbs, problems with certain kinds of <u>**PRONOUNS**</u> occur when they don't agree in number or when the pronoun's <u>**ANTECEDENT**</u> is unclear. Another problem is a shift in <u>**POINT OF VIEW**</u>.

PRONOUN ANTECEDENTS

The word *antecedent* means the word in a sentence that comes before the pronoun and to which the pronoun refers. For example:

1. **Bobby** left *his* concert tickets on the kitchen table.
2. The **woman** in the office was working on *her* reports.
3. **Rafael** and **Maritza** parked *their* car on the street.
4. **Anyone** who has not registered yet must hand in *his/her* form today.
5. A **judge** must carefully examine the evidence brought before *him* or *her*.

Note the problem presented by some of the sentences in the examples above. When the <u>**ANTECEDENT**</u> of a pronoun is singular and masculine, as in sentence 1, the follow-up pronoun *his* is appropriate. When the antecedent is singular and feminine, as in sentence 2, the follow-up pronoun *her* is appropriate. Sentences 4 and 5, however, are not as straightforward. When the antecedent is singular but can be masculine <u>or</u> feminine, what do we do?

American schools once taught that sentences like numbers 4 and 5 should use the singular masculine pronoun. Feminists and others protested that automatically following up with the masculine pronoun for gender-neutral words like *doctor, lawyer, engineer* and *judge* created a bias in our language, indicating that women never held these kinds of jobs.

So what do we do with a sentence like 5? How about this?

- A judge must carefully examine the evidence brought before them.

Making the follow-up pronoun plural solves the gender-bias issue, but it presents a new problem—logic. A <u>singular</u> antecedent is followed by a <u>plural</u> pronoun. That's just not logical, yet frequently people talk this way ("The bus driver put their warning lights on"). The appropriate alternatives are as follows:

- A **judge** must carefully examine evidence brought before *him or her*.

Now we're correct, but a lot of sentences like that in an essay can get pretty cumbersome. The best alternative when possible is to make the antecedent plural.

- **Judges** must carefully examine the evidence brought before *them*.

If it is possible, making the antecedent plural eliminates both the gender and the logic problem.

EXERCISE 7   IDENTIFYING ANTECEDENTS: Draw a line under the pronouns and their antecedents in each of the following sentences. Each sentence contains one pronoun with its antecedent.

1. By the time Ludwig van Beethoven was six years old in 1776, the boy's mother knew that she had given birth to a musical prodigy.

2. Beethoven's mother and father encouraged Ludwig to develop his musical talent.

3. Beethoven's parents knew that they needed to provide young Ludwig with music lessons.

4. Young Beethoven was told by a court organist, "Ludwig, you will be a second Mozart."

5. When Beethoven's magnificent Ninth Symphony was first played in 1824, the composer had gone completely deaf and was unable to hear it.

PRONOUN AGREEMENT

English is probably the fastest-changing language in the world, and we can see this in the way we deal with INDEFINITE PRONOUNS.

These indefinite pronouns are singular:

anybody	nothing	another	each one	something
everything	either	whatever	no one	whoever
nobody	neither	one	someone	
somebody	each	anyone	everything	
anything	none	everyone	whichever	

Some of these words don't sound singular. *Everybody, everything, everyone,* maybe even *anybody* and *anyone* probably sound like they should be plural, but they're not. *Everybody* literally means "every single body." *None* means "not <u>one</u>." *Anybody* means "any <u>one</u> body." Therefore, in both writing and in speech, they should be singular.

- *Everybody* who needs help should bring **his** or **her** essay to the writing center.
- *Anyone* planning to leave in the morning should put **his** or **her** luggage in the corridor tonight.

As explained previously, when the antecedent is a gender-neutral noun and we're not careful, we run into a gender-bias problem. The same thing occurs when the antecedent is an indefinite pronoun:

- *Someone* left **his** books on the table.
- *Anyone* who wants to go should bring in **his** money.
- *Everybody* [literally, "every single body"] who wants to sign the petition should raise **his** hand.

"One" literally means one and "body" means a single body. If you follow that old rule of always following an indefinite pronoun with a masculine pronoun, you solve the agreement problem, but you also get a language filled with gender bias.

We can't always follow an indefinite pronoun with *his* or *him*, so what do we use instead—*her? His or her? His/her?* Make up a word, like *sher* (his and her) or *sheit* (he, she and it)? How about *their*?

- *Someone* left **their** books on the table.
- *Anyone* who wants to go should bring in **their** money.

Problem solved. But, now we have a logic problem. "When **one** is in trouble, **they** (?) should dial 911." It's illogical to have a <u>singular antecedent</u> (one) followed by a <u>plural pronoun</u> (they), but frequently this is heard in our spoken language. *Someone...their* or the *Anyone...their* combination is becoming so frequently heard in spoken language that it has become generally acceptable. It is quite possible that this will become accepted usage in ten or twenty years (even though it's illogical).

But what about our written language, which we hold to a different standard of formality? What's the answer to this pronoun agreement problem? Unfortunately, we don't have a good answer. The most widely used method for this problem is to use *his or her* or *his/her*. Whenever possible in your speech use the appropriate grammatical form—and in your written language <u>always</u> use the his/her combination or rewrite the sentence so that the antecedent is plural.

Change	Someone left *their* books on the table.
To	Someone left *his* or *her* books on the table.

Better yet, Anne left *her* books on the table. (The information is more specific <u>and</u> the pronoun problem is solved.)

Or	The students left *their* books on the table.
Or	The students left *the* books on the table.

NOTE: Sometimes the context of the sentence indicates the gender of the antecedent, so it's easy to use the appropriate pronoun. For example:

- One of the players on the women's softball team left her glove on the bus. ("One" is an indefinite singular pronoun, but you wouldn't use "his/her" in this context.)

- Someone left his coat in the men's locker room. ("Someone" is an indefinite singular pronoun, but you follow up with the masculine pronoun here because of the context of the sentence.)

EXERCISE 8   USING INDEFINITE PRONOUNS: Underline the appropriate pronoun in each of the following sentences.

1. Neither Elizabeth Dole nor Geraldine Ferarro has declared (their her his/her) candidacy.

2. Each of the fraternity members brought (their his his/her) own beer to the party.

3. Somebody on the men's baseball team forgot (their his his/her) jacket.

4. Anyone who needs a ride to the conference should leave (their his his/her) telephone number with the secretary.

5. Either Fred or Ethel will return your call and let you know whether (they he he/she) can pick you up.

6. Each of the proposals that Stanley offered has (their its) drawbacks.

7. If anybody calls, tell (them him him/her) I'll be back in about an hour.

8. Alvin Ailey was the only one of the dancers who went from being just a cast member to having a troupe of (their his his/her) own.

9. A doctor who decides to specialize should plan on spending the next four years of (their his his/her) life attending classes and working in a hospital.

10. One of the reporters left (their his his/her) notebook on the train.

PRONOUN REFERENCE
A pronoun is unclear when the reader can't easily identify the antecedent:

- Henry was fortunate enough to have seen Wojo's work while *he* was still alive. (Who was still alive—Henry or Wojo?)

- Dexter looked at the specimen through a small microscope; then he put *it* in his backpack and left the laboratory. (What did Dexter put in his backpack—the specimen or the microscope?)

- *They* should make sure we have good food in the college cafeteria. (Who should make sure—the cafeteria staff? The college administration? The students?)

Here's how they should read:

- Henry was fortunate enough to have seen Wojo's work while Wojo was still alive.

- Dexter looked at the specimen through a small microscope; then he put the specimen in his backpack and left the laboratory.

- The company that has the contract to run food services should make sure we have good food in the college cafeteria.

EXERCISE 9   CLEAR PRONOUN REFERENCES: Rewrite
each of the following sentences so that the pronoun reference is clear.

1.   Both the mother and her daughter knew that she liked surprises.

    _____

2.   The scientist told his assistant that he had won the award.

    _____

3.   Meribel looked at a new car and a used car and then decided to buy it.

    _____

4.   Eve and Fern thought her story was stronger.

    _____

5.   They should do a better job of clearing the snow from the parking lot.

    _____

PRONOUN POINT OF VIEW
Pronouns should not shift inconsistently from first person (I, we) to third (it, he,
she, they), or to the second person (you).

- As we drove along Route 66, you could see the magnificent
  mountains in the distance. (I have never been on Route 66, so I
  couldn't have seen the mountains. Replace *you* with *we*.)

- When the fire fighters arrived at the scene, you couldn't see through
  the smoke. (I wasn't at the scene of the fire. Replace *you* with *they*.)

EXERCISE 10   PRONOUN POINT OF VIEW: Cross out the
inconsistent pronoun and replace it with the appropriate one.

1.   After we got to the party, you couldn't hear yourself think because
    the music was so loud.

2.   I haven't had much success with that new "miracle diet" because you
    still need will power when it comes to eating chocolate.

3. I like to get to the clubs early because you can see all of the bands setting up.

4. After her music video made it onto MTV, Stella enjoyed being a rock star, but she didn't like all of the autographs they had to sign.

5. Yesterday, on my way to class I ran into some fog that was so thick you couldn't even see the car in front of you.

EXERCISE 11   PRONOUN POINT OF VIEW: Cross out the inconsistent pronoun and replace it with the appropriate one. You should find nine inappropriately used pronouns.

Soccer is the most widely played sport in the world. In the European and South American men's professional leagues, a soccer player who is fast and can score goals can name their own price when it comes to negotiating with club owners. They can make really big money in these areas of the world if their teams win a lot of games. Club owners typically look for a young player, often still in high school, who has a lot of skill and has the potential to greatly increase their skill level with professional experience. A player like LA Galaxy midfielder David Beckham (who also plays for the English national team), can basically name their own price in contract negotiations with owners. Players like Beckham are so popular in their areas of the world that he can't go to a restaurant without getting mobbed by fans and being harassed by paparazzi. I once saw Beckham walking through an airport in Spain, and I wanted to get his autograph, but you couldn't get near him because of the crowd that gathered around him before you could get within a hundred feet of him. Because of the enormous popularity of these professional soccer players, they try to get as close to them as they can.

CASE OF PRONOUNS

The CASE of a pronoun is the form that is used depending upon what its function is in a sentence. The three cases are subjective, objective, and possessive.

If a pronoun is used as a subject in a sentence, we use the SUBJECTIVE CASE.

- *She* is my best friend.
- Jena and *I* decided to make popcorn and watch TV last night.

If the pronoun is used as an indirect object, a direct object or an object of a preposition, then we use a pronoun in the OBJECTIVE CASE.

- Please give *me* the ball.
- The frisbee hit *him* in the head.
- Let's take a walk with *them*.

When the pronoun is used to indicate ownership, it is in the <u>POSSESSIVE CASE</u>.

- Jolene decided to put her books in *my* car.
- This sandwich is mine and that one is *yours*.

<u>REFLEXIVE PRONOUNS</u> are another type of pronoun indicating an action that reflects back on an antecedent.

- I know that I will hate *myself* in the morning.
- Kenny hit *himself* in the leg with the hatchet.
- Monica and Tanya decided to treat *themselves* to a massage and pedicure.

SUBJECTIVE CASE PRONOUNS		OBJECTIVE CASE PRONOUNS	
I	we	me	us
you	you	you	you
it, he, she	they		
him, her, it	them		

POSSESSIVE CASE PRONOUNS		REFLEXIVE PRONOUNS	
my/mine	our/ours	myself	ourselves
your/yours	your/yours	yourself	yourselves
its, his, her/hers		their/theirs	
himself/herself/itself		themselves	

PROBLEMS WITH SUBJECTIVE CASE PRONOUNS

When an objective case pronoun is put in the subject position in a sentence (usually to the left of the verb), we get sentences like these:

- *Me* and *her* went to the mall. (*Me* went to the mall? *Her* went to the mall?)
- Bob and *him* came over for dinner. (*Him* came over for dinner?)
- *Her* and Lannie want us to help them put up the posters. (*Her* wants us to put up the posters?)

> **NOTE:** When you're not sure which form of the pronoun to use, take out the other words in the subject ("*Me* and Ralph went with them") and see how the sentence sounds ("*Me* went with them").

PROBLEMS WITH OBJECTIVE CASE PRONOUNS

Another common misuse of the object pronoun heard in our language today is "between you and I." *Between* is a preposition, and the pronoun that follows it is the **OBJECT OF THE PREPOSITION**. Just as you would use *me* after other prepositions, like *for, with, or to*, you would use *me* after between.

- Do this <u>for</u> *me*.
- Go <u>with</u> *me*.
- <u>Between</u> you and *me* . . . .

> **AVOID** That money should have been given to you and *I*.
> **USE** That money should have been given to you and *me*.

Another somewhat unusual misuse that seems to have become popular in the last couple of years, especially on TV, occurs in sentences like these:

- Tomorrow night ESPN will present Sportsline, with Chris, Dave and *I*. (It should be *me*.)
- The grand jury decided not to indict *he* and his partner. (It should be *him*.)

This is another illogical misuse of a pronoun, but it's becoming more and more common, especially among TV sportscasters and newscasters. Apparently they think their version sounds more refined (?) educated (?) but to anyone who knows grammar, these mistakes are the equivalent of fingernails on a chalkboard.

A NOTE ON WHO/WHOM

Who is in the subjective case and *whom* is in the objective case. Typical usage is as follows:

- The student *who* sells the most tickets will win the bicycle. (*Who* is the subject of the adjective clause *who sells the most tickets*.)

- Franny, *who* was my closest friend in college, is now the CEO of a Fortune 500 company. (*Who* is the subject of the adjective clause *who was my closest friend in college* that describes Franny.)

- That student, *whom* you never met, won the bicycle. (*Whom* starts the adjective clause *whom you never met*, but it is not the subject of the clause — *you* is the subject. If you rearrange the words, *you never met whom*, you can see that *whom* is the object of *you met*: therefore, you use the objective case here.)

- Franny, *whom* you saw on television last night, was my best friend in college. (*Whom* is not the subject of this adjective clause—*you* is. *You saw whom on television last night: whom* is the direct object of *you saw* [*whom*].)

Most Americans no longer make much of a distinction between *who* and *whom* in their speech patterns. However, to be considered a careful, educated writer, you should still make the distinction between *who* and *whom*.

In speech, and certainly in writing, whom should always be used if it directly follows a preposition. For example:

- To *whom* should the package be sent?

Even if you can't always remember all of the rules, if you can remember the preposition-followed-by-*whom* rule, you will at least know the most common use of *whom*.

EXERCISE 12 WHO/WHOM: Put a C in the blank if the appropriate form of who/whom is used or an I if the inappropriate form is used in each of the following sentences.

_____ 1. All of the Navy fliers whom were at the dinner last night were aces.

_____ 2. The man with whom I live is my dear, dear uncle.

_____ 3. Who should I send the bill to?

_____ 4. Who said you could go with us?

_____ 5. Maria Mendoza, whom is my next-door neighbor, brought me apples.

_____ 6. For whom are you painting that mural?

_____ 7. Who is the best writer is your class?

PROBLEMS WITH POSSESSIVE CASE PRONOUNS

The most common problem here is confusion between <u>HOMONYMS</u> (words that sound alike but are spelled differently and have different meanings).

- *You're* not supposed to come to work late. (NOT *Your*)
- George and Leon put *their* clothes in the locker. (NOT *there*)

PROBLEMS WITH REFLEXIVE PRONOUNS

Like "Me and her went . . ." and "Between you and I . . ." misuse of certain reflexives has become popular in recent years.

- John and *I* will make the decision and let you know. (NOT John and *myself*)
- The letter was addressed to Leona and *me* (NOT Leona and *myself*.

Don't use reflexive pronouns when you should be using the objective case.

PRONOUNS VS CONTRACTIONS

Sometimes college-level writers will confuse contractions with certain possessive pronouns. Remember, possessive pronouns do not need an apostrophe — they are possessive simply by their spelling.

Possessive Pronoun	Contraction
its	it's
your	you're
their	they're
whose	who's

Don't write, "The dog slipped out of *it's* collar," when you mean "The dog slipped out of *its* collar."

USING WHO, WHICH AND THAT

These three words, known as **RELATIVE PRONOUNS**, sometimes cause agreement and usage problems. In current usage, *who* refers to people, *which* and *that* only to inanimate objects.

When *who, which*, and *that* are used to begin an adjective clause, they should agree with the closest noun preceding them. Some examples:

- Moesha is one of those **women** who **are** able to raise a family while holding a full-time job. ("Moesha is one of those women *which* are able to raise a family while holding a full-time job," wouldn't be appropriate because *women* denotes human beings. Also, the verb *are* agrees with *women*, not *Moesha* or *one*.)
- Antonio is the oldest of several cast **members** who **prefer** to play the parts of younger men. (The verb *prefer* agrees with *members*, not *Antonio*.)
- Incorrect coding was one of several **problems** that **were** stopping the program from running. (The auxiliary verb *were* agrees with *problems*.)

A LAST POINT ABOUT THE USE OF PRONOUNS

Pronouns that follow forms of the verb *to be* should be in the subjective case.

Therefore:

> It is *I*. (not "It's *me*.")
> It is *they*. (not "It's *them*.")
> It was *I* who called you last night. (not "It was *me* . . .")
> It was *he* who spread those nasty rumors about you.
> (not "It was *him* . . .")

To many people, the examples in the list above just don't sound right because we're so unaccustomed to hearing "proper" English used around us. English is a dynamic, constantly changing language, and what people were used to hearing fifty years ago many sound strange to us today. In spoken language, "It's me" is generally acceptable. In writing, however, you should apply the guidelines discussed above.

EXERCISE 13   CHOOSING THE APPROPRIATE PRO-

NOUN: Circle the appropriate pronoun in the following sentences.

1. The chairperson of the Student Government Association appointed Shahid and (I me) to the rules committee.

2. When Professor Tinsley asked, "Who's there?" I used my best grammar and correctly replied, ("It is me." "It is I.")

3. Tai'tia and Larry said (their they're there) too tired to go out with us tonight.

4. Kristen told Millie that it was (her they're Millie's) turn to do the dishes.

5. (Its Its' It's) never too late to make amends to someone you have wronged.

EXERCISE 14   CHOOSING THE APPROPRIATE PRONOUN: Circle the appropriate pronoun in the following sentences.

1. The newly licensed driver forgot to use (their his) directional signal and got a ticket.

2. We wanted to go to Philadelphia last night, but there was no way (we you) could drive in such a heavy rainstorm.

3. Most of the people (who whom) were at the concert last week have been fans of the group since they started five years ago in England.

4. Try to keep (your you're) temper under control at the party tonight.

5. Anyone who wants to go on the ski trip must make (his/her their) reservation by 5 o'clock today.

6. Shawna and (me I) will meet you at the south entrance to Veterans' Park.

7. As I was driving through Yosemite National Park, I was overwhelmed by all of the beauty around (you me).

8. A mother needs (her their) time to relax and get away from the children.

9. The director said that Hilma and (me I) can each play a leading role in the production.

10. The coach has chosen David and (me I) for the swim meet.

USING MODIFIERS

MISPLACED or DANGLING MODIFIERS are modifiers, usually prepositional or participial phrases or adjective clauses, placed too far away from the words they are intended to modify (misplaced) or have nothing in the sentence to modify (dangling).

These are misplaced modifiers:

- Standing on the corner, the car slammed into the crowd of people. (The car was standing on the corner?)
  Revised The car slammed into the crowd of people standing on the corner.
- Marcy has planned on being a nurse for several years. (Marcy has been planning for several years to be a nurse? Or will she be a nurse for several years and then go to another career?)
  Revised Marcy has planned for several years to be a nurse.

These are dangling modifiers:

- After examining all of the issues, a consensus was reached. (Who is examining all of the issues? Whoever it is, he or she isn't in the sentence.)
  Revised After examining all of the issues, we reached a consensus.

- While talking to my instructor, the sprinkler system suddenly activated. (Who was talking to your instructor? The sprinkler system?)
  Revised While I was talking to my instructor, the sprinkler system suddenly activated.

EXERCISE 15 MISPLACED MODIFIERS: Place a check mark ✔ next to the sentence that is clearer because all of the modifiers are closely connected to the word or words they modify.

1. _____ a. George Bernard Shaw was born in 1856 in Dublin, Ireland near the site of the famous Abbey Theatre, dying in 1950 at the age of 94.

   _____ b. George Bernard Shaw was born in Dublin, Ireland in 1856 near the site of the famous Abey Theatre and died in 1950 at the age of 94.

2. _____ a. Moving to London in 1876, five novels brought Shaw to the attention of English literary critics.

_____ b. After moving to London in 1876, Shaw wrote five novels that brought him to the attention of English literary critics.

3. _____ a. While in London, Shaw heard a lecture by Henry George that convinced him of the merits of socialism.

_____ b. While in London, a lecture by Henry George impressed Shaw and convinced him of the merits of socialism.

4. _____ a. In 1892, Shaw wrote his first play, *Widower's Houses*, which was produced at J.T. Grein's Independent Theater.

_____ b. Produced at J.T. Grein's Independent Theater, Shaw wrote his first play, *Widower's Houses*, in 1892.

5. _____ a. Devoting himself to the writing of dramatic works, *The Devil's Disciple* was successfully produced by Shaw in New York in 1897.

_____ b. Following the success of his play, *The Devil's Disciple*, in New York in 1897, Shaw devoted himself to the writing of dramatic works.

EXERCISE 16 MISPLACED MODIFIERS: Put a C in front of the sentences below in which the modifier is appropriately placed. Put an M in front of those that contain misplaced or dangling modifiers and rewrite the sentence to improve the clarity.

_____ 1. As a young girl, my mother took good care of me.

_____

_____

_____ 2. Thousands of veterans and visitors on both sides of the river welcomed the *USS New Jersey*, as the 45,000-ton behemoth passed under the Delaware Memorial Bridge, a beautiful sight to all who were there.

_____

_____

_____ 3. About 1,000 guests watched the battleship go up the Delaware River aboard the Twin Capes Ferry.

_____

_____

_____ 4. Two strange-looking men in white suits entered the chimpanzee house at the zoo.

_____

_____

_____ 5. Chattering loudly, Daniel was suddenly alerted by the chimpanzees to imminent danger.

_____

_____

KEEPING ELEMENTS PARALLEL

PARALLELISM occurs when two or more of the elements in a sentence follow the same grammatical pattern as the rest of the elements. Look at the power that parallel elements can bring to your sentences:

- I came; I saw; I conquered.
  Julius Caesar, quoted in Suetonius, *Lives of the Caesars*

- We must all hang together, or assuredly we shall all hang separately.
  Benjamin Franklin, at the signing of the Declaration of Independence

- But in a larger sense, we cannot dedicate — we cannot consecrate — we cannot hallow — this ground.
  Abraham Lincoln, The Gettysburg Address

- ... we shall fight on the beaches, we shall fight on the landing grounds, we shall fight in the fields and in the streets, we shall fight in the hills, we shall never surrender.
  Winston Churchill, speech to the House of Commons, June 4, 1940

When you use parallel construction in your sentences, you are arranging two or more grammatically equivalent elements into a balanced pattern. When one of the elements is another grammatical form, the parallelism breaks down; this is faulty parallelism.

For example, writers sometimes get into trouble by switching from the active to the passive voice in the same sentence:

- Fipster sent the package to Geneva Corp., *but it was never received by the owners.*

The first part of the sentence is in the active voice, but the second part switches to passive. Look at the revised version where both clauses are in the active voice:

- Fipster sent the package to Geneva Corp., *but the owners never received it.*

Another breakdown in parallelism occurs when verb tenses are switched in the middle of the sentence:

- I left class early, but I *don't* go directly home.

The first part of the sentence is in the past tense, but the second part is in the present tense. The sentence should be revised to look like this:

- I left class early, but I *didn't* go directly home.

Here are some other examples of problems in parallelism of verb tenses:

NOT PARALLEL I *would like* to attend, but I *will need* to bring my son.
PARALLEL I *would like* to attend, but I *would need* to bring my son.

NOT PARALLEL I *will* appreciate it if you *would* send me a ticket.
PARALLEL I *would* appreciate it if you *would* send me a ticket.

NOT PARALLEL In the story, Fletcher *leaves* Dallas and *went* to Denver.
PARALLEL In the story, Fletcher *leaves* Dallas and *goes* to Denver.
In the story, Fletcher *left* Dallas and *went* to Denver.

Yet another form of a break in parallelism is the mixing of unlike grammatical units. You don't have to know the terms used to describe the grammar, such as participial phrase or gerund, but your sentence sense should tell you that the elements within the sentence don't fit together. Look at these examples:

- I like *playing* video games, *watching* TV and *to read* a good mystery. (*reading*)

- During a typical day, an educator in the primary grades must teach lessons, grade papers and *should see* that the children play well together. (*see*)

- Jason is selfish, nasty, conceited and *enjoys making cruel remarks*. (Eliminate "enjoys making" and "remarks.")

EXERCISE 17 PARALLEL CONSTRUCTION: Rewrite each of the following sentences so that all of the elements are parallel.

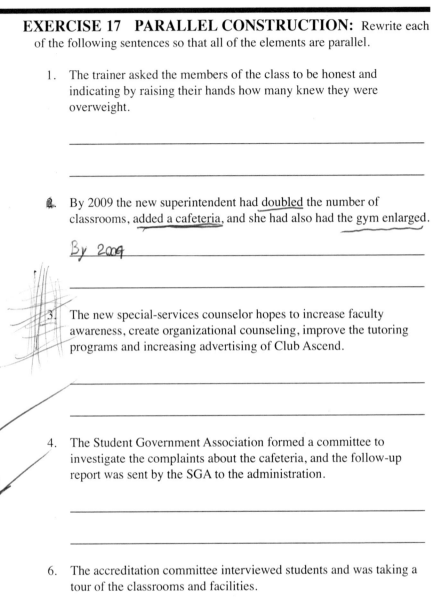

1. The trainer asked the members of the class to be honest and indicating by raising their hands how many knew they were overweight.

_____

_____

2. By 2009 the new superintendent had <u>doubled</u> the number of classrooms, added a cafeteria, and she had also had the gym enlarged.

By 2009 _____

_____

3. The new special-services counselor hopes to increase faculty awareness, create organizational counseling, improve the tutoring programs and increasing advertising of Club Ascend.

_____

_____

4. The Student Government Association formed a committee to investigate the complaints about the cafeteria, and the follow-up report was sent by the SGA to the administration.

_____

_____

6. The accreditation committee interviewed students and was taking a tour of the classrooms and facilities.

_____

_____

7. When I took a philosophy course, I had discovered a whole new

world of ideas that gave me a framework for living my life.

_____

_____

8. When I took biology, however, cutting up the pig, then to write a
    report about what I found didn't appeal to me.

    _____

    _____

9. A course in poetry can be interesting, enlightening and it can even
    entertain you.

    _____

    _____

10. Leaving your car in the student parking lot can be an adventure that
    is bringing you in contact with many strange and exotic life forms.

    _____

    _____

USING ADJECTIVES AND ADVERBS

ADJECTIVES modify (describe or give additional information about) nouns and pronouns. ADVERBS modify verbs, adjectives or other adverbs and usually end in ly.

COMPARATIVE AND SUPERLATIVE ADJECTIVES

The comparative and the superlative are forms of the adjective and the adverb. The comparative is used to compare one thing with another. The superlative is used to compare one thing with all others in a group of three or more.

- Ben is a *fast* runner. (one)
- Ben is a *faster* runner than Jared. (two)
- Ben is the *fastest* runner in his class. (three or more)

To form the comparative of a one-syllable adjective and some two-syllable adjectives, add *er* to the end of the word and use *than* somewhere in the sentence:

- Yogi is *smarter than* the average bear.

To form the superlative of a one-syllable adjective and some two-syllable adjectives, add est to the end of the word.

- Yogi is the *smartest* bear in the woods.

For some two-syllable adjectives and all longer adjectives, add *more* when comparing two things and *most* when comparing three or more.

- John gave us his *candid* opinion.
- John gave us a *more candid* opinion than Leroy did. (See how bad *candider* sounds?)
- John gave us the *most candid* opinion of all of the consultants.

Some adjectives have special forms of the comparative and superlative:

Positive	Comparative	Superlative
good	better	best
bad	worse	worst
little	less	least
much	more	most

COMPARATIVE ADVERBS To form a comparative adverb, use *more* before adverbs ending in *ly*.

- That star shines *more brightly* than the one next to it.
- Winchell walked *more steadily* than his inebriated friends.

GOOD AND WELL/BAD AND BADLY Two sets of adjectives/adverbs that frequently cause problems for college-level writers are *good/well* and *bad/badly*. *Good* and *bad* are adjectives; *well* and *badly* are adverbs.

USE	I played badly in last night's game.
AVOID	I played bad in last night's game.

USE	I did well on my test.
AVOID	I did good on my test.

USE	I felt bad when I heard about your brother's death. (*Felt* is a linking verb and is followed by an adjective.)
AVOID	I felt badly when I heard about your brother's death.

PAST PARTICIPLES USED AS ADJECTIVES

English has a form of verbs, called *verbals*, that look like verbs but really aren't—*infinitives, gerunds* and *participles*.

A participle is a form of a verb that functions as an adjective. The present participle ends in *ing* (a *dancing* bear) while the past participle ends in *d, ed* (a *potted* plant) or an irregular verb ending (a *broken* nose).

Sometimes we don't hear the endings on certain past participles, and they're written incorrectly in essays. For example,

USE   We looked at *used* cars yesterday.
AVOID   We looked at *use* cars yesterday.

USE   I like *hard-boiled* eggs.
AVOID   I like *hard-boil* eggs.

Watch for dropped endings of participles in writing and speech.

EXERCISE 18   PROBLEMS WITH PARTICIPLES USED
AS ADJECTIVES: Circle the misused participle in the following sentences and write the correct form in the blank.

1. Lillian was depressed because her iPod was broke.
    bro ken

2. My favorite part of Thanksgiving is the mash potatoes.
    _____

3. Each month Royce's church sends food and clothing to underdevelop countries in the far east.
    Undeveloped

4. Red's speckle complexion made him look like Howdy Doody.
    _____

5. I remember when teenagers thought rip pants were an essential part of their wardrobes.
    _____

6. The shock look on Sylvia's face told us we had managed to surprise her on her birthday.
    _____

EXERCISE 19   PROBLEMS WITH ADJECTIVES AND ADVERBS: Circle the appropriate adjective or adverb in the following sentences.

1. Liza said she didn't do too (good well) on the psychology mid-term.

2. The professor told the class that their grades were the (worse worst) she had ever seen.

3. LaToya feels (bad badly) every time she sees a homeless person on the street.

4. Jackson managed to pick the (most wet wettest) seats in the whole stadium.

5. On the other hand, if I bowl (badly bad), I might not even make the team.

EXERCISE 20   PROBLEMS WITH ADJECTIVES AND ADVERBS: Circle any misused adjectives and adverbs in the following sentences and write the correct form in the blank following the sentence.

1. I hope I do good on my math test tomorrow. _____

2. The lamp was already broke when I took it out of the box. _____

3. The owners needed to get a liquor license for their remodel restaurant. _____

4. Celeste felt badly when she lost the match. _____

5. "This is the worse meal I've ever eaten," said Michelle. _____

PART 5

PUNCTUATION

PUNCTUATION

Why is it important to follow established punctuation rules in your writing? Look at this sentence:

If Megan's father calls Mary Lynn should talk to him.

Do you understand who should talk to the father in this sentence? It's virtually impossible to figure this out because of the lack of punctuation. Look at these alternatives:

If Megan's father calls, Mary Lynn should talk to him.

If Megan's father calls Mary, Lynn should talk to him.

Here's another sentence that is unclear:

When the bank failed the test for insolvency was established.

Did the bank fail the test? Or did the bank fail (go out of business)? Look what happens when a comma is added:

When the bank failed, the test for insolvency was established.

Do you see the problems that arise when punctuation is either omitted or put in the wrong place? Look at the confusion caused by this sentence:

On our class trip we visited St. Louis, Missouri, Kansas City, Kansas, Oklahoma City, Oklahoma, Lincoln, Nebraska, and Boulder, Colorado.

Where did we go on our trip?! Look at this revision:

On our class trip we visited St. Louis, Missouri; Kansas City, Kansas; Oklahoma City, Oklahoma; Lincoln, Nebraska; and Boulder, Colorado.

Punctuation can be critically important to our understanding of the meaning of a sentence. At the very least, standardized punctuation often helps us to read a piece of writing faster and more efficiently.

As a college-level writer, you need to be aware of your punctuation. Although it may not seem important, one misplaced comma or semi-colon can sabotage the meaning of your sentence. Punctuation marks are like math symbols: use the wrong one and you'll get the wrong result.

COMMAS

The COMMA has six major uses:

1) To set off introductory material

Introductory adverb clause

Note that if the adverb clause comes at the end of the sentence, a comma is not normally used. You may see, however, that this is changing, and you will frequently see the comma used when the dependent clause is placed at the end. At this point, it's best to stick to the established rule and drop the comma when the dependent clause is at the end of the sentence.

- *If you see Todd in class today,* please tell him I want to talk to him.
  Please tell Todd I want to talk to him *if you see him in class today.*
- *Because I took 18 credits,* I'm having difficulty keeping up with my coursework.
  I'm having difficulty keeping up with my coursework *because I took 18 credits.*

Introductory prepositional phrase

The general rule is to place a comma after a prepositional phrase at the beginning of a sentence if the phrase is five or more words.

- *During the Giants-Bears game last Sunday,* Eli Manning threw three touchdown passes.
- *In the summer* I like to go to Long Beach Island with my friends.

Introductory participial phrase

Participial phrases consist of a group of related words that function as an adjective. Place the comma after the phrase.

- *Pleased with his grades,* Marvin treated himself to an ice cream sundae.
- *Falling faster and faster,* Kevin quickly pulled the ripcord.
- *Laughing, singing and dancing,* the partygoers stayed out until dawn.

Introductory infinitive phrase

Infinitive phrases consist of the word *to* plus a verb, such as "*To err* is human, *to forgive,* divine." Place a comma after the phrase.

- *To set the record straight,* Sammy decided to tell his version of the story.
- *To settle the bet,* Jitters and Hardboil played paper, scissors and rock.

EXERCISE 1   COMMAS WITH INTRODUCTORY ELE-
MENTS: Put commas in the appropriate places in the following sentences.

1. When Edgar Allan Poe was born in Boston in 1809 the United States was still a relatively new nation.

2. After both of Edgar's parents died in 1811 he was sent to Virginia to live with the Allan family.

3. Finding life with the Allans in Virginia too confining Poe decided to apply for admission to the University of Virginia.

4. During Poe's freshman year at the university he associated with a bad crowd and accumulated considerable gambling debt.

5. To avoid his stepfather's anger over his dismissal from the university Poe joined the Army as a common soldier.

6. Continuing his rebellion against established authority Poe was soon asked to leave West Point.

2)   <u>To separate complete thoughts</u>

Use a comma to separate the two complete thoughts in a compound sentence. Place the comma <u>before</u> the coordinating conjunctions (**FANBOYS:** *for, and, nor, but, or, yet, so*).

- Henry and Mona put the pillows and candles on the table**, *and*** then they invited Maude to join them.
- Eugene asked Marsha to go to the party with him**, *but*** she had made other plans.
- I don't want you to touch my monitor**, *nor*** do I want you near my CPU.

NOTE: If the second part of the sentence isn't a clause (doesn't contain a subject-verb unit), no comma is used.

- Henry and Mona put the pillows and candles on the table *and* invited Maude to join them.
- Marsha had planned to go to the party with Eugene *but* changed her mind.
- Don't touch my monitor *nor* my CPU.

EXERCISE 2   COMMAS TO SEPARATE COMPLETE THOUGHTS: Put commas in the appropriate places in the following sentences. Some of the sentences do not require commas.

1. The alarm was called in at 10:30 p.m. but the house was already engulfed in flames when the firefighters arrived.

2. A fine arts major is required to take a life drawing course and then follow up with an intermediate or advanced drawing course.

3. West State Street is five miles long and runs between Hamilton and Ewing Townships in central New Jersey.

4. Annabelle Lewis never seemed to me to be intelligent yet she always seemed to manage to get 90 or above on all of her tests.

5. Jared didn't invite Moesha to his party last month so she won't invite him to hers next week.

6. I can choose to accept the job at McDonald's or I can continue looking for a job more suitable to my considerable talents.

7. LaStrade wanted to track down the killer but he didn't know where to begin looking.

8. Albert wanted to apply for a job in the computer industry but he couldn't figure out how to put his résumé on the Internet.

9. Bernie made a left turn and drove another five blocks to get to the Honda dealership.

10. Mick Fleetwood is fifty-five years old but he can still play the drums like a much younger man.

3)   To set off words that interrupt the flow of thought

Nonessential adjective clauses
These clauses begin with **RELATIVE PRONOUNS** (*who, whom, whose, which, that*). If the clause is **essential** to the meaning or the identification of someone in the sentence, no commas are used. If the information in the clause is **nonessential** to the sentence, it is set off by commas.

- The woman *who owns the corner store in our neighborhood* loves children. (The subject could be <u>any</u> woman, so we need the adjective clause to pinpoint exactly whom we are talking about—thus, no commas.)
- Maria Sanchez, *who owns the corner store in our neighborhood,* loves children. (Maria Sanchez has already been identified, so the information in the adjective clause isn't essential.)
- The student *whose car was stolen from the east parking lot* was angry.(The adjective clause is essential so that we know which student was angry.)
- The student government president of our college, *whose car was stolen from the east parking lot,* was angry. (Since we know who the student is, the information in the adjective clause is nonessential.)
- The body *that was found in the East River* has not yet been identified. (*That* clauses are usually essential and not set off by commas.)
- The new student government constitution, *which we worked so hard to get passed,* failed by a 2-1 margin. (*Which* clauses are usually not essential and are set off by commas.)

Appositives
Appositives follow and rename an element in the sentence.

- J.D. Salinger, *the author of* <u>Catcher in the Rye</u>, is seldom seen in public.
- The author of <u>Catcher in the Rye</u>, *J.D. Salinger,* is seldom seen in public.

Note the similarity between the nonessential adjective clause and the appositive:

- Donald Shelton, *CEO of the Dallas Urban League,* came here to speak last week. (appositive)
- Donald Shelton, *who is the CEO of the Dallas Urban League,* came here to speak last week. (nonrestrictive adective clause)

Adjectives that follow the words they modify
Sometimes, instead of preceding the words they modify, adjectives will be placed after the word, usually for dramatic effect. Put these adjectives within commas.

- Arnold, *triumphant but tired,* dragged himself into the locker room.
- The old man, *sniffling, wheezing and coughing,* walked slowly down the street.

EXERCISE 3   COMMAS WITH INTERRUPTERS: Put commas where they are needed in the following sentences.

1. Garcilaso Inca De La Vega a Peruvian writer was the first significant native American historian.

2. Garcilaso who was born in Cuzco, Peru was the son of a Spanish conquistador and an Incan princess.

3. Garcilaso using the pen name *El Inca* wrote a history of DeSoto's conquests in North America.

4. *Los comentarios reales* an account of the Inca civilization before the invasion of the Spaniards was written in 1609.

5. *La historia general del Perú* which is a history of Peru after the Spanish conquest was published in 1617.

4)   To separate items in a series

Items in a series are separated with commas. Placing a final comma in the series (usually just before a conjunction) is the writer's stylistic option. The modern trend is toward fewer commas, so many writers don't put the comma before the conjunction unless the sentence would be unclear without it. Just be consistent.

- Bring a *hammer, chisel, hacksaw and nylon rope* to the "Get Out of Jail Free" party tonight.
- Next semester Alysha will take *chemistry, English, Spanish, psychology and modern dance.*
- The soldier walked along the base of the *high, moss-covered* wall of the fort.

NOTE: A comma is placed between items in a series only if the word *and* sounds natural in place of the comma.

- The soldier walked along the base of the high *and* moss-covered wall of the fort. (Sounds OK, so use a comma).
- The soldier walked along the base of the high stone wall of the fort. (The "high *and* stone wall" doesn't sound right, so no comma is used.)

EXERCISE 4   COMMAS WITH ITEMS IN A SERIES: Put commas where they are needed in the following sentences.

1. The four leading mathematicians of all time are Archimedes Euclid Newton and Gauss.

2. Sir Isaac Newton was a brilliant mathematician a noted and well-respected physicist and one of the foremost scientific intellects of all time.

3. In addition to his career as a scientist and mathematician, Newton was elected Warden of the Royal Mint in 1696 Master of the Mint in 1699 and Member of Parliament in 1701.

4. Among Newton's noted achievements were the calculations of the force needed to hold the moon in its orbit (inspired by the famous apple falling from a tree in his orchard) the centripetal force needed to hold a stone in a sling and the relation between the length of a pendulum and the time of its swing.

5. Newton spent the later years of his life revising his major works polishing his studies of ancient history defending himself against critics and carrying out his duties as an elected official.

5)   To set off direct quotations

Separate the speaker from his/her exact words with a comma.

- Jeremy said, "Don't come near me!"
- "Please put your name in the upper left-hand corner," said Professor Schwartz.
- "As you leave class today," the professor said, "put your essays on my desk."

NOTE: In American English, commas and periods are <u>always</u> placed inside the closing quotation marks, even if only the last word in the sentence is in quotes. Likewise, colons and semicolons are <u>always</u> placed outside of the close-quote mark. Question marks and exclamation marks can be in or out, depending on the context.

- Anita was so angry at Pauley that she called him a "muttonhead."
- Erin wrote a poem entitled "When Autumn Beckons."
- Are you the one who called me an "absent-minded egghead"?
- Alex asked, "Ariel, what size shoe do you wear?"

EXERCISE 5   COMMAS WITH DIRECT QUOTATIONS:
Put commas where they are needed in the following sentences.

1.   Larry said "Mary, where is Andrew?"

2.   "Well, Larry " said Mary "I think he's in the back yard."

3.   "I don't think so, Mary " said Larry. "I already looked out there."

4.   Mary replied "Gee whiz, Larry, he'd better be in the backyard because we buried him there last week."

6)   <u>To meet certain other conventions of writing (addresses; dates; num-bers; letter greetings and closings; direct address to a person)</u>

Addresses
Trenton, New Jersey 08690   Washington, D.C.   Atlanta, GA

> **NOTE:** No comma between state and Zip Code

Dates
December 7, 1941   November 23, 1963   February 15, 2001

> **NOTE:** In text place a comma after the year: *President John F. Kennedy was assassinated November 23, 1963, in Dallas, Texas.*

Letter Greetings and Closings
Dear Mom,   Sincerely yours,   Regards,

> **NOTE:** Use the comma after the greeting in a friendly letter. In business correspondence use a COLON after the greeting (*Dear Mr. Trump: Dear Senator Smith:*)

Numbers
          5,000   200,000   1,000,000

> **NOTE:** In four-digit numbers (*5307*) the comma is sometimes omitted.

Direct Address
*   Look, Stan, it's the Statue of Liberty!
*   I told you, Dolores, that you have to start coming to class on time, or you'll fail the course.

EXERCISE 6 COMMAS: Put commas wherever they are needed in the following sentences. In the blank beneath the sentence, put the letter(s) of the reason(s) why the comma should be added to the sentence.

A. introductory material
B. separate complete thoughts
C. interrupt the flow of thought

D. to separate items in a series
E. direct quotations
F. other conventions

1. Raoul said to Santiago "Whenever I read a story by Pablo Medina I feel as if I am a character in the story."   C   D

2. Professor Bennett who is my favorite teacher asked the students to bring a dictionary a newspaper scissors and paste to the next class.   E   B

3. Kamlesh was supposed to receive his bachelor's degree on May 26 1999 but he failed a course and had to go to summer school.   B

4. LaToya is a registered nurse but she has chosen to work in an HMO administrative position rather than a hospital.   C   B

5. The new guidelines which were intended to reduce paperwork have resulted in even more memos and the staff members are upset.   E

6. The article in yesterday's *New York Times* incorrectly said "The population of New Brunswick is 73 147."   A   D

7. Whenever Ramona parks her car in her garage she locks the car doors turns on her anti-theft device and bolts the garage door.   C   E

8. Leona who is the chief corporate financial officer thought that last month's telephone bill of $1 457 689 was a bit excessive.   E   B

9. Cheryl said "The staff would love to attend the conference at Yale but the SGA won't agree to allocate the money."   C   B

10. Supatra who attended the University of Virginia wanted to return to Bangkok but she was worried about finding a job.

SEMICOLONS

The SEMICOLON is an important punctuation mark for college-level writers. Its correct use in your writing indicates a certain level of sophistication. Conversely, its incorrect use can often lead to SENTENCE FRAGMENTS, so be careful when you use it.

The semicolon has two important functions: 1) to replace the coordinating conjunction (FANBOYS) in a compound sentence; 2) to separate items in a series that contain other internal punctuation.

Compound sentences

- Peter loves the opera, **so** he goes to the Met every Tuesday night.
  Peter loves the opera; he goes to the Met every Tuesday night. (The semi-colon replaces the , *so*.)

- I like watching silent movies, **but** Aimee is bored by them.
  I like watching silent movies; **however,** Aimee is bored by them.
  (A semicolon replaces the comma when an adverbial conjunction is used in place of a coordinating conjunction.)

Items in a series with internal punctuation

- On her latest business trip Barbara visited Tokyo, Japan; Melbourne, Australia; Beijing, China; and Auckland, New Zealand.

- Enrico has interview appointments with Marsha Stolts, who is the personnel director at Emco; Leo Tremaine, the chief of operations at Lanning Industries; and Ruth Ganges, a department director at Sellmor, Inc.

NOTE: When the semicolon is used to separate items in a series containing punctuation within the items, the semicolon before the final conjunction is **required**, not optional, as is the case with items in a series separated by commas.

EXERCISE 7   SEMICOLONS: Put semicolons in the appropriate places in the following sentences. Some of the sentences are correct as written and should be left alone.

1.   Trinidad and Tobago is an independent country in the Caribbean Ocean it consists of the southernmost islands of the West Indies.

2.   The country comprises the islands of Trinidad and Tobago and several smaller islands, the largest of which are Chacachacare and Little Tobago.

3.   Port of Spain is the capital other major cities include San Fernando and Arima.

4.   The country's flag is red with a black diagonal edged in white, running from the upper left to the lower right.

5.   Several languages are spoken in Trinidad and Tobago: English, the principal and official language Hindi, the language of the East Indian population and French and Spanish, the languages of the early European explorers who visited the country.

6.   The country is a member of the British Commonwealth of Nations during World War II the United States maintained a naval base there.

7.   The island of Trinidad is located just off the coast of Venezuela the island of Tobago is about 25 miles to the northeast of Trinidad.

8.   Christopher Columbus was the first European to sight Trinidad, landing there in June of 1498.

9.   Slavery was abolished in 1834, and three major groups of workers were brought in from other areas: fishermen, mainly Portuguese, from Europe laborers, predominantly Chinese, from Asia and clerks and office workers, mostly from India.

10. In 1958 Trinidad entered the Federation of the West Indies when Jamaica, with half the land and population of the entire group, withdrew in 1962, the federation was dissolved.

EXERCISE 8 SEMICOLONS: Where appropriate, replace the commas with semicolons in the following sentences. Some of the sentences are correct as written.

1. On August 4, 1892, someone killed Lizzie Borden's mother and father, the murderer hacked the Bordens to death with an ax.

2. The two elder Bordens were alone in their house at the time of the murders, Lizzie was working out in the barn.

3. When the bodies were found by police, Mr. Borden was on the couch in the living room, and Mrs. Borden was in an upstairs bedroom.

4. Each of the victims had been hit numerous times with both the sharp blade and the blunt end of the ax, each was found lying in a pool of blood.

5. While searching through the house looking for clues, police found blood splattered everywhere in the living room and in the upstairs bedroom.

6. The ax belonging to the family wasn't in its usual place in the cellar, police thought that it probably had been used as the murder weapon.

7. The Bordens, who were financially well off, kept their cash and jewels in a safe in the barn, nothing had been taken.

8. Because the murder weapon was never found and nothing was taken from the safe, suspicion immediately fell upon Lizzie.

9. Tried for murder in 1893, Lizzie Borden was acquitted of all charges, however, many people in the town still thought she was guilty.

10. From that case came the famous jingle, "Lizzie Borden took an ax and gave her father forty whacks . . . ."

QUOTATION MARKS

The primary use of **QUOTATION MARKS** is to set off the exact words used by a speaker or writer.

- Professor Callahan said, **"All research papers must be handed in by 5 p.m. today."**
- **"Don't call me—I won't be home until midnight,"** Darlene said.
- **"Oh Hans,"** Maria said, **"let's practice my putting skills."**

Note the distinction between a DIRECT QUOTE and an INDIRECT QUOTE (PARA-PHRASE):

Direct Quote:
Edward Teller said, "Hundreds of thousands of Japanese soldiers would have died in battle if the atomic bomb had not been dropped on Hiroshima."

Indirect Quote (Paraphrase):
Edward Teller said **that** hundreds of thousands of Japanese soldiers would have died in battle if the atomic bomb had not been dropped on Hiroshima.

> **NOTE**: In a research paper, you cannot take a direct quote and make it a paraphrase by deleting the quotation marks and adding a *that* without citing your source. If you do, it is considered **plagiarism**.

When you have a **quote within a quote**, use single quotation marks (apostrophe on the keyboard) within double quotation marks:

- Susan whispered to Ralphie, "Your old girlfriend Janice called me last night and said, 'Leave my Ralphie alone or I'll cut your ears off.'"

If you ever have a quote within a quote within a quote (not likely), alternate between double and single quotation marks:

- Mrs. Sternmeister told her class, "Sylvia Plath once said to me, 'The greatest poem ever written is Edwin Arlington Robinson's "Miniver Cheevy."'" (Note that the period goes <u>inside</u> all of the close quotation marks.)

EXERCISE 9   QUOTATION MARKS: Place quotation marks where appropriate in the following sentences.

1. Tommy said, I love reading novels by famous authors.

2. My favorite novel, he said, is *Grapes of Wrath* by John Steinbeck.

3. I like Steinbeck's writing style, Tommy said. I also like his ability to create memorable characters.

4. But his use of realistic dialogue is, to me, Steinbeck's greatest strength, continued Tommy.

5. My favorite line, said Tommy, is from *Grapes of Wrath* when Tom Joad says, We are all a part of the great oversoul, the great oneness of the universe.

EXERCISE 10   DIRECT/INDIRECT QUOTATIONS: Determine which of the following sentences contain direct quotes and which contain indirect. Add capitalization and punctuation in the sentences that contain direct quotes. Don't do anything to the sentences that contain indirect quotations.

1. Professor Ripley-Thorndike told his linguistics class that the origin of our alphabet has been the subject of debate for centuries.

2. The professor said, at one time or another the Egyptian, the Babylonian cuneiform and the Phoenician script have all been considered the prototype of alphabetic writing.

3. The professor continued, the fact is, however, that the earliest inscriptions in alphabet writing come from the region of the Holy Land as early as 1700 B.C.

4. Ripley-Thorndike said that the expansion of Islam from around 300 to 600 A.D. spread the Arabic alphabet from Arabia into parts of modern-day Europe and Africa.

5. Because of the influence of the Church of Rome, said Ripley-Thorndike, the Latin alphabet was adapted to most of the modern European languages.

Definitions

Use quotation marks when a word or phrase is named in *italics* and defined or translated.

- *Continuous* means "uninterrupted in time, occurring without breaks" while *continual* means "recurring regularly, intermittently; repeated at intervals."

Special emphasis

Use quotation marks to highlight words or to indicate that you don't agree with a certain perspective (irony).

- Pat Riley, former head coach of the New York Knicks, coined the term "threepeat" to indicate the winning of a third championship.
- The leaders of the Nazi party met at Wansee to decide upon a "final solution" to the "Jewish problem."
- Rube Goldberg's "inventions" were never intended to be taken seriously.

QUOTATION MARKS/ITALICS

In addition to their use in setting off the exact words of a speaker or writer, <u>QUOTATION MARKS</u>, used in conjunction with <u>ITALICS</u>, have certain uses in what are called "Manuscript Conventions."

The use of italics and quotation marks to set off titles in printed material helps the reader identify certain kinds of works, as listed below. The underlying logic of the convention is that longer works are italicized (Epic poem: *The Iliad* or <u>The Iliad</u>) while shorter works are put in quotes (Short poem: "Trees"; Novel: *Tristam Shandy*; Short Story: "The Sniper").

ITALICS	**QUOTATION MARKS**
Titles of	Titles of
books: *The Grapes of Wrath*	short stories: "The Telltale Heart"
epic poems: *The Iliad The Odyssey*	short poems: "Trees" "The Raven"
plays: *Enemy of the People The Wiz*	songs: "Purple Rain" "Blame It"
movies/DVDs: *Terminator Obsessed*	magazine articles: "US Economy
operas: *Madame Butterfly Tommy*	In Deep Trouble"
symphonies: *Fifth Symphony*	newspaper stories: "Two Teens
albums/CDs: *Purple Rain Intuition*	Arrested"
television series: *CSI: Miami*	book chapters: "Expository Writing"
	television episodes: "Death in the
	Streets"
Names of	
newspapers: New York *Times*	**EXCEPTIONS:** (Capitalize only;
magazines: *O Newsweek*	don't use italics or quotation marks.)
works of art: *Mona Lisa*	Historical legal documents:
ships: *RMS Titanic USS Maine*	Magna Carta
aircraft: *Spirit of St. Louis*	Declaration of Independence
Enola Gay Challenger	US Constitution
	Bill of Rights
Foreign Words and Expressions	Holy works: Holy Bible
très chic blitzkrieg carpe diem	Talmud Qur'an
Legal Cases:	
Roe v Wade __	
New York Times Co. v Sullivan	

Other Uses of Italics: Words Used as Words, Letters Used as Letters
Italics may also be used to highlight words or letters used as such:

- The word *success* has two *c*'s and two *s*'s in it.
- The runner-up in the spelling bee missed on the word *nickelodeon*.

Other Uses of Italics: To Indicate Emphasis   When used sparingly, italics (or underlines) may also be used to show emphasis. (Remember Voltaire's sage advice: "To esteem everyone is to esteem no one." Likewise, to emphasize everything is to emphasize nothing.

- If you were offended by my remarks, then that's *your* problem.

- Then Mark wanted me to pay him <u>five hundred dollars</u> for the scratch I supposedly put in the paint on his fender.

EXERCISE 11   QUOTATION MARKS/ITALICS: Put quotation marks and italics (underline) where they are needed in the following sentences. One of the sentences is correct as written.

1. Our World Literature I class read two epic poems: Beowulf and Paradise Lost.

2. We were also required to read portions of the Bible, the Talmud and the Qur'an.

3. In this week's issue of Newsweek, I read an article entitled Congress Debates NATO Bombings.

4. I like the song Cry Love on John Hiatt's CD, Walk On.

5. The Ruptured Duck was the name of one of the Boeing B-25 airplanes that bombed Tokyo in a famous raid during World War II.

6. Sunday's New York Times carried a story about the discovery of a rare copy of The Declaration of Independence.

7. Charles Darwin's best-known work, On the Origin of Species, was first published in the 19th century.

8. My journalism text, Modern Media, devoted several pages to a discussion of a famous defamation case, Rosenbloom v Metromedia,

9. The sinking of the battleship USS Maine and continuous agitation by William Randolph Hearst in the New York Journal led to the Spanish-American War.

10. We watched the classic old movie Bonnie and Clyde on a TNT network TV show called Dinner and a Movie.

11. Frieda and I went to the Rodin Museum in Philadelphia to see Rodin's two most famous works: The Thinker and The Kiss.

12. We have adopted the word blitz from German into English when we use it to describe a play in football, but we still consider blitzkrieg to be a foreign word.

13. Last night I watched an episode entitled Heads Up on that popular TV show, The Practice.

14. Our short story anthology, Modern Short Fiction, contains two works by Ernest Hemingway: The Killers and In Another Country.

15. Tonight's assignment is a long chapter—The War Years—in our textbook, The American Saga.

APOSTROPHES

The **APOSTROPHE** is used to show possession and contraction. The order of words in a sentence (**SYNTAX**) usually shows possession; even without an apostrophe, you would know that in the sentence *We took Bills car to the movies,* Bill owns the car. The apostrophe <u>is</u> useful, however, to distinguish numbers of owners: *That is the boy's car* = one owner; *That is the boys' car* = more than one owner.

In contractions, remember that the apostrophe takes the place of the letter or letters that have been removed (*they are = they're; 8 of the clock = 8 o'clock*). In the kind of formal writing that you do in college, contractions should be used sparingly. Use them only when not to would make your style too stiff and formal sounding or when you are writing dialogue.

When you use the apostrophe to show possession, a good rule to remember is that the apostrophe always comes after the ***word*** that is doing the possessing. For example, when you see "mens clothing," ask yourself who owns the clothing. Is the clothing owned by *men* or *mens*? Would you say, "The mens own the clothing"? No. So put the apostrophe after the word *men*: "men's clothing."

Look at another example: "the girls toys." Who owns the toys? The "girl"? Or the "girls"? If the "girl" is the owner, put the apostrophe after the word "girl." If the "girls" are the owners, put the apostrophe after the word "girls."

- **Examples of possessives that often present problems:**

child's toys
children's toys (the children own
the toys)
a person's choice
the people's choice
a day's pay
the Harts' house (all of the Harts
own the house)

the lady's room
ladies' room (the ladies own the
room)
a woman's shoes
women's shoes
a month's vacation
the Hart family's house (the family
owns the house)

- **In regular singular possessives put the apostrophe before the** *s*:

the boy's books
a day's pay

the girl's glasses
a parent's love

- **In regular plural possessives, put the apostrophe after the** *s*:

three boys' books
three weeks' vacation

those girls' glasses
my parents' house

- **When a word that you want to make possessive ends in s, you have the choice of using 's or just putting the apostrophe after the** *s*.

Jess' boots or Jess's boots   the princess' shoes or the princess's shoes

EXERCISE 12   APOSTROPHES: Put apostrophes where they are needed in the following sentences.

1. Hugh Mercer was born in 1725 in his parents home, but he lived in his uncles house for the first few years of his life.

2. Educated as a physician, Mercer served as a surgeons assistant in the Scottish army, but he wasnt happy living in Scotland.

3. In 1747 Mercers family helped him emigrate to America, where he

settled on another uncles farm.

4. In 1755 Mercer joined the British armys expedition to Duquesne, where he was assigned to help survey the settlers lands.

5. He then moved to Virginia and worked as a physician, specializing in childrens diseases and treating the colonists families.

6. At the Battle of Princeton, a British soldiers bullet cut Mercer down, and he died five days later despite his doctors heroic efforts.

COLONS

Like the <u>SEMICOLON</u>, the <u>COLON</u>, when used correctly by college-level writers, indicates a certain command or control of language. The colon is primarily used to introduce certain units, such as lists, or examples or explanations of something just mentioned. It is also often used to set off a long quotation, to separate hours from minutes and to follow the salutation in a business letter.

Lists
- When you report for your first day on the job, you should bring the following: a pencil, a ruler, a T-square and an eraser. (**NOTE:** The word "following" in a sentence often indicates that a colon is required.)

- While I was incarcerated, I read the following books: *Crime and Punishment, Gulag Archipelago* and *In the Belly of the Beast.*

Don't use a colon before a list when the items follow a form of the verb *to be* or a preposition. When you use a colon, you should hear a significant pause before the material that follows.

- To be a good football player, you should be fast, strong and intelligent.
NOT To be a good football player, you should be: fast, strong and intelligent.

- A complete sentence consists of a subject, verb and complete thought.
NOT A complete sentence consists of: a subject, verb and complete thought.

general guideline, use a colon only when the material to the left of it is a ,lete sentence.

- There are three officers: Bob, Andrew, and Max.
                                NOT
- The three officers are: Bob, Andrew, and Max.

- The recipe requires three ingredients: nutmeg, cinnamon, and sugar.
                                NOT
- The three ingredients required for the recipe are: nutmeg, cinnamon, and sugar.

Examples
- Sammy had several character flaws, but one stood out above all of the others: his vanity.

- Sammy had several character flaws, but one stood out above all of the others: he was extremely vain. (or *He was extremely vain*—if the follow-up unit is a sentence, you have the option of using a capital letter or not, depending upon your stylistic preference.)

Explanations
- When hot water is put into an ice-cube tray and placed in a freezer, an interesting phenomenon will occur: ice will form on the surface more quickly than if cold water is used.

Long Quotation (4 or more lines in the original text)
- One of the most famous openings in English literature occurs in Charles Dickens' *A Tale of Two Cities*: "It was the best of times, it was the worst of times, it was the age of wisdom, it was the age of foolishness, it was the epoch of belief, it was the epoch of incredulity, it was the season of Light, it was the season of Darkness, it was the spring of hope, it was the winter of despair . . . ."

Time
  12:45   8:30   11:43

Salutations
  Dear Mr. Tinsley: Dear Horizon Publishers: To Whom It May Concern:

EXERCISE 13 COLONS: Put colons where they are needed in the following sentences. Some of the sentences are correct as written.

1. We have a choice of three flights 8:47, 10:05 or 11:28.

2. When Latisha arrived at school, she saw Jerome, James, LeMonde and Michael.

3. In 1941 Winston Churchill told the London County Council, "We will have no truce or parley with Hitler or the grisly gang who works his wicked will. Let him do his worst—and we will do our best."

4. Marta has a favorite technique that drives her teachers crazy she snaps her gum incessantly.

5. The instructions said the following tools would be needed pliers, a screwdriver, a small hammer and a crescent wrench.

6. In 1935 the New York *Daily News* ran a famous photograph on its front page the execution of convicted murderer Ruth Snyder in Sing Sing's electric chair.

7. When we got to the library, we saw a strange sight Martin was actually doing his homework.

8. You should report to work at 7 45 a.m.

9. The American Medical Association says that one change in lifestyle can save hundreds of thousands of lives quitting smoking.

10. When you see Jackie, do me a favor ask her to meet me at the mall.

DASHES

The **DASH** is, in some respects, used much like the colon—it "points" to items in your writing to set them off. Unlike the colon, however, the dash is usually used for dramatic emphasis. Look at these two sentences:

- When we got to the party, our worst fear was realized: Bobby had forgotten to pick up the beer.

- When we got to the party, our worst fear was realized—Bobby had forgotten to pick up the beer.

Both sentences above are punctuated correctly, but the first one is a simple statement of fact while the second one conveys a more dramatic pause. Colons are used more in scientific/ technical/academic writing. Dashes are used more in creative/dramatic writing.

- I enjoy seeing my relatives—but not too often.

- Mary has many fine attributes—at the moment, however, I can't think of any.

> **NOTE:** On a word processor, a dash is two hyphens with no space between. This is a hyphen - . This is a dash—.

Use dashes sparingly. Since they are meant to have a dramatic impact, they shouldn't be used so often that they lose their effect. If you scatter them at random, your writing sounds as if you are on the edge of hysteria.

EXERCISE 14   DASHES: Put dashes where they are needed in the following sentences.

1. You have two chances to beat me slim and none.

2. After I finished the 10K race, I needed only one thing a bottle of oxygen.

3. Tony knew better than to fool around with the Mafia he was much too smart for that.

4. The word to describe your attitude "gracious" also describes your skill as a hostess.

5. Samantha was one of the nicest people in the class I don't know of anyone who didn't like her.

HYPHENS/PARENTHESES/BRACKETS/ELLIPSES/SLASHES

The **HYPHEN** is used to indicate that words are being combined to function as a single grammatical unit, usually an adjective (**COMPOUND ADJECTIVE**) or a noun (**COMPOUND NOUN**).

- Lucille loves watching world-class Greco-Roman wrestling matches.
- Big John served a three-to-five-year sentence in Attica Prison.
- Then John had an epiphany, went to college and excelled as a scholar-athlete.

The hyphen is also used in numbers written as two words, provided the number is below one hundred.

twenty-nine   thirty-three   ninety-nine   one hundred

PARENTHESES are used to set off additional or incidental information that breaks the flow of the sentence.
- Luther Burbank (1876-1949) made many discoveries in the field of plant genetics.
- Leroy's enormous size usually made even the toughest opponent (unless he was a skillful boxer) think twice before challenging Leroy to a fight.
- Alice broke the rule against leaving the base (Section 8-A in *Army Rules and Regulations*) once too often, and she was asked to resign her commission.

BRACKETS (also known as **SQUARE BRACKETS**) show that something in text has been added by someone other than the writer of the text.
- Sanford wrote, "The author [Fitzgerald] never intended Gatsby to be a heroic character."

In the example above, you are quoting Sanford, and you need to add Fitzgerald's name to Sanford's words so that _your_ reader knows whom Sanford is talking about. It also shows the reader which are the author's words and which are yours.
- Selwyn Raab, a reporter for the *New York Times*, wrote, "They [Carter and Artis] didn't know for hours why they had been picked up by the police."

In the example above, you need to clarify to whom the pronoun *they* refers.

The **ELLIPSIS** (plural: **ELLIPSES**) consists of three spaced dots . . . and indicates something has been cut out of a text.
- Selwyn Raab, a reporter for the *New York Times*, wrote, "The two men . . . were taken to Paterson police headquarters about four hours after the murders."

The original of the above read, "The two men, who had first been taken to St. Joseph's Hospital to see if a wounded victim could identify them, were taken to Paterson police headquarters about four hours after the murders."

Since you don't think the information given in the adjective clause is necessary to support the point you're making, omit the clause. But you need to indicate that something was there, so use the ellipsis.

In manuscript convention, you can have one ., which is a period; three . . ., which is an ellipsis; and four . . . ., which is an ellipsis plus a period. You can't have two **. .** or five or more **. . . . .** The ellipsis is written with one letter space between the word preceding the **.** and one letter space between each of the **.s**. The ellipsis is also used informally, like a dash, to indicate a pause for dramatic emphasis or to indicate suspended thought, but this should generally not be used in formal essays.

- I was just thinking . . . (long pause as if the writer is deep in thought).

Until the newspapers strongly protested, Hollywood press agents used to use the following technique when quoting critics in their ad copy for movies:

Original: "Ed Wood's *Plan 9 From Outer Space* is a classic example of a weakly written, poorly produced and terribly directed film."
"Revised": "Ed Wood's *Plan 9 From Outer Space* is a classic . . . film."

Using ellipses to alter the intent of the original is unethical.

The **SLASH** indicates alternative words (*either/or*) or to mark off lines of poetry in prose text.

To separate alternative words:

- A physician must be able to meet the psychological as well as the physical needs of his/her patients.

- No one was ever able to figure out how the strange Dovan/Clark partnership began in the first place.

To separate lines of poetry (put a space on either side of the slash):

- In "The Love Song of J. Alfred Prufrock," T. S. Eliot wrote, "Let us go then, you and I, / When the evening is spread out against the sky / Like a patient etherized upon a table;"

EXERCISE 15   OTHER PUNCTUATION: Put the appropriate punctuation marks in the following sentences. Do not change any capitalization. Every sentence needs the addition of at least one punctuation mark (counting sets of quotation marks or parentheses as one punctuation mark).

1. In the poem "Channel Firing," Thomas Hardy wrote, "The night your great guns, unawares, Shook all our coffins as we lay, And broke

chancel window-squares, We thought it was the Judgment-day."

2. Hack Wilson was a well known baseball player of the early 20th century.

3. Though John F. Kennedy was president for only a few years 1961-1963, his term in office had a major impact on American history.

4. The owner bartender made it clear to us that he could get along quite well without our business.

5. Twenty five of my closest friends will be invited to my birthday party.

EXERCISE 16 REVIEW—ALL PUNCTUATION: Put the appropriate punctuation marks in the following sentences. Do not change any capitalization. Every sentence needs the addition of at least two punctuation marks (counting sets of quotation marks or parentheses as one punctuation mark).

1. My friend Jeremy who always gets good grades never seems to study I know however that he has a photographic memory.

2. Don't worry about it Jeremy said to me one day.

3. Whenever he reads a play or novel for our literature class its a required course in our curriculum Jeremy immediately remembers all of the text.

4. One day our English professor John T. Ripper assigned us to read The Odyssey an epic poem.

5. Jeremy was assigned to memorize the dialogue for these three characters Odysseus the main character Penelope the wife of Odysseus and Circe the lady who turned men into pigs.

6. After he finished reading The Odyssey Jeremy decided it was so interesting that he read The Iliad another epic poem by Homer.

7. Jeremy said to me I finished the last chapter in twenty three minutes a new world's record.

8. Wow I said excitedly. Do you think we should try to get you into The Guiness Book of World Records

9. Jeremy hes very modest said no. I wouldnt want all of those paparazzi camped out in my driveway.

10. Thats Jeremy for you a scholar gentleman and true friend.

EXERCISE 17 REVIEW—ALL PUNCTUATION: Put the appropriate punctuation marks where needed in the paragraph below. <u>Do not change any capitalization</u>.

When the designers of the Titanic first began planning the gigantic ship they knew that they had to consider three important requirements the ship which was the largest passenger vessel ever contemplated had to be fast it had to have a double hull making it less likely to sink and it had to be elegant enough to attract rich passengers. This was such a well furnished vessel that even the sailors quarters had gold plated faucets on the sinks.

After setting a record six months, 14 days for completing the engineering drawings the members of the design team had their foremans pen plated with gold and framed. Then they attached an engraved silver plate with the following words To an esteemed colleague and a great leader

Some of the engineers who worked on the design of the giant passenger liner were featured in an article Building the Impossible in Liberty Magazine. One of the men Thomas Burnside was quoted as saying The Titanic will be unsinkable of this, you may be sure

Another one of the engineers quoted in the article said He Burnside knows what hes talking about this ship will still be sailing long after all of us are six feet under guaranteed

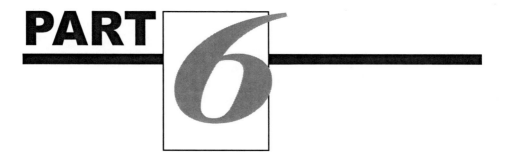

PART 6

USAGE

USAGE

Certain words in English are confused or misused according to current standards of "acceptable" usage. As noted earlier in the section on language, word use is not "good"/ "bad" or "right"/"wrong" as long as it communicates an idea. However, educated users of the English language expect to hear certain words used in a particular context—or more realistically, they expect <u>not</u> to hear certain words used in particular contexts.

"Standard" or "appropriate" usage is determined by the way in which generally acknowledged good writers (authors, editors, publishers, professors, teachers) use the language. As college students you should be aware of the distinction between spoken (colloquial) usage and the more formal, "edited" language of college-level essays.

Since English is such a fast-changing language, some of the words in the list below may be in a transition period, moving from "inappropriate" to "appropriate" usage. For example, while many people may say, "Rhoda's remarks really *aggravated* me" (used in the sense of "Rhoda's remarks *annoyed* me), most careful users of English won't like hearing *aggravate* used in that context. Eventually, however, if enough people use a word in a particular context, it will take on the meaning and become "acceptable."

Note: When words are crossed out (~~irregardless~~), it means they are generally considered inappropriate and using them in your speech (and, of course, your writing) may, in some people's eyes, mark you as not being well educated. Just as educated people do not expect to hear you say, "Hey, I seen you in the library yesterday" or "excape" when you mean "escape," they will be jarred if they hear the crossed-out words in the indicated contexts.

This list is intended to be a reference to help you pick the appropriate word for use in writing and, in some cases, in speech. **If the examples say "Sometimes Used" and "Preferred" you should be aware that the "Preferred" use is expected in college-level writing**.

accept except

> *Accept* means "to take or receive something offered"; "to agree or consent to."
> - Tom refused to *accept* responsibility for the mistake.
> *Except* means "other than"; "to omit"; "to exclude."
> - Everyone *except* Fran was allowed to go on the trip.
>
> **NOTE:** The usage problem most commonly associated with these words is *except* used when *accept* is needed to fit the context of the sentence.
>> **USE** We have decided to *accept* your offer of a settlement in the lawsuit.
>>> **NOT** We have decided to *except* your offer of a settlement in the lawsuit.

advice advise

Advice is a noun meaning "a recommendation offered as a guide to action or conduct."

- Take my *advice* and don't go to the party tonight.

Advise is a verb meaning "to offer an opinion or suggestion as worth following."

- I would strongly *advise* you not to go to that party tonight.

> **NOTE:** Pronunciation is the key to appropriate usage here. *Advise* is pronounced *ad vize*.
>
> > **USE** Take my *advice* and stay away from him.
> > **NOT** Take my *advise* and stay away from him.

affect effect

Affect is a verb meaning "to act on, to produce an effect or change in"; "to impress the mind or move the feelings."

- Prolonged alcohol abuse can *affect* your nervous system.
- The sad ending of that movie didn't *affect* me at all.

Effect is a noun meaning "something produced by a cause"; "result"; "consequence."

- Unfortunately, the new drug had no *effect* on the terminally ill patient.
- Last night's fire will have a negative *effect* on our production schedule.

Effect also may be used in some contexts as a verb, meaning "to bring about," "to accomplish."

- The board of trustees voted to *effect* a change in the grading policy.

> **NOTE:** The usage problem most commonly associated with these words in writing is the use of *effect* in a context where *affect* should be used:
>
> > **USE** Bobbi's resignation did not *affect* us at all.
> > **NOT** Bobbi's resignation did not *effect* us at all.

aggravate irritate

Aggravate means "to make worse or more severe."

- Rubbing an open wound with sand will *aggravate* the condition.
- Lula's attempt to settle the argument succeeded only in *aggravating* the situation.

Irritate means "to cause impatience or anger."

- Jena's inappropriate comments always seem to *irritate* (or *annoy*) Stacy.

> **NOTE:** The usage problem most commonly associated with these words in writing and in speech is the use of *aggravate* in a context where *irriatate* or *annoy* is more appropriate.

> **SOMETIMES USED** Your constant interruptions *aggravate* me.
> **PREFERRED** Your constant interruptions *annoy* me.

all right ~~alright~~

All right means "safe, sound"; "acceptable"; or "Yes, OK" and is used more in speech than in writing.

- That was a close call; are you all right?
- Your essay is all right, but you can do better.
- All right, I'll go with you.

When *all right* is used in writing, a*lright* is a variant spelling that is generally considered not acceptable for use in college-level writing, in the same category as *thru, nite*, or *tho*.

allusion illusion

Allusion means "a passing or casual reference"; "an indirect reference."

- Phelps made an *allusion* to Leland's weak acting ability but didn't come right out and say it.
- In my research paper I included a literary *allusion* from *Hamlet*.

Illusion means "something perceived in way that is different from reality"; "something imagined."

- Believe me, I have no *illusions* that you think I'm a good actor.
- We thought we saw the northern lights, but it turned out to be only an optical *illusion*.

a lot ~~alot~~ allot

A lot is an informal expression equivalent to "much" or "many." Though informal (and vague), its use seems to have become generally acceptable in college-level writing.

- Gina made a lot of money last year.

Alot is a misspelling of *a lot* and should not be used.

Allot means "to assign" "to apportion" "to distribute in certain proportions."

- Student Government *allots* a certain amount of money to each student organization.

amount number

Amount means "an aggregate quantity or measure" and is used when referring to something that can't be counted individually, as in *an amount of water, amount of sand, amount of love, amount of money*. (Even though one could argue that money can be counted, what we mean here is that while coins and bills can be counted, the collective noun *money* denotes something in bulk and is not countable.)

- No *amount* of pleading could convince Joan to change her mind.
- The *amount* of love I feel for you is immeasurable.

Number means "the sum of a collection of units" and is used when something can be counted, as in *number of drops of water, number of grains of sand, number of coins, number of people*.

- The *number* of errors in your last essay brought your grade down.
- Dan Smithson holds the record for the greatest *number* of fish caught in a one-hour period.

anyone any one

Anyone is an indefinite pronoun, like "everyone," "everybody," "anybody."

- *Anyone* with a problem should see the chaplain.

Any one (note the space between the words) means "one of many" and is followed by the preposition *of*.

- *Any one* of those solutions will work.

bad badly

Bad is an adjective.

- Adolph Hitler was a *bad* person.

Badly is an adverb.

- Our shortstop played *badly* in yesterday's game.

Use *badly* with action verbs	**Use *bad* with linking verbs**
I reacted *badly*	I feel *bad*
I sang *badly*	I look *bad*
I wrote *badly*	I smell *bad*
I hit *badly*	I seem *bad*
I shot *badly*	I am *bad*
they played *badly*	they sound *bad*

NOTE: The usage problem most commonly associated with these words occurs when the adjective *bad* is used to describe an action, such as "I did *bad* on the biology test yesterday." Conversely, using *badly* in a sentence such as "I felt *badly* when I heard your mother was ill," literally means that something is wrong with your sense of touch— maybe your fingers are numb.

because ~~being that~~ since

Because and *since* are used to introduce adverb clauses.

- *Because* PJ is my friend, I defended him.
- *Since* you weren't here, we went ahead without you.

Being that (or *Being as*), sometimes used in speech to begin the adverb clause, is considered by many careful users of English to be substandard and should be avoided in college-level writing.

| **SOMETIMES USED** | *Being that* you missed the meeting, we didn't have a quorum. |
| **PREFERRED** | *Because* (or *since*) you missed the meeting, we didn't have a quorum. |

beside besides

Beside means "next to"; "alongside of."

- I will walk *beside* you in the commencement procession.

Besides means "in addition to."

- *Besides* searching for solutions to the landfill problem, environmentalists are also seeking alternatives to incineration.

between among

Between is used when referring to two persons or things.

- Our recent disagreement has driven a wedge *between* us.
- We decided to split the money *between* the two of us.

Among is used when referring to three or more persons or things.

- We decided to split the profits evenly *among* the four partners.

bring take

Bring means "to carry, convey or conduct something toward the speaker."

- Please *bring* the pitchers of beer to our table.

Take means "to remove or carry off" (in a direction away from the speaker).

- Mervish has had enough beer; please *take* him home.

can may

Can means "having the ability, power or skill to."

- I *can* lift those weights with no problem.
- Dominick *can* eat more clams than anyone I know.

May is used to express permission, opportunity or possibility.

- Yes, you *may* use my weights for a while.
- *May* I borrow your car tomorrow?

NOTE: The usage problem most commonly associated with these words occurs when *can* is used when *may* would be more appropriate to the context of the sentence.

SOMETIMES USED	*Can* I ride to school with you tomorrow?
PREFERRED	*May* I ride to school with you tomorrow?

complement compliment

As a verb, *complement* means "to add to or to complete."

- An off-white veil *complemented* the bride's gown perfectly.

As a noun, *complement* means "something that adds to or completes."

- A light blue scarf was the perfect *complement* for my spring wardrobe.
- A cappuccino would be the perfect *complement* to an excellent meal.

As a verb, *compliment* means "to pay a kindness"; "to say something good about someone."

- Lateesha *complimented* Barry on his good taste in art.

As a noun, *compliment* means "an expression of praise, commendation or admiration."

- I love being paid a *compliment* by someone who knows what she is talking about.

---

could have ~~could of~~
might have ~~might of~~
should have ~~should of~~
would have ~~would of~~

Note that the underlined forms above are never appropriate. They come from hearing the spoken contracted forms: *could've, might've, should've, would've,* as in, "You should've been there—we had a lot of fun." The contraction sounds like *should of,* but those two words cannot be written together correctly.

USE I *should have* known better.
NOT I *should of* known better.

The following words use Greek and Latin plurals and are frequently misused in American English. Note the distinctions in the examples.

criterion criteria

Criterion means "a standard of judgment"; "an established rule against which things are tested."
- The most important *criterion* for this job is getting to work on time.

The plural form of *criterion* is *criteria.*
- You must meet the *criteria* for advancement before we can raise your salary.

medium media

Medium means "an agency, means or instrument."
- A newspaper is a *medium* of mass communication.
- Currency is one *medium* of exchange.

The plural form of *medium* is *media.*
- The *media* have brought the criticism on themselves.
- Some critics say the *media* have more influence than the congress.

phenomenon phenomena

Phenomenon means "an observable fact, occurrence or circumstance."
- A comet streaking across the night sky is a remarkable *phenomenon* to see.

The plural form of *phenomenon* is *phenomena.*
- Comets and meteors are heavenly *phenomena* that frightened early humans.

NOTE: The usage problem most commonly associated with these words occurs when a writer or speaker uses the plural form when the singular should be used as in "An important *criteria* in our decision is the candidate's educational background," or "A total eclipse of the sun is a fascinating *phenomena*." We also frequently hear members of the mass media make a statement like "The media is a powerful force in American culture."

---

disinterested uninterested

Disinterested means "unbiased by personal interest or advantage."
- A baseball umpire is interested in the game but must maintain a *disinterested* position to assure fairness to both teams.

Uninterested means "having or showing no interest"; "indifferent."
- Phillips seemed to be totally *uninterested* in the conversation of his two dinner guests.

According to *The Random House Dictionary of the English Language,* "These two words are not properly synonyms. *Disinterested* today stresses absence of prejudice or of selfish interests. *Uninterested* suggests aloofness and indifference."

> **NOTE:** The usage problem most commonly associated with these words occurs when *disinterested* is used when *uninterested* fits the context of the sentence.
>
> **SOMETIMES USED**   Shannon couldn't care less about the news — she's totally *disinterested* in current events.
>
> **PREFERRED**   Shannon couldn't care less about the news — she's totally *uninterested* in current events.

everyday every day

Everyday, written as one word, is an adjective that means "ordinary," or "regular" and is placed in front of a noun.
- Coming late to class has become an *everyday* occurrence.
- The Cost-Cutter stores are known for their *everyday* low prices.

Every day, written with a space between the words, means "daily."
- More and more students seem to be coming to class late *every day*.
- I go to my local Cost-Cutter store *every day*.

> **NOTE:** The usage problem most commonly associated with these words occurs when *everyday* is used when *every day* is needed to fit the context of the sentence.
>
> **USE** I go to work *every day*.   I see Tim at school *every day*.
>
> **NOT** I go to work *everyday*.   I see Tim at school *everyday*.

fewer less

Fewer is used when the items can be counted (see *number* in *amount/ number* above).

- *Fewer* students were in my English class on Wednesday than on Monday.
- With each day that passes I see *fewer* reasons to try to reconcile with Jack.
- *Fewer* people were at last night's concert compared to the one a month ago.

Less is used when the item denotes bulk, not countable units (see *amount* in *amount/number* above).

- Every month I seem to bring home *less* money.
- It takes *less* effort to do the job right than to do it wrong and then fix it.
- We should make *less* coffee for the next meeting.

good well

Good is an adjective. It should not be used as an adverb.

- Jackson is a *good* player.
- I earned a *good* grade on my last test.

Well is an adverb.

- Sanford performed *well* on his SATs.
- The meeting went *well* last night; we finished in less than an hour.

Well is also used as a predicate adjective when talking about health.

- I don't feel *well* today.
- How are you? I am *well*, thank you.

hanged hung

Hanged is used when talking about a form of capital punishment.

- The convicted murderer was *hanged* in the courtyard.

Hung is the past tense form of *hang* and means "suspended"; "attached"; "fastened."

- Alice *hung* the painting on the wall.

For some reason, perhaps the speed at which we speak, some writers run the following underlined words together. If you are using a word processor, it should catch the underlined words below as spelling errors. If you're handwriting, watch for them.

high school ~~highschool~~	**even though** ~~eventhough~~
in fact ~~infact~~	

---

imply infer

Imply means "to suggest without express statement"; "to hint."
- Harry implied that I wasn't doing my job.
- I didn't mean to imply that you were lazy.

Infer means "to surmise"; "to draw a conclusion from certain evidence."
- I *inferred* from Harry's attitude that he thought I wasn't doing my job.
- I *infer* from your remarks at the staff meeting that you think I'm lazy.

> **NOTE:** As a general rule, the speaker *implies* and the listener *infers*. The usage problem most commonly associated with these words occurs when *infer* is used and *imply* better fits the context of the sentence.
>
> **USE** Suzi's remarks seemed to *imply* that Shelley shouldn't be on the team.
>
> **NOT** Suzi's remarks seemed to *infer* that Shelley shouldn't be on the team.

in into

In is a preposition used to refer to inclusion within a space.
- Mr. Murray likes to take a walk *in* the park every day.
- I saw Freddie *in* the clothing store yesterday.

Into is used to indicate movement from one point to another.
- Mr. Murray left his house and went *into* the park.
- Freddie walked *into* the clothing store yesterday just as it was being robbed.

> **NOTE:** The usage problem most commonly associated with these words occurs when *in* is used while *into* more appropriately fits the context of the sentence.
>
> **USE** Sharrif walked *into* the room at exactly 9 a.m.
>
> **NOT** Sharrif walked *in* the room at exactly 9 a.m.

invite invitation

Invite is a verb that means "to request participation in something, especially a gathering or a celebration."
- I was *invited* to attend Monica and Dave's wedding.

Invitation is a noun that means "the written or spoken form with which a person is invited."
- I received an *invitation* to Monica and Dave's wedding.

> **NOTE:** The usage problem most commonly associated with these words is that *invite* is sometimes used as a noun.
>
> **USE** We need to send an *invitation* to Joey.
>
> **NOT** We need to send an *invite* to Joey.

its it's ~~its²~~

Its is a possessive pronoun. Possessive pronouns don't need apostrophes—they're already possessive by their spelling.

- The dog licked *its* fur.   **NOT**   The dog licked it's fur.

It's is the contraction for *it is*.

- It's not too late to repent, sinner.

Its' is not a word.

later latter

Later means "after the usual or proper time"; "to be continued at another time."

- I'll see you later.
- We all agreed to meet later in the day.

Latter means "the second mentioned of two things."

- We never knew whether he was courageous or crazy, but personally I think it was the *latter*.
- Thomas Jefferson said, ". . . were it left to me to decide whether we should have a government without newspapers or newspapers without a government, I should not hesitate a moment to prefer the *latter*."

lead led

Lead, as a verb (pronounced "leed"), means "to guide" or "to direct."

- The general will *lead* his troops into battle.

Lead as a noun (pronounced "led") is a soft, malleable, heavy metal.

- Fishing sinkers are usually made of *lead*.

Led is the past tense form of the verb "to lead."

- The general *led* his troops into battle.

NOTE: The usage problem most commonly associated with these words occurs when *lead* is used in writing in place of the past-tense *led*.

> **USE**   General Patton *led* the Sixth Army across France.
>
> **NOT**   General Patton *lead* the Sixth Army across France.

lie lay

Lie means "to recline" or "to rest."

- I like to *lie* on the beach during the summer.
- I think I will *lie* down and take a nap.

Lay is an action verb that requires a direct object and means "to place in a horizontal position"; "to set down."

- Lester asked Annie to *lay* the newspapers on the table.
- The installers will *lay* the wall-to-wall carpet in the apartment.

Lay is also the simple past tense of *lie*.

- I *lay* [not *laid*] down for a nap yesterday after lunch.

NOTE: The usage problem most commonly associated with these words occurs when *lay* is used while *lie* is the appropriate form of the verb.

SOMETIMES USED	Sandy got a terrible sunburn while she was *laying* on the beach.
PREFERRED	Sandy got a terrible sunburn while she was *lying* on the beach.

like as as if

Like is a preposition that means "similar to."
- My life is like a soap opera.

As and *as if* are subordinating conjunctions used to start clauses.
- As I said, my life is like a soap opera.
- As if I didn't have enough problems, now you tell me you're having an affair?

NOTE: The usage issue most commonly associated with these words is the use of *like* as a subordinating conjunction.

SOMETIMES USED	*Like* I said, you're really beginning to annoy me.
PREFERRED	*As* I said, you're really beginning to annoy me.
SOMETIMES USED	*Like* Buffy said, we should all meet at the mall.
PREFERRED	*As* Buffy said, we should all meet at the mall.
SOMETIMES USED	*Like* you indicated by your remarks, we need to work harder <u>and</u> smarter.
PREFERRED	*As* you indicated by your remarks, we need to work harder <u>and</u> smarter.

loose lose

Loose is an adjective that means "free from anything that binds or restrains."
- The bolts holding the gas tank to the frame of my car are *loose*.
- The president called his ambassador a "*loose* cannon."

Lose is a verb that means "to come do be without something, usually by accident or theft."
- I'm afraid I might *lose* my wallet, so I chain it to my belt loop.

NOTE: The usage problem most commonly associated with these words occurs when *loose* is used when *lose* more appropriately fits the context of the sentence.

USE	The boss said we might *lose* our jobs.
NOT	The boss said we might *loose* our jobs.

maybe may be

Maybe means "perhaps"; "possibly."

- *Maybe* we'll see you at the game tomorrow.
- When Art asked Selena if she would come to his party, she said, "*Maybe*."

May be is a verb that means "It might happen."

- We *may be* at the game if we can buy a ticket.
- Selena told Art, "I *may be* at your party if I can get a ride."

moral morale

Moral is an adjective meaning "pertaining to right conduct or the distinction between right and wrong."

- Whether to tell your friend she looks fat or to tell a "little white lie" is the type of *moral* choice with which we are sometimes confronted.

Morale is a noun meaning "a condition associated with confidence, cheerfulness or enthusiasm."

- The *morale* of the team was at its lowest point after they lost their tenth straight game.

NOTE: The usage problem most commonly associated with these words occurs when *morale* is used when *moral* is more appropriate to the context of the sentence.

USE   I sometimes wonder if Steve has any *morals* at all.

NOT   I sometimes wonder if Steve has any *morales* at all.

only

Only can be used as either an adjective or an adverb. When it is used as an adverb, be careful of where you place it within the sentence; it belongs immediately before the word, phrase or clause it modifies. Also, *only* has no superlative form; that is, English does not have a generally recognized word *onliest* that is sometimes heard in speech.

Used as an adjective: I lost my floppy disk, and the research paper that I handed in was my *only* copy.

Used as an adverb:

We were late by *only* a few minutes.

IS BETTER THAN

We *only* were late by a few minutes.

OR

We were *only* late by a few minutes.

Sherry can forget about her job and relax *only* on Sundays.
> **IS BETTER THAN**

Sherry *only* can forget about her job and relax on Sundays.
> **OR**

Sherry can *only* forget about her job and relax on Sundays.

passed past

Passed is the past tense of the verb "to pass" and means "went by" (or in football, "threw").

- We *passed* your house last night.
- The quarterback *passed* when he should have run.

Past as an adjective means "gone by or elapsed in time" and as a preposition means, "beyond in time," "after."

- We drove *past* your house last night.
- The quarterback threw the ball *past* the wide receiver's outstretched hands.

NOTE: The usage problem most commonly associated with these words is *past* used in a sentence when *passed* is needed:

USE   That car *passed* us as if we were standing still.

NOT   That car *past* us as if we were standing still.

---

pay back   payback
work out   workout
pay off   payoff
lay off   layoff

Note that the words on the left side, with the space between, are verbs. When the same words are put together and written as a single word, they're nouns or adjectives.

USE   I will *pay back* the money that I borrowed.

NOT   I will *payback* the money that I borrowed.

I *work out* every day.
I go to the gym every day for a *workout*.
Acme Industries announced they will *lay off* ten people.
Acme Industries sent out *layoff* notices to ten people.

---

persecute prosecute

Persecute means "to pursue with harassing or oppressive treatment"; "to annoy persistently."

- Historians have documented the many ways in which the Nazis *persecuted* Jews and other groups during World War II.

Prosecute means "to institute legal proceedings against."

- The sign in the store read, "If you shoplift, you <u>will</u> be *prosecuted.*

principal principle

Principal means "first or highest in rank, importance or value," "the main body of capital, as distinguished from income or interest."

- The *principal* reason you weren't chosen for the job was your lack of experience.
- The *principal* of the local high school was indicted for embezzlement.

Principle means "an accepted or professed rule of action or conduct"; "a fundamental, primary or general law."

- I make it a *principle* never to lend money to friends or relatives.
- As a general *principle*, I don't talk to strangers.

quiet quite

Quiet means "freedom from noise or unwanted sound."

- The usher told the candy-eating viewer to be *quiet* or feast elsewhere.

Quite means "completely, wholly or entirely."

- Are you *quite* sure you want to withdraw such a large sum of money?

NOTE: The usage problem most commonly associated with these words is the use of *quite* when the more appropriate word would be *quiet*.

USE   Max said, "Gee, it sure is *quiet* in here."
NOT   Max said, "Gee, it sure is *quite* in here."

regardless irrespective ~~irregardless~~

Regardless means "heedless"; "unmindful"; "careless."

Irrespective means "without regard to something else"; "ignoring or discounting."

Irregardless is considered a made-up word consisting of the *ir* part of *irrespective* combined with *regardless*. It should not be used.

USE   *Regardless (or irrespective)* of your objections, we're going ahead with the plan.
NOT   *Iregardless* of your objections, we're going ahead with the plan.

rob steal

Rob means "to take something from someone by threat or unlawful force."

- Sylvester was *robbed* at gunpoint last night.

Steal means "to take without permission or right."

- Sylvester locks his bicycle at night because he is afraid someone will *steal* it.

NOTE: The usage problem most commonly associated with these words is the use of *rob* when *steal* more properly fits the context:

USE   Somebody *stole* some money from the bookstore.

NOT   Somebody *robbed* some money from the bookstore.

sight cite site

Sight, as a verb, means "to see, notice or observe."

- The sniper *sighted* his enemy on the other roof top.

Sight, as a noun, means "a view, a glimpse."

- After the brawl, Stan was not a pretty *sight*.

Cite is a verb that means "to quote, especially as an authority"; "to mention in support"; "to refer to as an example."

- When you do a research paper, you must *cite* your sources carefully or run the risk of being accused of plagiarism.

Site, as a noun, means "the position or location of something, as a town or a building, especially in relationship to its environment.

- The construction crews arrived at the *site* for the new housing development.

sit set

Sit is an intransitive (linking) verb that means "to rest in a seated position."

- Let's *sit* down and talk this over.

Set is a transitive (action) verb that means "to put in a particular place."

- Please *set the* lamp on the table in the corner.

NOTE: Remember that *sit* and *lie* go together as in *sit down* and *lie down*. Just as you would not say, "I think I'll go into the living room and *set* down for a while," you shouldn't say, "I think I'll go into the bedroom and *lay* down for a while."

stationary stationery

Stationary means "standing still"; "not moving"; "fixed."

- The supports were nailed down to keep them *stationary*.

Stationery means "writing materials, especially writing paper."

- Cliff gave Barbara fancy *stationery* for their "paper anniversary."

statue statute

Statue means "a three-dimensional work of art often carved in stone, wood, or other material."

- One of Michelangelo's most famous works is his *statue* of David in Florence, Italy.

Statute means "an enactment made by a legislature and expressed in a formal document"; "a law."

- Under the new *statutes*, a person convicted of first-degree murder must serve at least 30 years in prison with no possibility of parole.

---

supposed to ~~suppose to~~
used to ~~use to~~

Supposed to means "required to," or "expected to" or "ought to."

- I was supposed to attend the meeting, but I forgot.

Used to can mean either "once" or "previously," or it can mean "become accustomed to."

- I used to live in that neighborhood, but I moved away when I was a teenager.
- I can't get used to this new teacher; I don't like his mannerisms.

NOTE: When *supposed to* or *used to* are used in the contexts cited above, they **must** have the *d* on the end.

    USE   I was *supposed* to give the money to Rachel, but I forgot to do it.

    NOT   I was *suppose* to give the money to Rachel, but I forgot to do it.

---

teach learn

Teach means "to impart knowledge of or skill in."

- I used to *teach* swimming at the YMHA summer camp.

Learn means "to acquire knowledge of or skill in by study, instruction or experience."

- Peter has never been able to *learn* how to dance.

NOTE: The usage problem most commonly associated with these words occurs when *learn* is used in a context where *teach* is needed to fit the context of the sentences.

USE   I had lousy teachers who never *taught* me about grammar.

NOT   I had lousy teachers who never *learned* me about grammar.

that which who

These are called relative pronouns. Use *which* and *that* to refer to inanimate objects. Use *who* to refer to people.

- Damien is the student *who* earned a perfect score on the last test.
- Tyrone and Damien are the two baseball players *who* were honored at the dinner.
- Liga's car, *which* was totally destroyed in the accident, was uninsured.

themselves ~~theirselves~~

Theirself is considered substandard usage. Don't use it.

USE They had only *themselves* to blame for the loss.

NOT They had only *theirselves* to blame for the loss.

then than

Then refers to time.

- We drove for eight hours, and *then* we stopped at the campsite.

Than is used to indicate a comparison.

- Marcia is taller *than* Tyrone.

NOTE: The usage problem most commonly associated with these words occurs when *then* is used when the context of the sentence requires *than*.

USE George's car is much faster *than* John's.

NOT George's car is much faster *then* John's.

there their they're

There as an adverb means "in that place—as opposed to here."

Their is a plural possessive pronoun.

They're is a contraction of "they are."

- Please put the new couch over *there* against that wall.
- The children were told to put *their* toys back on the shelves.
- *They're* happy to be back in the United States.

NOTE: The usage problem most commonly associated with these words is the use of *there* as the possessive pronoun.

USE Ed and Bill put *their* books in the locker.

NOT Ed and Bill put *there* books in the locker.

to too two

To as a preposition indicates "motion or direction toward a point."

Too is an adverb meaning "in addition to"; "also."

Two as a noun is a cardinal number expressed by the symbol 2.

- Janet an Ken walked *to* the store on the corner.
- Lauren wanted to go *too*.
- Janet said, "*Two* is company, three is a crowd."

unique

Unique means "existing as the only one or as the sole example."
- Mortenson's proposal presented a *unique* solution for solving the problem.
- All human beings are *unique* individuals.

> **NOTE:** The usage problem most commonly associated with this word is the modifying of *unique* with "more" or "most." Traditionally, something either is or isn't unique; it is one of a kind or it is not one of a kind.

SOMETIMES USED After Bobby modified his car, it was the most *unique* vehicle in the school parking lot.

PREFERRED After Bobby modified his car, there was none other like it in the school parking lot—it was *unique*.

was were

Sentences that begin with *If* clauses and make a statement contrary to fact or a condition that hasn't happened use *were* instead of *was*. *Were* is also used in sentence that express a wish. The following are the most common examples:
- If I *were* you, I wouldn't do that. (You're <u>not</u> me, so this is a statement contrary to fact.)
- If I *were* to win the lottery, I would be happy. (This is a condition that *might* occur but hasn't.)
- The actress said, "Sometimes, I wish I *were* dead." (This is a wish, not reality.)

Some other common examples:
- If I were rich, . . .
- If I were in charge of this company, . . .
- If I were the president, . . .
- I wish I were as thin as . . .
- I wish I were as lucky as . . .
- I wish I were as strong as . . .

whose who's

Whose is a possessive pronoun.
- I don't know *whose* coat this is.
- *Whose* coat is this?

Who's is a contracted form of *who is* and in college-level writing should be used only in reporting dialogue.
- Mariah asked, "*Who's* going to the game with us?"

EXERCISE 1 CONTEMPORARY USAGE:

In the appropriate blank put the letter of the word or word group that appropriately completes each sentence.

____ 1. Smith and Co. refused to (A. accept B. except) our shipment and sent it back.

____ 2. I graduated from (A. highschool B. high school) in 1998.

____ 3. (A. Everyone B. Every one) of the new tires had a major structural weakness.

____ 4. (A. Irregardless B. Regardless) of the outcome of the suit, the company will survive.

____ 5. The fox stuck (A. it's B. its) nose into the steel trap.

____ 6. Between you and (A. I B. me), he's not the man for the job.

____ 7. I want to (A. lay B. lie) on the beach this summer.

____ 8. (A. Whose B. Who's) car is blocking my driveway?

____ 9. Shop Rite says that it sells products at (A. everyday B. every day) low prices.

____10. You may (A. loose B. lose) your job if you miss too many days.

____11. The eighteen-wheeler (A. passed B. past) us on the turnpike at a high rate of speed.

____12. The (A. principle B. principal) of the high school was indicted for embezzlement.

____13. Tell him to (A. sit B. set) the package on the loading dock.

____14. Leslie's gum chewing (A. aggravates B. irritates) her supervisor.

____15. The employees demand that (A. their B. there) lunch break be lengthened.

____16. Abdul is taller (A. then B. than) Patrick.

___17. Stanhope is the employee (A. who's B. whose) job is in jeopardy.

___18. Some people say the media (A. has B. have) too much power.

___19. The law will not (A. affect B. effect) our operations.

___20. The teacher said that I made (A. alot B. a lot) of mistakes.

EXERCISE 2 CONTEMPORARY USAGE: In the blank put the letter of the word or word group that appropriately completes each sentence.

___ 1. (A. Anyone B. Any one) who misses the departmental final may take an alternative examination in the testing center.

___ 2. (A. In fact B. Infact), he's worse than that -- he's an imbecile.

___ 3. "I'm going to (A. lie B. lay) down for a nap," said Alice.

___ 4. My teacher asked me to (A. bring B. take) the attendance sheet to the main office.

___ 5. Arnold likes to (A. workout B. work out) for three hours each day.

___ 6. Whatever you decide will be (A. alright B. all right) with Mr. Forbes.

___ 7. Elvis (A. should of B. should have) stopped taking all of those drugs.

___ 8. Sally goes to work (A. everyday B. every day).

___ 9. The sword went right (A. through B. thru) Smedley's lung.

___ 10. "I would (A. advise B. advice) you not to go," said Benny.

___ 11. I did (A. good B. well) on that test.

___ 12. The FTC disputes the claim that Lite Beer has (A. fewer B. less) calories than regular beer.

___ 13. We are not (A. suppose to B. supposed to) take more than an hour for lunch.

____ 14. General Lee (A. led B. lead) his troops to victory at the first battle of Manassas.

____ 15. I did not intend to (A. imply B. infer) that you were not doing your job.

____ 16. Samantha says she can't get (A. use B. used) to her new boss.

____ 17. The soldiers put (A. theirselves B. themselves) in danger.

____ 18. (A. Like B. As) I told you before, don't touch me.

____ 19. Slater walked (A. in B. into) the spinning drum and was fatally injured.

____ 20. The (A. amount B. number) of mistakes that I made on the test caused me to fail.

____ 21. The person (A. who B. which) is selected for the job must be a hard worker.

____ 22. Mary said that she felt (A. badly B. bad) about missing the deadline.

____ 23. (A. Being as B. Since) Steffans isn't here, we'll table the motion until the next meeting.

____ 24. When we were in France, we visited the (A. sight B. site) of the Allied invasion of Normandy.

____ 25. We (A. maybe B. may be) at the party tonight, but we'll probably leave early.

INDEX

742